QUEST FOR EMPIRE

✠ ✠ ✠

Spanish Settlement in the Southwest

DONALD CUTTER
&
IRIS ENGSTRAND

FULCRUM PUBLISHING
GOLDEN, COLORADO

To Charlotte and Paul, for their enduring patience, encouragement, and support.

Copyright © 1996 Donald Cutter and Iris Engstrand

Inset cover photo—Santiago Matamoros (Moorslayer), seventeenth-century woodcut, courtesy Museo de Franz Mayer, México, D. F.
Cover background—Mapa de la Nueva California al Exmo Señor Principe de la Paz, courtesy Servicio Histórico Militar, Madrid, Spain

Book design by Bill Spahr

Library of Congress Cataloging-in-Publication Data
Cutter, Donald C.
    Quest for empire : Spanish settlement in the Southwest / Donald Cutter and Iris Engstrand.
    p.   cm.
    Includes bibliographical references and index.
    ISBN 1-55591-230-3 (Hardcover)
    1. Indians of North America—Southwest, New—First contact with Europeans. 2. Indians of North America—California—First contact with Europeans. 3. Southwest, New—Discovery and exploration. 4. California—Discovery and exploration. 5. Spain—Colonies—America—Administration. 6. Southwest, New—History—To 1848. 7. California—History—To 1846.   I. Engstrand, Iris Wilson.
II. Title.
E78.S7C87   1996
979'.02—dc20   95-52889
                                                          CIP

Printed in the United States of America

0 9 8 7 6 5 4 3 2 1

Fulcrum Publishing
350 Indiana Street, Suite 350
Golden, Colorado 80401-5093
(800) 992-2908

CONTENTS

ILLUSTRATIONS

FIGURES

MAPS

Acknowledgments

*I*n addition to the many writers of southwestern history who have contributed indirectly to this work, the authors would like to thank especially Douglas Cutter for his many hours of skillful assistance in collecting data, checking sources, suggesting refinements, and proofing the manuscript. His help has been invaluable. Also deserving of special appreciation are Valerie Schoenherr, whose careful editing strengthened this work immeasurably, and Cynthia van Stralen whose thorough proofreading made our task easier. We would like to thank Stephanie Gould for her patience and expertise in preparing the various maps; Harry Crosby for his excellent photographs; and Jack S. Williams for his original sketches of presidio life. We also appreciate the help of Steven Schoenherr, Michael Weber, Harry Kelsey, Eric Biggs, and Ray Brandes for making illustrations available.

We would like to acknowledge as well the work of Fulcrum editors Alison Auch, whose precise guidelines and insightful suggestions kept us on track, and Sam Scinta whose work and support insured the book's fruition. Our gratitude goes also to Bill Spahr for his excellent design and to Robert Baron for his faith in this project from the very beginning.

INTRODUCTION

$\mathcal{T}$his book covers Spain's quest to establish an empire in the far Southwest—California, Arizona, and New Mexico—from the sixteenth to the nineteenth century. In the areas of Arizona and New Mexico, oriented toward Mexico's northern frontier of Sonora and Nueva Vizcaya, primary attention has been given to Spanish activities such as exploration, missionary work, ranching, agriculture, mining, and Indian control. The focus in California, connected to Arizona and New Mexico during the Spanish period by a common language and a common colonial government, has been upon coastal exploration, trade and seagoing activities, as well as military, civilian, and mission establishments.

The emphasis in this book is on Spain's entry into a Southwest occupied by indigenous peoples—not as a matter of right, but as a matter of fact. The nature of the encounter varied greatly from one area to another because of Native American cultural differences, because the region was so geographically diverse, and because the motives of the newcomers ranged from a lust for gold to the saving of souls according to Christian doctrine. At times the entering Spaniards treated the natives with kindness, while at other times and places they acted with unpardonable cruelty. The natives, in turn, reacted with friendship, indifference, or violence. This interaction resulted not in the success or failure of either group, but finally in the development of an ethnically merged people living in a relatively isolated portion of what is now the United States.

The region studied includes that which today is a part of northern Mexico as well as the western United States, and one that has had a common and sustained Hispanic input in such measurable terms as population origins, place-name geography, land titles, and Spanish language use. It covers those areas where Spanish colonial efforts and institutions have had lasting impact, including Baja California. Expeditions of discovery along the Pacific Coast and related maritime activities, especially the Manila galleon trade, are also included to show Spain's efforts to gain a foothold in North America. The documentation is extensive. In addition to citations for quoted materials, we have included bibliographic essays for each chapter, a commentary on general sources, and a comprehensive list of references at the end of the book.

Arguments for treating Spain's entire northern frontier from Florida to California as a single unit have been advanced from various sources, principally because the area reflects a common Hispanic cultural contribution to U.S. history. Despite such an attractive argument, the documentation is so separate, the colonial administration so distinct, and the environments so dissimilar that historians are often discouraged from entering both fields. Nevertheless, David J. Weber, in *The Spanish Frontier in North America* (New Haven: Yale University Press, 1992), has admirably covered the entire area, providing a synthesis of major stature. Weber has also contributed a collection of essays entitled *Myth and the History of the Hispanic Southwest* (Albuquerque: University of New Mexico Press, 1988). Another important work is by Bernard L. Fontana, who treats the region from California to Florida in *Entrada: The Legacy of Spain & Mexico in the United States* (Tucson: Southwest Parks and Monuments Association, 1994).

The existence of manuscripts and publications primarily in Spanish complicates southwestern investigation. Historical research involves cultural, linguistic, paleographic, and archival considerations that derive in great measure from non-English sources, resulting in the need to have good translations of extensive material. Historical writing about Spain in the Southwest has nevertheless been enhanced by a large number of English translations of important documents or collections of documents, the origin of which is naturally Spanish. Also necessary in researching the Spanish period in the Southwest is the specialized effort involved in archival research in non-English materials. An early smalls volume that helped many students of the Southwest in their efforts to attain research skills was J. Villasana Haggard's *Handbook for Translators of Spanish Historical Documents* (Austin: University of Texas Press, 1941). Utilized for many years and helpful in standardizing translation efforts, it also imparted paleographic skills necessary to decipher difficult documents. More recently, Thomas C. Barnes, Thomas H. Naylor, and Charles W. Polzer have teamed up to produce *Northern New Spain: A Research Guide* (Tucson: University of Arizona Press, 1981). This handbook for researchers provides a guide to collections, a breakdown of archival sources both at home and abroad, information on paleography, weights, measures, coinage, racial terminology, Indian names, and a good bibliographical section on guides to archival collections.

Though some may claim that the abundance of southwestern study has made a far-off corner of Spain's colonial empire into one of the most studied parts of Latin America, there is still much to be done. The field offers seemingly inexhaustible possibilities. Furthermore, a study of the Southwest aims in great measure to enrich the comprehension of America's national heritage as well as illumine Spanish colonial history. The Spanish Southwest is an area where cultural pluralism is commonplace and where Cortés, Cabrillo, Coronado, Oñate, Vizcaíno, Kino, and Serra replace Pilgrims and Puritans, Quakers and Cavaliers as figures of primary importance in an aspect of national history that in its beginnings predates Jamestown and Plymouth Rock.

ABOUT THE COVER

The image of Santiago Matamoros (Moorslayer) on the cover is a seventeenth-century woodcarving of unknown origin from the Museo de Franz Meyer in Mexico City. According to Spanish legend, the body of Saint James the Apostle was discovered about A.D. 813 in an isolated valley in western Galicia. A hermit was directed to the spot by a bright light radiating from a star; therefore the saint became known as Saint James of the Starry Fields (Santo Iago de los Campos Stellae or Santiago de Compostela). The first battle in which the saint, galloping out of the clouds on a white stallion allegedly lent assistance to the Christians, was at Clavijo, when the Spaniards defeated the Moslems (collectively called Moors) in 844.

After that time, Pilgrims from all parts of western Europe began making their way along the road to the shrine of Santiago, a symbol of the *Reconquista*, Spain's eight-century fight against the Moors. The military/religious Order of Santiago, which became the largest and most prestigious of Spain's orders of knighthood, was founded in 1170, illustrating the close relationship between the church and the military. Soldiers took religious vows while monks, abbots, priests, and bishops joined armies and engaged in fighting. This phenomenon had important consequences in the New World.

There are thirteen well documented New World cases in which Santiago apparently intervened on behalf of Spaniards in combat. Nine episodes took place in New Spain and the one mentioned in this work occurred at the Battle of Acoma Pueblo in New Mexico in 1598. Although an Old World figure, Santiago continues to occupy an important place in the religious life of the Hispanic Southwest. There are a number of present-day *santeros* continuing the ancient tradition of hand-carving statues of a mounted Santiago. One of the prime examples is preserved in the Santuario de Chimayó north of Santa Fe where thousands of pilgrims travel annually during Holy Week. The feast of Santiago on July 25 is commemorated today in many villages throughout the Spanish Southwest.

THE LAND AND ITS PEOPLE

THE FIRST CONTACT

*F*ittingly, the documented history of Spain's quest for empire in the far Southwest begins with a dramatic moment that brought together for the first time local residents and Spanish explorers. Though the exact moment can never be determined, it was probably at some time in 1535. The Native American participants in that fateful encounter are unidentified, but the group of four aliens is well known to history. One man was Alvar Núñez Cabeza de Vaca, former treasurer of Pánfilo de Narváez's disastrous 1527 colonizing expedition to occupy Florida, and leader of the visitors. White companions were Alonso Castillo Maldonado and Andrés Dorantes, two more survivors of the Narváez fiasco. Cabeza de Vaca was also accompanied by a dark man, Esteban or Estevanico, a Moor from Azamor in North Africa and a slave of Dorantes, but by that time he had temporarily transcended his former status. All had survived the Spanish colonization debacle in Florida, and escaping from it, had washed ashore on the Texas coast.

By resourcefulness, good fortune, and application of clever psychology—particularly by Cabeza de Vaca—these men made their way generally westward and had obtained high status among the regional Indians. By the time of the first confrontation in the area under consideration here, the Cabeza de Vaca party was quite large and included Indian adherents who considered the Spanish leader to be a great medicine man and healer.

For the local Indians it was a new day. They had heard reports of the foreign itinerants, but now the Spaniards were visible in the flesh. The impact was obviously great, for even a half-century later these same Indians or their descendants told Spanish explorers the story of the long-remembered meeting. As far as the Spaniards of the 1530s were concerned, it was just another incident in an eight-year odyssey filled with far more exciting and dramatic events. Their long journey finally ended when in the spring of 1536, the barely recognizable travelers arrived at the northern Spanish outpost of Culiacán in Sinaloa.

Like many firsts, this occurrence did not lead to immediate action. Nevertheless, the reports made by Cabeza de Vaca set off the chain of events that altered life in the far Southwest, though they did so only slowly. This endeavor was just the prelude to more complete exploration culminating in the lengthy presence of Spain in the area—the focus of this story.

But what of the physical scene upon which coming events were to transpire? And what of the native people who were the non-Spanish actors on the mostly desert landscape?

GEOGRAPHIC ISOLATION

Difficult approaches by both land and sea created natural barriers that gave California and the southwestern region of the United States a distinct identity. Distance, desert, and mountain—factors of physical environment—separated the area from the mainstream of world travel. Common problems imposed by the area's geographic remoteness determined, in part, the culture of its aboriginal inhabitants and established the settlement pattern of its later colonizers. During its early history, California's cultural progress and economic development were conditioned primarily by its isolated position at the almost inaccessible edge of the North American continent. Arizona and New Mexico were equally difficult to reach because of difficult overland travel.

FEATURES OF CALIFORNIA'S LANDSCAPE

Nearly three-quarters of the total area of California is mountainous. Both Upper and Lower California lie along the Pacific Cordillera—a mountain belt extending from Cape Horn along the west coasts of both South and North America to Alaska, the Aleutian Islands, and even the Kamchatka Peninsula of the former Soviet Union. The mountains in the western part of California are mostly included within the Coast Ranges. Beginning with the Klamath Mountains of California's extreme northwest, they extend a thousand miles southeastward with slight interruption to the Peninsular Range, the backbone of Lower California. This narrow peninsula continues more than 700 miles southward, flanked on the east by the Gulf of California and by the Pacific Ocean on the west.

The uplifted Sierra Nevada dominates California's eastern side. Between the Coast Ranges and the Sierra Nevada is a fertile lowland—the 500-mile-long Central Valley, a prime agricultural area. California's northeastern corner is composed mainly of volcanic lava. Southern California is characterized by a diversity of regions, including the Mojave and Colorado Deserts, the Transverse and Peninsular Ranges, the Los Angeles Basin, the coastal plain, and a geologic depression known as the Salton Sink. Its desert region shares many similarities with Arizona and New Mexico. To the south, Baja California is a narrow appendage averaging sixty to seventy miles in width with its highest mountains and heaviest rainfall at either end. The region in the middle, dominated by the Vizcaino Desert, has but slight rainfall and is generally devoid of trees and springs, although the deep gorges contain scattered deposits of fertile soil.

Oceanic influences upon the Pacific Coast of California have been momentous. Prevailing westerly winds, low clouds known as *veloes*, and frequent fog all affected climate and became important sources of moisture for the land. The rivers emptying into the Pacific cut across the coastal plain and created the few natural harbors and fertile coastal valleys. Under Spain, interior inroads were made in Baja California, but only Alta California's coastal areas were occupied. Not until near the end of the Mexican period, in 1839, did people begin to move into the Central Valley. Communication by sea, moderate temperatures, and available, fertile land made living close to the ocean desirable.

Flora and Fauna

California's natural environment, varying considerably in rainfall from north to south, in fact greatly resembled the geographical conditions of the Iberian Peninsula. Originally California was one-fifth coniferous forest with needleleaf evergreens, especially redwoods, Douglas fir, and ponderosa-Jeffrey pines dominating the mountain regions. California's oak woodlands, coniferous woodlands (sagebrush interspersed with piñon pine and juniper bushes), and treeless grasslands were used by the Indians for food gathering and by Spaniards for grazing animals. The remainder of California—about 43 percent—was covered by chaparral (a collective name for manzanita, scrub oak, ceanoths, and chamise), sagebrush, and scattered desert shrubs of creosote, burroweed, and shadscale.

California's diversified physical environment and abundant natural resources that supported a dense Indian population also made possible a wide variety of fauna. Common among California's native animals were the black-tailed deer and muledeer, which frequented coastal and inland mountains, and the burro deer found along the Colorado River. Wapiti, usually called elk, big-horned mountain sheep, and prong-horned antelope roamed the northern mountainous areas in large herds. Native bears included the California grizzly, or golden bear and the California black bear of the Sierra Nevada. Valuable fur-bearing animals included beaver, muskrat, mink, otter, pine marten, wolverine, and sea otter. Other animals common to California's wilderness were jack rabbits, cottontail rabbits, gray squirrels, chipmunks, opossums, coyotes, badgers, raccoons, porcupines, weasels, and foxes.

Approximately 600 species of birds spend at least part of the year in California and thick flocks of duck and geese migrate from central Canada and the Far North. A thousand miles of coastline furnished feeding grounds for many shorebirds, which included snipes, sandpipers, seagulls, and rails. Common among upland birds were the California valley quail, desert quail, sooty or blue grouse, sage grouse, Pacific band-tailed pigeon, and western mourning dove. Predatory birds included eagles, hawks, owls, crows, magpies, ravens, jays, herons, and cormorants; California's songbirds numbered over 500 species.

Earthquakes

At the time of human arrival, California, geologically speaking, was quite young. Volcanic activity, fault movement with earthquakes, and high, immature mountains continued to be three surface manifestations of a continuing geologic process. California's location on the circum-Pacific seismic belt exposes it to 80 percent of the world's earthquakes, and approximately once a year the state experiences earthquakes of destructive magnitude. California's aboriginal inhabitants had some ideas about earthquakes. In Baja California, Indians told the Spanish missionaries that persons should not build walls over four feet high. If this were done, they said, a demon would shake the earth and knock down the wall. Other Indians thought that a giant tortoise supported the earth, and when the beast took a step, the earth trembled. When the first Spaniards traveled overland in California, they experienced earthquakes of frightening force but, in search of fertile agricultural lands with a nearby water supply, did not heed the Indians' warning about the fragile nature of the earth's crust. Ironically, several mission sites and subsequent settlements would be subjected to major earthquake damage in the years to come.

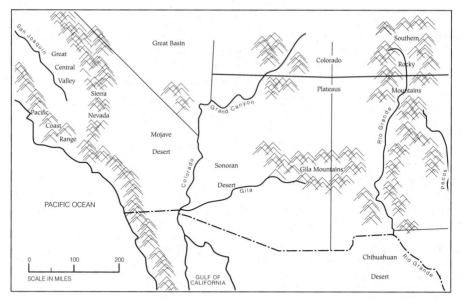

Map 1.1. Geographic features of the Southwest. Map by Stephanie Gould.

CALIFORNIA'S NAME

The name California originated from a popular Spanish romance of chivalry called *Las Sergas* (exploits) *de Esplandían* that inspired the early explorers. Written by García Ordóñez de Montalvo shortly after the voyages of Columbus, one portion featured a fanciful island called California, presumed to be located very near the terrestrial paradise. Published perhaps as early as 1508, *Las Sergas* enjoyed widespread popularity, running into several editions to describe the many adventures of its knightly hero, Esplandían. A kind of early-day "paperback," the book was available in Seville to soldiers and sailors embarking for the New World, and could also easily be obtained in Mexico City by explorers on the Pacific Coast. In chapter 157 of *Las Sergas,* Ordóñez explained how the Christians at Constantinople were forced to oppose the "frightful and unexpected help" given to the Turks by Queen Calafia and her Amazon troops from the island of California. No doubt the name was taken from that fictitious island.

GEOGRAPHY OF ARIZONA

Arizona, the northern portion of New Spain's province of Sonora during Hispanic times, became a part of the United States in 1846, though this sparsely populated territory was not admitted to the Union as a state until 1912. Its name was derived from a silver mining region called Arizonac. The state, which is the sixth largest in the United States, measures 392 miles from north to south and 338 miles from east to west at its widest point, containing 113,956 square miles of land. It is today bordered on the east by New Mexico, on the north by Utah, on the northwest by Nevada, on the west by California, and on the south by the Mexican state of Sonora.

Because of Arizona's location—isolated from settled areas by deserts, deep canyons, and high mountains—it developed slowly during the Hispanic and early American periods, essentially from 1540 to 1900. Nevertheless, the area was inhabited by a considerable number and variety of Native Americans during pre-Hispanic times. Descendants of these native inhabitants continue to reside in Arizona.

Arizona contains two major physiographic provinces with a transitional zone in between. To the south is the Basin and Range Province that contains the Sonoran Desert. Often called the Lower Desert, it stretches as a giant, imperfect crescent northwest to southeast, straddling Arizona's border with Mexico and reaching more than halfway along the Colorado River border with California and Nevada. Its upland portion is the heart of Arizona, where the majority of its wealth and population is concentrated. This area houses the two largest metropolitan areas, Phoenix and Tucson, as well as most of the state's major mines, industries, and agriculture. The Basin and Range Province has been divided further into the Mexican Highland section to the east and the Mojave Section to the northwest.

Fitting into the concave portion of that crescent, likewise oriented northwest to southeast, is the Colorado Plateau Province. Geographers sometimes distinguish a separate third area called the Intermontane Province, a tumbled, mountainous segment that ranges in altitude from 3,000 to 5,500 feet, is forested by ponderosa pine, which is transitional geologically as well as in flora and fauna. It marks the crumbling-off of the higher Colorado Plateau Province that rises from about 5,500 feet altitude to 9,000 feet and stretches northward to near the Continental Divide at the Four Corners where Utah, Colorado, and New Mexico join Arizona, and stretches westward to the edge of the Great Basin in southern Utah. The Colorado Plateau Province has been divided into the Navajo Section, containing the Painted Desert and Petrified Forest, the Grand Canyon Section, the Flagstaff Section, and the Tonto Section. The Tonto Section, which is separated by the Mogollon Rim from the north, contains the transitional intermontane region.

Water Resources

In terms of rainfall, Arizona is a desert, lying squarely within the arid designation of fewer than twenty inches of rainfall a year (except for a few isolated areas and mountain peaks). Twenty inches of rain is the accepted borderline between desert and temperate lands; with that much or more, crops will grow to maturity with regularity. Although an arid land, Arizona has a well-defined river system, even though fewer than a dozen of its rivers flow the year around. Most contain water only after torrential thunderstorms of summer or gentle winter rains; nevertheless they are rivers that define avenues of travel, cultivated crops, and habitable places.

Over 90 percent of Arizona's land area eventually drains into the Colorado River and then into Mexico to the Gulf of California, or Mar de Cortés, some eighty miles south of Yuma. The major internal river system in Arizona—the Gila—bisects the Lower Desert as it runs almost directly from east to west to its confluence with the Colorado River at Yuma, where it begins to flow southward to the gulf. The Gila River rises in the mountains of western New Mexico; on its left or southern bank, as it meanders slowly toward the west, it is fed by the San Simon, the Santa Cruz, and a small, constant flow from the San Pedro. All three of these rivers enter into Arizona from Mexico, flowing first northward to the immense alluvial trough through which the Gila moves westward.

From northern and higher mountains the Gila accumulates the bulk of its flow, in turn taking in the San Francisco River near the New Mexico border; then the San Carlos, coming quickly out of mountains in eastern Arizona; Mineral Creek, and finally, west of Phoenix, the Gila joins up with the Salt River, which is a larger stream than its parent. The Salt is formed of the White and Black rivers in the snow-covered White Mountains, picks up additions from Carrizo, Cherry, and Tonto creeks, and then adds the healthy Verde River thirty miles east of Phoenix. Together this system drains about a third of Arizona, meeting domestic, industrial, and irrigation demands of the great Salt River Valley, population center of the state. During the Hispanic period, the Gila, especially after its confluence with the Salt, was a respectable river, filled with fish and beaver, a dependable highway and route of exploration and conquest in the great westward flow of population to the Pacific shores.

Midway up Arizona's western boundary in the northwest corner of the Sonoran Desert, the combined flow of the intermittent Big Sandy and Santa Maria rivers—neither ever more than a mere trickle except in the rainy season—forms the Bill Williams Fork (not a river), which formerly emptied into the Colorado.

One other river of some consequence in the Arizona system drains the portion of the Colorado Plateau south of the Grand Canyon that slopes northward away from the Mogollon Rim and the heights of the White Mountains. The Little Colorado River trickles off the north and east slopes of that range, gathering water from tiny creeks such as the Puerco River and Zuni River to flow northwestward to join the great Colorado in the middle of the Grand Canyon. There the Little Colorado dumps its muddy waters into the clear, cold main stream.

Sonoran Desert

The Sonoran Desert, numbered among the dozen largest deserts in the world, is divided into seven regions, although only two—the Lower Colorado Valley and the Arizona Upland—are found in Arizona. The other regions are in Sonora or Baja California, Mexico. The Sonoran is an arboreal desert, characterized by a variety of trees and sturdy plants rooted deeply to take advantage of the torrential summer rains and the more gentle winter rainfall.

Indians who inhabited the Sonoran Desert made use of some 100 trees, plants, and grasses that yielded them food in some form. The most dependable desert food source in Arizona is the sugary seedpod of the mesquite, which gave the Pápago (bean-eater) Indians their name. Desert plants have little exposure above ground but have extensive root systems much larger than the visible foliage. Root systems reach far down for water, storing a reserve supply within underground stems or above the ground under waxy covers, safe from searing heat and evaporation. Some cactus varieties—the saguaro and organ-pipe types especially—have accordion-style trunks that are in effect expandable tanks of pulp filled with water to tide them over dry spells. Where water is more abundant, the desert growth multiplies, and with it the number of animals who make their living in austere surroundings.

NEW MEXICO GEOGRAPHY

Topographically, New Mexico drains from north to south, from high upland mountains and plateaus with elevations up to 12,000 feet to the minimum elevations along the southern (Texas) border at 3,100 feet. The topography is superficially simple with two almost parallel streams, the Río Grande and the Pecos, leading southward. To the west is the Continental Divide, an important, but at times almost imperceptible watershed line that divides the waters that reach the Pacific Ocean from those which end in the Atlantic via its tributary bodies of water. The divide, much closer to the former than to the latter ocean, is the spine of the Western Hemisphere, reaching majestic heights in the Andes of South America, the Sierra Madre Oriental of Mexico, and the Rockies of the United States and Canada. However, the divide breaks down considerably in western New Mexico, forming a geological flattening that had historical significance by making the continent easier to cross in that area. About one-third or about 30,000 square miles of the Llano Estacado or staked plains lies in eastern New Mexico.

Water Resources

The major rivers of New Mexico are the Río Grande, Pecos, Canadian, San Juan, and Gila. The Río Grande travels approximately 1,800 miles from its source in southwestern Colorado flowing southward across New Mexico and forming the southern boundary of Texas from El Paso to the Gulf. The Pecos River runs roughly parallel and to the east of the Río Grande through New Mexico and joins the Río Grande after it turns to the southeast in Texas. The Canadian arises in the Sangre de Cristo Range and flows east into Texas, cutting a deep gorge in the High Plains region. The San Juan flows southwest from Colorado and then westward along the northern border of New Mexico into Arizona and the Colorado River. Finally, the Gila rises in the Mogollon and Black Range Mountains and flows in a southwesterly direction into and across Arizona, joining the Colorado near Yuma.

Climate and Rainfall

Both great distance from either ocean and lack of appreciable bodies of standing water have influenced regional rainfall and climate. Rainfall is deficient and what does come is usually late in the year and therefore less valuable. This lack is compensated for by the annual snowpack in the upper elevations which, when melting, provides an important source of water. Historically its paucity has made water a transcendental element and its use and control have been the subject of concern from pre-colonial times. The Indians, particularly the Pueblos, had already developed agricultural expertise, but contact with the Spanish settlers resulted in increased need to share, store, and distribute this precious resource.

Boundaries

New Mexico has undergone various geographical changes, and though we generally restrict it to today's nearly rectangular boundaries, it was not always that shape. As an indefinite place name, the ill-defined area was first called Nuevo Mexico in a document written in 1561 by Franciscan Father Jacinto de San Francisco. The circumstances surrounding his use of Nuevo Mexico indicates it as an already established toponym, but just what the area included and since when it had been so known will probably never be determined. Application of the name seems to have been in hopeful anticipation of finding another Mexico, a second center of high culture duplicating the earlier find by Cortés and his men. It probably specifically referred to the relatively high culture area of the Pueblo Indians located well upstream on the Río Grande.

By the time of Spanish occupation the name was well established, though the limits were not. In the beginning, the amorphous boundaries were as unknown as the great *tierra incognita* in which the area lay. Following occupation there were no known borders except to the south where Nueva Vizcaya's jurisdiction ended. New Mexico, for practical administrative purposes was the area along the Río Grande with its headquarters first at San Juan de los Caballeros, and next at nearby San Gabriel de Chama; both locations were in what later became known as the Río Arriba. By 1610, the capital was moved for a final time to the newly founded Villa de Santa Fe to the southeast.

Over time, New Mexico expanded and contracted both its effective and its theoretical boundaries. At its greatest, it embraced the land as far west as California and as far east as Texas and even French Louisiana. To the south the boundary fluctuated between just north of the Río Grande crossing at El Paso to just south of that key spot. But to the north, New Mexico was seemingly limitless, at least on paper.

Colonial period development of Sonora, which embraced much of what is today Arizona, coupled with later political decisions that occurred after the Southwest became part of the United States, changed and gradually reduced the size of New Mexico. Arizona became a separate state, while El Paso (then called Franklin) was to become part of Texas. New Mexico was further limited by the creation of the state of Colorado when the occupied northern portion of the former was detached. When that embryonic neighboring state lacked sufficient population for admission to the Union, a substantial, overwhelmingly Spanish-speaking southern area was added to the Centennial State and the boundary between New Mexico Territory and Colorado was set at the 37th parallel. Since 1876, there have been no northern territorial changes and New Mexico has assumed its present northern boundary.

INDIAN MIGRATION

Archaeologists generally agree that proto-Asiatic people first migrated into the Western Hemisphere across the Bering Strait from Siberia to Alaska sometime between 50,000 and 20,000 B.C. Following large game, they took advantage of the natural bridge between the land masses created at different periods during the Ice Age. They continued southward from the Arctic Ocean through Canada, some branching off eastward of the Rocky Mountains and others, between 12,000 and 9000 B.C. continuing to California along the Pacific Coast. These Indians were probably organized into bands of a few extended families that numbered fewer than fifty people. In the earlier period, they relied heavily on large game for food, but by 3000 B.C. Indians had diversified and were utilizing a variety of plant and marine life. This led to a population increase and settlement in permanent villages.

After 3000 B.C., other economic changes took place and the archeological remains of mortars, pestles, grinding stones, and mullers indicate that Indians then relied more heavily upon plant sources. By the time of European contact, the population of Upper California is estimated to have reached somewhere between 135,000 and 350,000. They spoke some 135 different dialects that have been organized into six major linguistic groups: Algonkian, Athapascan, Penutian, Hokan, Ute-Aztecan, and Yukian. Approximately 13,000 to 60,000 Baja California Indians belonged to three major families—the Guaycura and Pericu, not related to each other or any mainland family, and the Cochimí, an ancient division of the Yuman group of Hokan-speaking native. During the pre-contact period, sometime between 2000 and 1000 B.C., a native group of cave-painting dwellers lived in the mountainous areas of the mid peninsula. Although their brilliantly executed murals were familiar to the Cochimí of the later period, none of the Indians knew anything about these prehistoric artists.

CALIFORNIA INDIAN CULTURES

Perhaps the easiest way to understand the Indians of California is through their culture or manner of living. This lifestyle directly reflected the potential food supply, climate, terrain, and availability of water. Though primarily hunters and gatherers, some practiced a form of proto-agriculture, which included environmental manipulation to the extent of scattering wild seeds, flooding certain areas, pruning or breaking of branches, or burning native vegetation to encourage growth of wild grasses. By the sixteenth century, even though they lacked the wheel or beasts of burden, the Indians had taken advantage of their environment and utilized effectively certain natural resources. They excelled in basket weaving, boat construction, the making of moccasins and sandals, preparation of animal skins for blankets and winter wear, and production of vegetable fibers for garments and other uses. The rendering of acorns as healthful food supply was also a highly developed skill involving the removal of the poisonous tannic acid. Acorn eating was probably the most characteristic feature of the domestic economy in the pre-contact period.

THE DESERT COCHISE PEOPLE

Beginning about 5000 B.C. the Cochise Culture was the best representative of the Southwestern Desert Culture. While the earliest of these people knew and hunted the now-extinct animals, the eventual loss of the big game forced them to turn to smaller quarry, the animals of today. They also turned to a greater dependence upon plants for sustenance. Adapting their way of life initially to gathering, they developed appropriate stone tools for collecting and preparing vegetal foods. Campsites of this period have produced large quantities of such tools; among these was the functionally related pair of grinding stones that served as the prototype of the mano and metate associated with the farming societies of later times.

The Cochise people eventually turned to intensive agricultural endeavors around 3000 B.C. as primitive forms of corn, or maize, and other new food crops were introduced from cultures to the south. Because corn does not reseed itself but must be planted and tended, these desert dwellers began also to restrict their nomadic ways; sedentary life was dictated by the length of the growing season. The desert supported a two-crop maize economy, so from the time corn seeds were planted in the early spring or late summer until harvest, animals attracted by growing plants—rabbits, rats, go-phers, deer, and others—had to be frightened away or were killed to add flavor and some protein to the mass of vegetables and carbohydrates eaten. The capacity to store surplus food was also essential to the success of the system. At this time, two other vegetal plants—squash and beans—were introduced to enrich and stabilize the economy, and the natives remained sedentary.

THE HOHOKAM CULTURE

The Hohokam Culture, based almost exclusively on irrigated agriculture, evolved in the Sonoran Desert area. Traces of an extensive network of irrigation canals have been found along the Salt and Gila Rivers near Phoenix, and some of these canals match modern ones in size. No Indian achievement north of Mexico surpasses the Hohokam canal system for planned expenditure of effort and for the inter-community effort that produced it. These people were master-farmers, producing via water control corn, beans, squash, and cotton in an arid land. In fact, their irrigation system may have existed as early as 300 B.C.

By developing such an intricate system of canals, the Hohokams were able to choose the location of their villages. Hundreds of people lived at a settlement called Los Muertos that was six miles from the Salt River and sustained by a thin lifeline of a canal. In other areas, far from live streams, control of the surface runoff was the key to successful living. Gathering ditches cut across numerous small natural drainages on mountain slopes, collected the water, and directed it to fertile ground. In the early summer, be-fore the corn was ripe, most of the able-bodied Hohokams trekked to the mountains rimming the desert to harvest the maguey, the plant that produces pulque and tequila in Mexico. Its sugar-laden flowering heart was harvested and roasted to the consistency of preserves to provide a food staple for colder months of the year and for times of low-yield irrigated crops.

The River Hohokams developed their sophisticated system of water diversion and delivery working only with stone hoes and tools of wood and bone. Nevertheless, their bountiful crops provided more leisure time for creative endeavors than was possible among other groups, and they had abundant animals to fill their cooking pots. The Desert Hohokams created decorated pottery and fine basketry; etched shells with fruit acid; built semipermanent homes; made attractive mosaic and turquoise ornaments, beads and other personal decorations; and crafted mirrors and cosmetic palettes. They constructed ball courts similar to those in Mesoamerica, and evolved a social system with separate warrior groups trained for and capable of repelling the thrusts of the aggressive Athapascan raids.

THE MOGOLLON CULTURE

Occupying an area to the east as far as the Río Grande Valley in New Mexico and to the northwest in west-central Arizona where origins of the Verde River mark the west-ern limits of the Mogollon Rim, this mountain-midland province came to support a modified lifestyle called the Mogollon Culture. It was developed by migratory desert dwellers who readily borrowed cultural elements from other peoples they contacted to the east, west, and north. This culture occupied roughly the 10,000 years of evolution and human expansion between the origins of the Cochise people and the classic period of the River Hohokams who dominated the Sonoran Desert after the introduction of maize, beans, squash, and pottery several centuries before the dawn of Christianity. The Desert Culture was followed in time by the Mogollon Culture, with migratory bands from both of these life-styles gradually moving up onto the Colorado Plateau where they would develop the Anasazi Culture.

Fig. 1.1. View from Acoma Pueblo. Photo by Iris Engstrand.

The Mogollons made their greatest contribution to human progress in the desert with architecture. Improving vastly upon the very simple and temporary circular pithouses of Cochise people and the Desert Hohokams, the Mogollons began building clusters of dwellings of a more permanent nature. They began scooping out pits several feet deep, piling dirt around walls reinforced with heavy poles instead of flimsy brush. A strong centered pole supported a conical roof. Permanent firepits and then storage bins and pits were added, where surplus supplies of food could be stored in jars and baskets, to relieving the Mogollons of the need to seek food during the harsh days of winter. That time instead could be devoted to improving their skills in tanning hides, basketry, and pottery arts; it could also be used for religious ceremonials.

By deepening and enlarging pithouses for ceremonial purposes, the Mogollons created the first *kivas,* or underground religious centers, in the Southwest. Humans had learned to survive by storing the surplus of crops and had constructed proper facilities for expression of their religious faith and aspirations. The material goods of the Mogollon culture were mostly rough tools of stone, tips for arrows, metates for grinding corn, thin rock slabs for tilling the soil, small stone bowls for pulverizing pigments, and similar items. The people excelled at producing a tubular stone pipe and, after A.D. 700 wore cloth of cotton.

THE ANASAZI CULTURE

Between 5000 B.C. and A.D. 1400, the Colorado Plateau supported the dynamic Anasazi Culture. The Navajos provided that name, meaning "ancient ones," for the early basket-maker and pueblo people who inhabited the enormous rocky province that stretches across northern Arizona, Utah, New Mexico, and southern Colorado.

Its cultural epicenter is located near an area called "Four Corners," the only place in the United States where four states' borders come together: Utah, Colorado, New

Mexico, and Arizona. The heartland of Anasazi achievement was in the drainage basin of the San Juan River, slightly east of Four Corners, with two concentrations of amazing size and sophistication. One was at Pueblo Bonito in the Chaco Canyon area of northwestern New Mexico and contiguously around the Mesa Verde cliff dwellings in southwestern Colorado. The second, in Arizona, had slightly less imposing structures and population concentrations in Canyon de Chelly and in the Tsegi Canyon-Kayenta area with the dramatic Inscription House, Keet Seel, and Betatakin sites. The earliest phase of Anasazi tradition is described by anthropologists as Basket Maker, in tribute to the excellence and variety of woven and plaited items created by these people, as opposed to the pottery that neighbors were making.

By about A.D. 600, cotton cloth appeared in the area and the Anasazi moved out of the caves in which they first found shelter. They built crude, shallow pithouses, frequently roofed with a combination of logs and mud mortar, easily recognizable as an introductory phase of the mud-and-log dwellings of the Navajos (the Anasazis' successors as principal residents of the Colorado Plateau). These early Basket Makers began building dwellings closer to fields of flint corn, and later beans and squash and perhaps cotton, planted in deep alluvial valleys that had been created by the timeless erosion of soft sandstone of the plateau. In time, some of these buildings were deepened and lined with masonry, becoming centers for communal affairs and progressively religious ceremonial chambers similar to those the Mogollons also were developing. These were the first kivas of the pueblos, the urban communities created as the Anasazis conjoined homes into extensive apartment structures. In some cases, pueblos covered several acres and included housing facilities for thousands of persons. With this remarkable and creative lifestyle, the Anasazis entered the second aspect of their rich tradition. Their culture, dating from about A.D. 800 has been designated the Pueblo tradition, *pueblo* being the Spanish name for town.

Developing great skill as masons, the Anasazi added contiguous rooms to dwellings and kivas until their multistoried apartment and plaza compounds had grown into small cities. Along with architectural achievements, they became pottery makers of remarkable decorative and utilitarian skill. Anasazi Culture encompassed a vast area east of the Colorado Plateau, occupying much of the middle and upper Río Grande Valley, and in Arizona spread southward over the ebbing Mogollon world. Branches of the Anasazis who lived along the Little Colorado River and blended with Mogollon, Hohokam, and Pueblo Cultures were identified as the Sinagua and Salado Cultures. They were to reach into the Sonoran Desert to be absorbed or interwoven with the late River Hohokam Culture.

In the late thirteenth century, the great Anasazi Culture declined, though the reasons for its demise remain unclear. Drought and internal epidemics are cited; the complacency and eventual nonproduction resulting from cultural superiority have also been advanced as possible contributory causes. The dynamic and vibrant Anasazi Culture flourished for several centuries, leaving elaborate ruins as monuments beyond the mortal span of human life. Even before severe drought swept over the Southwest in the last quarter of the thirteenth century, some Anasazi sites had been vacated. The lack of rain is given as another major cause of decline of all three cultures in Arizona during that era. An additional factor contributing to the dislocation and diffusion of the Anasazi and also the Mogollon cultural patterns was the gradual impact of a vast migration of hunting newcomers from the north and east, threatening rather than destroying the sedentary villagers and their fields. Some anthropologists believe that the first intruders were Shoshoneans from farther north in the Rocky Mountains. As the newcomers advanced, many Anasazis and Mogollons moved away, entire villages trekking eastward to resettle in the Río Grande Valley. Others found mountains and mesalands easily defensible, and became entrenched as enduring pueblo communities of Acoma, Zuni, and Hopi; isolated enclaves of Anasazi people becoming in time the modern Pueblo culture of great virtue and surpassing artistic skills, often said to be the epitome of all Native American achievement.

Newcomers to the Desert

Whether or not Shoshoneans (also called Ute-Aztecans) began the devastating invasion, the occupation of Arizona north of the Gila and east of its union with the Salt was to be fulfilled in the sixteenth century by bands of Athapascan hunters. These people had arrived in North America many thousands of years after the primary immigration of humans across the Bering land bridge during the waning Ice Age. Archeological discoveries along the Aleutian Islands suggest that this final great migration from Asia may have been accomplished by island-hoppers who, upon reaching the North American mainland, moved down into the Athapascan Valley of the Canadian Rockies before flooding onto the Upper Great Plains. Eventually they migrated southward in the buffalo country east of the Rocky Mountains and stayed there until overwhelming resistance from other migrants, possibly the Comanches of the Upper Plains, turned them westward across the backbone of the continent.

These newcomers, who swept over the remaining Anasazis and Mogollons and their Sinagua and Salado subcultures, were eventually to become the Apaches and the Navajos. In fact, the Athapascan language used by people in British Colombia is close to that spoken by these two interrelated groups of the Southwest with only slight dialectic differences, reflecting a common root of language and culture.

Ultimately, Mogollon Culture lost its separate identity, yielding to intrusions and finally disappearing entirely two centuries before the arrival of the Spaniards. To the north, the Anasazi Basket Maker culture had gradually grown into the monumental Pueblo period, whose enduring qualities and architectural style survive in many places. Meanwhile, to the south and west the River Hohokams were achieving the highest level of prehistoric progress in Arizona, even though they had not learned to make metal tools. Nevertheless, some relatively advanced bands in Mexico manufactured and traded into Arizona small copper bells, whose presence in ruins gave rise to a belief that Arizona copper deposits were mined in pre-Columbian times. The natives did dig for some turquoise and sulfites, but only for ornamental and cosmetic uses, not for smelting and making tools. The only domestic animals raised by Native Americans in Arizona were dogs and turkeys, both food items. The wheel was unknown. The bow-and-arrow was the most advanced weaponry; no metal existed to ease the struggle for existence.

The center of Arizona population today is in the Salt River Valley, just as it was in prehistoric days before the arrival of the Athapascans and Europeans. The valley was and is such a center because here, near the confluence of the Salt, Gila, and Verde Rivers, fertile soil and a dependable water supply are brought together under the life-giving sun.

When Salado bands moved southward from the Anasazi region, bringing more sophisticated pottery designs and architectural skills that resulted in great buildings such as Casa Grande and Pueblo Grande, the Hohokams absorbed these newcomers without disastrous conflict. The Hohokams evidently continued their custom of cremating their dead, while the newcomers practiced inhumation (to the confusion at times of present-day archeologists who find Salado and Hohokam material intermingled). Now totally eradicated by suburban dwellings, their largest urban center was Los Muertos, stretching several miles south and southeast of the modern city of Tempe. As at Los Muertos, much of the early farming and older residential sections of Phoenix were built on the ruins of similar Hohokam canal systems and colonies. The Casa Grande, most impressive of Hohokam-Salado structures, stands on the south bank of the Gila, about twenty-five miles east of Snaketown. Pueblo Grande, a house structure eclipsed in size and grandeur only by Casa Grande, stands guard over a Hohokam complex that includes the Park of the Four Waters, one of several remaining sections of canals constructed by the Hohokams with their stone hoes and carrying baskets.

This great farming center thrived for a thousand years, but was abandoned in the late thirteenth century, possibly the result of a devastating drought that swept the Southwest. Whatever the case, the ancient Hohokams departed. Archeologists believe they merely moved out of the Salt River drainage into the Gila River Valley, and that their skills have been preserved by the friendly Pima Indians who were living there when the first Europeans arrived. By the time the early Spaniards arrived in the mid-1500s and early 1600s, however, the local Indians apparently knew nothing of the people who had built the great structures like Casa Grande or the amazing cliff dwellings.

INDIANS OF THE HISPANIC PERIOD

While archeologists cannot agree on the arrival date of the Athapascans—estimates range from the tenth to the sixteenth century—the catastrophic impact of their takeover is unquestionable. The Athapascans, divided into numerous small Navajo and Apache family bands reaching from Four Corners to Mexico, dominated the eastern half of Arizona and New Mexico. Their only unity was in language and the commonalty of a nomadic, raiding culture with little in the way of fine arts but with advanced skills in martial pursuits. They had by the sixteenth century forced older groups into settlement patterns that have been modified little through succeeding centuries. People generally believed to be descendants of the Hohokams, largely the peaceful Pápagos and Pimas, occupied the Lower Desert and river valleys. The Desert Hohokams are thought to have become the Pápagos, and the River Hohokams, the Pimas.

The semi-nomadic desert people encountered by the first missionaries as they entered northern New Spain in the region of Sonora and southern Arizona were called *pavi au'autam* or "bean-eating people." This was transformed into Pápago by the Jesu-

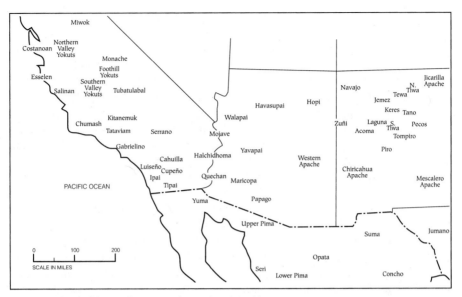

Map 1.2. Indians of the Southwest. Map by Stephanie Gould.

its, a designation that was used throughout the Spanish period. These people, who lived in the area that became known as the Papaguería, called themselves Tohono O'odham, the Desert or Thirsty people, to distinguish themselves from the Pimas, who were called 'Akimel O'odham, or River People. The O'odham or Pápagos belonged to the Piman language family of the Sonoran division of the Ute-Aztecan language.

Along the Colorado River were tribes of possibly earlier origin—at least, they spoke dialects of Ute-Aztecan derivation—believed to have come out Mesoamerica prior to the Hohokams. There were the Cocopahs, living near the mouth of the Colorado River, the Quechans or Yumans near the confluence of the Gila with the Colorado, and the Chemehuevis and Mojaves, sharing the middle portion of the western river boundary. To the east were the Cocomaricopas and farther north, near the big bend where the Colorado emerges from the Grand Canyon and turns south, were scattered bands of Havasupai and impoverished Paiutes, closely related to inhabitants of the Great Basin. The lifestyles of these people living along the Colorado River had not changed greatly from either the meager economy of the Cochise or the earliest patterns of desert dwellers from which the more progressive Mogollon and Hohokam cultures also developed.

Life was very simple for these people, depending basically upon gathering, with a rudimentary agriculture in the river floodplains. In the center of Arizona's vast desert and stretching toward the Colorado River were the Yavapai and Walapai (Hualapai) peoples, also living by a combination of hunting-and-gathering patterns virtually unchanged by the centuries. Slightly to the southeast were the Mojave.

Agriculture, supplemented by gathering and the little hunting possible in an arid land, was the mainstay of human survival in this region. Along the southern river valleys, farming progressed with meritorious engineering skill. Brush dams, canals, and well-tended irrigation patterns produced bountiful crops of corn, squash, beans, and cotton. Along the Colorado River and on scattered patches of ground in many areas the inhabitants simply poked seeds into wet soil after spring rains or floods, relying upon water absorbed by the earth to bring their plantings to maturity. Variations in the river's flow, however, made such cropping patterns unpredictable, and frequently resulted in deprivation and starvation, or equally destructive raids upon neighbors.

The Athapascans and western desert people lived very much as the desert dwellers had when they emerged from the original lifestyle of the Cochise people. They erected temporary brush huts and moved in small bands in a repetitious seasonal pattern, usually in a prescribed and restricted area, gathering roots, seeds, fruit and nuts, and trapping or shooting animals that lived in the varied environments of different altitudes. Once corn was established as the basic food staple, even wandering bands would plant tiny fields at some fertile spot, returning after a few months of gathering wild plants to harvest the corn, if it had not already been consumed by deer, antelope, or rabbits and other rodents. These little hidden patches of corn and the early summer migration of both mountain and river-valley residents to the flowering maguey forests on the slopes of the midland mountains, brought the bands into competition for food and often conflict over women and children sought as mates and slaves. Seasonal raiding excursions by mountain people to the river valleys at harvest time also destroyed peace in the land. The farming people defended their crops and habitations so vigorously that the Apaches came to characterize the Hohokams and their Pima and Pápago descendants as fierce warriors, although these people when encountered by entering Europeans were described as gentle and peaceable.

THE PIMA CULTURE: MODERN DESCENDANTS

When the written record for the modern Pimas begins, they occupied at least seven *rancherías* separated from each other by distances of from ten to nearly forty miles. Theirs was a digging-stick economy, like that of the rest of the Pimans, relying on irrigation with the waters of the Gila, the Salt, and the Santa Cruz. Diversion dams of logs and brush were built in the Gila River and an extensive system of canals and feeders distributed the water to fields.

These peaceful, agricultural Pimas, who lived in mud-plastered, woven-stick houses along the Gila, Santa Cruz, and San Pedro Rivers, were the first to come into contact with the Jesuit missionaries sent by Spain. Although friendly, they were the most aggressive, no doubt because they frequently had to repel Apache raids. West of them were the people whom the Spaniards called Pimas Gileños. To the southwest, in the desert, lived the Pápagos, closely related but living in a more primitive fashion, because of the lack of irrigation water in their country. The Pimas traded with the Pápagos for commodities scarce in their homeland such as mescal and chiltipiquines, a small wild pepper much used for seasoning in the Southwest.

Gathered wild plants were an important source of supplementary or emergency food. Hunting was of less importance, with deer being the largest game taken, although mountain sheep may have been important in pre-historic times. Rabbits were the animals most frequently sought. Fishing, usually with nets, provided additional animal protein but evidently was not regularly practiced at all settlements. Exploitation of those resources, as

well as war-making and religious requirements (wood for bows and hawk and eagle
chicks for ritual paraphernalia and observances), led the Pimas to travel beyond the
river valleys on the bajadas and the slopes
leading up to the mountains, even in the face
of possible danger from raiders.

Pima settlements were largely self-sufficient economically and politically. Each
settlement had a civil leader and one or more
shamans. Each shaman was credited with
only one specialty, with different shamans
being consulted for curing, control over
weather, or promotion of success in war. The
basic unit of social structure was the patri-
lineal extended family, composed of a couple
(or surviving member), married sons, and
unmarried daughters. Social organization
above the family level included clans organized into moieties, but their function had
become obscured or forgotten, or was perhaps concealed from the investigators when

Fig. 1.2. Tohono O'odham woman with Ollas
(Papago). Courtesy Arizona Historical Society/
Tucson. 13803.

inquiries about them finally came to be made. Because clan affiliation descended in the
male line, children of non-Pima fathers did not acquire it; hence it at least served a kind
of legitimizing function. A form of ritual kinship similar to the Spanish *compadrazgo*
also united the individual with a group beyond the family, but there was no evidence of
age-grading or rites of passage except possibly a puberty ceremony. A couple getting
married simply took up residence together; and divorce and remarriage were equally
informal. Ideally, parents were supposed to arrange marriages for their children, but in
practice considerable liberty of choice was allowed. Consanguinity was reckoned over
five generations, thus providing a set of incest rules.

In summation, at the beginning of their recorded history, the Pimas lived in a
loosely organized society, with an economy that was stable when compared with the
hunters and gatherers around them and that was capable of providing them with surpluses. They were on amicable terms with the Pápagos to the south but, because they
were allied with the Yuman peoples called Cocomaricopas who lived nearby on the
Gila and Salt Rivers, the Pimas were at odds with other Yumans, notably the Quechan
of the Colorado and the Yavapais. Pima surpluses were already attracting the attention
of the Apaches to the east adding another pressure to Pima life; still there had not yet
developed the tensions among Pima communities that were to come later.

OTHER NATIVE GROUPS IN THE SOUTHWEST

Another group of Native Americans encountered by the first Spaniards occupied
the area not far from the picturesque Canyon de Chelly. In historic times at least, the town

builders of this part of Arizona were mostly Hopis, belonging to the Shoshonean (Ute-Aztecan) language group of North American Indians. Apparently they too were the victims of some great drought or other disaster. Therefore, like other Pueblo tribes of southwestern Colorado and northern New Mexico, they retreated from larger towns in the arid plains to build on mesas and other uplands, where springs supplied them with water for their crops. Some of these peoples even may have rendered their former holdings worthless by cutting down the timber, thus reducing the soil moisture and encouraging erosion. Then again, hostile tribes may have driven them to more secluded and more easily defended townsites. Oraibi, Montezuma's Castle, and others are all mesa or cliff towns which indicate the struggle of Indian farmers to survive in spite of both climatic and human foes.

West of the Pima tribes were the Cocomaricopas, who spoke a Yuman dialect, and at the mouth of the Gila and along the Colorado were the Yumas proper. Farther north were the Mojaves, also of Yuman stock, and on up the Colorado and its tributaries were the Yuman Hualpais, Havasupais, Chemehuevis, and Yavapais. The Navajos and Apaches, both speaking Athapascan languages, ranged over the northeast corner and the southeastern one-third of the state respectively. They closely resembled each other in appearance as well as in speech, and were undoubtedly once a single people. When and why they split up is unknown, but a Navajo word *Apachu* (meaning enemy or robber) hints that the separation was not a friendly matter. The Navajos in early days apparently occupied the same region as they do now—that is, northeastern Arizona and northwestern New Mexico. The first European traders knew them as not only clever thieves and bold, crafty fighters, but also as keen traders. In fact, some anthropologists believe that the acquisitive Navajos became separated from the Apaches chiefly because they appreciated the advantages of permanent property more than their cousins did.

At the time when white men first encountered the Apaches, these Native Americans were engaged in driving the more sedentary Sobaipuris, who spoke a Piman language, out of southeastern Arizona. Consistently nomadic, the Apaches lived mostly by hunting. Like other wandering tribes of the Southwest, they supplemented their diet with mesquite beans, acorns, pitaya, and grass seeds of various kinds, although they seldom took the trouble to cultivate any of these as permanent sources of food. There were a number of Apache tribes, divided more by geography than by dialect or appearance. Five of these roamed over parts of Arizona, which formed the western limits of a range originally extending as far east as central Texas. The Chiricahuas occupied the southeastern corner of the state as well as southwestern New Mexico, Sonora and Chihuahua. The Tonto, Coyotero, San Carlos, and Cibecue groups were mostly to be found in the mountains farther north. Like other Apaches, those of Arizona lived in very small communities. Despite their seeming lack of organization, they continued to make themselves feared by constantly raiding the valley-dwelling Pimas and other more peaceful peoples. In the early sixteenth century, the area between the Little Colorado and Gila Rivers was uninhabited, becoming known as El Despoblado. By 1775, however, it had become a stronghold of the Western Apaches who were continuing to raid the settlements in the Gila and San Pedro Valleys.

When the Spaniards first entered Arizona, the natives almost all had weapons such as the bow—with or without poisoned arrows—lance, war club, and shield. They knew and used among themselves a kind of universal sign language. Even though a crude pictographic communication was used by some groups, they never actually progressed much beyond the symbolic decoration of pots and baskets. The families of almost any tribe were divided into clans usually named for animals, and the headmen of the more vigorous clans customarily led the warriors in times of conflict. Except in a few groups where there was a tendency toward matriarchy, women were mainly child-bearers, food gatherers, and the servants of men. The religion of these peoples centered around the spirits supposed to live in trees, winds, mountains, water, or other elements of the life around them. They had only vague notions of their origins, usually claiming to have come down from the north or up out of the earth. They had no concept of the outer world from which the Spaniards eventually arrived.

THE EARLY INHABITANTS OF NEW MEXICO

The known prehistory of the original inhabitants of New Mexico dates back to approximately 12,000 B.C. Archeological sites such as Sandia Cave and Folsom and Clovis sites indicate that early people hunted big game, including mammoth, and lived in open cave shelters. During the last phase of the Ice Age, around 8000 B.C., as the bigger game disappeared, people began subsisting on smaller game and gathering wild foods. The Archaic period, around 3000 B.C. witnessed the advent of agriculture. Although hunting and gathering were still practiced to supplement their diet, ranges were curtailed enabling people to remain near their planted food sources. During this period, cultural differences became evident between southern nomads, the Cochise, and their northern counterparts, the San José.

As these groups became more agriculturally based, they developed a sedentary lifestyle and an acumen for pottery making, a concept borrowed from Mexican and Arizonan cultures. These early sedentary peoples developed into two distinct groups, the Mogollon Culture of southern and western New Mexico, and the Anasazi in the north. The first group to make pottery in New Mexico were the Mogollon who introduced this art and technology to the Anasazi around A.D. 200 or 300. Both groups developed villages of communal living and a more sophisticated sense of religion, building ceremonial lodges. In the 1000s the Anasazi surpassed the Mogollon in terms of architectural developments and development of large communities. Chaco Canyon and Aztec Ruins National Monuments are testaments to the advanced culture developed by the Anasazi in New Mexico.

A drought during the late 1200s that may have caused the aforementioned decline of the Anasazi appears to have forced the Indians into different areas. As a result of these migrations, many pueblos that have survived into the present had their beginnings. The Zuñis, Keres, Tiwa, Tewa, Piro, Tompiro, Tano, and Towa Pueblos can all trace their origins to the 1300s. By the time the Spanish entered New Mexico in the sixteenth century, they found villages which featured a rectangular plaza bordered by terraced buildings. After the Spaniards' difficult experiences with the "wild Indians" of the Gran Chichimeca of Mexico, the Pueblos' advanced societies made the Spaniards think they had indeed found the "Nuevo Méjico."

The Navajo and Apache, sometimes enemies, sometimes friends and trading partners with the Pueblos, were Southern Athapaskan-speaking peoples who entered the

Southwest from the Great Plains shortly before the Spanish. Ethnohistorical evidence suggests that the first Apacheans who migrated to the area were bison-hunting nomads. The Comanches, also important players in the history of the Hispanic Southwest, did not arrive until the 1700s.

Pueblo Indians of New Mexico

The Pueblo Indians form a distinctive and identifiable unit in comparison with neighboring indigenous groups. Pueblo ancestors occupied the greater Southwest as hunters and gatherers for thousands of years, but the gradual introduction of agriculture from the south led to the cultivation of corn, beans, and squash. As they became settled, they built adobe houses rising for several stories around central plazas. They later cultivated cotton, made pottery, adopted irrigation techniques, and began to trade shell, copper, and turquoise ornaments.

Even though there is general cultural unity among the Pueblos, they can be divided into four linguistic stocks: The Hopi villages in the west are of the Ute-Aztecan family; the Zuni belong to a stock perhaps distantly related to California Penutian; and the Keresans, partly in the west (Acoma and Laguna) and partly in the Río Grande valley, belong to no known stock. The fourth linguistic affiliation is with the Kiowa-Tanoan family represented in the Río Grande valley by three Tanoan subgroups—Tiwa in the north and south, and Tewa and Towa in the center.

The advanced culture of the Pueblos became of interest both to Franciscan priests active on the northern mission frontier as well as to laymen. First, they had a thriving agricultural economy, potentially capable of producing enough food to make exploitation attractive. This was achieved by judicious use of the water of the area's principal stream, the Río Grande, and by diversification of crops. Second, the Indians were congregated in compact villages, a factor facilitating not only exploitation but also favorable to the establishment of missions for Christianization. Third, the local Indians were much more culturally advanced than were the nomadic "wild tribes," the Chichimecas of North Mexico. Cultural advance was evident in the technical skills of building, irrigation, agriculture, weaving of cotton blankets, and development of various arts and crafts, all factors which could be capitalized upon to introduce the Indians to Spanish civilization and its possible advantages. A fourth factor of importance was the already established Pueblo communal life in villages well located for protection and for utilization of land and water resources, which though not abundant, coincided with existing village locations.

But there were also drawbacks that made the area less desirable. The most obvious was its great isolation, being situated nearly a thousand miles beyond the northern cutting edge of Spanish civilization. Logistic support would be difficult, particularly if the area's resources did not live up to initial expectations. Isolation was compounded by poor communication with the existing northern frontier and even more so with the capital of New Spain. Long, dry stretches, largely devoid of natural highways such as navigable rivers, sparse population, and even limited capacity to support intervening occupation hampered serious consideration of colonization. The Pueblo Indians did not prove to be ideal subjects for conversion to Spanish Catholic Christianity. They had a satisfactory religion and therefore had little reason to change. They were not, however, totally unwilling to accept certain aspects of Christianity; nevertheless, their reception was neither whole-hearted nor at the expense of their own religion. Rather, what they accepted was in addition to their rites, rituals, and beliefs, which had served them and their ancestors well. Native priests did not demand any great sacrifices from the people, nor was there a large religious hierarchy to be supported. It has often been said, rather tritely, that to the Pueblos, life and religion were one and the same thing, a simple explanation of interrelations of much greater complexity.

European Impressions of Native Americans
When the first Europeans arrived in the Southwest, their view of the Indians resulted primarily from the nature of their initial contact. Adventurers lusting for wealth in Sonora and the Southwest thought the natives to be fierce and hostile; explorers along the Alta California coast described them as simple and friendly; missionaries in Arizona found them inquisitive and eager for conversion; while sophisticated travelers called them ignorant and superstitious. Many early visitors judged the natives' nudity to indicate a near animal-like existence, and others felt the aboriginal inhabitants had not taken sufficient advantage of such an ideal climate, abundant natural resources, and fertile soil. Because there are no first-hand accounts written by Indians during the contact period, it is necessary to evaluate as many of the European and later American observations as possible, as well as consider the anthropological evidence, when forming an idea about Indian life during the Spanish and Mexican periods. It is only from this kind of study, which includes a wide variety of commentaries, that a balanced and historically useful picture of Spanish-Indian relations can emerge.

——————— *Chapter One* ———————
BIBLIOGRAPHIC ESSAY

A good general summary covering the geography of the area stretching from California to New Mexico, called in this book the "far Southwest," is Warren Beck and Ynez D. Haase, *Historical Atlas of the American West* (Norman: University of Oklahoma Press, 1989). The same authors have also produced a specialized *Historical Atlas of California* and *Historical Atlas of New Mexico* (Norman: University of Oklahoma Press, 1974 and 1985). An excellent treatment of Arizona geography is Roger Dunbier, *The Sonoran Desert: Its Geography, Economy, and People* (Tucson: University of Arizona Press, 1968), and for detailed maps, the *Historical Atlas of Arizona* by Henry P. Walker and Don Bufkin (Norman: University of Oklahoma Press, 1979) is useful. A concise overview of California geography is found in David Hornbeck and Phillip Kane, *California Patterns: A Geographical and Historical Atlas* (Palo Alto, Calif.: Mayfield Publishing, 1983) and Andrew Rolle, *California: A History,* fourth edition (Arlington Heights, Ill.: Harlan Davidson, 1987). Pertinent to Arizona are Bert Fireman, *Arizona: Historic Land* (New York: Alfred Knopf, 1982) and Jay J. Wagoner, *Early Arizona: Prehistory to Civil War* (Tucson: University of Arizona Press, 1975). For New Mexico, Marc Simmons, *New Mexico: An Interpretive History* (Albuquerque: University of New Mexico Press, 1990) and Warren Beck: *New Mexico: A History of Four Centuries* (Norman: University of Oklahoma Press, 1962) are valuable. Recently published is Robert C. West, *Sonora: Its Geographical Personality* (Austin: University of Texas Press, 1993).

A basic source for the native peoples of the Southwest is the *Handbook of North American Indians* under the general editorship of William C. Sturtevant and published by The Smithsonian Institution, Washington, D.C., in 1978 and 1979. Relevant volumes are Volume 8 of *California* edited by Robert F. Heizer, and Volumes 9 and 10, *Southwest*, edited by Alfonso Ortiz. Volume 8 includes pertinent articles about California natives by Heizer, William F. Shipley, Sherburne F. Cook, Campbell Grant, Lowell J. Bean, and other leading anthropologists. Volume 9 contains the prehistory of the Southwest with introductions by Ortiz and Richard B. Woodbury. Separate articles are by Paul S. Martin, George J. Gumerman, Emil W. Haury, Charles C. Di Peso, Albert H. Schroeder, Fred Plog, and others. Volume 10 covers western Arizona, specifically the Havasupai, Walapai, Yavapai, Mojave, Maricopa, Quechan, Cocopa, Pima, Pápago, and Lower Pima tribes. Articles by Bernard L. Fontana and Paul Ezell are particularly valuable.

Recent works are R. G. Matson, *The Origins of Southwest Agriculture* (Tucson: University of Arizona Press, 1991); Linda S. Cordell and George J. Gumerman, eds., *Dynamics of Southwest Prehistory* (Washington, D.C.: Smithsonian Institution Press, 1989); Patricia L. Crown and W. James Judge, eds., *Chaco & Hohokam: Prehistoric Regional Systems in the American Southwest* (Santa Fe: School of American Research Press, 1991); Kathryn Gabriel, *Roads to Center Place: A Cultural Atlas of Chaco Canyon and the Anasazi* (Boulder, Colo.: Johnson Books, 1991); Stephen Trimble, *The People: Indians of the American Southwest* (Santa Fe: School of American Research Press, 1993); and David Rich Lewis, *Neither Wolf Nor Dog: American Indians, Environment & Agrarian Change* (New York: Oxford University Press, 1994).

A useful older work is Thomas Weaver, ed., *Indians of Arizona: A Contemporary Perspective* published by the University of Arizona Press in Tucson in 1974. It contains separate articles by Haury, Fontana, Gordon V. Krutz, Frank Lobo, Emory Sekaquaptewa, Barry Bainton, and Ruth Hughes Gartell. Edward H. Spicer's *Cycles of Conquest: The Impact of Spain, Mexico and the United States on the Indians of the Southwest: 1533–1960* (Tucson: University of Arizona Press, 1962) is extremely helpful. Henry Dobyns has written a number of articles concerning native peoples from a historical point of view. For California see George Harwood Phillips, *Indians and Intruders in Central California, 1769–1849* (Norman: University of Oklahoma Press, 1993); Albert Hurtado, *Indian Survival on the California Frontier* (New Haven: Yale University Press, 1988); and James J. Rawls, *Indians of California: The Changing Image* (Norman: University of Oklahoma Press, 1984). For New Mexico, see Ward Alan Minge, *Acoma: Pueblo in the Sky* (Albuquerque: University of New Mexico Press, 1976); Alfonso Ortiz, *The Tewa World: Space, Time, Being and Becoming in a Pueblo Society* (Chicago: University of Chicago Press, 1969); Alfonso Ortiz, ed., *New Perspectives on the Pueblos* (Albuquerque: University of New Mexico Press, 1972); Elsie Clews Parsons, *Pueblo Indian Religion*, 2 vols. (Chicago: University of Chicago Press, 1939); and Donald Worcester, *The Apaches: Eagles of the Southwest*. (Norman: University of Oklahoma Press, 1979). A popular treatment of the Piman peoples is Ruth Underhill, *The Papago Indians of Arizona and Their Relatives the Pima* (Lawrence, Kans.: The Haskell Institute, 1941). See also Edward F. Castetter and Willis H. Bell, *Pima and Papago Indian Agriculture* and *Yuman Indian Agriculture* (Albuquerque: University of New Mexico Press, 1942 and l951).

For further reading see: James Axtell, "Europeans, Indians, and the Age of Discovery in American History Textbooks," *American Historical Review*, 92 (June 1987): 621–32; Sherburne F. Cook, *The Conflict between the California Indian and White Civilization*, (Berkeley: University of California Press, 1943–1946); Gary B. Coombs and Fred Plog, "The Conversion of the Chumash Indians: An Ecological Interpretation," *Human Ecology*, 5 (December 1977): 309–28; Frederick J. Dockstader, *The Kachina and the White Man: The Influences of White Culture on the Hopi Kachina Cult*, 1954, rev. ed. (Albuquerque: University of New Mexico Press, 1985); Edward P. Dozier, *The Pueblo Indians of North America* (New York: Holt, Rinehart and Winston, 1970); Paul Ezell, "The Hispanic Acculturation of the Gila River Pimas," *American Anthropologist,* 63 (October 1961):1–171; Erna Fergusson, *Dancing Gods: Indian Ceremonials of New Mexico and Arizona* (Albuquerque: University of New Mexico Press, 1931); William W. Fitzhugh, ed., *Cultures in Contact: The European Impact on Native Cultural Institutions, A.D. 1000–1800* (Washington, D.C.: Smithsonian Institution Press, 1985); Robert F. Heizer, "The Impact of Colonization on the Native California Societies," *Journal of San Diego History*, 24 (Winter 1978):121–39; Keith W. Kintigh, *Settlement, Subsistence, and Society in Late Zuni Prehistory*; Anthropological Papers No. 44 (Tucson: University of Arizona Press, 1985); E. Charles Adams, "Passive Resistance: Hopi Responses to Spanish Contact and Conquest;" Georgia Lee and Norman Neuerburg, "The Alta California Indians as Artists before and after Contact," in *Columbian Consequences*, vol. l (Washington, D.C.: Smithsonian Institution Press, l989); and Carrol L. Riley, "The Road to Hawikuh: Trade and Trade Routes to Cibola-Zuni during Late Prehistoric and Early Historic Times," *Kiva*, 41 (winter 1975):137–59.

Chapter Two

SPANISH BACKGROUNDS AND EARLY EXPLORATION

SPAIN AND THE FAR SOUTHWEST: GEOGRAPHIC SIMILARITIES

*T*he fact that California, Arizona, and New Mexico, all characterized by contrast and inhabited by a substantial native population, should have been first explored and settled by Spain effectively determined the course of the region's early recorded history. Spain's diverse environment—a high mountainous plateau cut by deep flowing rivers and large semi-arid regions with a minimum of rainfall—challenged the people's resourcefulness and helped condition their role as New World colonizers. The Iberian Peninsula, like northern Mexico and the southwestern portion of the United States, was isolated. Nevertheless, it was subject to and conditioned by an ongoing series of invasions.

Spain's geographical position at the extreme west of the Mediterranean Sea and the extreme south of the European continent had been significant in shaping the country's historical destiny. The Pyrenees Mountains, standing high along the French border, hindered contact from the north and a coastal perimeter of mountains blocked easy entrance to the interior from the sea. Spain's temperate climate and fertile land, however, attracted a host of outsiders.

THE AGE OF DISCOVERY

By the time of the Spanish discovery of America, Spain had prepared for deeds of epic proportions with the year 1492 marking a crucial turning point in history for the Spanish people. On January 2, 1492, the last Moorish stronghold of Granada fell to the Catholic sovereigns Fernando and Isabel; the war against the Moslems was over. The victory was the climax of eight centuries of effort to establish Christian hegemony on the Spanish peninsula. Spain's Roman heritage and the Reconquest had created fervent religious crusaders, zealous military leaders, and a number of fearless adventurers fighting to gain a better position in life. It had also created a nation with vast experience in racial, if not religious, blending.

For seven centuries Moslems and Christians had lived side by side, often in peace and harmony, and there was considerable cultural exchange between the two major peninsular groups. As a result, a variety of laws, customs, and institutions had become an integral part of Spanish society, which in turn were used in the colonization of America. Spain's meticulously organized rules for New World administration had roots in Roman, Visigothic, and Moslem law, as well as in the local fueros of Castile. Tolerance and even encouragement of intermarriage with converted Native American peoples

Fig. 2.1. Christopher Columbus (artist unknown). Courtesy Museo Naval, Madrid.

was in accord with the customs of the Iberian Peninsula. Spanish laws reflected the humanitarian zeal of a crusading Christian nation—a nation of people ready for the conversion of an entire continent of pagan inhabitants. The Reconquest also prepared Spaniards to found new settlements—primarily towns—in previously unoccupied territory.

Columbus

With the final expulsion of the Moors, Queen Isabel could turn much of the energies of Castile to new projects; the queen was the foremost sponsor of Christopher Columbus in his initial voyage of discovery. This marginally equipped expedition, which set sail from southern Spain on August 3, 1492, was one of the most heroic ventures in Western history. In that undertaking, a handful of men impelled by dreams of future wealth embarked upon the navigation of alien waters to find new trade routes and possibly new lands. The territories they discovered became part of the Crown of Castile. Other Europeans must have touched the shores of America before the Spanish expedition, but Columbus provided the first permanent link between the Old World and the New. In reality, however, the epochal meaning of his discovery eluded the famous navigator; he called the new land "the Indies" because he thought he had found India. Even though historians have written that Columbus died without understanding the nature of his discoveries, he did make several references in his later writings that he was on to something new. He made four momentous voyages that greatly enhanced the geographical understanding of the Caribbean Sea region.

Spain gave to the New World a curious blending of medieval civilization and Renaissance ideas. The Reconquest had kept the crusading spirit and the idea of a universal church firmly alive in Spain, along with a strong belief in mythical elements known to the realm of fable and romance popular during the Middle Ages. Some of the Spanish conquerors were Renaissance men in their fondness for grandeur, wealth, and fame; but there existed a strong continuity between medieval developments and the early institutional and cultural life of the Ibero-American colonies.

In this context, Columbus was not so much the first modern explorer as the last of the great medieval travelers, no doubt inspired more by legends of fabulously rich islands off the coast of Asia than by a desire to colonize new lands. Even while navigating through the Caribbean Sea and along the continental mainland, he thought he was visiting islands depicted in medieval maps at the edge of the Orient in the vicinity of Cathay. On his third voyage of 1502, Columbus was certain that he had found the site of the Terrestrial Paradise. He showed the Orinoco delta on the Venezuelan coast to be the mouths of the four rivers of Genesis, which proceed from the Tree of Life. His description of the fabulous wealth of Paradise did nothing to lessen the notions of subsequent explorers that somewhere in America would be found all the mythical beings, monsters, griffins, gilded men, and golden cities known to the medieval world. Recall that California was surrounded by the legend of Queen Calafia and her Amazon women. In fact, one of the most significant forces that propelled Spanish explorers into the Southwest was the idea that somewhere beyond the Sonoran frontier were cities of gold that held a host of hidden marvels, of untrodden mysteries.

Spaniards of the sixteenth century, inspired by legends of golden cities and novels of chivalry, searched the most unlikely corners of the American continent in their quest for riches. Even the natives, so erroneously called Indians, became a principal mystery that perplexed the Spanish nation. Speculation ran from suppositions that they descended from the lost Ten Tribes of Israel to an idea that somehow the native peoples were an offshoot of the Welsh nation. Fact had to be sorted from fiction before the Indians' capacity for Christianity and European civilization could be understood, and before Spanish theologians could determine what the right kind of relationship would be to establish with them.

Papal Donation, 1493

In 1492 Alexander Borgia, a Spaniard, was elected pope. This gave Fernando and Isabel a strong ally in Rome and, at the same time, established the nature of Spanish control in America. The Papal Donation of 1493, by which Pope Alexander VI divided the New World between Spain and Portugal, gave dominion over the Indies to the Crown of Castile and imposed upon it the obligation to spread Christianity throughout the new land. Each Spaniard, made to feel individually responsible for conversion of pagan natives, was forced to question the basic nature of the Indian to determine how he or she could best be Christianized and brought to a "civilized" way of life. Conquistadors asked whether conversion should be attempted by peaceful persuasion or whether war could be waged to compel Indians to serve God and the king. Unfortunately, certain of the New World adventurers were unconcerned about the inability of the natives to understand what was required of them for obedience to the church and king, often resulting in wars waged against Indians who were totally ignorant of what was expected of them. Their reluctance or refusal to obey often led to their capture and enslavement.

Priests, in an effort to temper the cruelties of the conquistadors, asked how natives could be made to change from what they were to what Christianity dictated they ought to be. Among the documents of the conquest are opinions on these questions together with numerous proposals by missionaries and various officials for the protection and welfare of the American Indians. In comparison to other European colonizing nations, only the Spaniards, legalistic and fervently Catholic, asked these questions with such general concern. The pattern was set by Queen Isabel who, until the day of her death, regarded the welfare of the American natives as Spain's major responsibility in the New World.

Castilian Grammar, 1492

Another historic event of the year 1492 was the publication of Antonio de Nebrija's Castilian *Gramática,* the first grammar of a modern European language ever written. This book marked the clear supremacy of Castile and its language not only on the Iberian Peninsula, but also assured its dominant position in America. As soon as schools were founded for the natives, the Castilian language was taught. When it was discovered that the infinite number of Indian dialects made instruction in their native language nearly impossible, missionaries also introduced Castilian as a means of communication.

Thus, at the end of the fifteenth century, Spain stood at the pinnacle of its destiny—in a perfect position to profit from the discovery of a New World. Spain was able to follow through and become, for a time, a decisive factor in Western history. All the elements were present: the political and religious solidarity achieved by the marriage of Fernando and Isabel, the military and religious energies released by the final expulsion of the Moors, the crusading and colonizing zeal encouraged by both church and state, the fortunate accident of Isabel's faith in Columbus, and the intense pride, courage, and spirit of the Spaniard himself. These circumstances set the pattern of New World conquest, and determined the kind of settlement that would result from the first European contact.

In the conquest of America, Spain gave language, religion, laws, and customs to a score of nations that, through the ages, have risen and prospered. Whatever the effect of the country's later role in world progress, Spain's encounter with the American continent caused an irreversible and ongoing impact upon history. It shifted the center of contact from the known world, and turned the eyes of Europeans from the crusades of the East to the conquest of the West. For the Indians, however, it was a different story. Their lives—for better or for worse—were unalterably changed, and their history often became one of accommodation and survival.

THE LEGACY OF COLUMBUS

After two failed attempts to place colonists on the Island of Española, Columbus founded Santo Domingo in 1496, the first permanent settlement in the New World and present-day capital of the Dominican Republic. Discovery of some placer gold nearby destined it to become the earliest important city and seat of Spanish rule in America. The mines were soon exhausted, but Spanish colonizers built new towns and introduced sugar cane, citrus fruits, cattle, sheep and horses. In need of workers, they subjected the natives to strenuous exploitation both in mining and agriculture, which, along with disease, killed many of them within a short time. From this tragedy came governmental reform concerning treatment of Indians, plus the practical realization that if such a policy were continued, there soon would be no labor supply. Española thus became a proving ground for Spain's colonial system, and more humane methods of rulership were designed for use throughout the Indies. On the mainland it became a major objective to avoid the mistakes of the West Indian islands. The Spanish crown issued instructions for a well-regulated system of government and passed detailed laws about the occupation of new lands, foundation of towns, protection and conversion of Indians, and use of native labor.

Caribbean Settlement and Beyond

The Island of Española became a base for further expansion in America. Between 1508 and 1511, the Spaniards settled the islands of Jamaica, Cuba, and Puerto Rico; and expeditions were sent along the coasts of Florida, Mexico, and northern South America. Columbus's dream to find a route to India, still zealously pursued, received welcome encouragement when Vasco Nuñez de Balboa crossed the Isthmus of Panama in 1513 to find el Mar del Sur, a great uncharted ocean lying apparently due south. This discovery inspired other Spanish explorers to seek a way into the "new ocean" from the Atlantic; they were certain that once they sailed through or around the giant American land mass, they could at last head directly for the Orient.

Ferdinand Magellan, Portuguese by birth, first navigated the fierce, stormy strait at the southern tip of South America in 1520, and experienced waters so dangerous that he called the peaceful ocean that he entered afterward the "Pacific." His successful crossing to the Philippines ended with his death in a battle with the natives, leaving Juan Sebastián de Elcano to lead to completion the first circumnavigation of the globe. Spain's success increased the search for a still shorter route to the Orient—a search for some North American waterway that would save the long journey southward and passage through the difficult strait discovered by Magellan. The first rounding of Cape Horn, however, would not be made until the Dutch, looking in 1616 for an easier route into the Pacific, would name it for their home town of Hoorn.

Spanish sailors who searched for a northwest passage were inspired by those medieval legends that told of great wealth hidden in remote areas of the globe. In their quest for an all-water route leading directly to Cathay, ship captains speculated that rich cities and a host of other marvels were situated along its banks; these rumors in turn caused speculation about the location of other legendary lands. In addition to the Island of California, the most popular alleged repositories of wealth included the Seven Cities of Cíbola, supposedly founded by seven bishops with gold and treasures taken during the Reconquest (they were thought at first to be in the Atlantic); and the Kingdom of Gran Quivira, a land where even household utensils were of gold. These tales, plus a fear that England or Russia might first find the elusive Northwest Passage or "Strait of Anián" as they eventually called it, pushed Spanish explorers far into the interior of the North American continent, northward along the Pacific Coast, and ultimately to the shores of Alaska and Siberia.

HERNÁN CORTÉS CONQUERS MEXICO

The conquest of Mexico, perhaps more than Balboa's momentous discovery or Magellan's courageous voyage, is first in the direct chain of events that led to the discovery and settlement of California, Arizona, and New Mexico. Reports of substantial Indian wealth existing inland from the Mexican gulf coast inspired Diego de Velázquez, governor of Cuba, to outfit some ships under Hernán Cortés, a man he thought ambitious and brave enough to tackle the powerful Aztec Indians of central Mexico. Cortés, a native of Spain's rugged western province of Extremadura, led an expedition that faced unparalleled dangers, but reaped greater rewards than any Spain had yet known. Its success, like that of its leader, resulted from the combined elements of luck, cleverness, and courage.

The story of the conquest can be followed in Cortés's own letters and through the eyes of Bernal Díaz del Castillo, a tough old soldier of Spain who personally accompanied Cortés during the entire venture. Although Díaz wrote his *True History of the Conquest of New Spain* nearly a quarter of a century later, he had an excellent memory and reconstructed scenes with vivid detail. He described Cortés, who had served in the Indies since 1504, as valiant, fair, and just—a man who had the gift of leadership and who inspired a handful of fellow adventurers to plunge with him into unknown jungles and bring a powerful civilization under submission. The Indians of Mexico viewed him differently.

In defiance of Cuba's Governor Velázquez, who fruitlessly tried to recall Cortés at the last moment, the expedition left the island in February 1519 with 11 ships, 600 men, 18 horses and 10 small cannon. Landing on the Mexican coast, Cortés, then a rebel, founded La Villa Rica de la Vera Cruz (The Rich Town of the True Cross), a town whose name left no doubt as to the dual purpose of Spanish conquest and whose municipal council elected Cortés captain-general—a legal device used to gain the king's protection and avoid recall by the governor of Cuba.

DEFEAT OF THE AZTECS

A shipwrecked Spaniard, Jerónimo de Aguilar, and an Aztec slave girl living with the Mayas, first aided Cortés in his conquest of Mexico by acting as interpreters. The girl, called Doña Marina by the Spaniards and La Malinche by Mexicans, reported that the Aztec empire was riddled with dissension and its subject peoples, burdened with tribute, would serve as allies on a march against the Emperor Montezuma's island capital on Lake Texcoco (site of today's Mexico City). When the Spaniards looked down from the high mountains surrounding the Valley of Mexico, they were amazed to see six lakes and thirty white-plastered cities gleaming in the sun. On an island in the largest lake stood Tenochtitlán, the greatest and richest city of the Aztecs, and seat of government for a nation of some 300,000 people. The Venice-like capital, laced with canals and connected to the mainland by three narrow causeways, seemed almost impenetrable to the Spanish troops.

The overwhelming odds against the Spaniards were lessened by the Aztec belief that Cortés might be the legendary feathered serpent, Quetzalcoatl, a powerful God who had promised to return from across the sea as a white, bearded man. Montezuma's confusion and unwillingness to anger such an important God caused him to hesitate; and the emperor quickly fell into Spanish hands. In addition, the Aztecs, never having seen horses, thought that Cortés's mounted soldiers were terrifying creatures—certainly Gods as well. The Spaniards were better armed, with steel hand weapons, crossbows, guns, and cannon, but their psychological advantages were perhaps greater. When Montezuma was eventually killed by his own people, the remaining Aztecs failed to maintain enough military pressure to defeat the Spanish troops and their Indian allies. They were plagued by European diseases of epic proportions that spread throughout their island confines. By August 1521, the conquest was ended and Cortés, despite heavy losses, became master of the ruined Tenochtitlán. The final bloody siege cost the lives of an estimated 150,000 Indians. The bold conqueror proclaimed Spain's authority, banned human sacrifices, destroyed pagan idols, cleansed the temples of blood, and took over the Aztec treasury.

By defeating the powerful Aztec nation, which held political, economic and military control in central Mexico from the Gulf to the Pacific and as far southeast as Guatemala, the Spaniards were able to spread their victory over a large, densely populated area. Cortés's group of 400 to 450 solders initiated the thrust whereby the Spanish empire extended its control over an estimated fifty million Indians in central and southern Mexico. For three years after the fall of the capital, Cortés devoted himself to rebuilding Tenochtitlán and pacifying its subject areas with a moderation and political wisdom unique among conquerors. He established municipalities, appointed officers, promoted agriculture, and issued general ordinances affecting all lines of activity. His policy of expansion was governed by conciliation, using force only as a last resort. A little known aspect of Cortés's story is that with the exception of the initial Aztec conflict at Tenochtitlán, the majority of present-day Mexico came under Spanish rule with a minimum of bloodshed.

Search for Another Mexico

The gold, silver, and jewels of the Aztec empire naturally led the Spaniards to believe that other areas of Indian wealth must lie to the south and north of the Mexican capital. By 1522, Cortés reached the Pacific at Michoacán and founded the port city of Zacatula. He ordered construction of four ships for northward exploration, but a lack of supplies and skilled labor slowed progress. Essential European items such as iron work and rigging had to be transported slowly overland from Veracruz. Four ships were nevertheless completed by 1527—just in time to comply with a royal order sending three of them to the Moluccas to strengthen Spanish claims in the East Indies. Rival leaders then forced Cortés to return to Spain in 1528 to defend himself against charges of seeking independence from the crown. Found innocent at the royal court and placated with the title of Marqués del Valle de Oaxaca, Cortés returned to Mexico in 1530 as lord of a vast feudal estate south of the capital. He quickly renewed his dreams of exploration into the Pacific and to the north of Mexico City.

CARLOS V, HOLY ROMAN EMPEROR COMES TO POWER

As early as 1524, royal authority was strengthened as the king's officers assumed financial control of Mexico. Carlos I of Spain, grandson of Fernando and Isabel, had succeeded to the Spanish throne through his mother Juana; and to territories in eastern France, the Netherlands, Austria, and Bohemia through his father Philip the Fair of the Austrian Hapsburg family. Carlos, who became Carlos V, Holy Roman Emperor in 1519, took advantage of his inherited strength to maintain an absolute monarchy. Because Cortés's success began to rival the king's own power, Carlos V curtailed the conqueror's authority in all areas.

A royal *audiencia* for the governing of Santo Domingo had been set up in 1524 to insure the power of the crown, and in keeping with this purpose, the Spanish government supplanted Cortés very gradually with officials of its own. Expediency dictated the series of steps by which his presence in New Spain was rendered unnecessary; a program that ultimately forced the establishment of a viceroyalty. At the same time as Cortés's appointment to governor and captain-general of New Spain, October 15, 1522, the central government took over the management of its most vital concern: finance. Royal officials arrived in Mexico in 1524 and displaced the appointees of Cortés in the administration of the royal treasury. Two years later a more serious blow was struck when the licentiate Luis Ponce de León arrived. He instituted the *residencia* of Cortés, suspended him from the exercise of judicial functions, and assumed the governorship for the duration of the legal process. Cortés was left with only the management of the Indians and military leadership as captain-general. The subsequent deaths, in rapid succession, of the judge of residence and his successor, Marcos de Aguilar, brought the royal treasurer Alonso de Estrada into power. Numerous affronts, culminating in orders to desist from exercising his office as captain-general, finally drove Cortés to Spain to seek the restitution of his former commands and proper reward for his services.

Royal Audiencia of Mexico and Nuño de Guzmán

In the meantime, the emperor and his advisors, partly influenced by the complaints of Cortés's enemies, had determined to remedy the situation by establishing an audiencia in Mexico similar to the court set up in Santo Domingo in 1524, but with greater powers. They feared that the presence of Cortés might hamper the activities of this body, and so requested his presence back in Spain, an invitation that accorded exactly with his own plans. The first audiencia, appointed December 13, 1527, was composed of four licentiates, Francisco Maldonado of Salamanca; Alonso de Parada, who had resided in Cuba; Diego Delgadillo of Granada; and Juan Ortiz de Matienzo, a Viscayan. Nuño de Guzmán, the governor of Pánuco, was appointed president and, as the first two died soon after they reached Mexico, he was left with only two *oidores* to aid him in managing the affairs of New Spain.

The judges arrived in New Spain in December 1528, and Guzmán assumed his duties as president the first day of the next year. His role has been described as an orgy of extortion, misgovernment, and cruelty (though a more complete study of the documents in his case may show him to have been no worse than a number of the more successful empresarios of his age with whom history has dealt less harshly). Thus Cortés was disappointed once more in his great ambition to be made governor of New Spain. His new commission was to explore in the South Sea; his continuance as captain-general of New Spain, a grant of 23,000 Indians in *encomienda,* and the title of Marqués del Valle de Oaxaca were the greatest favors he could induce the crown to concede.

Nuño de Guzmán likewise saw the end of his brief day of authority. When he heard that he was to be deprived of the presidency and his audiencia was to be removed from office, he adopted a bold course. Using his position, he collected all the soldiers he could find, cavalry as well as crossbowmen, and departed for Jalisco on the west coast of Mexico. The conquest of the province of New Galicia was the result of this expedition. Unfortunately for Guzmán, no "New" Mexico existed there and he looked in vain for the plunder that would earn forgiveness for his deeds of misrule. For a time he was able to maintain a precarious position with the crown based on the possibility of new wealth through conquest. Active rivalry with Cortés, whose plans he had anticipated, and defiance of the new audiencia, which had been instructed to conduct his residencia, mark the period until the establishment of the viceroyalty in 1535. Guzmán's promises of success brought him appointment as governor of New Galicia, a guarantee of favor from the second audiencia, a continuation of his previous salary until the arrival of the new government, a loan of money on security, and permission to undergo residencia in *absentia*. At the same time, Cortés was instructed to stay out of New Galicia and confine his discoveries to the South Sea.

Guzmán's endeavors were not entirely without justification. With the help of his able lieutenant, Cristobal de Oñate, the permanent Spanish settlement of New Galicia was begun. Several Spanish towns, among them the villas of Santiago de Compostela, Espíritu Santo (Guadalajara), and La Purificación, were founded.

Viceroyalty of New Spain

Carlos I selected the first viceroy of New Spain with great care. Antonio de Mendoza, descendant of a highly respected Castilian family, had been trained as a diplomat and entrusted with missions requiring the utmost in loyalty and ability. As the king's most powerful official in New Spain, the viceroy served as president of the audiencia, governor, and captain-general of an area that extended throughout present-day Mexico, the southwestern United States, and coastal regions of the Pacific Northwest. Viceroy Mendoza proved to be worthy of his heavy responsibility and earned the admiration and respect of his subordinates. Only Cortés, who saw Mendoza as a competitor, was dismayed by the viceroy's arrival.

The viceroyalty of New Spain expanded upon the general features of Spanish colonial policy as initiated on the Island of Española. Since the Indies were assumed to be the exclusive possession of the Spanish sovereign, the king was absolute proprietor of all new lands, and sole political and religious head of all provinces created from them. Every privilege and position—whether economic, political, or religious—came from him. The prominent role of the church also helped characterize Spanish policy. The crown relied heavily upon ecclesiastical authority in questions pertaining to salvation of Indian souls, distribution of native lands and labor, settlement of disputes between Spaniards and Indians, and general transmission of all the elements of Spanish civilization that would make the natives as much a part of the Spanish empire as if they were born in Spain.

Quest for New Riches

As Mendoza and Cortés struggled for power in Mexico, the men of the conquest dreamed of new riches. Since reports of the fabulously wealthy Inca empire had reached Mexico, the Spanish adventurers were quick to imagine "un otro Méjico" or "another Mexico" lying somewhere nearby. Their first thoughts turned to the ocean, where they, too, hoped to find the mythical island ruled by an Amazon queen. It is thought that Cortés hoped to find both the famous golden island and that long-sought Strait of Anián somewhere to the north of the Mexican coast. Diego Hurtado de Mendoza commanded two new ships that sailed from Zacatula in 1532 to pursue these objectives, but the expedition ended in mutiny. In his effort to penetrate the mysterious Pacific, Cortés outfitted a second venture under his distant cousin Diego de Becerra, a haughty and disagreeable man who was put to death by his crew. Fortún Jiménez, first pilot and leader of the mutiny, took over command of the ship *Concepción* and sometime in late 1533 or early 1534 reached what he thought was an island, but was actually the peninsula of today's Baja California. Jiménez anchored in a bay, which he named La Paz, and

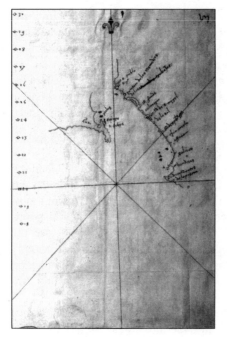

Map 2.1. Cortés's map of Baja California. Courtesy Museo Naval, Madrid.

the Spaniards went ashore. A sudden attack by hostile Indians brought the death of Jiménez and twenty of his men; the rest escaped to the Mexican port of Jalisco. The survivors reported that the natives of their newly discovered island were primitive savages, but had collected an abundance of pearls. Pearls alone gave Cortés sufficient incentive to plan his own expedition, and he was joined by a rush of volunteers who knew the captain's reputation for finding wealth.

Cortés Reaches Baja California

Three vessels reached the Bay of La Paz on May 3, 1535, and Cortés named the bay Santa Cruz, founding Baja California's first settlement on the dry, rocky coast. Native hostility and a lack of food made it necessary for two ships to return to the mainland for supplies; one of these was wrecked in the Gulf of California then called the "Red Sea of Cortés." On a second attempt to obtain supplies, only the ship that Cortés himself commanded made it back across the treacherous, stormy waters to La Paz; in the meantime, twenty-three of his men died of starvation on Baja California's inhospitable shore. Cortés took the one remaining vessel and returned to Mexico to get further relief. Finally, toward the end of 1536, prospects of success seemed so remote that Cortés sent ships to pick up the surviving colonists. Thus ended the first in a long succession of attempts to settle Baja, or Antigua, California, as it became later known.

Ulloa Searches for the "Northern Mystery"

In 1539 Hernán Cortés issued instructions to the final expedition which, under his direction, would pierce the Mysteries of the North. Three vessels commanded by Francisco de Ulloa sailed from the port of Acapulco in July of that year; one, the tiny *Santo Tomás,* was wrecked in the stormy waters of the Gulf of California before reaching La Paz. Ulloa's fleet, reduced to the 120-ton *Santa Agueda* and its consort, the *Trinidad,* a 35- to 40-ton vessel not more than forty feet in length, left La Paz and headed across the choppy Red Sea of Cortés to the mainland shore. Ulloa cruised northward to the port of Guaymas, which he named el Puerto de los Puertos (the Port of Ports), and farther on, expecting to find a passage around the California "island." Instead, the ships encountered violent tides caused by the Colorado River descending into the sea at the head of the narrow Gulf. The bleak shoreline—a lonely desert broken by stark mountains—offered few prospects for golden cities, so Ulloa turned southward, becoming the first Spaniard to know that Baja California was not an island. (His translated journal was published in London in 1600 by Richard Hakluyt.)

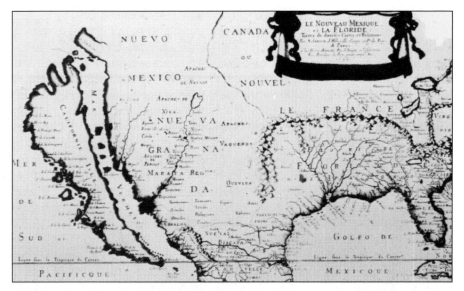

Map 2.2. Early map (1656) showing California as an island.

Ulloa took possession of the land he found for Cortés in the name of the Emperor Carlos V, King of Castile, and then sailed along the eastern shore of the peninsula until again reaching La Paz. Ulloa tried to round the southern tip at Cape San Lucas but for eight days, violent winds and tempestuous rains kept his ships beating up and down the Gulf Coast. The two vessels finally rounded the Cape by the end of January 1540, and then sailed up the western shore as far north as the Isla de Cedros (Island of Cedars) so named because "... on the tops of the mountains therein, there grows a stand of these Cedars being very tall, as the nature of them is to be." (Hakluyt, *Third and Last Volume of the Principal Navigations, Voyages, Traffiques, and Discoveries of the English Nation*, p. 418) After three months Ulloa sent the larger Santa Agueda home and continued his explorations northward in the Trinidad to perhaps Point San Antonio, just south of latitude 30°. Lack of evidence about Ulloa's eventual return to Mexico has led some to believe that the small vessel was shipwrecked on the California coast somewhere near present-day Oceanside. Mention of Ulloa in Mexico as late as 1543, however, indicates his later presence there.

Ulloa's revelation that Baja California was a peninsula aroused little attention and the "island" of California persisted on maps as late as 1784. His expedition, the last with which Cortés had any official connection, faced severe storms to explore both the eastern and western coasts of the peninsula. His discovery of an island of cedars, however, compensated little for expected cities of gold. Disappointment was great and Cortés, angered by his lack of authority and frustrated by Viceroy Mendoza's constant opposition, sailed for Spain in 1540. The great conqueror argued his claims before the royal court, but his lawsuits dragged on before an unsympathetic officialdom. Years of effort gave him little satisfaction and finally, in 1547, death claimed the unhappy Cortés, first of the Spanish explorers to open the way to California and the Spanish Southwest.

THE TRAVELS OF CABEZA DE VACA AND ESTEBAN

Cortés might have earlier given up his search for golden lands but for the return to Mexico of Alvar Nuñez Cabeza de Vaca in 1536. During a remarkable eight years' wandering over what is now the southern United States and northern Mexico, Cabeza de Vaca, shipwrecked on the Florida coast in 1528, said he had seen no great wonders but had heard the Indians tell of large cities further to the north—perhaps the Seven Cities of Cíbola.

As mentioned in Chapter 1, Cabeza de Vaca was accompanied on his long journey by fellow Spaniards Alonso del Castillo Maldonado and Andrés Dorantes, and the Moorish servant Esteban, belonging to Dorantes. They were the only survivors of an attempt by Pánfilo de Narváez to find riches in Florida in 1528. After drifting across the Gulf of Mexico in small, roughly constructed boats, they spent several years as captives among the Indians in Texas. They had finally managed to escape and made their way westward across Texas, parts of New Mexico, and Arizona, and finally southward through Sonora to Culiacán, the northernmost Spanish settlement on the Pacific Coast. From there they traveled to Mexico City and lived as guests of Viceroy Mendoza for several months. Cabeza de Vaca left a lengthy and detailed account of their wanderings in books *La "Relación" o "Naufragios,"* which has been published in numerous editions.

Viceroy Mendoza, caught up in the spirit of discovery, wanted Cabeza de Vaca to return to the north, but the explorer declined and instead traveled to Spain in 1537 where he was appointed adelantado of the Río de la Plata territory in South America. The viceroy then attempted to purchase from Dorantes the Moorish servant Esteban in order to use him as his own guide to the northern region. Apparently Dorantes himself had wanted to lead this expedition, but was passed over by the viceroy. Nevertheless, he finally agreed to let Esteban serve the viceroy without payment because of the good that might accrue to the Indians and to the treasury of New Spain. Meanwhile, both Castillo Maldonado and Dorantes remained as settlers in New Spain, and Dorantes, who received a grant of a pueblo, served the viceroy during the 1541 Indian uprising known as the Mixton War.

Thus, for the first fifteen years after the conquest of Mexico, no further areas of great riches were discovered. To the south, the expeditions of Francisco Pizarro had successfully conquered much of the Inca empire of Peru and Ecuador and had found valuable treasures of gold and silver. Rumors of more gold and silver to the north and south of the Inca empire were being circulated throughout the Spanish empire. Those who had traveled southward from Mexico to Guatemala and northward to Sonora were convinced that there was certainly "another Mexico" or "another Peru" just beyond the areas already explored. Viceroy Mendoza, although hopeful that the stories of rich Indian villages to the north were true, decided to be cautious and verify the facts before sending out a major expedition to follow the travels of Cabeza de Vaca and his men.

FRAY MARCOS DE NIZA SEARCHES FOR CÍBOLA

In 1538, Fray Antonio de Ciudad Rodrigo, provincial of the Franciscan Order, is reported to have sent two Franciscan Friars, Juan de la Asunción, and Pedro Nadal, northward from Culiacán to convert the Indians of Sonora to Christianity. Just how far these two missionaries actually traveled is uncertain, but they claimed to have gone

800 miles, which would have placed them in Arizona. The friars heard further reports about people to the north who lived in large houses and were said to be civilized and rich; curiosity about these people aroused further interest.

Viceroy Mendoza, eager to add valuable territory to his domain, decided to send out a truly trustworthy person, the vice-commissioner-general of the Franciscan order in New Spain, Fray Marcos de Niza, to verify Cabeza de Vaca's story about the possibility of rich towns to the north. Fray Marcos had visited Peru and had written some essays on the Indians of that country. He received the viceroy's instructions in September 1538 to explore to the north, study the Indians' lives and languages, observe the country carefully, note everything of value in it, and look for possible mission locations: He began his account with the hope that he would be favored by the Virgin Mary and St. Francis in his quest.

Traveling northward in the company of Fray Onorato (who turned back because of illness), Esteban, and a number of Indians who had been followers of Cabeza de Vaca, Fray Marcos left Culiacán on March 7, 1539. In accordance with a prearranged plan, Esteban was sent on ahead to gather information and send back reports by Indian messenger. After 150 miles, he was to wait for Fray Marcos. In the meantime, if he had news of a populous or rich country, he was supposed to send back a great cross as high as a man; if his discoveries were of medium importance, he was to send a white cross of two-hands' breadth. Apparently Esteban was enjoying his position of leadership and wanted to keep Fray Marcos happy, so he sent back large crosses from time to time indicating that further ahead were the elusive seven cities, one of which was named Cíbola.

Fray Marcos followed along by way of northeastern Sonora, crossing from the sources of the Río Sonora to the San Pedro River. He met Opata and Sobaipuri Indians who apparently told him about Cíbola and about a country near there called Totonteac, probably meaning the Hopi country or Tusayan, as it was later called. As he came down the San Pedro Valley, Fray Marcos found more and more evidence of trade between the Sobaipuri Indians and those of Zuni or Cíbola. Eventually he met an exiled native of Cíbola who told him that it was indeed a great city and that there were some very large houses of stone with doors decorated with turquoise.

No more crosses came from Esteban after Fray Marcos entered this valley. Only indirect messages indicated that Esteban had entered a despoblado beyond which lay Cíbola. It was probably early in May when Fray Marcos reached the point where Esteban entered the area, no doubt somewhere near the mouth of the San Pedro River or possibly farther up the Gila.

Esteban's Death

At this time Fray Marcos received news from an Indian who had been in the company of Esteban that the Moor was in trouble. Apparently the Indians had warned Esteban not to enter Cíbola, but he continued toward the town anyway. The Indian messenger told Fray Marcos that a crowd of people had attacked Esteban and his followers. The priest continued on toward Cíbola but when he was within a day's journey of the place, he met two of Esteban's men who reported that all had been killed except themselves. Fray Marcos allegedly came within view of Cíbola but decided not to enter the city, which may have been the Zuni pueblo of Hawikuh, largest of the Seven Cities.

Fray Marcos had continued his journey as far north as he thought safe in view of the death of Esteban. No one is exactly sure how far he traveled or what he actually saw, but he made the return journey by the same route and returned to Culiacán in July. He was in Mexico City in August 1539 with the incredible tale that from a distance he had seen the fabulous Cíbola, a city larger and finer than Mexico. Scholars have since been divided as to whether Fray Marcos actually came within sight of Cíbola, or whether fear of meeting Esteban's fate led him instead to fabricate that entire portion of his report to the viceroy. Fray Marcos may in fact have traveled much farther to the east than other writers have assumed. But even though Fray Marcos's journey raises more questions than it answers, it matters little at this point because the result was the same. Both Viceroy Mendoza and Cortés, even before the return of Fray Marcos, had organized expeditions to follow up anticipated discoveries. So eager were they to come upon new riches that their competition turned to increased rivalry.

Viceroy Mendoza, with a strong interest in the northern frontier, laid plans for its investigation. In the beginning, the viceroy had intended to accompany the large-scale exploring expedition he had envisioned, and his financial backing plus the general excitement created by the confidential report of Fray Marcos brought forth many volunteers.

THE CORONADO EXPEDITION

The expedition would be led by the able Francisco Vázquez de Coronado, a native of Salamanca, whom Mendoza had appointed Governor of Nueva Galicia in August 1538. A man who enjoyed both wealth and position, Coronado had recently married Beatriz de Estrada, daughter of Alonzo de Estrada, royal treasurer of New Spain, and was eager to accompany Fray Marcos to Mexico City. It was about 50,000 ducats (approximately one million dollars) of his wife's fortune that Don Francisco pooled with another 60,000 ducats invested by the viceroy to bankroll the planned trip. Recruitment proved to be easy, and soon more than 300 Spaniards and 800 Indians, provided by Mendoza, joined the expedition. Many paid their own way—even the Indian aides were volunteers. The group took on the appearance of a medieval crusade as with great pomp and ceremony the colorful entourage departed from Compostela, near modern Tepic, and headed for the anticipated prize. A first-rate group had been assembled, with only the viceroy missing, as he was needed at home in Mexico City. Among the men who left chronicles of the venture were Pedro de Castañeda, a Castilian colonist who joined the expedition at Culiacán, Juan Jaramillo, a captain in the army, and Fray Marcos as official guide.

A number of notable participants set out on February 23, 1540, including Fray Marcos, Tristán de Luna y Arrellano, Hernando de Alvarado, García López de Cárdenas, Pedro de Tovar, and Pedro de Castañeda. Melchior Díaz joined later while Hernando de Alarcón took charge of the vessels that were being sent by sea. These were to travel up the east coast of the Gulf of California and were intended to support the land group by paralleling the march of Coronado and his party. Adding international flavor to the expedition were five Portuguese, two Italians, one Frenchman, a German, and a Scot. Although there were few women, at least three of the soldiers brought their wives.

The viceroy himself accompanied the expedition to Compostela, where he found the army being entertained by Cristobal de Oñate, Coronado's substitute as governor of the province of Nueva Galicia. On February 22, 1540, there was a grand review of the army consisting of 200 horsemen, 70 footsoldiers, several friars, and nearly 1,000 Indians. It had been furnished with some small cannon, more than 500 horses and mules, and many cattle, sheep, hogs, and goats. It was an optimistic and well equipped group that set off from Compostela, near Tepic.

Coronado took great pains to outfit himself in the finest tradition of the day, taking along a great number of changes of clothing. His personal entourage included Black servants, arms, horses, mules, a head groom, and lesser grooms. Expedition supplies included many bales of trade goods (though none of these were carried by Indian burden bearers as had been customary in the early colonial period in Mexico).

Expedition methods became routine. Scouting parties formed the vanguard to determine the lay of the land, reconnoiter future stopover sites, and obtain whatever support the land and its natives might offer. The advance party moved rapidly, while the train including the mobile commissary of sheep, goats, cattle, and pigs went as fast as possible, but obviously set the true pace of the large group. Following north through Sinaloa and Sonora, the itinerary led the explorers on a divergent course from that of their maritime support group under the direction of Alarcón, who had been to the head of the Gulf of California on a previous expedition in 1539.

Hernando de Alarcón, 1540

So great were the expectations of obtaining wealth that Coronado invested his entire personal fortune in the venture and Mendoza authorized its eager volunteers to be equipped at royal expense. The three sea vessels commanded by Hernando de Alarcón left Mexico in May 1540, with instructions to explore the upper part of the Sea of Cortés in addition to making overland contact with Coronado's soldiers. On August 26, Alarcón's men became the first Spaniards to sail the Río Colorado, which they named the Buenguía. During this time they came in contact with the Cocopah, Chicama (Halyikuami), Coano (Kohuana) and Cumana (probably Kumeyaay) Indians. At one point the Indians lined the shore until there were more than 250 waving bows and arrows, carrying banners, and showing signs of hostility. But by holding up gifts, Alarcón was able to convince the Indians of their friendship. The Spanish leader described the natives as being large, well proportioned, of good features, and having faces marked with charcoal. They wore pendants of shells and bones and wore their hair cut short in front and long in back. Since they seemed to worship the sun, Alarcón said that he and his men were in fact Children of the Sun. Another successful device was the distribution of holy crosses which were in such great demand that he could not make them fast enough out of available sticks. After exploring in the area and finding no evidence of any other Spanish parties, they returned to the Gulf to check on the ships.

Alarcón again decided to push northward in hopes of learning some word of Coronado. On September 14, he and his men returned to the Cocopah villages bearing seeds to plant as well as other gifts. Further north they picked up one of several Spaniards who had been left behind at Coama and found that he had been treated well. Farther up the river they learned that two Indians had come from what they called the "wicked land of Cumana" (possibly Kumeyaay) with news that an uprising was planned but had been forestalled. Two days later, the travelers came to some very high mountains and a narrow canyon that forced Alarcón to return downstream at a point just south of the Gila near present-day Yuma, Arizona. He decided to plant a large cross and carve a message on it indicating that they had reached that spot but had turned back. The group sailed downstream and the swift current took them to the mouth of the river after four days. Then, with all members of the party safely on board, they returned to Mexico where Viceroy Mendoza expressed displeasure at their failure to meet Coronado on land.

The Grand Canyon

Meanwhile, the remainder of the large expeditionary group entered what is today Arizona, crossed the *gran despoblado,* the unoccupied area of central Arizona, and reached the outliers of Pueblo Indian civilization. Under Pedro de Tovar and the priest Fray Juan de la Padilla, the Spaniards had established friendly relations with the Hopi Indians, who told them of a large river with a fertile valley that was some twenty days' journey northwestward. To learn more of the mysterious large river, Coronado sent Captain García López de Cárdenas with twenty-five men, including Pedro de Sotomayor, who kept a diary. They left Hawikuh on August 24, 1540, and traveled northwestward to the land of the Hopis. Twenty days later, they came to the banks of the river, which flowed through a vast gorge. The country was elevated, very cold, and full of low, twisted pines. They spent three days looking for a passage down to the river, which the Indians said was one-half league wide. Judging from Cárdenas's comment upon contemplating that great scenic marvel, it seems that the gorge "from whose brink it looked as if to the opposite side it must be more than three or four leagues by air line" was discovered in the vicinity of Grand View. (Narrative of Pedro de Castañeda, in Hodge, ed., *Spanish Explorers in the Southern United States, 1528–1543,* p. 116) An attempt was made to descend the chasm, one which led to a realization that what from the top seemed to be small crags were pinnacles larger than the Giralda, the well-known ancient Moorish bell tower landmark of Sevilla. An abrupt change in weather motivated the party to comment on one extremely cold night that although it was the warm season, no one could live in the canyon because of the cold.

Efforts to descend to the bottom of the canyon were useless, so after two months, the explorers returned to Hawikuh. They had discovered the Grand Canyon of the Colorado and another group of Coronado's men had visited the Moqui pueblos of Arizona. They gained valuable knowledge of geography, but found no great wealth in the area of Arizona. Historic injustice is evident today at Grand Canyon National Park where one of the earliest-built extant hotels is named in honor of Pedro de Tovar, a Coronado party officer who never set eyes on the great chasm, while true discoverer García López de Cárdenas is nowhere remembered.

Pedro de Tovar

While López de Cárdenas was busy exploring the unpopulated areas of the Colorado River and its Little Colorado tributary, his colleague Pedro de Tovar had been sent by his commander to visit Tusayán, the name for Hopi villages at that time. Led by Zuni guides, the Spaniard and his cavalry party traveled to their destination by way of the Petrified Forest, visiting the seven Hopi towns starting from east to west.

The main body of the Spanish explorers had explored in the direction of the reputedly rich cities of Cíbola, and when they realized that Fray Marcos had been over-optimistic in his early report to the viceroy, there was collective dissatisfaction. One of the journalists asked that God protect Fray Marcos from all the curses that were hurled at him that day. So, rather than stay much longer with the Coronado expedition, Marcos considered returning to Mexico City. With his departure somewhat later, the only person with any prior knowledge of the area left the expedition.

Melchior Díaz

In the meantime, Coronado moved his main army slowly northward through the Yaqui River Valley. In September, before entering the barren lands of New Mexico, he dispatched Melchior Díaz, an experienced frontier soldier, to look for Alarcón at the head of the Gulf. Díaz was to go first to the town of San Gerónimo de los Corazones near present-day Ures in Sonora. He was to find Alarcón and then look for the source of the river with the "grand canyon" discovered by López de Cárdenas north and west of Cíbola. Díaz, with twenty-five horsemen, reached the mouth of the Colorado and followed its course to the point where Alarcón had given up. Here he came in contact with the Cocopah Indians, a powerful and vigorous people who carried firebrands with them for warmth on their journeys; for this reason, Díaz named the river Río del Tizon. The Indians told Díaz of recent white visitors in ships and, finding a cross and Alarcón's letter explaining his return, Díaz decided to continue up the river.

Contemporary accounts indicate that after five or six days' travel, the party reached an area—possibly near present-day Blythe, California—crossed the Colorado in Indian basket-like rafts, made watertight with pitch, and journeyed into the inhospitable Colorado Desert. Forced back by lack of water, Díaz and his men appear to have crossed the sand dunes of Imperial Valley on a shortcut to Yuma, Arizona. Hostile Indians harassed the group in their trek to reach Sonora. Unfortunately Díaz, while chasing a greyhound, accidentally impaled himself on his own lance, and the intrepid explorer died of his wounds twenty days later, on January 18, 1541. Even though Díaz left no statement of his discovery, it seems certain from supporting journals that he was the first Spaniard whose expedition entered Alta California and whose death directly resulted from his penetration into the territory.

Fray Marcos Goes to Mexico City

Another portion of the Coronado group set out toward Mexico City, including the discredited Fray Marcos who no doubt felt that his personal safety was in jeopardy. He departed with Juan Gallego, one of the best officers, who was entrusted with taking presents and news back to the viceroy. The messages from Coronado were both written and verbal, and the presents included items of small bulk and considerable curiosity. There were twelve "small mantas such as the people of this country ordinarily wear ... and I selected them because I do not think anyone else has ever seen any [such] needle work in these Indies, unless it was done since the Spaniards settled here," he wrote. Additional presents included a cowhide, some turquoises, fifteen Indian combs, some panels decorated with turquoises, and two wicker baskets. "And lastly, I [Coronado] send you samples of the weapons used by the natives of this country in battle—a shield, a mallet, and a bow with some arrows, among them two with bone points, the like of which have never before been seen ... ." (Bolton, *Coronado on the Turquoise Trail: Knight of Pueblos and Plains*, p. 145)

Bigotes

Since winter was approaching, it became necessary for the group to scout out the land in search of a place to pass the ensuing cold period. They also decided to launch a major sub-expedition to the east to investigate areas that native informants had discussed with the Coronado party. Bigotes, a bewhiskered Indian leader from Cicuyé Pueblo was the bearer of much information and it was determined that his city was worth investigation. The front-running party was entrusted to Captain Hernando de Alvarado, who was commissioned to visit Bigotes's pueblo near modern Pecos, inform the natives to the east of Coronado's arrival at Cíbola, explain why His Majesty in Spain had sent him to these regions, and explore what was beyond in the direction of the Great Plains. Alvarado first traveled northward and became the European discoverer of the northernmost pueblo, that of Taos. From there he returned to the area that the Spaniards referred to as Tiguex, identified as the modern Bernalillo area. His departure for the Buffalo Plains to the east was via the Manzano Mountains, and from there northward to where he came upon the tiny Galisteo River. Passing through Cerrillos, the party of cavalry soldiers entered the Pecos River valley via Glorieta Pass and hit the river, which Alvarado followed southward. He next picked up the Canadian River and several days further on Alvarado and his men had contact with one of the objects of their trip, the bison. Castañeda wrote:

> Now that I wish to describe the appearance of the bulls, it is to be noticed that ... they have very long beards, like goats, and when they are running they throw their heads back with the beard dragging on the ground. ... The hair is very woolly, like a sheep's, very fine, and in front of the girdle the hair is very long and rough like a lion's. They have a great hump, larger than a camel's. The horns are short and thick, so that they are not seen much above the hair. In May they change the hair in the middle of the body for a down, which makes perfect lions of them. ... They have a short tail, with a bunch of hair at the end. When they run, they carry it erect like a scorpion. It is worth noticing that the little calves are red and just like ours, but they change their color and appearance with time and age. (Hodge and Lewis, *Spanish Explorers in the Southern United States, 1528–1543*, pp. 382–83)

Alvarado also gained the impression through his contact with an untrustworthy interpreter-guide, that to the northeast of where he was along the Canadian River at about the Texas Panhandle, existed the wealthy country called Quivira. Instead of going in that promising direction, however, Alvarado determined to return directly to Tiguex, at which point he anticipated a rendezvous with the major portions of the expeditionary force.

El Turco

Meanwhile, the group determined to spend the winter of 1540–1541 at a spot near Bernalillo, some twenty miles north of what is today Albuquerque. Almost upon arrival at the site of winter quarters at Tiguex, Coronado was reunited with Captain Alvarado and met El Turco, a native guide, both members of the group that had just returned from the first visit to the Plains. The story of the buffalo was interesting, but the idea that the guide knew of a rich civilization in that direction fell upon even more receptive ears. Quivira, near El Turco's homeland, was described by him in grandiose and attractive terms. It had copious rivers with fish as big as horses and with many large canoes propelled by up to twenty oarsmen. The lord of the land took his siesta under a tree from which the sweet sound of numerous bells served to amuse him. The common table service was generally of silver, while the pitchers, dishes, and bowls were made of gold.

Although Bigotes of Cicuyé denied that there were such riches in that direction, Coronado and his men preferred to believe this better storyteller, a Pawnee Indian who looked like a Turk, who lied in a "straightforward manner," and seemed to be able to distinguish gold from other metals. El Turco's yarns would be repeated and savored for the entire winter before they would become unraveled by the test of an actual visit to the land that promised so much.

The winter of 1540–1541 proved to be severe, particularly for men who were arriving from more southerly and much warmer climes. The local Indians were at first quite cooperative, but the Spanish need for supplies and shelter resulted in dispossession of the natives and appropriation of Indian food supplies, provisions that had been carefully stored for winter use in an economy that had only slightly more production than consumption. The early cordiality disappeared and tension mounted. Perhaps most resented by the Tigeux people were the harsh methods of the Spanish visitors in their demands for supplies and the inconsiderate manners of the soldiers. But in the final analysis, the fact that they had little surplus forced the various pueblos to withhold any assistance. Particularly noteworthy were the cases of Arenal and Moho, villages that are not now clearly identifiable. In the case of Arenal, the Spanish records show that the matter culminated with the report that Indians from the village had killed one and wounded another of the men who had been guarding the horseherd. They also ran off a substantial number of horses, killing several while escaping with the others.

Following the horse tracks, the pursuers had forded the Río Grande at a place where the Indians had also crossed with horses they had rounded up in the fields. This leaves the impression that the local natives had fast learned about the management of animals, which up to a very few months earlier had been unknown to them. Prompt action by the Spaniards under López de Cárdenas led to recovery of many mounts, but the hostility of the Indians, warranted or not, led to reprisals by the visitors. Such actions resulted in a unanimous agreement that war should be waged on the offending pueblo. Close order fighting, a physical siege of the town, a severe battering of its walls, and the lighting of fires to create a suffocating smoke, all combined to finally defeat the natives. The victors carried out severe punishment of the Arenal Indians, some being killed as they tried to escape, others taken prisoner, and still others carried outside the pueblo, tied to stakes, and burned to death.

Siege at Tiguex

The second and much longer-lasting episode concerned the capital of the Indian province of Tiguex, Moho. Matters came to a head as the result of mutual distrust and reciprocal duplicity between the Indians and the Spaniards. In what was perhaps intended to be a friendly meeting between the most important Indian leader and López de Cárdenas, the latter was attacked and almost became a prisoner, being rescued at the last moment just as he was being carried off. The upshot was a prolonged Spanish siege that was eventually successful, but not until after some loss of personnel (whereas at Arenal the casualties had been only a few wounded). The attack on Moho lasted several months, during which time the Indian water supply was severely depleted. This lack of water eventually resulted in the native decision to surrender—not because they were militarily defeated, but because the upcoming growing season made it necessary for them to prepare their future crops. The long siege lasted until the end of March 1541.

Search for Riches Continues

With the arrival of spring and after hearing stories of an advanced civilization to the east of the pueblos, the explorers headed out over the mountains and on to the Buffalo Plains. Tales continued to abound about the rich city on the Plains—Gran Quivira—making everyone eager, for the story was sufficiently convincing to inspire the Spaniards to further conquest. They left behind a garrison at Tiguex and crossed by way of the Galisteo Valley to the Pecos River valley following the outbound itinerary Alvarado had made in 1540. The large party stopped at Cicuyé Pueblo, later known as Pecos, which they noted as consisting of some fifty houses. It was the strongest and easternmost of the pueblos, standing at the edge of the Buffalo Plains and was described in the most glowing terms. The friendship of the Cicuyé Indians, however, was later found to have been very superficial, for they were really part of an intensive effort to get the Spaniards out on the plains where they would become lost.

Coronado's party was delayed in crossing the Pecos, as they searched for a place to build a bridge to permit access to the east bank. (Obviously that stream must then have been flowing abundantly, possibly owing to the very heavy snowfall of the winter of 1540–1541.) The site of this first bridge in New Mexico was near what is today Anton Chico. Once the large caravan of people, livestock, and baggage was across, the party moved leisurely into the Llano Estacado, or Staked Plains, and followed the crossing by spending some time in the canyons and mesas of West Texas. There has been some difference of opinion regarding exactly how far the explorers went at this point. The consensus of researchers indicates Palo Duro Canyon in the north Texas Panhandle as the southeastern extent of reconnaissance.

The group then shifted interest to a more northerly area, still following the general direction of Indian guides, particularly that of El Turco. Sub-groups were sent out from the main body but returned and reported seeing nothing but cattle and sky. Losing their bearings amidst the endless sea of grass, the travelers lamented that the country "they travelled over was so level and smooth" that one could see "the sky between their legs, so that if some were at a distance, they looked like smooth-trunked pines whose tops joined, and if there was only one bull it looked as if there were four pines."

(Castañeda in Hodge and Lewis, *Spanish Explorers in the Southern United States, 1528–1543*, p. 383) When looking across the backs of the animals, the curvature of the earth made it possible to see only sky on the other side.

Fig. 2.2. Buffalo (wooly cow). From Francisco Hernández, *Nova Plantarum, Animalium et Mineralium Mexicanorum Historia*, Madrid, 1651.

When no evidence of any advanced civilization was found, suspicion mounted that El Turco was a false guide. Finally, on the limitless Great Plains, somewhere in what is today Kansas, Spanish patience dwindled. Their disillusionment was confirmed when the party passed for a second time a pile of buffalo chips that had been assembled as a trail marker. Faced with the proof of his perfidy, El Turco confessed that he had been hired by the Pueblo Indians to take the Spaniards out on the Plains and lose them. He was repaid for his duplicity with death by strangulation—no one came to his defense. However, the Indians who had hired him had achieved part of their goal—El Turco had led the strangers on a wild goose chase. As far as the Spanish exploring party was concerned, at this point there was a choice of continuing on with reduced hope of success or of retreat to their base camp on the banks of the Río Grande. The latter option was selected, and the return trip was rapid. En route back to base camp, the party erected a cross, presumably of wood. They carved some letters at the base with a chisel noting that Francisco Vázquez de Coronado had reached that place.

While returning to the Tiguex headquarters, at some spot on the Llano Estacado the leader of the group suffered a serious accident. When riding along at moderate speed, a stirrup broke and Coronado catapulted forward to the ground, striking his head. The severe impact of this accidental fall altered his perception of the exploratory mission. For example, before, he had cared little that his wife, Doña Beatriz, would be missing him, but now he was a changed man who was very concerned about her. Because of this shift there was a division among his followers about future action. Some were extremely insistent upon staying on in New Mexico, among these being some of the Franciscans who wished to remain in the area and go out to the Buffalo Plains again to try their hands at conversion of the natives. The result was that the official body of the expedition left New Mexico to retrace its route southward. Those who insisted on staying were left behind with the senior member of the party, Andrés Do Campo, a Portuguese officer (and one-time gardener), who became head of a detachment assigned to guard three Franciscans who chose to continue evangelization of the area.

The Horse in North America

With the departure of Vázquez de Coronado, one potentially culture-altering element, the horse, was withdrawn from the area. According to legends, the horse was introduced into North American Indian society as a result of the extended period of contact between the natives and the Coronado Expedition of 1540–1542. The later widespread extent of "horse Indians" seems to make such an early culture change appear logical.

However, there is little chance that such was the case. These early Spanish explorers brought with them very few mares, with one muster list of animals showing only two among the large number of mounts. As a percentage figure, it was probably less than .5 percent. Furthermore, the Spaniards' horses were extremely well guarded, both day and night. There is limited evidence of Indian capacity for stealing horses at that time, and certainly the loss of any significant number of mounts would have been noted in the expedition journals. The record notes that a few horses strayed off and that several others were killed in the Battle of Tiguex; still, later accounts of sixteenth and early seventeenth century expeditions into the Southwest and the Great Plains make no reference to any mounted Indians—certainly such a novelty would have brought forth considerable comment. The spectacular acculturation of the Plains Indians to a horse-oriented life was no doubt based on animals descended from stock that strayed or were obtained from the Spanish settlements after the permanent colonization of New Mexico and Texas in the seventeenth century. Anthropologists tend to date the emergence of the "mounted Indian" at about 1640 or 1650.

Father Juan Padilla Continues the Quest

With plans to cease exploration and return home, Coronado was faced with those protesters who were opposed to giving up so easily after so much planning and effort. Both soldiers and missionaries were among those who wanted to stay on in anticipation of more favorable results; they felt that with greater effort in other directions, success would crown their endeavors. With the advantage of hindsight, it is obvious that, despite the dismal results achieved up to that point, the stories of advanced civilizations and receptive groups of converts had not yet been eradicated from their minds.

In an effort to advance evangelization of the northern frontier, Vázquez de Coronado supported the three Franciscan priests who wanted to stay behind, providing them with a small contingent of military troops for their defense. Of the three, one priest in particular stands out—Father Juan Padilla. He was particularly interested in dealing with the Plains Indians, to which end he and some soldiers and a couple of *donados* (Indian lay brothers) returned to Quivira on the Buffalo Plains east of New Mexico. There Father Juan was well received by most of the Indians, though finally he met a mysteriously hostile group. Seeing that his small party was about to be attacked by those Indians and realizing his dire predicament, Father Padilla sacrificed himself while entreating his companions to flee for their lives. Padilla gave his life for his faith, and was the protomartyr of New Mexico's history, though he was soon joined by the two other Franciscans, Father Juan de Ubeda and Father Juan de la Cruz, who died at Cicuyé (Pecos) and Tiguex, respectively.

Father Padilla's arrow-filled body was later recovered by a Spanish party and was buried, as tradition indicates, in the floor of San Agustín Church at Isleta Indian Pueblo. In fact, the story of Juan Padilla's remains is one of long standing, recounting that, every twenty years, his bones attempt to leave their place of burial to be reunited with his spirit, which wanders in a separate existence on the lonely Buffalo Plains. The legend rests on controverted evidence, since the Father Padilla whose grave is at Isleta Pueblo is a later Franciscan, and the movement of the extant bones is not as regular as the legend suggests, but rather seems to respond to rises and declines of the water table of the nearby Río Grande. Notwithstanding these objections, the legend continues and forms one of the many religious stories that make up the folk beliefs of the region.

The stories of the survivors of the attack that took Father Padilla's life are also interesting. Andrés do Campo, military leader of the small party, emulating the successes of Alvar Núñez Cabeza de Vaca, roamed around in the interior, won some successes and fame as a medicine man, and finally returned to Mexico after as much as five years of wandering. He followed an itinerary almost directly southward, but since he had no such literary bent as the earlier itinerant, nor was he as well placed socially or politically, the result is that few have heard of his solo saga, one filled with adventure and discovery.

The two Indian lay brothers, Lucas and Sebastián, apparently from the Guadalajara area of Jalisco, escaped from the same Plains Indian attack. They stayed together, but they never had contact with do Campo, the Portuguese officer. The donados also made their way back to Mexico by a similar route. Many years later they were both reported to be living in the Nueva Galicia area. There was no follow-up information or other impact reported from the stories of Andrés do Campo or the donados, save for their report of Father Juan Padilla's death.

Coronado, the leader of Spain's first great reconnaissance of the Southwest, returned a failure but was stoutly defended by almost all his fellow explorers. Of course, his greatest shortcoming had been his inability to find those rich cities that were still thought to exist somewhere in the Mysterious North. After a prolonged inquiry concerning the expedition, Coronado was exonerated of any blame and spent the remainder of his life, some twelve years, involved in the government of New Spain's capital city of Mexico. In 1549, with the passage of time, and still maintaining a friendship with Antonio de Mendoza, Vázquez de Coronado received a royal grant of an encomienda of Indians as a reward for his meritorious services in discovery and conquest, a gesture that the old explorer did not consider to be total vindication for losses earlier sustained. Gradually Coronado's health declined, and on September 22, 1554, he died in Mexico City. He and his wife are buried there in the Church of Santo Domingo not far from the central plaza.

Was, as some have thought, his expedition a pointless jaunt, not only a disappointment but also a financial disaster of the first magnitude? The answer is no. It was a necessary prelude to eventual Spanish settlement and it established for the first time an appreciation of the vastness of the continent. For the native Indians, it foreshadowed the disruption of their previous existence. Interest in the interior, however, did decline for several decades and exploratory emphasis was shifted to seeking a short water route to the Orient, an almost equally elusive goal. Still, Coronado's failure ended the era of great conquerors who risked their lives and private fortunes for the promise of vast feudal estates and the tribute of wealthy subject peoples.

JUAN RODRÍGUEZ CABRILLO TAKES THE HELM

Viceroy Mendoza, disillusioned by the meager results of Coronado's effort, resolutely turned to the sea with yet another plan to find northern riches and the elusive Strait of Anián. Pedro de Alvarado, governor and adelantado of Guatemala, appeared at the port of Acapulco in 1540 with a fleet of thirteen vessels and offered his services to the crown for Pacific exploration. A powerful lieutenant who had served Cortés throughout the conquest of Mexico, Alvarado in 1523 had led an army of 400 Spaniards and 20,000 Indian allies into the fertile highlands of Guatemala on a brutal campaign of conquest, forcing the Indians to submit. At Alvarado's right hand during the siege stood Juan Rodríguez Cabrillo, navigator, horseman, captain of crossbowmen, and eventual discoverer of Alta California. With victory achieved in 1524, Alvarado founded Santiago de Guatemala and became captain-general of a province stretching from southern Mexico to the boundary of Panama; Cabrillo was appointed second-in-command of Alvarado's Acapulco fleet.

Though certain details of the background and life of Juan Rodríguez Cabrillo prior to his arrival in Mexico have come to light in recent years, his exact age and place of birth are still unknown. Rodríguez Cabrillo's original journal of exploration has not been found, but documents in the Archives of the Indies in Seville and in the General Archives of Central America in Guatemala give an account of his service to Spain, his family and estates in Guatemala, and his activities in California. His surname, which in its correct form would be Rodríguez or Rodríguez Cabrillo, indicates that his nationality is Spanish; he always signed himself Juan Rodríguez in the Spanish way.

The record of Cabrillo's life begins in 1510 when as a boy of about 12 he arrived in the New World. He participated in the conquest of Cuba under Diego de Velásquez and then traveled to the Mexican coast with the expedition under Panfilo de Narváez to proceed against the defiant Cortés. Cortés left part of his army under Alvarado at Tenochtitlán and returned to Veracruz to face the new threat from his home base. Defeating the Spanish force in a surprise move, Cortés won the soldiers to his side with promises of gold and prepared them to attack the Aztec island capital. Cabrillo thus became a part of Cortés's reinforced army and, because Alvarado had failed to contain the Aztecs, served through the bloodiest battles of the conquest. Bernal Díaz del Castillo recorded that Cabrillo "was a good soldier in the Mexican campaign ... who later, as a resident of Guatemala, was a very honorable person, and was captain and admiral of thirteen ships on Pedro Alvarado's behalf, and he served his majesty well in everything which presented itself to him ... ." (Diaz, *A True History of the Conquest of New Spain, 1517–1521*, p. 283)

Juan Rodríguez Cabrillo first engaged in farming and mining in Guatemala on the estates granted to him by Alvarado. In 1536 he was charged with the construction of a fleet of ships capable of exploring the most dangerous and remote areas of the Pacific. Assembling materials for such ships was so difficult that Cabrillo established headquarters in Honduras to get supplies by sea from the Atlantic. At a great sacrifice of lives, thousands of Indians transported the heavy metalwork, rigging, and other equipment across swamps and mountains to the Pacific Coast at Acajutla in present-day El Salvador. Construction of Alvarado's fleet proceeded slowly as tools were scarce and Cabrillo insisted upon high standards of quality, but thirteen ships were finally completed at government expense by 1540, although one, the *San Salvador,* was built by Cabrillo with his own funds. When the vessels were ready to sail, Alvarado asked his master shipwright to join the expedition in his own *San Salvador,* as admiral of the entire fleet. Cabrillo agreed and the ships reached the Mexican port of Navidad, near Colima, on Christmas Day, 1540.

Viceroy Mendoza and Alvarado entered into a partnership for Pacific exploration, which included the use of Cabrillo's own ship. They planned to divide the fleet into two parts: one to investigate islands far to the west, and the other to explore the North

American Pacific Coast northward "until its end and secret were sighted." (Kelsey, *Juan Rodriguez Cabrillo*, pp. 79–81) Just before departure, however, Alvarado left his ships in Cabrillo's charge while he fulfilled the viceroy's request to help put down the uprising known as the Mixton War. Ironically, this 1541 battle cost Alvarado his life—he was crushed to death by his falling horse. Viceroy Mendoza then took possession of Alvarado's fleet and, showing high regard for Cabrillo, commissioned the Guatemalan to sail the *San Salvador,* a caravel, and *La Victoria,* a small, open sailing launch, northward along the Pacific Coast in search of the Strait of Anían. The remaining vessels were dispatched to the Philippines under command of Ruy López de Villalobos.

Cabrillo's Voyage to Upper California

Fig. 2.3. Juan Rodríguez Cabrillo. Façade, San Diego Museum of Man. Photo by Iris Engstrand.

Because of Alvarado's untimely death, with two and possibly the least adequate vessels of Alvarado's fleet, Cabrillo's expedition set sail from the Port of Navidad on June 27, 1542, to explore the remote, uncharted areas of the North Pacific. Upon leaving the major port, both the flagship, probably not more than sixty feet long, and its consort were under-equipped and poorly provisioned, yet Cabrillo's men faced the possibility of death by thirst, starvation and scurvy with courageous indifference. The goal that had inspired so many before them—finding the Northwest Passage and a shortcut to Oriental riches—propelled these Spanish adventurers into unknown waters further to the north than any yet sailed by European ships.

Cabrillo's two ships entered the Bay of Ensenada, Baja California, on September 17, 1542. The expedition remained in port five days and then continued on, covering daily fifteen to twenty miles. Within three days they sighted the three Coronado Islands, called by Cabrillo Las Islas Desiertas and placed at 34° north latitude (about 2° too far north). From these waters the Spanish seamen noticed the smoke of coastal Indian fires and, as they approached the mainland, saw a promising green valley backed by high mountains. On September 28, 1542, Cabrillo headed the *San Salvador* and *La Victoria* into San Diego Bay, dropped anchor on the lee side of Point Loma, and formally discovered Alta California—as distinguished from Baja California. The Spaniards stepped ashore and were greeted by friendly Indians whom Cabrillo described as "well built" and clothed in animal skins. The admiral bestowed the name of San Miguel Arcangel upon his newly discovered "closed and very good port," but it was changed by Sebastian Vizcaíno, a later navigator who chose to honor San Diego de Alcalá instead. (Bolton, ed., Cabrillo Account, *Spanish Exploration in the Southwest*, p. 23)

Three Indians timidly approached Cabrillo's ship, indicating by signs that they knew of other similarly dressed white men, carrying crossbows and swords, traveling far inland. Cabrillo understood from the Indians' gestures that these strangers, probably a detachment from Coronado's expedition, wielded lances from horseback and had killed many Indians. For this reason the California natives were afraid, but the Spaniards gave them presents and calmed their fears. When Indians wounded three seamen on a night fishing party near the shore, Cabrillo ordered his crew not to fire on them but instead to win their confidence. Spain's first visitors to California, called Guacamal by the Indians, thus set a precedent of friendly treatment that was followed with few exceptions during the entire Spanish occupation of the territory.

Sailing from San Diego after six days' rest, the expedition sighted the Channel Islands of San Clemente and Santa Catalina. The *San Salvador* and *La Victoria* headed toward the mainland and Cabrillo sighted the bay of San Pedro (his Bahia de los Fumos); they continued a course along the coast and visited the Indian fishing village Cabrillo called Pueblo de Canoas. Heavy winds from the northwest near Point Concepción forced the ships to find shelter in a small port of San Miguel Island. On this island, which they named Isla de la Posesión, misfortune marred their enviable exploring record. While going ashore, Cabrillo fell on the rocky beach and broke his arm. Ignoring his wound, Cabrillo ordered his men to continue their mapping and coastal explorations and, despite winter storms and adverse winds, they reached an area near San Francisco Bay by mid-November. Here they turned southward and set their course for the safety of San Miguel. By the end of December, however, gangrene had severely complicated Cabrillo's injury—finally causing his death on January 3, 1543. The crew buried their leader on the barren, windswept island of La Posesión and renamed it Isla de Juan Rodríguez. Shifting winds and sands have covered all traces of the grave.

Cabrillo's final words reflected the dauntless spirit of the early Spanish explorers. He instructed his chief pilot Bartolomé Ferrer not to give up their projected reconnaissance of the northern coast, and the two ships again sailed into the open sea, making their way northward against heavy gales. Finally driven dangerously near the shore at a point somewhere near the Oregon boundary, they prayed for protection and were saved by a sudden change of wind. The expedition's journal describes few recognizable landmarks, making their exact course difficult to follow. Their estimated latitude of 44° was probably 2 degrees too high, but leaves no doubt about their courage in facing the perils of unknown waters.

Cabrillo's crew, weakened from exposure and scurvy, responded gratefully to Ferrer's order that the *San Salvador* and *La Victoria* return home. They reached the port of Navidad on April 14, 1543, with the sad news of Cabrillo's death and the discouraging results of their discoveries. They had found no Strait of Anían, no fabulous Indian civilization, no weapons of gold from an island of Amazons—nothing to enrich nor even excite the expectant viceroy of New Spain. Mendoza closely guarded the charts of the explorations, and Cabrillo's own journal, kept a secret, as yet has not been found. The name of this intrepid explorer—first European to walk the shores of the Alta California coast—was soon forgotten and eventually not even his place names were left to honor his expedition. Sixty years later Vizcaíno followed Cabrillo's same course and, unable to recognize certain landmarks, or perhaps disregarding instructions, renamed the places discovered and charted by his predecessor.

─────────────────────── *Chapter Two* ───────────────────────
BIBLIOGRAPHIC ESSAY

For general background on Spanish history, see Pedro Aguado Bleyes and Cayetano Alcazar Molina, *Manual de Historia de España,* Tomos I, II, and III (Madrid: Espasa-Calpe, 1964); Claudio Sánchez Albornoz, *Spain: A Historical Enigma,* 2 vols. (Madrid: Fundación Universitaria Española, 1975); Stanley G. Payne, *A History of Spain and Portugal,* 2 vols. (Madison: University of Wisconsin Press, 1973); J. H. Elliott, *Imperial Spain, 1469–1716* (Harmondsworth, England: Penguin Books, 1975); Henry Kamen, *Spain, 1469–1714: A Society of Conflict* (New York: Longman, 1991); and John Crow, *Spain: The Root and the Flower: An Interpretation of Spain and the Spanish People* (Berkeley: University of California Press, 1985). For New World interpretations see Hubert H. Herring, *A History of Latin America from the Beginning to the Present* (New York: Alfred A. Knopf, 1965) and J. H. Elliott, *The Old World and the New* (Cambridge, Mass.: Cambridge University Press, 1970). Exploration and discovery is covered in Juan Dantin Cereceda, *Exploradores y conquistadores de las Indias Occidentales 1492–1540: Relatos geográficos* (Madrid: Consejo Superior de Investigaciones Científicas, 1964) and Manuel Ballesteros Gaibrois, ed., *Bibliotheca Indiana: Viajes y Viajeros por Norteamerica* (Madrid: Aguilar, 1958).

As a result of the Columbus Quincentennial celebration in 1992, a number of new works were published. A three-volume study edited by David Hurst Thomas under the general title of *Columbian Consequences* contained some new interpretations. Volume I, *Archeological and Historical Perspectives on the Spanish Borderlands West* and Volume III, *The Spanish Borderlands in Pan American Perspective,* are the most pertinent to this study (Washington, D.C.: The Smithsonian Institution Press, 1989–1991). An older standard work on Columbus is Samuel Eliot Morison, *Admiral of the Ocean Sea* (Boston: Little Brown, 1942). New contributions include David Henige, *In Search of Columbus: The Sources for the First Voyage* (Tucson: University of Arizona Press, 1991) and Oliver Dunn and James E. Kelley, Jr., eds. and trans., *The "Diario" of Christopher Columbus's First Voyage to America, 1492–1493, Abstracted by Fray Bartolomé de Las Casas.* (Norman: University of Oklahoma Press, 1991). The books on Hernán Cortés and the conquest of Mexico are many. Especially significant are Salvador de Madariaga, *Hernan Cortés, Conqueror of Mexico* (New York: Macmillan Company, 1941); Henry R. Wagner, *The Rise of Fernando Cortés* (Los Angeles: The Cortés Society, 1944); Bernal Diaz del Castillo, *A True History of the Conquest of New Spain, 1517–1521,* translated by A. P. Maudslay with an introduction by Irving Leonard (New York: Farrar, Straus and Giroux, 1966); A. R. Pagden, trans. and ed., *Hernán Cortés: Letters from Mexico* (New York: Orion Press, 1971); and Miguel Leon Portilla, ed., *The Broken Spears: The Aztec Account of the Conquest of Mexico* (Boston: Beacon Press, 1992). Francis J. Brooks, "Revising the Conquest of Mexico: Smallpox, Sources and Populations," *Journal of Interdisciplinary History,* 24 (summer 1993):1–29 gives an excellent argument that accounts of smallpox's destruction of lives are exaggerated. W. Michael Mathes, ed. and trans., *The Conquistador in California: 1535: The Voyage of Fernando Cortés to Baja California in Chronicles and Documents* (Los Angeles: Dawson's Book Shop, 1973) talks about the later activities of Cortés.

Primary sources for the study of Spanish penetration into the southwestern part of the United States are to be found in the Archivo General de Indias in Sevilla; on microfilm copies in The Bancroft Library at the University of California, Berkeley; the library of the Arizona Historical Society and University of Arizona Library, Tucson; in the State Archives of New Mexico in Santa Fe; and in the Center for Southwestern Research at the University of New Mexico in Albuquerque. Additional materials can be found in the published *Documentos Inéditos del Archivo de Indias,* Francisco de Oviedo's *Historia General y Natural de las Indias* (tomo III, lib. xxxv., ed. 1853), and in the twelve volumes of Antonio de Herrera, *Historia general de los hechos de los Castellanos en las islas i tierra firme del mar oceano* (first printed in Madrid from 1601 to 1615), edited by Antonio Ballesteros and Beretta (Madrid, n.p., 1934–1953). There is also a guide to the major documents of the conquest period edited by Henry R. Wagner, *The Spanish Southwest, 1542–1794: An Annotated Bibliography* published in two volumes by the Quivira Society (Albuquerque, 1937).

A good English version of Cabeza de Vaca's journey is Cleve Hallenbeck, *Alvar Nuñez Cabeza de Vaca: The Journey and Route of the First European to Cross the Continent of North America, 1534–1536* (Glendale, Calif.: The Arthur H. Clark Co., 1940). In Spanish is Martin A. Favata and José B. Fernandez, eds., *La "Relación" o "Naufragios" de Alvar Nuñez Cabeza de Vaca* (Potomac, Md.: Scripta Humanistica, 1986). Early articles on the controversial Fray Marcos de Niza were written by Percy M. Baldwin, "Fray Marcos de Niza and His Discovery of the Seven Cities of Cibola," *New Mexico Historical Review,* 1 (April 1926):193–223 and Carl O. Sauer, "The Credibility of the Fray Marcos Account," *NMHR,* 16 (April 1941):233–243, whereas the most recent and complete analysis of the journey is in a new edition of Cleve Hallenbeck's *The Journey of Fray Marcos de Niza* with an introduction by David J. Weber (Dallas: Southern Methodist University Press, 1987). See also David J. Weber, "Fray Marcos de Niza and the Historians," in *Myth and the History of the Hispanic Southwest* (Albuquerque: University of New Mexico Press, 1988).

Frederick Webb Hodge edited the narratives of both Alvar Nuñez Cabeza de Vaca and Pedro de Castañeda's narrative of the expedition of Francisco Vázquez de Coronado in *Spanish Explorers in the Southern United States, 1528–1543* and Herbert E. Bolton edited *Spanish Exploration in the Southwest,* both published in New York by Charles Scribner's Sons in 1907 and 1908. George Winship's "The Coronado Expedition," *Fourteenth Annual Report,* Bureau of American Ethnology, Part I (Washington, D.C.: Government Printing Office, 1896), contains several original narratives. It has been republished as *The Journey of Coronado, 1540–1542,* with an introduction by Donald Cutter (Golden, Colo.: Fulcrum Publishing, 1990). Relatively modern works are A. Grove Day, *Coronado's Quest: The Discovery of the Southwestern States* (Berkeley: University of California Press, 1940) and Herbert E. Bolton, *Coronado on the Turquoise Trail: Knight of Pueblos and Plains* (Albuquerque: University of New Mexico Press, 1949). George Hammond and Agapito Rey edited and translated *Narratives of the Coronado Expedition, 1540– 1542* (Albuquerque: University of New Mexico Press, 1940) and edited *The Rediscovery of New Mexico 1580–1594* (Albuquerque: University of New Mexico Press, 1966) using documents in the Archivo General de Indias for the journeys of Espejo and Oñate. Also useful are Baltasar de Obregón, *Historia de los descubrimientos antiguos y modernos de la Nueva España* edited by Mariano Cuevas (Mexico: Secretaría de Educación, 1924); Angélico Chávez, *Coronado's Friars.* (Washington, D.C.: Academy of American Franciscan History, 1968); and Charles Gibson, *The Aztecs under Spanish Rule: The Indians of the Valley of Mexico, 1519–1810* (Stanford: Stanford University Press, 1964). Recent articles on Coronado are Joseph P. Sánchez, "Old Heat and New Light Concerning the Search for Coronado's Bridge: A Historiography of the Pecos and Canadian Rivers Hypotheses," *NMHR,* 67 (April 1992):101–14; Albert H. Schroeder, "The Locale of Coronado's 'Bridge,'" *New Mexico Historical Review,* 67 (April 1992):115–22; Richard Flint and Shirley Cushing Flint, "Coronado's Crosses: Route Markers Used by the Coronado Expedition," *Journal of the Southwest,* 35 (summer 1993):207–216; and "The Coronado Expedition: Cicuye to the Rio de Cicuye Bridge," *NMHR,* 67 (April 1992):123–38.

Jack D. Forbes has provided excellent information from the Native American point of view in *Apache, Navaho and Spaniard* (Norman: University of Oklahoma Press, 1960). He also wrote "Melchior Diaz and the Discovery of Alta California," for the *Pacific Historical Review,* 27 (November 1958): 351– 57. Viceroy Mendoza's life is detailed in Arthur Scott Aiton, *Antonio de Mendoza: First Viceroy of New Spain* (Durham: Duke University Press, 1927); the voyage of Ulloa in Richard Hakluyt, ed. *Third and Last Volume of the Principal Navigations, Voyages, Traffiques, and Discoveries of the English Nation* (London: George Bishop, 1600), and Maurice G. Holmes, *From New Spain to the Californias by Sea, 1519– 1668* (Glendale, Calif.: Arthur H. Clark, 1963); and the life of Juan Rodríguez Cabrillo in Harry Kelsey, *Juan Rodriguez Cabrillo* (San Marino: The Huntington Library, 1986). See also Kelsey, "Mapping the California Coast: The Voyages of Discovery, 1533–1543," *Arizona and the West,* 26 (winter 1984):307– 324. An interesting sidelight is Stephen T. Garrahy and David J. Weber, "Francisco de Ulloa, Joseph James Markey, and the Discovery of Upper California," *California Historical Society Quarterly,* 50 (March 1971):73–77. Also important are Philip Wayne Powell, *Soldiers, Indians and Silver: The Northward Advance of New Spain, 1550–1600* (Berkeley: University of California Press, 1952), and Albert H. Schroeder, "A Reanalysis of the Routes of Coronado and Oñate onto the Plains in 1541 and 1601," *Plains Anthropologist,* 7 (February 1962):2–23. A recent work is Douglas Preston, *Cities of Gold: A Journey Across the American Southwest in Pursuit of Coronado* (New York: Simon and Schuster, 1992).

Chapter Three

CONQUEST AND CONFLICT: 1542–1607

THE MANILA GALLEON TRADE

*R*odríguez Cabrillo's failure to find the Northwest passage combined with Spain's need for more trade brought renewed efforts to conquer the Philippines. Visited by Ferdinand Magellan in 1521, the islands nominally belonged to Portugal by the Papal Donation of 1493. Ruy López de Villalobos had nevertheless taken possession of the Philippines for Spain in 1542 but, unable to overcome native hostility, was eventually captured by the Portuguese. Activity in crossing the Pacific had slowed because none of the explorers had yet found a successful return route to New Spain. Vessels sailing eastward from the islands were quickly becalmed; the only certain way was around Africa to the Atlantic. Clearly a return route would have to be found.

Philip II (1556–1598) inherited the Spanish empire at the time of its greatest extension but was also left its most serious problems. While the New World viceroys strengthened Spain's hold in the Indies, the home country lagged behind the rest of Europe. And as the Protestant movement gained force, Spain doggedly clung to the dream of a Catholic Europe and wasted vast resources on useless battles. The government subsidized an enormous priesthood for many whose only wish was to avoid hard work. To achieve total Catholic unity, Philip II expelled the last of the Moors—industrious subjects living in former Moslem areas of Granada—and carried on a religious "cold war" with much of Europe. The constant financial drain upon the country caused by foreign enterprises, and heightened by frequent English raids on the Spanish treasure fleet, made new sources of income vital. Thus Philip II ordered New Spain's Viceroy Luis de Velasco (1551–1564) to outfit an expedition for Pacific conquest.

The crucial navigational problems of the Philippine route were entrusted to Andrés de Urdaneta, who late in life had become an Augustinian monk. Philip II thought Urdaneta, an experienced mariner, would be indispensable to the voyage, and so appointed him chaplain of the expedition. The fleet reached the islands in February 1565, and about 400 ground troops under military commander Miguel López de Legazpi began their conquest on Cebu. Urdaneta, after studying the winds and currents, took three vessels and headed northward to the Japanese currents. He plotted a great circular route, reaching the Pacific Coast at about Cape Mendocino; when the vessels sighted California they turned southward and sailed for Acapulco. Urdaneta received credit for discovering a feasible, although long and difficult, trade route that opened the way for Spain's famed Manila Galleons. In the meantime, Legazpi's troops occupied Cebu, overcame native and Portuguese resistance, and eventually took over Luzon. Legazpi, given authority by Viceroy Velasco of New Spain, founded the town of Manila in 1571.

A regular trade route established with one or two annual galleons was opened between Manila and Spain via Mexico. Each ship, usually weighing from 400 to 600 tons, carried a crew of about 115 men; each was fitted out at royal expense and commanded by an officer of the king. Profits were high, but miserable conditions on board ship caused heavy losses from death and desertion. The inadequate water supply often turned brackish and even the vermin-invested food frequently ran out before shore was reached. Provisions were sacrificed for trade goods that included silks for Spanish shawls, velvet, gold and silver brocades, jewelry, perfumes, exotic preserves of orange and peach, cedar chests, fine thread, ornaments of all kinds, and the highly prized pepper and other spices—in great demand for the preservation and palatability of meat that suffered from lack of refrigeration.

Prices for these Oriental commodities were high, bringing as much as 25,000 dollars in profit to the captain on a single trip. Consequently Spanish seamen, given permission to carry a small share of goods, were willing to endure incredible hardships. Many, used to the hot Philippine climate, died from the severe cold encountered in northern latitudes; others, weakened by exposure to wind and rain, were swept overboard by huge waves that threatened to submerge the shaky crafts. But the worst danger was from disease. For example, scurvy and beriberi resulted from the lack of fresh provisions containing the necessary vitamins C and B. The number of deaths often reached 50 percent of the crew members and few persons, if any, reached Acapulco without some suffering from the ravages of these diseases. Symptoms included bleeding gums, open sores, loss of teeth and nails, and general debilitation. For this reason the California coast was looked to as a potential stopping-place where the weak and dying galleon crews could obtain relief. Colonial administrators even suggested further exploration of California to find a suitable natural harbor where port facilities could be established, but plans were slow in developing.

DRAKE'S VISIT TO CALIFORNIA

For fifty years Spain had enjoyed almost free occupation of the Pacific Ocean, but in 1578 Francis Drake, an English navigator later knighted for his daring exploits, shattered Spanish confidence. England, by this time under the clever, energetic, and devoutly Protestant Elizabeth I, represented a thorny challenge to Philip's Catholic empire. The English queen encouraged revolt within the Spanish Netherlands and nodded approval as Elizabethan privateers preyed on Spanish shipping in the Caribbean. Drake's expedition, which sailed from Plymouth harbor in November 1577, originally planned to explore the coast of South America from the Río de la Plata around to the limit of Spanish settlement on the Chilean coast, and then return by the same route. Drake later claimed Queen Elizabeth's special charge was for him to annoy the King of Spain in his Indies.

Drake's flagship, the *Pelican*, successfully weathered sixteen treacherous days in the stormy Straits of Magellan and, separated from its fleet, emerged alone into the Pacific. Drake renamed his ship the *Golden Hind* and began a series of raids along the Chilean and Peruvian coasts, capturing unsuspecting Spanish vessels with ease. Finally, the eighty-foot *Golden Hind*, more heavily laden with treasure and provisions than a Manila galleon, sought shelter on the northern Pacific Coast. The English reached the California shore somewhere near San Francisco Bay on June 17, 1579. Drake called the country Nova Albion for two reasons: " ... one in respect of the white bancks and cliffes, which lie toward the sea; the other that it might have some affinity, even in name also, with our own country, which was sometime so called." (Drake, *The World Encompassed*) Since Drake's original journal has disappeared and because his chaplain's diary was called unreliable by Drake himself, considerable mystery surrounds the precise location of the English visit.

Present-day Drakes Bay, situated at 38° latitude and sheltered from northwesterly weather by the Point Reyes headland, fits in most completely with the sixteenth-century accounts of Drake's thirty-six day encamp-

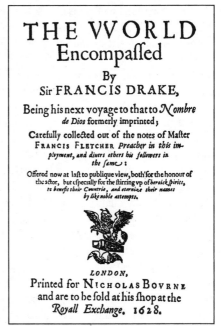

THE WORLD
Encompassed
By
Sir FRANCIS DRAKE,

Being his next voyage to that to *Nombre de Dios* formerly imprinted;

Carefully collected out of the notes of Master FRANCIS FLETCHER *Preacher in this imployment, and diuers others his followers in the same*:

Offered now at last to publique view, both for the honour of the actor, but especially for the stirring vp of heroick spirits, to benefit their Countrie, and eternize their names by like noble attempts.

LONDON,
Printed for NICHOLAS BOVRNE and are to be sold at his shop at the *Royall Exchange.* 1628.

Fig. 3.1. *The World Encompassed* frontispiece.

ment in California. According to Drake's chroniclers, they sailed northward toward Oregon, but "drew back ... till we came within 38 degrees towards the line. In which height it pleased God to send us into a faire and good Baye with a good winde to enter the same." A slightly different narrative, prepared by Drake's nephew, read: "In 38 degrees 30' we fell with a convenient and fit harborough June 17 and came to anchor therein, where we continued till the 23rd day of July following."

Drake careened the *Golden Hind* for cleaning and repair in a sheltered cove. The mouth of Drake's *estero*, adjacent to the bay, is free of ocean surge and offers excellent shore and tidal conditions for the hazardous operation of careening described in Drake's accounts. Further, the Indians with whom Drake came into friendly and frequent contact have been identified as Coast Miwok, inhabitants of the Drakes Bay region. Nevertheless, no certain identification has been made of Drake's exact landing site.

Drake took possession of the country for England, recording his claim on a plate of brass, inserted with a sixpence by his blacksmith, and nailed to "a great and firm poste." The inscription read in part: " ... June 17, 1579, by the Grace of God and in the name of Her Majesty Queen Elizabeth of England ... I take possession of this Kingdome ... now named by me and to be known unto all men as Nova Albion. Francis Drake." (Drake, *The World Encompassed*, p. 285) Since no archeological remains of Drake's visit have been uncovered anywhere in the area, the alleged discovery of Drake's "Plate of Brass" at Drakes Bay in 1933, and its discovery or rediscovery in 1936 near Corte Madera Creek inside San Francisco Bay, have done little more than add a note of additional confusion. Following internal and external analysis, a metallurgical study, and identification of the writing as Elizabethan in style and spelling, the plate was duly authenticated shortly after it was found. However, after additional and more sophisticated tests were made during the l980s, few persons remained who believed the artifact was genuine.

The uncertainties of Drake's landfall lend credence to arguments advanced for Bodega Bay, Tomales Bay, a bay on one of the Channel Islands, or perhaps even a cove inside San Francisco Bay as the English campsite. This controversy should not, however, obscure Drake's ability and character. Contemporary accounts agree that he was an exceptional navigator and capable of seeing what was necessary for the good of his country. He lived in times when the challenge of England was to weaken Spanish control in the New World. Drake's claim to California came to represent little more than a token gesture to honor Queen Elizabeth, but the presence of English ships posed a new threat to Spain's Pacific dominions. Drake, knowing the difficulty of returning through the Straits of Magellan and aided by captured Spanish charts, sailed the *Golden Hind* around the world, arriving at Plymouth safely in the summer of 1580. Other Englishmen would strike at Spain from the sea, leaving the interior regions of California and the Spanish Southwest entirely to Spaniards and Indians for the next two centuries.

EARLY SETTLEMENT IN NEW MEXICO

Because of the failures of Coronado and others to find riches in the north, nearly forty years passed before another Spaniard actually entered the Southwest. Then, in 1563, a young Spanish conquistador, Francisco de Ibarra, by way of New Mexico, founded the city of Durango as the capital of the province of Nueva Vizcaya (which for more than 200 years included Arizona and New Mexico.) Also in 1563, a group of Spaniards went north to work in the mines of southeastern Chihuahua and founded the town of Santa Barbara. From there, slave-hunting parties looked for Indians to work in the mines.

As a general area, but without boundaries, New Mexico received its name before any extensive re-exploration. As discussed earlier, the first known use of the toponym is found in a report by Franciscan Father Jacinto de San Francisco written in 1561. In the context of that early use, it probably meant "another Mexico" or a "second Mexico" rather than in the sense of a contrast between old and new, such as was later the case with Old and New California. Father San Francisco's report had no known impact on subsequent occupation of the area, for it was not until 1581 that any concrete plans for exploration or re-exploration developed. In that year, encouraged by local residents who were also interested in the frontier of Nueva Vizcaya, Agustín Rodríguez, a Franciscan lay brother, was able to enlist the cooperation of two other Franciscans, Fathers Francisco López and Juan de Santa María, who joined a party that he was forming. Only nine soldiers were willing to go, to which were added nineteen Indian servants. The party obtained the services of an aging frontier soldier of long experience, the sexagenarian Francisco Sánchez "Chamuscado," with the final name perhaps being a nickname for the old officer. Equipped with ninety horses, perhaps the first into the area since the visit of the Vázquez de Coronado expedition four decades earlier, 600 head of stock, and appropriate trade items, the party set out from the northern outpost of Santa Barbara. Obviously with such a large train, speed was not an important consideration, nor did it seem that the party was intending to live off the land.

The expedition followed a circuitous route via the Flórido and Conchos Rivers to La Junta (its junction) with the Río Grande, at what is today Ojinaga. At that relatively large river—one which over the years has been given many names such as the Concepción, the Magdalena, the Turbio, the Guadalquivir, and the Bravo—they headed north by following it upstream, going as far as present-day Bernalillo. The Rodríguez-Chamuscado visitors gave the area their own name—the Kingdom of San Felipe—in honor of the King's saint and doubtless in an effort to gain royal attention. As a religious symbol during exploration, the Franciscans distributed crosses to the local natives.

From the Río Grande the party made side trips, first over the Manzano Mountains to the Pecos River and then beyond to the Buffalo Plains—included within the Great Plains geomorphic province. En route, they noted salt deposits, the importance of which was not lost on these early explorers. Salt was always important to frontier advance and doubly so for mineral frontiers, for in addition to its preservative qualities, it was used in mineral reduction processes. Later, salt became an export item from New Mexico to the mining areas of Chihuahua to the south. The Rodríguez-Chamuscado expedition probably followed the Salt Trail as used for centuries by the Río Grande Pueblo of Isleta to get salt from the Estancia Valley.

In an effort to impress the local Indians, the Franciscans posed as Children of the Sun, which was a useful but theologically unsound concept. It was not an unknown ploy and probably was in response to their preconceived notion of the Indians' interest, as had been the case with Hernando de Alarcón four decades earlier along the banks of the Lower Colorado River. At some point during the course of the expedition, Father Santa María determined to set out on his own for home. Martyred somewhere in the Manzano Mountains, he became an early addition to the martyrs of New Mexico and was soon followed in this "greatest glory" of the missionary priesthood by Fathers Rodríguez and López, his two companions.

The Rodríguez-Chamuscado group originally had determined to stay in New Mexico to form an outpost for Christianity at Puaray, a location thought to have been a short distance south of Bernalillo. Even before the decision by some to stay on in New Mexico, the remainder of the party had decided to return to Chihuahua. In so doing, they apparently went west of the Río Grande into the Magdalena Mountains, though this is unclear. On the way home, the party's military leader, Chamuscado, fell ill and was treated by a normal blood letting, from which, or despite which, he died and was buried at Julimes, Chihuahua. The subsequent report of the expedition, as well as the general narrative is based on the *Relación* of the 24-year-old notary and soldier Hernán Gallegos. From this and from oral reports came a confused story of the expedition having found eleven silver mines, presumably in the Magdalenas. The rumors were sufficiently plausible to make the search for these mines one of the motives for a follow-up expedition.

THE ESPEJO-BELTRÁN EXPEDITION

Rescue expeditions have almost always been popular and well subscribed. Such was certainly the case with a sortie organized the following year, 1582, by Durangan priest Bernardino Beltrán. The fate of Fathers Rodríguez and López was as yet unknown, though it was rumored that they, like Santa María, had been killed. Pending approval for a full-scale rescue effort, Father Beltrán got permission to proceed without official funding. At that juncture an offer was made by Antonio Espejo to finance the operation and defray the cost of a squad of fourteen or fifteen soldiers as an escort.

Espejo's participation in the expedition is somewhat curious. He just happened to be in the area, was a lay officer of the Inquisition, and appeared to be interested in the expedition as a philanthropist. Though he may have had benevolent motives, it seems more likely that he saw an opportunity for profit, so in the guise of a benefactor, he seized the chance that otherwise would have eluded him. This hypothesis is in part substantiated by his insistence once the party was under way that there be an election to determine who should lead. It is not surprising that since the soldiers were in his pay, he was officially elected.

The Espejo-Beltrán party departed from San Bartolomé (now Allende) in November 1582 via the Flórido, Conchos, and Grande Rivers. Nearing the target area, they renamed the land that later became New Mexico, giving it the name Nueva Andalusia, doubtless from Espejo's area of origin in Spain. Early on, the travelers received reports confirming the suspected demise of the two Franciscans for whom they were searching. And, even after so many years, Indian informants also gave the party news of Cabeza de Vaca, of Chamuscado, as well as of the activities of slavers in the area.

Having assumed that Rodriguez and his companions were dead, Espejo decided to explore the country rather than return, and so journeyed to Acoma and then westward to the Zuni towns. From there Beltrán and about half of the Spaniards returned to Santa Barbara, while Espejo and nine others traveled northwestward looking for a lake of gold said to lie in that direction. Beltrán and the others knew, however, that Coronado had covered that country and found nothing. After four days, Espejo's group reached the Hopi towns, but were told they would be killed if they came closer. Espejo continued to advance, however, and was met about two miles outside of town by some 2,000 natives bearing provisions. Espejo reassured them that the Spaniards wanted to trade and gave them gifts. The situation actually turned into a profitable occasion with the Indians building a corral for Espejo's horses, since they were afraid of the animals. The Spaniards traded with these Indians of Awatobi for six days. Espejo received various kinds of ore and 4,000 cotton *mantas*.

Leaving five of his men to carry the bulky blankets to Zuni, Espejo and four companions traveled due west for forty-five leagues in search of some rich mines. They found them and were able to extract ore that contained silver. Espejo then sought behind the mountains a large river the Indians had told him of. More than eight leagues in width, it led to a rich and fertile plains country; at this point, Espejo was probably in the vicinity of Bill Williams Fork near Prescott, Arizona. The large river was no doubt the Colorado. He then left the area and returned to Zuni, finding Beltrán's party still there. The whole group left for the south and reached Santa Barbara on September 20, 1583.

Upon returning to the Río Grande, Espejo found Father Beltrán, but almost immediately the priest decided that he would set out for home and this time made good his determination to return to Durango. Espejo was not in accord, but rather decided to revisit the area to the east of the Manzanos and Sandias in the direction of the Pecos

River. After hitting the Pecos, he followed it downstream to its junction with the Río Grande, whence he returned home, his story and ore specimens led to great interest in the area of Arizona. (Present knowledge of the 1582 expedition is based on the account thereof kept by Diego Pérez de Luján, an expedition member.)

Gaspar Castaño de Sosa's Venture

Reports from the Espejo-Beltrán expedition sparked renewed interest in the northern frontier, resulting in various candidates applying for license to colonize the area. Among the applicants was Espejo, whose application was turned down for unknown reasons. Two contracts were let, but neither reached fruition, and an authorized visit to New Mexico did not occur for over fifteen years.

In the meantime, as the bureaucracy took its time, others proceeded illegally to attempt colonization, which the area seemed to invite. In 1590, Gaspar Castaño de Sosa, lieutenant governor of the northeastern frontier province of Nuevo León, in the absence of Governor Luis de Carbajal, took 170 colonists overland from Almadén in an unauthorized colonization venture. Lack of prosperity in Almadén was cited as the principal motive, and even the few reluctant local residents were convinced to join up belatedly following a doctored assay of an ore sample reputedly brought from New Mexico and produced at the proper moment.

A direct route was taken from Almadén to the Río Grande that was followed upstream to the mouth of the Pecos. In so doing, the renegade lieutenant governor became the first person to take four-wheeled wagons into what is today a part of the United States, though he did so with extreme difficulty owing to the rough terrain. The Pecos was ascended and a settlement was begun at or near Pecos Pueblo. A second community was established on the Río Grande at Santo Domingo Pueblo, a more central location.

The Castaño de Sosa colonization effort was short-lived. The viceroy of New Spain sent a prominent mestizo frontier captain, Juan Morlete of Mazapil, to apprehend Castaño and to return the colonists to Nuevo León. Morlete set out from Almadén with a small army of forty-three. His outbound route is not known, but the success of his mission was complete. At Santo Domingo, Morlete arrested Castaño and together all returned south, probably using the route of today's Inter-American Highway. For his unauthorized colonization effort, Castaño de Sosa was tried for invading the lands of peaceful Indians, raising an unauthorized army, and illegally entering into New Mexico. Found guilty, he was sentenced to exile for a period of six years in the Philippine Islands, during which time he was killed by galley slaves while on a trip to Molucca.

Francisco de Leyva de Bonilla

In 1593 there was another illegal entry, this time directly from the south via the frontier province of Nueva Vizcaya. The leader was Francisco de Leyva de Bonilla who approached the area as head of a retaliatory sortie against marauding natives of the Nueva Vizcaya frontier. His group spent an entire year at San Ildefonso Indian Pueblo and subsequently went out exploring on the Buffalo Plains. Almost from the beginning of the enterprise, Leyva had been unpopular. During the plains exploration the leader was murdered by Antonio Gutiérrez de Humaña, who then led the party into what is today

Kansas and Nebraska, as far as the Platte River. On the banks of that stream, at an unidentified spot, almost the entire party was killed by local natives. (Knowledge of this is sparse, based on the account of an Indian survivor named Jusepe or José.)

The importance of these precursory expeditions lies in their collective impact on the natives. They were the prelude to permanent colonization that would ensue shortly and was destined to alter Indian life permanently. Interest in New Mexico had reached higher levels of administration and there would be no turning back. Various candidates wishing to lead a permanent occupation effort presented plans for extension of Spanish control into the northern frontier region—that area substantially beyond the frontier line of mineral exploitation. Among the several applicants who emerged were the former benefactor Espejo, Juan Bautista de Lomas y Colmenares, Juan de Oñate, and Francisco de Urdiñola.

Considerable time elapsed between the preliminary sortie and final approval of the plan that brought about the desired goal of occupation. During that interval there was not only considerable jockeying for position, but also an important change in viceregal administration. This change brought Gaspar de Zúñiga y Acevedo, count of Monterrey, to New Spain as viceroy (1595–1603), though his interests lay more in increased exploration along the west coast and into the Pacific Ocean area. After nearly canceling all plans for movement toward New Mexico, a project espoused by his predecessors, he finally approved the plan presented by Oñate, though in a somewhat curtailed version. The delay also resulted in a loss of enthusiasm on the part of some of the would-be colonists and the diminishing personal resources of Juan de Oñate—the man named for the important assignment of colonization. In order to assure himself of adequate preparations by the chosen entrepreneur, the viceroy sent some royal inspectors to ascertain the status of preparations.

Explorers Along the California Coast

While plans were slowly being laid for an official *entrada* into New Mexico, New Spain's concerns were focused on the Pacific. In 1584, Francisco Gali, a prominent and highly regarded navigator and cosmographer, was in command of a Manila galleon that made a much greater sweep northward than usual on his return voyage, reaching almost to Alaskan waters. His coastal landfall on the California shore was very high, and he thought he saw evidence of a strait. Some traditions have him the discoverer of the Hawaiian Islands, or Islas de la Mesa. In any case, he was slated to make a follow-up voyage to the Pacific, but there is no indication of his having done so.

A second English interloper ravaged the Pacific Coast in 1586–1587. Thomas Cavendish, a native of Suffolk, assumed a pirate's role in a series of destructive raids—robbing, looting, and burning Spanish ships, amassing considerable treasure. His greatest prize was the capture of the great *Santa Ana*, a Manila galleon said to have been carrying more than 1,000,000 dollars in gold in addition to its regular cargo of silks, perfumes, jewelry, and other valuable commodities. Cavendish first sighted the galleon off Cape San Lucas where its pilot, Sebastián Rodríguez Cermeño, set a final course for the run to Acapulco and home. Without warning, the slow-moving *Santa Ana* fell easy prey to Cavendish's two ships, the *Desire* and the *Content*. Spanish joy at sighting the Baja

California coast turned to dismay as Cavendish systematically looted the galleon, put the people ashore (with provisions) and set fire to the "Great St. Ann." Cavendish headed into the Pacific and continued his voyage around the world, returning to England as a swashbuckling hero. The Spaniards rescued the *Santa Ana's* burning hulk, repaired the hull and eventually reached Acapulco.

While Cavendish was active in the Pacific, another Manila galleon commander of 1587, Pedro de Unamuno, had orders to search for the legendary islands of Rica de Oro and Rica de Plata and the Armenian Islands. He also had orders to explore the California coast, seeking a port of rest and refreshment. Unamuno landed at Morro Bay, just north of San Luis Obispo, where he performed a symbolic act of possession. In an attempt to explore inland, his party was attacked by the local Indians, probably the Chumash, and he was in too weakened a condition to carry out retaliation. The result of his visit was a set of official orders prohibiting further inland exploration and was a definite temporary deterrent to colonization.

The threat of English piracy gave New Spain's long-delayed plans to occupy California an added thrust. Cermeño, pilot of the tragic *Santa Ana*, was given command of the galleon *San Agustín* and instructed to look for possible California ports on his way back from Manila. Cermeño anchored in today's Drakes Bay (which he named San Francisco) early in November 1595. Fearful of taking the clumsy galleon too close to the rocky coast, he ordered his crew to build a large open sailing launch for detailed exploration. Cermeño, constantly apprehensive about the *San Agustín's* cargo, unhappily watched a fierce storm wreck his ship on the last day of November. The Spanish seamen completed and provisioned the open launch, and Cermeño, with all seventy passengers and crew, headed southward. Over constant protest, the captain continued surveying and mapping, noting particularly the entrance to Monterey Bay. When the launch reached Cedros Island, malnutrition, scurvy, and exhaustion finally forced him to stop work. Thankful for the safety of Acapulco, Cermeño recounted his epic tale of hunger, misery, and discouragement; but untouched officials, prejudiced by conflicting stories, reprimanded him for losing the ship and owners of the lost cargo threatened to sue for damages. The final result was a royal order that Manila galleons no longer be used for exploration and survey.

Sebastián Vizcaíno, 1602

The voyages of Drake and Cavendish were soon followed by the formation of the British East India Company (1600), creating further conflict with Spanish merchants in the Orient. In the wake of the English came the Dutch, whose ships passed through the Straits of Magellan at the end of the sixteenth century. With a view toward Spanish needs for protection and supplies on the Pacific coast, Viceroy Gaspar de Zúñiga approved a new California expedition under Sebastián Vizcaíno, an experienced participant in the galleon trade but not a professional mariner.

Vizcaíno, an ambitious and capable Basque merchant of Acapulco, had survived the capture of the *Santa Ana* (having organized the group that put out the flames on the burning galleon) and later headed an attempt to colonize Baja California. In 1595 Vizcaíno received a twenty-year monopoly on pearl fishing at La Paz in exchange for the crown's usual one-fifth of all pearls, gold, and silver found. He sailed from Acapulco the next year with three vessels, four Franciscan priests, and a good-sized number of colonists; but the settlement, founded on Cortés' abandoned site, failed. Storms prevented pearl fishing, Vizcaíno's explorations northward in the Gulf uncovered nothing of value, and Indian hostility endangered the Spaniards at La Paz—all returned to Mexico in 1597.

Vizcaíno, still believing that pearls, gold, and silver must exist somewhere in California, finally convinced the viceroy to give him another chance at colonization. Viceroy Monterrey recommended Vizcaíno's new expedition for royal approval primarily to establish the true value of pearl fishing and to increase understanding of the defense and security of Manila galleons. Royal instructions to the viceroy set Vizcaíno's objective specifically as "the discovery and demarcation of the ports, bays, and inlets which exist from Cape San Lucas, situated at 22 degrees 15', to Cape Mendocino, at 42 degrees." (Instructions to Sebastián Vizcaíno March 18, 1602, Archivo General de Indias, Guadalajara 133) Vizcaíno was warned "not to allow anyone to go inland in search of Indians, nor even find out if Indians were there, since the intent and principal purposes [of coastal charting and soundings] did not require it." He was to follow Cabrillo's route and not change any of the place names already given.

Vizcaíno sailed from Acapulco on May 5, 1602, with the *San Diego, Santo Tomas,* and *Tres Reyes,* a small auxiliary and, on board, a cosmographer, three Carmelite friars, and a company of nearly 200 men carefully selected for their nautical experience. The ships took four months to reach Alta California, while Vizcaíno, claiming difficulty in recognizing localities, permanently renamed all of Cabrillo's landmarks except Magdalena Bay. He modestly bestowed the new name La Bahia de Sebastián Vizcaíno upon Baja California's great coastal indentation, which stretches sixty miles northward from Cedros Island. Upon approaching Cabrillo's Islas Desiertas, he called them San Martín, but the name suggested by the Carmelite Father Antonio de la Ascensión—Los Cuatro Coronados took precedence.

Vizcaíno entered Cabrillo's Bay of San Miguel on November 10, 1602, noting its good anchorage and abundant natural resources. "On the 12th of said month, which was the day of the glorious San Diego, almost everyone went ashore; they built a hut, said mass [and] celebrated the feast of San Diego ... ." (Bolton, ed., *Diary of Vizcaíno* in *Spanish Exploration in the Southwest, 1542–1706.* p. 80) About 100 Indians with bows and arrows appeared on a nearby hill, but did nothing until the Spanish, with offerings of presents, assured them of friendship. At the crest of Point Loma, Father Ascensión recorded the discovery of "another good port" (Mission Bay) and made a quick survey of the region. The priest thought the land fertile, the variety of fish most numerous, and the existence of gold assured by some sparkling iron pyrites he found. After ten days' rest, the Spaniards set sail from their naturally protected port; Vizcaíno called the bay San Diego de Alcalá to honor the Spanish Franciscan brother who had been canonized in 1588.

The expedition continued northward, stopping briefly at Catalina Island, and then passing through the Santa Barbara Channel (renaming Cabrillo's island burial place San Miguel). On December 16, 1602, they anchored in the bay whose name would honor the count of Monterrey, viceroy of New Spain. Vizcaíno's unqualified praise of Monterey as the "best port that could be desired" [and] "sheltered from all winds" (Bolton, ed., *Diary of Vizcaíno* in *Spanish Exploration in the Southwest, 1542–1706.*, p. 91) resulted in its selection as Spain's first capital of California. Unfortunately, the actual infrequency of these ideal weather conditions made the port unrecognizable by California's first overland explorers who searched for Monterey in 1769.

Although one ship returned to Mexico, the remainder of the expedition explored further northward. Departing from Monterey on January 3, 1603, they reached Drakes Bay in two days (naming the headland Point Reyes); a week later they sighted Cape Mendocino and here, Vizcaíno decided to head back to Acapulco. The ships could not stop at any place along the coast since none of the men, all ravaged by scurvy, had the strength to pull up an anchor once dropped. Vizcaíno entered Acapulco on March 21, 1603, with his glowing reports about Monterey, and at first was well received.

Viceroy Monterrey was impressed by the bay named for him, but his successor, the Count of Montesclaros (1603–1607), distrusted Vizcaíno, ridiculed the idea of a California port for provisioning Manila galleons, and discouraged further exploration. The galleon problem was solved instead by improvements in design and construction, which added space for carrying needed provisions. Stopping along California's unfamiliar coast within so few days of home caused an unnecessary risk to the cargo.

In her search for a golden island, Spain had found instead the realities of California's rugged coast. There were no apparent treasures to attract adventurers willing to invest their private fortunes in a colonizing venture, and the crown lacked sufficient motive to pursue exploration. As a result, no sea expeditions stopped on the shores of Upper California for more than 165 years. Advancement northward from Mexico was left to the slow but steady progress of overland parties. To this end the central corridor of advance was the most inviting route and New Mexico was the target area.

OÑATE AND THE CONQUEST OF NEW MEXICO

A nearly constant factor to be considered in any treatment of Spanish New Mexico is the "time lag component." Often conditions were no longer propitious for the main purpose of an expedition, for a rescue mission, or for a military reinforcement. By the time news traveled southward from New Mexico, was digested, became the subject of some official action, and a response finally arrived, the motive was nearly forgotten. The time lag factor can be seen in the case of Juan de Oñate and the initial conquest of New Mexico. Perhaps as early as 1592, Oñate made his first efforts to become governor of the frontier province that had attracted unofficial and even illegal interest. Since the fate of early interlopers Leyva and Gutiérrez was as yet unknown, Oñate's instructions included bringing those renegades to justice.

For Oñate himself, although near to the heart of a sluggish bureaucracy, negotiations for a contract for pacification and conquest of New Mexico were very slow. It was not until September 21, 1595, that viceregal approval was granted to begin the conquest. What seemed to be the starting point for occupation proved to be only the beginning of a further discouraging sequence of almost endless delays. In retrospect, it seems incredible that any delay should have been forthcoming. Juan de Oñate was a first-rate candidate for the appointment. He was the son of one of the first conquerors who had accompanied Cortés, Cristóbal de Oñate. The senior Oñate had been Vázquez de Coronado's lieutenant governor in Nueva Galicia, following which he had been one of the four principal discoverers and developers of the great Zacatecas silver mines of central Mexico. His likeness was one of four on the coat-of-arms of the city that grew up around those mines. Juan, born in Zacatecas, was consequently the son of one of North America's first millionaires.

Juan de Oñate married well; his wife was the daughter of another of the four discoverers of the Zacatecas silver mines: Juanes de Tolosa. Her mother was Leonor Cortés, a daughter of Hernán Cortés and a granddaughter of Montezuma. The younger Oñate was a miner and frontier captain involved in the opening of new lands under authorization of Viceroy Luis de Velasco and was wealthy in his own right. In addition, he had wealthy friends, important relatives, and supporters on many sides.

Rumors from the north concerning advanced Indian civilizations fell on the alert ears of Juan de Oñate, who determined to petition for this new area of service to the crown. Upon approval of his contract, Oñate began recruitment of officers and men. His two chief officers were two of his nephews, Juan and Vicente de Zaldívar, the former his *maestre de campo* and the latter as *sargento mayor* and recruiting officer. Another early appointment was Captain Gaspar de Villagrá, a soldier-poet.

Epic Poem of Villagrá

Villagrá wrote and subsequently published a book-length epic poem, the history of New Mexico in verse. He wanted to record the undertaking for posterity, for as he said:

> *No greater misfortune could possibly befall a people than to lack a historian properly to set down their annals; one who with faithful zeal will guard, treasure, and perpetuate all those human events which if left to the frail memory of man and to the mercy of the passing years will be sacrificed upon the altars of time. ... Thus, that the many sacrifices and heroic deeds of those who conquered and converted the many tribes and people of New Mexico may not be forgotten, as have the chronicles of those who preceded them into these regions, I take my pen, the first to set down these annals, more in response to that sense of duty I feel than in confidence in my ability. I ask that my many shortcomings be charitably overlooked.*
> (Prologue to Villagrá, *Historia de la Nueva México*, 1610)

Villagrá's poem is one of the earliest contributions to southwestern literature. It is a glorification of the activities of the Spanish conquerors of New Mexico, and as such it takes considerable liberty with the facts as recorded by others, but it is not out of keeping, except possibly in merit, with the abundant epic poetry of the conquest.

Recruits for Colonization

Recruitment for the projected colonization effort was easily accomplished, with the greater number of the volunteers coming from the frontier area. The contract between Oñate and the government, as represented by the viceroy, gave Oñate sweeping powers as well as specific obligations. Among the latter were the requirements of recruiting

200 men, fully outfitted, and providing quantities of flour, corn, jerked beef, plus wheat for sowing. Livestock was to be provided as follows: 1,000 cattle, 3,000 sheep, 1,000 rams, 100 black cattle, 150 colts, and 150 mares. Other items to be supplied at Oñate's cost were medicine, shoes, tools, paper, sackcloth, and a blacksmith's bellows. For his own use, he agreed to provide 25 horses, 25 mules, several *carretas* (two-wheeled carts), weapons, and a great quantity of personal clothing.

On his part, Oñate received important governmental powers, which of course were only of value in case of success. He was to be governor and captain-general of the new territory, the appointment being valid for two generations. These powers and titles vested the nominee with political, military, and economic leadership and power. In addition, King Philip II provided the colonizer with three field pieces, 30 quintals of gunpowder, 100 quintals of lead, and a dozen coats of mail armor (these latter to be paid for by Oñate). Evidence of his status was his right to commandeer carts, provided that he paid for them at a fair price.

Oñate sought the right to allot Indians as laborers and to create encomiendas. He also requested that all first settlers be recognized as *hidalgos*, with all of the rights and privileges of those minor nobles in Castile. He requested thirty leagues of land, the title of marquis, 8,000 ducats yearly salary, the office of *alguacil mayor*, extensive authority in making appointments, and sweeping mining and fiscal powers. He was, however, denied the marquisette and his salary demand was reduced to 6,000 ducats. Oñate's powers were also restricted to those permissible under the recently enacted royal ordinances of 1573.

The completion of Luis de Velasco's term as viceroy dealt a nearly fatal blow to Oñate's grandiose plan for New Mexico. When Velasco was promoted to the vice regency of Peru and was replaced by the count of Monterrey, a new consideration of the contract terms was necessitated. Despite the outgoing viceroy's recommendation, the count of Monterrey had doubts about Oñate. A desire for independence on Oñate's part, as well as efforts by his enemies to discredit him, brought about a decision by the new viceroy to curtail substantially the original contract. These changes were opposed vigorously by Oñate and his friends, but despite recruitment and preparations for departure, Oñate was left frozen in position in southern Chihuahua until further orders. Finally, the serious challenge to Oñate's contract was overcome and an inspection was made at year's end of 1596. It indicated that all was in good order, yet the departure was again delayed.

It was not until over a year later—after a rigorous final inspection held at the unlikely spot of San Bartolomé between December 22, 1597, and January 8, 1598— that the go-ahead signal was given. Only 129 men answered the first muster, and although there is no list of the accompanying family members, the great caravan was far short of the initial requirement.

Oñate finally began his journey, but did not follow the previously used entry route into New Mexico. Instead he sent Vicente de Zaldívar on a preliminary scouting mission who deemed it unnecessary to follow the Río Conchos to its junction with the Río Grande and then proceed upstream on the latter. Rather, he found it was logical and possible to make a time-saving short cut directly northward via the sand dunes of Samalayuca and hit the river at the major crossing, today known as El Paso.

Symbolic Act of Sovereignty

Just before arriving at the river crossing, the men performed the significant and well-established symbolic act of sovereignty as a token of possession of the new land. Since medieval times such symbolism was an essential formality in justification of the right to rule. Though some historians have felt that the act was directed principally toward the local Indians, this was not the case. When Oñate took possession with the prescribed ritual involved, he was doing so to meet legal requirements so that other "Christian princes" would be prevented from laying claim to that area. Indian acquiescence was not considered because, according to European standards, they did not have sovereignty. Furthermore, any natives witnessing the act of possession would have had no idea of what was going on.

Without their consent, save for the absence of any negative action, the natives became subject to Spanish rule. The Spaniards' act of possession implied that the land was ownerless, that it was available for the taking, and therefore subject to their control. In possession-taking, Spain combined medieval ritual with papal authority, imbuing the act with both temporal and spiritual validity. Though most European nations avoided any religious component, all respected and expected regard for acts of sovereignty, though in the disputes the original date and the geographical extent of any single act came into question. The act of possession was the outward symbolism probably sufficient in itself to create sovereignty, but it was perfected and assured by continuous occupancy.

More complicated was the matter of title to the land involved. The sovereign made the rules, but in turn was constrained by (1) concepts of aboriginal occupancy and possession, and (2) the crown's own laws in dealing with property rights. The famous *Recopilación de leyes de los reinos de las Indias*, a compilation in 1680 of the laws passed for the Indies, contains many of the basic rules concerning Indian rights, which are protected therein in large measure. There always existed a dichotomy between the role of the crown as protector of Indian rights and the absolute power that the sovereign exercised. In the case of Spain, the Indian position concerning land was by and large more favorable than under the other colonial powers—as the laws had years to evolve. It should not be assumed, however, that the natives were at all times aware of their rights or that these laws were always enforced in a frontier setting such as New Mexico.

The Franciscans and the Colonists

Franciscans had early demonstrated a strong interest in New Mexico and, as would be expected, the religious aspect of this conquest had not been forgotten. (For Franciscan backgrounds, see Chapter 8, p. 188.) Grey-robed (later brown-robed) Franciscans, led by Fray Rodrigo Durán as commissary, joined the group. The importance of the Franciscans from the very start of the colonization project is important to regional history, because no other regular clergy were assigned at any time to New Mexico. This became an exclusively Franciscan missionary field and continued to be so throughout the colonial period. Since almost no secular clergy were sent to New Mexico during Spanish control, Franciscan ideals, theology, traditions and morals were those in evidence, not only among the Indians, but also, the colonists' religious matters.

The retinue of founding colonists set out with eighty-three wagons and 7,000 head of livestock. The group moved slowly north, stopping to talk with the leaders of each successive Indian pueblo en route. By mid-June Oñate had reached his goal. He chose the Pueblo Indian village of Caypa as his headquarters and renamed it San Juan de los Caballeros, perhaps because all of his followers had been made hidalgos. It did not last long as a seat of government; that function was moved to nearby San Gabriel de Chama at the confluence of the Chama and Río Grande, founded on the site of the native village of Ohke. This second location had lasted as headquarters for Spanish operations for about a decade when the seat of government was transferred under the leadership of Oñate's successor, Pedro de Peralta, to its permanent location at Santa Fe, which since 1610 has been the capital of New Mexico. Archaeological investigation carried

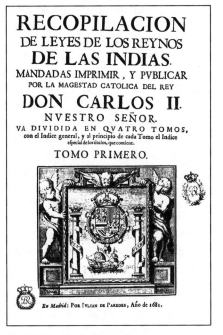

Fig. 3.2. *Recopilación* frontispiece.

out at San Gabriel recovered material evidence of the early Spanish occupation site in the form of broken bits of armor, shards of Majolica, and other intrusive items. These are the oldest clearly Spanish artifacts that document New Mexico's early history. The amount of evidence recovered has been small, reflecting the fact that not much gear was broken to the point that it was discarded.

Once the initial seat of government was established, Oñate's job began in earnest. New Mexico's first church was built at San Juan, and Oñate and his lieutenants went out to explore his new domain. The friars, ten in number, were assigned to strategic areas to begin the spread of the gospel to Indians, who were not very receptive to their overtures. As previously indicated, the Pueblos had what for them was a satisfactory native religion, one mainly animistic in nature. It did not require great economic support, nor did it have a large clerical component. In general it was a simple, straightforward religion with appropriate rites and celebrations beseeching the Gods for good weather, good crops, and successful hunting. Though all aspects of life were religiously oriented, it was not a harsh religion.

As a result of Indian satisfaction with their existing religious orientation, Franciscan efforts met with little initial response. Later, there was some amount of outward success evident as the Pueblo Indians conformed to Spanish religious requirements. Yet, beneath it all, the Pueblos retained, and continue to retain, much dedication to their original religion. Many Pueblo Indians even today are involved in the practice of Christianity but only in combination with their own religion. Such ideas have never been completely accepted by the non-Indian population of New Mexico, yet as early as the colonial period, this dual religion phenomenon was clearly evident. One Spanish tactic was the use of syncretism, the inclusion of new religious forms, but with the maintenance of the old. This inclusion was effective if the dates of both Christian and non-Christian celebrations coincided.

The religious life of New Mexico was complicated not so much by a Pueblo Indian unwillingness to embrace Christianity but rather by their reluctance to make it their exclusive religious faith. The clarity of their logic was to them incontestable, just as the lack of exclusive orientation in matters of religion in the Judeo-Christian tradition was untenable to the friars. With such opposite views there was frequent opportunity for religious differences.

Another significant contribution of Oñate was to gather together the Indian leaders and distribute to them rods of office, the symbol by which they were vested by Spain with the power to rule. Good psychology was employed in making the old leaders into the new leaders. The result was only partial disturbance of the native power structure, and it remained unchanged except at the top where Spanish officialdom held the ultimate authority. In fact, the rod of office has been passed down for nearly four centuries from outgoing to incoming native governor, early each year. For political-symbolic reasons, the Spanish rods of office were replaced during the Civil War with silver-headed canes bearing the engraved inscription "A. Lincoln, Prst. U.S.A.," plus the name of the pueblo. Canes are of great ceremonial importance and some pueblos still have canes dating back to the Spanish period (recognized by their length of thirty-three inches, the Spanish *vara*, rather than thirty-six inches, the length of the American yard). The rod of office is the political tradition of longest duration in New Mexico's history and is probably the most ancient in the United States. It is so important that without physical transfer of the cane, the incoming Pueblo governor is not fully vested with authority.

Zaldívar's Expedition
The disappointment brought about by lack of wealth in New Mexico was great. One of Oñate's responses was to send out reconnaissance expeditions. In the fall of the first year of Oñate's occupation, 1598, his nephew, Vicente de Zaldívar, led an expedition over the mountains and out on the great plains to explore. They found only countless bison or buffalo, but as a potential economic asset, the American bison was attractive to the point that Vicente Zaldívar tried to bring one back alive. He became the first of many people who have visualized creation of large herds of domesticated buffalo, a dream that was as impossible in the sixteenth century as it has been ever since. In the end, the party had to be content with bringing back a supply of buffalo beef, after having killed some of the huge beasts with gunfire. Direct acquisition of meat, cured and dried as jerky, and trade for such provender was for almost three centuries part of Hispanic New Mexico's food supply. Curiously, though the North American range of the bison was extensive, New Mexico was outside the normal range of that indigenous mammal upon which both local Indians and Spaniards depended in some measure during the colonial period. The expedition by Vicente de Zaldívar to the Buffalo Plains failed to find any other items of exploitable use.

Several trips west of the Río Grande Valley were made without finding traces of any rich cities, but it was during such ventures that parties under Vicente's brother Juan de Zaldívar visited the Sky City of Acoma. That pueblo, perched some 357 feet above the surrounding plain on a great sandstone mesa, was not only a magnificent site, but also an important native defensive position. Juan's first visit there was friendly, but during a second one, the Spaniards demanded food and were refused by the natives. This led to hostilities during which Juan de Zaldívar was killed. By modern standards there was no justification for peremptory requisition of Acoma's food supply, but by sixteenth-century reasoning, those royal Indian subjects were required by the crown to supply food to its military representatives while they were on campaign.

A Spanish retaliatory expedition of revenge, led by brother Vicente de Zaldívar, was planned; Oñate's logical rationale was that such an example of treachery should not go unpunished. The castigation of the Acomans was not easily accomplished, however, particularly since the Indians had great confidence in their ability to defend their stronghold. The account of the Battle of Acoma is filled with drama and inventive storytelling in which the miraculous took place. Acoma's defense of its citadel was spirited, matched only by Spanish determination that the native fortress should fall. Spanish attempts to scale the great rock were met by native skill in planned defense. But by superhuman efforts, a great leap, and placement of a tree trunk across an otherwise impassable chasm, the Spanish soldiers reached the summit, clearing the way for cavalry troops. Artillery had been in play for two days and had done some damage, but once the field pieces were hoisted to the mesa top on the third day, the matter became decisive. The final stage of the battle on the elevated mesa was one of great carnage, leaving the pueblo almost totally destroyed.

In recounting the story, one of New Mexico's great legends appears. In the aftermath of combat, it was felt that the hero of the hour had been an especially effective horseman on a white charger who was everywhere in battle. Then it was recalled that the party had no white horses, and the timely intervention soon became clear to all. Santiago, St. James, patron saint of Spain and particularly of the military, had put in an unexpected appearance and had been responsible for the overwhelming success that day. Without any pretense of understanding just what had happened, it might well have been morally satisfying to believe that Santiago Matamoros (the Moor-slayer) had lent sanctity to their overwhelming rout of the Indians, who were surrogate Moors, while the Spanish army, particularly the cavalry, was the Christian troop.

The punishment meted out to the defeated Acomans was severe. It was meant to serve as an example to other native groups of the consequences of defiance of Spanish orders. Besides almost total destruction of the pueblo and the death in battle of 600 to 800 natives, an additional 600 were taken prisoners. Some of these Indians were enslaved; others were mutilated by having a hand or foot cut off, and children were taken to live in Spanish households. Spanish revenge was excessive, but neither Oñate nor Vicente de Zaldívar was in any mood for tolerance. Nevertheless, the harsh measures taken at Acoma came back to haunt Oñate when he was later called on by higher authorities to justify irregularities of his administration.

While other expeditions were made by Oñate and his lieutenants, many of his settlers were complaining about conditions in the new province. Some of the disgruntled attempted to leave and a few made good on threats to desert. Oñate tried his best to prevent discouraging reports from being carried back to Mexico City, going so far as censoring the outgoing mail. There did seem to be some hope for stabilization of the faltering colony when in 1600 a reinforcement of eighty people arrived, including seven priests. But resentment continued to be high, particularly when Oñate was away on exploratory trips. This was especially true in 1601 when the governor spent five months out on the Buffalo Plains in a fruitless search for the fabled city of Gran Quivira. All that his returning party could show for their efforts was failure and a few wounds from a battle with the "Quivirans," probably the Kansa Indians.

Despite efforts to prevent bad reports concerning the province, Oñate was unable to stop all information from leaking out. In an heroic effort to do something of note and thereby save his deteriorating position, Oñate made plans for a trip west in quest of the South Sea, now known as the Pacific Ocean, and in search of mines.

Oñate and Espejo's Silver Mines

Oñate then turned his attention to finding Espejo's silver mines, exploring to the west on various occasions. His captain, Marcos Farfan, and eight men traveled all the way to the mountains near modern Flagstaff and crossed the upper Verde River between Bill Williams Mountain and Prescott. Farfan and his men staked out over sixty claims and brought back ore specimens alleged to be rich in silver. Even though Oñate was excited about the discovery, it took him six years to get an exploring expedition together. Finally, on October 7, 1604, with thirty soldiers, two Franciscans, and a number of Indian servants, he left his settlement on the Río Grande and started for the west.

During this long period of early exploration, Spanish pathfinders and authorities in Mexico and Spain labored under the delusion that the North American interior was a great deal narrower than it really is. The inability to establish longitude was perhaps the most difficult problem that they faced; nevertheless, this difficulty was combined with hopeful anticipation, such as that expressed by Oñate at the point of maximum penetration to the east. At that time he regretted that the sad condition of his animals and the anxiety of his men prevented him from going to the North Sea (the Atlantic), which he felt was not far away.

Explorations to the West

In the opposite direction, in quest of the western ocean, a party of thirty soldiers and two Franciscans accompanied Governor Oñate who set out first to the Pueblo villages at Zuni, followed by a visit to the Moqui (Hopi) towns. Moving westward and following the route taken several years earlier in a similar sortie by Vicente Zaldívar, they traveled down the Santa María River to another which they called the Río San Andrés (Bill Williams Fork). By following this river downstream, they reached the Río Colorado, which Oñate called Río de Buena Esperanza. Near the junction of the rivers they met the Mojave Indians; from there they descended the river along the east bank and emerged upon a wide river bottom, thickly inhabited. They reported each Indian always carried a lighted torch, with them so they thought the river should be named El Tizón. The Indians told Oñate and his men that there was a sea ahead with coral and pearls, encouraging the men to hurry on. They passed the mouth of the Gila, which they called Río del Nombre de Jesús, and reached the mouth of the Río Colorado on January 25, 1605. From that point, Oñate and his men descended the great river to its mouth at the head of the Sea of Cortés (the Gulf of California), making contact with many new Indian groups en route. Here, he felt that he had discovered an important port that might lead to commerce with the Orient when in fact he had mistaken the head of the Gulf for the open sea, believing that California in the distance was a huge offshore island. His enthusiasm for occupation of the "port" that he had discovered was doubtless conditioned by his desire to have made a significant discovery.

At the point of his greatest penetration, on January 25, 1605, Oñate performed the act of sovereignty in taking possession of the region at the mouth of the Colorado River.

Fig. 3.3. Yuma Indian. Courtesy Arizona Historical Society/Tucson. 25970.

In line with great expectations was the report by Father Francisco de Escobar of hearing about (but not seeing) men with ears so long that they dragged the ground and were used at night to wrap around themselves in lieu of a blanket. Other natural curiosities were also reported. On the road back to New Mexico, following generally the outbound westward trip, the party stopped at what is today El Morro National Monument in western New Mexico where they chiseled on the sandstone of Inscription Rock the following carving which is visible today on that registry of early travelers:

Pasó por aqui el Adelantado Don Juan de Oñate al descubrimiento del Mar del Sur a 16 de abril de 1605.

It translates: "The Adelantado Don Juan de Oñate passed by here on 16 April 1605 from his discovery of the South Sea." This ancient inscription, which has near it dozens of later carvings, is the oldest local written evidence of Spanish occupation of New Mexico and is the most famous inscription on New Mexico's great stone autograph album, as writer Erna Fergusson has called this frequently visited rock.

Little else is known of Oñate's return journey to New Mexico except that his party endured many hardships and hunger, reaching the village of San Gabriel on April 25, 1605. Oñate had traveled a longer distance through Arizona than any previous Spanish visitor, and his explorations made the region better known to Europeans than it had been before. Arizona's mineral wealth was definitely revealed, but the cost of getting there made it difficult to follow up any discoveries.

While Oñate was trying to recoup his lost fortune and prestige on exploratory trips, word was gradually passed southward toward the viceregal capital that conditions in New Mexico were difficult. Oñate, try as he might, could not quell such rumors. The result in Mexico City was increased misgivings as reports of Oñate's mismanagement spread. The final outcome was that the viceroy decided to replace Oñate who was ordered back to the capital, some 400,000 dollars poorer from his misplaced investment. After more than a decade as governor, Oñate decided to resign rather than be discharged. It was then August 1607, and Oñate placed his son Cristóbal in charge, but the viceroy decided otherwise, appointing instead Pedro de Peralta to take over the office. The Villa of Santa Fe was founded as the capital of New Mexico shortly afterwards and the new governor was more interested in building up his own province than in exploration to the west.

When Oñate reached Mexico City he was required to face charges, basically those of abuse of his authority. There were twenty-nine charges of which twelve were substantiated, including showing cruelty toward the Indians, passing a death sentence on some of his own men, belittling the clergy, illegally cohabitating, making false reports on the value of New Mexico, and perhaps worst of all of speaking ill of the viceroy. A lengthy hearing dragged on for about seven years, after which he was found guilty on sufficient charges to be permanently banished from New Mexico, exiled for four years from Mexico City with prohibition from getting within five leagues of the city, fined 6,000 pesos, and dispossessed of his title of "adelantado for two lifetimes." By 1617 Oñate mounted an appeal based on his long and faithful service to the crown, as well as his expense on behalf of the king. It was during this appeal that his wife died at their Zacatecas home, and Juan decided to go to Spain to present his case directly to King Philip III. The first step in his vindication was a decision of the Council of the Indies absolving Oñate of any blame and reimbursing him the 6,000-peso fine.

Another major step in personal revindication was Oñate's efforts to become a knight of the highly prestigious order of Santiago. Don Juan apparently initiated his efforts while still in Mexico. In the long process of testimony, during which he was continually referred to as adelantado of New Mexico, all of his merits and none of his shortcomings were brought out by witnesses in Burgos, Madrid, and Granada. In the latter location some twenty witnesses testified to some aspect of his fitness. The interviews began in September 1625 and probably continued into the following year, by which time the aging conquistador was certainly physically present in Spain. The composite of the testimony sheds more light on Oñate's genealogy than on activities of his long career in New Spain. Summarized, his merits of service to the crown were well known, as was his lineage and his continuous dedication to the king. He was well on the way toward becoming a knight of the great military order of Santiago.

In Spain, at age 73, Oñate assumed a position as visitor general of mines, while pressing his candidacy for entry into the order of Santiago. In his new work, he was clearly a concerned public servant, and it was during one of his visits to the mining area of southern Spain that he suffered his demise. He died in June 1626 in Guadalcanal, and according to one source the cause of death was a mine cave-in. His last will and testament show him as a great deal more than an impoverished and discredited conquistador.

A considerable amount of Oñate's worldly goods, about 20 percent of his accumulated wealth, was bequeathed to the Colegio Imperial, a Jesuit school in Madrid, with certain stipulations attached to the donation. Ten thousand ducados were earmarked for a chapel in the new church of the school, a chapel to which his body was to be brought from Guadalcanal for final burial, and on the walls of which the Oñate coat of arms was to be placed. An endowment fund of 200 ducados was established for a chaplaincy, thereby guaranteeing for him three masses per week therein. Additional funds were set aside for the support of students in various categories, and if any of Oñate's descendants were to apply for admission, they were to receive preference. Finally, a high mass was to be said regularly and daily prayer was to be offered for Oñate.

The school, a significant Spanish educational institution that still exists in the heart of Madrid, enjoys an excellent reputation. Though the school does not have its own records of the generosity of Oñate, nor are the terms of his endowment in perpetuity as stipulated in his will being carried out 350 years later, the physical evidence of his interest is there, linking Spain to the land on which Oñate spent much of his first fortune. In addition, the old founder of New Mexico left a huge sum to his heirs who became wealthy as a result.

Chapter Three

BIBLIOGRAPHIC ESSAY

A good source for the establishment and maintenance of New Spain's Philippine trade is the pioneer and still standard work by William Lytle Schurz, *The Manila Galleon* (New York: E. P. Dutton, 1939). Sir Francis Drake's exploits are well chronicled through such works as W. S. W. Vaux, ed., *The World Encompassed by Sir Francis Drake, Being His Next Voyage to That to Nombre de Dios, Collated with an Unpublished Manuscript of Francis Fletcher, Chaplain to the Expedition* (1589. Reprint, London: The Hakluyt Society, 1854); Henry R. Wagner, *Sir Francis Drake's Voyage Around the World: Its Aims and Achievements* (San Francisco: J. Howell, 1926); Robert F. Heizer, *Francis Drake and the California Indians* (Berkeley: University of California Press, 1947), and *Elizabethan California* (Ramona, Calif.: Ballena Press, 1974); as well as the more contemporary work edited by Norman J. W. Thrower, *Sir Francis Drake and the Famous Voyage, 1577–1580: Essays Commemorating the Quadricentennial of Drake's Circumnavigation of the Earth* (Berkeley: University of California Press, 1984). Controversy over the *Golden Hind's* landing site abounds. The *California Historical Quarterly* devoted the fall 1974 issue to the question, "The Francis Drake Controversy: His California Anchorage, June 17–July 23, 1579," including articles by Robert Power, V. Aubrey Neasham, and Raymond Aker; while Warren L. Hanna has written *Lost Harbor: The Controversy Over Drake's California Anchorage.* (Berkeley: University of California Press, 1979). Harry Kelsey produced "Did Francis Drake Really Visit California?" *Western Historical Quarterly*, 21 (November 1990):445–62. A fine overview of Sebastián Vizcaíno and subsequent Spanish exploration is W. Michael Mathes, *Vizcaíno and Spanish Expansion in the Pacific Ocean, 1580–1630* (San Francisco: California Historical Society, 1968).

The early settlement and exploration of New Mexico is illustrated through Herbert E. Bolton, ed., *Spanish Exploration in the Southwest, 1542–1706.* (New York: Scribner's, 1908) and George P. Hammond and Agapito Rey, *The Rediscovery of New Mexico, 1580–1594: The Explorations of Chamuscado, Espejo, Castaño de Sosa, Morlete, and Leyva de Bonilla and Humaña* (Albuquerque: University of New Mexico Press, 1966). Read in conjunction with the following articles, these accounts provide a good basis for understanding the period. See also Agapito Rey, "Missionary Aspects of the Founding of New Mexico" *New Mexico Historical Review,* 23 (January 1948):22–31; G. R. G. Conway, "Antonio Espejo as a Familiar of the Mexican Inquisition, 1572–1578" *New Mexico Historial Review*, 6 (January 1931):1–20; Carroll L. Riley, "Early Spanish-Indian Communication in the Greater Southwest" *NMHR,* 46 (October

1971):285–314; Winifred Creamer "Re-examining the Black Legend: Contact Period Demography in the Rio Grande Valley of New Mexico" *NMHR*, 69 (July 1994):263–278; and Cheryl J. Foote and Sandra K. Schackel, "Indian Women of New Mexico, 1535–1680" in *New Mexico Women: Intercultural Perspectives*, ed. by Joan M. Jensen and Darlis A. Miller (Albuquerque: University of New Mexico Press, 1986).

There are several useful sources regarding the last conquistador, Juan de Oñate, including the standard work by George P. Hammond and Agapito Rey, eds. and trans., *Don Juan de Oñate: Colonizer of New Mexico, 1595–1628*, 2 vols. (Albuquerque: University of New Mexico Press, 1953); also George P. Hammond, *Don Juan de Oñate and the Founding of New Mexico* (Santa Fe: El Palacio Press, 1927); and Marc Simmons, *The Last Conquistador: Juan de Oñate and the Settling of the Southwest* (Norman: University of Oklahoma Press, 1991). Further insight into Oñate and his additional expeditions can be found in Hammond, "Oñate's Effort to Gain Political Autonomy for New Mexico," *Hispanic American Historical Review*, 32 (August 1952):321-30; Albert H. Schroeder, "A Re-analysis of the Routes of Coronado and Oñate onto the Plains in 1541 and 1601," *Plains Anthropologist*, 7 (February 1962):2–23; and Susan C. Vehik, "Oñate's Expedition to the Southern Plains: Routes, Destinations and Implications for Late Prehistoric Cultural Adaptations," *Plains Anthropologist*, 31 (February 1986):13–33. Eric Beerman discusses Oñate's final days as inspector of mines in Spain in "The Death of an Old Conquistador: New Light on Juan de Oñate," *NMHR*, 54 (October 1979):305–19.

A primary document and considered as the first example of colonial literature in the Spanish Southwest is Gaspar Perez de Villagrá, *Historia de la Nueva México, 1610*, translated and edited by Miguel Encinias, Alfred Rodríguez, and Joseph P. Sánchez (Albuquerque: University of New Mexico Press, 1993). It is an epic poem describing the reconquest of New Mexico highlighted with a description of the battle at Acoma. See also Donald Cutter, "With a Little Help from Their Saints," *Pacific Historical Review*, 53 (May 1984):123–40.

Chapter Four

A Struggle for Power:
Issues Between Church and State

Missions of New Mexico

After Oñate's resignation as governor of New Mexico in 1607, Spanish officials questioned whether continued efforts to colonize the area merited the effort and expense. To the delight of the Franciscans, the crown honored its ecclesiastical obligations to the reported 7,000 baptized Indians in the territory. With the arrival of the newly appointed governor, Pedro de Peralta, in 1610, New Mexico became a government-funded mission zone. The reasons for permanent settlement of the region, however, were more than spiritual: as long as Spain retained the unprofitable province, it could lay claim to the vast, heretofore unexplored regions that lay to the north. Nevertheless, from 1610 until the Pueblo Revolt of 1680, the missions were the reason for New Mexico's very existence. This seventy-year period represents the Golden Age of missions in New Mexico—one in which they held a spiritual monopoly.

A New View

In traditional treatments of the period between the founding of New Mexico and the watershed dates of the Pueblo Revolt of 1680 and the reconquest twelve years later, nearly all attention has been given to the heavily documented problems between the clergy on the one hand and the governors and their various supporters on the other. Nevertheless, a much different view of the pre–Pueblo Revolt period than that traditionally held is found in three important, but for many years rare, documents of that period written by two on-the-spot Franciscan priests assigned to the promising mission field of New Mexico. These were Alonso de Benavides, a native of San Miguel in the Azores who wrote two reports, and Gerónimo de Zárate Salmerón. Their accounts, considered to be treasures of early documentation, reflect little of the acrimony of the seventeenth century power struggle for control of the young colony. Instead they are glowing reports of the potential of the new frontier province. They also contain an undisguised plea of greater support of the important evangelization to which these order priests were so greatly dedicated. If there were any inaccuracy it was not born of internal conflict, but rather as the product of their salesmanship and their rosy vision, unfettered by dedication to fine detail.

Father Alonso de Benavides

Benavides's background as a Franciscan began in 1602 in Mexico City when he was in his mid-twenties. He saw religious service in Puebla, Cuernavaca, and Temanatla

Fig. 4.1. María de Jesús de Agreda preaching to the Chichimecos of New Mexico, by Arthur de Castro. From Henry Wagner, *The Spanish Southwest*, II, 344.

prior to his appointment in 1623 as custos and commissary of the Holy Office of the Inquisition for New Mexico where he arrived in 1625. His stay in the province was not long; he left in 1629 with the intention of returning but never did. His role in the dissemination of the story of María de Agreda follows and adds to his importance as a regional figure. His later life was involved in higher clerical activities in Rome, then back to Spain and Portugal. Consecrated archbishop of Goa in India, Benavides died in 1635 en route to that important assignment.

Father Zárate Salmerón

The Zárate Salmerón account is not the introspective work of a humble, discalced Franciscan in a far-off province chronicling the prosaic events of a distant mission field; it is the clarion call of the missionary, stimulating the Spanish crown through the beating of drums and the blowing of trumpets. Attempting to appeal at once to the cupidity of the Spanish monarchy with its ever-present and insatiable need for money, and to the great papal surrogation of power in the Royal Patronage that made the crown responsible for conversion of the infidel, the account alternately tries to stimulate the acquisitive tendencies of the monarch and challenge his conscience to obey the biblical commission of spreading the gospel to every living creature. At times, the literate Franciscan becomes carried away by his somewhat fanciful and occasionally prophetic descriptions of the wealth in mines to be uncovered in the northern area of New Spain.

Even the imaginary geography of that time, including such places as Quivira and the Strait of Anían, was not as yet dispelled, and the priest's account continually reflects the expectation of important things to be encountered over an expansive northern landscape. At the same time, Father Gerónimo seems properly preoccupied with the welfare of such a great harvest of souls, which he asserts lacked only the laborers to bring them into the fold. Intended as a stimulus to positive action to be taken by the Spanish crown for the purpose of assuring the future of New Mexico, the devout Franciscan brings to bear on his subject any information that might lead to that end, however speculative and remote the material. As a result, he was interested in an area extending from California to Newfoundland and beyond, but always as an attempt to clarify the relationship of those areas to the place of his missionary activity in the several pueblos where he served in New Mexico.

Father Zárate Salmerón resided in New Mexico for only five years, from 1621 to 1626, but during that period he accomplished much. He is credited with building a *convento* and a temple, of baptizing over 6,500 Jemez Indian converts, and of writing a *doctrina* in the language of his parishioners, evidence of a linguistic facility that was infrequently demonstrated by frontier missionaries and one that doubtless cost many hours of study to obtain. In addition to these activities he gathered the information for his *Relaciones* which he wrote after his departure—a fact that might account for some of the errors contained therein. And though his account, motivated by strong spiritual zeal for expansion of the Franciscan missionary work, did not have all the effect that he had hoped, it certainly did paint the area in the brilliant tones of later day publicists; for to the seventeenth-century priest the province was truly a land of enchantment. Salmerón's ministry was rewarded with success and the future seemed unusually promising.

Thus during this period when there was increasing strife between church and state, there is also evidence that things were not as dark as has been pictured in the rather one-sided surviving documentation contained in Inquisition and other judicial records. The major works previously mentioned from that pre–Pueblo Revolt period written by Alonso de Benavides and Gerónimo de Zárate Salmerón, though recorded some years apart, have the common basic theme of presenting New Mexico in a much more cheerful light. Both the *Mercurio Volante* of the former and the *Relaciones* of the latter contained general descriptions of the history and geography of the area, with particular emphasis on potential but as yet unrealized mineral wealth that both priests felt could be exploited with the help of royal intervention. More central to the thinking of both of these early boosters was the great number of Indian souls that could be won for Christianity if the king in his piety and generosity would underwrite a full-scale colonization-missionization effort.

Much of the information contained in these publicity releases of the two Franciscans was based on wishful thinking and on highly generalized reports. There is no reason to believe that direct action was taken specifically as a result of these enthusiastic proposals, but at least they provided some information of a positive, albeit fanciful, nature. To capture the royal attention that they sought, both priests emphasized the precious metals and even pearls to be found and, of course, the revenue in the *quinto*, the royal tax of 20 percent, that would therefore accrue to the crown.

María de Agreda: The Lady in Blue

One topic treated in the documents of both Benavides and Zarate Salmerón was a subject of contemporary interest, one that forms the basis for one of the Southwest's most intriguing legends. It is the account about the Woman in Blue, the Lady in Blue, or the Blue Lady. The story as far as the Spaniards were concerned begins with annual visits of some Jumanos Indians from the Great Plains to the pueblo and mission at Isleta. These visitors indicated that they had been told by a lady dressed in blue to go to New Mexico, talk with the priests, and ask for missionaries to come among them to bring them salvation. They specifically wanted Father Juan de Salas to go with them to baptize their people. The story was repeated at later times, at various places, but always in a missionary context.

At about the same time, Father Benavides, the custodian of the New Mexico Franciscans, who had been very skeptical about the original story, was about to make a

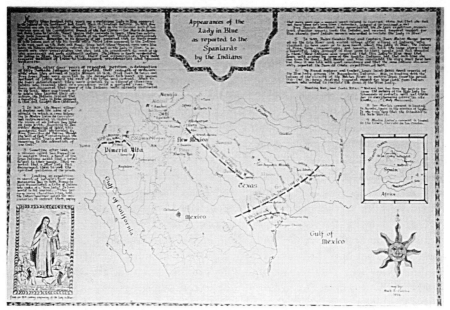

Map 4.1. Lady in Blue map. Courtesy Mark Carrico.

trip to Spain. While there he heard the story of the Lady in Blue from the other side. This version tells of frequent visits to the Indians of what is today West Texas by a now identified visitor, María de Jesús. The mother superior of the Agreda convent in the Spanish province of Soria, de Jesús was a cloistered nun who had been born in that province in 1602. By the mystical gift of bilocation, in ecstasy she had been repeatedly transported to the Southwest where she appeared to the Indians and gave them the instructions that brought them to Isleta. Alonso de Benavides later visited Agreda, talked with María de Jesús, and became convinced of the truth of her account, that indeed over a period of some eleven years the angels had repeatedly carried her to the lands of the Indians.

For the much longer period of twenty-five years Indians brought the story to the Franciscans, complete with detailed descriptions of the mystical visitor, a beautiful young nun. When shown pictures of various religious women of that day, the Indians always identified their visitor—the one from Agreda. They told of earlier visits, and when questioned why they had not told of these visits at the time, the Indians logically said that they had not told because no one had asked. Clearly the story was being repeated for the same reason that Benavides and Zárate Salmerón had indicated when writing their reports—to stimulate mission activity.

There is no logical explanation for this great regional legend. Some feel that it was just a pious hoax. Yet this seems too facile an explanation since the Indians were those who first told the story, and it uniformly found doubters among the Franciscans. When confronted by Father Benavides, María was specific in details of Indian customs and of specific times of meetings between Indians and Franciscans, meetings she observed in her bilocated state, but during which she was not visible to the Franciscans. She also knew certain Indians, indicated by recognizable names. In many ways the story is believable, but the matter of bilocation is an insuperable hurdle. When questioned, María de Agreda admitted to the gift of having traveled from Spain with angelic help, and that she had even made several trips in ecstacy on the same day. She went so far as to specify the dates of the first and last visits that she had made; her total number of visits was about 500.

Several aspects of the story are of interest. The first is that divine intervention took place in times of stress and at places very distant from great groups of fellow Spaniards. Second, it was generally restricted to pious persons who had a direct interest in the results. Third, the story of the Lady in Blue was long-lived, with the area of her appearances as widespread as from East Texas to western Arizona. Even as late as the eighteenth century, the story was told by Indians who said that their elders had seen this figure and had, as a result, taken a fancy to blue cloth. There is also some confusion involved with another religious woman of the era, María de Carrión de los Condes, also reported to have had the gift of bilocation and to have visited in some of the same or similar areas.

As in all stories that are passed on orally and make good listening, some inconsistencies appear. For example, when dealing with the Jumanos Indians of West Texas, María de Agreda spoke to them in Spanish, yet they each heard her in their own language. On the other hand, Indians along the Colorado River in western Arizona could not make out anything that she said. Father Eusebio Francisco Kino, the Jesuit apostle to the Pima Indians of Sonora-Arizona encountered the story of the Blue Lady in 1699 while exploring in la Pimería Alta. Kino's military companion with whom he frequently traveled, Lieutenant Juan Mateo Manje, was more prone to credit the Indian story as true than his priestly companion. Their informants, the Yuma Indians, told the story in a variant version. Many years before the 1699 visit, a beautiful white woman had appeared to them, carrying a cross. She was dressed in white, gray, and blue, with her head covered by a cloth or veil. Twice the Indians had shot at her with their arrows and left her for dead, but she revived and flew off. Later she returned to continue her preaching.

This story was heard more than once, which led Manje to surmise that the visitor had been María de Jesús de Agreda, who sixty-eight years earlier had been on the eastern border of New Mexico. This is chronologically possible since Manje's informants were about 80 years old and the events being recounted had occurred in their youth. Manje had one misgiving that he expressed: He felt that if God had performed the greater miracle of transporting María all the way from the Sorian village of Agreda to Arizona, He would have also provided her with adequate means of communicating with its pagan inhabitants. Father Kino treated the incident much more casually than Manje, but did mention that there was a tradition that María de Agreda had visited New Mexico.

The Lady in Blue Continues On

The Lady in Blue story continued to surface. In 1719 Father Juan de la Cruz, writing to Viceroy Marqués de Valero, said that María de Jesús once mentioned the Jicarilla Apaches, who lived to the northeast of the settled area of the province, as a good possible source of souls for future conversion. As a priest, he was most interested as some of the Jicarillas had come to him at the frontier mission of Taos.

The noteworthy California Franciscan, the famous and devout Junípero Serra, was heavily influenced by María de Jesús's writings. While serving in the Franciscan missions in the Sierra Gorda, he took with him one of her books, *La Mística ciudad de Dios*. Later, in 1773, when Serra made a well-known visit from California to Mexico City to see Viceroy Bucareli, the priest told him of the story of the nun from Agreda. On the basis of a statement by Serra's biographer and companion, Father Francisco Palóu, Serra said that María had once written that the mere sight of a Franciscan was sufficient to convert pagans. The biographer indicated that this was the reason that Viceroy Bucareli insisted on those friars accompanying Spanish exploratory expeditions being sent at that time from San Blas by sea to northern latitudes.

In far-off California, shortly after the founding of Mission San Antonio de Padua, an old Indian woman told of having heard her parents speak of a man who came to their land in Franciscan garb who did not walk, but rather flew. Her story, repeated elsewhere, led the California Franciscan to connect the tale with one told by María de Jesús about two friars who had been sent north by St. Francis. They had much success, but were finally martyred. Palóu, when he wrote his biography of Serra, included a copy of Benavides's letter to the Franciscans of New Mexico, together with the letter of encouragement from María de Jesús herself. There can be no doubt that the abbess of the Agreda convent, whether or not she ever visited New Mexico and the Southwest, continued to have some influence in the missionary field, both from her writings and because she remained a subject of speculation for 175 years.

Madre María de Jesús

Of the historical Madre María de Jesús quite a bit is known. As mentioned, she was a native of Soria, an area of Spain known for its austere and dedicated religious activity, a zone where miracles were not unknown nor unexpected. María was carefully trained in a prayerful and devout life by extremely observant parents. In 1618, María's parents established for discalced Franciscan nuns a convent in Soria that still exists. María, two sisters, and later even her mother became members. Shortly thereafter María de Jesús took final vows and by 1625 she was elevated to abbess, a position that she held until her death in 1665. Of her life in Agreda we have the information supplied by Father Benavides, but her principal importance does not rest on either her claim of bilocation or of her reported influence on the natives of the Southwest. She later became involved in an exchange of letters with King Felipe IV of Spain who was likewise an aesthetic person. María was author of the somewhat controversial book *La Mística ciudad de Dios* as well as other writings that bordered either on genius or heresy. After her death, she was proposed for canonization in the Catholic Church, and even reached the stage of being named Venerable Madre María de Jesús. The final hurdle for sainthood, however, has never been passed, probably on the basis of her lack of orthodoxy.

FRANCISCAN PROBLEMS IN NEW MEXICO

From the beginning of their ministry in New Mexico, the Franciscans felt that their numbers were far too few for the job to which they had been called. They believed there had been insufficient attention to conversion of the local Indians under the governorship of Juan de Oñate. They, almost alone, were convinced of the value of New Mexico, especially its spiritual worth, and argued strongly for its continued support, though logic would have dictated early abandonment. The colony's great need not only to be self supporting, but also to contribute to Spain's material prosperity, perhaps caused these clerical informants to exaggerate considerably New Mexico's potential wealth.

Custodian Estevan de Perea

During this early period, the provincial capital was moved to Santa Fe and the missionary-spiritual center located at Santo Domingo. Stabilization of existing mission fields occurred and converts reached about 10,000 divided among the eleven mission centers. By 1616 the area of New Mexico was administratively elevated to a custody—La Custodia de la Conversión de San Pablo—with its first custodian Estevan de Perea. In

Fig. 4.2. The oldest house in the United States. Photo by Donald Cutter.

an early struggle between church and state, governor of New Mexico Juan de Eulate was accused by the Franciscans of exploiting Indian residents to the detriment of the province's spiritual advancement.

Benavides's period as custodian reflected a spectacular increase in missionary success, and as mentioned, the period from 1610 until 1680 is considered the Golden Age of New Mexico religious history. By 1629, numbers had increased to twenty-five missions, fifty priests, and over 60,000 Indians. These early missions, as depicted by Benavides, were ideal, with well-built churches, choirs, schools of primary letters, instruction in Christian doctrine, and practical experience in trades, arts, and crafts. Under Perea, who succeeded as custodian, the evangelization of the province peaked.

Almost from the beginning of Spanish occupation of New Mexico and certainly before settlement had achieved uniformly strong footing, there appeared the previously mentioned major problem that threatened the existence of the new colony. Eventually an underlying cause of the Pueblo Revolt of 1680, this was the struggle between the church, as represented by the Franciscan fathers, and the state, as personified by a series of appointed governors. That such infighting, backbiting, and lack of cooperation ever should have existed belies the often-made statement that in colonial Spanish America church and state were one. This conception in large measure has been ascribed to the Royal Patronage that gave the king of Spain the role of vicar of the pope. Somehow this frequently repeated shibboleth was often untrue or its implications were taken lightly by those concerned with the governance of the frontier province.

The main point of contention, viewed in retrospect, was that neither side was convinced that the other was capable of being in charge. The Franciscans were certain that the major reason for Spain's presence in New Mexico was to Christianize the natives. The governor, his assistants, the military, and his frequent supporters, the settlers, believed that the frontier province was there as an outpost of Spanish empire, to be made profitable for both themselves and the crown. The missionaries were not opposed to economic prosperity. However, they were in favor of any affluence, being a prerogative of the church and of benefit to their Indian wards to whom the crown had sent the Sons of St. Francis as ministers, both spiritually and materially.

STRUGGLES BETWEEN CHURCH AND STATE

The contest for control surfaced frequently, took various forms, but in general was a bitter struggle with few tricks left unplayed by either side. It is hard to take sides in the polemic that developed, for neither party was totally right nor completely wrong. Perhaps the system was wrong, for the crown seemed to permit small successes and great failures without stepping in and solving the existing problems. Its piecemeal, teeter-totter approach permitted the problem to exist much longer than it should have. Both sides used whatever tactics necessary, but the end result of such bickering was a lesson learned by the pawns in the struggle, the Indians, who were eventually convinced that the Spaniards were divisive, disunited, and more concerned about prerogatives than about good government.

It is possible that history has not truly done justice to the period from 1610 to 1680. It is also likely that the view of this period is distorted because there is a paucity of documentation to bring to bear on those seven decades. The Revolt of 1680 brought with it an almost complete destruction of local records, some done by the insurgent Indians and some by the Spaniards prior to their hasty flight toward El Paso. The records that do survive are those of such importance that at least one copy made its way out of the province to become lodged in archives of greater importance—the viceregal, Inquisitorial, Franciscan, or archiepiscopal files.

The records of the day-to-day activities of early New Mexicans, the land deeds, local reports, routine correspondence, and minor transactions of society are absent, forcing the researcher to attempt to recreate history from mainly judicial records, a risky proposition at best. This is not to suggest that the other problems did not exist nor that they were unimportant. It is merely to indicate that many other events were transpiring of which we have little documentary knowledge, save for those that seeped through the accusations and recriminations of the parties to law suits, residencias, and adverse reports.

The controversy between church and state may have reached its peak in seventeenth-century New Mexico. Similar struggles occurred throughout the empire, but rarely did they reach the intensity of the controversy in this region. Basic disagreements were over the treatment and use of the Indians, and the position of the church as a privileged institution. New Mexico was primarily a mission area, so the church was extremely influential and the friars zealously defended their rights to protect the missions. Governors resented Franciscan interference in political affairs. Since no bishop had jurisdiction over New Mexico before 1680, the Franciscans exerted unusual control. They quickly denounced any infringement on Indian rights, but according to the colonists, the missionaries in fact exploited the natives.

The governor often had to protect the missions from civilian entrepreneurs while promoting the economic development of the province. When exploitation of Indians provided the only source of wealth, friction with the clergy resulted. Some governors contributed to the problem by conducting slave raids against nomadic tribes, and by violating laws forbidding them to trade with natives. Some governors were intemperate and immoral.

Between its founding and the 1680 outbreak of rebellion there were some twenty-five governors of New Mexico. Most of them were out of touch with the Franciscans, and very few were the cream of colonial administrative personnel. In fact, from their on-the-job performance, it is clear that the position was a matter of making things work despite limited resources and infrequent help from the viceregal capital. And, too many governors envisioned their position as one in which they might enrich themselves personally to the detriment of the inhabitants of the province. Some have become infamous for their misdeeds, and justly so. Others ran afoul of the missionaries who threatened and cajoled them by employing various ecclesiastical powers to coerce conformity with the mission program. Perhaps the most noteworthy, though not the best, of the pre–Pueblo Revolt governors were Luis de Rosas (1637–1641); Bernardo López de Mendizábal (1659–1661); and Diego de Peñalosa (1661–1664).

Governor Luis de Rosas, 1637–1641

Between 1610 and 1650 the intensity of the conflict between church and state gradually increased, almost resulting in civil war. Of special difficulty was the governorship of Luis de Rosas, whose four-year term was particularly chaotic. Rosas has been characterized as an outspoken, hard-hitting soldier, fearless in action. He possessed the qualities useful in a leader of a faction, but he was unsuited for civil administration of a province where passions had already been deeply aroused before his arrival. Rosas was admired by some and hated by others because his straightforward character and direct and positive approach left no room for neutral ground.

In the struggle that reached crisis proportions between 1639 and 1642, Franciscan custodian Juan de Salas did not have effective use of the Holy Office of the Inquisition, but made use of all other avenues available to him. Rosas found himself universally opposed by the Franciscans and also by an anti-Rosas faction that included some of his officers. By 1641 accusations of malfeasance were brought forward, including charges dealing with the exploitation of the converted Pueblos and other allegations relating to Rosas's policy toward the nomadic tribes.

Forced Indian Labor

In the first category was Rosas's continuation of his predecessor's policy requiring Indians to weave mantas and other textiles. He also established an *obraje*, a workshop, in Santa Fe, where natives, including some Christian Indians, were forced to labor under conditions of virtual servitude, an endeavor in which Rosas participated personally. He also employed considerable Indian labor in planting great quantities of seed for food crops and was charged with using the frontier villages as commercial centers for barter and trade with the nomadic Indians. Still, Rosas felt that some of his trading activities were hampered materially by the opposition of some local Franciscans. He even went so far as to have one priest arrested for interference. More flagrant, in the eyes of the priests, was the governor's promise to the Pecos Indians allowing them to revert to their "pagan and idolatrous customs if they could furnish more mantas and hides." (Scholes, *Church and State in New Mexico, 1610–1650,* p. 300)

Rosas was accused of making unjust war on the "Utacas" Indians who lived beyond the Pueblo area, and subsequently employing the captives of those "wars" to work in his Santa Fe workshop. Much more serious were complaints about Rosas's policy regarding the Apaches, who were already recognized as a difficult problem. Trading relationships between the Apaches and the frontier Pueblos of the Pecos and Tompiro groups had deteriorated. In part this had been due to acts of treachery and was compounded by the governor's failure to protect the exposed pueblo villages when raids were made from the plains to the east.

In personal trade dealings with non-Pueblo Indians, Rosas was reported to have made unjust demands. He forced some to bring him feathers and hides, and robbed them of the clothing from their very backs. The Franciscan protests against Rosas were motivated by the Pueblo Indians' growing resentment of any contacts with other Indians, but the governor paid no attention to these priestly complaints. More personal, according to the clerical party, was Rosas's determination to destroy all ecclesiastical privilege and authority. He was charged with making statements implying doubt concerning the just authority of the church as a whole. He was even known to become abusive during a church service, an action which brought him close to excommunication, having told the Father to shut up and branding what he said as a lie.

The Santa Cruzada (Holy Crusade) in New Mexico

The matter over which Rosas and the clergy had their final showdown was the status of the representatives of the Santa Cruzada in New Mexico, insignificant as such a thing ought to have been in a far-off province. It came down to a matter of ecclesiastical jurisdiction with Fray Juan de Góngora the focal point as not only custodian, but also as commissary subdelegate. The governor sought to have Custodian Juan de Salas issue an order for Góngora to withdraw from New Mexico, but Salas refused to do so on the grounds that Rosas had no jurisdiction over a representative of the crusade. Thereupon Rosas, on his own authority, banished Father Góngora.

From that point until his death over three years later, Rosas was continually under ecclesiastical censure, and as a result became increasingly hostile to the clergy and to any one who supported the Franciscans. Rosas, finding the *cabildo* of Santa Fe resistant to many of his plans and projects, purged that body of his opposition and named more compliant members. However, it must not be supposed that everyone was against Governor Rosas, for there were some important members of high-ranking families that sided with him. Documents indicate that epithets directed against Rosas were based mostly on personal and political passion. Nevertheless, Rosas succeeded in antagonizing a group of powerful soldier-citizens who had been cut to the quick by his arbitrary governmental policy, and probably by various acts that affected their pride. The net result was a clerical-military coalition that in the final years of Rosas's regime played a key role in provincial politics.

In Rosas's defense were statements that the friars had for many years wielded a strong hand in New Mexico, being litigious, causing disturbances, and even denouncing the governor and certain citizens as heretics. It was one round after another of tattling and name-calling. With control of the sacraments and in extreme cases excommunication, the church held a trump card, the fate of one's immortal soul. Detractors felt that the clergy used these powers all too freely, including withholding the sacrament of penance, especially during Lent, unless the penitent signed papers praising the clergy and denouncing civil authority.

What made the clerical position even stronger was that all of its several jurisdictions enjoyed the privileges of the ecclesiastical fuero, which allowed them to stand trial, if any, in a clerical court rather than a civil one. Summarizing the many complaints against the clergy, the fundamental issues were that the church was controlled by a single order, the Franciscans; that they exercised wide and thoroughgoing powers over the citizens in every phase of their spiritual and moral life, with no appeal except to Mexico or to the governor, the crown's representative in New Mexico; and that there was a strong economic basis for the conflict.

Friar Juan de Vidania

A proposal by the governor to establish as prelate Friar Juan de Vidania, an expelled Jesuit and a newcomer to the province, brought forth great protests over his qualifications. He was soon in league with Governor Rosas and became his researcher for seeking precedents to justify the governor's policies. To the Franciscans, Vidania was a traitor and a scoundrel, and together with Rosas the two were branded as an unholy pair. They both held firmly to the position that Father Salas's failure to have presented his papers of appointment as legal prelate deprived him of authority as such, and that his orders and censures had no validity. Vidania was a tool of the governor and by so acting defied the Franciscan hierarchy.

After much difficulty and planning, the Franciscans attempted to heal the breach by sending an innocuous delegation of two to visit the governor in Santa Fe. Rosas was so personally offended that he began to berate the Franciscans and beat them with a stick, breaking it over the head of one. He finally placed them both under guard. After much humiliation, the two were expelled from the villa. The following day Father Vidania said Mass for the governor and his henchmen and gave them absolution for their deeds. The outcome was to make any reconciliation impossible and the groups remained at odds for the next twelve months.

Supported by the renegade priest, Rosas continued to act in a high-handed manner. One result was that an increasing number of soldiers abandoned any support of the governor and swung their weight to the side of the church. Of course, Rosas took legal action against these defectors, most of whom were being tried in absentia. The clergy then assumed the position that Rosas had forfeited all right to exercise the prerogatives of his office while Rosas did all possible to punish any of the clergy that he could, and made raids on several of the convents. He was in turn held in diminishing regard by the citizens, and it was under such circumstances that the local natives became less subordinate and more restless. The Indian attitude was compounded by a plague that spread among their people, taking a reported toll of 3,000 persons, which was over 10 percent of the Pueblo Indian population. The inroads of Apache raiders were also felt during this critical period, and it was estimated that over 20,000 *fanegas* of corn were burned by such marauders, causing great dissatisfaction among the natives and probably making them think of the old days and old ways.

After a long wait to hear the judgment of the government in Mexico City, the day came. Father Salas was succeeded by a priest sent from New Spain and vested with wide powers to govern the local church. Salas remained on as commissary of the Inquisition, whose powers had been largely in abeyance during the troublesome times. By mid-April, a new governor, Juan Flores de Sierra y Valdez, relieved Rosas of his office.

Governor López de Mendizábal

Several subsequent New Mexico governors stand out, partly because they were sufficiently literate to generate a mass of documentation, and partly because they played noteworthy—though not creditable—roles. The first was Bernardo López de Mendizábal who entered office in 1659. Born in the province of Chietla in New Spain and educated in Jesuit schools in Puebla and Mexico City, he was one of the better educated of those serving as governor of the province. Presumably his Jesuit training made him anti-Franciscan, since it is certain that he did not hold the sons of Saint Francis in high regard.

From the beginning of his term in office, López antagonized both the Franciscan friars and many of the soldier colonists. He introduced innovations in the system of Indian labor, increasing the wage scale for household servants and farm laborers and reducing the number of Indians in service at the missions. Instead of supporting the friars in their campaign against Indian ceremonial dances, he authorized the public performance of these pagan ceremonies in all the pueblos. He called into question the authority of the custodian as ecclesiastical judge, and in the summer of 1660 actually forbade the prelate to exercise such authority pending a decision from the viceroy on the subject. Resentment against López's governmental policies was accentuated by his personal conduct, negligence in the observation of his religious obligations, and by tactless remarks that many persons regarded as bordering on unorthodoxy and heresy. The gossip-mongering servants at the Casa Real made things worse by reporting incidents that many believed to be evidence that both the governor and his wife were practicing Jews.

López was described as a petulant, strutting, ungracious criollo with a sharp tongue and enough education to make himself dangerous. At odds with the important clergy from the very beginning, he not only defamed them, but also attacked their use of free Indian labor employed in services to the church. He accused the priests of oppressing the mission Indians and making unwarranted use of religious powers. However, the governor himself was accused of mistreating and overworking the Indians in his own commercial interests. His residencia at the end of his term in office was a real showdown. A thirty-three count indictment was prepared, which he denied, but he was nevertheless placed in confinement from which he never emerged. López was subsequently found guilty on sixteen of the charges, including granting permission to the Indians to again perform their ceremonial dances, which according to the friars were "evil and idolatrous." And, not only was López de Mendizábal being put in his place, his wife of Italian descent was also a target of their wrath.

Doña Teresa de Aguilera

Doña Teresa, who followed a custom of bathing and changing linen on Fridays, was accused of Jewish inclination. In addition, she had the reputation of primping on Saturdays, as if she were especially celebrating that day. The fact that the governor and his wife liked to sleep alone in their bedrooms commanded attention as well. Doña Teresa was also accused of reading a book in a foreign tongue, and "was even heard to laugh as she did so." (Scholes, "Troublous Times in New Mexico," pp. 383–84) The book in question was Ariosto's *Orlando Furioso*, a natural choice for a person who had been reared in Italy, had learned the Italian language, and enjoyed reading works in it. Still, Doña Teresa's literary interests were a mistake in an isolated frontier province where there were very few people who could read their native Spanish and even fewer probably who could read and laugh at the same time. Finally, Doña Teresa de Aguilera was also tried before the Inquisition and prepared a lengthy document in defense of charges against her.

Governor Diego de Peñalosa

Next in office was Diego Dionisio de Peñalosa Briceño y Berdugo, an adventurer born in Lima, Peru, in 1624. He was the great-great-grandson of Pedro Arias de Avila, the ill-thought-of conqueror of Panama and the nemesis of Vasco Núñez de Balboa. He was also reported to be the great-grandson of Admiral Diego de Ocampo and of Pedro de Valdivia, the conqueror of Chile. Diego was tutored by an uncle and had academic training with the Jesuits, and as a precocious lad of 14, received his first of many political appointments based on his nobility. By the time he was 18, Peñalosa was a *regidor* in La Paz, and subsequently served in various bureaucratic jobs as a result of his family connections. While serving as *provincial alcalde* of the Santa Hermandad, there were serious complaints against him, resulting in a summons by the viceroy of Peru to appear before him. Instead, Peñalosa escaped by taking refuge in the Augustinian College, after which, with the aid of friends he fled on a ship bound for Panama. However, the ship sank and Peñalosa lost most of his substantial worldly fortune, which he was carrying with him. From the isthmus he went to Nicaragua where he had an uncle who was a bishop. The next stop on his lifelong odyssey was in Mexico where he obtained office as an alcalde mayor. It was from that position in 1660 that Peñalosa was given the appointment as governor of New Mexico to succeed the disgraced López de Mendizábal.

Peñalosa's chief aim as governor was personal profit and gain. Through fraud, he took advantage of his position as an investigator to acquire a large amount of property belonging to López de Mendizábal. When he learned that the latter was about to be arrested, he seized more of his belongings. As agent of the Inquisition, Father Alonzode Posada, demanded return of López's property, but Peñalosa refused. The governor became angry and bitter toward the prelate, resulting in strained relations between them during the spring and summer of 1663. In the autumn, Peñalosa seized a colonist who had taken refuge in the church. Posada demanded return of the prisoner, and was ready to impose excommunication if the governor failed to comply. Peñalosa then arrested the prelate and threatened him with exile from the province. Finally, the governor repented and negotiated a peaceful settlement with the church.

In the beginning of his tenure, Peñalosa had played an enthusiastic role in the gathering and manufacture of evidence in the residencia he held for López de Mendizábal. He had even cooperated at first with the custodian of the Franciscans, but it was not to last long, and in a brief while he was also in trouble with the Inquisition. Among other things, the governor was accused of obstruction of Inquisition business and disrespect for the tribunal's authority. His moral standing was low. "His language was the filthiest, his jokes the most obscene. With undisguised glee, he often made the friars the butt of his crude humor." (Scholes, *Troublous Times in New Mexico, 1659–1670*, p. 384) Peñalosa was reputed to have made extravagant statements, scandalized the populace with the levity that characterized his conversations on religious topics, and by his coarseness of speech. When opposition became severe, he left New Mexico hurriedly in 1664.

After his return to Mexico City, Peñalosa was arrested by the Inquisition. The formal accusations against him numbered 237 and it took a full two days just to read them. In the twenty months between accusations and trial, Peñalosa must have had time for thought; nevertheless the final sentence was severe. He had to perform the *auto de fe*, a public acknowledgement of his guilt; he was fined and saddled with a lifelong exclusion from public office and perpetual banishment from New Spain and the Antilles. Treatment of his expedition of 1662 and subsequent career follow.

EXPEDITIONS FROM NEW MEXICO

If too much attention is paid to the bitter struggle between church and state, it might give the false impression that nothing else was happening in the troubled colony of New Mexico. In fact, the hope of finding riches had never been completely forgotten, nor was the possibility of expanding the frontier and opening trade with the non-Pueblo Indians totally neglected. It was the latter of these two possibilities that brought the governors considerable criticism from time to time.

The post-Oñate era witnessed an extension of the frontier during a period of gradual but unspectacular progress. In 1613 Chililí was founded in the Estancia Valley to which the native mission settlements of Abó, Quarai, and Tabira were later joined. Pecos, at the site of Cicuyé was settled in 1617, and existing Indians were attracted to the missionary activity. Of special note were the substantial and uncharacteristic stone churches that were built in the Estancia Valley area and environs. These same buildings and their productivity soon became the target of marauding Apache Indians, and their prosperity was short-lived. They became what one writer has called the Missions that Died of Fear, and their occupants, mostly Tompiros, retreated to the relative safety of the Río Grande Valley from Isleta southward.

Father Juan de Salas

During the seventeenth century before the Pueblo Revolt, both religious and commercial interests stimulated a series of sorties to the east of New Mexico. In 1629 Father Juan de Salas paid a visit to the Jumanos Indians, with whom he spent time in missionary activity. Just who the Jumanos Indians were is a puzzle that has never been fully solved, but they were found seemingly everywhere in the Southwest, leading to their characterization as the ubiquitous Jumanos, since they were identified on the High Plains, the Low Plains, and even west of the Río Grande in a few documents. They were not, as some have supposed, the Comanches, but they had regular contacts with that nation. Whoever they finally turned out to be, they were of maximum interest to the Spaniards during the seventeenth century. Salas found them some 120 leagues east of Santa Fe when he went there with a military escort.

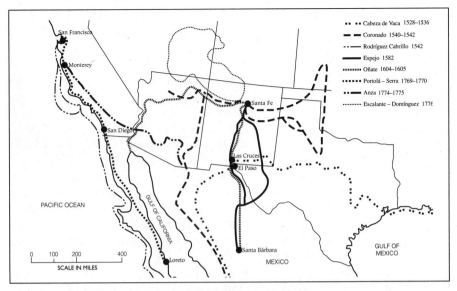

Map 4.2. Spanish routes in the Southwest. Map by Stephanie Gould.

Fathers Perea and López

Also in 1629, Fathers Esteban Perea and Diego López made a trip in the same easterly direction from Santa Fe. In 1632 Fathers Salas and Diego Ortega again visited the Jumanos, this time finding them on one of the branches of the Upper Nueces (or perhaps the Colorado) of Texas. The Jumanos were reported to have requested that missions be established for them, but it is uncertain whether they viewed missions as spiritual institutions or as good places to do business in trading their buffalo products. Two years later Alonso de Vaca in a follow-up visit went "300 leagues east of New Mexico to a great river near Quivira." (Bolton, ed., "Introduction," *Spanish Exploration in the Southwest, 1542–1706*, pp. 313–14) Except for its discovery of fresh water pearls, nothing else is known of this expedition that would have penetrated some 800 miles eastward. In 1650 there is a report of a little known trip from New Mexico to Central Texas to visit the King of the Texans (Rey de los Tejas). Finally, in 1654, Diego de Guadalajara made the last of a flurry of expeditions from New Mexico into Texas. There was seemingly insufficient motive for any greater activity, but this would not last long, for about twenty years later the French Sieur de La Salle made his intrusion into Texas. His expedition in turn stimulated great Spanish interest in the area, but it was activity that came from New Spain rather than from New Mexico.

Diego de Peñalosa, 1662

Even the La Salle venture had some possible New Mexico antecedents. By his later admission (though it is not based on clear documentation), Governor Diego de Peñalosa in 1662 led what may have been a major expedition to the east, consisting of eighty soldiers, 1,000 Indian allies with bows and arrows, and two priests. The Franciscans were Father Miguel de Guevara, guardian of the Convento de Santa Fe, and Father

Nicolás Freytas, who held the same title at San Ildefonso. Also reported to have been included was Don Tomé Domínguez de Mendoza, a prominent resident who went as *maestre de campo* on the sortie that departed on March 6, 1662. Father Freytas, to whom the account of the Peñalosa expedition is ascribed, left descriptions of travel through and to areas of beautiful rivers, marshes, and springs, and of passing through forests and groves of fruit trees in lands of fine grapes. Many mulberry trees in the area gave promise of sediculture, and the land abounded in small and large game. At his destination Peñalosa was welcomed by the natives of Quivira with great love and respect. Demonstrating his Christian zeal (which was otherwise notably absent), the leader inspired the natives to build a portable altar for religious services.

Peñalosa's greatly esteemed visit was rewarded by many presents of ermine, buckskin, chamois, marten, otter, beaver, and sable, to which was added foodstuff, including game. Peñalosa's status with the Quivirans was further enhanced by punishment meted out by the Spaniard to their ungrateful rivals and neighbors, the Escanxagues. For their hostile reception of the visitors, these opponents were severely beaten in a three-hour battle. In the end, over 3,000 Indians were killed as the Spanish arms far outweighed inferior native weaponry. In addition to the friendly Quivirans who lived near the banks of the Mischipi River, the Spaniards summarized the area's attractiveness by commenting on its obvious assets. The men of the expedition, who were from the various nations of Europe, Asia, Africa, and America, unanimously agreed that the country was the most fertile, pleasant, and agreeable that they had seen. On the trip Peñalosa was able to visit Gran Quivira and the Kingdom of Texas, claiming it to be the greatest land of all.

Four months later, 400 Quivirans returned the visit, according to an unsubstantiated report. The visitors were led by a prominent cacique from the plains "150 leagues away," accompanied by 7,000 Indians with dog trains loaded high with chamois, buckskin, and other pelts. They came to visit their friend Peñalosa and to thank him for the punishment that he had given to their enemies, the Escanxagues.

Upon inspection of the account of Peñalosa's great trip, it seems to be a paraphrase of one made by Oñate over a half century earlier. Whatever the importance of his Indian relations were as far as New Mexico was concerned, the governor was soon under indictment by the Council of the Inquisition. Forced to stand trial in Mexico City, Don Diego was thoroughly discredited. He went off to England, there attempting to convince the court that he could lead a project to invade Texas (as yet unoccupied by the Spanish) and from there go overland and seize the mines of Mexico. His quixotic scheme of self-aggrandizement rejected, Peñalosa crossed the channel to France where he got a better hearing from the king. There is reason to believe that Peñalosa's attractive story, then well rehearsed, was the basis for the grand plan of which La Salle became the commander, but from which Peñalosa was ultimately excluded. The controversial governor eventually died in Paris in 1687.

MISSIONS IN SONORA AND ARIZONA IN THE MID-1600s

By the mid-1600s, since there did not seem to be evidence of abundant wealth in the areas of Sonora and southern Arizona, the major overland thrust to the north was being carried on through the church. Because New Mexico had been the special missionary field of the Franciscans, the Jesuits were given charge of the provinces of Sinaloa and Sonora, which were in turn a part of a region the Spaniards called Nueva Vizcaya. By 1644 there were thirty-five Jesuit missions in Sonora and thirty years later they were in the valleys of Sonora and San Miguel.

After several decades of expansion among the Yaquis and Opatas, the Jesuits traveled into the hot, dry land of desert valleys and the scattered mountain ranges called La Pimería after the Pima Indians. The region called La Pimería Alta was divided between Sonora in Mexico and Arizona in the United States, stretching 50,000 square miles north from the Altar and Madgalena River valleys to the banks of the Gila, and from the San Pedro River Valley west to the Gulf of California and almost to the Colorado River. Since the early 1640s, the Indians of this area had resisted penetration by the Spaniards. The Jesuits, however, were certain that the Pimas would welcome missionaries. They began making plans to enter both Baja California and northern Sonora by the 1680s.

────────────── *Chapter Four* ──────────────

BIBLIOGRAPHIC ESSAY

Early attention to the pre–Pueblo Revolt era was almost the exclusive domain of France V. Scholes during the mid-twentieth century. His many contributions have been most useful, forming the basis for interpretation of the seventeenth century. A recent work that gives a general introduction to issues in the history of early New Mexico is William H. Broughton, "The History of Seventeenth-Century New Mexico: Is It Time for New Interpretations?" *New Mexico Historical Review*, 68 (January 1993):3–12. For primary materials, see France Scholes, ed. and trans., "Documents for the History of the New Mexican Missions in the Seventeenth Century," *NMHR*, 4 (January and April 1929):45–48; 195–201. Also important are Lansing B. Bloom, ed. and trans., "Fray Estevan de Perea's *Relación*," *NMHR*, 8 (July 1933): 211–35 and "The Royal Order of 1620 to Custodian Fray Esteban de Perea," *NMHR*, 8 (July 1930):288–98. See also France V. Scholes, *Church and State in New Mexico, 1610–1650* and *Troublous Times in New Mexico, 1659–1670*, vols. 7 and 11, Historical Society of New Mexico Publications in History (Albuquerque: University of New Mexico Press, 1942); "The Supply Service of the New Mexican Missions in the Seventeenth Century," *NMHR*, 5 (January, April, October 1930):93–116; 186–210; 386–404; "Civil Government and Society in New Mexico in the Seventeenth Century," *NMHR*, 10 (April 1935):71–111; and, with Lansing B. Bloom, "Friar Personnel and Mission Chronology, 1598–1629," *NMHR*, 19–20 (October 1944; January 1945):319–36; 58–82. For Spanish legal backgrounds see James Muldoon, *The Americas in the Spanish World Order: The Justification for Conquest in the Seventeenth Century* (Philadelphia: University of Pennsylvania Press, 1994).

For the subject of Father Alonso Benavides and the issue of María de Agreda, a number of works are available. Of primary importance are *Fray Alonso de Benavides' Revised Memorial of 1634*, edited and translated by Frederick W. Hodge, George P. Hammond, and Agapito Rey (Albuquerque: University of New Mexico Press, 1945); *The Memorial of Fray Alonso de Benavides, 1630*, translated by Mrs. Edward E. Ayer and edited by Frederick W. Hodge and Charles Fletcher Lummis (Chicago: R. R. Donnelley, 1916); and Carroll L. Riley "Las Casas and the Benavides Memorial," *NMHR*, 58 (July 1973):209–22. See also T. D. Kendrick, *Mary of Agreda: The Life and Legend of a Spanish Nun* (London: Routledge & Kegan Paul, 1967); John Kessell, "Miracles or Mystery: María de Agreda's Ministry to the Jumano Indians of the Southwest in the 1620s," in Ferenc Morton Szasz, ed., *Great Mysteries of the West* (Golden, Colo.: Fulcrum Publishing, 1993); Clark Colahan, *The Visions of Sor María de Agreda: Writing Knowledge and Power* (Tucson: University of Arizona Press, 1994); and, for a popular treatment of María and her friendship with Philip IV, see Frances Parkinson Keyes, *I, the King* (Greenwich, Conn: Fawcett Publications, 1966).

In the area of Indian relations prior to the Pueblo Revolt, see Frank D. Reeve, "Seventeenth Century Navajo-Spanish Relations," *NMHR*, 32 (January 1957):36–52; Alicia Ronstadt Millich, *Relaciones by*

Zarate Salmerón (Albuquerque: University of New Mexico Press, 1966); John P. Wilson, "Before the Pueblo Revolt: Population Trends, Apache Relations and Pueblo Abandonments in Seventeenth Century New Mexico," in *Prehistory and History in the Southwest,* edited by Nancy Fox (Santa Fe: Ancient City Press for the Archaeological Society of New Mexico, 1985); and James E. Ivey, "The Greatest Misfortune of All: Famine in the Province of New Mexico, 1667–1672," *Journal of the Southwest, 36* (spring 1994):76–92. For a controversial view of the Pueblo world at the time of Spanish conquest, see Ramón Gutiérrez, *When Jesus Came the Corn Mothers Went Away: Marriage, Sexuality, and Power in New Mexico, 1500–1846* (Stanford: Stanford University Press, 1991) and, commenting on the former, Albert L. Hurtado, "The Underside of Colonial New Mexico: A Review Essay" in *NMHR*, 68 (April 1993):181–188.

See also Angélico Chávez, *The Missions of New Mexico* (Albuquerque: University of New Mexico Press, 1956); Myra Ellen Jenkins, "Spanish Colonial Policy and the Pueblo Indians" in *Southwestern Culture History: Collected Papers in Honor of Albert H. Schroeder,* edited by Charles H. Lange (Santa Fe: Ancient City Press, 1985); and Eleanor B. Adams and France V. Scholes, "Books in New Mexico, 1598–1680" in *NMHR*, 13 (July 1942):226–255. Richard N. Ellis, ed., has included several essays on this period in his *New Mexico Past and Present: A Historical Reader* (Albuquerque: University of New Mexico Press, 1971). For glimpses of day-to-day activities throughout the colonial period, see Marc Simmons, *Coronado's Land: Essays on Daily Life in Colonial New Mexico* (Albuquerque: University of New Mexico Press, 1991).

On the governorship of Diego de Peñalosa is John G. Shea, *The Expedition of Don Diego de Peñalosa, Governor of New Mexico from Santa Fe to the Rio Mischipi and Quivira in 1662 as described by Father Nicholas de Freytas* (Albuquerque: Ham and Wallace, 1964). See also Jill D. Sweet and Karen E. Larson, "The Horse, Santiago, and a Ritual Game: Pueblo Indian Responses to Three Spanish Introductions," *Western Folklore,* 53 (January 1994):69–84.

THE PUEBLO REVOLT AND RECONQUEST OF NEW MEXICO: 1680–1700

*I*n the fall of 1680, the most important, and for Spain the most disastrous, event in New Mexico's colonial history occurred. The culmination of smoldering discontent erupted in the Pueblo Revolt. There is no doubt as to its significance, for it serves as a watershed period in the history of New Mexico. Before was the age of the conquistador, and afterward local history became increasingly characterized by accommodation and adjustment between the local Indians and the returned New Mexico residents who came accompanied by new Spanish colonists.

CAUSES OF THE PUEBLO REVOLT

The causes of the great revolt—which was not confined only to New Mexico, but reflected a general uprising—are more easily identified with hindsight. It was not the amount of external pressure on the province that was the proximate cause for rebellion, but rather internal disquiet that finally neared a breaking point in the summer of 1680. Earlier evidences of Pueblo Indian unrest could have been noted in a consistent pattern of outward religious conformity, the natives' facade for preserving their ancient religion despite harsh measures taken against those who continued to practice what most Spaniards considered to be "idolatry." Such Indians were branded as apostates, heretics, or backsliders by Spaniards whose intolerance of other religious practices was deeply implanted in their Iberian experience. Other Indians were quick to note a strong rivalry between the church and the populace.

There can be no doubt that the Franciscans had worked zealously to stamp out every vestige of native rites, but their efforts were not supported by all colonists. The governors had pursued a vacillating policy. Some, as we have seen, supported the clergy. Others, in order to ingratiate themselves with the natives, had permitted "pagan" dances, thereby bringing down the wrath of the ceaselessly intolerant clergy. On several widely spaced occasions there were minor revolts against Spanish overlordship, and these ought to have been portents of things to come. As early as eleven years before the general outbreak, the provincial predicament was clearly stated by Father Juan Bernal:

> This kingdom is seriously afflicted, suffering from two calamities, cause
> enough to finish it off, as is happening in fact with the greatest speed.
> The first of these calamities is that the whole land is at war with the
> very numerous nation of the heathen Apache Indians who kill all the
> Christian Indians they encounter ... .

*The second calamity is that for three years no crop has been harvested.
Last year, 1668, a great many Indians perished of hunger, lying dead along
the roads, in the ravines, and in their hovels. There were pueblos, like Las
Humanas, where more than four hundred and fifty died of hunger. The
same calamity still prevails, for, because there is no money, there is not a
fanega of maize or wheat in the kingdom. As a result, the Spaniards, men
as well as women, have sustained themselves for two years on the cowhides
they have in their houses to sit on. They roast them and eat them. And the
greatest woe of all is that they can no longer find a bit of leather to eat, for
their livestock is dying off.* (Kessell, ed., *Kiva, Cross and Crown: The
Pecos Indians and New Mexico, 1541–1840,* p. 212)

Not only had those years been bad, half of the provincial population had averted
starvation in the great famine of 1668 by eating animal hides and the straps of the
carretas, prepared with herbs and roots. In the following year there was a great pestilence during which many people and much livestock perished. Finally, in 1672 Apache
hostility reigned, as those Indians sacked, robbed, pillaged, and otherwise intimidated
the province.

POPÉ'S ROLE IN THE REVOLT

The best known, most universally accepted, and most general explanation of the
causes of the Pueblo Revolt ties it to the leadership provided by a San Juan medicine
man, Popé. In 1675, five years before the actual event, the charismatic Popé had been
arrested along with forty-six other native leaders on charges of sorcery and witchcraft.
Governor Juan Francisco Treviño, determined to take strong measures to stamp out
such superstitious practices, ordered three captives hanged as examples to their
coreligionists. Other leaders were severely punished, including the San Juan medicine
man himself. In protest of this chastisement of their religious leaders, a delegation of
some seventy Tewa warriors appeared in the capital and put pressure on Governor
Treviño in an unsuccessful effort to obtain release of the accused.

Popé was eventually released from custody and proceeded to plan vengeance against
the Spaniards. From the vantage point of his home pueblo of San Juan in Río Arriba,
the incensed medicine man began preparations to throw off the Spanish yoke of subju-
gation. Slowly hatching a plan that included eradication of all vestiges of Spanish occupation, Popé nursed his feelings in the friendly atmosphere of his own people. His plan
for a general revolt was only in the embryonic stage when Maestre de Campo Francisco
Xavier continued the persecution of Popé by driving him out of his home village. He
then moved to the northernmost pueblo of Taos, where he found another willing audi-
ence for his great project.

At Taos, Popé consolidated his support. Three infernal spirits from the underground Lake of Copala and named Caudi, Tilina, and Tleume, were reported to have
directed Popé's activities; however, they never emerged from the subterranean kiva
where the Indian messiah of San Juan received regular visits from these underworld
phantoms. This supernatural assistance resulted in widespread acceptance of Popé's

plan, based in part upon the medicine man's intimacy with beings who were alleged to be capable of emitting fire from their extremities. Popé believed and persuaded others that he was the chosen one to deliver the Pueblo Indians from the evil consequences of Iberian control. With great capacity for appealing to his listeners, he convinced the restive Pueblos that it would be possible to drive out the Spaniards by inflicting a devastating defeat on them in a well-coordinated offensive. Even in this early stage of the plan, the Indian uprising had certain non-Pueblo overtones of military strategy borrowed from the same Spaniards that the Indians sought to destroy completely.

Particularly active in planning the revolt were the chiefs and medicine men of the northern villages who, little by little in the congenial surroundings of the kivas, shaped the expulsion operation. Popé's scheme for general revolt was not divulged to all Indians, nor was it intended to make all privy to the elaborate plan until just prior to the fateful day of attack. Ex-post-facto accounts by Indian deponents later asserted that the conspiracy and rebellion had not, in general, been voluntary on the part of all the pueblos. Rather, Popé had held them in fear and obedience because, as they believed, he had talked with the devil, a superior authority. Many natives were persuaded that Popé's word was more potent and more to be believed than the word of any Spaniard, whether governor, priest, soldier, or civilian. Among the "devil-inspired" actions of Popé was that of killing his own son-in-law, Nicolás Bua, Spanish-appointed governor of San Juan Pueblo. Fearful that necessary secrecy might be compromised by Bua, Popé killed him rather than run the risk that the San Juan chief might turn informer.

The Knotted Cord

One of the best known and oft-told aspects of the actual revolt is the tale of the knotted cord. Popé took a maguey fiber rope and tied knots in it to represent the number of days until the strategic blow was to be delivered. This calendar string was sent through the pueblos as far south as Isleta; swift runners carried the portentous cord under pain of death for revealing its secret to any non-Indian. The planned date for the strike was August 11, 1680, and the concurrence of almost all of the people was reached, except for the Piros who were not made aware of the plan.

Despite strict security measures, the Indian plan was discovered two days before the target date. It is even possible that the original date had been established for as late as August 13, but premature divulgence altered the Indian timetable and threw off schedule the synchronization that was so essential. Some Spanish sources indicate that warnings were heard, perhaps as many as twenty days ahead of the attack, and that such advice was also given to the Spaniards by friendly Indian leaders on more than one occasion in the days just preceding the outbreak.

Otermín Learns of the Plan

Governor Antonio Otermín learned from Indian chiefs at Tanos, San Marcos, and La Ciénaga that two Indians had brought an order from the conspirators that the revolt was about to begin. Otermín then had the messengers arrested, whereupon they testified that they had been given a cord with two knots, symbolic of the two days before hostilities would commence, and that they had been entrusted to carry the cord in all

Fig. 5.1. Acoma Pueblo. Photo by Iris Engstrand.

secrecy to the headmen of those three groups. The captured messengers also admitted that the chiefs of one of the pueblos, that of San Cristóbal, had been unwilling to receive the message that they carried, an indication that there was no unanimity. Neither of the young prisoners knew many details of the plot except for their own indirect participation in it, having been sent by two Indians of Tesuque Pueblo who had entrusted them with "a deerskin thong with two knots." Though this statement raises a question about what the legendary knotted string was made of—maguey or deerskin—the cord's message was always clear.

The young Indian captives said that the conspiracy originated in the north, and involved a letter from an Indian lieutenant of Po he yemu, who was a legendary God. The informants reported that they had heard that this Indian lieutenant of Po he yemu was tall, black, and had large yellow eyes, and that he was greatly feared. The appearance of a mystical lieutenant of a long-departed deity seems curious, and is not substantiated by any other testimony. However, emphasis upon Popé as virtually the sole perpetrator of the entire affair is also a convenient way of shifting the responsibility for instigation of the revolt. In any case, the time the Spaniards returned to Santa Fe during the later reconquest of New Mexico, Popé was conveniently dead, and it was easy to shift upon his fallen corpse the principal burden of guilt. The rather fanciful idea that an intrusive man became the head of such a major revolt is weakened by the near impossibility that an outsider could have achieved such a role of leadership in traditional Pueblo Indian society, particularly when there were already meritorious leaders of more tangible form.

What role, if any, some frequently mentioned native leaders had in the planning and early execution of the revolt is quite vague. Governor Luis Tupatú of Picurís Pueblo, regularly cast in the role of a principal leader, seems only to emerge in that category after the shock phase of expulsion was completed. Alonso Catatí, Lorenzo Tupatú (brother of Luis), and El Saca likewise do not appear to have been important in the initiation of the move to expel the Spaniards. In fact, the well-accepted explanation later fostered by Otermín that at one hour of the same day the revolt began all over the province does not do justice to the exact truth.

Following the capture of the young messengers, the natives of Tesuque were confused. In fear that their plans had been discovered, they determined to hasten the outbreak as the only hope for successful consummation of the revolt. As a result, they decided to put the operation plan into force in advance of the intended date, with the first attack occurring on August 9. On the following day, the important towns of San Juan and Taos began their offensive action; and, during the same afternoon, the more distant pueblos such as Santo Domingo, Jémez, and some of the other Río Abajo villages joined after having received news of the premature start of hostilities.

On the eve of the great rebellion against Spanish authority, there were an estimated 17,000 Pueblo Indians of which about 6,000 were considered to be "warriors," an extremely high percentage of the total population (and perhaps an exaggeration in subsequent accounting for the loss of Spanish prestige and possessions). Against this numerous, though untrained host, the same sources indicate that the colonial forces numbered only 170 effectives, doubtless an underestimate.

The hotbeds of revolt, the large pueblos of Taos and Picurís, were soon in action. The northern Hispanic settlers were surprised by the premature outbreak and probably by the fact that Apache allies had joined the rebel Taoseños. Both of these factors contributed to the Spanish incapacity to mount an effective defense. According to the preliminary Indian plan, every man, woman, and child was to be killed, settlers and Franciscan missionaries alike, and their goal was almost reached, with seventy-odd people killed and only two escaping. These were the Sargentos Mayores Sebastián de Herrero and Fernando Chávez, who made their way past the other rebellious pueblos and joined a group of refugees who had taken up defensive positions far to the south near Isleta village.

At Picurís Pueblo the Indians made a clean sweep of the Spaniards, including the two missionaries. The plan was working as anticipated. Houses were looted, cattle and horses were driven off from the *haciendas* and *estancias*, the churches were burned, and the sacred contents thereof were profaned and destroyed. All that remained to be done was the final act of assembling at Santa Fe for one last attack, after which they would return to their ancient customs.

There is much more documentary detail concerning the death of the Franciscans, who as a result of having died at the hands of those whom they had come to convert to Christianity, won at that moment the greatest glory of the missionary priesthood, the crown of martyrdom. Those who died in a vain attempt to protect the priests were merely casualties. A list was made of the twenty-one religious who met their deaths in the uprising on the northern frontier of New Spain, which included the father custodian of the Province of New Mexico, Fray Juan Bernal. Most of the martyrs had been in the province for fewer than ten years, and the names of all are listed in Hackett's *Revolt* of the Pueblo Indians of New Mexico and Otermín's Attempted Reconquest, 1680–1682 (vol. I, pp. 109–11), though there is no such listing of the 380 non-clerical dead.

In attempting to eradicate every vestige of Hispanic overlordship, the revolt spread southward to the Queres and Jemez, then to the Tigua pueblos of the Río Abajo and finally west to Zuni. Even the ever-resistant but normally peaceful Hopi killed their four missionaries and destroyed the churches that had been built there. The little defense that could be mounted by the besieged and thoroughly frightened Iberians centered around Santa Fe in the north and around the southern pueblo of Isleta, but there was neither communication nor any possible coordination between these two isolated surviving detachments.

SUMMARY OF THE DESTRUCTION

The destruction wrought in the surprise attack by the nearly unified Indians caused the entire province from Taos to Isleta to be devastated and depopulated in two brief days. Residences were looted of household goods, livestock were driven off, and many homes were set afire. The churches also suffered either arson or extreme forms of vandalism. A Spanish source reported that they were stripped of their sacred vessels, robbed of their holy vestments, and "in every way as completely and foully desecrated as Indian sacrilege and indecency could suggest." This Spanish report of the Indian activity branded the natives as "blind fiends of the devil who set fire to the holy temples and images, mocking them with their dances and making trophies of the priestly vestments" and other paraphernalia of worship. (Hackett, *Revolt of the Pueblo Indians of New Mexico and Otermín's Attempted Reconquest, 1680–1682*, vol. I, pp. 177–78)

Indian hatred of the Spaniards was so great that in the pueblo of Sandia images of saints were found among excrement, two chalices were found in a basket of manure, and the paint on a carved crucifix had been taken off by lashes. The natives also placed excrement at the Holy Communion table at the main altar, and hacked off the arms of a sculptured image of Saint Francis.

Those Spaniards who had not been killed in the first attack took refuge at Isleta in the south, or at the capital city where they were rallied together by Governor Otermín. The group at Isleta under Lieutenant Governor Alonso García were fully convinced that they were the sole survivors of the battle. García and his soldiers had been instrumental in successful rescues of isolated Spaniards at several places and had united these and other groups at Isleta for a defensive stand. With the arrival of a few stragglers from various points, the refugee numbers at Isleta swelled to about 1,500, including seven Franciscan missionaries. Early reports indicated that there were only 120 men there capable of bearing arms, and gave the discouraging information that an equal number of Spanish soldiers had been killed, though this latter figure seems to be a considerable exaggeration.

Loss of lives was accompanied by loss of arms, ammunition, and military mounts. In fact, dubious intelligence information indicated that the Pueblo Indians had captured more than 200 firearms and a large quantity of ammunition. In any case, the odds for survival were strongly against the besieged at either location and yet each could not help but think of their fellow countrymen perhaps in a more difficult situation. Of the two groups, the Spaniards at Isleta had the distinct advantage of being far from the storm center of revolt. Also, a great, relatively unpopulated zone lay to the south as their route of escape, if (as was soon to be the case) such course of action were to prove advisable.

The obviously disastrous days of the initial blow of rebellion were followed by a period of Spanish insecurity, procrastination, and hopeful waiting. In the northern area, with survival dependent on the supposedly impregnable capital of Santa Fe, matters became increasingly more urgent and distressful. The governor did not at first grasp the seriousness of his predicament and confined his immediate efforts to the job of defending the capital. By August 13, he at last ordered all settlers to leave their homes and hasten to Santa Fe, but few ever got his message. Those who were in a position to obey his order were from La Cañada, while a few others from nearby Cerrillos had already started to the capital in advance of any notification.

Otermín, oblivious of the great destruction elsewhere and in expectation that others would be joining him in both defensive operations as well as in his anticipated recovery of control, made plans for operations on a local scale. The flurry of activity was great, but Otermín's hopes for increased strength from other areas was not realized; to the contrary, he gradually became aware that he was in dire straits. Contemporary documentation depicts his final realization that a state of active siege was being conducted by a "horde of savage demons, who, having killed as many of the settlers elsewhere as possible, now danced in their glee around the besieged refugees who had taken safety in the government buildings [*casas reales*].The natives had reason to believe that even these strong buildings would fall as had the other buildings in the neighboring jurisdictions." (Hackett, *Revolt of the Pueblo Indians of New Mexico and Otermin's Attempted Reconquest, 1680–1682*, vol. I, p. lxiv)

With the arrival of three soldier stragglers from the north—who had narrowly escaped death en route to the expected safety of Santa Fe—Otermín soon realized the even greater magnitude of the disaster, therefore increasing concern over his own position. Fruitless hopes of help from the Río Abajo had buoyed up the governor, who meanwhile tried to prepare his local resources for an inevitable showdown at the capital. By then the odds of battle were stacked against even a strong showing by the badly outnumbered Spaniards, who at this point were fewer than 1,000 strong, with fewer than 100 capable of bearing arms. In addition, a disproportionate number of women and children made defense more difficult. It was against this weakened resistance that the Indians intended to level Santa Fe, kill the governor and his minions, and "return undisturbed to their ancient liberties and the adoration and obedience of the Gods of their fathers." (Hackett, *Revolt of the Pueblo Indians of New Mexico and Otermin's Attempted Reconquest, 1680–1682,* vol. I, p. lxiv) To add to the Spanish wounds, the natives were proclaiming that God and the Virgin Mary were dead, that they had seen them die, and that the Indian God whom they obeyed never died.

Reminiscent of a more famous leader, Hernán Cortés in the conquest of Cholula, Otermín rose to the occasion by placing pieces of ordnance in the doors of the government building, charged and mounted on their carriages, and aimed at the street entrances to repel any attack. The anticipated siege began on August 15. A local Indian messenger sent by the Spaniards to deliver a message to the hostile besiegers returned instead as one of the rebel leaders. He informed the governor that the Indians could not turn back at this point because the revolution had gone too far. The native delegation brought with them two crosses, one red and the other white, and Otermín was to choose between them—if he wanted war, as represented by the red cross, he could so elect. If, however, he desired peace, then he must choose the white cross and agree to depart forthwith.

In a brave, futile, and quixotic response, the Spanish leader told the apostate Indians that he desired to avoid war because he had not sought it; and that if the Indians would become peaceful, he as governor would pardon the crimes that they had committed. It hardly seems possible that even Otermín believed his own statements. Certainly the Indians did not, as they derided and ridiculed his reply. In the ensuing hours, the Spanish defense, spirited by dint of its extreme necessity, seemed temporarily to gain the advantage, overcoming the Indians and retaking a great number of animals. At the last moment, however, the timely arrival of an awaited contingent of Teguas, Taos, and Picurís Indians who attacked the capital from the other side, caused Otermín to turn his attention to that quarter. Lack of water and the excessive number of Spaniards and their animals confined to close quarters and surrounded by a determined enemy, caused the first non-military casualties as animals began to die of thirst.

The Spaniards then decided to engage the enemy in open battle rather than to die cooped up in the government buildings. After preliminary planning, at daybreak on August 20 a small Spanish force rushed from the casas reales where they had been besieged. Invoking the aid of the Virgin Mary, they took the Indians by surprise, "running over them, trampling them under the hooves of the horses and dislodging them from their positions in the streets and nearby houses." (Hackett, *Revolt of the Pueblo Indians of New Mexico and Otermín's Attempted Reconquest, 1680–1682,* vol. I, p. lxiv) Otermín's figures for the skirmishes of that morning were over 1,500 Indians put to flight, 300 left dead in the streets, and forty-seven captured. This human toll was accompanied by recovery of some firearms and more than eighty head of cattle.

Despite such reported initial military success, time was running out for the besieged Spaniards. They were still greatly outnumbered, though according to their count of casualties they had lost only five men, four soldiers, and perhaps most significant, the maestre de campo, Andrés Gómez who held a position of extreme importance to any military operations. Among the substantial number of Spanish wounded was the governor, who suffered a painful though not dangerous flesh wound in the chest. If such disproportionate losses are true there are various explanations: The Spaniards were in a defensive posture, always a tactical advantage in early phases of siege; they fought using modern techniques of battle; and finally, they were the ones keeping the statistics.

For any long-range operations the Indians had many key advantages, including those of supply, reinforcement, freedom of movement, and extreme motivation, factors whose importance not lost on either side. Under the circumstances, despite great religious faith on the part of the Spaniards, the best they could hope for was an honorable withdrawal from a clearly unequal contest.

From some Indians who had been taken captive, Governor Otermín learned for the first time that the Pueblo Indians had some outside help from their old enemies, whom the Spaniards customarily referred to as the "infidel Apaches." There is some doubt as to the traditional relationship between the Pueblos and various Apache groups. The Apaches historically were friends and trading partners of the Pueblos, but the wedge of Spanish occupation changed that relationship, though it was then reestablished. Be that as it may, the Pueblos could count on a little help from their friends, principally those referred to as the Apaches de Acho. Those allies could hope to share the booty and establish a good trading relationship with the Pueblos, who would enjoy the spoils of a successful war.

Otermín became increasingly worried about the extremity of his position, and justifiably so. He looked around and saw shortages of water and food plus the weakened condition of his animals, coupled with the improbability of any reinforcement. He was trying to defend the shell of what had been the principal city of the province, but houses had been burned, the casas reales as places of refuge were overcrowded, and it was even necessary for survival's sake to diminish his effective military garrison on a regular basis to take the water-starved animals out to the nearby Santa Fe River to drink. With most of the remaining people already in favor of flight, could Otermín justify holding out?

Gaining unanimous consent of alcaldes, Franciscans, soldiers, leaders, and followers, Otermín decided to abandon the Villa de Santa Fe on August 21, planning to march south-southwest to Isleta. It was an opportune time for withdrawal since the Indians were nursing their recent wounds, were not fully ready for such a surprise move, and could not yet fully count on Apache help. Otermín issued orders to the secretary of government and war, Francisco Xavier, to gather together all of the property of the governor's own hacienda and distribute it equally among the people at the casas reales in order to provide protection and sustenance for the march ahead. "These provisions, as distributed to the one thousand and more men, women, and children, consisted chiefly of wearing apparel, such as shoes, shirts, uniforms, overcoats, and other supplies, together with all the horses that were left, for the use of the people in leaving the province." (Hackett, *Revolt of the Pueblo Indians of New Mexico and Otermín's Attempted Reconquest, 1680–1682*, vol. I, p. lxvi) These were made as gifts, free of any charge, with the total value of the items distributed estimated by the secretary as 8,000 pesos.

Retreat to the South

Distribution having been completed, the group departed from the capital the same afternoon so that they could camp out that night in open country. Since many refugees were going to be on foot, it was deemed best to take advantage of every moment in making a strategic withdrawal. All were still hopeful that aid would be forthcoming from the military and civilian populations that were thought to be awaiting their arrival at Isleta far to the south.

In heading southward, the Spaniards were menaced but never attacked by Indians who shadowed them. At Sandia Pueblo there was a near encounter that resulted in damage inflicted on local assets by both Indians and Spaniards. En route farther south, stops were made at the estancia of Doña Luisa de Trujillo—where in 1706 the town of Albuquerque was founded—and at the hacienda of the Gómez family. It was at about this time that, to his disappointment, Otermín finally learned that Lieutenant Governor García and all the people who had earlier escaped from Jémez, Zía, and the Río Abajo had long since vacated their initial point of refuge at Isleta. Knowing nothing of the reason for García's rapid departure, and quick to cast blame on the lieutenant governor, Otermín had no alternative but to continue his march of evacuation.

Upon reaching Isleta, the governor learned that not only had the Spaniards left, but many of the Isletans had also gone along with García and his party as they headed for El Paso, where some of them established permanent homes at a New Isleta Pueblo. Today, Indian residents of Isleta del Sur still trace their origins back to the time of the revolt and have in recent years reestablished relations with their northern counterparts after a separation of nearly 300 years.

The activities of the survivors south of Santa Fe form a significant part of the story of the Pueblo Revolt. On the day after the main attack in the south, many down-river survivors straggled into Isleta. The lieutenant governor was instrumental in assuring the safe flight of some of the area's isolated groups, having formed rescue parties that scoured the country as far north as Santo Domingo. As a result, many men, women, and children escaped the fate of their neighbors. After observing the effectiveness of Indian operations in the Río Abajo area, García came to the conclusion that the rebellion had totally destroyed all Spanish life to the north. He had received an erroneous report of the death of his superior and decided that having no word of any Spaniards still living, he needed to call a meeting of the local survivors. One leading figure, Maestre de Campo Juan Domínguez de Mendoza said that in his opinion they should march out in good military order to meet the wagons of a caravan that was supposedly coming north with supplies. If that help materialized, he reasoned that with a resupply of ammunition, the survivors should go back upstream to ascertain the fate of their northern counterparts.

There were no dissenters concerning the general decision to evacuate the area, so García took steps to legalize his action by calling a junta and by drawing up an official document expressing individual and collective opinion. The document indicated that the Spanish position was extremely bad, the rebels being in possession of much of their arms and livestock, including horses.

It was not unusual for a commander in García's position to take such steps; the super-legalistic Spaniards in the conquest of the New World were ever mindful of the need to justify almost every act. For example, no sooner had Otermín realized that his second-in-command had abandoned Isleta, than the governor took the legal step of issuing an order of arrest against García. The charges were that without orders or notice, García had marched out with a number of Spanish soldiers, going six leagues beyond the settled part of the kingdom to a place they called Fray Cristóbal. Needless to say, García hastened to defend himself in an elaborate statement in which he indicated that he was motivated by reports of the death of the governor, and outlined his actions based on that supposed knowledge. He indicated that he personally was not in favor of leaving and was determined not to abandon his home. Instead he wanted to fortify himself there and learn for certain about his lordship the governor, but the roads were infested by the enemy. He begged in light of such overwhelming evidence that he be free and absolved of the arrest and charge.

García's defense was quite persuasive. He pointed out that he had no source of resupply, even though some Pueblo Indians from Socorro and Sevilleta were friendly and desired to join the Spaniards. He mentioned the long-expected supply train that had left from Mexico a year earlier and had been organized by Father Francisco Ayeta, *custos* and procurator general of the Franciscans of New Mexico. Ayeta also had been active in attempting to obtain a substantial military reinforcement for the understaffed province.

Long before the outbreak of revolt, in an effort to provide for safe arrival of Ayeta's caravan of supplies, Otermín had sent an officer with a troop of thirty men to meet the convoy and escort it to Santa Fe from the river's crossing at El Paso. And, it is very likely that the absence from Santa Fe of these thirty soldiers, a substantial fraction of the total military force in New Mexico, emboldened the Pueblos. It certainly left the defending Spaniards shorthanded at the time of the August uprising.

Though García exhibited great desire to march north to ascertain the fate of his governor, "or to lose his life in the attempt," there was no chance to put such a heroic and illogical plan into effect. (Hackett, *Revolt of the Pueblo Indians of New Mexico and Otermín's Attempted Reconquest, 1680–1682*, p. lxxiv) García's officers had been effective when they pointed out that his people were naked, on foot, and without shoes. Furthermore it was not certain how the retreating Spaniards would be received by the Mansos Indians with whom they were planning to take refuge, and even en route there was the possibility of an Apache attack. But, García's situation, though critical at all times, was not nearly as bleak as the governor's, for most of the Indian warriors of the Río Abajo jurisdiction had gone off to Santa Fe to participate in the main event.

Following contact between Otermín and García, it was only a matter of days before the survivors were united, and only a short while longer until the badly needed supplies of the expected caravan relieved the tremendous shortage from which all were suffering. Finally, after a review of the supporting documents, Otermín declared his lieutenant governor a free man, absolving him from all blame for having abandoned the province without first obtaining superior authority.

Once united, there was some doubt about the next move, but this was resolved by Otermín making a personal trip down to Salineta, a place just four leagues north of Guadalupe del Paso. Otermín ordered a full review of his people and their equipment, which resulted in a long muster list. Though it included 1,946 persons, only 155 of them were men capable of bearing arms. This total figure represents a considerable shrinkage from the more than 2,500 reported to comprise the surviving Otermín and García divisions a few weeks earlier. It is thought that several hundred of the refugees went directly to Nueva Vizcaya without passing muster at La Salineta. They probably never intended to return to New Mexico under any circumstances, and during the years of waiting at El Paso for the reconquest of New Mexico many of those who reported in at La Salineta also slipped away to the south. Doubtless those who had little to gain by a return to the Upper Río Grande were those who defected, whereas those who were substantially invested in the province were more willing to run the risk that return would entail.

An early matter requiring a decision was whether to attempt an immediate recuperation of the lost province, though this was not an inviting prospect. There was obvious danger, and to many the idea seemed rash. But the position of the refugees in El Paso was not very good either, nor was La Salineta an appropriate place. Otermín agreed to the request of his people to establish the exiles near Nuestra Señora de Guadalupe (the small mission founded in 1659 at El Paso by priests from New Mexico), at three camps called Real de San Lorenzo, Real de San Pedro de Alcántara, and Real del Santísimo Sacramento.

Another matter then came to the attention of the group. It was possible that the entire New Mexico province, including the populace at El Paso, might be recalled and the area of New Mexico written off as a lost cause. Father Ayeta's timely arrival had temporarily saved the day, but it was not enough to keep a large and unproductive colony from great suffering. Some people, specifically those from the Isleta area southward, had been able to bring with them some of their assets. As a result, they were in a much more favorable economic position than those who came from the far north with only the clothing they had on their backs. In fact, a certain amount of animosity developed between the "have's" and the "have not's," and life at El Paso was not fully harmonious.

Seeing the great suffering of the colony, and particularly the need for a replenishment of church ornaments, vestments, and supplies, Father Ayeta became what Herbert E. Bolton once called "the Paul Revere" of New Mexico. The Franciscan decided to ride virtually non-stop to Mexico City to prevent any move toward abandonment of the province over which he had spiritual oversight. In a tour de force of equestrian skill, or at least of persistence, the highly motivated priest rode the 1,200 miles to Mexico City in a period of twelve days to save the province—not from approaching redcoats, but from bureaucratic economy.

Otermín Attempts a Reconquest

At El Paso the defeated Spaniards nursed their wounds, solidified their position, and subsequently attempted a premature reconquest in 1681 under the direction of Otermín. Yet it only resulted in a realization that retaking the area was not going to be easy and that the Indians had in no way regretted the expulsion of the Europeans. Years of hopeful waiting passed, several governors came and went, trade continued as usual with Indians of the Texas plains to the east, but the population of El Paso decreased and certainly thoughts of return became dim.

By September 1680, the active phase of the revolt was completed. The natives expelled the Spaniards from their northernmost province; still, independence proved to be only temporary for the Indians. They had suffered losses in the battles and some 317 Indians from the Río Abajo pueblos of Isleta, Sevilleta, Alamillo, Socorro, and Senecú had departed, whether willingly or unwillingly, with the fleeing Spaniards. One demographic impact of the revolt was the marked reduction of native population, especially adult males. Another result was the locale change of a considerable number of

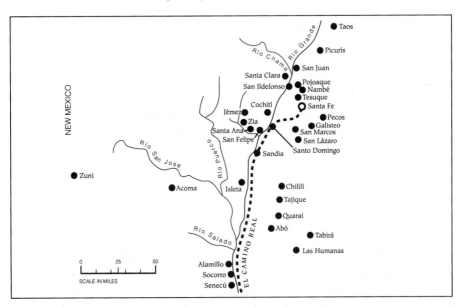

Map 5.1. New Mexico pueblos, circa 1650. Map by Stephanie Gould.

Pueblo Indians, some taking residence with other friendly groups never to return to their pre-revolt homes, and others having their old homes moved to new places as circumstances dictated.

MIXED NATIVE REACTION TO THINGS SPANISH

Some documentary evidence and a considerable amount of oral tradition gives some idea of the success of efforts after 1680 to obliterate all vestiges of Spanish colonialism. Some church items that were saved secretly by Indians friendly to the Spaniards were, however, subsequently returned during the reconquest. More important was the widespread Pueblo resistance to destruction of cultural items that had been adopted during more than eight decades of Spanish control. It was impossible to kill livestock, especially horses, to uproot plants and trees, and to do other things to bring about a total return of Pueblo culture as it existed before the time of Juan de Oñate. Acculturation had taken root so firmly that in many regards there was no turning back. The messianic deliverer had been able to take the first step, war; but the second step, complete return to a more primitive economy, was much harder to accomplish. That the old religion had been totally reinstituted did not mean all aspects of the new religion were rejected. Pueblo Indian culture has to the present been capable of comfortably embracing two religious orientations—Catholic and Native American—by taking the best of both philosophies and making life fuller and richer.

Despite the anticipated and unrestrained happiness that freedom from Spanish control promised, the new liberation brought different restrictions. According to later informants, Popé and his associates came down to Santa Fe accompanied by war captains and other Indians and proclaimed that the Devil was very strong—much better than God, who was just a piece of rotten wood. He encouraged the people to burn all the remaining images and temples, rosaries and crosses, and even to break up the bells. The Indians were told to discard their baptismal names and call themselves whatever they wished. They were told to leave their Christian wives and take any wife they chose. Upon pain of severe punishment, they were not to mention in any way the names of God, the most holy Virgin, or the saints. Popé asserted that the commands of the Devil were better than the laws of God. Orders were also issued not to speak Spanish in any pueblo. These orders were not too difficult to follow, but an order to burn any seeds that were Spanish must have been impossible to enforce. Had Popé extended, as would have been logical, the idea of obliterating all vestiges of Spanish occupation to include the slaughter of all European domestic animals, he would have had great trouble.

Just how long Popé held sway as absolute leader of the Pueblo people is uncertain, but his blaze of unrestricted glory was doubtless brief, perhaps only a little more than a year. He soon shared the spotlight with others, such as Picurís chief Luis Tupatú and Queres governor Alonso Catití, a mestizo. But just what happened to Popé and why is unclear. Spanish sources reported him to be alive until about 1690, though there is no verification of his death. Other sources indicate a much earlier death. Whatever the case, his fame came from leading the rebels to the immediate goal of independence, which was a considerable achievement. But the capacity to succeed in revolution does not automatically bring success in time of peace, and it was impossible for Indian New Mexico to return to the pre-Oñate, pre-Coronado days. The area was out of necessity forced to maintain troops on a wartime footing, or at least in preparedness against an imminent attempt at reconquest. If nothing else, Popé and his demise provided a convenient scapegoat for both the Indians and the Spaniards upon whom to cast the principal blame for the Pueblo Revolt when, after the reconquest, the Europeans returned to an altered New Mexico. One considerable gain for the Indians was that the detested institution of encomienda was a permanent casualty of the revolt.

THE EMERGENCE OF EL PASO

An important development resulting from the revolt was the emergence of El Paso as a second center for New Mexico. Though there had been a small mission founded there in 1659 to begin work among the Mansos Indians, the arrival of the refugees and the economic impact of their subsequent settlement transformed the river crossing into an important area—and for a while the only area still occupied by New Mexicans. That it was part of New Mexico was soon made official when Governor Otermín was placed in charge, and the area was no longer administered from Nueva Vizcaya. And even long after the revolt's impact had vanished, the existence of El Paso helped to secure for New Mexicans a less isolated feeling, since there was now a town about halfway between them and Chihuahua City.

THE NEW MEXICO RECONQUEST

Years of waiting at El Paso were hard on the New Mexico refugees, so much so that the area's population gradually dwindled. The reduction in forces can be attributed to the uncertainty about ever going back, the less desirable living conditions in El Paso, and an almost constant harassment of the weakened colony by the surrounding Indians, with Mansos, Sumas, and Gileño Apaches being the principal irritants. In far-off Mexico City and in even farther-off Spain, the fate of New Mexico hung in the balance. It had always cost the government much to maintain a show of Spanish force in the Upper Río Grande, a situation that would not change during the colonial period. However, the fact that New Mexico was an unprofitable enterprise did not set it apart from any of the other northern frontier provinces. They were all financial losers. But the Franciscan missionaries could not bear to see the eternal loss of so many souls that they had been at great pains to preach to, catechize, baptize, and train in the rudiments of the Catholic faith and the associated "civilized" life. The priests were outspoken about the need to return, evidenced particularly by the custos, Father Ayeta, who with his earlier phenomenal ride to Mexico City brought attention to the area at a most critical time. Ayeta must have been an unusually effective salesman, for in the years 1596–1683 the royal treasury expenses on behalf of New Mexico had exceeded receipts by a greater than 90-to-1 ratio.

The history of New Spain in the seventeenth century mirrored the history of the Iberian Peninsula. It was a time of economic depression caused by a sharp decline of the Indian labor force, reduced production of precious minerals, and serious problems of defense throughout the Southwest. During the same period the home government, plagued by chronic fiscal crises, levied new taxes on both the peninsular realms and the Indies in order to sustain a small, isolated outpost on a faraway frontier. Approximately 70 percent of the total cost needed to support New Mexico was for maintenance of the missionary effort among the Pueblo Indians. The amount of money spent in New Mexico provides incontrovertible evidence of the vitality of the religious motive of Spanish enterprise in the New World.

Many of the colonial exiles at El Paso were yearning to return home to New Mexico, for even though it had not always been a happy home, it was the only real home that many of them knew. Their lands, their houses, and their other assets were there. Furthermore, Spanish pride required that the Pueblo Indians be chastised and put back in their assigned place. Finally, the area still provided a buffer zone that had to be occupied in order to keep other nations out of more valuable areas to the south.

Originally it was felt that the return, usually called the *reconquista*, would be prompt and rapid in execution. Neither was to be the case. El Paso became the capital of New Mexico for a period of twelve years of waiting for the reconquest. When that time finally came, El Paso played the role of staging base through which the return was funneled, and for many years afterward it was New Mexico's second city.

Whether from ignorance of his position's weakness, the overconfidence he felt resulting from Spain's backing, his underestimation of Indian strength, or some combination of these factors, General Otermín planned for an almost immediate reconquest, one that would begin the year following the uprising. The expedition was made up of nearly 150 soldiers supported by over 100 Indian allies, and consisted of a surprisingly large support group of remounts, carretas, and pack animals. But there was less than universal enthusiasm for the campaign, as reflected by frequent desertions even before the operation began.

First Attempt at Reconquest

The first attempted reconquest was a total failure, though the advance party under Juan Domínguez de Mendoza, a man who had played a very creditable role in the evacuation, got as far as some of the southern pueblos. Those Indians protested their innocence or at least demonstrated their repentance and were appropriately forgiven, though there is reason to believe that they were just buying time. Following the governor's orders, Domínguez de Mendoza burned some of the villages and destroyed food supplies. As it turned out, this was not only tactically unsound, it showed something less than good sense, since those foodstuffs could have been taken off to El Paso where the Spanish refugees had been suffering from a severe food shortage.

In retrospect, some had thought that if Domínguez de Mendoza had been more forceful in these initial contacts, he might have accomplished the reconquest rapidly. Even at that early time, some Pueblo Indians had not found their independence to be the great boon they had hoped. They were already somewhat divided by factionalism and certainly felt that the Spaniards would return someday. It was this constant expectation of a day of reckoning that forced the Pueblo leaders to stay on a war-readiness footing, one which, as time went by, became an increased burden to their new economy.

Otermín and Domínguez de Mendoza were liberal with pardons, but they should have realized that Indian repentance and promises of submission were not very sincere. The two officers, accompanied by Father Ayeta, contented themselves with surveying the damage of the Pueblo Revolt and taking notes for extended reports that they intended to make. Not having used his time well—though Domínguez de Mendoza entered as far as Cochiti—nor having any real hope of reconquest or even of food for the winter, Otermín returned south in December. He did return with some Indian reinforcements, for the natives of Isleta who had given the governor a good welcome were afraid of local reprisals. Some 385 left their New Mexico homes to take up residence with some of the other Isletans who had gone south the year before with the retreating Spaniards. Otermín would not get another chance to recoup his and Spain's lost fortune.

Otermín did return to El Paso with some news concerning New Mexico under Indian control, and from this and his failed operation plan of reconquest a revised version of the native revolt emerged. The news may not have been accurate in detail, but was passed on as official intelligence, probably combining wishful thinking with fact and serving to cover any inadequacies of the governor's actions from the outbreak of the revolt until his return from the abortive reentry. The information gathered during the attempted reconquest indicated that, within a year of the successful culmination of the revolt, Popé was deposed as a result of his cruelty, despotism, and greed. Popé was reported to have made a tour of inspection, Spanish style, of the pueblos. He was also reported to have demanded heavy tribute, taught the natives the old, nearly forgotten dances, and insisted that he be accorded such preferential treatment as the Indians had previously given to the Spanish governor.

Otermín's sources indicated that the rebel Pueblos had been fighting among themselves and were threatened by Apache and Ute attacks. Luis Tupatú, a Picurís leader who seemingly had not participated much in the revolt, had been chosen as the new leader, but had not been strong enough to keep the disparate Pueblo nations secure and united. Further information indicated that Don Luis, as he was called, was forced by circumstances to divide the liberated area. He took personal control of the area from La Ciénaga north with Alonso Catatí, the Cochití mestizo, assuming charge from that point southward. Of the two, Luis Tupatú was considered the principal or high chief. A report indicated that Don Luis demonstrated interest in things Spanish and even talked of a Spanish return. Of the pre–Pueblo Revolt villages, all were still occupied except for Sandía, Alameda, Puaray, Isleta, Sevilleta, Alamillo, and Senecú. A story also circulated that there were several Spaniards still alive in the Pueblo area.

Otermín Inquiry

In his inquiry into the great revolt, Otermín came to the conclusion that the causes had been the forced labor system, religious oppression, and cruelties suffered at the hands of several Spanish officers, particularly from Otermín's secretary of government and war, Francisco Xavier. Xavier's strong-armed participation was greatly resented to the point that the Indians requested that he leave. In an attempt to mask his own incompetence, Otermín placed the greatest blame for the failure of his early reconquest on Juan Domínguez de Mendoza, whom he charged with lack of decisive action in field operations. Domínguez countered with the assertion that lack of support and a non-aggressive reoccupation plan, coupled with Indian resentment of Otermín's orders to burn Senecú, Socorro, Alamillo, and Sevilleta Pueblos, were the real reasons.

The cabildo of El Paso sided with Domínguez de Mendoza and secretly sent off charges concerning Otermín and Xavier, but these efforts were largely dismissed by authorities in Mexico City. As a result, Domínguez was harshly criticized, and he suffered a further blow to his prestige when Otermín's successor in office, Domingo Jironza Petriz de Cruzate, cleared Otermín of any improprieties.

Usually referred to by his maternal surname of Cruzate, Domingo Jironza Petriz de Cruzate was sent in 1683 to replace Otermín. For the next six years, save for a brief interregnum, he was in charge of the restive colony, attempting an unorganized, unsuccessful reentry during his first year. Greatly bedeviled by raids on his colony by nearby natives, the new governor later divided his efforts between unsuccessful sorties into New Mexico and campaigns to punish some of the local offenders.

Domínguez de Mendoza, 1684

As evidence that certain activities continued as before, despite the set-back that the Spaniards had suffered, the energetic Domínguez de Mendoza left El Paso in 1684 on a trading and exploring expedition into central Texas. Accompanied by Fray Nicolás López, Domínguez planned a visit to the ever-present Jumanos in the same region he had explored some thirty years before. Particular attention was to be given to the Nueces River region from which they were to bring back samples of pearls reported to exist there, and they were to be especially vigilant concerning overall possible economic advantages that might be gained. They were also to check on the disposition of the local Indians and to ascertain as much as possible about their way of life. This frequent concern for Indian customs is a partial reason for such success as the Spaniards had in missionization.

The 1684 expedition to Texas can be classified as a religious expedition with commercial overtones. This is particularly evident in the orders requiring the soldiers to show the greatest respect for the religious members of their party, a stratagem beneficial to future mission activity. Unlike many of the sorties, this was not a quick hit-and-run affair, since the party was out for six months. The itinerary took the group from El Paso to the Pecos River, and from there overland to the Conchos, then the Nueces, and back to the Colorado of central Texas. Domínguez de Mendoza was responsible for building a temporary chapel on the banks of the Colorado, while his clerical companions busied themselves in baptizing Indians. Some 4,000 buffalo were killed by the party and they took the meat back to El Paso to help relieve the extreme food shortage. After a most successful stay in central Texas, the Spaniards departed, promising that they would return the following year. Once back in El Paso, the party reported on the desirability of potentially occupying the area, but this idea was never carried out from New Mexico as a base. In large measure this was a result of rumors of possible French intrusion, the impending La Salle expedition to the Texas coast.

The Cruzate Grant

During the following year, 1685, Governor Cruzate made another unsuccessful Spanish attempt at reconquest. Not to be discouraged, he tried again in 1689. By this time it was clear that if New Mexico were to be reoccupied, the Indians would need to be brought into a more satisfactory relationship with their future Spanish neighbors. In the New Mexico State Records Center, there exists a series of archival documents dated in 1689 in which Spain formally recognized in legal form the Pueblo Indian rights to their lands, though there has been considerable controversy over whether these documents are genuine or fraudulent.

The questioned documents are land grants recognizing the areas of the various pueblos, even mentioning one that failed to survive the reconquest period. The obvious rationale was to bring the Pueblo people back into the Spanish fold and to give them assurance that their land would not be taken. By this time the Indians knew quite a bit about the Spanish penchant for legalism, a concept that they either already possessed or had grasped firmly in the pre-revolt period. A sample of the documents, whether real or bogus, is given below, for even if not genuine, they were acted upon as such, and therefore have had importance.

> At the town of Our Lady of Guadalupe del Passo del Río [Grande] del Norte, on the twentieth day of the month of September in the year one thousand six hundred and eighty nine, the Lord Governor and Captain General Don Domingo Jironza Petriz de Cruzate stated that whereas in overtaking the Queres Indians and the apostate and the Theguas and those of the Thanos nation in the kingdom of New Mexico, and after having fought with all the Indians of all the other Pueblos, an Indian named Bartolomé de Ojeda of the pueblo of Zia who distinguished himself most in battle, being everywhere, finding himself wounded by a ball and an arrow surrendered; that which has been said being true, I ordered that under oath

he state the condition of the Pueblo of San Felipe, that apostatized and took
part in the wars of that kingdom of New Mexico and who were very
rebellious Indians.

   Asked if this Pueblo would rebel again at any future time as it was
customary for them to do, the deponent answered no; that although it was
true that all the Indians were connected with those of Zia in what had
taken place in the year previous, he judged it was impossible for them to
fail in giving their obedience. Therefore the Lord Governor and Captain
General Don Domingo Jironza Petriz de Cruzate granted them the
boundaries herein set forth: On the north the large grove [Bosque Grande]
that faces east, and on the east one league, and on the west one league, and
on the south a little grove which is in front of a hill called Cullevra
[Culebra] opposite the fields of the Santa Anas. His Excellency so provided,
ordered, and signed before me the present Secretary of Government and
War. To all of which I certify.
[signed] Domingo Jironza Petriz de Cruzate
Before me
[signed] Dn. Pedro Ladrón de Guevara
Secretary of Government and War (Ms., New Mexico State Archives, Santa Fe)

Attacked at a much later date by persons who might have had some personal gain by alleging that these documents were not genuine, there is as much evidence to consider them valid.

   The most serious challenge to the validity of the Cruzate grants is based on the fact that the grant to Laguna Pueblo predates its official founding by the Spanish, the official date being 1699. This is a serious question. When all the grants were written in 1689, however, the Spanish were not physically present in what is today New Mexico, but were still at El Paso. From there, as seen, they made some unsuccessful attempts to reconquer the lost province, each time being forced to return to El Paso to regroup. Apparently as part of the peaceful persuasion program, the reconquerors came prepared to support their efforts by granting written titles to various Indian groups. Among the areas where Indians had gathered during the era of freedom was the shallow freshwater lake not far from Acoma Pueblo—hence the name Laguna for the polyglot population of dispersed Indians. That the Spaniards foresaw the utility of providing written assurance to the Indians argues well for their foresightedness. One sign of this advance preparation was a similar document granting lands to the Pueblo of San Cristóbal, an Indian village that disappeared during the period of Spanish absence from New Mexico. This San Cristóbal document is similar to the others, though obviously it was never utilized for its intended purpose once the Spaniards returned after the reconquest. It is hard to imagine why anyone manufacturing bogus grants would take the trouble in the nineteenth century, as alleged, to invent a spurious grant to a long-forgotten pueblo. If the Cruzate grants are false documentation, the person allegedly fabricating them had fine command of early seventeenth century paleography, spelling, and geographical detail. This person would also have been very clever to have slipped them into the governmental archives, and would have been possessed of great patience to await their discovery at a much later date, and to what end?—that the Indians might have a solid written basis for the land that they had been in quiet possession of for centuries?

Diego de Vargas and the Reconquest

Cruzate left an impression on New Mexico, but he did not get the job of reconquest accomplished. The crown then turned to a man of energy, confidence, and financial resources. A native of Madrid and descended from the noble Vargas line, Don Diego José de Vargas Zapata y Luján Ponce de León y Contreras, was described by his biographer as "a strutting aristocrat hungry to perform glorious deeds in an inglorious age," and "capable, cocksure, and visibly daring." (Kessell, *Kiva, Cross and Crown*, p. 243) Vargas was also a veteran of frontier Indian warfare and as soon as he assumed command of the struggling garrison at El Paso, conditions became better. He started by pacifying the El Paso area by putting down rebellious groups in the vicinity, a measure that he was able to accomplish while at the same time giving his troops the confidence they needed for his envisioned campaign against the Pueblo Indians. Given authority for the reconquest, Vargas devised a plan that was daring almost to the brink of foolhardiness, but one that worked. He marched his small force of fewer than 200 soldiers up the Río Grande into the jaws of danger. Vargas's strategy was to use with maximum effect his small army, and when reaching one of the pueblos, he laid siege not with gunfire, but by having everyone sing praises five times to the Blessed Virgin. This was followed by attempts by the missionaries and by the leader to convince the Indians to once more become vassals of the crown, a duty from which they had strayed. If repentant, the Indians were to be absolved of their sins. The strategy was so bold that it succeeded on multiple occasions; the Pueblos were caught off guard by Vargas's bravado, particularly by his plan of entering directly into the capital.

Amid a flourish of trumpets and drums, Vargas proclaimed that he had come not to punish, but to pardon and convert. He promised the frightened Indians that if they would leave the pueblo peacefully and re-enter as loyal Spanish vassals, all would be well. Vargas won the Indians over by his bold yet gentle manner, and in a regal ceremony, the Spaniards unfurled their banner, making New Mexico once more part of Spain's empire.

Don Diego toured the province, repeating the promises and getting assurances of peace, following which he returned to El Paso to celebrate Christmas 1692 and to prepare to return the next year with colonists for the difficult task of resettlement. His first entry, a strictly military operation, had been bloodless and imminently successful. News of the Vargas reconquest set off a wild celebration in Mexico City. Bells rang, the clergy sang hymns, and the viceroy ordered that an official history be written to commemorate the event.

Vargas Returns to New Mexico

In the fall of 1693, with the expectation of a successful outcome, Vargas brought with him families, friars, and high hopes. In the meantime, some of the Pueblos had renounced their quickly given allegiance, and though Vargas was able to reestablish headquarters at Santa Fe, his efforts to persuade all of the Indians to submit were futile.

Instead, he had to spend nearly an entire year in campaigns. He was fierce in battle, but once peace had been restored, he issued pardons and sought reconciliation. The viceroy had given strict instructions that only criminal violations of the law should be punished, avoiding indiscriminate reprisals for purposes of revenge. The reconqueror showed discernment when he left the Indian ceremonial centers—the kivas—undisturbed instead of destroying them as his predecessors had done.

Following the reconquest of New Mexico, there was a great need for replacement colonists for those who had been killed in the Pueblo Revolt and for those who, after over a decade of residence as refugees in the El Paso area, had permanently settled as *vecinos*. It had long been thought that there was little opportunity to reconstruct any appreciable list of the recolonizers of the province, but a muster roll, discovered in 1978 by Dr. Clevy Lloyd Strout at the Gilcrease Institute in Tulsa, Oklahoma, enumerated a substantial group of settlers who were conducted to Santa Fe in 1695 by Juan Páez Hurtado. The importance of this document is great from both genea-

Fig. 5.2. Diego de Vargas. Courtesy Museum of New Mexico. 11409.

logical and cultural perspectives. It contains important information on the people, their social status, and their area of origin or of recruitment, giving new insight into the ethnic composition and the cultural baggage that was transported with them to their new home.

PAEZ HURTADO EXPEDITION TO SANTA FE

The general orders issued by Viceroy Conde de Galve to the reconqueror, Diego de Vargas authorized him to name Páez Hurtado to lead an expedition of needed settlers to the reconstructed Santa Fe. Páez was at the time serving as presidial commanding officer at El Paso del Río Grande del Norte, today's Ciudad Juárez, Chihuahua, on the modern international border. His orders directed him to proceed to Durango and then to Zacatecas for the purpose of enlisting families for resettlement.

Páez Hurtado had a difficult task in obtaining volunteers to go to a frontier that had been the scene of the bloody Pueblo Revolt only fifteen years before. For lack of funds, the Durango officials were of little help, so Páez changed his area of recruitment to the great silver area of Zacatecas-Sombrerete, with most success in Zacatecas proper. Viceroy Conde de Galve helped tremendously by sending a letter ordering royal officials in Zacatecas to furnish money for the recruited families. These funds were for living expenses until such time as the expedition was actually to start its northward march, as well as for expenses incurred on the trip itself. Unfortunately, Páez himself was not mentioned in the royal orders and the group of men under his military command, as well as necessary helpers that he had with him, had to get along with substandard fare.

For the families involved, the Viceroy's instructions allotted 320 pesos for each family of four or more persons, and 300 for those of three or less. A daily living allowance of 12 reales was also set aside. Forty-six families were represented totaling 146 persons. The eldest future colonist was 54 and the youngest were four children of only one year of age. Only a few colonists were from Europe, though most were listed as Spaniards. The preponderance of those recruited were from Zacatecas, Sombrerete, and nearby Llerena, all in central Mexico. Most of the identifiable classes of Mexican society were represented, though the preciseness of class structure was not observed as closely on the frontier as in the capital. Whether all of the settlers were to have the same status of hidalgo as had been offered to those recruited by Diego de Vargas is not known. But since no New Mexico resident seems to have taken seriously the instant nobility of any offer, it is hardly of consequence. The amount of money invested by the crown and the efforts of Páez Hurtado were a substantial contribution to the future of the reestablished colony. In addition, the demographic implications were considerable, especially in facilitating the racial mixture of the new citizens with existing Pueblo Indians.

Despite the outward evidence of peace, all was not well, for inside each of the pueblos there were those still opposed to the return of the Spaniards. Furthermore, the arrival of so many mouths to feed, plus the continuing scarcity of food—an alleged important cause of the great revolt—were problems that were not easily solved. Some of the dissatisfied Pueblo Indians fled from the scene to take up residence with their sometimes friends and sometimes enemies, the Navajos and the Apaches (principally the Jicarilla Apaches). With this background, in 1696 the northern Pueblos became once more the center of anti-Spanish sentiment, and in that year, after some three years of Spanish reoccupation, there was a second Pueblo Revolt.

The second Pueblo Revolt, brief as it was, still brought death to twenty-one civilians, as well as martyrdom to five missionaries who joined a substantial list in New Mexico's relatively brief history. (Certainly the number of missionaries who died for their faith in New Mexico was high in comparison to those who lived out a full life in other frontier areas). Vargas was not nearly as charitable with second-time offenders as he had been three years earlier, and subjugated them with great vigor. This Pueblo Indian Revolt represented the final effort of the Pueblo Indian medicine men and war chiefs to eliminate the yoke of Spanish rule; from then on, Spanish authority was complete and New Mexico could turn to peaceful activities such as economic reconstruction and reestablishment of the missions. Basic agricultural pursuits that had been abandoned during the war were difficult to revive, and the missions, which were mostly in a shambles, could not be rebuilt without adequate supplies.

By the end of the century most of the old areas had been reoccupied and the Indians had been reorganized, with some old villages abandoned and some new ones established. Others received over a period of years the return of fugitive Indians who had avoided the pain of reconquest by taking refuge outside the sphere of Spanish control. Title to Indian lands was made more certain by formal recognition, and assistance was given to both Indians and Spanish settlers in making the province more secure. As poor repayment for his labors, Vargas was relieved of his duties as governor and replaced by Pedro Rodríguez Cubero, who arrived in July 1697. The new governor's presence set off a struggle that left Vargas vilified and held in Santa Fe for nearly three years. The reconqueror was finally able to get away, win vindication in the viceregal capital, and return to New Mexico as Marqués de la Nava Brazíñas. During a second term as governor, Vargas became ill on a campaign against the Apache Indians. He died at Bernalillo on February 8, 1704, as he was being carried back toward the capital. His passing marked the end of an era during which local problems were central to the existence of New Mexico, a focus that was soon replaced by concern instead for outsiders and what effect other nations might have on the destiny of New Mexico.

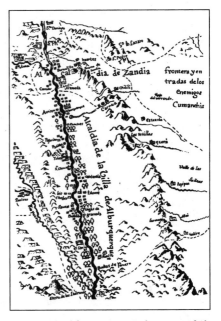

Map 5.2. Detail from Miera y Pacheco map of Albuquerque. From Marc Simmons, *Albuquerque,* p. 63.

Before the death of Vargas, as well as shortly thereafter, several towns of Spanish settlers were founded for the much-needed strengthening of the province's defensive posture. The first of these, though only in its infancy, was Bernalillo. When Vargas marched north with the reoccupants of New Mexico, some were given permission to drop out not far from what would later be Bernalillo. Most were probably old settlers who were anxious to return home to the haciendas and ranches they had abandoned in 1680. It was not, however, until 1695 that any official town was created. From what was a nucleus of small family-operated farms, the population pattern spread, particularly downriver.

In April of the same year, in an effort to buttress the northern portion of New Mexico in the Río Arriba area, Vargas created the Villa de Santa Cruz de la Cañada, not far from the cluster of Indian pueblos in that area. The housing of some sixty-six families recently brought to New Mexico from the south gave stability to the north. An additional forty-four families were settled in May at the provincial capital of Santa Fe.

FOUNDING OF ALBUQUERQUE

Though it was not of great consequence at the time, and its foundation was not during Vargas's lifetime, the greatest event in the readjustment of the Spanish population of New Mexico was the founding of Albuquerque, to the south of Bernalillo. A new governor, Francisco de Cuervo y Valdés, was responsible for establishing the city. He noted to the viceroy: "I certify to the king, our Lord, and to the most excellent señor viceroy: That I founded a villa on the banks and in the valley of the Río del Norte in a good place as regards land, water, pasture, and firewood. I gave it as patron saint the glorious apostle of the Indies, San Francisco Xavier, and called and named it the villa of

Alburquerque." (Simmons, *Albuquerque: A Narrative History*, p. 81) It was thus named in honor of the reigning viceroy of New Spain, Francisco Fernández de la Cueva Enríquez, duke of Albuquerque. Even today, the city continues to be nicknamed the Duke City.

Governor Cuervo y Valdés had assembled thirty-five families—a total of 252 persons—for Albuquerque. Juan de Ulibarrí had scouted the area for the proper site, and Captain Martín Hurtado had led the settlers to the Bosque Grande de San Francisco Xavier on what earlier had been an exposed rancho, where the new town was founded with all of the formalities required. It was an important step for the future of the state of New Mexico because the Villa of Albuquerque would become the most populous city in New Mexico, far outstripping all others from the Hispanic period. The town, as is characteristic of settlements in semi-arid environments, eventually started to spread out north and south along the margin of the Río Grande, which provided life-giving support. With Albuquerque's occupation, the last major town-founding effort of the immediate post-reconquest period was complete.

INTERPRETATIONS OF THE PUEBLO REVOLT

The Pueblo Revolt of 1680 had profound regional importance, so it is not surprising that there have been many interpretations of its causes. Alleged reasons have been psychological, physical, ecological, religious, economic, mystical, and fanciful; but almost all have as a common denominator an Indian desire to return to the pre-contact period. Such native dreams almost universally were doomed to failure despite some early successes in throwing off the yoke of European control. The process of acculturation had been both rapid and insidious, and the idea of a Messiah who would be the great deliverer was never as happy an event in fact as it was in prospect, for the theory of return to previous ways failed to materialize in practice. And, though the Pueblo Revolt is an excellent case study, it is not an isolated example of an attempt to recapture a lost lifestyle.

One of the underlying causes that reaches back to the very beginning of Spanish control in New Mexico was the institution of the encomienda, a subject much discussed by Latin Americanists. The encomienda, from the Spanish verb *encomendar* (to entrust), was utilized to achieve several goals, including Indian control, economic exploitation, and indoctrination. The theory and the practice of the encomienda were not closely related. In theory, it was a means whereby native people under the guidance of trustworthy Spanish citizens were to be instructed in the ways of becoming not only good vassals of the crown but also Christian citizens. In practice, especially since receipt of an encomienda resulted from having performed meritorious service for the crown, it became an opportunity to become wealthy at the expense of the labor of the Indians. At an earlier date the institution was misunderstood to be a grant of land, as well as of the Indians resident thereon. More careful study has made it clear that land itself was not involved, but rather the service of the residents of such lands. Ultimately, the measure of such holdings was the number of Indians assigned to a kind of trusteeship that evolved, even if this had not been the original intent of the system.

Certainly by the time New Mexico was occupied and the encomienda implemented, the system had changed considerably. The active agent in granting encomiendas was the governor, who in the beginning was also adelantado, both of which offices brought the privilege of granting Indians in such trusteeships. In theory, gentile (non-converted) natives were not subject to distribution, but the practice and theory were also at variance on this matter. In New Mexico the encomienda took the form of tribute, and converted heads of households were required to pay on an annual basis one fanega (about 1.5 bushels) of corn and one blanket. Such a tax, which by modern standards would be minimal, was resented by the Pueblo Indians, who previously had no taxation. The result was a heavy tax on an economy that had produced only slightly more than its subsistence requirements.

In addition to the tribute payments, Spanish *encomenderos* in New Mexico were granted the right to use a limited amount of Indian labor on their farms and ranches, with such Indians being paid a small wage and given subsistence. Statistically there were not a great number of encomenderos in the province. One source indicates between fifty and sixty in the area in 1638, with this number reduced to thirty-five a few years later. A single encomendero might be assigned Indians from several pueblos, whereas in some cases both the tribute and labor of a single pueblo were shared. Encomiendas could be granted for the lifetime of the grantee, or for two generations or even three, but completion of such periods did not complete the obligation of the Indians, who might then be granted to a new encomendero.

Based on the few existing records of the pre-1680 period, it can be supposed that the encomienda system was marginally successful as an economic institution favoring the colonists. It had some influence on acculturization of the Indians, but it was understandably disliked by the Pueblos. Also, the institution was under attack constantly by the Franciscan clergy who resented the excessive use of native labor for personal gain by citizens who gave little thought to their own responsibility implicit in the protective system. Yet the encomenderos believed that clerical concern was motivated by a Franciscan desire to use the labor of these same Indians for the benefit of the church. Whatever the case may have been, Indian labor in clerical hands did contribute to the construction of churches, some of which still remain and a few of which have been set aside in recent times as part of the Salinas Pueblos National Monument.

Despite such a contribution to our modern heritage, labor, either forced under the encomienda system or exacted as a religious duty, was not willingly given in the pre–Pueblo Revolt era. It is of interest, however, that modern Pueblo Indians carry out communal labor in the preservation and maintenance of their village churches, vestiges of the Spanish era both in the physical structures and in the supporting system of labor.

One of the promises made by the *reconquistadores* of New Mexico was that there would be no more encomiendas after the Spaniards returned. It is not clear whether this came about at the request of the Indians, or whether it was as an offer made to placate the Pueblos and attract them back. What is obvious is that it became an important point in reestablishing control. After the successful reconquest, the encomienda and the tribute involved therein were dead issues. Curiously, however, the reconqueror, Don Diego de Vargas, was rewarded by the crown in 1698 by an annual grant of 4,000 pesos, money to be collected from the Indians as tribute. Neither Vargas during his lifetime nor his heirs subsequently, were able to collect the tribute and the grant was replaced in 1737 by a pension paid to his heirs.

Another ascribed cause for the Pueblo Revolt was a gradual decline in Pueblo Indian population. This decrease was the result of mortality from a series of epidemics in the area. While the causes of some of these epidemics are fully clear, other plagues are not easy to identify since the symptoms given in the documentary record leave appreciable doubt. Population statistics during the colonial period are not completely reliable sources; most listings suffer from one or multiple defects, and must therefore be used with great caution. The agency (the person or institution involved in creating any population data) is an intangible factor. A priest might wish to give the impression of a larger population in an effort to obtain greater assistance for conversion or he may wish to convey the idea of decline to be blamed on the military or the citizenry. The greater or shorter lapse of time between enumerations made a difference not only in global data but also in specific sub-items, an extremely variable factor. Whether the Indians were counted by pueblo, by linguistic orientation, or by the administrative sub-unit (*alcaldía mayor*) to which they belonged, was not standardized.

Further problems result from discrepancies in the age at which, for census purposes, individuals become adults, the percentage of Indianness they need to be considered Indian, or, as in some cases the matter of the degree to which they live or fail to live an hispanicized existence. *Genízaros*, generally detribalized non-Pueblo Indians, or at times any Indian not living a primitive life, are often included in a census. With passage of time these Indians become elevated in political status to that of *gente de razón*, or civilized people, probably the highest level attainable. Even with these problems inherent in census reports, there are obvious facts. The first is that by the time of the revolt, the Pueblo Indians had declined substantially in numbers, but they had not become militarily impotent as is clear from their success.

An early estimate of Pueblo population calculated as many as 80,000, but later estimates gave a much reduced figure of 34,000. Intermediate figures place the Pueblo population at around 60,000. A substantial population reduction occurred in the years before 1638 as a result of the prevalence of smallpox, and of the sickness which the Mexicans call *cocoliztli*. Another epidemic of 1640 is reported to have claimed the lives of 3,000 Pueblos. Plagues reduced the count to 20,181 (excluding children) in 1664. The year of 1670 was one of famine and plague and just before the Pueblo Revolt, a Franciscan priest estimated the Indian population at a mere 17,000. It is uncertain what the extent of the famine might have been, but it is almost certain that the inadequate resources being produced locally ended up in the hands of encomenderos and government officials, thereby leaving less than normal for the local natives.

The Pueblo Revolt of 1680 dealt a blow to the winners as well as to the losers. Both armed conflict and disease during the rebellion and during the interlude of Indian control were causes for a greater absolute loss of Indian lives as compared to non-Indians. Furthermore, upon reentry by Spanish military and colonists, some natives fled to the remote security of the Moqui villages in what is today eastern Arizona, some doing so permanently. Others departed in the opposite direction for the Great Plains. Setting aside statistical changes resulting from the mestizo (and therefore non-Indian) classification, it seems that in the post-revolt era, population remained stable at the small figure of about 10,000 to 11,000. A much later smallpox epidemic occurred between 1780–1781 during which over 500 Pueblo Indians are said to have died. Inadequate medical knowledge coupled with use of home remedies were the feeble local resources for attempting to combat disease. The eighteenth-century smallpox epidemic was the most disastrous. It caused loss of life among both Spaniards and Pueblo Indians, with the latter being hardest hit. In addition to death, there were severe dislocations in society and in the missionary program. The epidemic began in the late spring of 1780, and of all the towns, Albuquerque suffered most with thirty-one deaths. Santa Fe and its military garrison recorded an additional nineteen. Among the Indian pueblos, San Felipe had 130 deaths in February 1781 alone. At nearby Santo Domingo the epidemic carried off 230 and Santa Clara, to the north, lost 106.

Hubert Howe Bancroft, writing in the 1870s, claimed a total mortality of 5,025. Just how many persons contracted smallpox is unknown, but probably many were immune until a new generation appeared which, without the immunity obtained from exposure, would suffer. Census figures, however, do not bear out such large mortality; to the contrary, during the latter part of the eighteenth century there appears to have been substantial population growth. The novelty of the entire period from conquest to the end of the colonial period was the capacity of the Pueblo Indians to maintain their cultural and ethnic identity in the face of so many forces working toward conformity.

— *Chapter Five* —

BIBLIOGRAPHIC ESSAY

Despite considerable research, including the dozens of articles and documents published since 1926 in the *New Mexico Historical Review,* there are significant aspects of New Mexico history for which there is inadequate information, and for which there is no remedy. One negative result of the Pueblo Revolt, which was irreparable and has prevented historians from giving a balanced account of the region's history from its founding until 1680, was the almost total destruction of the existing New Mexico archives at that latter date. This destruction was bilateral—the Spaniards upon retreat from Santa Fe took time to destroy at least some of the public record upon which later historians would have depended for recounting the story of regional development. Though there is no quantitative measure, it is reasonable to suppose that even the documents that may have been saved from the revolt suffered some loss, deterioration, or disposal in the exodus to El Paso. The rest of the destruction was the responsibility of the Pueblo Indians themselves. In their eagerness to wipe out vestiges of Spanish control, they destroyed, among other things, the remaining written record. The only documents that survive from the pre-1680 era are those of such importance or such type of activity that the originals or copies were sent off to Durango, Guadalajara, or Mexico City. The existence of those records, without support from local archives, have conveyed what is probably a false impression of much of that period as reflected in residencias, in Inquisition activities, and in accusations and counter-accusations.

A good general source on the events leading to and the aftermath of the Pueblo revolt is John Kessell, *Kiva, Cross and Crown: The Pecos Indians and New Mexico, 1541–1840* (Washington, D.C.: National Park Service, 1979). Kessell, along with Rick Hendricks, Meredith D. Dodge, Larry D. Miller, and Eleanor B. Adams, has also edited *Remote Beyond Compare: Letters of don Diego de Vargas to His Family from New Spain and New Mexico, 1675–1706* (Albuquerque: University of New Mexico Press, 1989); with Rick Hendricks, *By Force of Arms: The Journals of don Diego de Vargas, New Mexico, 1691–93* (Albuquerque: University of New Mexico Press, 1992); and with Rick Hendricks and Meredith D. Dodge, *To the Royal Crown Restored: The Journals of don Diego de Vargas, New Mexico, 1692–94* (Albuquerque: University of New Mexico Press, 1995). See also J. Manuel Espinosa, ed. and trans., *First Expedition of Vargas into New Mexico, 1692* (Albuquerque: University of New Mexico Press, 1988); and *The Pueblo Indian Revolt of 1696 and the Franciscan Missions in New Mexico* (Norman: University of

Oklahoma Press, 1988). The latter book gives a good background for the entire Pueblo-Spanish confrontation. Marc Simmons has written "The Pueblo Revolt: Why Did it Happen?" *El Palacio*, 86 (winter 1980–81):11–15.

A number of documents were edited by pioneer historian Charles Wilson Hackett in *Historical Documents Relating to New Mexico, Nueva Vizcaya and Approaches Thereto*, 3 vols. (Washington, D.C.: Carnegie Institution, 1923–1937) and *Revolt of the Pueblo Indians of New Mexico and Otermin's Attempted Reconquest, 1680–1682* (Albuquerque: University of New Mexico Press, 1942) translated by Charmion C. Shelby. Jane C. Sánchez has written "Spanish-Indian Relations during the Otermín Administration, 1677–1683" in *NMHR*, 58 (April 1983):133–51. Clevy Lloyd Strout discovered an important document at the Gilcrease Institute in Tulsa and published it as "The Resettlement of Santa Fe, 1695: The Newly Found Muster Roll" in the *NMHR*, 53 (July 1978):261–70.

Studies from an Indian point of view include Stefanie Beninato, "Popé, Pose-yemu, and Naranjo: A New Look at the Leadership in the Pueblo Revolt of 1680" in *NMHR*, 65 (October 1990):417–35 and Angélico Chávez, "Pohé-Yemos's Representative and the Pueblo Revolt of 1680" in *NMHR*, 42 (April 1967):85–126; Chavez also wrote *Our Lady of the Conquest* (Santa Fe: Historical Society of New Mexico, 1948). For a general Indian perspective see Joe Sando, "The Pueblo Revolt" in *Handbook of North American Indians*, vol. 9.

Two articles of further interest are Lansing B. Bloom, "The Vargas Encomienda," *NMHR*,14 (October 1939):366–417, which describes how the Vargas pension went to his heirs in 1737; and Ernest J. Burrus, "A Tragic Interlude in the Reconquest of New Mexico," *Manuscripta*, 29 (November 1985):154–65, which shows conditions among Spanish refugees four years after their flight from New Mexico. A work that covers the later years of the reconquest is J. Manuel Espinosa, *Crusaders of the Rio Grande: The Story of Don Diego de Vargas and the Reconquest and Refounding of New Mexico* (Chicago: Institute of Jesuit History, 1942). For the founding of Albuquerque, see Marc Simmons, *Albuquerque: A Narrative History* (Albuquerque: University of New Mexico Press, 1982).

Chapter Six

MISSIONARY, MILITARY, AND TRADING VENTURES: 1680–1724

RELIGIOUS ENTHUSIASM

*T*o understand Spain's efforts to penetrate into northern Sonora and the southwestern regions of the present United States, it is necessary to recognize the forces that compelled the soldier or missionary to risk his life for a vision—for an unknown destiny. The stoic philosophy of individual Spaniards often included a near contempt for personal safety, an aspiration to greatness, an uncompromising self-pride, a need for action and enterprise, and above all, a willingness to dream. In addition, there were many Spaniards, brought up with the heritage of the reconquest of the Iberian peninsula, who considered the salvation of non-Christian souls a moral duty. The Spanish missionary, whose religious enthusiasm carried him to the remote regions of North and South America, was fired by incredible zeal—his journey into heaven would be assured by what he believed to be God's work on earth. The number of Franciscans to achieve martyrdom during New Mexico's early settlement provides strong evidence of the religious zeal of these dedicated clergymen.

The fact that the Spanish people had turned so readily to Christianity during the Roman period led to the expression that "Spain was perhaps Christian before Christ." With passion and vivid imagery, Spaniards made God a concrete presence in their religious ritual. Moorish and Jewish influences brought to the Iberian Peninsula a sensuous feeling for religion that seemed not to penetrate the Protestant countries. From the reconquest, Spain gleaned the concept of religion as a way to nationalism; militant friar and Spanish soldier fought the infidel side by side. Spain alone waged the two most successful crusades in history: the crusade against the Moslem Moors and the crusade to conquer and Christianize the Indians of the New World. But then as now, the spiritual conquest of the Indians was misunderstood, and the greed of a few has discredited the Christian motives of many.

Juan de Solorzano y Pereyra: In Defense of Spain

Spain cannot be absolved of guilt for exploiting the Indians, but the excessive charges of avarice and cruelty levied by other European countries, especially against missionaries, are undeserved. Juan de Solorzano y Pereyra, an eminent Spanish legal scholar of the seventeenth century, prepared a defense of Spanish policy in the Indies applicable to the mission period. He said:

> *Although heretics and other rivals of the glories of our Spanish nation have recognized the validity of its titles to the New World ... they try to discredit*

these titles, saying in the first place that we were impelled more by greed for gold and silver of its provinces than by zeal for the propagation of the Gospel. ... Even if we concede that greed for gold and riches ... may have prevailed among some, this blemish does not lessen the merit of the many good men who took part so sincerely and apostolically in the conversion of the New World. Nor does it lessen the merit of the zeal and concern repeatedly displayed by our Kings in their sagacious decrees and instructions. (Solorzano, *Politica Indiana*, I, 117–27, passim quoted in Hanke, *Latin American Civilization*, p. 165)

The story of Spain's attempt to bring the aboriginal inhabitants of the Americas into full participation within the Spanish empire gives ample proof of the validity of Solorzano's observations. For a century and a half, Spanish kings, viceroys, and private parties had sent expeditions to northern Mexico to establish sovereignty, until they realized that the country could not be settled, much less evangelized, by groups of colonists or by military force. Finally, Jesuit missionaries—the Black Robes—succeeded in gaining a foothold in the river valleys flanking Mexico's west coast. Their Christianizing endeavor was an epic of individual courage, crusading spirit, and disdain for the comforts of life. By gathering Indians into self-sufficient mission towns, the Jesuits tried to shield them from exploitation by miners and ranchers and from corrupting examples of European civilization. Efforts by the three major mendicant orders—Franciscans, Dominicans, and Augustinians—who had been involved in missionary work since the conquest, were marked with equal fortitude.

Society of Jesus

Ignacio Loyola, a Spanish Basque of noble birth, organized the Society of Jesus along military lines in 1534 to fight the spread of Protestantism in Europe. He won papal approval for his new fraternal order from Pope Paul III in Rome in 1540. Loyola emphasized education among his "soldiers of God," and the first Jesuits were university men from some of the best families in Europe. Candidates were chosen on the basis of physical and mental fitness, suitability for a life of rigorous discipline, complete obedience, and unswerving devotion. As a religious order, they were generally better trained than the friars of the mendicant orders and soon became the custodians of learning in the New World. Because of their ambition, inflexibility, and direct allegiance to the papacy, the Jesuits also made enemies easily, even among the clergy. As they began to criticize the lifestyle of the landed aristocracy and the entrenched colonial bureaucracy, they sowed the seeds of later discontent. Nevertheless, a fearless protection of their Indian charges was uppermost in their New World program.

The first Jesuit missionaries landed on the coast of Brazil in 1549, just nine years after the order's formal recognition. They arrived in La Florida in 1566 and finally, a select fifteen reached Mexico in 1572. They devoted most of their first two decades to founding secondary schools (*colegios*) in the cities and it was not until 1591 that the Black Robes entered the mission field on the northwestern frontier of New Spain. In that year, on July 6, Fathers Gonzalo de Tapia and Martín Pérez opened the first permanent Jesuit mission in New Spain when they began to convert the Indians of the frontier province of Sinaloa. Father Tapia became the protomartyr of his order in New Spain. As the reign of Philip II came to an end in 1598, the Black Robes began seeking converts among the mountain tribes of the Sierra Madre Occidental in Sinaloa. From there the Jesuits advanced steadily northward, river by river, into the frontier regions and by 1604, had advanced to the Río Fuerte. The first mission was set up in modern Sonora in 1613 on the Río Mayo. Four years later, in 1617, the Yaqui Indians, who had defeated Spanish military expeditions in the area, invited the Black Robes into their country to found another mission. From there, the missionaries advanced into Opata country in 1628, where they remained for several decades.

Fig. 6.1. Solorzano frontispiece.

Mission Policy

In conformance with general Spanish mission policy, the Black Robes induced the scattered Indians to settle in small, permanent villages called *reducciones* where they could be taught the rudiments of a civilized and Christian life. Those Indians already settled were instructed in their native towns and allowed to retain their existing class structure. It was planned that native leaders would assume roles similar to their old ones within the Spanish municipal organization. Under the "Laws of the Indies," control by the missionaries was to be temporary—ideally to last only ten years. To accomplish secularization, it was planned that religious duties would be turned over to a parish priest and mission lands distributed among converted Indians. In many cases, however, the missionaries insisted that independence was not practical, especially within ten years, and conflicts between secular and religious authorities became a major issue in later years. Spanish law also provided that the royal treasury bear the expense of the missionary's initial equipment and transportation, pay him a small annual salary, share the cost of mission buildings, and furnish a small military guard.

As soon as the fathers could enlist Indian support, the missions were supposed to become self-sustaining economic units through farming, stock-raising, and some manufacturing. The missionaries were also explorers, geographers, and diplomatic agents among various Indian tribes. In times of attack by unconverted Indians or foreigners, they mustered the allegiance of their neophytes in defense of these frontier outposts. In certain areas the missionary tasks were complicated by poor land, a lack of natural resources, and a lack of interest by the native Indians. The Jesuits nevertheless were convinced that the missions were an improvement over the native Indians' previous lifestyle.

Map 6.1. Peninsular Spain. Map by Stephanie Gould.

Francisco Eusebio Kino, S.J. in California

Because the Society of Jesus in 1671 had received a bequest from Alonso Fernández de la Torre for the founding of a mission in California, the Spanish crown decided to proceed to the peninsula on an expedition organized around religious goals. Because it had become apparent that a permanent base in California would not result from private enterprise, Don Isidro Atondo y Antillón, an experienced seaman and soldier, gained royal support to establish a colony somewhere near La Paz. Francisco Eusebio Kino and fellow Jesuit Matias Goñi were assigned to accompany the expedition to the peninsula. They were joined in 1684 by Juan Bautista Copart, in whose hands Father Kino completed his final vows as a missionary in August of that year.

Kino, born Eusebius Chinus or Chini on August 10, 1645, grew up in his native village of Segno, near Trent in the Austrian Tyrol. At the age of 18, as he suffered from a severe illness, he vowed to become a missionary upon his recovery. Educated in mathematics and astronomy at Trent, Italy, he joined the Society of Jesus at Landsberg, Bavaria, on November 20, 1665. Young Eusebio hoped to travel to the Orient as a foreign missionary, but fate dictated a different career. Finally in 1678, a year after his ordination, two appointments were received from the King of Spain—one for the Philippines and one for Mexico. Kino, as he came to spell his name, and a friend both wanted the Philippine assignment, so they drew lots. Kino lost.

After traveling to Spain and remaining in Cádiz for more than two years awaiting a ship to the New World, Kino finally reached Mexico in the late spring of 1681. This was a sad time for the northern mission frontier as the Indians had begun a series of hostilities that would last for several years, starting with the Pueblo Revolt of 1680. The Pueblos, aided by the more nomadic and hostile Apaches, managed in a few months to kill twenty-one missionaries and an estimated 380 colonists. The news of the Pueblo Revolt, however, did not dim Kino's enthusiasm for accompanying the Atondo expedition to Baja California as royal cosmographer, though his participation actually encompassed much more. The group landed at La Paz in April 1683, took formal possession of the land, and started a settlement near the bay. After several months, hostile Indians and insufficient supplies forced the settlers to move the colony further north—near a river they called San Bruno. While the new settlement was under construction, Atondo, with Kino as his cartographer, explored the mountainous region to the west. The two men finally crossed the giant barrier of the Sierra de la Giganta and became the first Europeans to reach the Pacific shores by an overland route. To their delight, they met friendly, cooperative Indians who showed them sea shells; of particular interest were some large blue abalone shells that would later significantly influence Kino's geographical concepts.

Nowhere on the arid, rocky southern peninsula of Baja California had Atondo found lands sufficiently fertile to sustain a colony or mission. As supplies from Mexico ran low, two-thirds of the settlers fell ill with scurvy; little hope remained for the enterprise. Atondo abandoned the attempt and in May 1685, ordered the entire expedition back to the mainland. His report to the viceroy indicated that the peninsula could not be Christianized by means then available and, with Kino's recommendation, proposed that the Jesuits be given an annual subsidy

Fig. 6.2. Statue of Padre Kino in Tucson. Courtesy Arizona Historical Society/Tucson. 97302.

of 30,000 pesos for full responsibility for the conversion of the California natives. Carlos II, considering the more than 200,000 pesos already spent on the unsuccessful Atondo-Kino venture and the urgent demands upon the treasury elsewhere in New Spain, issued a royal decree in December 1685 suspending Father Kino's project. The barriers to California settlement thus gave the movement toward Arizona an added thrust.

Kino at La Pimería Alta

Despite his urgent requests to be permitted to return to Baja California, Father Kino was reassigned to La Pimería Alta, the land of the Pima Indians of northern Sonora and southern Arizona. The imaginative Jesuit never gave up his dream of returning to the peninsula, and in fact hoped to found a base among the Seri Indians on the mainland coast from which to continue his plan to missionize California. Eventually, however, he had to see his mission program undertaken by Father Juan María Salvatierra, a fellow Jesuit of noble Spanish and Italian ancestry.

Kino arrived at Oposura (now Moctezuma) in Sonora in late February or early March 1687. Because of the Pueblo Revolt, the Indians along the northern frontier had been restless and were thought to be plotting further attack. Since the 1640s, when the Pimas living along the Río Magdalena had repelled Don Pedro de Perea and his New Mexican friars, these Indians had been known for their hostility and treachery. The resident priest at Cucurpe, an Opata Indian mission, thought Father Kino seemed like the ideal person to go among them and convert the Pimas to Christian ways. On March 13, 1687, on a promontory near the *ranchería* of Bamotze, or Cosari, in the San Miguel

River Valley, Kino founded the mission of Nuestra Señora de los Dolores. The Pimas flocked in for gifts and the teachings of the mysterious but kindly Black Robe. They helped plant fruit trees and wheat, and this mission became Kino's headquarters for the next twenty-four years.

Kino was successful in converting Indians from the very first. He sent native runners with promises of gifts to those who would listen. He baptized their children and showed them the material benefits that Christianity could bring. However, once the mission was established, Kino, an irrepressible expansionist, wanted to continue on to new fields. He first entered what is now Arizona in January 1691 with Juan María Salvatierra, then a father visitor sent by the father provincial of New Spain to investigate rumors circulated in Spanish circles that the Pimas were incorrigible liars and thieves. Since Kino was planning to convert the northern Pima tribes, Salvatierra decided to accompany him on a tour of La Pimería Alta. Received enthusiastically by hundreds of peaceful natives, the father visitor was impressed by the advantages of a mission in the region. The two Jesuits traveled to the headwaters of the Río Altar, where a delegation of natives appeared carrying wooden crosses. If Salvatierra had any doubts about their desire for conversion, they were dispelled. The timing was perfect.

Together Kino and Salvatierra rode north across the international border west of present-day Nogales, then east through the mountains, and finally down an arroyo into the valley of Guevavi. Instead of turning south to the Indian village of Guevavi, the natives guided them north toward the ranchería of Tumacácori. On the east bank of the river, which Kino called the Santa María, a congregation of Indians awaited them. At the ranchería of San Cayetano de Tumacácori, there were some Sobaipuri (or Northern Piman) headmen from the north who had constructed three huts (*ramadas*)—one in which to say mass, another in which to sleep, and the third for cooking. There were more than forty houses and the Indians were friendly and industrious. The valley was fertile and the natives seemed particularly eager to hear the word of God.

Salvatierra believed in Kino's mission. They then turned back along the same river following it to the ranchería of Guevavi, where the people had built a cluster of huts that came to be known as *gi vavhia,* or Big Well or Big Spring. The water from the river was used to irrigate the Indians' maize and give life to the giant cottonwoods and willows that provided shelter and shade. The people accepted gifts and through interpreters listened to what the Jesuits said. Kino thought the prospects for mission work seemed rather good in the Santa Cruz valley, so he planned to return the next year. Work in Sonora, which was successful, kept him busy so he did not visit Arizona again until late 1694 when Kino traveled down the Santa Cruz and Gila valleys. He probably passed by Tucson since he saw the ancient ruined city of Casa Grande and went to a point almost as far as the junction of the Gila and Salt rivers. Kino's diary states:

> *By November 1694 I came with my servers and a few judges from this Pimería to the Casa Grande, which is what the Pimas call it, which is near the ample Gila River, which flows from New Mexico and has its origins near Acoma. This east flowing river and Casa Grande lie 43 leagues northeast of the Sobaipuris of San Francisco Javier del Bac. ... All the*

people are affable and gentle, and they gave us news of the two friendly
nations that are further downstream to the west and to the northeast on the
Río Azúl, and further ahead on the Colorado River are the Opas and
Cocomaricopas, who although quite different speak a similar tongue. ... The
Casa Grande is a four-story building, as big as a castle or like the biggest
church in the area of Sonora; it is said that it was abandoned by the
Ancestors of Moctezuma, who pressured by the local Apaches left toward
the East of Casas Grandes, and from there moved south by southeast where
they founded the grand city and court of Mexico. Next to Casa Grande are
13 minor ruins, in worse shape, of many houses that are recognizable as
once having been a city. On this and later occasions, I have learned, heard,
and at times seen, that further East, North, and West there are seven or
eight of these ancient Casas Grandes and the ruins of entire cities with
many metates and broken pots, charcoals, etc., and these are certainly the
seven cities referred to by the apostolic fray Marcos de Niza, who, in his
lengthy travels came all the way to Bacapa, rancheria of these coasts 60
leagues distant from the Casa Grande of the Southwest, which is about 20
leagues from the Gulf of California ... . (Capitulo VIII, p. 107)

Rebellion in 1695

In 1695, problems began at the mission of Tubutama in the Altar Valley where Father
Daniel Januske was stationed. Father Januske asked some Spanish soldiers to come to
his settlement to punish two Pimas who were causing trouble and, he believed, threatening his life. The soldiers complied and punished the Indians in front of everyone.
Father Januske made another mistake when he hired an arrogant Opata Indian as an
overseer of the mission's herds and fields. The Pimans at the mission disliked the Opatas
and when Father Januske was away in March 1695, the Pimans murdered the overseer
and two other Opatas who happened to be there at the time. They also burned the
priest's house and the church, destroyed sacred artifacts, and killed mission cattle. They
then headed south, enlisting more Pimas, and continued on to the mission settlement
at Caborca, where they killed Father Francisco Javier Saeta, resident Jesuit missionary
who had just come from Mexico City in October 1694. Father Saeta became the first
martyr in La Pimería Alta.

As a result of Saeta's death, Gabriel del Castillo, a native of Madrid who had been
governor and captain general of Nueva Vizcaya since 1693, ordered an unprecedented
response to quash the rebellion, but the soldiers could find no organized resistance.
Father Kino was then asked to assemble the leaders who had not taken part in the
uprising, and a meeting among Pimas, Kino, Spanish soldiers, and Seri Indians took
place at the rancheria of El Tupo (then called La Matanza). All went well until the first
guilty man was pointed out. Instead of being arrested, he was beheaded by one of the
soldiers. At that point a riot broke out, and most of the fifty Pima Indians killed were
peaceful ones. The Pimas in retaliation burned the remaining mission buildings at
Tubutama and Caborca along with churches at Imuris, Magdalena, and San Ignacio.
Once more a meeting was arranged at El Tupo to arrange for peace. Kino was able to

restore order, but the initial Spanish response to the rebellion would be long remembered by the Indians.

Campaign of 1695

The entire story of the campaign, preserved in a 200-page daily journal, is an excellent source of detail about the military activities, the soldiers who took part, the conduct and responses of the Indians, and the actions of the Spanish leaders. The following excerpts give a good picture of what was occurring in the area of what is now Arizona during the final decade of the seventeenth century:

> On July 26, 1695, Generals Don Domingo Terán de los Ríos and Juan Fernández de la Fuente, in accordance with the above official statement, had Alférez Francisco de Acuña of the flying company under the command of General Don Domingo Jironza Petriz de Cruzate appear before us. Because he understood the Pima language well, we appointed him to act as our interpreter because of his loyalty, knowledge, and understanding. We also appointed two Christian Pimas to be present. One was named Cristóbal and the other Francisco. They were to tell him everything that was asked the witness in the Opata language and also interpreted their answers in that language. A soldier of the company of General Juan Fernández de la Fuente was also appointed as interpreter in the Opata language. He was Cristóbal Granillo. When all interpreters were present they were given a formal oath in the name of Our Lord God and of the cross. They promised to interpret well and faithfully as far as they understood, without adding or omitting any words or statements. Next we ordered the fettered Pima captive brought before us. Through the interpreters he was asked whether he was a Christian or a pagan. He said he was a Christian named Xavier, that Padre Eusebio Francisco Kino had baptized him in the pueblo of Nuestra Señora de los Dolores, and that he was a native of Bosane... . (Archivo de Hidalgo del Parral, microfilm 1695, ff. 5–208; quoted in Naylor and Polzer, eds., "Campaign Against the Pimas," *The Presidio and Militia on the Northern Frontier,* pp. 613–16)

Continuing their interrogation, the Spaniards tried to elicit additional information from the Pima Indian:

> They asked if he knew the causes for the Indians' rebellion in the pueblos and settlement previously mentioned. Why had they murdered Padre Francisco Xavier Saeta in the pueblo of Caborca and the Opata Indian, Antonio, the mayordomo of Padre Daniel Janusque the missionary, at Tubutama? Why had they also wanted to kill this padre? Xavier replied that they never wanted to kill the padre of this pueblo because he was well liked. They wanted to kill only the three Opatas because they did not belong to their tribe. Antonio, the mayordomo of the padre, had whipped

the chief of the settlement, a pagan, who had given the messages to their
kinsmen in the rancherías of Quisore and Araupo and this pueblo
[Tubutama] while they were all together in the estancia saying that they
were going to kill the Opatas. When they were all gathered together to kill
these Opatas, the padre and his mayordomo came and spoke with them. He
told them he intended to leave and not return because they had been killing
his cows and livestock, and he knew they did not like him. He was going to
take everything he had and go at once. Then he left for the hills with an
Indian boy. Some wanted to chase and kill the padre but the chief told them
not to follow him or kill him because he liked the padre very much. After
they let him go, the people began to shoot arrows at the mayordomo
because he had seen the chief kill a cow and give it to the assembled
Indians. They reproached him and started to shoot at him. At this point
seeing he was wounded, Antonio fled on horseback toward the pueblo while
the chief and the others followed him. He hid in the house of a friend where
they later found him dead. They took Antonio's body and threw it into an
arroyo. They also killed the other two Opatas and discarded their bodies.
(Naylor and Polzer, eds., "Campaign Against the Pimas," pp. 615–16)

Xavier said that a compadre of his had hidden an Indian named Angel
and his wife to keep them from being murdered. They were from the Zuris
pueblo and spoke the Pima language well. He took them out at night to
escape to their own pueblo. Meanwhile, the chief broke the doors of the
padre's house and went in with the other Indians, taking everything,
including the vestments, and distributed the booty among them all. (Naylor
and Polzer, eds., "Campaign Against the Pimas," *The Presidio and Militia*
on the Northern Frontier, pp. 613–16)

Kino and the Pima Indians

The constant raids and depredations of the Apaches kept the Pima nation, the Spanish military, and Padre Kino in a constant state of worry. After the death of Padre
Saeta, Kino and his companion Captain Juan Mateo Manje, expected to hear the war
cries of either the Apaches or the Pimas and to endure a similar attack. Captain
Manje later wrote that Dolores and its occupants were not attacked because of the
continuous prayers of Padre Kino and because the mission church was well painted
and adorned. Kino finally convinced General Juan Fernández de la Fuente, commander of the presidio of Janos, that the Pima nation was not in revolt, but that
Indians were fleeing in fear of suffering the same punishment that had been meted
out to both the innocent and guilty for Padre Saeta's murder. Kino was then commissioned by the general to arrange a truce with the Pima leaders, and the Indians met
with him and the Spanish authorities at Tupo on August 30, 1695. The meeting was
successful and peace was restored. The friendship of the Pimas at this time was so
great that when Padre Kino traveled to Mexico in November 1695, he took with him
the son of El Coro, a converted Sobaipuri leader. The viceroy and ecclesiastical authorities were delighted to meet the young Pima Indian and believed that he was

proof of the good work being done by the Jesuits. For this reason the viceroy promised to send five additional priests to La Pimería Alta.

Kino's Preliminary Work

In early 1696, Kino set out to bring the Sobaipuris of the upper San Pedro River rancherías into the mission system. First, he drove cattle up to Bac and distributed them among the Indians of the Santa Cruz settlements. These cattle would be the nuclei for mission herds that would furnish food to mission residents and to Kino's men on journeys of exploration. Thus, the mission cattle ranches preceded the missions themselves. Second, Kino set up altars in the open or under protective shades built by the Indians, said Mass, and talked about Christian living. Third, he organized a large delegation of Sobaipuri headmen as well as headmen from the upper Santa Cruz valley to go to the Jesuit rector of the district at Bacerac and ask for missionaries.

Kino returned to Mexico City in late 1696 and then made the journey back to Arizona in 1697, when he traveled northward again along the Santa Cruz River. On September 27, 1698, Kino and his military escort leader, Captain Diego Carrasco, made the first known written reference to Tucson, Arizona, calling it San Cosme de Tucson. Kino greeted the native peoples of Tucson again on March 7, 1699. Lieutenant Juan Mateo Manje, his military escort on this journey, mentioned passing four settlements, one league apart, between San Agustín de Oiaur and San Xavier del Bac. The people of Tucson, like those in a modern Pápago Indian ranchería, were scattered through the brush in clusters of houses near the Santa Cruz River. Manje remarked that the five or six leagues between Oiaur and Bac contained numerous cultivated, ditch-irrigated fields. It is possible that the natives of Tucson raised maize, beans, squash, melons, wheat, cotton, amaranth, chenopodium, devil's claw, and tobacco on the fields irrigated from the river; they also depended upon the semi-arid desert for some of their vegetable foods and all of their meat.

Father Kino established the first Jesuit missions in what is today the state of Arizona. In 1701 he assigned priests to the Pima settlements of Guevavi and Bac in the Santa Cruz River valley. The first missionary to reach his post was Father Francisco Gonsalvo, a 28-year-old native of Valencia who had little lasting effect on the Pima culture. He had trouble with natives in the area who began to kill his livestock. After just over a year, Gonsalvo became ill and, reaching the house of Father Agustin de Campos at Mission San Ignacio de Caborca, died on August 7, 1702. He was buried at the mission cemetery there. His colleague, Father Juan de San Martin, who was born in 1670 in Caravaca in Murcia, arrived in Mexico City at the age of 18. He entered the Jesuit order and studied in the capital for a dozen years. Father San Martin reached Guevavi in the summer of 1702 and directed the building of a small house and church. He then laid the foundations for a large church and house but, like Gonsalvo, became ill and left the mission. More fortunate than his fellow Jesuit, San Martin recovered his health and served in other areas on the frontier. Father Agustin Campos, the priest at Caborca until 1736, was born in Sijena in the province of Spanish Huesca in 1669. He had been a Jesuit since he was 15 years old and began his ministry at San Ignacio in 1693 when he was 24.

Baja California Connection

By 1700, Father Kino began making plans to establish a connection between Arizona and the missions of Salvatierra in Baja California. Between 1698 and 1701, Kino had made nine exploratory journeys by horseback to establish that California was definitely a peninsula and its missions did not have to be supplied across the treacherous Sea of Cortes. In 1701, in the company of Salvatierra, he headed toward the Gulf across country which looked "more like ashes than earth," and where the ground was peppered with boulders of black solidified lava. Upon reaching the point where the headwaters of the Gulf converged with the mouth of the Colorado, Kino concluded and later confirmed that no island existed as was currently thought; indeed, he could finally believe the explanation of the Yuma Indians that the blue shells

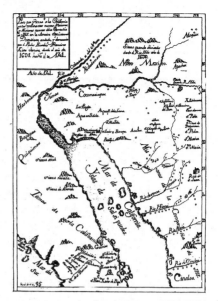

Map 6.2. Travels of Father Kino, 1698–1701. Courtesy Archivo General de Indias, Sevilla.

which they carried had been brought to them by land from the Pacific. Kino's maps of La Pimería Alta and the California peninsula of 1702 showed conclusively that Francisco de Ulloa's geographical concept of 1539 had been correct.

Settlement of Baja California, 1697

Father Kino's good friend and companion Father Salvatierra took command of the California mission field under a royal order of the aging Hapsburg, Carlos II, in February 1697. Because chances for success were so slim, royal approval came only after the Jesuit determination to be entirely self-supporting. Through the work of Honduran-born Father Juan de Ugarte, a professor of philosophy in the Jesuit colleges of Zacatecas and Mexico City, sufficient funds for the California project were raised through donations from individuals and organizations in both Old and New Spain. These gifts formed the beginning of the Pious Fund, a substantial sum of money designated for the support of California missions and permanently maintained throughout the Spanish and Mexican periods.

The decree of 1697 ordered the Jesuits to bear all costs of their California expedition without help from the royal treasury. In exchange, the missionaries were given extraordinary authority: permission to control their military protectors, enlist soldiers and guards, select and remove officers, and appoint civilian officials for the administration of justice. They were to take possession of new territory in the name of the king. Father Kino planned to go with the expedition when supplies and men were finally ready, but at that time trouble among the Indians of La Pimería Alta required his attention. So in October 1697, Salvatierra sailed with Captain Luis de Torrey y Tortolero, four soldiers, and three Indians. Unfortunately, the accompanying long-boat loaded with livestock and provisions sank in a storm before reaching the peninsula, but Salvatierra's small party arrived safely at Bahia de la Concepción (near present-day Mulege). The party soon moved southward to find better land, passing San Bruno—Kino and Atondo's sadly abandoned site—to San Dionisio Bay, where they discovered a natural spring not far from shore. Friendly natives called the place Concho, meaning colored mangrove tree. Here, on October 19, 1697, they erected a temporary chapel, planted a large cross in front, took formal possession of the land, and named it for their patroness Our Lady of Loreto. They were soon joined by Father Francisco Piccolo.

Search for an Overland Route

As the new century began, there were about seventy colonists at Loreto, yet all supplies still had to come from Sinaloa and Sonora on leaky, second-rate vessels whose chances for survival in the stormy Gulf were limited. The barren, unproductive peninsula made dependence upon these ships so great that Salvatierra journeyed to La Pimería Alta in 1701 to join Father Kino in his search for a possible overland route from Sonora to California. During Salvatierra's absence, Father Ugarte, discouraged by his failure to obtain government aid for California, arrived in San Dionisio Bay after a three-day sail across the Gulf on the rotting hulk of a makeshift vessel. Ugarte decided his help was better placed with Salvatierra and Piccolo, and thus relieved the latter to rejoin his Indians at San Javier. Ugarte remained at Loreto until Salvatierra's return from Mexico, at which time the three Jesuits began to work as a team, alternating between the two missions and the mainland.

Funds and supplies continued to run so low on the peninsula that the Jesuit fathers were literally on the verge of starvation. Father Salvatierra jokingly referred to his rations as a "rat-diet," but eventually the realities of the situation darkened his humor. In 1700 he prepared an account listing the missionaries' achievements, describing their tremendous difficulties, and asking for payment of the soldiers by the crown, as was normally done at other frontier posts. The royal fiscal in Mexico rejected the petition for aid since the Jesuits in 1697 had agreed to bear all mission costs. Father Ugarte, then soliciting funds in Mexico, tried to explain the difference between creating a colony and maintaining it indefinitely. Finally Father Piccolo traveled to Mexico and presented a similar report in 1701.

Help for California

Amidst the crisis, Carlos II died without an heir, and his young Bourbon successor, Philip V, grandson of Louis XIV, reversed the penny-pinching trend toward missions. Even though the succession of a French monarch caused a war with England, it had a positive effect in California. A new royal decree of July 17, 1701, pledged 6,000 pesos a year not only to save, but to encourage and extend the California missions; the king also ordered a full report of the existing conditions of the missions and their supply vessels. The offer did have an important positive psychological effect, even though the missions actually had been saved by the generous donations of Don Joseph de la Puente, Don Juan Cavallero y Ocio, and other private gifts that formed the Pious Fund. Philip V then requested a second report in February 1702 that Father Piccolo answered by painting a favorable picture of Lower California. The zealous priest's enthusiasm for royal support led him to exaggerate the fertility and advantages of the rocky peninsula, and he failed to mention the general lack of water, frequent droughts, occasional destructive flash floods, winds of hurricane force, or swarms of locusts. It was because of the hostile nature of the land that the dreamed-of connection with Kino's missions of Sonora and Arizona would never actually be realized. The Jesuits in Baja California would struggle for decades to make it a mere two-thirds of the way up the peninsula.

Father Kino as a Diplomat

In addition to his work as a mission builder and explorer, Padre Kino met many difficult situations as a diplomat. The Apaches, subdued temporarily by El Coro in 1695, became aggressive again in 1703 and commit-

Fig. 6.3. Apache Indian, circa 1882. Courtesy Arizona Historical Society/Tucson. 3972.

ted so many raids that the Spanish authorities believed La Pimería Alta might be lost. Kino made several visits to Apaches in order to keep the peace. Although the Apaches were considered the enemies, the Pimas were also blamed for the problems. Because of his skill in diplomacy, Kino was able to keep the friendship of the Pimas, especially through the help of his friend El Coro, and maintain his mission.

War of the Spanish Succession

Plans for a civilian town in northern Sonora never came to fruition. In 1701, Philip V's succession to the throne of Spain had set off the War of the Spanish Succession. The attacks of Great Britain against France and Spain took a large share of the Spanish military forces leaving few extra soldiers to work on a distant missionary frontier. Even after the war came to an end and was settled by the Treaty of Utrecht in 1713, the Spanish government had little money to spare for the New World colonies. And, Spain's family ties with France through the Bourbon monarchies would cause Spain further financial stress as inter-colonial wars continued throughout the whole of the eighteenth century.

Father Kino left few records of his actions between 1707 and 1710, but in 1710 he wrote a lengthy report that summarized the results of his work in La Pimería Alta to that time. In it, he urged the king to consider the great advantages to be gained by the continued colonization of Alta California and the establishment there of a civilian villa. Despite Kino's efforts, the missions within the present state of Arizona did not thrive. The first priests at San Xavier del Bac and San Gabriel de Guevavi were also the last during Kino's lifetime and for over two decades thereafter. Nevertheless, Kino was the first who brought cattle, sheep, goats, horses, and mules to La Pimería Alta for the use of the Indians, and more than twenty ranchos owed their establishment to his care and foresight. He also introduced new varieties of fruit, vegetables, grain, and sugar cane among the Pimas, and helped them hold their own against raids by warlike neighbors. The seemingly tireless Jesuit explored almost every part of Arizona south of the Gila River prior to his sudden death on March 15, 1711, which occurred as he was helping to dedicate a beautiful new chapel consecrated to San Francisco Xavier at Magdalena in Sonora. Padre Agustin de Campos gave the loyal Jesuit his last rites and said the ceremonial mass. Father Kino was buried in the chapel at the pueblo of Magdalena, today's Magdalena de Kino, on the right side from the Altar, where the second and third chairs are situated. His writings about the Pima lands made the country known to the outside world, bringing settlers to the area.

WOODES ROGERS, 1709

Spanish control through missionary activity was hard work, but other problems existed in Spanish settlements. Residents along the Pacific Coast were not often visited by foreigners, though English and Dutch privateers looking to prey upon Manila Galleons appeared at irregular intervals. After the Jesuits took over in Baja California, the Dutch pirates went on to other areas; nevertheless, the celebrated English privateer, Woodes Rogers, commanding three ships and a small bark, reached Cape San Lucas in November 1709, with plans to capture the returning Manila galleon. Although the English did not visit the area of the missions, they spent some two months in a bay called Puerto Seguro, and carried on friendly relations with the natives. Rogers and fellow officer Edward Cooke recorded their observations about the local Indians and their lifestyle. Rogers commented:

> The Natives we saw here were about 300, they had large Limbs, were straight, tall, and of a much blacker Complexion than any other People that I had seen in the South Seas. Their hair long, black, and straight, which hung down to their Thighs. The Men stark naked, and the Women had a Covering of Leaves over their Privities, or little Clouts made of Silk Grass, or the Skins of Birds and Beasts. All of them that we saw were old, and miserably wrinkled. We suppose they were afraid to let any of their young ones come near us, but needed not; for besides the good Order we kept among our Men in that respect, if we may judge by what we saw, they could not be very tempting... .
>
> Some of them wear Pearl about their Arms and Necks, having first notch'd it round, and fasten'd it with a String of Silk Grass; for I suppose they knew not how to bore them. The Pearls were mix'd with little red Berries, Sticks, and Bits of Shells, which they look'd upon to be so fine an Ornament that tho' we had Glass Beads of several Colours, and other Toys, they would accept none of them. They coveted nothing we had but Knives, and other cutting Instruments, and were so honest, that they did not meddle with our coopers or Carpenters Tools, so that whatever was left

ashore at Night, we found it untouch'd in the Morning. (Rogers, *A Cruising Voyage Around the World,* pp. 229–30)

After cruising off Cape San Lucas for nearly two months, the English privateers spied the 400-ton *Nuestra Señora de la Encarnación y Desengaño,* carrying twenty guns and a cargo of treasure. Rogers, commanding the *Duke,* pulled within range of the Philippine ship on the morning of January 2, 1710, and in less than two hours had captured the galleon. Rogers lost part of his upper jaw when a bullet hit him in the face but managed to continue directing the battle for more than two days. The pirates departed after spending thirteen days in port to repair their ship and reached England with their prize in October 1711.

MISSION PROGRESS AFTER KINO'S DEATH

After Kino's death, the continual efforts of Padres Agustín de Campos and his co-worker Luis Xavier Velarde kept the missionary work in La Pimería Alta going. Between 1716 and 1720, Father Campos baptized 1,004 Indians, most of them children. Serving at Caborca until 1736, he carried on the work begun by Kino and organized expeditions to the west and to the north. Father Luis Xavier Velarde, who succeeded Kino at Dolores, Remedios, and Cocospera, was also well qualified to save souls, even though he did not like to travel long distances, preferring instead to welcome visitors from the north. Velarde was born on August 25, 1677, in Valladolid, Spain, and entered the Society of Jesus on April 20, 1697. He did not arrive in La Pimería Alta until 1713, two years after the death of Kino, but knew of the good work that his predecessor had done. Velarde remained in charge at Dolores until his death in December 1737.

One of the major problems the missionaries always faced was Old World diseases killing the Indians in large numbers. Many of the children baptized by Father Campos on one expedition were dead by the next, killed by smallpox, measles, or typhus. Campos and Velarde worked hard to keep the Pimas happy, but understood neither the cause nor how to control disease. In 1720 two additional priests arrived—Fathers Luis María Gallardi and Luis María Marciano—though they too were unfamiliar with how diseases spread or how to cure them.

The Pimas of the north continued to travel south to the established missions. At Imuris, near San Ignacio on January 17, 1722, Father Campos first baptized and then married Native Americans María and Ignacio of Guevavi. On March 5, 1722, Campos, accompanied by native officials and Fray Joseph Durán de la Peña of the order of San Hipolito, rode into Guevavi and baptized eighteen children. The next day the priest's entourage, joined by natives from Guevavi and other rancherías, traveled along the river to San Cayetano de Tumacacori. In that village twenty-seven infants were baptized and given Christian names. The native Indian governors of Guevavi and San Cayetano both took part in the rite as godfathers. At San Xavier del Bac, twenty-five leagues further north, nearly 100 children lined up for baptism. After completing the ceremony, Campos and his group doubled back along the river to a point several leagues north of Tumacácori through Sopori and Arivaca to Tucubavia, where thirty-one years before Father Visitor Salvatierra had been impressed by some small wooden crosses.

Fig. 6.4. Mission San Francisco Javier Biaundó, founded in 1699. Photo by Harry W. Crosby.

Here Father Campos baptized as many Indians as he could and wrote to his superiors of the need for more priests. He also suggested to the viceroy that a presidio be planted on the lower Gila to serve as a link with California; from the Gila, the Jesuits could possibly penetrate the Hopi pueblos farther north.

Opposition to the Missionaries

The early 1720s were difficult for Sonora. Certain elements of the civilian and military population opposed the mission system, and as early as 1706, Juan Mateo Manje, Kino's traveling companion, praised the Jesuits for their work but proposed that the missionary phase should be regarded as over. In line with the general feelings of the miners and hacendados of Sonora, he proposed that the mission lands should be distributed among the Indians, that the missions be secularized, and that Indians be impressed for work in mines and on ranches under the *repartimiento* system. Jesuit influence caused Manje's imprisonment in Parral for making such proposals, although he was ultimately released. Nevertheless, the twenty-year exemption of Indians in missions from tribute and repartimiento under Kino's original *cédula* had expired and, in 1722, citizens of San Juan Bautista petitioned for the complete removal of the Jesuits and the division of mission lands and cattle among the Indians. Don Gregorio Alvarez Tuñón y Quirós, captain of the presidio at Fronteras, and certain others, were apparently hopeful of taking over Indian lands and labor and petitioned to have the Jesuits removed and their missions secularized.

MISSION PROGRESS IN BAJA CALIFORNIA

After years of struggle, the Jesuits had successfully planted orchards, gardens, fields of grain, sugar cane, and cotton; introduced herds of cattle, sheep, horses, and mules; and managed to build a series of connecting roads throughout the southern and central peninsula, some of which are still used today. Father Ugarte, who headed the missions after Salvatierra's death in 1717, founded the first school and hospital, continued his work of preaching, teaching and exploring, and even sailed a home-built ship to the headwaters of the Gulf in 1721. Ugarte was respected by the California Indians until his death at Mission San Javier in 1730.

By 1720 the Jesuits had expanded to the south, where they discovered San Bernabe Bay, visited previously by Alonzo González in 1644. They found it to be a convenient port where the Manila galleon could take on fresh provisions before the last leg of its journey to Acapulco. They established four missions in this area—La Paz and Santiago in 1721, San José del Cabo in 1730, and Santa Rosa de Todos Santos in 1733. This period marked a major advancement for the Jesuit mission system, but brought great pressure upon the rapidly diminishing Pericu Indians. And, as a result of punishment for polygamy, two Pericues initiated a revolt in the southern area.

Indian Attack of 1734

In October 1734, a hostile group of Indians destroyed all four settlements, killed two priests—Nicolas Tamaral of San José del Cabo and Lorenzo Carranco of Santiago—and numerous Christian natives. Father Ignacio Napoli, founder of Mission Santiago, reported the priests' martyrdom in a letter as follows:

> ... all the Indians that I asked said that the reason they had for killing the priests was the hatred they held for them because, after being baptized, they were not allowed to have multiple wives as they had been accustomed to before, and that they were obligated to pray and go to Mass... .

When the Pericues attacked the crew of the galleon *San Cristobal* that had anchored in the bay, the Spanish government at last considered it worthwhile to station a permanent military garrison at Loreto. Manuel Bernal de Huidobro, governor of Sinaloa, arrived at Loreto with Spanish troops and Indian auxiliaries in December 1735. All the southern missions, then under military protection, were rebuilt and reoccupied.

JUAN BAUTISTA DE ANZA TAKES OVER

Not until late 1726, when Visitador General Pedro de Rivera dismissed Don Gregorio Alvarez and replaced him with a new captain, Don Juan Bautista de Anza, did the missionaries of northern Sonora and Southern Arizona relax. Anza became a staunch supporter of the Jesuits as was Bishop Benito Crespo of Durango. The bishop urged the viceroy and the father provincial to send three additional ministers to La Pimería Alta. While the case for more missionaries was being considered, Fathers Campos and Velarde carried on as usual, christening twenty-five natives at Tumacácori during Holy Week of 1726. Just north of San Cayetano at a place on the Santa Cruz River, the hardworking padre baptized a baby. Father Campos recorded the name of the ranchería as Tubac, a site destined to become an important presidio during the 1750s.

To attract the Indians of the north to the missions, Father Velarde ordered a supply of gifts for them from Mexico City. He reported fifty-seven marriages of natives from

Fig. 6.5. Tumacácori. Drawing by Jack S. Williams.

Santa María and Guevavi performed between November 1, 1725, and April 20, 1729; he also indicated that 276 children from those and other nearby areas had been baptized, even though most of them had died of measles. Despite the problem of disease and the criticism of the Pimas by outsiders as ungrateful and unworthy, the viceroy was prepared to continue support for the missions. Royal cédulas dated October 10, 1728, allowed the viceroy to request on April 27, 1730, the establishment of three new Jesuit missions in northern Pimería Alta. Although this was good news for the Jesuits, it was not without problems. The condition of the already established missions had deteriorated since Father Kino's death and it would require a great effort on the part of the new padres to follow in the footsteps of their famous predecessor.

Beyond New Mexico's Borders

Because of a desire to curb the potentially hostile actions of the natives of the Great Plains, Spaniards began to look to the area north and northeast of their newly established settlements. Their interest was an obvious extension of the exploratory impulse that had brought the colors of Imperial Spain as far north as they had already come.

Flight of Pueblo Indians, 1696

Immediately following the reconquest, some Navajos who were engaged in distant trade with Plains tribes informed the Spanish of a French-Pawnee alliance that did not bode well. As a consequence of the Pueblo Indians' second revolt in 1696, which originated in the northern pueblos of Taos and Picurís, some of the Indians of those villages gathered together their possessions and fled to the open plains. Governor Vargas followed in pursuit and learned from local sources and from physical evidence of abandoned goods that the escape had been a headlong flight. A considerable number of the disorganized natives were then captured and taken off to Pecos Pueblo, but their principal chief, Lorenzo Tupatú, got away. In commemoration of an important victory over the natives, a large cross was erected at the spot where the Indians eventually surrendered. An early winter added significantly to problems with the natives which Vargas summarized as follows:

> *On the seventh day of the month of November, 1696, I, the governor and captain-general, arrived at this village of Pecos with the commanders and some*

of the officers of the army to send relief to the army force which I left at the foot of the mountain of this village at a distance of eight leagues. Having been on the march since the twenty-eighth up to this day in the fury of snowstorms and driving hurricanes which obliged me to stay two days unable to move from the spot, I as well as all the people ran great risk in going on foot because the snow was so deep, the frost and winds moreover making a tempest. Every day dawned upon many horses dead and others in like manner benumbed by it and frozen, so that they were almost gone. When the count was taken we had lost more than two hundred horses and five mules belonging to the soldiers and my own; the Indian allies lost more, the Pecos as well as the Tiguas of Tezuque who came on the campaign. We went through most of the places in a melting snow, serving roasted corn to the people for food and also the flesh of the horses that died. The delays of the campaign were due to accidents caused by the storm.
(Thomas, *After Coronado: Spanish Exploration Northeast of New Mexico, 1696–1727*, p. 15)

Francisco de Cuervo y Valdés and Juan de Ulibarri, 1706

After a lapse of ten years, in 1706 a new well-documented Spanish expedition penetrated the area of the plains to the northeast. However, the remaining Picurís from the flight of 1696 were as yet dispersed and still under the leadership of Lorenzo Tupatú. The group's status was that of "slaves" to the Cuartelejo Apaches, as their captors were now called in the extant documentation.

Lorenzo Tupatú sent a message to the new governor of New Mexico, Francisco de Cuervo y Valdés, asking for forgiveness and implying a desire to be rescued. The response to his request was Spanish organization of an expedition under the command of Juan de Ulibarri for insuring the return of the Picurís to their village. For that purpose, Ulibarri was sent northeastward to the plains to investigate. He got as far as El Cuartelejo, in what is today southern Colorado, where he visited the Cuartelejo Apaches. Those Indians, probably the immediate ancestors of the modern Jicarilla Apaches, became for many years persons of increasing interest to the New Mexicans. At one time rudimentary plans were made to occupy their area, with intent to use the mission and the presidio as institutions of control. Such plans were short lived, later replaced by attempts to attract the Cuartelejos to residence closer to Santa Fe. The rumors that motivated the Ulibarri sortie were perhaps the result of the activity of one Derbanne, a French trader whose activities had brought him close to El Cuartelejo. Fortunately, a good diary permits the first satisfactory insight into the Indian area of the northeast, a view reflecting Ulibarri's observations while on the Plains.

Ulibarri's Observations

Among the twenty soldiers, twelve vecinos, and one hundred Indian allies or auxiliaries, Ulibarri had with him two especially noteworthy persons. One was the Indian scout and fighter, the veteran José Naranjo. The other was a survivor of the La Salle fiasco in Texas, Juan L'Archeveque. The latter originally had been caught in Texas, sent off to Mexico City, then transported to Spain. There, nobody knew what to do with him, so he was shipped back to New Spain and eventually ended up in New Mexico, where he married and became a trader. He then became the progenitor of a soon-to-be numerous New Mexico family, with the name often spelled Archibeque and even Archibeck.

Ulibarri's itinerary, beginning on July 13, took him to Taos via Picurís where he was given a supply of provisions. From Taos, following the Río de San Fernando into the mountains, he crossed over and emerged near Cimarron. With the aid of friendly natives, the party made its way northward and picked up the Purgatoire River, following it to near what is today Trinidad, Colorado. From there a direct course north took Ulibarri to the Arkansas River, known to the natives as the Napestle but called by the explorer the Río Grande de San Francisco. The river was characterized as being four times as large as the Río Grande del Norte and as having the broadest valley discovered in New Spain, consisting of fertile lands producing plums, cherries, and wild grapes. The area visited was the present site of Pueblo, Colorado. A few days of travel generally eastward—punctuated by searches for scarce water because it was the dry season—brought the group to one of the outliers of the Cuartelejos, where the Spaniards were received cordially with exchange of presents. In the days that followed, the main Cuartelejo group was visited and preliminary contact was made with the objective of their search, the dispersed Picurís. The Cuartelejos regaled the visitors with buffalo beef, corn, tamales, and plums.

When Chief Lorenzo Tupatú and the Spaniards met, Don Lorenzo was given an explanation of the visit's purpose.

> *After they understood everything, they cried for joy. We continued thus until we arrived at the plaza which the rancherías formed. The Reverend Father Domínguez de Aranz took up in his hand the most holy cross and intoned the Te Deum Laudemus and the rest of the prayers and sang three times the hymn in praise of the sacrament. After these holy ceremonies were over, the royal Ensign Don Francisco de Valdés drew his sword, and I, after making a note of the events of the day and the hour on which we arrived, said in a clear, intelligible voice: "Knights, Companions and Friends: Let the broad new province of San Luis and the great settlement of Santo Domingo de El Cuartelejo be pacified by the arms of us who are the vassals of our monarch, king and natural lord, Don Felipe V—may he live forever." The royal Ensign said: "Is there anyone to contradict?" All responded, "No." Then he said, "Long live the king! Long live the king! Long live the king!" and cutting the air in all four directions with his sword the ensign signaled for the discharge of the guns. After throwing up our hats and making other signs of rejoicing, the ceremony came to an end. (Thomas, After Coronado: Spanish Exploration Northeast of New Mexico, 1696–1727, p. 69)*

There yet remained the touchy matter of obtaining the release of the Picurís who were slaves of the Cuartelejos, negotiations for which entailed much gift giving as well as Spanish assurance of good intentions and complete friendship. In his journal, though perhaps not reflective of good psychology in actuality, Ulibarri wrote that he had told the Cuartelejos that they had deceived the Picurís and enslaved them when they were really asking for protection. Ulibarri wrote further that he advised the Cuartelejos not to show the slightest objection to handing over the slaves, for otherwise they would experience the severity of Spanish military might. The Cuartelejos were willing, for they said they would give up all the Picurís, not only those who were present but also those who were scattered about in the other rancherías. In exchange, they wanted the Spanish troops to accompany them on a sortie to attack the enemy Pawnee Indians. Ulibarri let them know that on a future occasion he might be able to do so, but that he was now required to take back to New Mexico the prisoners that had been turned over to him.

Juan Tupatú

It took some time to gather the former prisoners, but among them was a very young chief, Juan Tupatú, nephew of Don Lorenzo and son of the important leader of the Pueblo Revolt, Luis Tupatú, whom "since the year '80 of the general revolt of this kingdom, all tribes as well as the apostates and likewise heathen acknowledged as their king, as everyone knows." (Thomas, *After Coronado: Spanish Exploration Northeast of New Mexico, 1696–1727*, p. 71) This statement contradicts conventional history that indicates that Popé of San Juan Pueblo was the first leader, or it may only mean that Popé was no longer important, reportedly long dead.

The recovery of the prisoners was quickly accomplished, save for six persons who were scheduled for return the following year, in part because they were too far away. They were to be escorted to Picurís the next year by one of the principal Cuartelejo captains, Ysdelpain. The total number, both adults and children, recovered in 1706 by the Ulibarri party was reported as "sixty-two persons, small and grown, of the Picurís who were living as apostates, slaves of the devil, and as captives of the barbarity of the Apache. Among them were two of the most noteworthy Indians of the entire kingdom and provinces: they are Don Lorenzo and Don Juan Tupatú, his nephew. I assisted them with particular care in their sustenance, loaning them riding horses until they arrived at their pueblo." (Thomas, *After Coronado: Spanish Exploration Northeast of New Mexico, 1696–1727*, pp. 74–5) The return trip was without incident, carried out over the outbound itinerary. Only the poor condition of many of the mounts slowed the progress somewhat. The return of the long- absent members to their pueblo was a source of rejoicing, after which Ulibarri went to report in person to Governor Cuervo.

THE COMANCHES AND THE FRENCH

With the beginning of the eighteenth century a new force became evident in the Spanish-Indian contest for control. This was the Comanches, whose earlier home had been in southern Wyoming amidst other Shoshone groups. Earliest mention of the Comanches is their connection with the Utes, with whom they had an alliance during at least the first half of the 1700s. Early in the century both groups had attempted to make friends with the Spaniards, but the Comanche orientation toward raiding and running off livestock caused relations to become strained, particularly when the

Comanches attacked the Jicarillas, a group that usually enjoyed good relations with the Spanish crown. In the years 1719–1720, French trader Charles Claude Du Tisne was trading with the Osage and was reported to have failed in an attempt to reach a more westerly group, the Comanches, which had been his initial intention. This is an early mention of Comanches as Plains rather than Rocky Mountain Indians. Du Tisne's activities resulted in renewed though short-lived interest in possible Spanish occupation of the barracks-like Indian town of El Cuartelejo.

Governor Valverde's 1719 Expedition

By 1719, another French Indian trader was in contact with the Osage and was reported as attempting to reach the Comanches. A more ambitious response to this new French challenge resulted when New Mexico governor Antonio Valverde y Cosío planned a major effort to the northeast, including one expedition that he personally commanded. The governor made ready a September 1719 expedition for an attack on the offending Comanches, with the ever-present rumors of French designs on New Mexico adding incentive. Furthermore, the Comanche-Ute alliance brought the Spanish to the point of taking up arms against their erstwhile friends, the Utes. The proposed campaign found a multitude of volunteers from among the civilian and Indian populations, who when added to the military component resulted in a campaign party of over 600, mostly Indian auxiliaries. The group was well supplied with riding animals, sheep, and great quantities of pinole, chocolate, tobacco, and gifts to be given en route to friendly, cooperative Indians.

Valverde followed the same outbound route as had been used by Ulibarri thirteen years earlier as far as La Jicarilla (now Cimarron). There tales of Comanche and Ute depredations were immediately heard, including a report of the wanton destruction of a sophisticated agricultural operation developed by the Jicarillas. Valverde reported a very rosy view of Jicarilla Apache progress, including favorable comments on their industry, methods of irrigation, and friendly attitude.

Heading northward to what is today near Trinidad, additional native auxiliaries in the form of Plains Apaches joined the group, ready for action. The subsequent route of march was northward to the Napestle (the Arkansas River), and beyond, putting the group firmly in enemy territory. Following along the Napestle toward the east, Valverde's party found an abandoned Comanche camp. After meeting with friendly Apache groups and obtaining from them critical information concerning French help given to other Plains Indians, Valverde felt that his mission had been accomplished; before leaving he offered Spanish aid and protection to his hosts against the French and their allies.

When the viceroy received the latest news about the French he became alarmed. He wanted Valverde to establish a presidio at distant El Cuartelejo to hold back any French intrusion. At the same time he wanted the governor to induce the Apaches to become sedentary around the stronghold that he envisioned. Rather than go personally to carry out the viceroy's orders, which he disagreed with because the fort would be too isolated at 130 leagues away, Valverde planned to send his Lieutenant General Pedro de Villasur. The governor expressed his opinion that La Jicarilla, only forty leagues distant, would be a much more suitable place for the Spaniards to support any dependent Indian population, far better than El Cuartelejo.

The Villasur Expedition, 1720

The Villasur expedition was envisioned as a major reconnaissance. By 1720 standards, his was a large group, consisting of forty-two soldiers, three civilians, seventy Indian allies, and the earlier mentioned Father Juan Mínguez as chaplain. Juan L'Archeveque went as interpreter for French contacts, while José Naranjo served as Indian interpreter. The party left New Mexico and headed northward, hitting the South Platte River, which was followed to its forks into what is today Nebraska. There Villasur and his men had contact with hostile Pawnee and allied Indians. Those Indians stampeded the Spanish horses, and in an early morning attack the Spaniards suffered a major defeat with all but thirteen of the party killed. To the Spaniards, the methods and success of the native offensive strongly suggested French participation, a suspicion that has never been proved. Among those killed were Villasur himself, Father Mínguez, and L'Archeveque.

Government economy measures and the loss of troops put a halt to what had promised to be a concerted move to the northeast. Therefore, instead of a move out to the Plains, efforts were renewed to persuade the Jicarillas to become both more sedentary and more dependent on Spain by arranging their relocation to a place more suitable for colonial subjects. An area near the northern Spanish outpost of Taos was suggested but was subsequently rejected by the Jicarillas.

Meanwhile, in 1724 one of the most successful and best known of the French traders in the trans-Mississippi West, Etienne Venaird (also known as Sieur de Bourgmond), had penetrated the area as far as Comanche territory, probably as far as Central Kansas. The importance of this action was not lost on the Spaniards, as the Comanches were becoming closer neighbors and a greater potential threat to the province of New Mexico. The effect of Comanche pressure caused a readjustment of Indian orientation, including a willingness of the Jicarillas to now move much closer to Spanish outposts. This move was the result not only of the Comanche threat but also to some extent of Ute pressure.

Chapter Six

BIBLIOGRAPHIC ESSAY

The sources for the history of the Jesuits in New Spain and the northern frontier of Sonora and Baja California are numerous. The American Division of the Jesuit Historical Institute at the University of Arizona in Tucson has compiled a wealth of information in its Documentary Relations of the Southwest (DRSW) project. The index of manuscripts of the Provincias Internas is divided into eighteen volumes under places, persons, ethnic, military and archives, and key words. Entries on Arizona per se are limited until the latter part of the eighteenth century. An excellent source for biographical information on the Jesuit missionaries is Francisco Zambrano, S.J., and José Gutiérrez Casillas, S.J., *Diccionario Bio-Bibliográfico de la Compañía de Jesús en Mexico* (Mexico: Editorial Jus, 1977). Documents covering this and later periods of the eighteenth century can also be found in the Archivo General de la Nación in Mexico, D.F., The Bancroft Library, and in the William B. Stephens collection of the University of Texas Library in Austin. For the latter, see Carlos E. Castañeda and Jack Autrey Dabbs, *Guide to the Latin American Manuscripts in the University of Texas Library* (Cambridge, Mass.: Harvard University Press, 1939). Defending Spain's policy in the New World is Juan de Solorzano y Pereyra, *Política Indiana* (Madrid: Matheo Sacristan, 1736; reprinted Madrid: Compañía Ibero Americana de Publicaciones, 1930.)

General works on the Jesuits in New Spain include Francisco Javier Alegre, S.J., *Historia de la Provincia de la Compañía de Jesús de Nueva España,* edited by Ernest J. Burrus, S.J. and Felix Zubillaga, S.J., 4 vols. (Rome: Institutum Historicum, 1956–1960); and Andrés Pérez de Ribas, *Historia de los Triumphos de Nuestra Santa Fe entre Gentes las mas Bárbaras y Fieras del Nuevo Orbe* (Madrid, 1645 and reprinted in Mexico: Editorial Layac, 1944). The University of California Press in Berkeley published several works by Jesuit historian Peter Masten Dunne including *Pioneer Black Robes on the West Coast* (1940), *Pioneer Jesuits in Northern Mexico* (1944), and *Black Robes in Lower California* (1952). An excellent modern work is Harry Crosby, *Antigua California: Mission and Colony on the Peninsular Frontier, 1697–1768* (Albuquerque: University of New Mexico Press, 1994).

Basic to an understanding of New Spain's northern frontier are Edward Spicer, *Cycles of Conquest: The Impact of Spain, Mexico and the United States on the Indians of the Southwest 1533–1960* (Tucson: University of Arizona Press, 1962); Henry F. Dobyns *Spanish Colonial Tucson: A Demographic History* (Tucson: University of Arizona Press, 1976); Thomas H. Naylor and Charles W. Polzer, eds., *The Presidio and Militia on the Northern Frontier of New Spain* (Tucson: University of Arizona Press, 1986); and John L. Kessell, *Mission of Sorrows: Jesuit Guevavi and the Pimas 1691–1767,* with a foreword by Ernest J. Burrus, S.J. (Tucson: University of Arizona Press, 1970), and his "Friars versus Bureaucrats: The Mission as a Threatened Institution on the Arizona-Sonora Frontier, 1767–1842," *Western Historical Quarterly,* 5 (April 1974):151–59. Ernest J. Burrus edited *La Obra Cartográfica de la Provincia Mexicana de la Compañía de Jesús 1567–1967* (Madrid: Ediciones José Porrúa Turanzas, 1967) and *Correspondencia del P. Kino con los Generales de la Compañía de Jesús, 1682–1707* (Mexico: Editorial Jus, 1961), and translated *Kino's Plan for the Development of Pimería Alta, Arizona and Upper California* (Tucson: Arizona Pioneers Historical Society, 1961). Kino's diary is published in Spanish in Manuel Ballesteros Gaibrois, ed., *Bibliotheca Indiana:Viages por Norteamérica* (Madrid: Aguilar, 1958), pp. 95–255. Father Burrus also wrote *Kino and Manje, Explorers of Sonora and Arizona: Their Vision of the Future: A Study of their Expeditions and Plans* (Rome: Jesuit Historical Institute, 1971). Charles W. Polzer, S.J. has edited "The Franciscan Entrada into Sonora, 1645–1652: A Jesuit Chronicle," *Arizona and the West,* 14 (autumn 1972):253–78, and Thomas E. Sheridan provides a modern perspective with "Kino's Unforseen Legacy: The Material Consequences of Missionization among the Piman Indians of Arizona and Sonora," *Smoke Signal,* nos. 49–50 (spring and fall 1988):151–67. See also James E. Officer, "Kino and Agriculture in the Pimeria Alta," *The Journal of Arizona History,* 34 (autumn 1993):287–306, and John Augustine Donohue, *After Kino: Jesuit Missions in Northwestern New Spain 1711–1767* (Rome and St. Louis: Jesuit Historical Institute, 1969).

Herbert E. Bolton's *Rim of Christendom: A Biography of Eusebio Francisco Kino, Pacific Coast Pioneer* (New York: Macmillan, 1936) is also valuable. Bolton also prepared the *Guide to Materials for the History of the United States in the Principal Archives of Mexico* (Washington, D.C.: Carnegie Institution, 1913), which inspired Charles E. Chapman's *Catalogue of Materials in the Archivo General de Indias for the History of the Pacific Coast and the American Southwest* (Berkeley: University of California Press, 1919).

Alfred Barnaby Thomas, *After Coronado: Spanish Exploration Northeast of New Mexico, 1696–1727* (Norman: University of Oklahoma Press, 1935) is a valuable source for this period of New Mexican history, especially for the French advance on New Mexico. The Villasur story is also covered in Elizabeth John, *Storms Brewed in other Men's Worlds: The Confrontation of Indians, Spanish and French in the Southwest, 1540–1795* (College Station: Texas A&M University Press, 1975); in Thomas Chavez, "The Segesser Hide Paintings: History, Discovery, Art," *Great Plains Quarterly,* 10 (spring 1990):96–109, and in Robert S. Weddle, *Wilderness Manhunt: The Spanish Search for LaSalle* (Austin: University of Texas Press, 1973).

As mentioned previously, Marc Simmons covers the founding of Albuquerque and its subsequent history in *Albuquerque: A Narrative History* (Albuquerque: University of New Mexico Press, 1982). Edward K. Flagler in "From Asturias to New Mexico: Don Francisco Cuervo y Valdés," *New Mexico Historical Review,* 67 (April 1994):127–144 talks about the governor who was primarily responsible for the city's founding. His little known predecessor, the man who replaced Diego de Vargas, is covered in Rick Hendricks, "Pedro Rodríguez Cubero: New Mexico's Reluctant Governor, 1697–1703," *NMHR,*

68 (January 1993):13–39. For women's settlement during the reconquest period see Salomé Hernández, "*Nueva Mexicanas* as Refugees and Reconquest Settlers, 1680–1696" in *New Mexico Women: Intercultural Perspectives*, ed. by Joan M. Jensen and Darlis A. Miller (Albuquerque: University of New Mexico Press, 1986) and Rosalind Z. Rock, "'Pido y Suplico: Women and Law in Spanish New Mexico, 1697–1763," *NMHR*, 65 (April 1990):145–59.

For an account of the Woodes Rogers expeditions, refer to Woodes Rogers, *A Cruising Voyage Around the World* (New York: Dover Publications, 1970). Finally, for a good overview of key aspects of Latin American history, see Lewis Hanke, ed., *History of Latin American Civilization, Sources and Interpretations*, vol. 1 (Boston: Little, Brown and Company, 1967).

EXPANSION AND CONSOLIDATION: 1735–1768

JESUIT TRAINING

*D*uring the late 1720s, a group of Jesuits from various parts of Germany, Italy, and Spain assembled for missionary work in New Spain. They gathered in Spain where they resided in the large Jesuit hospice in Sevilla or at the Puerto de Santa María in Cádiz while awaiting for possibly a year or two transportation with the convoy to Veracruz. Father Kino, at an earlier time, had spent a considerable length of time in Cádiz perfecting his Spanish and learning techniques useful for missionary work. Jesuit study included astronomy and mathematics, as well as learning to make compasses or sundials, sewing clothing, making bottles, soldering tin, working with a lathe, and developing skills that they would need when trying to build a mission among the natives.

A list of the twenty-six Jesuits who were a part of the 1730 group can be found in the Archivo General de Indias in Contratacion, legajo 5550. Before they were allowed to embark, each one of the Jesuits appeared before a board of examiners.

When the ship *La Potencia,* alias *El Blandón* departed in 1730, all twenty-six Jesuits were aboard. It must have been an interesting group with Germans, Italians, and Spaniards getting along in such close quarters. They arrived in Havana harbor on February 2, 1731, where they remained for two months. In April the missionaries sailed to Veracruz, where Father Fernando Consag, a native of Hungary, described the port as being very unhealthful with considerable sickness. He thought the name Veracruz to be appropriate because so many Europeans died there from *el vómito negro* (black vomit) and other stomach ailments. The missionaries were not sorry to begin their overland journey to Mexico City.

NEW ASSIGNMENTS IN LA PIMERÍA ALTA

After a short stay in the capital, three of the newly arrived Jesuits—Phelipe Segesser, Swiss; Ignacio Xavier Keller, Moravian; and Juan Bautista Grazhoffer, Austrian—received word that they were assigned to La Pimería Alta. They packed their belongings and started out on the road north to Durango where they would meet with Bishop Benito Crespo. They had each received the customary royal gift of vestments and altar furnishings for the proposed churches to be built in the frontier regions of Sonora and Arizona. After meeting with the Bishop in Durango and visiting with Father Gaspar Stiger, on his way to a Tarahumara mission, the three departed for La Pimería Alta in August 1731.

The small company traveled northward to the mining center of Parral and then headed west to Casas Grandes and the presidio of Janos. They continued due west to

Fronteras, where Captain Juan Bautista de Anza was in charge. One more half-day's ride brought them to the Opata mission of Cuquiarachi where their superiors were waiting. On October 7, 1731, they met Father Visitor Cristobal de Canas, Father Rector Luis María Gallardi, and Fathers Agustín de Campos and Luis María Velarde. The Jesuit leaders assigned the newcomers to the three vacant missions of Guevavi, San Xavier del Bac, and Santa María Soamca, warning them that their jobs would be extremely difficult and that the dwellings of the missions were dilapidated at best. Each of the new missionaries was directed to spend several months in the company of one of the older Jesuits to learn the Pima language and customs. Captain Anza would help them at their new sites.

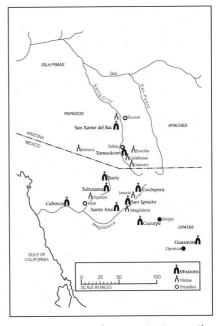

Map 7.1. Missions and visitas in La Pimería Alta after 1767. Map by Stephanie Gould.

An anonymous missionary report of 1730 had complained that the Spanish officials and settlers were criticizing and interfering with the work of the missions and that the padres could do nothing to please their neighbors. The report stated that the Pimas were ungrateful, immoral, and shiftless, and that the missionized areas centering around Dolores, San Ignacio, Tubutama, and Caborca had lost population and were, as compared with regions to the south, weak mission fields. In 1730, these four areas combined contained fewer than 1,500 people living under the mission system. The least populous of the four was Kino's home area where only 135 Indians were reported in Dolores, Remedios, and Cocospera. The most populous was Caborca, where 723 Pimas were reported in the mission pueblos. Epidemics, Apache raiding, and declining vigor in the Jesuit program had all contributed to the loss of population.

Nevertheless, when the new padres arrived in 1732, there was a feeling of optimism. The focus of missionary activity definitely shifted to the Arizona area again. The Pimas of the upper Santa Cruz and the Sobaipuris farther north around Bac received the new missionaries with apparent eagerness and began again to gather around the missions. The Jesuits never established themselves on the Gila and did not build a church in Pápago country, although one was completed at its edge at Sonoita.

FATHER JOHANN BAPTIST GRAZHOFFER AT GUEVAVI

Father Grazhoffer, tall with brown hair, was born in Bleiburg, Carinthia, in southern Austria on June 5, 1690. He entered the Society of Jesus in Bohemia on October 27, 1710. During his apprenticeship with Father Gallardi at Tubutama, Father Grazhoffer suffered from a serious bout of fever, but by the spring of 1732 was ready to begin his ministry. He joined Segesser, Keller, Captain Anza, a military escort, Eusebio Aquibissani, the native designated by the Spaniards as captain general of the Pimas, and various Indians at a place called Quino. The priests had carpenters' axes, blacksmiths' tongs, and sickles with them to begin building new mission structures. They also had magnificent damask vestments in five colors and silver vessels for the altars. They celebrated mass at dawn on May 3, 1732, the day on which a new era for La Pimería Alta began.

The Santa Cruz river, on which all three of the missions are located, rises in the Huachuca Mountains, extending south past the village of Santa María Soamca, the site of present-day Santa Cruz. Father Kino called it el Río de Santa María, although later it was called by the local names of Río de Soamca, Río de Guevavi, Río de Tubac, and finally, in the late 1780s, Río de Santa Cruz. The ground was dry and dusty, but the cottonwoods and willows along the river made the place habitable.

Hundreds of Pimas, painted and wearing blankets and feathers, came to Guevavi to see what was happening. On May 4, the Spanish expedition made its grand entry into the village. Father Grazhoffer no doubt thought that with luck, a fine adobe house and chapel would soon replace the temporary shelter, and mission fields and orchards would be added to the small plot of wheat to provide food and clothing for the neophytes. The mission finally became known as "La Misión de los santos ángeles Gabriel y Raphael de Guevavi o Gusutaqui." Later the archangel San Miguel was added to the mission name to invoke further protection. The Pima name Gusutaqui, meaning big water, was first recorded by Captain Juan Matheo Manje in 1699 and appeared off and on as a synonym for Guevavi.

Captain Anza formally introduced the Pima Indians to their new padre with an appropriate ceremony. A symbolic replanting of the Holy Cross and the firing of muskets marked the occasion. The natives reciprocated with races, dancing, and singing. The report of Father Canas to the Bishop of July 31, 1732, located in the Archivo General de Indias in Sevilla (Guadalajara 185) describes the reception:

> Through a skillful interpreter the Captain delivered to more than a thousand Pimas who gathered that day ... a pious and effective oration explaining to them the cause, purpose, and motive of his coming, which was to present to them, in the name of the king our lord, Philip V, whom God guard, a Father Minister to teach and impress upon them Christian obligations, to baptize their children and instruct adults so that they might gain the same benefit and partake of the rest of the services offered, as do the natives in the other missions. At this all showed great happiness and obedient. (Quoted in Kessell, *Mission of Sorrows: Jesuit Guevavi and the Pimas 1691–1767*, p. 49)

Next, the native leader "Don Eusebio" Aquibissani, namesake of Father Kino who was called captain general of all the Pimas, then talked to the Indians gathered at the celebration. The Pimas at Guevavi may have resented Aquibissani, since he had been chosen by the Spaniards, but listened anyway. An old and popular Christian Indian by the name of Francisco retained the vara of authority as governor of Guevavi.

When Father Grazhoffer began to work among the Pimas, he no doubt found them very different than the descriptions left by Father Kino. Kino always saw them as gentle, friendly, sincere people who lived up to their word even though other reports described them as sly and crafty. He never criticized their drunkenness or all-night parties, nor did he seem to worry when on one occasion the Pimas of Quiburi were dancing over the scalps of fifteen enemies whom they had killed a few days before. He never mentioned their polygamy or other characteristics that would make them less desirable as subjects of the Spanish king. Kino's tolerance had made him welcome everywhere.

When Father Grazhoffer settled in at Guevavi as the resident priest, he expected the Indians to conform to Christian ways on a permanent basis. The Indians became sullen, though they cooperated in the building of the mission. A small house had already

Fig. 7.1. Pima woman. Courtesy Arizona Historical Society Library/Tucson. 22950.

been built under the direction of Captain Anza and soon a well-roofed ramada over the altar provided shade during services. Four visitas were established—Sonoita to the northeast; Arivaca to the west; Tumacácori, north downriver; and beyond that, Tubac. Padre Grazhoffer estimated that some 1,400 souls were living under his jurisdiction. There were also some civilians in the area, including Nicolas Romero and a member of the Romo de Vivar family. Because they lived so far from a secular priest, they came to the mission at Guevavi for their spiritual needs.

Celebration and Death

In midsummer of 1732, Father Grazhoffer joined his companions Fathers Ignacio Keller, from Santa María Soamca, and Philip Segesser von Brunegg, from San Xavier del Bac, to celebrate with Fathers Canas and Gallardi, and Captain Anza, the feast day of Ignacio Loyola. They were guests of Father Campos at San Ignacio, and the weather was excruciatingly hot. They remained for eight days and performed the spiritual exercises of their founder San Ignacio de Loyola. Segesser must have recalled his cool and refreshing hometown of Lucerne, Switzerland while he stayed on at San Ignacio to care for the aging Father Campos. He then divided his time between his own mission at San Xavier del Bac and San Ignacio.

Later in May 1733, Segesser found Father Grazhoffer very ill at Guevavi. His condition continued to worsen until the dedicated Jesuit died in the arms of Segesser on May 26. Father Segesser accused the Indians of poisoning Grazhoffer and they later admitted they had, though one can only speculate about the reasons. As a result, Segesser was appointed to Guevavi and Father Gaspar Stiger was transferred from Tarahumara Alta to San Xavier del Bac.

FATHER STIGER AT SAN XAVIER DEL BAC

The first resident priest of San Xavier del Bac, Francisco Gonzalvo, had died in 1702 and despite the plans of Father Kino, no permanent priest was stationed there until 1732, when the Spanish crown could support additional priests. Padre Segesser had been assigned to Bac in 1732 but spent most of his time caring for the ailing Father Campos. Segesser commented little about the Sobaipuris of the area who were to some extent sedentary irrigation farmers. The Piman community of Tucson may have at that time suffered a decline in inhabitants from Old World diseases.

Padre Stiger, born on October 20, 1695, at Oberreid near St. Gallens in the Diocese of Constance in northern Switzerland, entered the Society of Jesus on October 9, 1725. He reached New Spain in 1729 and went first to the Tarahumara mission of Carichic. When he arrived at Bac, he had a difficult time with the native religious leaders, especially in 1734 when, during his absence, the natives broke into his house, stealing everything, including the beautiful vestments in five colors, and other items that had been sent by the viceroy. Captain Anza intervened and the natives finally came back, returning much of what they had stolen, though the vestments were torn. Padre Stiger continued to minister to his flock even though the native *hechiceros* placed curses upon him.

FATHER PHELIPE SEGESSER AT GUEVAVI, 1734–1762

Father Segesser, the third of seventeen children, was born on September 1, 1689, to the provincial governor of Lucerne and entered the Society of Jesus on October 14, 1708. He had blue eyes, light brown hair and was of medium build. He made his profession in 1726, just prior to his departure for the New World. When he took over at Guevavi, he had little success. He managed to plant some fruit trees, as he had done at Bac, and tried to enlist the aid of the natives of Sonoita. When he rode over to see why they had not come to help, he found them drunk; he had arrived during the annual rain ceremonial, the beginning of the native year, just before the summer planting in July. For several weeks the women had harvested the fruit of the giant saguaro and made a kind of crimson-colored drink. Because it spoiled quickly, they had to drink it quickly, causing general drunkenness. Although they invited him to partake, Father Segesser declined and decided to wait until another day to ask them to work.

Unfortunately, as time went by, more and more Indians died of disease or were unable to adjust to the new way of life. The Pimas seemed to drink more frequently, and the bishop threatened them with excommunication. But Father Segesser knew their difficulties and was lenient. After a few months at Guevavi, the Jesuit also began to experience bouts of illness. At Bac he had been perfectly healthy, but now he had become weak. Segesser suspected the village *hechiceros* who he believed had poisoned Grazhoffer. Finally Father Keller came to act as nurse and sent Segesser south to Mission Cucurpe. After five months, Segesser was well enough to return to Guevavi.

As July 31, 1734, approached, Segesser arranged to join Father Keller at Soamca to celebrate the feast of San Ignacio. Stiger, at that time absent from Bac, could not join them. Then, without warning, the Indians of Soamca deserted them, and Segesser hurried back to Guevavi to find that his natives had fled into the hills driving the cattle and horses before them. The same thing had happened at Bac, except the Indians had broken into Stiger's house. The cause of their departure had been a rumor that Captain Anza was coming to kill all of the Pimas; once the rumor was quelled, conditions returned to normal and the Indians came back.

When Segesser became ill again at Guevavi, Anza took him to his own house at Fronteras where the captain's wife nursed him back to health. This time Segesser did not return to Guevavi but went to the mission of Tecoripa in La Pimería Baja. For several years afterwards, Guevavi was cared for by Gaspar Stiger of San Xavier del Bac. The hechiceros put several curses upon him, but he managed to remain healthy until his transfer to San Ignacio to replace the aging and increasingly senile Father Campos. Segesser remained at San Ignacio until his death on April 24, 1762.

FATHER IGNACIO XAVIER KELLER AT GUEVAVI

Father Keller, tall and fair, was born on November 11, 1702, in Olomouc, Moravia, and joined the Society of Jesus on October 17, 1717. With the transfer of Stiger, all of northern Pimería Alta was under Keller's jurisdiction. Throughout 1736 and 1737 he rode to Guevavi to preach and offer baptism. On one occasion he baptized three baby Pima girls and one a boy he called a Nijorita or Nixora. A Nixora was the name for an Indian sold by other Indians to the gente de razón. They lived as virtual slaves and this boy, Francisco, was probably the property of Vicente Figueroa, his godfather at the baptism. Keller also baptized some of the other civilians on his visits to Guevavi, including a son of Luis Pacho and Juliana Romero, a daughter of Juan Nuñez and María Rosa Samaniego, and a son of Agustín Fernández and María Antonia Romero.

Apparently more settlers were moving in along the river south of Guevavi and, at the encouragement of Father Keller, these people acted as godparents to the natives. Unfortunately, the *compadres* did not take their responsibilities too seriously since some of the soldiers became godfathers to dozens of natives, seldom seeing either the children or their parents after the initial baptismal ceremony.

BOLAS DE PLATA, 1736

Meanwhile, to the southwest of Guevavi, an event occurred toward the end of October 1736 that not only gave Arizona its name but also sparked the first mining rush into the region that today bears that name. Near the mining camp of Arizonac or Arizona, belonging to Captain Don Gabriel de Prudhom Heyder Butron y Muxica, the son of a Yaqui Indian prospector found the first of some amazing *bolas de plata* or *planchas de plata*. The size of the balls grew greater with every telling. Finally, Captain Juan Bautista de Anza, as *justicia mayor* of Sonora under Bernal de Huidobro, the new governor of Sinaloa, arrived at the scene and prepared to write a report to Bishop Benito Crespo of Durango. He conducted an investigation to determine what the silver balls represented, but most of the silver was already gone. (The documents concerning the strike, located in the Seville archives, have created in recent times interest in the silver.) Anza reported that between the mission of Guevavi and the ranchería of Arissona, there was discovered chunks of silver, one containing more than 100 arrobas. Anza himself only saw ten or twelve arrobas but indicated that there were mines being discovered in the hills. The chief concern of Anza was that the crown should receive its quinto real of the metal taken.

The fame of the *bolas y planchas de plata* spread throughout New Spain. The tiny ranchería of Arissona, a *visita* of the mission of El Saric a few miles southwest of present-day Nogales, was becoming very popular. The name Arissona was soon more common than La Pimería Alta for the region. It has been suggested that the word "Arizona" was of Pápago origin, and since the Pápagos were a part of the Pima nation, the word could have been picked up by the Spaniards. The word in Pápago means a small, ever-flowing stream and was a logical name for a village on just such a stream. The tiny ranchería became known as Real de Arissona and possibly reached a population of 10,000, becoming the first boom town and the first ghost town in the area.

The miners kept pouring into the area in search of the elusive silver, and Captain Anza was continually concerned about payment of the equally elusive royal fifth. Finally the mines were closed by royal order in 1741, when most of the silver was gone; nevertheless, prospectors continued to search the area, and every once in a while a small strike would be made. The name Arizona became synonymous with quick wealth.

NEW PRIESTS FOR LA PIMERÍA ALTA

In contrast to those who had gone before, the next two priests at Guevavi each lasted more than three years. The first was Alexandro Rapicani, born in the town of Zeven in the Duchy of Bremen on November 3, 1702, of a Swedish mother and a Neapolitan father. He had blonde hair, blue eyes, and a fair complexion. Father Rapicani bid farewell to his Jesuit classmates in Westphalia in April 1735 and journeyed to Genoa. From there he sailed to Cádiz, where he remained at the spacious Jesuit hospice at nearby Puerto de Santa María until arrangements could be made for his passage to New Spain. Here Father Rapicani met Father Andrés Xavier García, superior of the group, and Father Jacobo Sedelmayr of Bavaria, with whom he would embark with more than forty other members of the Jesuit mission of 1735. They sailed on November 22 aboard the *Santa Rosa,* which on February 18, 1736, ran aground within sight of San Juan de Ulua in Veracruz harbor. The unfortunate Jesuits had to abandon ship and some lost trunks containing their few precious belongings.

At Puebla de Los Angeles, on the road to Mexico City, the Jesuits were greeted at the cathedral by Bishop Benito Crespo recently promoted from the See of Durango. The bishop told the new arrivals the names of all the German missionaries in his extensive province and was able to give the name of the province where each was born. Ironically, the bishop, who had devoted so much of his life to the Indians of La Pimería Alta, died in a devastating plague in 1736.

FATHER RAPICANI AT GUEVAVI, 1737–1740

The transfer of Mission Guevavi to Father Rapicani was made on June 1, 1737 by Father Ignacio Keller in the company of Father Rector Gaspar Stiger. The inventory showed how poor the mission was at that time: The house contained kitchen utensils such as copper pots, a large skillet, majolica and earthenware plates, a large cup, two napkins, and a chocolate cloth. The mission owned 240 cattle, 150 sheep, 50 goats, 8 oxen, 12 horses, 10 mules, and a few mares. The income, the annual royal stipend, was 350 pesos.

The Mission San Xavier del Bac had stood without a resident padre for most of its existence. Since there were not enough missionaries to serve the frontier area of Arizona, Father Rapicani also took over Bac as a visita of Guevavi; sometimes he received an extra 200 pesos per year for this added responsibility. The inventory at Bac also showed a few poor items in the padre's house, most of which had been nearly ruined during the uprising of 1734. There were the same number of cattle, sheep, and goats as at Guevavi (which indicates that the figures were merely estimates), but fewer horses, mules, and mares, and no oxen.

Father Keller continued his work in La Pimería Alta, and on January 19, 1738, he baptized six persons in the ranchería of Gusutaqui. During the following week Father Keller visited San Xavier to celebrate another twenty-three baptisms and then returned to Gusutaqui on February 22. In late April 1740, Fathers Rapicani and Sedelmayr traveled to San Ignacio to experience the annual eight-day spiritual exercises and then, on May 1, 1740, they professed at a public mass solemn vows of poverty, chastity, obedience, and willingness to go wherever the Pope might send them. As professed fathers, they had reached the culmination of all their years of study and probation.

HOSTILITY ON THE FRONTIER

During the six weeks prior to May 1740, there had been outbreaks of violence among the Yaqui Indians and neighboring tribes. There were rumors of widespread unrest and the blame lay with Governor Bernal de Huidobro, who held jurisdiction over the five northwestern coastal provinces—Rosario, Culiacán, Sinaloa, Ostimuri, and Sonora (including La Pimería Alta)—since 1734. The governor, whose autocratic methods were popular neither with the Jesuits nor the Indians, caused unrest throughout the area. Then, in addition to a difficult situation, another tragedy occurred on May 9, 1740—the death of Captain Anza, friend and protector of the Jesuits. It happened near the mission of Father Keller at Soamca.

Father Keller, knowing that Apaches had recently scouted the area, warned Captain Anza to be on his guard. Despite taking certain precautions, Anza rode on ahead of his troops when the danger seemed less imminent. In his path, hidden by chaparral, the Apaches lay in ambush. When Anza approached, the Indians began to fire and in an instant, the veteran soldier was dead. The Apaches then claimed their grisly trophy: Anza's scalp. Unfortunately for the Jesuits, they lost one of their strongest supporters; Anza's place would be difficult to fill. By June, Yaqui and Mayo rebels had severed all communications between Sonora and the south and were inciting rebellion to the north.

Governor Bernal de Huidobro called upon his sargento mayor of the Province of Sonora, Don Agustín de Vildósola, a close friend and associate of Anza who was in charge of settling Anza's estate. During the summer of 1740, Vildósola and his men successfully defended Sonora and sent a detachment of men among the Pimas to locate Apache infiltrators. Soldiers later executed four Yaquis and an Apache whom they suspected of plotting a rebellion of the whole of La Pimería Alta. By this time, Father Rapicani, who did not get along well with Vildosola, was transferred to the Opata mission at Batuc.

Father Joseph de Torres Perea at Guevavi and Bac

Joseph de Torres Perea was born in the Mexican village of Chalchicomula, Puebla, in 1713. He entered the Society of Jesus in 1729 and by 1737 was studying theology at the Colegio Máximo in Mexico City. Soon after his ordination, Father Joseph set out for the missions of the north, traveling through Mayo and Yaqui country. On January 31, 1741, Father Torres Perea reached Arispe on the upper Río Sonora and presented himself to Father Visitor Carlos de Roxas. Father Roxas assigned the young priest, just in his late 20's, to the missions at Guevavi and San Xavier del Bac.

Father Joseph began his activities immediately. In addition to his duties at Guevavi, its four visitas, and San Xavier, the energetic Jesuit offered his services to the rancherías scattered throughout the area. His first marriage ceremony was a gala affair when Joseph Tutubusa, native governor of Tumacácori, married Martha Tupquice of San Xavier on May 23, 1741. Among the witnesses were Ignacio Jocumisa, the governor of San Xavier, Domingo Cussu, and several settlers with Spanish names.

Non-Native Settlers

The silver discovery had brought in many new settlers, and some stayed to plant crops and let cattle graze in the hills. Don Nicolas Romero continued to preside over a large and expanding family at Buenavista, and other families with names such as Tapia, Grijalva, Bohorquez, Barba, Amesquita, Gallego, and Samaniego arrived. Others settled north of Guevavi at Tubac. Father Rapicani had performed a double marriage ceremony on February 14, 1740, for Francisco de Ortega and Gertrudis Barba, and Luis Villela and Rosalia Duran, all of whom he called *vecinos de Tubac*. By the fall of 1741 Father Torres Perea baptized the son of the Villelas who was named Miguel Ignacio Villela Duran.

At Arivaca, Don Antonio de Rivera maintained an estancia with a large household of Yaqui and Nixora servants. Near Sopori, between Arivaca and Tubac, could be found the estancia of Captain Don Bernardo de Urrea from Culiacán. He served three times as interim governor of Sonora. All of these gente de razón settlers belonged to the parish of Nacosari, 120 miles southeast of Guevavi. Because of its distance, they usually asked Father Joseph to perform the necessary services of baptism, marriage, or last rites.

Father Joseph's Work Continues

Father Joseph carried on his duties with considerable success. He tried to choose native leaders who had the respect of the village and could act as intermediaries. He did his best to educate them and seldom found it necessary to administer corporal punishment. When it did become necessary, he gave punishment through the native governor, who exercised a position of power as a symbol of authority, carrying his vara and occupying a special place in the church. The Pimas themselves seldom used corporal punishment, except for the occasional execution of an evil shaman. Among the Pimas, the Jesuit way was slowly accepted.

A week before Christmas of 1741, Father Joseph traveled along Sonoita Creek to call upon and marry native governor Antonio of Sonoita. On the road, he realized the need for another presidio in the area, especially since word of Apache raids on cattle had been heard. Coincidentally, plans were being made for the founding of a new presidio of fifty men to be placed nineteen leagues southeast of Guevavi and five south-east of Soamca at a place known as San Mateo de Terrenate. Because it was to protect Guevavi, it sometimes became known as the presidio of Guevavi even though it was some fifty miles away.

During the next two years, Father Joseph spent much of his time riding among the various villages performing marriages and baptisms. Sadly, in January 1744, he had to record five deaths from an illness described as yellow vomit. Later, in the spring, he was able to write a complete report about conditions at Guevavi, in which he complained that Guevavi's climate was unhealthful and the natives ate raw fruit, washing it down with almost-poisonous water. They also practiced the unsafe custom of bathing any time, even just after a meal, which was considered a serious cause of indigestion. Father Joseph also thought it was dangerous for the women to bathe immediately after giving birth and carry on as before. Also, the mothers' milk seemed to dry up very soon, causing their babies to die. Another problem at Guevavi was the work of the hechiceros who had cast "an evil spell" and made the women sterile. Naturally, in the villages where there had been more Spanish contact there was more disease and there-fore more death. It was difficult for the Jesuits to understand why God would punish their work by causing their native charges to die.

Since Guevavi's founding in 1732, there were recorded 978 baptisms, and only twenty-three families who were living at the mission. Father Joseph reported that the children were changing their pagan ways and were attending daily instruction; in addi-tion, the natives had given up their orgies of drinking and danced only occasionally. They believed in Christian marriage and were obedient to the padres.

CONDITIONS AT SAN XAVIER DEL BAC

In March 1744, Father Torres Perea reported on the condition of San Xavier del Bac. He complained that toward the north there were no longer Christians, only gentile nations. Since the mission's founding in 1732, the baptismal register showed 2,142 without counting those who had been baptized by other fathers before. There were more than 400 families living within the mission area, but they were mountain dwell-ers who were little amenable to Christian ways. Only two priests had resided there, one whom the Indians claimed to have bewitched in 1734. They profaned the vestments and chalices, but after that, claimed Torres Perea, they had surrendered and lived qui-etly. They were ministered to by the father at Guevavi, and even though they had been baptized, they did not follow proper procedures such as crossing themselves. They mostly married according to their pagan rites and would then tell the padres that they had been married by previous padres. The church records showed that only thirty couples had been married out of 400 families.

In February 1744 Father Torres Perea moved to Caborca and Father Ildefonso de la Peña, another Jesuit born in Mexico, came briefly to Guevavi. Another visiting cleri-cal inspector, the Swiss-born father visitor Juan Antonio Balthasar, also arrived at Guevavi in May 1744. Writing his own description of the natives at San Xavier del Bac, he mainly complained that the Indians continually abandoned the mission. What the fa-ther visitor failed to understand was that this was their normal economic pattern.

The regular seasonal movement of the Pimas to take advantage of economic re-sources was a major stumbling block to the missionaries, who wanted them to be sedentary. Water supply largely determined their moves, and the Pimas spent winters either at villages with wells located near permanent springs in the mountains, or on the Magdalena-Concepción, Santa Cruz-Gila, or Colorado Rivers. In the summer, they car-ried water in baked clay vessels to the thick stands of giant cactus for the mid-season fruit harvest. When summer thundershowers filled earth tanks in the valleys between the streams, some moved to their field villages to plant maize and other crops. Despite the closeness of fields and permanent domestic and irrigation water at Bac and the village of Tucson, their residents had to travel to find stands of giant cactus, oak groves, and yucca for edible fruit and nuts. They also moved out to good deer and mountain sheep hunting areas.

Because of these native cultural patterns, Father Balthasar claimed that Bac needed military troops to force the Northern Pimans to live in the pueblo, to labor constantly in the fields, to punish the medicine men, and to deport undesirable residents to Mexico City. Father de la Peña departed with Balthasar and during the summer, Father Keller was once again placed in charge of Guevavi and Bac.

THE ELUSIVE MOQUIS (HOPIS)

The Spaniards had tried to bring the Moquis (Hopis) into the Spanish cultural fold since the days of Juan de Oñate in New Mexico. They had hoped not only to convert them to Christianity, but also to establish trade and organize them as a part of the Spanish empire. The Hopis were an independent and peaceful people but were ada-mantly opposed to accepting the padres and their teachings; they did not cherish the memory of Coronado or Tovar. After the settlement of New Mexico, the Franciscans succeeded in establishing three missions at Awatobi, Oraibi, and Shongopovi, and two visitas at Walpi and Mishongnovi, which lasted from 1629 until the Pueblo Revolt. When the churches were destroyed, two friars were killed and two were thrown over the cliff. For nearly a century, that stopped Spanish attempts to found missions among the Hopis.

The project of extending Spanish missions from La Pimería Alta to the Moqui province had interested the Jesuits since they had first arrived in Arizona. They had been attempting since Kino's day to extend their work beyond the Gila, but had greatly underestimated the distance to the Hopi villages and therefore did not truly under-stand the distance to New Mexico. Furthermore, both the Franciscans in New Mexico and the Jesuits in Arizona wanted to control the Hopi mission field, resulting in a dispute between the two orders. The Jesuits also realized that the Gila basin was a natural route for overland communication with California and hoped it would provide a connection between their mission fields. The Franciscans considered the Hopis to be a link with New Mexico.

Because of various arguments put forth by the Jesuits, the king in 1719 approved their request to minister to the Hopis. However, the difficulties of reaching the field and a lack of manpower prevented action by the Jesuits until the royal order was re-newed in 1741. Padre Ignacio Keller traveled up to the Gila in 1745 in an attempt to penetrate the country northward, was attacked by the Apaches, had one of his soldier guards killed, lost most of his horses and supplies, and was forced to return. In the same year Padre Jacobo Sedelmayr of Tubutama arrived at the Gila by way of Sonoita and set out to find the Hopis. He reached the Gila in the region of Casa Grande, but the Indians there refused to guide him northward on a direct course. Sedelmayr therefore went down the river on the north bank, exploring the Big Bend area for the first time, and crossed over to the Colorado.

Father Sedelmayr left the Gila at a warm spring called Agua Caliente and saw another spring called San Rafael Otaigui where the trail struck the Colorado, perhaps near modern Ehrenberg. He went up the river near the junction of another "río azul" (probably Bill Williams Fork) and learned that the Moquis were not more than two or three days' journey away, having frequent trade with the Colorado tribes. But the padre decided not to continue and returned southward.

In 1744 a new royal cedula had called for more information from the Franciscans and Jesuits about where the Moquis actually were. As a result, a new royal cedula of November 23, 1745, put the Franciscans of New Mexico in charge, although they did not follow up on their mandate until after the expulsion of the Jesuits in 1767. In the meantime, Father Sedelmayr made two more entradas to try to reach the Hopis in 1748 and 1750. In the first, from Tubutama, he reached the Gila at a point near the ranchería called San Felipe Uparch and went down the river, noting the painted rocks at the point where in 1744 he had turned off to the northwest. Here he named the warm spring ranchería Santa María del Agua Caliente and noted that it was a fine site for a mission.

Father Sedelmayr then remained on the northern bank of the Gila traveling toward Yuma country. Apparently the Yumas were unfriendly; it had been a year of drought and none of the Cocomaricopa tribes were in a mood to accept visitors. The padre's second tour was made at the end of 1750, when he traveled farther down the Colorado to the Quimac or Quiquima rancherías. Since he found the natives to be hostile, he returned to Tubutama across the desert by way of Sonoita.

FATHER GARRUCHO AT GUEVAVI

Father Joseph Garrucho, born Giuseppe Garrucio on the Island of Sardinia on March 27, 1712, entered the Society of Jesus in January 1731 and sailed for Spain from the port of Alghero, Sardinia, in late October 1740. Once in Spain he awaited transportation to the New World. Father Garrucho and twenty fellow Jesuits finally sailed on the *San Francisco* in 1744 only to be captured by English pirates. Since the Spaniards were close to the north coast of Cuba, almost within sight of land, the English decided to put the Jesuit passengers ashore. Fathers Garrucho and a companion landed in Puerto del Príncipe (today Camagüey) and were welcomed by the residents for a twenty-day ministry. The two then set out for Havana and booked passage to the mainland.

After meeting his superiors in Mexico City, Father Garrucho was sent to meet Father Keller on the Sonoran frontier in 1745. Once acquainted, the two priests traveled to Guevavi where they saw little more than an adobe house, a roughly built church, chicken coops, and a corral. Father Garrucho was nevertheless filled with optimism and began to minister to the Indians' needs, providing baptism, instruction, marriage rites, and Christian burial. On May 5, Father Garrucho made his first entry in the mission register as resident padre, noting the death of a girl servant formerly employed by Captain Urrea. The next day he performed a marriage and on the seventh, baptized four children. Juanico Cipriano Cavosstuitoc, then native governor of Guevavi, served as godfather for one of the children.

Father Garrucho soon experienced some of the problems faced by his predecessors. Almost immediately, all but two houseboys and a settler deserted the mission. Captain Pedro Vicente de Tagle Bustamante, and a detachment of soldiers from the presidio of San Felipe at Terrenate came to the mission to find and punish the Pimas. Father Garrucho protested against force, using instead gifts and flattery to convince the Indians to return. When they came back, they remained friendly but began to die from illness. Measles and smallpox, the twin scourges of the missions, caused continual deaths. In October 1747, Father Joseph returned from Bac to find ten children dead, all of whom he buried in his church. Nevertheless, he continued to recruit more Pimas from the surrounding territories, and to lose more to disease.

Father Garrucho seemed to get along well with the residents of the district, even though it was a constant battle to keep the Spaniards from encroaching upon Indian lands. It was especially difficult since the Jesuits controlled the best land available and the settlers had problems in obtaining enough of their own for cultivation. They later claimed that the priests had turned the area into their private domain.

Don Joachin de Casares, a master builder from Arispe helped Father Garrucho plan the building of a new mission church. The new structure, about fifteen by fifty feet, was built by native laborers on the edge of the mesa. Mud mortar provided the foundation and the walls were of sun-dried adobe three feet thick, plastered with mud, whitewashed, and finally decorated inside in various colors. A door through the west wall of the church led to a patio enclosed on the other three sides by rooms containing quarters for Father Joseph, the Indian school, a kitchen, a refectory, and whatever storage and other rooms space permitted. Although the work proceeded slowly, the new church was finally completed.

FATHER FRANCISCO XAVIER PAUER

Franz Pauer, a Moravian born in the town of Brno in Czechoslovakia on January 6, 1721, joined the Society of Jesus in October 1737. He studied at the Jesuit College of Olomouc in Father Keller's hometown, and left there on the first of February 1749. He reached the Jesuit hospice at Cadiz in early May where he remained for more than one year. Coincidentally, he was in the southern port at the same time as a group of Franciscans, including Father Junípero Serra, who were also awaiting departure for Mexico. Pauer sailed for Veracruz on June 16, 1750, and disembarked in late August. After a short stay in Mexico City, he set out on muleback in the company of ten other Jesuits along the coastal route from Guadalajara to Sinaloa, a difficult journey at best. He was assigned to relieve Father Garrucho at San Xavier de Bac early in 1751.

During the last week in May 1751, Father Pauer baptized eight children at San Ignacio and then rode up to San Xavier to become that mission's first resident priest in fifteen years. Unfortunately, Father Pauer reestablished missionary work at Bac on the eve of a major nativistic movement among the Northern Piman Indians. The crisis arose in part from competition between clerics and civil-military officials jealous for control of native labor and because Indian resentment over the Spanish intrusion had been building up for several years. The outbreak of hostilities became known as the Pima Revolt of 1751.

MISSION PROGRESS IN BAJA CALIFORNIA

In the meantime, Jesuit missions in Baja California had made considerable progress. Despite an uprising in 1735 on the southern peninsula, the fathers had continued to found missions to the north and south of the presidio and mission at Nuestra Señora de Loreto. There was some communication across the Gulf of California, or Sea of Cortés, but the crossing was generally difficult. For this reason, the Jesuits continued to move northward with hopes of joining their brethren via an overland route.

Father Fernando Consag, a native of Hungary, arrived in Baja California in 1732 and embarked upon a remarkable career of missionary work and exploration centered at Mission San Ignacio, about forty miles inland from present-day Santa Rosalia. Father Consag, in an attempt to communicate with the missions of Arizona, journeyed overland to the upper Gulf coasts as far as the mouth of the Colorado River in 1746. His party discovered the Bay of Los Angeles and recommended its use as a port of supply from the mainland. The bay was just north of the dreaded Salsipuedes ("get out if you can") area of the Channel Islands. Consag's diary and accompanying map gave a detailed description of this portion of the Gulf and once again confirmed the findings of Ulloa, Kino, and Ugarte. His report showed the feasibility of an overland connection with Arizona, but the Pima Revolt of 1751 made communication virtually impossible at this time. In 1753 Consag made a new exploration of the western coast to about 30° north latitude in the company of Captain Fernando de Rivera y Moncada, the newly appointed commandant of the presidio of Loreto. Still, the overland journey to Yuma remained difficult and impractical.

A CONFLICT BEGINS: GOVERNOR DIEGO ORTIZ PARRILLA

Diego Ortiz Parrilla, appointed governor and captain-general of the provinces of Sonora and Sinaloa on June 23, 1749, had a long career of service. He fought Apaches on the northern frontier of New Spain beginning in 1750. Ranking as a captain, he successively commanded the presidios of San Saba, Texas, and Santa Rosa. Promoted to lieutenant colonel, he served with the Veracruz dragoon regiment prior to serving in Sonora. After supervising construction of the San Miguel de Horcasitas (Pitic) post, he led an expedition against hostile Seri Indians on Tiburon Island and on the Gulf of California coast. To campaign against these Indians, who objected to their lands being given to Spaniards at Pitic, Ortiz Parrilla recruited Northern Piman warriors. They were led by Spanish-speaking Luis Oacpicagigua of Santa Gertrudis del Saric, a mission located at the headwaters of the Altar River.

The Pimans fought so well that they returned home feeling less awe for the Spaniards than they had before and, rewarded by the military authorities for their contributions to the Seri campaign, felt less inclined to follow the Jesuits authoritarian rule. The padres, on the other hand, were upset to find that Governor Ortiz Parrilla had given the ambitious Luis Oacpicagigua the title captain-general of all the Pimas without consulting them. The Jesuits had for months expressed concern that the governor's flattery of the Indians would make them difficult to control.

As a part of the annual fall offensive against the Apaches in 1751, a contingent of Pimas joined with the soldiers of the San Phelipe de Terrenate presidio on a campaign to search and destroy hostile Indians down the Río San Pedro and back through the Chiricahua Mountains. Luis Oacpicagigua set forth with a large band of warriors and passed through the mission of Guevavi, where Father Joseph fed them for three days. When the warriors were ready to leave, Garrucho sent them on their way with fifteen head of mission cattle. When the Indians reached Soamca, their reception was less cordial. Father Keller, instead of offering praise to the Indians, apparently insulted Luis and ill feelings began to fester.

On September 29, 1751, a great fiesta was held at Guevavi to honor San Miguel. The new church was filled to overflowing. Most of the residents, including Don Nicolás de Romero and his family, Miguel Valenzuela, recently retired from the Terrenate garrison, and Juan Manuel Ortiz from the mining camp of Aguacaliente, attended. In addition, Don Gabriel Antonio de Vildosola, son of Don Agustín, former governor of Sonora, was there. Vildosola, born in the Basque town of Villares in 1722, had come to the New World with his father and was owner of the nearby hacienda de Santa Barbara. Also attending were Father Juan Nentuig, a Bohemian Jesuit assigned to Saric, Father Francisco Xavier Pauer from San Xavier del Bac, and others.

In the midst of the celebration, an Indian known as Pedro Chihuahua, who considered himself the right-hand man of Luis, came looking for the padres. He was carrying the vara of the sergeant major of the Pima nation that had been given to him by Governor Ortíz Parrilla without the knowledge of the padres. Father Garrucho either told Pedro that he was not authorized to parade around with the vara and took it away, warning the Indian that if he set foot in Guevavi again he would receive 100 lashes. Pedro was not happy with this treatment.

THE PIMA REVOLT OF 1751

On November 21, 1751, the Sunday activities of Mission Guevavi were interrupted by the arrival of Juan de Figueroa, mission foreman at Tubac, who had been beaten almost to death by furious Indians. The natives of Guevavi grabbed their weapons and fled while they could, paying no attention to Father Garrucho. Don Antonio de Rivera, a settler who happened to be in Guevavi that day, rode out with a dozen others to Arivaca to be met by about 200 menacing Indians, only to find that Juan María Romero, the mission foreman, Joseph de Nava, and several others were dead. The natives throughout the region had become disillusioned with Jesuit activities.

Before Indians at San Xavier del Bac decided to revolt, Father Pauer received a warning from the native governor and escaped with his Spanish foreman and three or four soldiers stationed at the mission. At Tucson, the natives debated for several days before committing themselves to the rebel cause. Warnings were sent to Father Keller at Soamca, and he passed the news on to Father Stiger at San Ignacio, which became an armed camp. The worst news was that Luis Oacpicagigua, who had changed his last name to Bacquioppa, meaning "enemy of adobe houses," had allied himself with the Apaches and that Jesuit Fathers Tomas Tello at Caborca and Henry Ruhen at Sonoita had already been martyred. Father Garrucho prepared to abandon the mission at Guevavi. He would never return, and in fact was blamed by Governor Ortiz Parrilla for causing the rebellion. Seeking asylum at the presidio of San Phelipe de Terrenate, the refugees learned that Pedro Chihuahua had been executed by Don Pedro Menocal, captain of Fronteras.

Once they learned that their padre was not coming back, the natives of Guevavi split up. Some joined Luis, while others merely went into the mountains. In December 1751 bands of natives ransacked the padre's house, smashed the *santos*, killed the chickens and pigeons, and did as much damage as they could. San Xavier del Bac suffered a similar or worse fate. Finally Governor Ortiz Parrilla realized that Luis was not the loyal supporter that he had previously thought, although he court-martialed Captain Menocal for executing Pedro Chihuahua without direct orders. He sent out a peace mission to Luis, who was willing to talk after losing a fight to eighty-six Spaniards in early January 1752. His conditions for peace included the removal of Father Keller from La Pimería and having Father Garrucho, then serving the Opatas at Oposura, return the Pima houseboys he had taken with him.

On March 18, 1752, Luis Oacpicagigua arrived alone at Tubac, where the governor's representative, Captain Joseph Díaz del Carpio and his men were camped. He surrendered, and forty of the former rebels appeared at Tubac while more than 100 returned to Sonoita. Others returned to Guevavi, but they resisted the return of a missionary. The governor decided that the Jesuits were to blame and summoned several settlers to testify against them. The Jesuits, who knew that the settlers had been threatened with banishment to San Juan de Ulua, concluded that the governor was a man of little character who had a deep dislike of the Jesuits. The priests blamed Ortiz Parrilla for giving Luis so much power that he considered himself the rightful owner of everything in La Pimería Alta. Only after he was made captain-general did he begin to plot against the padres.

After a thorough investigation, the Spaniards concluded that the Pimas generally desired mission life, especially the cattle herds and the religious rituals considered as curing techniques, but the Jesuits could not keep up with their demands. The situation also benefitted from relatively limited contact with other Spaniards, who remained at the extreme southern part of the Pima area. It was mainly in the south that Pimas experienced forced labor and left the area. At any rate, the hostility toward the Spaniards was not great and a favorable attitude toward the missions prevailed. Because the Upper Pimas did not constitute a tribal unity and because the mission program affected the Pimas in an irregular manner, there was no widespread conformity. Since it took nearly fifty years for mission activities to reach as far as San Xavier del Bac, there was a very uneven acculturation, with some Pimas in intensive contact since 1687 and others with practically no contact at all. Because of better living conditions near a mission center, some of the Pápagos from the poorer desert areas chose to join the program.

PRESIDIO AT TUBAC, 1752

As soon as Governor Ortiz Parrilla had received news of the revolt, he requested authorization to recruit and equip a new frontier garrison to control the northern Pimas.

Fig. 7.2. Tubac ruins. Courtesy Arizona Historical Society/Tucson. 5512.

By the spring of 1752, he received the authority and raised a company of fifty men who took up temporary quarters in Santa Ana, a Spanish settlement south of San Ignacio. They waited while the governor held a meeting of military officers and veteran missionaries Sedelmayr, Segesser, and Stiger at San Ignacio to choose the best site. They favored one site on the Río Santa Cruz and another on the Río Altar. Father Sedelmayr considered Tucson, a place with abundant water and pasture, some four or five leagues north of San Xavier del Bac as a prime location. An additional military presence would prevent problems among the northern Pimas and nearby Pápagos. Father Segesser favored Tucson for the same reasons and because the presidio could control the rancherías of the Apaches farther upstream and in the nearby mountains.

The governor finally chose Tubac on the west bank of the Río Santa Cruz in early June 1752. The presidio was founded by Captain Juan Tomas Belderrain as the Real Presidio de San Ignacio de Tubac sometime after the governor's decision, although the date of actual construction is unknown. The garrison apparently had moved to Tubac by March 1753, when natives in the area whose lands had been taken for the presidial soldiers moved to Tumacácori, one league south of Tubac on the same side of the river. The new mission visita of San José de Tumacácori was dedicated with suitable pomp on March 19, 1753. The old village of San Cayetano which Kino had known on the east side of the river was abandoned. Some residents apparently moved to Tucson, and that area began to rival Bac in population.

The presidio of Tubac, situated on a low rise in the Santa Cruz valley, featured high walls and enclosed dwelling places built of adobe blocks. On one side was a corral for the horses that regulations required to be ready for immediate action. Above the presidio and on the east were the Santa Rita Mountains. Directly to the west were those of

Tumacácori, and even though this was high desert country, the mountains were often capped with snow during the harsh winters. There were four roads leading to the presidio—one went south to the mission at Tumacácori and from there to central Sonora. The one to the north ran to the mission of San Xavier del Bac and the little settlement of Tucson. The road to the east went only as far as a small mission visita at Sonoita, and the road to the west led over the mountains and then south to the settlements of Tubutama and Altar in Sonora.

RETURN OF FATHER PAUER

While the Jesuits were deciding upon replacements for the Pima mission, Father Keller filled in during 1753, looking after three missions and two presidios. Early in December, Keller baptized Juan Antonio, the son of Captain Belderrain and Doña María Theresa Butron Prudhom y Muxica, the daughter of Baron Prudhom, formerly of Arizonac. The godparents were Don Gabriel Antonio de Vildosola and his wife Doña Gregoria de Anza, sister of Juan Bautista de Anza the younger and Francisco de Anza.

The new interim governor Don Pablo de Arce y Arroyo had complied with the viceroy's orders to preserve maximum harmony with the Jesuit fathers and had begun to listen to requests that priests return to the frontier. Ironically, Luis Oacpicagigua himself appeared in November 1753 to ask for a missionary. He said that Caborca and Guevavi were ready to receive a missionary but that San Xavier del Bac was still unfit because there was no church, no house, and no harvest. The governor assured Luis that he would write to Father Visitor Carlos de Roxas immediately to see what could be done. He also alerted Captain Belderrain to the possibility that Father Pauer might soon be back at Guevavi.

Father Keller told the Indians on December 8, the fiesta of the Immaculate Conception, that their priest would arrive soon. When Father Pauer arrived in late December, he was surrounded by the Indians who had rejected him just two years before. Pauer, who had studied in Father Keller's hometown, must have felt a comradeship with the older padre and hoped that his career would span as many years. On New Year's Day 1754, Pauer began a visit to his large area, first baptizing thirty-four Pima children at Tubac, twenty-nine of whom had been brought by their parents from San Xavier del Bac. He christened another twenty-eight children at Tucson, four at Tubac, ten at Guevavi and by the end of the week had baptized ninety-nine natives, two fewer than Garrucho during his first three years.

Work proceeded well for Father Pauer at Guevavi in the spring of 1754 until he heard reports that Luis Oacpicagigua was fanning the flames of rebellion once again. Bands of Pimas were wearing Apache war caps, stealing stock, and murdering settlers. Governor Arce y Arroyo and Father Visitor Roxas hastened north to assess the threat. They called a meeting at San Ignacio attended by Jesuits Pauer from Guevavi, Keller from Soamca, Luis Vivas from Tubutama, Stiger from San Ignacio, and Ildefonso Espinosa, a new man on his way to Caborca. Espinosa, 34 years old, would later be sent to the north. Also present were the frontier captains of Sonora—Belderrain of Tubac, Elías González of Terrenate, and Vildosola of Fronteras. Two suspects were brought in for questioning—Luis Oacpicagigua of Saric, who insisted that he had been a good Indian, and Luis of Pitic, who said that he had not only been good but had also helped to rebuild the burned churches and returned stolen furnishings.

While the suspects were in jail, Luis of Pitic tried to commit suicide but was saved just in time. He said he knew his crimes were bad and the Devil had told him to end his life. He confessed that he and Luis Oacpicagigua had fought together in the Seri campaign and that the latter had plotted revenge against the Spaniards for the killing of Pimas at El Tupo in 1695. He said that after the 1751 revolt, Oacpicagigua had not been content with the amnesty and was planning further rebellion. The Spaniards decided that jail was the best place for both Luises.

Pauer Goes to Tucson

For Father Pauer, the journey to Tucson, the northernmost part of his territory, was difficult. He baptized forty-three persons in Bac and Tucson in August 1754 but could not return to Bac until February 1755. In the meantime, Pauer had gone to Mission Nuestra Señora de la Asunción de Arispe located on a plateau west of the Bacanuche River. Here, he made his final profession before Father Rector Carlos de Roxas on February 2, the feast of the Purification of the Blessed Virgin. After his visit to Bac in 1755, Pauer returned to Guevavi and was found at Tubac to baptize the son of Captain Belderrain on March 19, the day of San José. The baby was called Joseph Antonio, the same as the previous baby born just sixteen months earlier and who must have died. Father Pauer became the boy's godfather.

After 1755, Tucson and Bac cease to be mentioned in Guevavi's records because a resident missionary was finally appointed in mid-April. Ildefonso Ignacio Benito Espinosa, born on February 1, 1720 in the Canary Islands, entered the Society of Jesus and traveled to New Spain in 1750. He was sent first to Caborca, then to San Ignacio to regain his health, and finally to San Xavier del Bac. He apparently did not stay long at Bac on his first trip because it was reported in mid-1756 that Espinosa had charge of Cocospera Mission while Father Pauer still cared for both Guevavi and Bac.

GOVERNOR OF SONORA JUAN ANTONIO DE MENDOZA, 1755

A new governor had been appointed for Sonora in the summer of 1755. He was Colonel Don Juan Antonio de Mendoza, an energetic Castilian who planned to defeat the Seris, Apaches, and rebel Pimas and move the missionary frontier further to the north. Colonel Mendoza toured the area and planned to install Espinosa at San Xavier del Bac in 1756. Already rumors were spreading that the Gila River Chief Jabanimo intended to rebel with some Pápagos. Father Pauer traveled north to tell the native leader to reassure the authorities of his peaceful intentions. Pleading that he was too old to make the journey, Jabanimo sent one of his sons to declare the rumors false. The son admitted that some Pápagos at Ati wanted to take advantage of Jabanimo's leadership of the powerful Gileño Pima tribal army to avoid moving; Espinosa may have been pressing the desert dwellers to migrate to his Santa Cruz river mission to make up population losses there. Jabanimo's son said that his father would not accede to the wishes of those from Ati.

Conditions then seemed under control until the annual harvest festival in October 1756. Espinosa evidently tried to terminate native ritual elements and restrain the Pimas from holding their customary dances and festivities, including the ritual intoxication to bring rain. The natives at Tucson and Bac bitterly resented Espinosa's attempt to change their centuries-old aboriginal religious rites and beliefs, so they went to war thinking that they could remove Father Espinosa and destroy the mission at San Xavier.

Spanish accounts attribute the violence of 1756 to the Gila River Chief Jabanimo. One report stated that Jabanimo assaulted the mission of Bac with his band of rebel Pimas and was aided by the Indians of the pueblo itself. They sacked the padre's house and tried to kill Espinosa, who managed to escape with his life. Ensign Juan María de Oliva rode to the rescue with fifteen soldiers from Tubac, and Colonel Mendoza quickly organized a punitive expedition of soldiers from the various presidios. With Captain Elías González from Terrenate as his second in command, he rode north during November through San Ignacio, where he acquired the services of a chaplain, Father Bernardo Middendorff, a Jesuit from Westphalia.

FATHER BERNARDO MIDDENDORFF, 1756

Father Middendorff belonged to a large reinforcement of forty-two Jesuits who had left Spain on Christmas Day 1755 and arrived in New Spain on March 19, 1756. Shortly after reaching Mexico City, Middendorff set out from the capital and spent four months on the road to Sonora, where he and his companions suffered from a painful diarrhea. After spending three weeks at Matape to recover, they proceeded to Ures and Middendorff continued on to San Ignacio to become the chaplain for Mendoza's expedition. Picking up Espinosa at Tubac on their way north, they reinstated him at San Xavier. From there Mendoza followed the enemy's tracks to the banks of the Gila. After an indecisive battle, they returned to San Xavier del Bac and finally to San Ignacio.

Father Middendorff became the first Jesuit to live north of San Xavier del Bac in the Tucson area. Beginning in January 1757, Middendorff worked to extend Spanish control to the northern limits of the frontier. Accompanied by ten soldiers, the German Jesuit contacted the northern Pimas living scattered in the brush and hills in their traditional rancherías. Seventy families were attracted to a mission setting by gifts of dried meat, and the prospective converts included a few Christians who had been baptized at Bac by Espinosa. Middendorff had considerable difficulty communicating with his prospective charges because he had not, as had previous German Jesuits, learned the Piman language at San Ignacio before attempting a major conversion. He had to instruct the natives through an interpreter. In addition, Middendorff had barred the Indians from their vices, of nightly dancing and carousing. Finally, one night in May, he reported that 500 heathen Indians attacked his village and destroyed everything. Middendorff was lucky to escape with his life to Guevavi, and Tucson once again reverted to the status of a visita of San Xavier del Bac under the charge of Espinosa. Meanwhile, south of Tubac, Father Pauer with more success had completed a new adobe church at Tumacácori measuring about sixty by twenty feet and served the residents of the area for over sixty years.

Despite its failure, Middendorff's five-month effort did bring the Tucson people into daily contact with the Spanish soldiers and a missionary. It gave them a fuller understanding of daily mass, baptism, marriage, and last rites. Upon his departure, the northern Pimas could settle into a more relaxed frame of mind with the option of traveling to Bac if need be where, despite serious illness, Father Espinosa continued to serve until his transfer to Caborca and Ati in 1765.

Changes in Personnel

Upon serving nearly three decades on New Spain's northern frontier, Father Keller, after tending a dying Pima, passed away sometime after mid-August. On September 7, 1759, Captain Juan Tomás Belderrain died at Guevavi, just five weeks after the birth of a daughter. Named Father Rector of La Pimería Alta by his superiors, Father Pauer was transferred to San Ignacio and his replacement, a thin and ailing Jesuit named Miguel Gerstner arrived at Guevavi.

Miguel Gerstner, a native of Evenshausen in the southwestern German duchy of Franconia was born on March 17, 1723, and admitted to the Society of Jesus in July 1744. After serving in the Jesuit province of the Upper Rhine River, he volunteered for the Spanish missions. Continually ill from the time of his arrival in La Pimería Alta, Gerstner found life on the Sonoran frontier difficult and not always rewarding. His first entry into the mission books at Guevavi recorded a burial on January 12, 1760, and Father Pauer's last was dated January 15. The two priests must have had some time to discuss problems of mutual concern.

Shortly after his arrival, Father Gerstner rode north to investigate the death of Eusebio of Tumacácori at the hands of revengeful Pimas. When he arrived at Tumacácori, he had to speak through his interpreter but was nevertheless able to take care of the native needs. He christened four children and married three couples. Then, instead of returning to the safety of Guevavi, the determined Jesuit rode to Sonoita, his most distant visita and baptized six children, three of whose parents lived in the San Xavier-Tucson area. The native governor, Gregorio, stood as godfather for a little boy, and Lieutenant Joseph Romero, Gerstner's escort, accepted the same responsibility for a Nixora. His duties complete, the padre rode back to Guevavi and must have felt considerable success at having ridden over his entire territory without incident.

─── *Chapter Seven* ───
Bibliographic Essay

Primary sources for this period are documents from the Archivo General de Indias, *Contratación* and *Guadalajara* and the syntheses provided by John L. Kessell in *Mission of Sorrows: Jesuit Guevavi and the Pimas 1691–1767* (Tucson: University of Arizona Press, 1970) and Francisco Javier Alegre, S.J., in *Historia de la Provincia de la Compañía de Jesús de Nueva España* (Rome: Institutum Historicum, 1956–1960). Also important are Juan Matheo Manje, *Unknown Arizona and Sonora, 1693–1721,* translated by Harry J. Karns and Associates (Tucson: University of Arizona Press, 1954); Henry F. Dobyns, *Spanish Colonial Tucson: A Demographic History* (Tucson: University of Arizona Press, 1976), and James Officer, *Hispanic Arizona, 1536–1856* (Tucson: University of Arizona Press, 1987). The pioneer work of Hubert Howe Bancroft, *History of Arizona and New Mexico, 1530–1888* (San Francisco: The History Company, 1889) gives a good summary of the period while Peter Masten Dunne, ed. and trans., *Jacobo Sedelmayr: Missionary, Frontiersman, Explorer in Arizona and Sonora* and *Juan Antonio Balthasar, Padre Visitador to the Sonora Frontier, 1744–1745* (Tucson: Arizona Pioneers' Historical Society, 1955 and 1957) offer detailed glimpses into Jesuit activities.

Theodore Treutlein has edited and translated *Missionary in Sonora: The Travel Reports of Joseph Och, S.J. 1755–1767* (San Francisco: California Historical Society, 1965) as well as Ignaz Pfefferkorn's *Sonora: A Description of the Province* (Albuquerque: University of New Mexico Press, 1949). John A. Donohue, *After Kino: Jesuit Missions in Northwestern New Spain 1711–1767* (Rome and St. Louis: Jesuit Historical Institute, 1969) and Ernest J. Burrus, ed. *Misiones Norteñas Mexicanas de la Compañía de Jesús 1751–1757* (Mexico: Antigua Librería Robredo, 1963) are significant along with Russell C. Ewing, "The Pima Outbreak in November, 1751," *New Mexico Historical Review*, 13 (October 1963):337–46 and "Investigations into the Causes of the Pima Uprising of 1751," *Mid-America*, 23 (October 1938):138–51.

For New Mexico during this time period is Alfred Barnaby Thomas, ed. and trans., *The Plains Indians and New Mexico, 1751–1778: A Collection of Documents Illustrative of the History of the Eastern Frontier of New Mexico* (Albuquerque: University of New Mexico Press, 1940); Donald Cutter, "An Anonymous Statistical Report on New Mexico in 1765" in *NMHR*, 50 (October 1975):347–52; and Henry W. Kelly, "Franciscan Missions of New Mexico, 1740–1760," 15/16 (October 1940; January and April 1941):345–68; 41–69; 148–83. See also Russell M. Magnaghi, "Plains Indians in New Mexico: The Genízaro Experience," *Great Plains Quarterly*, 10 (Spring 1990):86–95.

For Baja California, the most complete one-volume work is Harry Crosby, *Antigua California: Mission and Colony on the Peninsular Frontier 1697–1768* (Albuquerque: University of New Mexico Press, 1993). A number of individual stories are contained in the Baja California Travel Series published in Los Angeles by Dawson's Books during the past several decades. See, for example, Ernest J. Burrus, trans. and ed., *Wenceslaus Linck's Diary of His 1766 Expedition to Northern Baja California* published in 1966. For Upper California, see Donald Cutter, "Plans for the Occupation of Upper California: A New Look at the 'Dark Age' from 1602–1769," *Journal of San Diego History*, 24 (winter 1978):78–90.

PRELUDE TO CHANGE:
THE MID-EIGHTEENTH CENTURY

PUEBLO AUXILIARIES IN NEW MEXICO

*T*hroughout the eighteenth century, Indians constantly contributed to the stabilization and pacification of the Spanish Empire in America. In New Mexico, Spain's northernmost province, Pueblo Indian support of Spanish control, especially through their service as military auxiliary troops, helped reconquer, control, and defend the province. Gradually they aided in bringing peace to this remote area. This was done not only actively and directly through military aid, but also indirectly by attracting those tribes that resisted Spanish control, and leading them to the well-established Spanish-Pueblo alliance. This contribution by the Pueblos has not been well understood or sufficiently appreciated by historians or by the general public. The dramatic and destructive Pueblo Revolt and the Reconquest of New Mexico have captured much attention, while the more harmonious aspects of native and Spanish relationships are little known.

The use of auxiliaries was nothing new. During the New World conquest, Spain was quick to make use of Indian allies, perhaps the best example being Cortés and his use of Tlascalans in the conquest of the Aztec capital of Tenochtitlán. Subsequently, more auxiliaries were used, consisting of allies from friendly tribes used against hostile groups. Following the Pueblo Revolt and after restaging at El Paso, friendly Pueblo Indians, many of whom had fled the area of conflict in 1680, aided in the restoration of Spanish control. They were employed during the long years of waiting in El Paso as scouts, guides, interpreters, and finally as soldiers in both the early abortive attempts to rewin New Mexico as well as in the Reconquest under Diego de Vargas.

During that time, increasing numbers of Pueblo Indians rallied under the banner of Vargas, to the point that he was able to employ the ancient Roman tactic of divide and conquer to enhance his chances for success.

Pueblo military parties also conducted their own campaigns independent of Spanish participation. The native troops fought well, usually performing better than their Spanish counterparts. Repeated raids by hostile Indian groups that surrounded the province on all sides made necessary extensive campaigns both to protect existing settlements from attacks and to punish those who had made attacks. Cultural and economic differences between the Spaniards and Pueblos on one hand and the nomadic Indians on the other complicated the situation. The raiders depended upon the productivity of the sedentary people of the Río Grande Valley, and obtained by plundering what they were unable to get by trading. In addition to food and livestock, the invaders took captives from the Pueblos and stole horses and weapons from the Spaniards.

Pueblo Indians could be counted on to report raids or the approach of marauders to local or provincial authorities. Upon receipt of such information, the Spaniards had to determine their course of action, frequently calling top military personnel together to determine what should be done. As time went by, such high-level meetings were considered both time consuming and unnecessary since the course of action was already clear. Campaigns were authorized by the provincial governor who was also the senior military leader. Local Spanish officials working with the Indian leaders recruited the Christian Indians and coordinated the logistics. Usually all auxiliaries from a district were under the overall command of a *capitán mayor a la guerra*. When all troops had finally been brought together, a final review and muster was held at the *plaza de armas*, the rendezvous point, normally the Pueblo nearest the target area. For campaigns against the Utes, it was Taos, Abiquiu, or San Juan. Western campaigns left from Jémez, Laguna, or Zuni; while other rendezvous points were Sandía, Isleta, or Acoma. Pueblo auxiliaries performed various functions, since they constituted about 50 percent of the effective force, but late in the eighteenth century their number reached as high as 85 percent.

Certain reasons can be suggested to explain the satisfactory performance of Pueblo auxiliaries. They knew the terrain, were familiar with much of the culture of the potential enemy, and frequently had a working knowledge of his language. They possessed a great willingness to serve and were most frequently involved in the midst of combat, not showing the least reluctance to participate or to follow orders. Reports from the field and post-action reports cited them for overall competency as well as for their loyalty.

Spanish and Pueblo Unity

Activities such as the close association of Pueblo warriors and tribal leaders with Spanish settlers and soldiers hastened the process of acculturation. Serving as companions in arms and risking their lives side by side reduced a great deal of hostility. The well-developed system of using Pueblo Indian auxiliaries established unity in a province that had known much disunity in the pre–Pueblo Revolt era. With the province's limited resources, Spain could not have controlled New Mexico had not the Pueblos been unified and supportive of Spain's interests. In order to achieve such unity, liberal and meaningful rewards were offered to the Pueblo Indians, including titles, recognition, privileges, gifts, and most important of all—the spoils of battle. The Indians were also trained to ride horseback and to bear arms—another extremely useful reward. Any royal edicts prohibiting such activities were obviously disregarded. Yet there is no official documentary substantiation of local officials either asking for or receiving such a dispensation in favor of the Pueblo Indians. It was something that just occurred normally, a necessity that made legal activities that were not legal under the law. The documentary evidence is clear: the Pueblos were both mounted and armed with guns during the eighteenth century.

One effect of similar Pueblo and Spanish goals was that some formerly hostile tribes gradually joined the alliance, having seen the advantages that accrued to their traditional enemies, the Pueblos. This did not always mean peace on the frontier, but reflected something that had long been evident. The arrival of the European did not bring war, death, and destruction to otherwise peace-loving native people living in harmony with nature and with each other. The real effect was to give certain native groups a new, powerful ally with whose intervention ancient grievances could be rectified. This was the case with other groups who, seeing that chances were poor against their ancient Pueblo enemies now fortified by Spanish help, decided to even the score with other traditional enemies further removed from the Río Grande. It was a system that decreased the number of distinctly enemy Indian nations, but at the same time probably increased the bitterness felt by those left out of the new power bloc. Toward the end of the eighteenth century, Spain actually subsidized her allies by providing them arms, horses, and even cash payments for assistance leading to control of the frontier.

As suggested previously, the Spanish system stepped up cultural interchange between two groups of people. Some of this was in the form of military and cultural borrowing as exemplified by the use of the horse and the gun. Other evidence is easily found in the Pueblo Indian adaptation to agricultural pursuits such as horticulture, including vineyards, orchards, and field crops, as well as a great dedication to sheep raising. Another area of cultural exchange is found in the statistical growth of the Hispanic population, whereas Indian population figures remained almost static. In view of the almost non-existent Spanish migration into the province, it is likely that *mestizaje* was rapidly occurring. Some of this was probably mere detribalization of Indians who later passed as gente de razón. Principally it was the result of intermarriage, mostly of male Spaniards with female Indians, to produce a mestizo race. Many of New Mexico's old Spanish families without doubt have blood ties to native Indians as is evident from their physical and facial features. Being Indian was more a reflection of a way of life than it was genetic. The reverse process, cultural borrowing by the Spaniards from the Indians can be seen in folk medicine, folklore, architecture, and in some of the foods eaten both then and now. A measure of the cultural interchange was found in the close similarity of the economic pursuits of both groups.

On the negative side, there were drawbacks to the utilization of Pueblo auxiliaries. The greatest single weakness was the relative lack of success, with the number of truly successful military campaigns being in the minority. Long delays in getting personnel into action prevented any real retaliatory action against offending groups who by that time had scattered. Delay even resulted in the need to deploy the waiting forces against later attackers rather than against the original targets. Another negative factor was that use of Pueblo Indians against outlying groups probably had the effect of increasing in some of them the hatred that they had for the Spaniards. The system of rewarding Pueblo warriors with booty, and rewards given for captives and for visual evidence in the form of heads and ears, probably led the enemy to choose resistance rather than capitulation.

Yet another drawback was the absence of Indians who were away on campaign at ill-chosen times, leading to decreased attention to harvests and other economic pursuits. Furthermore, it reduced the capacity to defend the pueblo against attacks by either the same enemy or by other enemies. The economic impact was negative in that it drained the pueblos—particularly the one serving as a rendezvous point—of their supplies.

As is often the case with mercenaries, the Pueblo warriors were at times hard to control. Enthusiasm for campaigning was boundless. In cases of counterattack by the enemy, some of the Pueblos reverted to an earlier response pattern, that of fleeing in a disorganized retreat. Even with these drawbacks, the technique of using Pueblo auxiliaries was both practical and pragmatic. Without their assistance the Spaniards would have had little chance for success.

FRENCH TRADERS

As successful as the New Mexican military defense was becoming with the use of auxiliaries, there was a problem that was potentially more menacing to regional security. This was the threat of European intrusion into the isolated frontier. As early as 1719, there were rumors of French trading activity, though it was confined to the Indians of the Great Plains. After a lapse of nearly two decades (which at times were punctuated with anxiety about French intentions), it became clear that the French wanted to open trade with Santa Fe. In 1739 a party of nine French traders arrived unexpectedly in New Mexico. Headed by Pierre and Paul Mallet, the group had set out from Illinois, had picked up the Missouri River and moved south to the Platte, following it to where it emerges from the Rockies. Following southward along the front range of that great cordillera, the small group of Frenchmen entered New Mexico via Raton Pass, and on to Taos and Santa Fe, though they arrived without the merchandise they expected to trade. Received with some caution, the group stayed for many months awaiting a viceregal decision regarding their status. When it came, they were encouraged to depart, though two party members remained behind in Spanish territory. Four others, including the Mallet Brothers, descended the Canadian River, the Arkansas, and the Mississippi, finally arriving at New Orleans. The effect of these first "callers" in New Mexico was to alert local authorities and for them to reissue directives against trade with foreigners. But for the French, this seemed to be an invitation for the opening of trade, particularly since the Mallets reported rich silver mines to exist in New Mexico.

The British, as a result of intercolonial wars, finally eliminated France as a political and economic rival for supremacy in North America. While there, the French had been difficult competitors in trade. First, they had an advantage in better and more attractive goods, items that the Indians wanted. Fur traders coming from the East were more aware of Indian needs, thereby almost instinctively recognizing which items of commerce would have acceptance. A shorter trade line in bringing merchandise for barter assisted the French in keeping more up-to-date in their offerings, whereas the Spanish traders often had merchandise that traded poorly, and they were slow to respond to changes in fashion.

More critical was the Spanish policy, long followed, of not providing effective arms to the Plains Indians. Under extreme pressure, and at times extralegally, some faulty, outdated guns were traded from Spanish sources. But by and large, arms on the Plains were French supplied. Spanish policy was motivated by a realization that arms supplied one day to friendly Indians, might by unfavorable changes in circumstances, be turned back on the suppliers, an idea apparently not equally clear to French and English traders. Also, the French brought merchandise out to the Indians, whereas the much less numerous and less mobile Spanish traders, being more aloof, often waited for Indian groups to come to the New Mexican frontier towns to carry out barter. As a result, French fur traders frequently obtained the cream of the crop. Finally, Spain had much more limited markets for fine furs and even for the coarser ones, since their trade route lay directly to the south and its warmer climate.

As long as France, by means of roving traders, was present in western North America, Spain needed to engage in the game of Indian trade, poorly equipped as they were to be truly competitive. The full extent and impact of the Indian trade of the eighteenth century is difficult to assess. What is clear is that the frequent European wars, motivated in large measure by dynastic struggles for supremacy, had their distant counterparts in North America. Depending on the lineup for these wars, frontier defense and trade was greatly affected. The climactic struggle as far as French presence in North America was concerned was a war that broke out in 1755 in which Spain and France were united. Known in America as the French and Indian War, its concluding treaty signed at Paris in 1763 eliminated France from North America and turned over to Spain all French holdings west of the Mississippi, though some inhabitants were reluctant to switch their allegiance. French residents remained despite cessation of French political control, with the result that many, especially frontiersmen, became Spanish. With them Spain inherited the trade contacts that the French had carefully developed earlier in the century. It then became acceptable for these Frenchmen (now Spaniards) to engage in commercial relations with the Indians, with the newly founded city of St. Louis as the depot for the changing market.

The Search for Silver, 1765

With the French no longer a threat, Spanish attention was turned to an area previously unexplored—northwestern New Mexico. As a result of a small incident around 1765, great interest was generated in a search for silver in northern New Mexico. At the recently founded, mostly genízaro frontier outpost of Santa Rosa y Santo Tomás de Abiquiu, a Ute Indian had come to town bearing a small ingot of silver that he had traded to the village blacksmith José Manuel Trujillo. Rumor was that the ingot had come from a place where in otherwise sterile land silver could be extracted by digging with minimum effort. The Ute's piece of metal may not have been large, but was of sufficient size that the blacksmith had fashioned of it two rosaries and a crucifix. If silver were thus available, perhaps the Indians could be persuaded to divulge the location of such a potential bonanza to traders who might bring interesting goods to them. As a result of some fact and some rumor, Abiquiu became the center of preparations for a northwestern sortie. None of the over 600 local residents could have been oblivious to the excitement in the air in late June 1765. Some of the leading residents were preparing for a new adventure, hoping to find mineral wealth that had eluded Vázquez de Coronado, Espejo, Chamuscado, and Oñate. A search for wealth, an occupation discarded for many decades, was to be revived. Any such trip had to be officially sanctioned, although there is some evidence that local traders had made occasional unlicensed contacts at an even earlier date.

Juan María Antonio Rivera Searches for Silver

An existing decree mandated that no citizen nor Indian, nor any other class of people could enter Indian country without a specific license from New Mexico's governor, who at that time was Tomás Vélez Cachupín. But from the Palace of the Governors in Santa Fe, Cachupín had granted the necessary permission, and there is some possibility that he himself was invested in the effort, even though this would have been illegal. The group was a mere handful of men mounted on their best horses and led by their resourceful commander Juan María Antonio Rivera, a civilian. As companions, Rivera had Gregorio Sandoval—who was possibly associated with the much better known Domínguez-Escalante expedition a decade later into the same general area—Antonio Martín, Andrés Sandoval, and a Ute interpreter by the name of Joaquín or Juachinillo. It is curious that the Indian was a member of the party since two years earlier in an important legal case, he had been accused of witchcraft, a not uncommon accusation of that period. Juachinillo's transgression was that by sorcery he had upset the stomach of the local Franciscan missionary, and his suspect status as a warlock was worsened by his social and legal status as a genízaro.

Rivera, for reasons explained later, did not carry out a single expedition, but rather two in the same year. As the party went along they bestowed place names to salient spots, some of which became permanent. After several days of travel, on July 3 the party arrived at the Río de los Pinos, still so called. Ancient Anasazi ruins of advanced Indian culture bore mute testimony of a civilization long past but not yet obliterated. Of even greater interest to the explorers was what appeared to have been a retort for purifying metals, which the explorers hoped had been for gold reduction. They loaded some of the burned adobes on their pack animals as physical evidence of their discovery.

Next, Rivera and his party moved to the Río Flórido and the Río de las Animas (both still so named). At the former they again found remnants of ancient civilization and at the latter they found the ranchería of the principal Ute chief Coraque, who was accompanied by three of his subordinate captains. Dealing with Indian leaders normally required established formalities; in this case preliminaries involved bestowing of gifts—tobacco, maize, and *pinole*—which was followed by questions and explanations. The Spaniards told Chief Coraque that they were looking for a Ute Indian who, when he had been to Abiquiu, had promised to divulge the sources of silver and other metals. This Indian, Cuero de Lobo, was unavailable, reported to have gone off to see his mother-in-law in the land of the Payuchis (the Southern Piaute), located to the west.

The party continued on to the Dolores River where the members were told that if they returned later in the year the silver deposits would be shown to them. With a mixture of hope for the future and disappointment with the present, the explorers broke camp on the Dolores and headed back to Abiquiu without any silver, but with reports of an immense river far ahead of their maximum point of penetration. Thus ended phase one of the 1765 exploration.

The hot days of summer had given way to the crispness of autumn, and the ancient cottonwoods along the Chama River at Abiquiu were becoming golden when there was renewal of the activity akin to that of three months earlier. Governor Vélez Cachupín had determined to send Rivera and his men back with more specific instructions, including orders to proceed farther than they had in June and July; however, the effort was to be at their own expense of both mounts and supplies.

The Search Continues

The governor wrote precise instructions. Rivera was to seek out the Payuchi Indian who had earlier offered to show the route to the Río del Tizón. This great watercourse (the Colorado River) had not yet been visited on its upper reaches, but was thought to be the same large river that had been given that name on its lower course in 1540 by Melchior Díaz. To ensure native cooperation, Rivera took some tobacco with him and orders to give the Indians no cause for displeasure. These instructions stated that once he had found the Tizón, he was to note the nations that inhabited it on both banks, learn if there were large towns on either side of the river, and ascertain whether or not there were white, bearded strangers dressed in the European manner.

If there were no danger in doing so, some of the party were to cross the Río del Tizón accompanied by the Payuchi, or by the interpreter, as well as by some of those party members who were experienced in trade with the natives. In so doing, it was thought necessary to pretend that they were not Spaniards, nor were they to give reason for anyone to believe that they were there for exploratory purposes, but rather that they were there for customary commerce and trade.

If the Tizón were as wide as the Payuchi said, but nonetheless crossable, the Spaniards were to find out if there were an impassable barrier to further penetration. Moving into the realm of legendary geography of the sixteenth century, the governor asked Rivera's party to determine if the Río del Tizón had its origin in the Great Lake of Copala, which the Pueblo Indians had always called Teguayo. Copala came from the origin myths of the Aztec, and Coronado had heard of Gran Teguayo early in his journey. The viceroy's guess as to the whereabouts of the advanced civilization that they were seeking existed in a north-northwest direction from Santa Fe. He knew that ancient and modern traditions indicated the existence there of a lake surrounded by many large towns, and that the people were ruled by a king or sovereign. He believed that the lake of Copala should be somewhat to the east of the proposed route of Rivera's march.

Since the area as far as the Dolores River was already known, Rivera was ordered to start his journal from that point onward and to omit inconsequential details. A final provision granted the explorers permission to explore the mountains known as La Plata (or La Grulla), later known as the Rocky Mountains, to see if they could find the rich mineral deposits thought to be there in accordance with earlier information. It would be well to check on such Ute stories of virgin silver "in order to stop unfounded rumors." (Ms., Instructions to Rivera, Servicio Historico Militar, Madrid)

Upon arrival at the Río de la Plata, Rivera's party met with their Moache Ute friend, attended by the customary gift giving. Arrangements were made for the services of guides who would lead the party to the Río del Tizón. Though there is a difference of opinion concerning the exact itinerary followed, on October 6, the party possibly crossed from southwestern Colorado into Utah just northeast of Montecello. Doubtless following Indian trails, the directions and distances suggest that the explorers followed Spanish Valley to what is probably Moab, Utah on the banks of the great river. They described the river as very deep and extremely wide, and the Indians substantiated their already established opinion that it was the Tizón.

As an essential, though inchoate, act of sovereignty, Rivera left on the meadow of the great Tizón, on the shoot of a white poplar tree, a large cross with the inscription "Viva Jesús" at its head and his own name and the date at the foot, so their arrival could be verified in the future. Rivera had thus carried out an oft-repeated political ceremony tinged with religious overtones as a requisite for strengthening Spanish claim. Unfortunately, as no immediate follow-up expedition was made to help identify the exact spot of possession taking, only an educated guess can be made (though ten years later there was a feeling by members of an exploratory expedition that they were near the spot where Rivera had taken possession).

Evidence that the local Indians still had great capacity for telling tall tales so associated with the earliest Spanish entries into much of North America, and illustrative of the fact that the Spaniards never ceased to be gullible and eager listeners, a Tabeguachi Ute came forth with a tale rivaling the late sixteenth century stories of Amazons and Patagonians. The informant now added a few more curiosities to the long list that had been earlier sought by European explorers. These were the child-eaters, the universally hated "straw-heads," and the men made of stone. These monstrosities all lay ahead if the Spaniards would first cross the huge river.

Consistent with the earlier stories of the fabulous in the conquest of the Americas, all of these people were formidable potential foes, capable of testing the mettle of the greatly outnumbered visitors. If the explorers continued on, at the end of a six-day, adventure-filled trip, they would find other Spaniards. The danger-infested highway started shortly after crossing the river, for about one day's travel beyond were a "type of people who when there was scarcity in hunting ate their own children for sustenance." (*Rivera's Journal*, Ms., Servicio Historico Militar, Madrid) Beyond them were the "strawheads," characterized by their hair. These were enemies of all the other nations. To pass through their country should take two days, but for safety sake it was better to do so rapidly and by night. Finally, there were to be found at the foot of a small mountain range by the shores of a very large lake the last obstacle, the people who were like rocks "and even more than rocks." The Indian informant capped off his description by saying that from there if one followed along the edge of the mountain range, one would come to the Spaniards who live on the banks of a small stream, and this would be their first town. "They were reported to have houses like the New Mexicans and they were thought to be Spaniards because they spoke the same language as the traders, and were very white, with heavy beards and dressed in buckskin, because they did not have clothing like the Spaniards of New Mexico." (*Rivera's Journal*, Ms., Servicio, Historico Militar, Madrid) If the rest of the Tabeguachi's story had not been so farfetched, it would be interesting to speculate on who the white Spaniards were in that area lying beyond the shining river.

Attempting to follow his orders as closely as possible, Rivera indicated that from the Tizón he was ready to return to Santa Fe. There is a report that Rivera's party, or at least some of them, crossed the river and went a day or two beyond. But for all practical purposes the goal of the Tizón had been achieved and the next thing to do was to return home with the news. But by what route? The 1765 explorers set off upstream eastward after their maximum penetration, doubtless trying to carry out their second-

Fig. 8.1. Parochial church at Arizpe where Juan Bautista de Anza is buried. Photo by Harry W. Crosby.

ary mission concerning elusive silver deposits. Riding two weeks on horseback with lightened loads, they could have covered much ground. If any positive signs of silver had been found, it was perhaps prudent not to commit such a fact to paper for fear of a rush into the area. That a rush did not occur is suggestive that nothing of monetary value was found, despite finds made after American occupation of major silver deposits in the area, or near the area, that they had just explored. It is also true that other activities soon captured the attention of New Mexico's populace, not the least of which were concerns about defense of its frontiers.

Of more lasting significance historically than their failure to find silver in an area rich in that metal, was that Rivera's outbound trip followed what later became part of the Old Spanish Trail from New Mexico into Colorado and Utah—a trail that later connected those areas with California. On this journey Rivera also bestowed several place names, including the San Juan River. Curiously, for a man who had been given an important mission, Rivera disappears from the archival record as abruptly as he appeared. Even his journal, though known to some Franciscans a decade later, also disappeared only to be rediscovered in 1974 in a military archive in Spain.

JUAN BAUTISTA DE ANZA THE YOUNGER

While life in New Mexico was beset with problems of greater importance than the result of Rivera's exploration, farther west significant events were taking place. Picking up the thread of Arizona's unfolding historical development, new personalities had reached the forefront. Early in 1760 there arrived as the new captain of the presidio of Tubac, Don Juan Bautista de Anza, the 24-year-old son of the deceased former captain and friend of the Jesuits. Not only did this young man carry his father's name, but also his ability, courage, solid disposition, rapport with soldiers, and skill with weapons. Born at the Fronteras presidio in 1736, young Anza grew up around soldiers and was a cadet from early adolescence. His grandfather served as lieutenant and captain at Janos presidio in Nueva Vizcaya and his father commanded the garrison at Corodeguachi and Fronteras. Young Anza entered military service at Fronteras in 1753 and became a lieutenant on July 1, 1755. He came to Tubac after five years at Fronteras, serving at the side of his brother-in-law Don Gabriel Antonio de Vildosola, Captain of Fronteras, and well known throughout the entire province. Anza had been trained by the best the Sonoran frontier had to offer.

Anza bought a house at Tubac and moved into it with his widowed mother Doña María Rosa Bezerra Nieto de Anza and immediately set out to fight some Pima rebels who were in the area south of the deserted visita of Arivaca. He soon found fellow soldier Miguel de la Cruz, dead, with his killers standing over him and about to remove his scalp. Anza took quick revenge and killed nine of the Indians including Ciprian, their leader, and son of former enemy Luis Oacpicagigua. After that time the padres of Guevavi had little to fear from the Pimas, but the 1760s would bring renewed warfare from the Apaches.

Frontier stabilization required continued effort, and to that end Jesuit Father Miguel Gerstner continued work on the new church at Guevavi and had the natives build a house at the visita of Calabazas. Baptisms were running ahead of burials and local fiestas were celebrated. A secular priest, Joseph Manuel Díaz del Carpio served off and on at Tubac as a chaplain for the men and signed several entries in the Guevavi baptismal book. His sister, Ana María Pérez Serrano, also visited Tubac from time to time and caught the eye of young Anza. The two were married on June 24, 1761, by Father Carlos de Roxas, who had baptized Juan Bautista twenty-five years before. The couple took up residence at Tubac, but the new Señora de Anza could not convince her brother Joseph Manuel to stay. As a result, Father Gerstner took up the additional duties of serving the garrison and vecinos. He also baptized many babies at Tumacácori, suggesting that it had become, by 1760, the largest and most active village. Unfortunately, the death rate was also high and the native population was declining overall.

FATHER IGNACIO PFEFFERKORN AT GUEVAVI

On May 25, 1761, Father Gerstner left Guevavi and rode over to Saric to begin work there. Though his health had never been good, he had survived. An old friend, Ignacio Pfefferkorn, born in Mannheim near Cologne, on July 31, 1726, the day of San Ignacio, took Gerstner's place at Guevavi. Father Pfefferkorn had shared the trip from Germany to La Pimería Alta with Gerstner and other Jesuits, including Joseph Och. They were given a frightening initiation into missionary life by Father Segesser at the mission of Ures when a band of Indians swept down upon them and pretended to attack. The padres were not amused when thrown to the ground while their mules took to the woods. Father Pfefferkorn, who later wrote a lengthy book on Jesuit activities in Sonora, traveled to Guevavi in hopes of finding purer air and more healthful water than he had found at Ati. He was probably disappointed.

Word soon reached Father Pfefferkorn at Guevavi that the Jesuit father visitor General Ignacio Lizassoain, a native of Pamplona, had begun his inspection of the missions in April 1761. Since the visitor general did not want to travel during the rainy season, he did not reach La Pimería Alta until November, and then did not go to Guevavi. Instead, he traveled to San Ignacio, where he received the other padres of the district. Father Pfefferkorn, after nearly six months at Guevavi, rode the sixty-five miles to San Ignacio to render his report on the mission's progress and potential. He presented the records of baptisms, marriages, and burials, and a census of the native population. He showed that at Guevavi there were 31 families, 5 each of widowers and widows, and 29 *doctrineros*—adults receiving instruction—with their children. Calabazas and Sonoita showed 36 and 34 families respectively with 30 and 19 persons receiving instruction. Tumacácori showed 72 families, 7 widowers, 8 widows, and 40 doctrineros. Unfortunately, there had been a number of deaths at Tumacácori that had gone unrecorded and when Phelipe, the popular native governor died, many of the Pápagos fled the area.

FORCED SOBAIPURI MIGRATION

At San Xavier del Bac, Father Espinosa was suffering a similar problem. Most of his neophytes had deserted him, and only the old and sick remained. The natives of Tucson had abandoned their village. Whether disease or fear of the Apaches had caused them to leave, one thing was certain, the mission area was in trouble. At San Miguel de Horcasitas, Father Visitor Lizassoain discussed the situation with Joseph Tienda de Cuervo, governor of Sonora since mid-January 1761. The governor, a Dutch native in the Spanish royal service, mainly had experience with the Seri Indians who had been driven off the mainland to Tiburon Island. He and Lizassoain reached a decision that was to have tragic consequences. They decided to use colonial troops to force the Sobaipuris to resettle at the existing Jesuit missions. However pious or well-thought-out the decision may have been, the movement actually weakened frontier defense and left the door open for Apache raids, as the Sonorans soon discovered.

The Sobaipuri migration of 1762 did help to assure the eventual biological survival of an aboriginal population in the Tucson area and diversified the social structure of the settlement. Captain Francisco Elías González, commander of the presidio at Terrenate, was ordered to carry out the move. The Sobaipuri migrants had only a limited choice of new homes, settling where Captain Elías would allow them. About thirty settled at Santa Maria Soamca Mission; others moved as close to their aboriginal lands as possible at Sonoita in the highlands west of the San Pedro River. In addition, there was a group of about 250 (although the missionary said 400) that settled in Tucson, where they were assigned adequate fields and water. Father Espinosa was quite ambitious in his plans to integrate the new settlers into life at Tucson and introduced them to sheep and cattle husbandry. The Sobaipuris, however, were not accustomed to this kind of life and failed to look after their cattle. In the following year, Apaches ran off Espinosa's surplus livestock at Bac, reducing his carefully raised herds from nearly 1,000 head to a mere 200.

The decision to move the Sobaipuris from the San Pedro River valley to the missions farther west caused the loss of Espinosa's stock. When they lived along the San Pedro River, they prevented Apache raids as the first line of defense. Their resettlement on the Santa Cruz River at Tucson made that previously protected area the front line of Apache attack. Apache thefts during 1763 increased in number until Anza asked the governor for permission early in 1764 to move the Sobaipuris once again.

GOVERNOR JUAN CLAUDIO DE PINEDA AT SONORA

The new governor of Sonora, Juan Claudio de Pineda, a native of Sort, in the Spanish province of Lérida, had served as a lieutenant in the Italian campaign in the 1740s and was then promoted to captain on December 17, 1759. Again promoted because of capable service, Pineda became a lieutenant colonel just a year later and, contrary to his wishes, was sent to New Spain as governor and captain-general of Sonora and Sinaloa. On his way he stopped in Mexico City and accompanied the viceroy to

Veracruz in 1762 to evaluate the English war threat. Pineda finally reached Rosario, Sinaloa in February 1763 and relieved Captain Urrea at San Miguel de Horcasitas on May 20. In 1764 Pineda inspected the frontier garrisons and reorganized the militia units. He concentrated his main efforts on the hostile Seris and offered a bounty of 300 pesos on the head of the Seri chief. Pineda later surveyed the port of Guaymas to select sites for a large Sonora expedition to defeat the Seris.

Governor Pineda did not agree with Anza that the Sobaipuris should be moved again—this time from Tucson to the Buenavista valley. Anza argued that the Indians lacked adequate irrigation water and fields at Tucson and that Father Espinosa was not able to hear their confessions. Father Rector Manuel Aguirre advised Pineda that instead of moving the Indians, he should send another priest to the people of Tucson. Aguirre also wanted to send the Pápagos to Buenavista as they had no fields to cultivate and because he had disagreed with the original decision to relocate the Sobaipuris at Tucson. He commented that the colonial authorities should have moved the garrison at Tubac to the San Pedro valley instead of moving the Sobaipuris to Santa Cruz. The Jesuit rector and the military governor could not agree.

Father Aguirre in the meantime asked for three more missionaries for the Sonora-Pimería province, especially for one at Tucson. Governor Pineda reminded the rector that the Jesuits were collecting too many stipends for missions without missionaries so they needed to fill empty posts. Aguirre kept trying while Father Espinosa fell seriously ill. Espinosa recovered his health temporarily by moving to San Ignacio but was back at San Xavier in extremely poor condition in mid-May 1765. Aguirre finally found José Neve, a young Mexican Jesuit, to assist him. Born in Calpulalpan in the province of Tlaxcala on June 10, 1739, Neve joined the Society of Jesus in 1755 and reached Sonora early in 1765. He began his work at Ati and was then sent to assist the ailing Espinosa at Bac. He nursed the partially paralyzed priest to a condition that would allow him to make the trip to San Ignacio. Espinosa was so ill that it took several months, until October 1765, before Neve finally got him to San Ignacio. Espinosa eventually recovered sufficiently to be transferred to Caborca in February 1766.

BACK AT GUEVAVI

Father Pfefferkorn found the air at Guevavi less than pure and healthful. Soon the summer heat and marshes along the river began to breed disease. Pfefferkorn became seriously ill and, in June 1763, rode or was carried off to Oposura, where he recovered and found time to amass material for his book (published in German in 1794) detailing his life among the Indians of Sonora. He included no direct references to his experience at Guevavi but did describe the dangers of the *toloache* plant, or sacred datura, whose juice caused hallucinations or sometimes, if improperly taken, death. Pfefferkorn and the other German padres had a difficult time in the heat of the Sonoran Desert.

FATHER CUSTODIO XIMENO TAKES OVER

Father Custodio Ximeno, a tall, dark Spaniard born in Valdelinares in the mountains of southern Aragon on May 1, 1734, replaced Father Pfefferkorn at Guevavi. Father Ximeno entered the Society of Jesus in September 1752 and attended the Jesuit

College at Zaragoza. Having been assigned to the Jesuit province of Mexico, he journeyed southward nearly 500 miles to Cádiz where he awaited a ship for New Spain. He sailed aboard the *Nuestra Señora de Begoña*, alias *El Vencedor*, and, after a short stay in Mexico City, set out for the northern frontier. Father Custodio and Father Francisco Xavier Villarroya, a friend since college days in Spain, set out together in mid-spring 1763 in the company of Sonoran governor Juan Claudio de Pineda.

Father Ximeno traveled to Guevavi while Villarroya went to Ati. Since the Apaches had been attacking frequently along the valley from Soamca through Guevavi to San Xavier del Bac, the two priests soon learned that the residents of the San Luis Valley had asked Captain Anza for permission to abandon their homes and move near to the presidios. Anza's own sister-in-law, Doña Victoria Carrasco, wife of Don Francisco de Anza, was buried in October 1763 at Guevavi, although Father Ximeno did not record the cause of her death. This may have influenced Anza's decision to allow the settlers to move to Terrenate and Tubac, almost within the shadow of the presidios' walls; Governor Pineda was not happy with the decision.

Father Ximeno became sick and feverish at Guevavi, but even so presided over the festivities for Guevavi's patron saint of San Miguel on September 28, 1763. He was joined by Father Visitor Manuel Aguirre from Sonora who had been to most of the missions as secretary to Father Lizassoain. Aguirre commented that Guevavi had a good church and vestments but that its livestock had been depleted by the Apaches. He also noted that Father Ximeno had not yet learned the Piman language and in fact wanted to abandon the mission because of the Apache danger. Father Aguirre argued against abandonment and believed that instead a new mission should be created with Tumacácori as its head and Calabazas as a visita. From Tumacácori, the missionary could minister to the presidio at Tubac. The annual stipend originally allotted to Kino's abandoned mission at Dolores could be used since it had been designated for the Sobaipuris. Father Ximeno continued to work at Guevavi while disease claimed the life of the natives both at Guevavi and Calabazas.

FATHER LINCK IN BAJA CALIFORNIA

Back in Baja California, the arrival in 1764 of additional Jesuits provided Father Wenesclaus Linck, a native of Bohemia, with the opportunity to make a series of exploratory expeditions. Father Linck, who had arrived on the peninsula in 1761, had founded Mission San Borja in 1762. An enthusiastic worker, he hoped to find additional mission centers to the north and northeast, to continue the search for an overland route connecting the Jesuit missions of La Pimería Alta with California, and to discover a suitable harbor for Manila galleons on the Pacific coast. His first endeavor, a hazardous journey to the island of Angel de la Guarda in the Gulf of California, proved that site to be totally deserted, without water, and with weather conditions that impeded easy departure from the island.

During 1765, Linck traveled almost constantly throughout the northern gulf area with a small contingent of explorers that included Captain Rivera y Moncada of the Loreto presidio, two Spanish soldiers, two German deserters from a Manila galleon, and sixteen Indians. Although covering considerable ground, they discovered nothing of significance. The tireless priest's most significant contribution resulted from his two-month 1766 expedition northward toward the Colorado River. Linck's key objectives were to prove for a final time that California was peninsular, and to examine new mission sites that would enable the Jesuits to advance into Alta California. He also planned to note native customs, social organization, war potential, languages, material conditions, food supply, and availability of water. The expedition, blocked by the Sierra San Pedro Martir, failed to reach the mouth of the Colorado, but Linck's party nevertheless completed its major goals. Upon his return, the dedicated father busily made preparations for a fifth expedition to the Pacific—never dreaming that his career in California would shortly be cut off. Two years later, Father Junípero Serra, en route to Alta California, would carry with him a copy of Linck's diary and establish Mission San Fernando de Velicatá on the site recommended by his Jesuit predecessor.

THE REFORMS OF CARLOS III

As discussed previously, the eighteenth century began with the accession of Philip V, the Bourbon grandson of Louis IV. Defiant of the Treaty of Utrecht signed in 1713 to end the War of the Spanish Succession, the Bourbon monarchs of France and Spain began preparations to challenge the growing world power of Great Britain. In 1733, they furthered their alliance by entering into the Family Compact for Mutual Defense. Because of this agreement with the French, Spain suffered substantial losses during the several eighteenth-century conflicts involving these three nations. As noted before, the final struggle, known in Europe as the Seven Years' War and in America as the French and Indian War, marked the end of French colonial power in the Western hemisphere; and the rival powers of England and Spain fell heir to the vast North American empire. By the terms of the Treaty of Paris signed in 1763, Spain relinquished Florida to England and received France's territory of western Louisiana in compensation. With the French barrier to English expansion thus removed, Spain's frontier on the Mississippi River lay exposed to possible attack through Canada and from England's thirteen colonies. In addition, the Pacific Coast territory was threatened by the Russian advance from Alaska, and the provinces of Sonora, New Mexico, and Texas were being overrun by increasingly hostile Indian tribes.

After 1763, poor and unprepared though it was, Spain was forced to make plans for a seemingly inevitable war with England, to occupy and control Louisiana, to colonize and establish a line of defense in Alta California, and to strengthen frontier posts against Indian retaliation and other possible attacks. At this crucial time, Spain either had to restore its colonial power or sink to the rank of a third-rate nation. All these demands could only be met by taking extreme measures. With his accession to the throne in 1759, Carlos III strengthened the reforms that had been instituted from time to time since the beginning of the century and established means for increasing national revenue.

A series of decrees enacted between 1764 and 1778 modernized commercial activities. These attempted to remove the monopoly enjoyed by the Spanish port of Cádiz and eliminate delays due to the *flota* system (an annual fleet of ships sailing together to Spain and providing an easy target for pirates). The decrees also targeted export duties on Spanish goods, restrictions upon colonial commerce, smuggling, and the English monopoly on the slave trade. At home Carlos III centralized the administration of government, reduced the public debt, funded roads and canals, encouraged scientific farming, reorganized the army, rebuilt the navy, and fostered emigration to the Indies. His reform efforts also found expression in the patronage of intellectual pursuits on the Iberian Peninsula and throughout the Spanish colonial world. During the twenty-nine-year reign of Carlos III, Spain tripled its revenues, increased its population by 50 percent, and improved its prestige among European nations. Nevertheless, the situation overseas called for a tremendous effort in militia reorganization.

The Bourbon reforms called for greater military efficiency and a new defense plan to stimulate recruitment of new military units. The crown appointed Lieutenant General Juan de Villalba y Angulo, captain-general of Andalucia and one of the most important officers in Spain, as commandant general and visitador general of the Army of New Spain in command of the Regimiento de America. This American Regiment consisted of Spanish troops and foreign mercenaries who were to serve as training units for the armies of New Spain. Villalba had formed the regiment by recruiting soldiers from Naples, Brabante, Flanders, Lisbon, and the North African post of Oran. Most of the troops, however, came from within the Spanish provinces of Sevilla, Granada, Castilla, Navarra, and others.

Villalba, with his staff and a contingent of troops left from Cádiz and arrived in Veracruz on November 10, 1764. Villalba first had to strengthen the coastal defenses of New Spain, especially those at Veracruz where invasion from the sea was commonplace. He then had to tackle the hostile Indian frontier stretching from the Gulf of Mexico to the Pacific Coast of California. Interior defenses had to be reorganized and regenerated through the examples of professional soldiers in the new American Regiment. In their assessment of existing defenses, Villalba and his staff reviewed proposals submitted by military advisors in New Spain.

THE MARQUÉS DE RUBÍ, 1766

Don Cayetano María Pignatelli Rubí Corbera y San Climent, the Marqués de Rubí, conducting an extraordinary inspection and evaluation tour from the Gulf of Mexico to the Gulf of California, arrived in New Spain on November 1, 1764, and accompanied the expedition of Juan de Villalba. Although Villalba was to cooperate with Viceroy Joaquín de Montserrat y Ciruana, the Marqués de Cruillas, an unfortunate personal antagonism grew between the two that restricted effective completion of the projects proposed by the king.

Coincidentally, Villalba's arrival preceded that of another highly regarded official, visitador general José de Gálvez, who reached Veracruz in mid-July 1765, also with a commission for reform and reorganization. About a month after setting foot on shore, Gálvez presented himself to Viceroy Cruillas and immediately afterwards to Villalba. Gálvez hoped to reconcile the differences between the two but instead found himself having difficulties with the viceroy. Although the missions of Gálvez and Villalba—who in turn commissioned Rubí—were similar, the former was to carry out financial and related administrative reforms, while the latter was to deal exclusively with frontier defense. Since Rubí was to inspect every frontier presidio and make recommendations for future defense, Viceroy Cruillas appointed Nicolas de Lafora of the Royal Corps of Engineers to serve as Rubí's technical advisor and to sketch a small map of each area visited.

New Mexico was the first objective of Rubí's inspection, with Santa Fe as his key stop. The party led by Rubí had been on the road for over four months from Mexico City when they arrived at El Paso. There the Marqués noted that the local complex consisted of the presidio, the pueblo of Guadalupe, and five mission towns situated downriver from the crossing. With a population of about 5,000, El Paso had been the anchor for the Reconquest of New Mexico after the Pueblo Revolt of 1680. Rubí also considered it to be a key to the defense of an extended region, both to the east and to the immediate west. He considered the town

Fig. 8.2. José de Gálvez, Spanish stamp issued 1967.

to be sufficiently populous to permit its defense to be turned over to a well-organized militia composed of local citizens. He felt that the existing regular army garrison might be better located to the south at Carrizal so as to plug a hole in the defense line and to be more effective in repelling the Apaches by preventing them access to northern Nueva Vizcaya.

After departure from the river crossing and about four day's travel northward from El Paso, the Rubí party was attacked by some Apaches who attempted to steal their horses. The natives failed in this, but they were able to run off most of the sheep. Determined soldiers gave chase, recovered many of the animals, and held off any further attack. On its way northward from that incident, the party passed some of the sites still abandoned from the Pueblo Revolt, finally reached the occupied area, and continued on to Santa Fe. The reigning governor was Tomás Vélez Cachupín, one of the colonial governors who served New Mexico the longest, having been appointed for two non-consecutive terms. Following such a long trip, the visitors were not impressed by the Villa de Santa Fe. They felt that the existing presidio was incapable of providing adequate defense, and that it should be replaced by a small, well-constructed fort in order to provide greater protection.

One of Rubí's general observations concerned the abandoned condition of the country between El Paso and the Río Abajo settlements of central New Mexico. His solution was to place a garrison at El Robledo, buttressed by a colony of settlers, thereby forming a strong point for protection of the caravans moving north along the Royal Road. This redeployment would be especially necessary if soldiers were withdrawn from El Paso in accordance with his plan. Though his recommendation to the crown was strong regarding settlement of El Robledo, nothing was done to implement it, and the long stretch of New Mexico's lifeline remained unprotected, exposed to attack.

Rubí, Lafora, and the tour continued on to Arizona. On December 19, 1766, advance riders announced in the village of Guevavi the approach of a Spanish nobleman and his entourage. At the mission they made preparations for his arrival, an important event at that distant outpost. After a short stay, the party left Guevavi to continue on to their destination, the royal presidio of Tubac, where they would remain two weeks. The Marques de Rubí thought that Anza, because of his energy, valor, zeal, and experience, was a valuable officer worthy of the king's recognition. Rubí noted that the presidio arsenal was well-stocked with Catalan carbines of superior quality and with swords, lances, shields, and other appropriate weapons. An inspection of the books showed that Anza governed with a generosity uncommon on frontier posts—giving his men discounts instead of overcharging them for necessary items.

Despite all of the compliments given to Anza, Rubí's report listed three complaints that had emerged from the soldiers' testimonies. One, expressed by the whole company, was the arbitrary duty assignments and unsystematic discipline that they blamed mostly on Ensign Juan de Huandurraga. A second complaint concerned the food. Before he left, Rubí standardized the quantities and prices and along with maize and wheat, each soldier was to receive a quarter of beef every fifteen days, if available, or mutton or salted meat could be substituted. The third complaint was that the soldiers had to spend time and energy herding horses and mules when the majority of the animals belonged to the local settlers and the Jesuit missionaries. In addition, so many animals resulted in overgrazing, to the detriment of presidial herds.

While the inspection was going on, Rubí's lieutenant, Joseph de Urrutia, made a sketch of the presidio and surrounding area. Urrutia would become, three decades later, captain-general of all Spanish armies and would pose for Goya at the Court of Madrid in 1798. Nicolas Lafora also received lasting fame with the publication of his full diary of the two-year inspection tour. Rubí said that Lafora's diary, observations, and maps helped him greatly in writing up his own *Dictamen*.

Shortly after the departure of the Rubí entourage, the situation for Father Custodio became depressing. Father Neve, the Mexican Jesuit at San Xavier del Bac was transferred and no replacement had arrived by mid-April 1767. Finally, 27-year-old Father Antonio Castro was given the assignment, but he probably never reached the mission. At that point it made no difference. The death-knell of the Society of Jesus, which had sounded in Portugal and France, finally had its repercussions in Spain and would soon reach the remote frontier of La Pimería Alta.

EXPULSION OF THE JESUITS, 1767

The viceroy's special courier rode swiftly over the seemingly endless hills separating Culiacán from the northern frontier. He fell ill at Alamos, but passed on the important documents in his pouch to another rider until at last, on July 11, 1767, three days behind schedule, Governor Juan Claudio de Pineda, governor of Spanish Sonora with headquarters at San Miguel de Horcasitas, opened the mysteriously sealed package. The order within, direct from the Conde de Aranda, president of the Council of Castile,

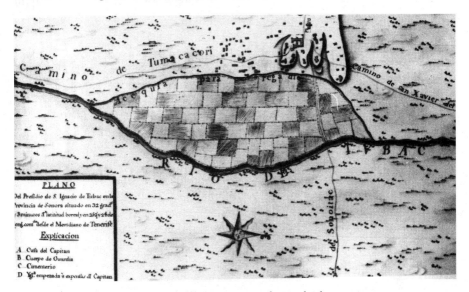

Map 8.1. Lieutenant Urrutia's 1766 map of Tubac. Courtesy The British Library.

would forever change the course of history. As had the Marqués de Pombal in Portugal eight years earlier, Aranda suddenly, and without warning, conveyed the shattering news that Carlos III, on June 25, 1767, had ordered the arrest of all Jesuits in colleges and missions in Spain's empire. The priests on the northern frontier, as well as elsewhere, were to be removed to Veracruz for immediate expulsion from Spain's overseas dominions.

The Society of Jesus, founded early in the sixteenth century by Ignacio de Loyola, had grown in a relatively short time into one of the most powerful of all the orders. Secondary education was almost entirely under Jesuit control. The order's expanding influence aroused the jealousy of both the secular clergy and other members of the regular clergy. In time, opposition toward the Jesuits spread to government officials and those favoring what became known as a policy of regalism. While the monarchs of Spain had followed a policy of royal absolutism with regard to the church since the early days of discovery and conquest, the use of royal control had grown more pronounced under Bourbon domination. Regalism became synonymous with an almost abusive use of the king's powers over ecclesiastical affairs. Since regalists were strongly opposed to the centralization of church authority in Rome, the Jesuits, who defended the supremacy of the popes over councils and kings, became the target of serious accusations. The Black Robes were expelled from Portugal in 1759 and from Bourbon France in 1764.

In Spain and its provinces, merchants and others complained that the Jesuits were involved in illegal commerce, undersold their competitors because of tax exemptions, and had amassed great wealth at the expense of Indians. Jesuits were accused of meddling in politics and had earned the opposition of many who resented their individualism, independence, and material wealth. The secularist bureaucracy introduced by the Bourbons in Spain had begun to destroy the traditional overlapping of civil and ecclesiastical authorities, and those in charge wanted to reduce the Jesuits widespread control over Spanish colegios—the bastion of secondary education.

Carlos III permitted the publication in 1765 of the anonymous *Tratado de la regalia de l'amortizacion* that questioned the right of the church to possess real property. It argued that in all temporal matters, the state was supreme. Its author was the Conde de Campomanes, *fiscal* of the Council of Castile, friend of Aranda, and of the same nationalistic, anticlerical leanings. Campomanes believed in a poor church that should confine its activities to prayer and penance. He had openly accused the Jesuits of fomenting riots and, as fiscal, signed on June 8, 1766, the first decree condemning the Jesuits as aspiring to universal power. By January 1767, the Council of Castile had formulated its opinion that the order should be expelled and produced a letter, later shown to be without foundation, that the Jesuits believed Carlos III to be illegitimate. The king finally became convinced that the order wanted to depose him and might even be plotting to have him killed. All of these circumstances combined to lend support to the plan of Aranda and Campomanes for immediate expulsion, a plan that was carried out with great secrecy.

The expulsion of the Jesuits did not depend much upon the order's activities in America, and still less upon the developments in New Spain. Even so, the missionaries played a measurable part in the overall drama. As mentioned before, the Jesuits had recently had difficulties with the military in La Pimería Alta, and the soldiers resented having to care for Jesuit herds. The governor of Sonora complained that missions without missionaries were receiving government stipends. In Baja California, the society's missionaries were charged with enslaving the soldiers, overworking the Indians, trading with the English, maintaining secret silver mines, and concealing the vast resources of the peninsula. These charges, exaggerated by the bitterness of prejudice and hatred, exerted undue influence because the missionaries' isolation kept their true condition a mystery.

José de Gálvez Begins Reforms

To carry out the crown's economic polices and institute certain political reforms in New Spain, Carlos III appointed José de Gálvez, an energetic young court lawyer, as his personal representative. Gálvez, born near Vélez Málaga of a poor Andalusian family with noble lineage, studied law at the University of Salamanca and first rose to prominence in the Spanish foreign office. His legal ability, efficient service, and knowledge of French favorably impressed Carlos III and won for him the high office of *visitador general* or inspector general of New Spain. In this capacity Gálvez was entrusted with sweeping power to carry out the king's reform measures overseas—completely overhauling colonial administration, revising outdated fiscal methods, developing new revenue sources, eliminating graft, and expelling the Jesuits. He arrived in Mexico in July 1765.

After removing the uncooperative Viceroy Marques de Cruillas, Gálvez received full support from the newly appointed Marques de Croix, viceroy of New Spain from 1766 to 1771. The new visitador immediately began to examine the area for new sources of income and looked toward the improvement of colonial government. Upon receipt in May 1767 of the king's directive to expel the Jesuits, Gálvez took immediate steps to supervise the controversial move. Although suffering and hardship would result for both the religious and their Indian charges, the visitador, never a fan of the society, carried out the eviction notice with little remorse or delay.

Views of the Conde de Aranda

The Conde de Aranda, a student of the Enlightenment and a strong opponent of Jesuit influence, had put forth his views on the future role of the church in his instructions accompanying the royal decree. Writing from his office in Madrid, Aranda urged that Spanish merchants settle within Indian villages and engage in reciprocal trade that would benefit all concerned. He also suggested that new clerics might go to the missions as individuals rather than as part of a missionary college or province.

Gálvez, moving conservatively at first, found this latter suggestion to be impossible and decided to make arrangements with the Franciscans to take over in the traditional fashion. Besides, Carlos III liked the Franciscans and was a tertiary of their order. Also, the friars were numerous, learned, and traditionalist. The visitador's long-range plans, however, called for an integration of the mission system into an autonomous commandancy general of the north, which would make the Indians useful tributaries of the crown and give Sonora a strong diocesan structure when the missions were turned into parishes. Gálvez met with Comisario General Fray Manuel de Najera, the highest Franciscan authority in New Spain, to decide which of the Apostolic Colleges serving as missionary training centers would be assigned to various areas. It was finally agreed that the College of San Fernando in Mexico City would send twelve replacements to Baja California; Santa Cruz de Querétaro would send fourteen to occupy a part of the missions of Sonora and La Pimería; and Guadalupe de Zacatecas would send twenty-five friars to Tarahumara and Chinipas missions.

New Instructions

In keeping with the reforms of Carlos III, the guardian of the College at Querétaro wrote out instructions for the padres to follow upon reaching their new missions in Sonora. These represented quite a change from previous Spanish policy toward the natives. The missionaries were instructed to learn about the geography and ecology of their new area and the lands beyond the frontier. They were strictly forbidden to prevent the Indians from communicating with the Spaniards, from trading freely with them, and from living among them. Spaniards could also live within Indian pueblos. Instead of following the policy of isolationism practiced since the decline of the encomienda system in the sixteenth century, the missionaries were urged to acculturate the natives to Spanish ways and teach them the Castilian language. The new instructions also demanded that the missionaries employ the aid of non-Indian teachers and establish formal schools in the mission villages to expedite the acculturation process. With this new policy in force, the hope was that settlers, soldiers, natives, and missionaries would all live in a cooperative frontier society.

The Final Blow

Governor Juan Claudio de Pineda had no choice but to order each of his captains to begin the expulsion. Instead of sending Captain Anza to round up the missionaries of La Pimería Alta, he sent him to Arizpe, the seat of the rectorate of San Francisco Xavier, to notify the elderly father visitor General Carlos de Roxas, the priest who had both baptized and married him, of the situation. Captain Bernardo de Urrea of Altar was given the duty to gather up the padres and take them to the mission at Tubutama, residence of Father Rector Luis Vivas, because it was centrally located. Father Vivas called in all the priests, and the soldiers who took the message from Altar allowed them no time to make arrangements for their absence. Father Custodio Ximeno at Guevavi was asked to surrender the mission records and his keys; the soldiers then shut the church furnishings in the sacristy and told the Indians not to disturb them. They told Ximeno that he could take his personal belongings—clothing, tobacco, handkerchiefs, his breviary and small prayer books—but they could not tell him the nature of his journey.

In the large church at Matape, sixty-five miles east of present-day Hermosillo, about fifty Jesuits were gathered together to hear the decree read formally. Ahead of them lay months of confinement at the port of Guaymas, a frightening, disease-ridden voyage on the Gulf, and a pitiful march across Mexico to Veracruz during which at least twenty died. Among those who survived and sailed aboard the Swedish ship *Princess Ulrica* on November 10, 1768, were Fathers Garrucho, Pauer, and Ximeno. Fathers Gerstner and Pfefferkorn crossed later.

THE END IN BAJA CALIFORNIA

Gálvez appointed Don Gaspar de Portolá y de Rovira, a native of Lérida in northern Spain and formerly of the Spanish Dragoons, as governor of Lower California with instructions to remove the sixteen missionaries working in California's fourteen centers. Portolá reached San José del Cabo at the southern tip of the peninsula on November 30, 1767, and for ten days marched northward along the rocky Gulf Coast. Whatever visions of gold, silver, and pearls he might have held gave way to grim reality as Portolá later wrote to the viceroy of Mexico: "His eyes saw nothing but stones and thorns, barren hills, dry rock, and waterless creeks." (Baegert, *Observations in Lower California*, p. 169) The governor was met by the conscientious Captain Rivera who confirmed the poverty of the entire region.

One by one the Jesuit missionaries—five Spaniards, five Germans, three Austrians, two Mexicans, and one Bohemian—gathered in sadness at Loreto to prepare for departure on February 3, 1768. Father Baegert, a grim realist, expressed the opinion of many of his co-laborers that "from a material point of view, no greater favor could have been done for them ... than to get them out of such misery and back to Europe, their homeland." But, he wrote, "I can assure the reader that there was not one among us whose heart did not ache at the thought of leaving California and who, even if the position of his brethren in the Spanish monarchy did not change, would not have gladly turned back in the middle of the homeward journey." (Baegert, *Observations in Lower California*, p. 165)

Looking Back

The padres of La Pimería Alta no doubt felt the same way as did their brethren in Baja California. If they had seemed harsh in their insistence that the Indians give up their old ways, it was only because they believed the new way was better. They taught the natives European methods of agriculture and gave them building skills, believing the natives needed help and guidance to insure themselves of a better life. And yet because of disease, the padres nearly brought extermination to many villages. They watched in horror as men, women, and children died from epidemics that seemed to sweep through the area. As a consolation they could offer only one thing—a Christian chance for everlasting life. Even if the bodies of their charges did not survive, the padres took solace in knowing that their souls were saved.

The Presidial Population

The missionaries and Indians were not the only ones affected by the Jesuit expulsion. Even though they did not participate in the daily activities of the missions, civilians, and soldiers had come to know the padres as the only priests in the area for baptisms, marriages, and other ceremonies. Although not especially numerous, there were families attached to the military presidios and some who had come to the area as independent ranchers or miners, who made up a growing population. Some of these families were first or second generation criollos who maintained close ties with persons and family members still residing in Spain. The elite were extremely cautious in seeking suitable marriage partners who could assure a purity of lineage. They were represented, for example, by the families of Elías González, Anza, Vildósola, and Díaz del Carpio. More commonly, however, the frontier families were mestizos, although some were classified as *castizos*, meaning a quarter or less mixture of Indian ancestry. The children of castizos were considered Spaniards and could be admitted to the holy orders and cloisters of the Catholic church.

Because of the importance of the presidios, the commanders of these posts were near the top of the power structure in deciding which merchants would supply the troops and what the price of horses would be. Even though food had to be sold at fixed prices, the commander could buy provisions as cheaply as the market would permit and in turn make a good profit. The wealth of the military elite allowed them to live in good houses, invest in mining and ranching ventures, educate their sons, obtain political favors, and arrange good marriages or careers for their children.

The most numerous group, the mestizos, lived under difficult conditions on the frontier. Their houses were usually of adobe and contained two, or at most three, rooms. Furnishings were sparse and typically included beds of stretched raw oxhide, a chest for clothes, benches for seats, and a small table. Two classes that included persons of African ancestry were the *mulatos* (Spaniards and African-Americans) and *lobos*, a mixture of Indians and African-Americans. These were considered to be among the lowest of classes.

Clothing was scarce on the frontier and varied according to wealth and status. The men of the upper class wore coats of red or scarlet trimmed with copper or silver buttons. They also wore long-sleeved blue shirts and trousers of heavy blue or red plush. Their hats were stiff and decorated with silver borders and red and blue cloth. Women wore pleated gowns, blouses that were closed at the neck and a *rebozo* which, depending on the occasion, was a shawl of cotton, mixed cotton or silk, or pure silk.

All classes enjoyed fiestas and observed weddings, baptisms, saints days, and funerals. Guests were served chocolate and tortillas and there was usually music, dancing, singing and some drinking. Everyday food consisted of beans, *posole*—corn soup, *pinole*—a cereal of ground corn, *atole*—a porridge made of the pith extracted from corn kernels, and tortillas. The settlers used corn as a base for tamales; for *puchas,* ring-shaped cakes of corn flour mixed with sugar, cinnamon and egg yolk; and *biscochuelos*, hard rolls made of corn flour, sugar, and milk. Chocolate was a favorite but it was expensive and few could afford it. Beef, mutton, and chicken were also scarce and reserved for special occasions.

For these frontier residents, the changeover from Jesuit to Franciscan missionaries meant little. They were more concerned about survival and protection from the danger of attack by hostile Indians.

Interim Period

Captain Bernardo de Urrea of Altar named Andres Grijalva, a civilian resident of the presidio at Terrenate, as comisario for the three missions of Soamca, Guevavi, and San Xavier del Bac after the Jesuit expulsion. Grijalva, in a spirit of generosity, told the natives that they were the absolute owners of the mission properties and could use them however they wished. He gave them the keys to the granaries and, much to the unhappiness of Captain Juan Bautista de Anza, the natives at Tumacácori consumed more than fifty fanegas of corn within a few days. For this reason, Anza had to take the keys back and warned Grijalva not to continue in such a disorganized manner.

Anza needed to protect the provisions in case of an Apache attack, which came soon enough. Early in the winter of 1767, an Apache war party rode down upon the horse herd belonging to the presidio at Terrenate, killing one soldier and taking captive a soldier and a settler. The Apaches, pursued by the soldiers, killed their captives and prepared to fight. The soldiers withdrew and fortunately there was no more bloodshed for the time being.

ORIGIN OF THE FRANCISCAN ORDER

The Franciscans who were assigned to replace the expelled Jesuits belonged to an order founded in thirteenth-century Italy by Giovanni Francesco (Frances) di Bernadone. Born in 1182 to a wealthy merchant of the mountain town of Assisi in central Italy. Francis, upon recovering from an illness, became animated with a great spirit of poverty, charity, and piety. He sold some of his father's wares and gave the funds to the parish church. Being renounced by his father, Francis took up residence with the Bishop of Assisi, swore obedience only to God, and decided to spread the word of the church as a common beggar—or mendicant. Objecting to a secluded, monastic life, Francis and two others founded a new order in 1209, vowing to own no material possessions in order to be free to travel to wherever their services were needed. They would accept only the use of property needed in their work rather than take title to it.

The Franciscans, recruited mostly from humble families, proved to be dedicated, energetic, and practical workers; the order adopted an enforced discipline and received papal sanction in 1223. Francis died in 1226 and was canonized as St. Francis in 1228. Some Franciscans sailed with Columbus on his second voyage to America and opened the first New World convent at Isabella on the Island of Española in 1493. They opened another in Santiago de Cuba in 1510 and by 1524 had established a custody in Mexico

City. Franciscans were serving in central Mexico, Texas, and New Mexico at the time of the Jesuit expulsion.

The Franciscan Apostolic College of Santa Cruz de Querétaro, the earliest in Mexico, was founded in 1683 by Father Antonio Linar. A direct link with the apostolic and primitive church, the mission program was inspired by early Christian theology that stipulated manual labor as a part of church doctrine. The missions would function as self-sufficient spiritual strongholds, providing an economic base and social life for previously dispersed population groups. The friars would aid the military in the pacification of the Indians and the military in turn would protect the friars. The Franciscans would hold the mission lands in trust for the Indians and instruct the natives that God would reward their services and devotion. The civil authority would regulate the collection of the tithes for the secular church.

On January 18, 1768, thirteen gray-robed Querétaran friars left the hospice in Tepic where they had been awaiting orders for their mission assignment. They were led by Father President Fray Mariano Antonio Buena y Alcalde, veteran of the missions in Texas and apostolic prefect for all the Franciscan colleges in America. They traveled the forty miles to San Blas on the west coast of Mexico full of optimism for sailing northward on the newly built *San Carlos* and the tiny *Lauretana*.

One friar, Antonio de los Reyes, traveled overland with Colonel Domingo Elizondo, whose Spanish Dragoons were bound for Sonora to campaign against the Seri Indians. Elizondo had already experienced the difficulties of sailing up the Gulf and preferred the long but certain trail. Unfortunately the ships, as had happened before in the unpredictable Gulf, were alternately becalmed and caught in furious *chubascos* until the *San Carlos* had to limp back to San Blas and start again. The unhappy friars, who spent forty days on the water going nowhere, were consoled by Father Junípero Serra and his group of friars from the College of San Fernando who were assigned to take over the Baja California missions. With six friars, the *Lauretana* put ashore at Mazatlan and made it to Sonora early in the spring of 1768. Seven weeks later, the others, including Father Buena, finally made it onto the beach at Guaymas.

FRANCISCAN ASSIGNMENTS

After presenting their credentials to Governor Pineda at San Miguel de Horcasitas, the padres received their assignments. Those from Querétaro were paired with the missions of La Pimería Alta as follows: San Ignacio—Fray Diego Martín García; Caborca—Fray Juan Díaz; Ati—Fray Joseph Soler; Tubutama—Fray Joseph del Río; Saric—Fray Joseph Agorreta; Soamca—Fray Francisco Roche; Guevavi—Fray Juan Crisóstomo Gil de Bernabe; and San Xavier del Bac—Fray Francisco Garcés.

After four days at San Ignacio in the south, Father President Buena decided to move his headquarters to Tubutama on the Río Altar where the last Jesuit superior had lived. From there he confirmed the arrival of Father Gil de Bernabe and Father Garcés at Guevavi and San Xavier del Bac, the two missions within the boundaries of present-day Arizona. By July 1768, Governor Pineda sent word to Andres Grijalva and the other comisarios to surrender the churches, sacristies, padres' quarter, and furnishings to the Franciscans by formal inventory.

Under the new instructions, the friars were strictly forbidden to follow any economic precedent set by the Jesuits. Pineda was careful to hold them to the annual royal stipend as their only sustenance; any supplies the padres needed were to be charged against their stipends. The friars were forbidden to use the material possessions of the missions even for the good of the Indians a difficult request as some of the orphaned children barely had enough clothes to wear or food to eat. The royal stipend was definitely inadequate.

There were no special funds for construction and maintenance of church buildings and most of those inherited from the Jesuits needed repair. For example, two beams supporting the ceiling of the church at Mission San Miguel de los Ures crashed to the floor on August 4, 1768, narrowly missing the parishioners. The church at Tubutama lacked a sacristy and bats were flying in the open windows. Since the royal stipend could not possibly cover building expenses, there was no way to repair, much less improve, the mission structures. Hospitality was certainly a problem when officials and other travelers who used the missions as stopping places needed to be fed. Because the friars could not use the common stores of the mission for that purpose, it came from their personal accounts.

THE BAJA CALIFORNIA MISSIONS

In July 1768, Gálvez had journeyed to Baja California to invest the Franciscans with the former Jesuit mission properties and to survey the region's economic possibilities. During his ten-month stay, Gálvez consolidated Indian pueblos, tried to stimulate Spanish colonization, and took measures to encourage mining. Establishing himself south of La Paz in the colonial village of Real de Santa Ana, the only town that had not been founded by the Jesuits, Gálvez issued his first decrees. His Instruction of August 12, 1768, set forth the means by which immigrants of European descent could receive urban and rural grants of land. They would be exempt from taxes for three years but were obligated within one to build and occupy their homes and to encircle their property with shade or fruit trees; they were to have at least twenty sows for breeding; a yoke of oxen; five sheep or goats; two mares; and five hens with a rooster. The colonists also would have to own a plow, an ax, a hammer, plus other equipment including weapons for protection. They would enjoy water and pastures in common.

In October, Gálvez put forth a plan that set a pattern for Spain's frontier settlements, with Indians organized in towns outside of the missions. Each head of a family would receive a house lot, free title to a piece of irrigated land, and temporary ownership of two others. They would build a house containing beds that were "clean and above the ground so as to keep them free of the contagious illnesses that harass them and of the stench that they acquire by sleeping on the floor and receiving humidity from the ground." (Ms., Instructions of August 12, 1768, Archivo General de la Nación, Mexico, D.F.) The Indians would plant corn, cotton, fruit trees, and prickly pear cactus. The women, instead of working in the fields, would learn cooking, weaving, and spinning from the priests. The men, in addition to farming, could devote themselves to business by carrying their products to the town's weekly market and selling them under the supervision of the royal judge. If they had no other duties, they could be assigned to work in the mines to benefit from another trade and source of income. Six or eight of the most capable Indians would be chosen from among the bachelors to learn mechanical arts and useful trades at the missions, while another four or six would learn about cultivating and raising corn so they could teach the others. Gálvez provided that Indian leaders would be freely and democratically elected by an assembly that would meet the first day of each year and in which all people over 25 years of age would participate.

PLANS TO SETTLE ALTA CALIFORNIA

After issuing plans for a civilian settlement, Gálvez sailed to La Paz in July 1768 to carry out his plans for the settlement of lands to the north in Alta California. With energy and optimism, the visitor general was fully prepared to launch a two-pronged land and sea expedition from Baja California to the ports of San Diego and Monterey.

Chapter Eight

BIBLIOGRAPHIC ESSAY

The most comprehensive work on the Pueblo Indian auxiliaries is Oakah Jones, *Pueblo Warriors and Spanish Conquest* (Norman: University of Oklahoma Press, 1966). See also Marc Simmons "Tlascalans in the Spanish Borderlands," *New Mexico Historical Review*, 39 (April 1964):101–110 and Alfred Barnaby Thomas, *The Plains Indians and New Mexico, 1751–1778* (Albuquerque: University of New Mexico Press, 1940). Robert Ryal Miller has edited and translated "New Mexico in Mid-Eighteenth Century: A Report Based on Governor Vélez de Cachupín's Inspection," *Southwestern Historical Quarterly*, 79 (October 1975):166–81. A general study of Europeans entering the area is William Brandon, *Quivira: Europeans in the Region of the Santa Fe Trail, 1540–1820* (Athens: Ohio University Press, 1990). On French traders is Donald J. Blakeslee, "The Mallet Expedition of 1739," *Wagon Tracks: Santa Fe Trail Association Quarterly*, 5 (February and May 1991):15–18; 14–16; Herbert Bolton, "French Intrusions into New Mexico, 1749–1752," in John F. Bannon, ed., *Bolton and the Spanish Borderlands* (Norman: University of Oklahoma Press, 1964).

For the expedition of Rivera see Donald C. Cutter, "Prelude to a Pageant in the Wilderness," in *Western Historical Quarterly*, 8 (January 1977):5–14 and G. Clell Jacobs, "The Phantom Pathfinder: Juan María Antonio de Rivera and His Expedition," *Utah Historical Quarterly*, 60 (summer 1992):200–23. For definitions of castes and class structure see Lyle McAlister, "Social Structure and Social Change in New Spain," *Hispanic American Historical Review*, 43 (1963):349–70; Robert Archibald, "Acculturation and Assimilation in Colonial New Mexico," *NMHR*, 53 (July 1978):205–17; and Oakah Jones, *Los Paisanos: Spanish Settlers on the Northern Frontier of New Spain* (Norman: University of Oklahoma Press, 1979).

Luis Navarro García in *Don José de Gálvez y la Comandancia General de las Provincias Internas del Norte de Nueva España* (Sevilla: Escuela de Estudios Hispano-Americanos, 1964) describes conditions on the frontier of Sonora throughout the eighteenth century. James Officer's *Hispanic Arizona, 1536–1856* (Tucson: University of Arizona Press, 1987) gives a summary of early exploration and settlement in Arizona, chronicles the later Jesuit years in some detail, and begins in depth in the later eighteenth century. John Kessell's *Mission of Sorrows: Jesuit Guevavi and the Pimas 1691–1767* (Tucson: University of Arizona Press, 1970) and Henry F. Dobyns, *Spanish Colonial Tucson* (Tucson: University of Arizona Press, 1976) continue to be valuable sources for this period. Also important are John Augustine Donohue, S.J., "The Unlucky Jesuit Mission of Bac, 1732–1737, *Arizona and the West*, 2 (summer 1960):127–39 for San Xavier del Bac and Jay J. Wagoner's *Early Arizona* (Tucson: University of Arizona Press, 1975) for missionaries and soldiers in the 1700s. See also Ignaz Pfefferkorn, *Sonora: A Description of the Province* (Albuquerque: University of New Mexico Press, 1949).

For military and related operations, see Janet R. Fireman's *The Spanish Royal Corps of Engineers in the Western Borderlands* (Glendale, Calif.: Arthur H. Clark, 1977). A short survey of the Rubí Inspection is in Marion Haskell, "A Review of Rubí's Inspection of the Frontier Presidios of New Spain, 1766–1768," Historical Society of Southern California *Annual Publications*, 11 (1918):33–44. See also Nicolás de LaFora, *Relación del Viaje que hizo a los Presidios Internos situados en la frontera de la America Septentrional perteneciente al rey de España*, edited by Mario Hernández y Sánchez-Barba in *Bibliotheca Indiana*, Tomo II, *Viajes por Norteamerica* (Madrid: Aguilar, 1958) and Nicolas Lafora, *The Frontiers of New Spain: Nicolas de Lafora's Description, 1766–1768*, edited and translated by Lawrence Kinnaird (Berkeley: University of California Press, 1958). Juan Nentvig, a Jesuit stationed in Sonora from 1752 to 1767 wrote an account of the area called *Rudo Ensayo, by an Unknown Jesuit Padre* (Tucson: Arizona Silhouettes, 1951) that has become fairly well known. Luis Navarro García, "El Marqués de Croix (1766–1771)," in *Los virreyes de Nueva España en el reinado de Carlos III*, edited by José Antonio Calderón Quijano, vol. I (Sevilla: Escuela de Estudios Hispano Americanos, 1967):161–381.

For the expulsion of the Jesuits see Alberto Francisco Pradeau, *La expulsión de los Jesuitas de las Provincias de Sonora, Ostimuri y Sinaloa en 1767* (Mexico, D.F.: Antigua Librería Robredo, 1959). Benno Ducrue's *Account of the Expulsion of the Jesuits from Lower California (1767–1769)* edited by Ernest J. Burrus, S.J. (Rome: Jesuit Historical Institute, 1967) has many parallels for the area of Sonora. Johann Jakob Baegert, *Observations of Lower California*, translated and edited by M. M. Brandenberg and Carl L. Baumann (Berkeley and Los Angeles: University of California Press, 1952) talks about Jesuit feelings upon leaving the area. Kieran McCarty, O.F.M., has told the transition story in *A Spanish Frontier in the Enlightened Age: Franciscan Beginnings in Sonora and Arizona, 1767–1770* (Washington, D.C.: Academy of American Franciscan History, 1981).

Of continued importance for Baja California is Harry H. Crosby, *Antigua California: Mission and Colony on the Peninsular Frontier, 1697–1768* (Albuquerque: University of New Mexico Press, 1994).

ALTA CALIFORNIA, ARIZONA, AND NEW FRONTIERS: 1769–1775

FRANCISCAN MISSIONARIES

*T*he spiritual vacuum created by the Jesuit expulsion from New Spain forced a general reshuffling of missionary forces. Gálvez had assigned Franciscans from the College of the Holy Cross of Querétaro to the missions of La Pimería Alta, and to Lower California went members of the College of San Fernando in Mexico City. From this latter college, José de Gálvez selected Father Junípero Serra, distinguished for missionary work in the Sierra Gorda region of Mexico, as president of the California missions.

FATHER JUNÍPERO SERRA AND THE CALIFORNIA MISSIONS

In California, Father Serra, the new mission executive, began a third phase of his apostolic career. Born on November 24, 1713, at Petra on Spain's Balearic Island of Mallorca, he was baptized Miguel Joseph at the local church. Later, as an undersized 16 year old, Serra entered the Franciscan Order at Palma de Mallorca on September 15, 1731, taking the name of Junípero to honor a brother companion of St. Francis. Although sickly as a child, he gained in health and strength at the convent and eventually earned a doctorate in sacred theology. Serra became a professor of philosophy and spent several successful years preaching throughout his native Mediterranean island, but a desire to work among pagan Indians came to dominate his thoughts. In response to the urgings of former students Francisco Palóu, Juan Crespí, and Rafael Verger, Serra traveled in 1749 to the Spanish port of Cádiz to join his fellow Mallorcans and other Franciscan missionaries embarking for New Spain. Soon after their arrival in Mexico, Serra and Palóu entered the mission field in northeastern Sierra Gorda, where the former served as father-president from 1750 to 1759. Afterwards Serra taught at the College of San Fernando in Mexico, served as a choir director, and traveled throughout New Spain as a commissioner of the Inquisition until his assignment to Lower California in 1768. Without hesitation, he accepted his appointment by Gálvez to head the spiritual conversion of Upper California. Despite physical handicaps and advancing age (55), during his final sixteen years spent in California, Serra never lacked the dynamic will or constant enthusiasm that characterized his entire career.

THE RUSSIAN THREAT TO CALIFORNIA

All efforts to send a colonizing expedition to Upper California after Vizcaíno's return in 1603 had met with failure. What new motive could fire into action the necessary official machinery that had neglected such an enterprise for 165 years? The North-

ern Mystery—with its tales of fabulous empires, golden cities, and a surplus of treasure—had by this time lost its appeal; even a belief that the English might discover the
still sought-after Strait of Anián stirred up little enthusiasm for northern settlement.
Conditions in 1768, under the aggressive policies of Carlos III, were ripe for progress,
but it was José de Gálvez who jolted New Spain's complacent bureaucracy out of its
lethargy. The determined visitador turned the king's request for an investigation of
Russian aggression in the North Pacific into an official sanction of his California project.

The Spanish crown had intelligence of Russian activities in the North Pacific ever
since the explorations of Vitus Bering in the years 1728 and 1741, but the threat of
Russian encroachment did not seem imminent.

It was not until late in 1767 that reports of Russian advancement made Carlos III
uneasy enough to advise the viceroy of New Spain to investigate the matter. Gálvez had
quietly planned the occupation of Upper California several months before news of the
king's concern reached Mexico, but he now magnified the Russian threat to gain needed
backing. Sidestepping usual procedures, the visitador convened a governmental junta
at the port of San Blas in May 1768, which approved his plan. With Viceroy Croix's
easily obtained official blessing, Gálvez sailed to La Paz in July, fully prepared to launch
a two-pronged land and sea expedition from Lower California to the ports of San Diego
and Monterey.

The Sacred Expedition, 1769

Because proposed occupation of the northern country was to be spiritual as well as
military—with the founding of missions and conversion of Indians equally as important as establishment of presidios—the attempt to settle Upper California became known
as the "Sacred Expedition." Gálvez left nothing to chance in planning the details of the
enterprise. Fortunately he had sufficient control of the means and methods to outfit
four divisions—two by sea and two by land—to start independently but to unite in San
Diego. The risks of total failure were thereby greatly lessened. Gálvez chose capable
and experienced leaders destined to contribute significantly toward the permanence of
California settlement. All received individual instructions about each phase of their
projected roles.

Paragraph two from Gálvez's instructions to Governor Portolá show exactly how
precise were the actions of the visitador:

> *The governor shall take with him for the march to Villacata only the*
> *supplies that are necessary. From there to San Diego, he will use the*
> *abundant provisions that I sent by launch and canoe to the Bay of San Luis*
> *de Gonzaga located in the interior of the Gulf [of California] in latitude 31.*
> *These are now making their second trip, the goods being sent to Captain*
> *Rivera for the overland expedition. Moreover, the two royal packetboats,*
> *the San Carlos and the San Antonio, which are going by way of the South*
> *Sea [Pacific], are carrying a large quantity of food of every kind in order*
> *that nothing will be lacking to those who travel by land ... .* (Ms., The
> Bancroft Library)

With regard to the Indians, the expedition members were always to "exercise the greatest care not to exasperate or alienate" them. Rather they were to "do everything possible to attract them, to obtain their good will ... through gifts such as knick-knacks or provisions." (Ms., The Bancroft Library) But Portolá was not to diminish his own supply of necessary food for the soldiers of both expeditions.

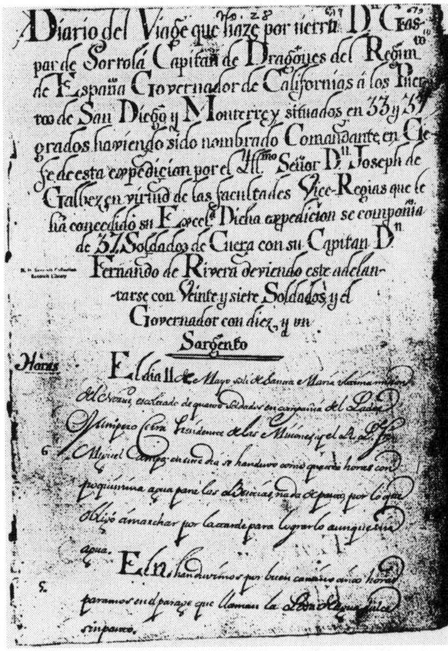
Diario del Viage que haze por tierra D.n Gaspar de Portolá Capitan de Dragones del Regim.to de España Governador de Californias á los Puertos de San Diego y Monterrey situados en 33 y 37 grados haviendo sido nombrado Comandante en Gefe de esta expedicion por el Ill.mo Señor D.n Joseph de Galvez en virtud de las facultades Vice-Regias que le ha concedido su Excel.a Dicha expedicion se componia de 37 Soldados de Cuera con su Capitan D.n Fernando de Rivera deviendo este adelantarse con Veinte y siete Soldados y el Governador con diez, y un Sargento

Fig. 9.1. Frontispiece of Portolá diary. Courtesy The Bancroft Library.

The *San Carlos* and *San Antonio*, two small packetboats commanded by captains Vicente Vila and Juan Pérez of the royal navy, were fitted out at San Blas, Mexico, for the seagoing division. These vessels, plus a special military force of twenty-five Catalonian volunteers (Compañia Franca de Cataluña) then serving in Sonora under Lieutenant Pedro Fages, were ordered to La Paz. The hastily constructed and still uncompleted *San Carlos*, the first to set sail, reached Lower California early in December 1768. Partially provisioned at San Blas, the vessel had to be unloaded, careened, finished, and reloaded at La Paz. Gálvez personally supervised and even lent a hand to all operations, and the ship was ready to depart on the morning of January 9, 1769. Father Serra said mass and prayed for those on board: Captain Vila; first mate Jorge Estorace; Lieutenant Fages and his Catalonian soldiers; cosmographer and engineer Ensign Miguel Costansó; royal surgeon Pedro Prat; the Franciscan Father Fernando Parrón; and a crew of thirty-one.

Gálvez saw his first California division sail from La Paz amidst joyous blessings, and even accompanied Vila as far as Cape San Lucas in the supply ship *La Concepción*. Despite its favorable send-off, the *San Carlos* ran into serious difficulties. Severe storms hampered progress, the water casks leaked, and many of the sailors became afflicted with scurvy. Vila's instructions were to keep out to sea until 34° and then head in for San Diego (thought to be at 33° 30' according to Vizcaino's 1602 narrative instead of its actual 32° 40'). This added more than 200 miles to the distance and increased the crew's exposure to cold weather. When the *San Carlos* reached San Diego Bay on April 29, 1769, after almost four months at sea, the stricken men had no strength to lower a boat; they were rescued by crew members of the *San Antonio* who preceded them into port on April 11.

The *San Antonio*, under command of the Mallorcan Juan Pérez, a former navigator on the Manila galleon route, had departed from La Paz on February 15 with Franciscan Fathers Juan Vizcaíno and Francisco Gómez, and a crew of about thirty men on board. Pérez, favored by good winds, also sailed to 34° and landed on an island in the Santa Barbara Channel to replenish his stores. The Spaniards obtained fresh fish and water from the friendly natives in exchange for beads. Naming the island Santa Cruz, Pérez turned southward and anchored the *San Antonio* safely in the harbor of San Diego after a voyage of fifty-five days. The Indians of the region at first mistook the vessel for a great whale, but upon discovering their error, regarded it as a forerunner of wonderful things—its arrival had coincided with an eclipse of the sun and an earthquake. Pérez was dismayed not to find the *San Carlos* already in port and called for a stay of twenty days before proceeding to Monterey. The tardy *San Carlos* arrived on April 29, just two days before the *San Antonio* was due to sail.

The men of the *San Antonio* built a tent on shore to shelter the sick and dying crew of Vila's ship. Dr. Prat and the three friars attended the scurvy-ridden soldiers and sailors as well as circumstances permitted, but the sickness spread throughout the camp until about one-half of the combined crews had succumbed. Since scurvy (caused by a lack of vitamin C) is not contagious, some other malady must have been present. Neither Costansó nor Fages could carry out their instructions for a preliminary exploration of the territory; indeed, for two weeks they did little more than help care for the sick and bury the dead. A third ship, the *San José*, had sailed for San Diego on June 16, 1769, but returned to San Blas for repairs. Departing again in May 1770, the vessel was lost with all on board and no trace of it was ever found.

Gálvez appointed Captain Fernando de Rivera y Moncada, commandant of the Loreto presidio, as head of the first overland detachment. It was scheduled to depart from Santa María, the northernmost Spanish mission where Rivera had explored with the Jesuit Father Linck. With twenty-five *soldados de cuera* (leather-jacket soldiers) from his Loreto garrison, Rivera started from La Paz in September 1768 on a northward mission-by-mission tour to recruit Indian auxiliaries and gather all available livestock and provisions. Nearly 400 animals were assembled at Mission Santa María, but pasturage was so scarce that Rivera transferred his camp to Velicata, about thirty miles to the north and inland from present-day El Rosario. The energetic captain informed Gálvez that his departure for San Diego would be in March 1769, so the visitador immediately ordered Father Juan Crespí, Serra's Mallorcan companion, to join Rivera. The expedition, which included forty-two Christian Indians, left for Upper California on March 29, and reached San Diego after fifty-one days and some 400 miles of marching. Several Indians died and the animals were weakened by lack of water and feed, but overall, the journey was successful. Rivera, aghast at seeing the hospital camp so near the ocean's edge, moved the patients to a nearby hill where the presidio was later built. Even the Laws of the Indies (Book IV, Title 7, Law 4) warned against the dangers of sea air.

Gaspar de Portolá, governor of Lower California and overall commander of the expedition, led the second overland party. Its members also assembled at Mission Santa María while supplies were transported inland from the Bay of San Luis Gonzaga. Portolá awaited Father Serra, religious head of the company, who was delayed by the gathering of church utensils and ornaments. A lame leg, injured on the road from Veracruz to Mexico, also hindered the priest's travel until, at times, his departure with the expedition seemed doubtful to everyone but himself. Serra finally started from La Paz at the end of March, stopping at Mission San Javier to appoint Father Palóu president of the Lower California missions. Despite his painful leg, he proceeded slowly to Santa Maria, and joined the worried Portolá on May 5. The entire company departed from San Diego six days later; upon reaching Velicatá on May 14, they remained long enough for Serra to found Mission San Fernando on that site.

Portolá's march essentially duplicated Rivera's, but without the burden of transporting so many domestic animals. After passing through the broad Tía Juana River Valley, the group entered San Diego on July 1, 1769. Portolá and Serra, pleased to join the others, were distressed to find the port a veritable harbor of sickness. Upon meeting with the sea and land commanders, the governor decided to send the *San Antonio,* with Juan Pérez and the remaining eight of his original twenty-eight man crew, back to La Paz to report on the condition of San Diego and to obtain additional supplies. Meanwhile, the *San Carlos* prepared to leave for Monterey as soon as there were enough healthy sailors to handle the ship. Portolá then planned his overland march to Monterey.

The Search for Monterey

The governor had instructions to proceed to Monterey without delay, take formal possession of the land, and establish a mission and presidio at the port. Portolá organized a company of sixty-three men, "or rather of skeletons," as he put it, "who had been spared by scurvy, hunger, and thirst … ." (*Diary of Portolá* as quoted in Chapman, *History of California: The Spanish Period*, p. 226) He left San Diego on July 14, 1769. The party included Fathers Crespí and Gómez, Miguel Costansó, Pedro Fages, the six Catalonian volunteers still able to march, Captain Rivera, Sergeant José Francisco Ortega, twenty-six leather-jacket soldiers (*soldados de cuera*), seven muleteers, fifteen Indians, and two servants. They began their northward trek through present-day Rose Canyon near La Jolla and, continuing along southern California's coastal plain, came to be pleasantly surprised by the fertility of the new country.

Information about the trip abounds in the diaries of Portolá, Crespí, and Costansó, who recorded daily distances and observations of the places visited and named. In the San Luis Rey Valley, friendly Indians approached the group and, according to Father Crespí, "the women were modestly covered, wearing in front an apron of threads woven together which came to the knees, and a deerskin behind. To cover the breasts they wear little capes made of strips of hare and rabbit skins twisted together … for modesty's sake and to protect them from the cold." "All the men," wrote Crespí, "go naked as Adam in Paradise before he sinned, and do not feel the least shame in presenting themselves before us … just as though the clothing given them by nature were some fine garment." (Bolton, ed., *Fray Juan Crespi: Missionary Explorer on the Pacific Coast*, p. 130) Costansó commented that the Indians were so impressed by the novelty of the encounter that they "never came to visit the Spanish without bringing a substantial present of game." (Teggert, ed., *Diary of Portolá*, p. 67)

The travelers turned inland from the coast where water for their animals was more plentiful. Near today's San Juan Capistrano, they passed through green valleys and saw springs of fresh water, live oaks and alder, wild berries, and an abundance of blossoming wild roses. Although not a true rose, they called the pale pink flower "Rose of Castile" because it reminded them of home. On July 28, they camped on the bank of a river which Crespí named Santa Ana, but Costansó called Río de los Temblores or River of Earthquakes. Numerous visitors from a nearby Indian village bid them welcome and, shortly afterwards, they experienced a series of four sizable tremors. The amazing frequency and violence of earth movements on subsequent days led the Spaniards to believe that large volcanoes existed in the nearby mountain ranges.

The party traveled on through the San Gabriel Valley and on August 2 camped near a river that they named La Porciúncula—today's Los Angeles River—watching its rapid descent from an opening in the mountains. According to Costansó, they forded the Porciúncula River and headed west for about three leagues along present-day Wilshire Boulevard to Ojo de Agua de los Alisos, a "natural spring among the alders." Its abundant water flowed southwest through a deep ditch and "the entire population of an Indian village was gathering seeds on the plain." Crespí described "some large marshes of a certain substance like pitch; they were boiling and bubbling ... there is such an abundance of it that it would serve to caulk many ships." (Bolton, ed., *Fray Juan Crespí: Missionary Explorer on the Pacific Coast*, p. 149) These were the asphalt beds now known as the La Brea Tar pits.

Their progress blocked by the Santa Monica mountains, Portolá's men directed their course inland, crossing over the hills into el Valle de los Encinos in the San Fernando Valley. Again the Indians showed extreme friendliness, offering their help as guides and exchanging pinole, nuts, and acorns in baskets made of sage and other grasses, for breads and ribbons. Turning northward, the Spaniards passed through la Cañada de Santa Clara and reached what they thought was Cabrillo's "Pueblo de Canoas." Further north the soldiers named an Indian town Pueblo de la Carpintería "because the natives were building a canoe." (Bolton, ed., *Fray Juan Crespí: Missionary Explorer on the Pacific Coast*, p. 164) They continued through a small valley they called Cañada de los Osos and followed the coast beyond San Luis Obispo until stopped by the rugged cliffs of the Sierra de Santa Lucía that drop abruptly into the sea. Rivera and Sergeant José Ortega, the best scout, searched an entire week for a pass which cut through "mountains so perilously steep as to be inaccessible, not only for men, but also for goats and deer." (Bolton, ed., *Fray Juan Crespí: Missionary Explorer on the Pacific Coast*, p. xxv)

The Spanish party crossed the treacherous ridge over the seemingly endless Santa Lucía range and finally descended into the valley of the Salinas River around today's King City. Scouts traveling ahead thought they saw the ocean a short distance away, but it took another six days' march to replace illusion with reality. They approached the Pacific coast with breathless anticipation—expecting to find Vizcaíno's sunny, sheltered harbor. Portolá reached the Monterey shore on September 30, 1769, but could not imagine that this open roadstead with its crashing surf and grotesque, wind-warped cypresses was the harbor that Vizcaíno had believed to be the best in California. He found the thick pine grove of Point Pinos, located the Carmel River, but his dreams of success were rudely shattered when the carefully described port did not seem to appear. The travel-weary governor made plans for the party to continue their journey.

San Francisco Bay

Assuming that Monterey lay further to the north, Portolá ordered his men to press on. Passing through abundant evergreen forests, they saw some giant trees which they called *palo colorado,* meaning red wood. From present-day Half-Moon Bay they could see the Farallon Islands out to sea, and Portolá clearly recognized the white cliffs of Cermeño's San Francisco Bay and the Point Reyes headland in the distance. He knew he had passed Monterey, but decided to make camp and explore a little further anyway. He sent Sergeant Ortega to scout ahead for a trail to Point Reyes and dispatched a group of hunters to look for game. Climbing to the top of the hill, the hunting party beheld "an immense arm of the sea, or estuary, which extended inland to the southeast as far as they could see." (Bolton, ed., *Fray Juan Crespi: Missionary Explorer on the Pacific Coast,* p. 229) They reported their discovery to Portolá on November 2, a few hours before Ortega returned with the news that his progress to Point Reyes was blocked by an estuary leading into a very noble and large harbor.

The uncharted bay was almost land-locked by the high mountains forming its gate into the open sea. Upon seeing the incredible body of water, Father Crespí described it as "a very large and fine harbor, so that not only the navy of our most Catholic Majesty but those of all Europe could take shelter in it." (Bolton, ed., *Fray Juan Crespi: Missionary Explorer on the Pacific Coast,* p. xxvii) But Portolá, the dedicated soldier, was mainly discouraged by his failure to find Monterey as his orders instructed. Further dismayed by the obstacle the great bay (soon to be named San Francisco) presented to further travel, he wrote in his diary that "they had found nothing" and ordered his sick and hungry men homeward. When the expedition reached Carmel Bay on the return trip, Portolá's men crossed Cypress Point peninsula and planted a cross on the still unrecognized shore of Monterey Bay. Beneath it they buried a letter reporting that "for lack of provisions" they were returning to San Diego on that day, December 9, 1769. (Ms., The Bancroft Library)

Mission San Diego

Two days after the departure of Portolá's expedition to Monterey, Father Serra convened his little band of half-starving Spaniards and Indians on the slopes of present-day Presidio Hill just above San Diego's Old Town. A crude cross marked the site thus chosen for Alta California's first mission, and the new outpost was officially dedicated on July 16, 1769, to the glory of San Diego de Alcalá. Problems for the settlement began at once. The originally friendly Indians who had shared food with the Spaniards became defiant, pestered the sick at night, and stole anything they could find, especially cloth. The natives used their rafts, which were skillfully made from cattail reeds and propelled by means of a double-bladed oar, to board the *San Carlos* in an attempt to steal the sails. They carried long harpoons with a sharp bone inserted at the point which they wielded with such great skill.

As the Indians watched the continual deaths from scurvy diminish the strength of the Spanish garrison, they planned an attack. During the first encounter, three natives and one of Serra's Indians were killed and several others, including Father Vizcaíno, were wounded. After the battle, Spanish soldiers built a stockade around the mission building to keep the Indians from entering. Things quieted down, although the priests had no success in gaining converts. They were mostly occupied in caring for the sick and doing their best to survive. The first six months in Upper California were marked by a constant struggle between Spaniards and Indians.

Fig. 9.2. Mission San Diego, six miles inland from the original founding site. Courtesy Seaver Center for Western History Research, Los Angeles County Museum of Natural History.

Portolá's expedition, exhausted from their long journey, at last reached Mission San Diego on January 24, 1770. When the governor told Serra of his failure to find Monterey, the father-president remarked wryly, "You come from Rome without having seen the Pope?" (Juan Manuel de Viniegra, quoted in Chapman, *History of California: The Spanish Period*, p. 227) Serra and Vicente Vila were readily convinced by Portolá's descriptions that he had indeed found Monterey, but failed to recognize it. Since provisions were low, the commanders decided to await the arrival of the ill-fated *San José* or the return of the *San Antonio* before making a return trip to the north.

The shortage of food at San Diego became extremely critical during the next few months. The Spaniards subsisted on wild geese, fish, and other food exchanged with the Indians for clothing, but the ravages of scurvy continued as its cause was unknown. A small quantity of corn they had planted grew well—only to be eaten by birds. Portolá sent Captain Rivera and a small detachment of men to the Baja California missions in February to obtain cattle and a pack-train of supplies. This eased the drain on San Diego's scant provisions, but within weeks, acute hunger and continuing sickness threatened to force abandonment of the port. Both Serra and Portolá, Spaniards of the most tenacious, unwavering faith in God and themselves, remained steadfast in their desire to fulfill the orders of their superiors. Yet the lives of their few remaining soldiers were at stake. Reluctantly, Portolá resolved that if no relief ship arrived by March 19, the feast day of the expedition's patron saint San José, they would leave the next morning because there were not enough provisions to wait longer and they did not want the men to die of starvation.

Father Serra immediately proposed a *novena*, a nine-day period of prayer that would end on the crucial day of San José. As the morning of March 19 slipped away, no ship came into sight, but at three o'clock in the afternoon, as if by a miracle, the sails of the *San Antonio* were discernible on the horizon. Joy filled the hearts of all in camp, even though the ship sailed past the entrance to San Diego Bay on its way to Monterey, where Juan Pérez assumed Portolá was waiting. The *San Antonio* lost an anchor in the Santa Barbara channel near Point Conception. Several crewmen, upon going ashore, learned from friendly Indians that Portolá's expedition to Monterey had long since retraced its route southward. Pérez then headed toward San Diego Bay and four days later joined the thankful survivors at the mission. Although many of its own sailors had died of scurvy, the *San Antonio* brought corn, flour, and rice to the starving men, thereby assuring the permanence of the settlement.

Map 9.1. Missions in Baja California. Map by Stephanie Gould.

The Spaniards had achieved their goal—the extension of Christianity to both Lower and Upper California. Standing fast in their devotion to church and state, they had survived in a wilderness. For the Indians, however, it was a new reality and the end of an era. The years of isolation were over and, for some Native Americans, the California dream would become a nightmare.

FATHERS GIL AND GARCÉS IN ARIZONA

At the same time that Alta California was being penetrated, the Franciscans were settling in at their new missions in the area of Arizona. It is difficult to speculate whether they were prepared for the hot, stifling desert conditions in the summer, the chilling winds of winter, or the lack of land suitable for cultivation. Juan Crisóstomo Gil de Bernabe, assigned to Guevavi, was born in 1728 in the Villa de Alfambra in Aragón. At the age of 17 or 18, young Juan, tall and lanky, entered the Franciscan seminary of Nuestra Señora de Jesús in Zaragoza. Sometime after his ordination, Juan set out for Monlora, one of his order's mountaintop retreats. There he remained in an ordered, meditative life, quite different from that of his patron St. Francis.

Late in 1762, two friars from the College of Santa Cruz in Querétaro, one of them a former professor of theology at the University of Zaragoza, were traveling from convent to convent to recruit missionaries for their provinces in New Spain. Juan Gil, hearing about entire pagan nations who were utterly ignorant of Christian teachings, begged to go. On January 15, 1763, he left the mountain top with his travel order for Cádiz safely in hand. Two days south of Zaragoza, he joined another friar bound for the missions, Father Francisco Tomás Hermenegildo Garcés of the Villa de Morata del Conde in southern Aragón. The two seemed to have little in common—Father Gil was sophisticated and well educated with a preference for meditation while Father Garcés, ten years younger, was more at home in the company of humble listeners to whom he could preach the Catholic faith. Nevertheless, the two Franciscans would become companions and neighbors on Arizona's southern frontier.

Father Francisco Garcés

Francisco Garcés, born on April 12, 1738, was educated by an uncle named Mosen Domingo Garzes, curate of the Villa de Morata del Conde. Young Francisco sought holy orders at age 15 at the Franciscan convent of San Cristobal de Alpartir and, after having been approved in philosophy, studied sacred theology at the convent of Calatayud. He was eager to go when the missionaries from Querétaro talked of the mission opportunities in New Spain. On August 1, 1763, after several months wait at Cádiz, Father Garcés and eleven other recruits sailed on the *Jupiter*. Father Gil and nine others disembarked on the *Mercurio*, an ill-fated ship that was wrecked off the shores of Yucatan. The Franciscans, along with the crew and 666 barrels of liquor, were finally rescued, and by early December 1763, the newly recruited priests were on the road to Querétaro to join Garcés and the others whose voyage had been more direct.

Unfortunate sea experiences plagued both the Aragonese friars. When they received their instructions to proceed northward to the former Jesuit missions early in 1768, Father Gil sailed on the *Lauretana* which, after forty days, landed short of its goal at Mazatlán, 500 miles south of Guaymas. Father Garcés spent a trying four months aboard the *San Carlos* as it floundered back and forth in its effort to reach Guaymas. Surviving seasickness, the padres took the overland trail to San Miguel de Horcasitas to receive their assignments from Governor Pineda. Juan Gil finally arrived at his Mission Guevavi in mid-May 1768 and found the little church adorned with two altars and one small side altar with paintings in gilt frames, while the sacristy contained three chalices, a silver baptismal shell, and vestments of all types and colors.

THE ARIZONA MISSIONS, 1768

From Guevavi, Father Gil could see the cottonwoods along the banks of the shallow northward-flowing river; above the pueblo to the south the mission Indians irrigated plots of maize. Father Gil and his military escort rode north downriver to call on the visita of Calabazas, which had a small, half-built adobe, and a dozen families. Ten miles farther on, the visita at San Juan Tumacácori had both a church and a cemetery and more natives than at either Guevavi or Calabazas—possibly more than 100. Here on May 20, 1768, the gray-robed friar baptized nineteen Pápago Indians, calling seven of them Isidro or Isidra in honor of the patron saint of Madrid and one he called Juan Crisóstomo. The third visita, San Ignacio de Sonoita, half hidden in the hills, stood directly in the path of Apaches raiding southwestward into the Santa Cruz Valley. And, though there should have been a detachment of soldiers at Sonoita, but there were not enough troops both to fight the Seris and guard against the Apaches. Clearly, Father Gil would have his work cut out for him.

San Ignacio de Tubac

At the presidio of Tubac lived nearly 500 people. In addition to the garrison of fifty-one men, including three officers and a chaplain, their dependents and servants, there were dozens of settlers, most of them gente de razón, who were refugees from the abandoned ranchos upriver. A 1767 census of Tubac settlers showed 34 heads of family, 144 dependents, plus 26 servants and their families for a total of well over 200. The presidial chapel, begun at Anza's personal expense, stood just to the northwest with the cemetery in front. The royal presidio at this time focused on keeping peace between the Pimas and Pápagos while defending the province against the Apaches.

San Xavier del Bac

When Father Garcés arrived at remote San Xavier del Bac at the end of June 1768, he was welcomed by the local Indians. He described them as being very wild, without religious concepts even in their own language. After six weeks, Garcés wrote to the guardian of his college that he believed the Piman Indians at Bac would be better adjusted in Tucson than in San Xavier since the Tucson social structure was influenced by the Northern Piman Indians who had migrated there. Encountering three Indians governors who were natives of three former pueblos, the Franciscan urged his superior to assign a full-time missionary to Tucson, because a third priest on the Santa Cruz River could take care of additional Indian needs.

Within two months of his arrival, Garcés decided that the mission was functioning well enough for him to embark upon the first of his exploring trips; it is for these that he is best known historically. Leaving on August 29, 1768, and guided by four Indians, Garcés traversed Pápago territory to the Gila River, preaching the gospel through an interpreter. Upon his return in October, having been gone nearly two months, he fell violently ill. Unconscious for twenty-four hours, Garcés later suffered severe chills when Father Gil had him carried the sixty miles to Guevavi to recuperate.

While Garcés was gone, an Apache war party of about 200 ran off the Terrenate garrison's entire herd of horses and then raided San Xavier del Bac, killing its native governor and carrying off the two-man soldier escort. The next day the Apaches struck 75 miles southeast, stealing 37 oxen and 180 head of cattle from Santa María Soamca. The few mission Indians, remembering a recent Apache attack in which ten of them died and three were abducted, let the animals go. After Garcés returned to Bac, Apaches raided again on February 20, 1769. Continuing their fierce raids well into the spring, the garrison at Tubac did not have the strength to retaliate.

New Restrictions Become a Problem

Apache raids were not the only problem that confronted the new Franciscans. When Father President Buena had been at Tubutama no more than a few weeks, he realized that the new way of running the missions was a disaster. The king's wish that the Indians of Sonora be given freedom to live and learn with non-Indians was not working. Buena complained to his superior that the natives lived in perpetual idleness without any form of discipline, and therefore would not pay attention to the teachings of the church. Besides, the annual subsidy of 360 pesos for mission expenses was not enough for the father to maintain himself and pay a cook, houseboy, and tortilla maker;

provide wine and wax for services; improve the mission; and offer the Indians material benefits. Father Buena also believed that each mission should have two friars to work in such a sparsely populated area.

Governor Pineda responded by suggesting that the friars cultivate some mission land and offered to supply some livestock at low prices, but because of the Apache danger, it was difficult to protect the herds. The padres all complained that the annual stipend scarcely covered church expenses and was barely enough to maintain one missionary. Worst of all, the padres had no material means to attract the natives and no authority to mete out discipline; they were dealing with a group of people who were culturally very different.

Governor Pineda, Father Buena, Captain Anza, and others all looked toward José de Gálvez, the king's brilliant visitador, as the man who was going to solve the problems of the Sonoran frontier. For eight months Gálvez had been struggling with the needs of Baja California and had launched the Alta California expedition, but now he was needed to bring the war against the Seris to a close and free up troops to deal with the Apaches. The missionaries also wanted advice on changing the way the missions were run. Gálvez finally left the Baja California peninsula for Alamos to inspect military operations in Sonora. Prior to his arrival he had written to Father President Buena asking that the Seris be offered a proposal that in exchange for peace, they would not be punished for past crimes. Buena failed to establish peace in his mission, but decided to discuss other matters with Gálvez. High on his list was the problem of Franciscan administration of the missions.

On June 3, 1769, in the company of Father Buena at Alamos, Gálvez eliminated the rule of the *comisarios* in La Pimería Alta, just as he had done in Baja California and southern Sonora. He wrote to Governor Pineda ordering the immediate surrender of mission temporalities, which belonged to the Indians, plus a complete list of gold and silver taken from each and a listing of all supplies furnished to the friars. The friars would finally be totally in charge.

According to the padres, ideas of the Enlightenment ultimately failed in the missions of La Pimería Alta. The Franciscans had tried to stand by while the Indians became independent, hardworking, taxpaying Christians, but European and native cultures had not yet become integrated. The Franciscans themselves, having taken vows of poverty, were not always astute businessmen and had their own problems in managing the mission temporalities, but they needed more power to bargain with the governing powers of New Spain. Despite the major cultural differences between Spaniards and Indians, the missions of southern Arizona, with certain adjustments, continued to function as frontier institutions, and Spanish settlement pushed its way further to the north and west.

Gálvez's Illness

Shortly after his arrival in Alamos, Gálvez began to suffer recurring attacks of fatigue accompanied by severe fevers and intermittent periods of irrational behavior. The revolt of Seri Indians on the Río Fuerte had put his plans far behind schedule and his offer of amnesty had brought few results. On his way to campaign headquarters at San

Miguel de Horcasitas (Pitic), Gálvez began to show signs of mental derangement that bordered on insanity. Stopping over at San Miguel de Ures, he seemed to recover temporarily, and on September 29, at the fiesta of San Miguel, Gálvez told a large crowd of natives about their obligations and duties to the new friars. He dictated a set of orders that left no doubt as to the relationship of the natives to the Franciscans.

First, all Indians were to begin attending Christian instruction daily. If they failed, they were to receive twenty-five lashes for the first offense and fifty for the second. The same punishment was to be applied to any Indian who refused to work. Gente de razón living at the missions were to recognize the padre as their proper priest and were not to apply to the secular priest for marriage or any other reason. Mission Indians were to think of themselves as sons of the mission (*hijos de la misión*), not as relatives of pagans. Spanish was to be spoken whenever possible and taught to the Indian children. The mission Indians were to give up their native surnames and assume those of the Spaniards. Finally, Gálvez suggested that the Seris, after their defeat, would also need a mission; Father President Buena accompanied the visitador to Pitic to confer with the governor on this issue.

After two weeks with Governor Pineda and Captain Domingo Elizondo, Gálvez suffered a collapse. Seriously stricken on the night of October 14, 1769, Gálvez insisted at various times that the Virgin Mary gave him divine instructions and that St. Francis of Assisi had brought him field reports. Governor Pineda and his staff diagnosed the malady as megalomania and, at the suggestion of Father Buena, decided that Gálvez should return to the mission at Ures for rest and recovery.

On one occasion at Ures, while under particular stress, Gálvez claimed to be, among other important personages, king of Prussia, Charles XII of Sweden, deputy of the admiral of Spain, St. Joseph, and finally the Eternal Father himself. He even signed one of his papers "Joseph de Gálvez, insane for this world; pray for him, that he be happy in the next." (Priestley, *José de Gálvez: Visitor-General of New Spain*, p. 280) When the visitador was coherent, however, Father Buena reminded him of the need for two missionaries at each mission and showed him letters from Francisco Garcés telling of the many pagans awaiting salvation beyond the Gila. When Gálvez was finally able to travel, Father Buena accompanied him as far as Chihuahua and further protected by the men who served him, Gálvez regained his health in Mexico City early in 1770. Within six months, and after hearing news of the successful settlement of Alta California at San Diego (July 1769) and Monterey (June 1770), he was able to return to Spain. Despite his illness, he had fulfilled his charges as visitador general with such success that Carlos III appointed him to the Council of the Indies. Gálvez advanced to its head as minister of the Indies in 1776. Throughout his life, he never forgot the kindness shown to him by Father Buena when he had been ill.

LA PIMERÍA ALTA, 1770

Meanwhile, conditions in La Pimería Alta had not improved, in fact they had become worse. An epidemic in March 1770, which had decimated the Seris, evidently spread north. In one week Father Gil at Guevavi buried eight mission Indians, including Governor Eusebio of Tumacácori. In addition, Apaches killed seven from Calabazas and to the west, Pápagos disguised as Apaches began stealing and slaughtering stock. The thought that the entire Pápago nation, estimated at 3,000, might join the rebel Pimas, Seris, and Apaches became cause for alarm. The whole situation was not at all conducive to peace.

Governor Pineda, who had become grossly overweight, then suffered a stroke, becoming partially paralyzed. He quickly ordered Anza and sixty presidial soldiers, who were fighting Seris under Colonel Domingo Elizondo on the Gulf of California, to join Captain Bernardo de Urrea of Altar to bring peace to Pápago country. His show of military strength was successful, and the Pápagos settled down.

On April 17, 1770, Anza left Tubac for San Xavier del Bac and Tucson. Three Sobaipuri families had already departed for the Gila River settlements and factionalism had reached a peak. Anza persuaded the natives still at Tucson to remain there and ordered the three migrant Sobaipuri families to return. Anza picked out a place for the people to construct a protective wall, which became the first major European-style construction at Tucson, and listened to the complaints of the Sobaipuris. The Indians said they had long wanted a church, but the missionaries had failed to provide one. They also wanted a food subsidy, so Father Garcés granted the Indians all their own wheat from the church field at Tucson—ten bushels—and half of that from Bac. With that, the natives agreed to stay and build a church.

Anza, on his way back to Pitic with the ailing Governor Pineda, killed some Apaches in a skirmish. In retaliation, the Apaches devastated Father Gil's visita at Sonoita and killed nineteen Pimas, including women and children. Among them were the native Governor Juan María and his wife Isabel. It was for this and other reasons that Father Gil decided to move his mission to Tumacácori, the largest of the mission pueblos and closest to help and the presidio of Tubac.

Father Garcés and the Opas

Father Garcés described these Indians as friendly and curious and commented that with their good lands, they grew cotton, squash, watermelons, maize and even wheat. The Opas were robust and stocky, comparatively light-skinned, and appeared to be hard workers. They lacked skills at warfare but were learning some fighting techniques from the Pimas. Even though they grew cotton, the women still wore a kind of skirt that consisted of a stick wrapped around the body from which were hung many ribbon-like strips that they obtained from the bark of the willow.

Father Garcés mentioned that the Opas were not densely concentrated even though there were many people and many pueblos. The Indians were amazed and happy that Father Garcés traveled alone and wanted to know what he wore under his habit. He told them about his religion and felt the natives had some knowledge of God because they called upon Him when they planted or when they were ill. He noted that the Indians wanted to steal whatever they could, but since he had little, they just looked over his things and left them alone. They shared their food and fish with him and, according to Garcés, were not stingy like the Pápagos, who were probably that way because of poverty.

After talking with a Cocomaricopa delegation from the Colorado River and promising them that he would return another day, Garcés headed back to San Xavier del Bac at the end of October 1770, which he reached after a trip of nearly 250 miles.

Change in Mission Personnel

In the meantime, Father Gil at Tumacácori had been very sick, somewhat in the same manner as the Jesuit Father Segesser before him. Father President Buena sent Fray Francisco Sánchez Zuñiga, a native of Hervas in northern Extremadura, to take his place. Father Sánchez Zuñiga had entered the Franciscan Order at the Recollect convent of Santa María de Gracia in 1761. He traveled to New Spain with thirty-seven other Franciscan missionaries in 1769, the same year that Father Junípero Serra reached Alta California. Father Sánchez Zuñiga was just 28 years old when he accepted his assignment at Tumacácori, a frontier mission where Apaches recently had killed five mission Indians, though Sánchez Zuñiga and the others had believed the assurance of José de Gálvez that the Apaches were under control. Unfortunately, Colonel Elizondo and his soldiers had been recalled from the area in fear of a British invasion. However, Presidio Commandant Anza knew the Apaches were not under control and asked the interim Governor Pedro Corbalán, who had replaced Pineda, for Indian auxiliaries from the missions of San Ignacio and Saric to serve on a voluntary basis. He also asked Father President Buena to supply provisions and animals from the missions since nothing was available in the Tubac area. In early August 1771 Anza rode out of Tubac toward the Gila River with thirty-four presidial soldiers and fifty Pima auxiliaries. On August 9, they surprised an Apache ranchería, killing nine and taking eight prisoners. The attack was successful, though in the meantime an epidemic struck the mission Indians at Tumacácori. In the end, Father Sánchez Zuñiga gave up his assignment to a recovered Father Juan Gil, and rode southward to relieve the priest at San Ignacio.

At the same time, Father Garcés took another trip to the Gila and Colorado Rivers, leaving San Xavier del Bac in early August 1771. He went to the pueblos of Ati and Sonoita and then decided to go on to Yuma. He continued westward until he reached the Río Azul, thought to be a branch of the Gila. As he traveled on toward the Colorado, he passed several rancherías where the Indians were friendly and wanted him to stay. He spent September west of the Colorado writing about various Indian groups, and on September 28, Garcés appears to have been near the mouth of the Colorado and may have reached the gulf. Finally, after visiting a funeral ceremony held by the Yumas for eleven of their men who had been killed in a fight with the Cocomaricopas and Gila River Pimas, he decided to return to Bac. His diary ends on October 28, 1771, at Caborca with the comments that his diet had consisted of many pitahayas, and that even though he was somewhat sick when he left, after all of his traveling, he was no better or worse off than before.

Father Garcés returned from his trip only to find two sick companions. He had to look after the ailing Father Gil as well as Father Juan Joseph Agorreta of Saric, who had begun to suffer with chills and fever while he was taking care of Gil. Garcés, however, who had been traveling for two months among the Indians, was healthy and looking forward to his next journey. As the winter of 1771–1772 approached, Anza and the commanders of Terrenate and Fronteras struggled against the Apaches while the padres, except for Garcés, struggled against illness. Father President Buena suffered from excruciating hemorrhoids and could no longer ride a horse, finally deciding to retire to the college at Querétaro. He appointed Father Juan Gil of Tumacácori as his successor who could now head for a more healthful climate.

Antonio Bucareli Becomes Viceroy

The 46th viceroy of New Spain, El Bailio Frey Antonio María Bucareli y Ursua, Laso de la Vega, Villacis y Córdoba, was born in Seville on January 24, 1717. His family was so distinguished that young Antonio was made a member of the military order of San Juan de Jerusalem at the age of 5 and at age 15 became a cadet in the brigade of Royal Carabineers. He fought with distinction in Italy and Portugal and reorganized the entire Spanish cavalry, becoming a lieutenant general of the Royal Army. In 1766 Bucareli entered the field of colonial administration when he became governor and captain-general of Cuba. Because of his meritorious service, he was promoted to viceroy of New Spain and took over from the Marqués de Croix in September 1771. Although instructed to carry on the campaigns of Gálvez and Croix, Bucareli decided first to get the facts.

Hugo Oconor

Bucareli sent the Irish-born Colonel Hugo Oconor (O'Connor), former commandant of the presidio of Adais and interim governor of Texas from 1768 to 1771, to assess the military situation in the north. Oconor had arrived in Cuba from Spain with the Regiment of Volunteers of Aragón and had served there until 1765 under his first cousin Alejandro O'Reilly. Known as El Capitán Colorado because of his ruddy complexion, Oconor was responsible for putting into effect the earlier recommendations of the Marqués de Rubí.

Bucareli decided to postpone the planned expansion of the Franciscan missions to the Gila River, but made sure that the missionaries of California under Father Junípero Serra were supplied with the necessary goods to maintain a settlement. The new viceroy took a more conservative view with regard to the padres' administrative control over the Indians. He agreed that the Marqués de Croix's enlightened reforms that gave the Indians more independence had not been successful.

New Missionaries

Several of the new missionaries who had come from Spain in 1769 were assigned to the northern frontier, including Fray Bartolome Ximeno who had grown up in the same general region of Aragon as had Father Garcés. Ximeno entered the Franciscan Order in 1759, just five years after Garcés. The two had met in Calatayud when Garcés was studying theology and Ximeno was making his novitiate. As he reached the mission of Tumacácori, Ximeno would find that his Aragonese companion was just a short distance away at Mission San Xavier del Bac. By November 1772, Ximeno was joined by Father Gaspar Francisco de Clemente, a native of the villa of Pancorvo in northern Spain. In 1764 Clemente had become a Franciscan in Vitoria and then served as a deacon in Santander until joining the group of friars traveling to New Spain in 1769. At the time of his arrival in Tumacácori, Clemente was just 27 years old.

For the first time, there were two friars to fulfill frontier mission duties, so Ximeno and Clemente began to improve the buildings. They tore down the brush huts, began to build adobe dwellings, and refurbished the Tumacácori church. They built a wall around the entire complex, hoping to protect themselves from Apache intruders. At Calabazas they installed a roof on the church and put the building into service.

The Death of Father Gil

As it turns out, this period was a tragic time for the Spaniards. Father President Juan Crisóstomo Gil became involved in a struggle with the military governor Mateo Sastre, his fellow Franciscan Antonio Maria de los Reyes, the supply officer of the college at Querétaro in Mexico City, and finally the Indians themselves. While Reyes wanted to adopt a new plan for administering the missions, Gil wanted more protection from the Apaches. Unless something were done to stop the Apaches, who were killing mission Indians and driving off the horses, all the new methods suggested by Reyes would not save the missions. Even the presidial soldiers could not protect their own herds.

Finally, on March 6, 1773, Father Gil led his neophytes away from Carrizal after hearing that rebel Pimas were going to kill everyone in the mission. That night they saw the mission burn. Returning the next morning to see what could be done, Father Gil was attacked by four youths who pounded him with rocks until he was dead. The people of Carrizal buried the body and put up a tent over his grave; by the time the soldiers arrived, the Indians had cut off the heads of two of the murderers and captured the alleged ringleader. Many of the natives wept for their priest, while the Franciscans had their first martyr on the Sonoran frontier. Coincidentally, Governor Sastre died a few days later, insisting that Father Gil was coming to absolve him for his sins. His attendants later decided that the martyred priest had stopped to console the dying governor on his way to heaven. A year later, Father Joseph Antonio Caxa was named to succeed Gil as Father President.

REGLAMENTO OF 1772

As already indicated, vast changes had been made in the colonial territories of North America after 1763. In fact, Spain had become heir to Louisiana in 1760, even before England received the cession of Canada from France. The control of additional warlike tribes brought increasing responsibilities to Spanish officials, while only the Mississippi River lay between Spanish territory and that of England. To meet the demands of this difficult situation, Spain's Indian policy had to undergo a fundamental change. Because the French had been accustomed to making annual gifts of guns, powder, and other articles to the friendly tribes, the Spaniards felt forced to continue this practice or make new enemies. It had long been a standard Spanish policy to prevent weapons from falling into the hands of Indians.

Changes under the Reglamento

As mentioned earlier, the plan of the Marqués de Rubí to relocate certain presidios was put into execution by the new Reglamento for Presidios adopted by the king on September 10, 1772. The northern provinces were set apart as a separate jurisdiction to be governed by a commanding general independent of the viceroy. The Reglamento was based upon Rubí's recommendations of 1768 as formulated by José de Gálvez and promulgated provisionally by the viceroy Marqués de Croix. Until a commanding general was named, Oconor was chosen to put the plan into action. Unfortunately, his total force of about 400 soldiers was insufficient to meet the ordinary demands of warfare without the additional burden of moving presidios to new locations.

Rubí had suggested spacing the frontier presidios at regular intervals to form a cordon of fifteen posts extending from the Gulf of California on the west to the Bahía del Espíritu Santo in Texas. He considered this line to form the true frontier of New Spain and in fact it continued to mark the limit of successful Spanish settlement, eventually approximating the border area between the United States and Mexico. In some cases the presidios were to be moved a great distance from the towns they were expected to defend, under the delusion that they would be better able to stop Indians from approaching the settlements.

Beginning with the four presidios of Sonora in the west, Altar was to be moved a little westward toward the Gulf of California, Tubac a little to the southwest, Terrenate a little to the east, and Fronteras a little to the northwest, into the valley of San Bernardino. The civilians who had settled around these presidios were to remain at the original sites and be reinforced for their own protection by other settlers, both Spaniards and Opata Indians. Santa Fe, New Mexico, was an outpost well beyond the frontier line.

In addition to repositioning the presidios, the Reglamento of 1772 elevated the frontier forces to a status equivalent to that of the king's regular army. They were now to perform the same duties, be subjected to the same discipline, and enjoy the same consideration in regard to promotions, honors, rank, recompense, and retirement. As a protection against the abuses of the past, they were to receive their salaries in advance and semiannually from one of three reasonably convenient disbursement offices, and both their pay and their provisions were to be managed by a company supply officer elected by themselves. The new regulation specifically deprived the captains of this formerly profitable business and held them responsible for the quality and moderate prices of the goods which the new supply officer would provide.

The new Reglamento also attempted to standardize the strength of the companies. Each presidio of the line, which included Tubac, was to consist of a captain, a lieutenant, an ensign (*alférez*), a chaplain, a sergeant, two corporals (*cabos*), forty common soldiers, and ten Indian scouts (*exploradores*). Beyond the line, the governors of New Mexico and Texas were to serve as captains for the companies of Santa Fe and San Antonio, respectively, and these two companies were to have two lieutenants, an ensign, a chaplain, and, respectively, seventy-six and seventy-seven noncommissioned officers and common soldiers. Behind the line, the flying company (*compañía volante*) of Nuevo Santander was also to be commanded by its provincial governor and was to remain at its current strength and distribution in the several towns.

The Reglamento of 1772 also attempted to standardize the pay scale, weapons, uniforms, and mounts of the troops, all of which were charged to their personal accounts as in the past. Each soldier was now to maintain a colt in addition to his string of six serviceable horses and a pack mule as provided in the Reglamento of 1729. Each of the ten Indian scouts was allotted three horses and was to share the service of five pack mules. In order to encourage better marksmanship, each soldier was to be issued cartridges prepared from three pounds of gunpowder every year, and regular target practice was to be held at the presidios. New recruits, who obviously needed the most practice, were to receive a double supply of cartridges during their first year. Only moderate amounts of ammunition were to be issued for actual combat, but an adequate reserve of gunpowder (eight pounds for each soldier) was to be maintained in the presidio under lock and key.

The remaining articles of the Reglamento of 1772 specified the qualifications for captains and subaltern officers, the procedures for monthly reviews of the companies, the strict accounting of vacancies and enlistments, the policy to be pursued in dealing with hostile and neutral Indian tribes as well as the civilian settlements at the presidios, the responsibilities of the new commandant inspector of presidios, and the duties of the other officers and common soldiers.

In 1774 Oconor sent Antonio Bonilla to inspect the Sonora military posts and to plan improved defenses there. In the course of his inspection, Bonilla examined the proposed site at Aribaca where the presidial garrison located at Tubac was to move according to the Rubí plan. Bonilla reported that the area was unhealthful, as Father Sedelmayr had noted twenty-two years before. Bonilla therefore recommended against moving the Tubac presidio to that site. At the same time, Captain Juan Bautista de Anza rendered Rubí's concept of the western section of the frontier line obsolete when he and Father Francisco Garcés succeeded in opening a land route from Sonora to Upper California. To protect the new supply route, Spanish posts farther north than Rubí's envisioned straight line from gulf to gulf became necessary.

THE ROUTE TO CALIFORNIA

One of the first developments under Bucareli's administration was the reassignment of the Franciscan missions of Lower California to the Dominicans. This religious order originated from the work of Domingo (Dominic) de Guzmán (1170–1221), a Castilian cleric sent in 1210 to convert Albigensian heretics in southern France. Dominic saw the need for creating a highly educated group of preachers to fight heresy with learning and logic. Members of the mendicant Dominican order, sometimes called Friars Preachers or Black Friars (from the color of their robes), took vows of poverty, chastity and obedience; they dedicated themselves to scholarship as well as to preaching.

The Dominicans had worked hard in New Spain and were anxious to participate in the conversion of California. The Franciscans strenuously resisted their efforts until the favorable reports from Upper California made retention of establishments on the lower peninsula less desirable. The final division of the missions was agreed upon between the two orders on April 7, 1772. The new boundary, marked with a cross about fifty miles southeast of San Diego, was close to the present international border. Father Francisco Palóu, a companion of Serra in Mallorca, received word of the transfer at Loreto and officially delivered the mission properties to his Dominican successor. Eight Franciscans, including Palóu, were released in the spring of 1773 for missionary service in Upper California.

While Viceroy Bucareli showed concern for religious matters and Indian welfare, his major policies were governed by military considerations. He had long known of California's strategic value as a buffer colony against foreign aggression by sea. In fact, rumors of an English voyage to the North Pole and the threat of Russian activities in the Pacific northwest led Bucareli to plan renewed naval exploration. Although this was a primary goal, Viceroy Bucareli also wanted to establish an overland trail from Sonora to

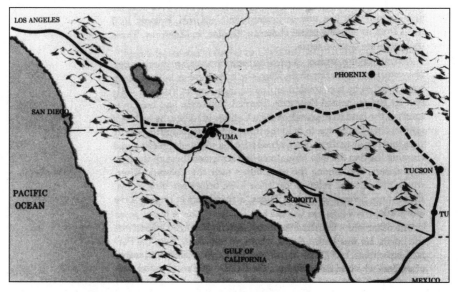

Map 9.2. Map showing Anza's routes in 1774 and 1775 (dotted line) from Tubac in Arizona to the San Gabriel Mission near present-day Los Angeles. Courtesy The Copley Press.

California. Long envisioned by Father Kino and his Jesuit missionaries, it became an official project of José de Gálvez and the Spanish government in the early 1770s. Difficulties experienced by sea and on the trail from Baja California had proven these routes impractical for families of settlers and large herds of livestock. A way to reach Monterey was needed to facilitate civilian settlement of Spain's isolated California province.

The man who had revived Kino's plan was the intrepid Father Francisco Garcés; the one to realize it was frontier Captain Juan Bautista de Anza, who had wanted to establish communication with California even during the Jesuit period. He had asked permission to cooperate with Portolá in the 1769 expedition to California, but pressure from the Seri Indians in Sonora had led Gálvez to refuse his request. Father Garcés had become conversant in the Pima language and familiar with the desert regions of the Gila and Colorado Rivers. On a journey in 1771, during which he covered some 800 miles, Garcés established an amiable contact with the Yuma Indians and their chief, whom he named Salvador Palma. He reported his success to Anza at Tubac, who in turn wrote to Viceroy Bucareli on May 10, 1772, telling of Garcés' visit to the strategically located Yumas and asking approval to open a trail to Monterey.

The viceroy, typically careful, sought the advice of engineer Miguel Costansó who had been in California with Serra, had designed the presidio of Monterey, and was familiar with the terrain. Although all reports were favorable, a governmental junta delayed approval until further information could be obtained. Father Serra, then in Mexico to present his suggestions for California's government, strongly urged the new route. A second junta provided the necessary resolution and Bucareli, anticipating the king's consent, advised Anza to proceed. By the time royal approval reached Mexico in early March 1774, the expedition was well on its way.

Shortly before Anza and Garcés departed for California, they were blessed by the fortuitous arrival of Sebastián Tarabal, a Cochimí Indian from Baja California who had run away from Mission San Gabriel. Attempting to return home with his wife and brother, Tarabal crossed the San Jacinto Mountains, the Borrego Desert, and finally the treacherous sand dunes near the Colorado River, from which he alone emerged lost but alive. The exhausted Indian reached Tubac and gave himself up to Anza; he was added to the expedition as a guide. Tarabal devoted himself to Father Garcés and became his constant companion during the next seven years.

The First Expedition, 1774

Anza's thirty-four-man party left Tubac on January 8, 1774, with ample provisions and animals. They reached the Yuma village at the junction of the Gila and Colorado without difficulty, but from there on the trail was rough. Chief Palma, whom Anza confirmed in office as governor of the Quechans and decorated with a red ribbon and royal coin, gave them help across the Colorado River. The men headed south in an attempt to avoid the seemingly interminable sand dunes. Abandoned by their local Indian guides, they became lost in the endless sand. After ten days they returned to the Colorado and again found the Yumas. Anza, leaving a portion of his party behind, followed Tarabal's lead on a more northerly course to the distant mountains. Passing through the San Carlos pass high above the Cahuilla Valley, the men rejoiced to see green valleys and snowy mountains. They camped along the San Jacinto River, later crossing present-day Ontario and Riverside, and finally entered the crudely fashioned gates of Mission San Gabriel on March 22. Garcés returned to the Colorado under orders from Anza and made the trip in twelve days. Anza continued on to Monterey, where he arrived on May 1. He turned homeward after just three days, since Fernando de Rivera y Moncada, the new governor, had not yet reached his post and was not soon expected.

Anza and his men traveled in the tracks of Garcés and arrived at the junction of the Gila and Colorado where they were received with great joy by Chief Palma and the Yuma Indians. The Indians made a raft and ferried them over to the place where Garcés had made camp. There, Anza found that his soldiers and muleteers had fled to Caborca, having heard that the captain had been killed. Anza and Garcés traveled together from May 15 to 21 when Garcés met two Halchidhoma Indians who invited the priest to visit the Upper Colorado. He joined them on a trip over the route used by Father Sedelmayr in 1744.

Garcés traveled to the vicinity of the Chemehuevi Mountains visiting the Halchidhomas and meeting some of their Yavapai friends. A Yavapai elder told Garcés that his people were especially friendly with the Quechans whom all the people called Cutchanas. The Halchidhomas impressed Garcés tremendously as their houses were better and larger than any he had ever seen and their fields were superior to those of the Quechans. Garcés was determined to contact some Mojave Indians upstream, but the Halchidhomas refused to help him because the Mojaves were enemies. In the meantime, Anza's weary company of twenty-five men had arrived at Tubac on May 26 after an absence of more than four months. Garcés did not return to San Xavier until July 10, 1774.

Anza's Second Journey to California

Pleased with Anza's success, Viceroy Bucareli promoted him to lieutenant colonel and granted his men extra pay for life. The two met in Mexico City in late 1774, where plans were being made to strengthen Alta California by sending settlers, soldiers, and livestock over the Yuma route. Anza and Bucareli drew up plans for a second expedition—a large-scale enterprise designed to help put California on a sound and permanent basis. During early 1775, Anza recruited mestizo settlers living in Sinaloa on the edge of poverty to settle in California by way of Arizona.

After gaining royal approval, Anza set out from Tubac on October 23, 1775, with a total of 240 men, women, and children and almost 1,000 animals. The expedition was accompanied by Father Garcés and Father Tomás Eixarch who would remain temporarily among the Quechans. The very pious Father Pedro Font from the Franciscan college at Querétaro kept a diary of the journey. With Sebastián Tarabal as guide and three Indian interpreters, the Spaniards proceeded northwest to the Gila, visiting the Gila Pimas and the Pápagos, as well as the Opas and Cocomaricopas. Though the Opas had suffered from attacks by the Yavapais, Anza thought they and the others had improved their standard of living. Hopi blankets were seen among the Gila Pimas, Quechans, and Kohuanas and the latter two groups had acquired cotton blankets made by the Opas and Gila Pimas.

After traveling some thirty miles up the Gila from the Colorado to Laguna Salada, the Spaniards met a Quechan messenger who could serve as a guide. Two days later, Salvador Palma and his brother extended official greetings. The expedition crossed the Gila about two and one-half miles from the Colorado and camped on what had been an island in 1774 but was now connected to the shore. Here the Cocomaricopas and Quechans entered into a final peace agreement. Chief Palma indicated to Father Font that missionaries should come to live with the Quechans. Palma had even selected the site for the Spaniards to use, Puerto de la Concepción, or today's Fort Yuma Hill.

Because the crossing of the previous year was unusable, Anza attempted the next day to find a ford. Less than a mile upstream from its junction with the Gila, the Colorado was divided into three branches, and the expedition was able to cross at that point the day after. In the meantime, a Halchidhoma messenger had arrived among the Quechans and was sent back to his people with greetings from the Spaniards. Anza's party camped on the California side of the river a few miles northeast of the residence and village of Palma. A house was constructed for Garcés and Eixarch close to Palma's home, and on December 3, the entire expedition moved from the riverbank to Axa Kwedexor, the new camp.

The Spaniards wanted to maintain Chief Palma's enthusiasm for the Europeans, and gave him many gifts for that purpose. According to Font, Palma donned the new suit that consisted of "a jacket with a yellow front and some decorations, a cape of blue decorated with gold braid, and a cap of black velvet adorned with imitation jewels and a crest like a palm." (Diary of Pedro Font in Pourade, *Anza Conquers the Desert: The Anza Expeditions from Mexico to California and the Founding of San Francisco, 1774 to 1776*, p. 126) This uniform no doubt aided the friendship between Palma and the Spaniards and helped raise the chief's standing among the Quechans.

On December 4, the expedition departed from Axa Kwedexor, saying good-bye to Garcés and Eixarch with their four servants. They traveled to the west, crossing a branch of the Colorado that made the Fort Yuma Hill–Axa Kwedexor area a long island. From this area the party traveled southwest and left the main stream of the Colorado. During the day, they passed through some friendly Quechan villages and after three or four leagues, they arrived at the Laguna de los Coxas (or Cojats). According to Anza, this area marked the end of the jurisdiction of Captain Palma and of the Yuma tribe.

On December 6, 1775, the expedition left los Coxas and journeyed twelve or thirteen miles over a winding route to the Laguna de Santa Olalla. This narrow lagoon was about three miles long and approximately six miles west of the main stream of the Colorado. On the 7th, Anza gave the men an extra ration of liquor, which Font thought was evil. Despite the harsh conditions, the priest complained that "anyone who gets drunk sins, and anyone who contributes to the drunkenness of others also sins." Anza showed no signs of repentance. (Diary of Pedro Font in Pourade, *Anza Conquers the Desert: The Anza Expeditions from Mexico to California and the Founding of San Francisco, 1774 to 1776*, p. 135) The resident Kohuanas were friendly, presenting the Spaniards with net-caught fish. The Spaniards spent several days there preparing to cross the desert, and on December 9 the party, split into three divisions, began marching toward San Sebastián. The journey was made successfully, despite unusual weather conditions coating the Coast Range with snow and dropping a heavy snowfall in the Imperial Valley. In the Yuma area, the older Quechans were surprised to see snow, and some of them, including Palma, said they had never seen such a thing nor known it to be so cold.

At San Sebastián, the Spaniards were greeted by twenty or thirty miserable and hungry Indians who, despite the cold weather, were in the habit of bathing every morning. On December 16, some Kumeyaay Indians from a rugged mountain range (the Superstition Mountains) about ten miles away succeeded in stealing three horses. In response, Anza sent out five soldiers who recovered the horses from two villages located at the foot of the mountains near a marsh with brackish water. Two of the horses were hobbled and one was tied to a mesquite when found, indicating that these Indians had handled horses before. Ironically, the weather ultimately forced part of the expedition to leave six horses behind in that same region.

The Anza party was fortunate in that it did not encounter major difficulties with the Indians, for on November 4 and 5, the Kumeyaay near San Diego had revolted against the missionaries, and anti-Spanish feeling had spread northward to the Indians of the San Gabriel area. As early as November 27, news of the attack on San Diego Mission had reached the Quechans, although when Anza received the information from Palma, he apparently disregarded it. In January 1776, the Quechans received more definite information when a Kumeyaay arrived on the Colorado River with word that two or three nations had united to fight against the Spaniards of the seacoast. Already they had killed a padre and burned his house, but to the Spaniards who had passed through, the Yumas had done nothing, knowing that they were the Quechans' friends. But if both groups of Spaniards united to attack them, the Kumeyaay would in turn attack the Anza party. The Kumeyaay "brought this message on behalf of his nation, because they well knew that they were very old friends" of the Quechans. (Forbes, *Warriors of the Colorado: The Yumas of the Quechan Nation and their Neighbors*, p. 464) The Quechans continued to remain pro-Spanish under Palma's leadership, although the attack at San Diego eventually may have helped to alter their feelings.

A cold Christmas Eve was spent in today's Anza-Borrego desert where a young soldier's wife gave birth to a baby boy. Father Font said three masses on Christmas Day to thank God for their safety. By early January, they knew they would reach their destination. Overall, Anza, a competent frontiersman, had led his mixed assemblage for three months over desert sands, across the swollen Colorado, and through rugged mountains to Mission San Gabriel—with a net gain of four persons. Eight children were born during the course of the expedition and the party's single loss was one woman who died in childbirth. Anza viewed the births with mixed emotions since the mothers could not ride horseback for a few days and delayed the entire expedition. Father Garcés, Sebastián Tarabal, and one other remained in the territory of the Yuma Indians and explored new areas to the north.

ANZA'S WORK IN CALIFORNIA

Shortly after his arrival at San Gabriel Mission on January 4, 1776, Anza received a call to assist Governor Rivera in strengthening Spanish control at Mission San Diego. As mentioned, during the previous November the non-mission Kumeyaay of the district, in collusion with some of the neophytes, had planned the simultaneous attack on both mission and presidio reported to Anza above. On November 4, 1775, hundreds of Indians, shouting their revenge, had approached the mission and set the buildings on fire. They dragged Father Luis Jaime from his quarters and beat him to death; his mutilated body was later found pierced with eighteen arrow wounds. One other Spaniard was killed and a third died of wounds after several days. The attack on the presidio, however, apparently miscarried and the arrival of reinforcements under Rivera and Anza brought the Indians under submission. With further danger averted, Anza departed for Monterey while Rivera remained at San Diego.

When the Indian leaders of the revolt were finally caught, Father Serra asked that they be forgiven and punished only moderately so they could eventually be converted to Christianity. Mission repairs were begun the following summer with the help of Diego Choquet, commander of the supply ship *San Antonio,* and his crew. Christian Indians, together with the sailors, the boatswain, and officers mixed clay, made adobe bricks, dug trenches, and gathered stone for the new church. There were no further uprisings at Mission San Diego.

Anza proceeded with a few families up the coast and, though slowed by driving rains, reached Monterey on March 10, 1776. His second-in-command, Lieutenant José Joaquín Moraga, arrived a few days later with the rest of the colonists. Anza, then suffering from illness, nevertheless proceeded to explore the San Francisco peninsula as instructed by Viceroy Bucareli. Unable or unwilling to await the arrival of Rivera, whom he was ordered to assist, Anza picked out a site for the presidio at a place called Cantil Blanco. In the company of Father Pedro Font, he selected a place for the mission along a small stream that he called Arroyo de Nuestra Señora de los Dolores. Anza then returned to Monterey and failed in several attempts to meet with Rivera. The governor, angry at Anza for proceeding alone with the San Francisco project, and severely ill himself, exchanged only a few words with the Sonoran captain before the latter departed for Tubac and his regular frontier duty.

Acting upon orders from Rivera at San Diego, Lieutenant Moraga, accompanied by Fathers Palóu and Cambon, led the settlers to a new site at the tip of the peninsula overlooking the entrance to the bay. Both the presidio, founded on September 17, 1776, and the mission, officially dedicated near the Arroyo Dolores on October 9, honored Saint Francis of Assisi, founder of the Franciscan order. When the news reached Mexico, Viceroy Bucareli joyfully celebrated completion of the San Francisco project. He then continued work on a plan to connect New Mexico with California by an overland trail.

Chapter Nine
BIBLIOGRAPHIC ESSAY

The basic documents covering this period are found in the Archivo General de Indias under the headings of "Guadalajara" and "Mexico." In addition, some are contained in the Archivo General de la Nación, Mexico, D.F., *Historia* and *Marina*. Additional manuscript and microfilm collections are contained in The Bancroft Library, University of California, Berkeley and the Huntington Library, San Marino, California. Luis Navarro Garcia, *Don José de Gálvez y la Comandancia General de las Provincias Internas del Norte de Nueva España* (Sevilla: Escuela de Estudios Hispano Americanos, 1964) is an important source for this period. Older standard works are Irving Berdine Richman, *California Under Spain and Mexico, 1535–1857* (Boston and New York: Houghton Mifflin, 1911); Herbert I. Priestley, *José de Gálvez: Visitor-General of New Spain* (Berkeley: University of California Press, 1916); Charles E. Chapman, *The Founding of Spanish California: The Northwestward Expansion of New Spain, 1687–1783* (New York: Macmillan, 1916); and Chapman, *A History of California: The Spanish Period* (New York: Macmillan, 1921).

A primary source for the Franciscan effort in Alta California is the work of Father Francisco Palou, a student and companion of Father Junípero Serra in Mallorca. Palou chronicled the history of this era in *Noticias de la Nueva California* completed in 1783, translated and published as *Historical Memoirs of New California* by Herbert E. Bolton, 4 vols. (Berkeley: University of California Press, 1926) and in his biographical study *Vida del Padre Serra* edited and translated by C. S. Williams in 1913, with a recent edition published by the Academy of American Franciscan History in 1955 edited by Father Maynard Geiger, O.F.M. The Franciscan father Zephyrin Engelhardt wrote *The Missions and Missionaries of California* in four volumes (San Francisco: The James H. Barry Company, 1908–1915) and prepared individual histories of sixteen of the twenty-one Franciscan missions in California during the 1920s. Geiger's *Life and Times of Father Junípero Serra* (Washington, D.C.: Academy of American Franciscan History, 1959) and Francis J. Weber's twenty-three volume *Documentary History of the California Missions* (Los Angeles, 1975–1987) are also useful for the missionary point of view. Philosophical backgrounds are given in Iris H.W. Engstrand "The Enlightenment in Spain: Influences on New World Policy," *The Americas*, 61 (April 1985):436–444 and Francis F. Guest, "Mission Colonization and Political Control in Spanish California," *Journal of San Diego History*, 24 (winter 1978):97–116. The Spanish search for Monterey is narrated in Herbert E. Bolton, trans. and ed., *Fray Juan Crespi: Missionary Explorer on the Pacific Coast* (Berkeley: University of California Press, 1927). *The Narrative of the Portolá Expedition 1769–1770* by Miguel Costansó is accessible in both Spanish and English through the collaboration of Adolph van Hemert-Engert and Frederick J. Teggert (Berkeley: University of California Press, 1910).

A number of newer works have focused on the difficulties faced by Indians in an attempt to adapt to mission life. See Robert H. Jackson and Edward Castillo, *Indians, Franciscans and Spanish Colonization: The Impact of the Mission System on California Indians* (Albuquerque: University of New Mexico

Press, 1995); George H. Phillips, "Indians and the Breakdown of the Spanish Mission System in California," *Ethnohistory*, 21 (fall 1974):291–302; Linda Sizelove, "Indian Adaptation to the Spanish Missions," *Pacific Historian*, 22 (winter 1978):393–402; Daniel Garr, "Planning, Politics and Plunder: The Missions and Indian Pueblos of Hispanic California," *Southern California Quarterly*, 54 (winter 1972):291–312; and Robert H. Jackson, "The Changing Economic Structure of the Alta California Missions—A Reinterpretation," *Pacific Historical Review,* 61 (August 1992):387–415. For an overall assessment of the mission enterprise, see *Columbus, Confrontation and Christianity: The European-American Encounter Revisted*, edited by Timothy O'Keefe (Madison, Wisc.: Forbes Mills Press, 1993) which includes articles by David J. Weber, James Sandos, Clara Sue Kidwell, and Iris H.W. Engstrand.

Valuable for Arizona is John L. Kessell, *Friars, Soldiers, and Reformers: Hispanic Arizona and the Sonora Mission Frontier 1767–1856* (Tucson: University of Arizona Press, 1976) while Henry Dobyns, *Spanish Colonial Tucson* (Tucson: University of Arizona Press, 1976) covers the Tucson area from the military and religious point of view. Basic to the study of the viceroyalty is Bernard E. Bobb, *The Viceregency of Antonio María Bucareli in New Spain, 1771–1779* (Austin: University of Texas, 1962). Max Moorhead, *The Presidio* (Norman; University of Oklahoma Press, 1975) contains the Reglamento of 1772 in addition to illustrations of the presidios on the northern frontier. In 1993 Fay Jackson Smith produced *Captain of the Phantom Presidio* (Spokane, Wash.: The Arthur H. Clark Co.). Joseph P. Sánchez, *Spanish Bluecoats: The Catalonian Volunteers in Northwestern New Spain 1767–1810* (Albuquerque: University of New Mexico Press, 1990) gives good coverage to those serving in the *Compañia Franca de Voluntarios de Cataluña*. See also Charles R. Carlisle and Bernard L. Fontana, "Sonora in 1773: Reports by Five Jaliscan Friars," *Arizona and the West*, 11 (spring and summer, 1969):39–56; 179–90.

For the visit of Hugo Oconor and the adoption of the regulations of 1772 see Enrique Gonzalez Flores and Francisco R. Almada, editors of *Informe de Hugo de O'Conor sobre el estado de las Provincias Internas del Norte, 1771–76* (Mexico, 1952); Donald Cutter, ed. and trans., *The Defenses of Northern New Spain: Hugo O'Conor's Report to Teodoro de Croix, June 22, 1777* (Dallas: Southern Methodist Press, 1994); Mark Santiago, *The Red Captain: The Life of Hugo O'Conor* (Tucson: Arizona Historical Society, 1994); Mary Lu Moore and Delmar L. Beene, "The Interior Provinces of New Spain: the Report of Hugo O'Conor," *Arizona and the West,* 13 (autumn 1971):265–82; and Sidney B. Brinckerhoff and Odie B. Faulk, eds. and trans., *Lancers for the King: A Study of the Frontier Military System of Northern New Spain, with a Translation of the Royal Regulations of 1772* (Phoenix: Arizona Historical Foundation, 1965).

For the Indian viewpoint on the expeditions of Juan Bautista de Anza to California and the journeys of Francisco Garcés to the Colorado River, see Jack D. Forbes, *Warriors of the Colorado: The Yumas of the Quechan Nation and their Neighbors* (Norman: University of Oklahoma Press, 1965). Herbert Eugene Bolton has edited and translated *Anza's California Expeditions* in five volumes (Berkeley: University of California Press, 1930) and published in Spain is Mario Hernández y Sánchez-Barba, *Juan Bautista de Anza, un hombre de fronteras* (Madrid: Editorial Gráfica Espejo, 1962). Original documents are found in the Archivo General de Indias, Provincias Internas. See also J. N. Bowman and Robert F. Heizer, *Anza and the Northwestern Frontier of New Spain* (Los Angeles: Southwest Museum, 1967) and Richard Pourade, *Anza Conquers the Desert: The Anza Expeditions from Mexico to California and the Founding of San Francisco, 1774 to 1776* (San Diego: The Copley Press, 1971).

Chapter Ten

FRONTIER REORGANIZATION AND EXPANSION: 1776–1778

THE PROVINCIAS INTERNAS

*P*rominent among the plans of former visitador general José de Gálvez was the administrative reorganization of the northern frontier provinces of New Spain. Setting up an independent commandancy general would remove some responsibility from the overworked viceroy and would provide better protection against Indian uprisings. Gálvez had formulated his idea for combining the Provincias Internas (Interior Provinces) of Nueva Vizcaya, Sinaloa, Sonora, the Californias, Coahuila, New Mexico, and Texas under a separate military and political government during his tour of New Spain in 1768. As the newly appointed minister of the Indies in 1776, Gálvez effected his plan for the commandancy general and gained royal approval on August 22 of that year. This move, made to relieve the viceroy of direct supervision over frontier defense, had the practical effect of creating a new viceroyalty. Although the main objective of the new entity was to strengthen the line of defense, the conversion of Indians was also named by the royal instructions as a primary goal.

TEODORO DE CROIX, COMMANDANT GENERAL OF THE PROVINCIAS

Gálvez appointed Teodoro de Croix, the 46-year-old nephew of his old friend and former viceroy, the Marques de Croix, as the new commandant general. Croix, born on June 20, 1730 in the castle of Prevote near Lille, France, enlisted in the Spanish army at the age of 17 and went to Italy as an ensign of the Grenadiers of the Royal Guard. In 1750 he transferred to the Walloon guard, ranking as a lieutenant in 1756. He was decorated in that year in Flanders, becoming a gentleman of the Teutonic Knights. He had become a captain by 1765 and as such accompanied his uncle to New Spain in 1766. While the Marques de Croix was viceroy, Teodoro held the position of governor of Acapulco and then inspector of troops. He worked for José de Gálvez during the expulsion of the Jesuits and campaigned with José's nephew, Bernardo de Gálvez, in Nueva Vizcaya, forming a friendship with the latter when both sailed for Spain in 1772 with their uncles. Coincidentally, both Teodoro and Bernardo returned to New Spain in 1776, the former to become commandant general and the latter to become acting governor of Louisiana on January 1, 1777.

Croix, as the new chief executive of the Provincias Internas, was independent of the viceroy and responsible directly to the crown through Gálvez as minister of the Indies. Judicial authority, however, still remained with the audiencia of Guadalajara. In practice the office faced some viceregal intervention and was less effective than hoped in keeping peace with the Indians. Croix's seat of government was designated to be in the small town of Arizpe on the Sonora river. It was a community that had no particular distinction other than its somewhat central location and long history. The Franciscans had actually begun proselytizing in the area about 1642, but the first mission, Nuestra Señora de la Asuncion de Arizpe, was a Jesuit establishment begun about 1648. The last Jesuit at Arizpe, Father Carlos Rojas, had served there over thirty-five years and greatly improved the church. Meanwhile, Pedro Corbalán became governor of Sonora in 1776 with jurisdiction over political and economic affairs, while Colonel Anza directed military affairs.

Gálvez's Plan

The major provisions of Gálvez's reorganization plan concerned warfare. For example, Article 4 reminded the commandant that in order to devote all of his attention to "the operations of war," he should "ignore legal details, leaving them entirely to the intendants and governors of the provinces. ..." (Gálvez, *Instructions for Governing the Interior Provinces of New Spain*, p. 30) Two subordinate officers, Don Joseph Rengel, commandant inspector in charge of Nueva Vizcaya and New Mexico, and Colonel Juan Ugalde, in charge of Texas and Coahuila, were appointed to help govern Sonora and the Californias. The governor of New Mexico would continue as sub-inspector of his troops in order to lessen the number of visits by Rengel and his aides. War was to generally be waged at all times against the Apaches, who were constantly on the attack. They were to be sought out and punished in order to pacify the whole area. Some 104 general provisions spelled out the duties of officers and soldiers throughout the Provincias. Some special provisions pertaining to Sonora, California and New Mexico were as follows:

106

Without prejudicing the movements and arrangements of war against the Apaches, necessary steps should be taken for restraining the Seris and Tiburones, endeavoring to bring these Indians back to their former peace; for even though the situation seems bad, with little hope of getting better, it is necessary to take time for the work of constraining them on the Island of Tiburon, attacking and conquering them again.

111

With the greatest efficiency and skill, you should dedicate yourself from now on to settling and establishing in the said pueblos of the Piatos and in all those of La Pimería Alta the greatest possible number of honest Spanish families, and those of other castes, who would be industrious and of good customs. This would work as an imperceptible control over or brake on the changeable Upper Pimas, who are not few in number and who are related to the pagan Pápagos and Pimas Gileños.

115

Without an urgent motive, you should not open communication by land with Upper California, for the parties that travel by this road, if they are small, are exposed, and if large, leave a serious shortage of men in Sonora for operations of war.

116
> And since there is a lack in California, you will charge Governor Pedro
> de Fages with maintaining the Indians of the Santa Barbara channel in
> their innocence, and those of missions San Diego, San Gabriel and San
> Francisco in their peacefulness, and the troops who serve in the present
> system to maintain the most just order, subordination and discipline to
> inspire respect and give a good example to the Indians, and to punish the
> excesses that they commit with prudence, prohibiting them from the use
> and handling of horses. (Gálvez, *Instructions for Governing the Interior*
> *Provinces of New Spain*, pp. 56–9)

California

The plan for the Provincias Internas also provided that the governor of the Californias should reside at Monterey and his lieutenant at Loreto, instead of the reverse, which had been practiced since Monterey's founding in 1770. Fernando de Rivera y Moncada therefore left Monterey and returned to his former, and perhaps friendlier, headquarters in Baja California. Governor Felipe de Neve, a native of the Andalusian town of Bailen and a cavalry major, had been governor of the Californias since March 1775. Neve left Loreto on an overland journey to Alta California to become acquainted with his new province before taking up residence at Monterey. At Loreto he had quarreled frequently with the Dominican missionaries of the peninsula over mission policy. A longtime supporter of civilian pueblos, Neve's relations with Father Serra and the Franciscans in Alta California were to show little improvement in questions regarding new missions.

Nevertheless, Alta California's settlement under Neve saw Spanish colonists make some headway in creating European institutions on the Pacific Coast. As in the plan for Arizona and New Mexico, native villages gradually gave way to Spain's threefold formula for frontier settlement: missions, presidios, and pueblos. Unlike these areas, however, there were few threats in Alta California from hostile Indians such as the Apaches, Comanches, or Seris. The eight missions, three presidios, and one pueblo established in California between 1769 and 1779 set a pattern for continued development. Although still isolated and sparsely populated, the province of California, joined to Arizona by the Yuma route, had assumed an aura of permanence.

Sonora

Commandant Croix first directed his major attention to problems in Texas and did not immediately visit the western portion of the Provincias as instructed by Gálvez. In fact, he did not reach Arizpe until November 13, 1779. Officially designating this small Sonoran town as the capital, he elevated it to the status of *ciudad* (city) and provided the town with an aqueduct. Croix hoped to make the settlement attractive to settlers. Engineer Manuel Mascaro would later draw up plans for the new town.

In the meantime, a number of changes were taking place in the mission district of La Pimería Alta. The Franciscans of Queretaro were able to negotiate the transfer of their eight missions in La Pimería Baja to the Franciscans from Jalisco. The Queretaran

friars arrived in La Pimería Alta in October 1776 and indicated their readiness to occupy the new missions planned for the Gila and Colorado Rivers. Since those missions
had not yet received official sanction, the fathers were sent to the existing missions.
Fray Juan Bautista de Velderrain, a Basque, 29 years old and a native of Cizurquil near
San Sebastián, was sent to Tumacácori to join fellow Basque Pedro Arriquibar. Velderrain
had taken his first vows in 1763 and, six years later at Vitoria, volunteered for the
college of Querétaro. His three years among the Seris in La Pimería Baja from 1773 to
1776 had conditioned him to face every kind of difficulty and had given him experience in building a church at Suaqui, Real de San Marcial. By early 1777, Father Velderrain
was transferred to San Xavier del Bac to work with Father Garcés.

THE DOMÍNGUEZ AND ESCALANTE EXPEDITION

The most ambitious exploring expedition seeking to penetrate the great unknown
area to the north and west of New Mexico was carried out in 1776 by a small group
under the leadership of Franciscan Fathers Francisco Atanasio Domínguez and Silvestre
Vélez de Escalante. Father Domínguez, the senior Franciscan, had at that date recently
arrived in the frontier province of New Mexico as commissary visitor of the Franciscan
missions there. Among his many instructions was that of discovering a direct route
from Santa Fe, capital of New Mexico, to the recently occupied northern province
along the Pacific Coast, that of California founded some seven years earlier by the
major effort placed in motion by José de Gálvez. Information concerning the little
known expanse of mostly arid land that lay between the two frontier provinces was
minimal. The previously mentioned exploration made earlier that same year by Father
Garcés was of some guidance and probably determined the explorers' choice of a more
northerly course than otherwise would have been expected. Escalante had received a
letter from Garcés in late July 1776 that had been sent to the Franciscan priest at Zuni,
reporting Garcés's difficult trek across Arizona and his failure to reach New Mexico.
They also had access to the journals kept by Juan María Antonio Rivera, which they
used during the first portion of their travels.

The 1776 explorers had decade-old knowledge concerning the upper waters of
the Colorado River, or Río del Tizón, as the area had been first visited by Rivera and
possibly by others since him. Diarist of the 1776 journal, the original of which seems to
have been lost, was Father Vélez de Escalante. (Modern usage usually refers to him as
Father Escalante.) Father Angelico Chávez, who was responsible for the most recent
transcription and translation of the journal in a bilingual edition indicates that although
Escalante was the scribe and author of the journal, his superior also contributed significantly to the final product. Although the original is missing, many contemporary copies exist, differing only slightly one from the other, and probably from that signed by
both priests at journey's end. As is the case with many journals of exploration, Vélez de
Escalante's account often reveals as much about the author and about Spaniards of that
day as it does concerning geography of the area explored or about the nature of the
people that inhabited the vast area.

Members of the Expedition

Escalante's knowledge of the area was greater than that of Domínguez, though the latter had gathered much general information for a study that was later translated and published as *The Missions of New Mexico, 1776*. Domínguez was 36 years old, born in Mexico City in 1740. He had become a Franciscan in 1757 and was a member of the Mexican Franciscan college of the Santo Evangelio in the viceregal capital. His younger companion, Escalante, a 26-year-old native of Treceño, near the Cantabrian coast in the Spanish province of Santander, had taken the habit of St. Francis in 1767 in Mexico City. He arrived in New Mexico in 1774, stationed first at Laguna and then transferred westward to Nuestra Señora de Guadalupe de Zuni until he was called by Domínguez for exploratory duty. He had some idea of the frontier in the direction of California, but probably only vague secondhand notions of the itinerary that was later chosen.

Accompanying the Franciscans were Juan Pedro Cisneros, alcalde mayor of the Pueblo of Zuni, and a group of citizens, all of whom apparently went as volunteers. Most important of those who joined the expedition was the retired militia captain Bernardo de Miera y Pacheco, a most noteworthy contemporary. Miera was multi-talented—engineer, merchant, Indian fighter, government agent, rancher, artist, and historically most significant, cartographer. Born in the Valle de Carreido in Spain's Montañas de Burgos, he had come in 1743 to El Paso, and subsequently to Santa Fe about 1755. He prepared a detailed map in 1778, doubtless based on previous notes and rudimentary maps. Of the expedition members, he was the person most frequently at odds with the priests over decisions made or routes proposed.

Other members of the expedition, which was entrusted to the patronage of the Virgin Mary and San José, were Joaquín Lain of Santa Fe; Lorenzo Olivares of El Paso; Andrés Muñiz of Bernalillo who "knew the language" (probably of the Utes) and served as interpreter; Andrés's brother Lucrecio from Embudo; Juan de Aguilar; and Simón Lucero. The latter four were either mestizos or detribalized Indians living in Spanish society. Uncharacteristically and curiously, none of those were listed as being soldiers or even of having earlier served in any military component save for Miera, and none later achieved any distinction in New Mexico society.

Purpose of the Expedition

Many times before departing from Santa Fe, the two Franciscan leaders reminded everyone of the exclusively religious character of the expedition. When they finally left the capital on July 29, 1776, they traveled twenty miles northwest to the Indian Pueblo of Santa Clara and from there to the town of Santo Tomás de Abiquiu on the Chama River, nestled just before the sandstone cliffs that lay beyond. This frontier town was the last outpost of Spanish civilization, a town comprising mostly detribalized Indians of non-Pueblo origin. Here was the point of final preparation for the long journey ahead that they hoped might carry them to the shores of the Pacific Ocean.

Geographical knowledge of the target area ahead was based on Indian information and on estimates of distance as calculated by priests, cartographers, and military engineers. It was fervently desired that the area involved would be peopled by groups of aborigines receptive to the gospel of Catholic Christianity and that the pleasant valleys that might be discovered would awaken royal interest and open a whole new field to conversion. But above all they hoped to discover the existence to the north of that fabled Strait of Anián leading through the North American continent from the North Sea (the Atlantic) to the South Sea (the Pacific). Recall that belief in the strait had led Juan de Oñate in the founding period to carry with him shipbuilding equipment with which to construct vessels once having encountered the desired waterway. Such an idea which today seems so fanciful, particularly in view of the fact that the explorers were on the flanks of the Rocky Mountains at an elevation of over 5,000 feet, was not finally eliminated from European thinking until the 1790s. But even if a great waterway admitting oceangoing vessels was not truly possible, discovery of a substantial river might at least permit facile transportation westward to some place like San Francisco, a bay that promised at least a gateway to the Pacific.

Although it was already August and several months too late for the project to have any reasonable hope of fruition, the landscape of higher elevations was still more like springtime with wild flowers and abundant pasturage as the small party moved on up the Chama River. The group was following about the same outbound march as had Rivera a decade earlier and apparently had one or more veterans of such early contacts with them as guides, interpreters, and companions. Passing by water holes and small streams, the party noted one area which was called Río de las Nutrias, a swampy area that had water all year long in banked ponds, or beaver dams, where those rodents were said to breed. In this regard, and because the word *nutria* is often repeated in the place-name geography and in Hispanic period documentation, it is of note that the New Mexicans used that word for beaver instead of the more appropriate *castor.* Nutria is else-where normally used for sea otter, a much larger animal, and at times for land otter. (New Mexican nutria became a source of great later interest to Rocky Mountain traders and trappers most of whom were either of French of Anglo-American background.)

Apparently the Domínguez-Escalante party had with it some measuring device, probably a sextant, more than likely employed for observations by former topographic engineer Bernardo de Miera. The sun's meridian transits, which were observed from the very beginning, regularly gave a calculated latitude some 36 minutes too high, possibly as a result of not compensating for the elevation from which observations were taken.

Crossing Colorado

The guides from time to time lost the trail, but in the area of the Navajo and later the San Juan Rivers, it was not hard to regain proper direction. Up to that point they had been following fairly closely the route taken by earlier visitors, since local place-names were already established. During the expedition special care was taken to determine potential sites for future Spanish occupation, with particular regard for agricultural potential and capacity to sustain population concentration. En route they crossed the Río de los Pinos, the Río Flórido, and the Río de las Animas, all three still so called. The group was especially interested in the abundant water of the Animas as it rushed down from the Sierra de la Plata. Where it was crossed by Domínguez and Escalante, near modern Durango, Colorado, it was noted as having greater flow and much more rapid current than the Río Grande. Pasturage in the region seemed quite abundant, particularly given the lateness of the year. Commenting on the name of the Sierra de la Plata it was said that "although years ago certain individuals [the Rivera party] from New Mexico came to inspect" the veins and outcroppings of metallic ore by order of Governor Tomás Vélez Cachupín and carried back metal-bearing rocks, "it was not determined for sure what kind of metal they consisted of. The opinion which some formed previously from the accounts of various Indians and from some citizens of the kingdom, that they are silver ore, furnished the sierra with this name." (Chávez and Warner, trans. and ed., *The Domínguez-Escalante Journal: Their Expedition through Colorado, Utah, Arizona, and New Mexico in 1776*, p. 12)

Among the early places the group visited was a site along the banks of El Río de los Dolores where it was noted; "Here there is everything that a good settlement needs for its establishment and maintenance as regards irrigable lands, pasturage, timber and firewood." It was also a place that had the vestiges of what in ancient times was "a small settlement of the same type as those of the Indians of New Mexico, as the ruins that we purposely inspected show." (Chávez and Warner, trans. and ed., *The Domínguez-Escalante Journal: Their Expedition through Colorado, Utah, Arizona, and New Mexico in 1776*, p. 14) Only a brief occasional reference was made to evidences of Anasazi ruins, even though they had traveled near many significant sites that in the twentieth century have become archaeological treasures and have been set aside as national and state parks. This site, now called Escalante Ruin, is the only place noted of Anasazi remains, which the journalist equated with the New Mexico Pueblo Indians.

At this time the Domínguez-Escalante party was overtaken by two Indians, Felipe and Domingo (a *coyote* and a *genízaro*), who had run off from New Mexico without permission, either to wander on the frontier or to overtake the missionaries. Even though they had no need for extra personnel, the priests took them on as companions to forestall the mischief, either motivated by ignorance or malice, that the two might do by wandering any further among the Utes. On August 16 half the horses were missing, having strayed off seeking water rather than passing the night at a dry camp. Shortly thereafter water was found at Agua Escondida, to meet the pressing need of the *remuda*, the accompanying horse herd.

Lacking confidence in their own knowledge of water sources, the priests tried to make contact with some nearby Utes who, by the evidence of some quite recent tracks, were known to be present but not visible. Following the Indian trail as far as the Río de las Paralíticas, the explorers came to the end of Tabeguachi Ute territory and to the beginning of the lands of the Muhuachi group of the same tribe. The trail became more difficult and the guides less adept, wasting time in steep ascents and descents. The party soon experienced the ill effects of such a late start in the season—a growing scarcity of grass and the dryness of the country.

The explorers then chanced upon a Tabeguachi Ute and, after some early unwillingness to communicate, he said that the Sabaguanas were all in their own country and that the Spaniards would soon meet them. His own people were scattered, wandering about the mountains. It was finally arranged for him to serve as a guide, for which purpose he would return the next day, the 24th. Apparently the Tabehuachi Ute thought that the Spanish party had come to trade and he came with his family and some other Indians bringing cured deerskins and other items to barter, including some manzanita berries thought by the visitors to be quite good. The Indians could not believe that the expedition was not there for commercial purposes, giving rise to the supposition that since Rivera's time there had been repeated trade contacts. Local fears about the purpose of the priestly visit were lessened by questions concerning Father Garcés and of his whereabouts. The Indians had no information, but they did become more friendly and seemed concerned about the priest. Following a good meal, an exchange was made of flour for jerked deer meat and manzanita berries. The original Indian, whom the Spaniards decided to call Atanasio, was hired as a guide for the price of two large knives (*belduques*) and sixteen strings of white-glass beads. These he gave to his wife who went off with all the other Indians except Atanasio, each to their own camp.

The party owed a considerable debt to friendly local Indians they hired as guides along the way. Since they knew the trail well, their intervention prevented the padres from making misjudgments about routes to be followed. With the new guide, travel became easier and the first night brought the travelers to a copious spring, abundant pasturage, and much firewood. The party experienced a heavy downpour, a frequent occurrence in the Rocky Mountains in August. The explorers were then on the Plain of Ancapagari, which in Ute means "Red Lake," and which has a modern spelling of "Uncompahgre." The nearby river was given the name San Agustín, after which they visited the San Xavier (today called the Gunnison). According to Escalante, it was also called the San Francisco Xavier. He asserted that it was at this point that Juan María de Rivera, after crossing the Sierra de los Tabehuchis, had carved a cross on a poplar tree, the letters spelling his name and the expedition's year. Andrés Muñiz, who went as interpreter, said that he had been in that same area in the preceding year, 1775, but had been a three-days' march behind his companions Pedro Mora and Gregorio Sandoval. The latter two had been with Don Juan María during his entire expedition of 1765. They had at that early date reached the great Río del Tizón and had been sent across it by Rivera to look for Utes on the side opposite the meadow where they had all stopped, and from which point they had returned. Journalist Escalante felt that this site on the Gunnison was what Rivera had been convinced was the Tizón, the Colorado. A difficulty then and now is that the upper tributaries of the Colorado are quite similar in size, making it difficult to determine precisely which is the main stream.

After a brief while, somewhat to the north, the travelers met some Sabaguana Utes who warned the Spaniards that if they continued in that direction they would run into Comanches who would kill them. But in order to get to their immediate destination of the Timpanogas Utes, it was necessary to go through Comanche country. Finally, a Laguna (Timpanogas) Indian, when regaled substantially, agreed to lead the Spaniards to the Indians who resided near a big lake. Domínguez tried through an interpreter to explain to the natives about Christianity and the customs associated with the Spanish faith. He was elated when all the natives "listened with pleasure," especially several Lagunas. As soon as the padre began instructing them, the new guide interrupted so as to predispose the Sabuaganas as well as his own fellow tribesmen "to believe whatever the padre was telling them because it was all true." (Chávez and Warner, trans. and ed., *The Domínguez-Escalante Journal; Their Expedition through Colorado, Utah, Arizona, and New Mexico in 1776*, p. 30)

By early September the explorers were still in Colorado, headed just slightly west of due north and traveling in extremely high altitude. Again the Spaniards were warned of the dire consequences they would suffer if they continued on their current course, with the Indians threatening not to trade sound horses for trail weary ones that the Spaniards wanted to replace farther along the trail. Even this was to no avail, with the Spaniards insisting that they could not give up without knowing the fate of Father Garcés who might be lost and wandering about.

Entering Utah

Satisfactory arrangements finally made, the party continued northward and finally hit the Colorado River on its upper course, hardly considering it to be that great stream and giving it the name San Rafael, though the Utes called it the Red River. The party did not recognize it as the Tizón of which so much had been said; however, it was noted as carrying more water than the Río Grande. From that point the party continued in a generally westward direction determined by topography, the relative competence of several guides, and the desire to make progress toward their still distant anticipated destination of Monterey in California. This portion of their itinerary took the Spaniards from the Colorado River drainage to the Great Basin, where there is no external drainage to the sea, and all of the considerable number of steams end in sinks, or large lakes such as Utah Lake and the Great Salt Lake.

As the party headed generally westward, on September 14 they checked their position while along the Green River, and were still getting regularly high latitude calculations. These were made with a quadrant and despite considerable effort the results continued to be poor. At that point, in commemoration of his participation in the expedition, Joaquín Laín found an appropriate tree trunk upon the northwest side of which he "dug out a small piece with an adze in the shape of a rectangular window and with a chisel carved on it the following inscription: 'Year of 1776,' and lower down in a different hand 'Laín' with two crosses at the sides, the larger one above the inscription and the other one beneath it." (Chávez and Warner, trans. and ed., *The Dominguez-Escalante Journal: Their Expedition through Colorado, Utah, Arizona, and New Mexico in 1776*, p. 44)

Smoke signals, appropriate for such climatic conditions and extensively used by Indians in the Southwest, at times indicated surveillance and later announced arrival of the exploring party in the area of central Utah. The Spaniards feared that their coming as strangers might be viewed with hostility. From an elevated point along their route the Spaniards caught sight of a large lake (Utah Lake) amid the spreading valley which they called Nuestra Señora de la Merced de los Timpanogotzis, the latter being an Indian name meaning fish eaters and one still used as a place-name in that area as Timpanogas. Following Spanish Fork (called by them the Vega del Dulcísimo Nombre de Jesús), they noted:

> *Through where we came we found the meadow's pastures recently burnt*
> *and other adjacent ones still burning. From this we inferred that these*
> *Indians had taken us for Comanches or other hostile people and, perhaps*
> *having seen that we brought horses, had tried to burn the pastures along*

the way so that the lack of them would make us leave the bottomland sooner. But since this is so large and extensive, they could not do it in such a short time, even though they had started fires in many places. This is why, while our small party stayed here, Padre Fray Francisco Atanasio set out for the first camps as soon as we halted, together with the guide Silvestre, his partner Joaquín and Andrés Muñiz the interpreter. Then, after racing the horses as much as they could, even to the point of exhaustion, so as to get there this afternoon, and for six and a half leagues north-northwest, they got to them.

Some men came out to meet them with weapons in hand to defend their homes and families, but as soon as Silvestre spoke to them the show of war was changed into the finest and fondest expressions of peace and affection. They very joyfully conducted them to their little humble abodes, and after he had embraced every single one and let them know that we came in peace, and that we loved them as our greatest friends, the padre allowed them time to talk at length with our guide Silvestre, who gave them an account so much in our favor of what he had observed and witnessed ever since he had become one of us, and about our purpose in coming, that we could not have wished for anything better. (Chávez and Warner, trans. and ed., *The Dominguez-Escalante Journal: Their Expedition through Colorado, Utah, Arizona, and New Mexico in 1776*, p. 54)

Silvestre, the guide, went on at length about the trip thus far and how despite having gone through Comanche country they had not been attacked as God had been with them. Once the ice was broken, Father Domínguez explained to the Timpanogas Utes that the Spaniards' greater purpose was the salvation of their souls. The priest indicated that if they would submit to Spanish control, Carlos III would send missionaries and other Spaniards to come and live among them and teach them how to farm and raise livestock.

A second purpose was indicated in the search for their Franciscan brother, Francisco Garcés, as well as the need for guides to help the expedition. The following day at a site where Provo River enters Utah Lake a large meeting was celebrated with the head chiefs and all the Spaniards present. The party told of the advantages of Christianity and the Indians offered all the land necessary for the Spaniards to build their homes whenever they wished. The local Indians would continually be on the lookout for Comanche intruders and would warn the Spaniards, with whom they would go out and punish such invaders.

There was no doubt that everyone there expected the Spaniards to return in the near future to carry out occupation of Utah Valley and that the local Indians were most anxious to receive the promised benefits, both temporal and spiritual, that would soon accrue. As the result of an earlier suggestion that the Timpanogas Utes give a visual token of their desire to have the Spaniards, a present was arranged that could be taken to the great chief of the Spaniards. It consisted of four male figures crudely painted with earth pigments and with red ochre on a deerskin. The figure representing the head

chief had the most red ochre (blood), because he had received the most wounds in
battles with the Comanches. Two other figures had less blood, and the final one, representing an important person who was not
a war captain, had no ochre. The token was
accepted and it was planned to bring it back
when they came to settle as a reminder of
the promises given and reciprocated. (Later
this token was given to the governor of New
Mexico by the Franciscans.) Once these formalities were completed, a new guide, José
María as he was immediately called, took
the place of Silvestre who had been guide
for many leagues of travel. The parting of
the old guide and priests was poignant.

Map 10.1. Domínguez and Escalante route. Courtesy Ted J. Warner, Provo, Utah.

It was at this point in late September that the priestly entourage was the closest to
the road that seventy-five years later would carry the greatest number of immigrants to
California, the same destination that was hoped for by Domínguez and Escalante. In 1849
and 1850 gold seekers would pass through the Great Basin in search of riches in the Sierra
Nevada of California, but at this point the priests were still over 750 miles short of their
goal, even if it were a straight, easy, and well-watered route, which it was not.

Escalante paused to make a geographical summary of Utah Valley and its lake, the
sizes of which he overestimated. He also indicated that the area consisted of very good
potential farm land for all kinds of crops. There was plenty of land for towns and
Indian villages, more so than along the Río Grande. He waxed eloquently on the many
advantages, the wildlife and fish, and even the temperate climate. Though it was not
seen, the Great Salt Lake, fifty miles northward via the Jordan River, is mentioned in the
account. That immense lake was and continues to be of extremely high mineral content, the opposite of Utah Lake, which is of fresh water. The nature of the larger lake's
water made it a less desirable place, inhabited at that time by the Puaguanpe nation,
who spoke a Comanche-related language, but who maintained generally friendly relations with the Lagunas (Timpanogas).

Their route took the explorers to Juab Valley and then to the Sevier River (Río de
Santa Isabel). Indians they met at that point on September 30 were more fully bearded
and spoke a Timpanogas language. These Indians may have accounted for an earlier
report of Spaniards said to live on the other side (northwest) of the Río del Tizón. It was
noted that "in their features they more resemble the Spaniards than they do all the
other Indians known in America up to now." (Chávez and Warner, trans. and ed., *The
Domínguez-Escalante Journal: Their Expedition through Colorado, Utah, Arizona, and New
Mexico in 1776*, p. 64) They were the "Barbudos" or "Bearded Utes," probably the Paiutes,
some of whom were so full-bearded that they looked like Capuchin priests or
Bethlehemites. The bearded ones were given some rudimentary, preliminary Catholic
instruction with the assurance that the Spaniards would soon be returning. The depar-

ture was accompanied by a tearful farewell when all natives cried copiously, evoking great sympathy from the priests who said that "even when we were quite a distance away we kept hearing the tender laments of these unfortunate little sheep of Christ, lost along the way simply for not having the light. They touched our hearts so much that some of our companions could not hold back the tears." (Chávez and Warner, trans. and ed., *The Domínguez-Escalante Journal: Their Expedition through Colorado, Utah, Arizona, and New Mexico in 1776*, p. 67)

Decision to Turn Back

On October 5, after only about ten days of service, guide José María deserted to return home and left the party without knowledge of the land. He was motivated in part by a fight that erupted between Juan Pedro Cisneros and his servant Simón Lucero over the latter's laziness and lack of piety for having refused to pray with his master. Ideas of heading westward seemed impossible as a result of the poor terrain in that direction. Furthermore, the last heat of fall had given way to cold winds and an early snowfall on that same day. Continued bad weather kept the party at a standstill for over two days. By October 8 the Franciscans finally recognized that they were not going to reach Monterey. This realization stemmed from "not having found among all these latter peoples any reports about the Spaniards and the padres" of California. (Chávez and Warner, trans. and ed., *The Dominguez-Escalante Journal: Their Expedition through Colorado, Utah, Arizona, and New Mexico in 1776*, p. 70) Furthermore, progress had been slowed by continued cold while their estimated longitude indicated that the party had only gone thirteen leagues (about 365 miles) west and certainly not yet half way. They were afraid of becoming snowbound in a wilderness, for everywhere around them there were mountains covered with snow and provisions were growing short. They calculated that even if they did arrive in Monterey that winter, they would not be able to get back to Santa Fe until June of 1777. They also expressed that the delay incurred by going all the way to California would bring postponement of the promised conversion of the Lagunas, and those Indians might become frustrated in their hopes, or might conclude that the priests had purposely deceived them.

The explorers then hoped to discover a shorter and better route to Utah Lake and to the bearded Indians than that via the Sabaguanas. Clearly, almost any route they might take would seemingly be better than the slow, steep, meandering itinerary that they had taken when their animals were fresh and their provisions plentiful. Little did they reckon with the great difficulty that lay ahead in trying to cross the immense chasm of the Río del Tizón (Colorado), or in negotiating other alternate routes in the unknown canyon lands. Apparently, prominent members of the party—Miera, Joaquín Laín, and interpreter Andrés Muñiz—were opposed to abandonment of the effort to reach Monterey. Miera thought that there would be great honor and profit in reaching the California capital, so much so that he tried to convince the others in the matter. Opposition was so great that rather than argue endlessly and fruitlessly, on October 11 it was decided to cast lots to see if their destination was to be southward to the Cosnina (Havasupai) villages or westward to Monterey. Monterey lost, and the party became unified in their immediate objective of heading south toward the Havasupai villages.

Many days were spent headed generally southward seeking the Colorado River. Water became scarcer, food provisions exhausted, and it became necessary to trade for food with the local Paiute Indians who had almost no meat. On October 23, still seeking the Colorado, the lack of meat forced the travelers for the first time to kill a horse for food.

Heading for Arizona

Headed southward near what is today Cedar City, the party encountered a large marsh and met some local Ute women who said that the big river was not far off. Even though it was in fact quite distant, the travelers were animated and continued with only moderate difficulty. By October 15 the explorers hit the small Virgin River near what is today the Utah-Arizona border. Here they learned of the immensity of the Grand Canyon of the Colorado and were forced to make a great detour from the route thus far projected. In the midst of the Canyonlands the Spaniards were dismayed by the stark barrenness found everywhere. The party finally reached the Río Grande de Cosninas (the Colorado) just below what would later be called Lee's Ferry, after a most troublesome descent into the deep canyon through which the mighty river passes. In their frustration, they named the site San Benito Salsipuedes (Get Out if You Can). Men sent in advance to swim across the river found it very difficult and hardly had strength enough to explore and return, losing their clothing in the effort.

They spent nearly two weeks trying to find the best place where both men and animals might cross in safety. By then it was very cold and rations were again low, requiring slaughter of a second horse for food. Travel difficulties were extreme since the group had to go up and down sheer cliffs. Rain, hail, flash flooding, and unexpected delays beset them. They finally crossed at a place where the river was its widest and gave some footing on intervening sandbars. The passage was made successfully at a point that is now 550 feet deep under the waters of Lake Powell several miles east of where the Glen Canyon Dam was constructed two centuries later. The priests ascribed a great deal of the difficulty to the fact that there was no guide, but all joined in praising God and firing off the muskets once the "Crossing of the Fathers" was behind them. Some space in the expedition journal was dedicated to what should have been done and would need to be done in the future. They deemed the area around the crossing unsuitable for any sort of settlement.

Hopi Villages

From that point on, it was a matter of following a trail in the direction of the Hopi (Moqui) villages with the first stop being at Oraibi (which, along with Acoma, has the distinction of being one of the oldest continually occupied towns in the United States). The Hopi natives were friendly, since their leaders had ordered them to give the Spaniards a good reception, sell them provisions, and cultivate their friendship. Nevertheless, they were not to have anything to do with efforts that the visitors might make to preach to the natives. As discussed, during the entire colonial period the Hopi were considered to be obstinate as a result of their total refusal to accept Christianity. Domínguez and Escalante had hoped by good example to "exert anew our efforts on behalf of the light and meekness of the gospel, as against the willful blindness and

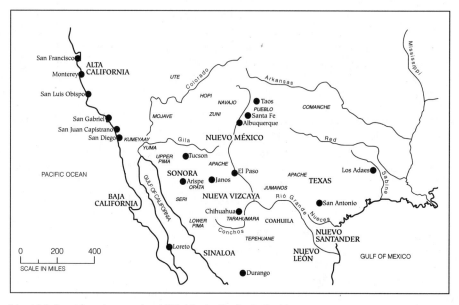

Map 10.2. Spanish settlement, circa 1776. Map by Stephanie Gould.

inveterate obstinacy" of those Indians. (Chávez and Warner, trans. and ed., *The Dominguez-Escalante Journal: Their Expedition through Colorado, Utah, Arizona, and New Mexico in 1776*, pp. 108–9) The outcome was a long parley during which the Hopi asked for aid against the inroads of the neighboring Navajo and a possible alliance with the Spaniards. Because the priests insisted that Christianity was a prerequisite for any help, assistance was denied. The Hopi answered that they desired only Spanish friendship, but by no means wanted to become Christians as the ancient ones had counseled them never to subject themselves to the Spaniards. This failure by the Franciscans to convince the Hopi was a final disappointment.

Return to Santa Fe

From the Hopi villages onward was familiar territory to the group, particularly to Escalante, and thus it was not long before they were at the Zuni villages where Escalante had been serving prior to inception of the expedition. A stay of about three weeks at Zuni gave the explorers time for recuperation and performance of clerical chores, following which they made their way to Santa Fe and reported officially to Governor Pedro Fermín de Mendinueta. It had been a long and arduous trip of 159 days during which the party had traveled over 1,700 miles, a distance which if better directed could have taken them as far as Monterey with much distance to spare. The expected follow-up to extend Spanish religious and governmental control into Utah and the Great Basin never materialized, though on the map of North America the area was considered part of Spain's colonial empire until 1821.

In summary, although the 1776 expedition has become well known historically, it was in great measure important for its negative result. The explorers had learned that any route to California would be not only long, but filled with difficulty. The Utah Valley, though promising and within seventy-five years destined to be the site of thriving white settlements, was not sufficiently attractive to overcome contemporary drawbacks of distance and of geography. When the expedition was over, Father Domínguez was recalled to Mexico City from his canonical visitation to answer charges leveled against him by some of his disgruntled colleagues, though none of them had anything to do with his exploration. He spent the remaining thirty years of his life in missionary assignments elsewhere on the northern frontier. Father Escalante remained in New Mexico for several years of missionary service among the Pueblos, but in 1780 requested permission to return to Mexico City for treatment of a severe ailment. En route, at Parral, he died in that same year. Father Garcés, the object of some search, had returned to work among the Yumas on the Colorado River.

As a permanent legacy of the notable expedition, place-name donors have been more generous with the junior priest, creating an Escalante Desert, Escalante River, Escalante Forest, Escalante Mountain, Escalante State Park, and a town of Escalante—all in Utah. The senior priest has had only limited and belated conservation of his surname. But of the actual place-names given by Domínguez and Escalante, no vestige survives nor was much note made of its achievements until some 200 years later.

Map of Miera y Pacheco

Some years after completion of the notable expedition, and based on his notes or his memory of the terrain traversed, and on other sources of information, Don Bernardo Miera y Pacheco drew a map. It was not a conventional map since it had illustrations and did not preserve proportion. It did, however, depict the area covered and clarified certain points. On it appears the Río de Buenaventura, clearly the Green River, one of the principal tributaries of the Colorado. Its existence in cartography, journals, and oral tradition later gave rise to a mythical river of the west, one which flowed instead to the Pacific Ocean. This may have resulted in confusion of oral information concerning the Bear River, the Snake River, the Great Salt Lake, and the Humboldt River, all combining some characteristics to create a river later sought by Hudson's Bay Company trappers and by U.S. Topographical Exploring Expedition officer John C. Frémont as late as mid-nineteenth century.

Although the results of the Domínguez-Escalante expedition to the Great Basin were for them very disappointing and none of their hopes for a short route to California or Franciscan missionary work were realized, 1776 did not mark the end of Spanish interest. As was seemingly the case before and after the Rivera expeditions of 1765, so too there were unrecorded and unofficial visits throughout the rest of the colonial period. The archival record offers little about these visitors, their motives, and their results, which is perhaps sketchy in proportion to the illegality of such activity.

SAN AGUSTÍN DEL TUCSON IS FOUNDED

During the next few years, problems on the northern Sonoran frontier occupied Spain's attention. Arizona was of growing interest, particularly with reference to its more realistic connection to the newly founded frontier province of Alta California. In

Fig. 10.1. Ruins of convento of San Agustín de Tucson photographed in 1891 by A. S. Reynolds (also called San José de Tucson). Courtesy Arizona Historical Society/Tucson. 20729.

January and February 1778, Father Garcés reported to the viceroy that Father Velarde had returned to Tumacácori and that his companion Father Velderrain at San Xavier del Bac was learning the Piman language. Since there were two priests in residence at the mission, Father Garcés decided to spend more time at the presidial garrison at Tucson, which had been moved from Tubac. At this time, the ambitious Franciscan traveler was urging and planning the establishment of new missions among the Yumas to answer the request of his Indian friend Salvador Palma.

The movement of the presidio from Tubac to Tucson had been recommended as early as 1772, but commandant inspector Hugo Oconor was busy worrying about the eastern sector on the Texas-Coahuila border. He did send Antonio Bonilla to inspect the Sonora military posts in 1774, at which time Bonilla recommended against moving the presidio to Aribaca, as stated by the plan of the Marqués de Rubí. Because of the opening of the Anza route to California, Oconor chose the Tucson site, which was further to the north. On August 20, 1775, in the company of Father Garcés and Lieu-tenant Juan Fernandez Carmona, Oconor certified the selection of the site, the bound-ary marking, and the fact that there was enough water, pasture, and wood. He desig-nated the presidio as San Agustín de Tucson situated at a distance of eighteen leagues from Tubac.

Two days after selecting the site of Tucson, Oconor inspected Santa Cruz and de-cided that the Terrenate garrison should move there. Three days later he selected the San Bernardino site for the fourth Sonoran unit. Oconor wrote to Viceroy Bucareli in early September 1775 again recommending that the Tubac garrison be moved to Tuc-son. Having received on December 2 the viceroy's approval dated the previous Octo-ber, Oconor ordered the move to take place on December 10.

JUAN MARIA DE OLIVA AT TUBAC

The Tubac garrison in the fall of 1775 was commanded by Lieutenant Juan María de Oliva in the absence of Juan Bautista de Anza, then on his way to California. Oliva, a 60-year-old veteran of the frontier had come up through the ranks of the Tubac garrison, where he had served since 1752. A brave frontiersman who had been wounded by Apaches four years before, he excelled as a field commander but was illiterate and therefore unable to handle the necessary paper work. Oconor recommended at that time that Oliva be retired with his salary and promotion to the rank of captain. This was approved by the vice-

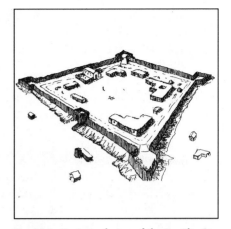

Fig. 10.2. Conjectural view of the Presidio San Agustín del Tucson. Drawing by Jack S. Williams.

roy, and the king signed the appropriate order on February 28, 1776. Oliva probably did not learn of his retirement until the beginning of August 1776 and may have retained command of the post for a time after that since Anza was still absent.

Since most of the officers were with Anza, the only person Oliva had available to fill the post upon his retirement was Anza's godson Ensign Juan Felipe Beldarrain, son of Tomas Beldarrain, the original captain of La Pimería Alta company and founder of Tubac. Unfortunately, the younger Beldarrain did not have the competence or social skills of his father.

THE PRESIDIAL POST AT TUCSON

For several years after the transfer of the presidial garrison from Tubac to Tucson, the soldiers lived on an open post. The fort was not immediately built, even though various Apache bands had been stealing horses and killing settlers in the district. When Don Pedro Allande y Saabedra took command on June 12, 1777, he found that there were no funds available for construction, no inventory of what belonged to the presidio, and no way to pay Indian laborers who already had put in time. Nevertheless, he ordered that a palisade of rough logs with four bulwarks, magazines, and a guardhouse be built without cost to the royal treasury. When he reviewed the troops, he was disgusted at their utter lack of even the basic necessities. He could only blame the illiterate Juan María de Oliva and his inexperienced assistant Ensign Juan Felipe Beldarrain who was inept in handling finances.

The post at Tucson was built as a compact village and would serve as the location for the present city. A stockade and then an earthen wall surrounded the buildings although both the soldiers and civilians built houses outside the wall. The presidio followed the royal plans based on the Roman design of earlier centuries. The common goal of resistance to the Apaches gave the residents a social solidarity and their Catholic faith also unified the group. The presidial chaplain was usually the best educated person in the district and most of the commandants had some formal education.

Once established, the post at Tucson had a major impact on the Native Americans who farmed along the river. The Northern Pimas were generally friendly and were involved in an exchange of food and goods. Since the area was basically very dry, they also participated with the Spaniards in dividing up irrigation water, which, under Spanish law, had to be shared equally among all users. The Pimas gathered around the mission at San Xavier del Bac on the opposite side of the river for their spiritual needs. The also cooperated in the defense of the area against their traditional enemies—the Apaches.

Water Rights under Spain

Water was so important in the dry area of northern Sonora and what became Arizona, that on many occasions the Spaniards adopted names for towns, presidios, and missions which the Indians used to honor water. For example, the Pima settlement Pitiquim, meaning "where the rivers come together" became Pitic. The word *bac*, meaning "water" in a number of Ute-Aztecan languages, was used in names such as Tubac, Bacanuche, Bacatete, and significantly, in San Xavier del Bac. Other places were given Spanish names for water such as Pozo Verde, Agua Prieta, Cienaguita, and Agua Caliente. Recall that even the name Arizona, according to some sources, came from the Pápago words *ali shonak* meaning "place of the small spring."

The Laws of the Indies or *Recopilación de leyes de los reynos de las Indias,* compiled in 1680, had a number of provisions concerning the use of water that had come down through Roman, Visigothic, and Moslem law. These all stressed the importance of sharing this precious resource. They extended the same general principles applicable in the Spanish peninsula but reflected an additional concern for the rights of Indians.

Book IV, Title 17, Law 9 (1532) instructed that "the Viceroys and Audiencias shall see to what shall be of good government in regard to the pastures, waters, and public buildings, and provide that which shall be convenient to the population and perpetuity of the land. ..." and Book IV, Title 17, Law 11 (1536) stated that "We order that the same system that the Indians had in the division and apportionment of water be observed and practiced among the Spaniards to whom lands have been distributed and assigned, and for this let the same natives supervise those who were in charge before, in whose opinion they should be irrigated, and each one be given the water he must have, successively from one to the other, with the penalty that he who wishes to get ahead and takes the water and uses it on his own initiative shall be deprived of it until all those farther down from him have irrigated the lands that have been assigned to them."

Despite some practices to the contrary, the lands previously cultivated by the Indians were not to be disturbed. According to Book IV, Title 12, Law 7 (1588), it was ordered that "the distributions of lands, both in new settlements and in places and districts already settled, shall be made with complete equity, without preference, personal exception, or injury to the Indians."

Because the Spaniards introduced into Sonora new food crops from Europe and central Mexico such as wheat, barley, oats, citrus fruits, apples, apricots, pears, grapes, garbanzo beans, carrots, radishes, and onions, more irrigation water was necessary than had previously been required by maize, beans, and squash. None of the new food crops could survive on desert rainfall alone. The new crops also brought in new insects that destroyed some of the natural desert vegetation. Patterns of land ownership tended to be different than in other areas, and because more land along the river was needed, tracts tended to be rectangular instead of square. Small diversion dams were built wherever possible to permit secondary canals to carry the water to fields away from the river. In the early period, however, Indian attacks were still the most significant threat and the area needed increased protection from the presidial soldiers.

CAPTAIN PEDRO DE ALLANDE Y SAABEDRA COMES TO TUCSON

Pedro de Allande y Saabedra was born in Spain of noble ancestry. He entered the royal army as a cadet in the Infantry of Navarre at the age of 14 and had spent twenty-two years in the service by the time he took command of the presidial company at Tucson. Allande had fought against the Portuguese, the Moors, and the Seri Indians on the Gulf of California coast between 1767 and 1777. He had become a lieutenant in the Dragoon Regiment of Mexico, but had been reprimanded in 1779 for using cruel and improper punishment to maintain discipline and for using soldiers and Indians for his own private use. He was assigned the command at Tucson on February 11, 1777, at the age of 35 or 36 and took over the post on June 12.

There were seventy-seven soldiers at San Agustín del Tucson in 1779, of whom only fifty-nine were effectives. Second in command under Captain Allande was Lieutenant Miguel de Urrea, a native of Sonora and son of Captain Bernardo de Urrea, a native of Culiacán, Sinaloa, who founded the presidio of Altar. Miguel had spent thirty-seven years of military service on the Sonoran frontier and was well acquainted with the Apaches and their raids. Because he was a criollo, Miguel was not promoted as rapidly as those officers born in Spain. He spent twenty-three years at Altar defending the area against the Seris, and was eventually transferred to San Miguel de Horcasitas. Urrea was assigned to Tucson five months after Allande took over command.

Since Juan Felipe Beldarrain had been arrested for mishandling funds, the first ensign of the Tucson company was Diego de Oya, then 57 years old, who had served in the Portuguese War. Oya had been in the military for nineteen years, five as a sergeant, when the king signed his commission of August 31, 1776. The second ensign was José Francisco de Castro, a 37-year-old native of Mexico, had also come up through the ranks. Castro had fought in the Caribbean and served as a sergeant with the Dragoon Regiment of Mexico under Hugo Oconor. His commission was signed by Carlos III on August 26, 1778.

The presidial troop consisted of thirty-seven troopers with two first corporals, a sergeant, and a master armorer. The light cavalry had seventeen soldiers under a sergeant and two corporals. There were also ten Indian scouts under a corporal. Five of the corporals and twenty-nine of the soldiers were Spaniards, one was Roman, and the rest were mestizos or Native Americans. Racial categories included in the list of troopers were Spaniard, coyote (a person of mixed Indian and Spanish blood normally with a dominance of the former), morisco, and mulato. Both of the latter categories had a certain amount of African blood. The Opata Indians serving in the heavy cavalry had acquired Spanish baptismal names and both Opata and Spanish surnames. Juan Bautista de Anza had attached twenty Opatas to the Tucson company in 1777 for service against the Seris, but these were dismissed when Adjutant Inspector Roque de Medina reviewed the troops in May 1779.

In October 1777, the Apaches ran off the last of the cattle and horses of the settlers still at Tubac and began grazing their own animals on Tubac's fields. They also stole maize from the planted fields (*milpas*) of the settlers, so Allande felt obligated to protect the civilians who were cultivating the soil and extending Spain's line of settlement. Allande also made grants of lands to retired soldiers to encourage permanent settlement of Spanish-speaking families

During 1779, Captain Allande made a concerted effort to defeat the Apaches. He hired Indian reinforcements and even paid for some out of his own pocket. In October the Apaches successfully ran off five horses and a mule. In response, the soldiers killed some Apaches and attempted to get the Pimas, Pápagos, and Gileños to campaign against them. On November 6, 1779, an Apache force estimated at 350 approached Tucson, but Allande formed a command of fifteen men to counterattack and with superior weapons managed to defeat the Indians. He cut off the head of a chieftain and carried it on a lance to scare the rest of the Indians, which worked, and the Apaches abandoned the attack. The Spaniards killed several other Apaches and gained the cooperation of the northern Pimas, who were beginning to serve in the frontier forces. The Pimas and the Pápagos had forty years of experience with the Spanish army and, like the Pueblo auxiliaries, had learned European patterns of warfare and organization. Many then learned the Spanish language and became acculturated into the new society.

The Tucson post played an important role in supporting Spain's overall plan for colonial expansion. Comandante General Croix asked that Tucson supply eleven of the troopers needed for two new settlements on the Colorado River planned since Garcés's first visit. The Tucson troops were led to the Colorado River in December 1780. There they were well received by the Yumas, but right away the situation began to deteriorate. The settlers paid no attention to Yuma land rights and the boundaries of their fields, letting their livestock graze on the cultivated areas and in general began making the situation difficult.

INDIAN ATTACKS AT THE MISSIONS

The mission settlements were frequently raided by Indians during the period from 1777 to 1780. Calabazas was attacked on June 10, 1777, the same day Captain Allande reached Tucson. Comandante General Croix reported to José de Gálvez that Apaches had sacked and set fire to the settlement, burning all of the houses, the church, and the granary with more than 100 fanegas of maize. The mission Indians put up a stiff defense, killing thirteen Apaches but at the cost of seven of their own gravely wounded. On June 13 the Apaches struck again, raiding a party of settlers from Altar who were rounding up stray cattle at the rancho of Ocuca. Eight settlers died there.

Teodoro de Croix was frustrated by the number of deaths. He thought Oconor's long report of his frontier administration did not tell the truth about frontier conditions and asked Bucareli for 2,000 soldiers to reinforce the Provincias Internas. Since this was unrealistic in view of economic conditions, Croix named Juan Bautista de Anza as Comandante de Armas for Sonora and told him to save the province.

THE NEW MEXICO MISSIONS

Unlike the successes enjoyed by their gray-robed brethren in California, the missionaries in late-eighteenth-century New Mexico faced trying times. From the Pueblo Reconquest forward, military considerations were given priority over spiritual ones. The presidio replaced the mission as the dominant frontier institution, leaving less authority and fewer funds for the Franciscans. In the spiritual realm, the missionaries suffered from a shrinking mission field, due in large part to Indian mortality. Pueblo populations dropped from a probable high of 30,000 at first contact with Europeans, to 10,000 by the end of the eighteenth century. The decrease in Pueblo population was not entirely due to disease, since many Indians simply realigned themselves with other groups. The Reconquest had a scattering effect for many Pueblos; those who feared Spanish reprisals abandoned their traditional communities. The Jémez, Tanos, and Zuni pueblos, severely depopulated already, joined together to form one pueblo each. The lower Río Grande Pueblos of Abó, Quarai, and Las Humanas, on the other hand, did not recover from these migrations and were never repeopled. Some joined the Hopis, who after 1700 no longer tolerated the Franciscans; others joined Apache tribes, among whom the padres never had much proselytizing success. A notable exception was a group of Indian refugees who formed a new pueblo at Laguna in the late 1690s.

Due to the high Indian mortality and relocation of certain native groups, Spanish population doubled that of the Pueblos by the end of the 1700s. For the padres this meant less time spent in missionizing endeavors and more time ministering to Spanish settlers. Even though the Franciscans fulfilled parish obligations, the bishopric in Durango wanted to break the Franciscan's spiritual monopoly by sending secular priests, but few would go. Nevertheless, with the padres' increased parish duties and fewer mission opportunities, New Mexico was an undesirable destination for enthusiastic, qualified Franciscans. Father Domínguez, who had served as special inspector to the New Mexico missions in 1776 prior to his journey to the west, wrote a scathing report on conditions of the missions and ministers, judging the buildings and friars substandard. To a new Franciscan recruit, the mission fields of La Pimería Alta and Alta California certainly seemed more promising.

———————— *Chapter Ten* ————————

BIBLIOGRAPHIC ESSAY

Documentary evidence for this chapter is found primarily in the Archivo General de Indias, Provincias Internas. For a biography of the first Commandant of the Provincias Internas see Alfred Barnaby Thomas, *Teodoro de Croix and the Northern Frontier of New Spain, 1776–1783* (Norman: University of Oklahoma Press, 1941). See also Lillian Estelle Fisher, "Teodoro de Croix," *Hispanic American Historical Review*, 9 (1929): 488–504. Sources of continued importance are John L. Kessell, *Friars, Soldiers and Reformers* (Tucson; University of Arizona Press, 1976); Luis Navarro García, *Don José de Gálvez y la Comandancia General de las Provincias Internas* (Sevilla: Escuela de Estudios Hispano-Americanos, 1964); James Officer, *Hispanic Arizona, 1536–1856* (Tucson: University of Arizona Press, 1987); Henry Dobyns, *Spanish Colonial Tucson* (Tucson: University of Arizona Press, 1976); and Jack D. Forbes, *Warriors of the Colorado* (Norman: University of Oklahoma Press, 1965).

Further travels of Father Francisco Garcés are in Elliot Coues, ed. and trans., *On the Trail of a Spanish Pioneer: The Diary and Itinerary of Francisco Garcés in his Travels Through Sonora, Arizona and California 1775–1776*. Two vols. (New York: Francis P. Harper, 1900). Max L. Moorhead has written

The Presidio: Bastion of the Spanish Borderlands (Norman: University of Oklahoma Press, 1975) and "Spanish Deportation of Hostile Apaches: The Policy and the Practice," *Arizona and the West*, 17 (autumn 1975):205–20. Odie B. Faulk comments on the effectiveness of the presidios in "The Presidio: Fortress or Farce?" in the January 1969 issue of *Journal of the West*, a special issue devoted to the military in the Borderlands. Also included in that issue is Max L. Moorhead, "The Soldado de Cuera: Stalwart of the Spanish Borderlands," and Paige W. Christiansen, "The Presidio and the Borderlands." Faulk's article is reprinted in David Weber, ed., *New Spain's Far Northern Frontier: Essays on Spain in the American West* (Albuquerque: University of New Mexico Press, 1979). See also Jack S. Williams, "Fortress Tucson: Architecture and the Art of War (1775–1856)," *The Smoke Signal*, 49–50 (spring and fall, 1988):168–88.

For the Domínguez and Escalante expedition, see Herbert E. Bolton, ed. and trans., *Pageant in the Wilderness: The Story of the Escalante Expedition to the Interior Basin, 1776, including the Diary and Itinerary of Father Escalante* (Salt Lake City: Utah State Historical Society, 1950); Walter Briggs, *Without Noise of Arms: The 1776 Domínguez-Escalante Search for a Route from Santa Fe to Monterey* (Flagstaff, Ariz.: Northland Press, 1976); and Fray Angélico Chávez, trans., and Ted J. Warner, ed., *The Domínguez-Escalante Journal: Their Expedition through Colorado, Utah, Arizona, and New Mexico in 1776* (Provo, Utah: Brigham Young University Press, 1976). For New Mexico see Eleanor B. Adams and Fray Angélico Chávez, eds. and trans., *The Missions of New Mexico, 1776: A Description by Fray Francisco Atanasio Domínguez, with Other Contemporary Documents.* (Albuquerque: University of New Mexico Press, 1975); Eleanor B. Adams, "Fray Silverstre and the Obstinate Hopi," *New Mexico Historical Review*, 38 (April 1963):115–16; and John Kessell, *The Missions of New Mexico Since 1776* (Albuquerque: University of New Mexico Press, 1980).

Elizabeth A.H. John, *Storms Brewed in Other Men's Worlds: The Confrontation of Indians, Spanish, and French in the Southwest, 1540–1975* (College Station: Texas A&M Press, 1975) has an excellent chapter on the Provincias Internas. Donald E. Worcester edited and translated *Instructions for Governing the Interior Provinces of New Spain, 1786* by Bernardo de Gálvez (Berkeley: The Quivira Society, 1951). Noel M. Loomis has provided "Commandants-General of the Interior Provinces: A Preliminary List," *Arizona and the West*, 11 (autumn 1969):261–268.

For water rights under Spain, a number of recent works have been published. A good survey is Michael Meyer's *Water in the Hispanic Southwest: A Social and Legal History, 1550–1850* (Tucson: University of Arizona Press, 1984); see also William B. Taylor, "Land and Water Rights in New Spain," *NMHR*, 50 (July 1975):189–212; Daniel Tyler, *The Mythical Pueblo Rights Doctrine: Water Administration in Hispanic New Mexico.* (El Paso: Texas Western Press, 1990); Richard E. Greenleaf, "Land and Water in Mexico and New Mexico, 1700–1821," *NMHR*, 47 (April 1972): 85–112; and Norris Hundley, *The Great Thirst: Californians and Water, 1770s–1990s* (Berkeley: University of California Press, 1992).

TOWNS, AGRICULTURE, AND TRADE: 1777–1800

THE LATE EIGHTEENTH CENTURY: AN OVERVIEW

S pain's work of national reconstruction under the Bourbon monarchy reached its peak during the final years of the reign of Carlos III (1759–1788), and the late eighteenth century witnessed the steady growth of industry, agriculture, trade, and colonial expansion. Programs for reform, administered throughout the empire by able ministers, brought financial recovery to the royal treasury. This spirit of progress had sparked the organization of the Provincias Internas and provided for the extension of New Spain's frontier line of defense from the Mississippi River to the Pacific Coast. The end of the American Revolution and the Treaty of Paris of 1783 returned Florida and Havana to Spain and gave the new United States of America freedom to move westward to the Mississippi. Spanish settlement of Baja California moved northward and new areas of Alta California were brought under control.

PROGRESS IN BAJA CALIFORNIA

Since the Dominicans had first taken up their mission work in Baja California in 1772, they had attempted to carry out royal orders to build five missions as soon as possible between San Fernando de Velicatá and San Diego. Foundations for the first establishment, Nuestra Señora del Rosario, were laid at a site called Viñaraco, meaning reed-grass, in 1774. The mission was located about three and one-half miles inland from the Pacific Ocean at 30° 3' latitude. The next mission, founded about three and one-half miles north of Rosario by Fathers Manuel García and Miguel Hidalgo in late August 1775 was named for Santo Domingo, founder of the order. This mission, like its predecessor, did not remain on its original site, but was moved further upstream because of a lack of water. The third mission, founded another fifty miles to the north by Fathers Hidalgo and Joaquín Valero on October 24, 1780, was named for the Dominican Saint Vicente Ferrer. This mission came under attack by the natives, but the most serious disaster was an epidemic of smallpox in that same year. The dread disease, which began at San Fernando Velicatá, spread southward as well as to the other northern missions by 1782. This delayed the founding of a fourth mission, San Miguel Arcangel, until March 1787, and the fifth, Santo Tomás was not completed until 1791. Conditions throughout the Baja California peninsula were wretched because of drought and widespread hunger, but the Dominicans continued in their attempts to inoculate against smallpox and alleviate starvation.

Fig. 11.1. Ruins of Mission Santo Domingo. Photo by W. Michael Mathes.

THE TUCSON PRESIDIO

In Mexico, Anza had taken Salvador Palma of the Yumas to the court of the viceroy and presented him at a marvelous reception. Bucareli requested that Anza, who was being considered as governor of New Mexico, be promoted to colonel which he became when he assumed that office. All seemed to be going well for Anza and Salvador Palma in the spring of 1777 as they left the capital to travel northward. Palma was confirmed in the cathedral at Durango and continued on to Culiacán.

When Anza reached San Miguel de Horcasitas in May 1777, he found that Sonora was besieged with difficulties. The transfer of the garrison from Tubac to Tucson and the movement north of Terrenate and Fronteras presidios had meant they were unable to protect the province. The posts were isolated and undermanned. The transportation of food and provisions was very difficult and about one-third of the troops were constantly engaged in freighting. The hostile Indians could do almost as they pleased. Croix told Anza that he could move the presidio from Tucson back to Tubac since little had been done in the way of construction at the new site. The Spaniards could then be in a better position to restore Calabazas and protect Tumacácori.

In November 1777, Captain Allande held a meeting of the people of Tumacácori and Tubac to present their reasons for wanting the presidio returned to its former site. They reported that in the valley around Tubac there were many acres of fertile land and even with a third of it lying fallow, the community raised 600 or more fanegas of wheat annually. If the system of irrigation put into effect by Captain Anza and maintained by Allande was kept in force, there would be enough water for all—one week for the settlers at Tubac and the next week for the Indians at Tumacácori. There was enough grazing land and wood available. Cottonwoods and willows grew along the river and there were pine trees in the Sierra de Santa Rita.

In addition to the possibilities for farming, there were three silver mines to the west near Arivaca. Beyond those mines were gold placers that had so far yielded about 200 pesos. Other mines to the east had yielded small results but there were too many Apaches in the area to allow for further exploration. Because of this danger and because of the burning of Calabazas, the people of Tubac asked that the presidio be returned, but the request was never approved. It was necessary to retain the presidio at Tucson at this time since it was the gateway to the north. Captain Allande assigned a detachment of only twelve to fourteen men to protect the old presidio of Tubac and the missions of Tumacácori, Calabazas, and San Xavier del Bac. It was not enough, but by this time Captain Juan Bautista Anza, long the protector of the frontier, became governor of New Mexico and left Sonora in March 1778.

ATTACK AT ATI, APRIL 1778

The worst fears of the friars and settlers were realized in April 1778. While Fray Felipe Guillén, the missionary of Tubutama was on a trip to his visita of Santa Teresa in the Altar Valley, he decided to call on Fray Juan Gorgoll at Ati. Halfway there he ran into seven hostile Indians fleeing from Ati where they had just killed four persons. They then not only killed Father Guillén, but cut his body into four pieces, hanging them separately in four trees. Fathers Gorgoll, Eixarch, and Barbastro laid their martyred brother to rest at Ati before the assembled Indians of Tubutama, Santa Teresa, Oquitoa, and Ati. The friars asked Croix for mission guards to prevent such an event from happening again. Croix replied to Gálvez that Father Guillén should not have been traveling through dangerous territory with only the escort of three Indians from his mission adding that the Apaches did not understand the sacrilege of killing a priest.

FRANCISCAN MISSIONARIES FROM NORTHERN SPAIN

Fray Pedro Arriquibar was accompanied at his mission of Tumacácori during most of his last three years by Joaquín Antonio Belarde, a blue-eyed, 26-year-old Basque from Vitoria. He had become a Franciscan at the Convento Grande de Vitoria in 1764 along with Gaspar de Clemente. Fray Joaquín was ordained by the bishop of Cádiz just before sailing to New Spain. He arrived in Sonora in 1773 and joined Matías Gallo among the Seris at Pitic. For a time, he substituted for Pedro Font at San José de Pimas and in the fall of 1776 was sent to San Xavier del Bac. From there, Belarde moved to Tumacácori to join Arriquibar in the fall of 1777. The two Basques worked together until the spring of 1779 when Belarde returned to San Xavier del Bac; he died of a fever at Cieneguilla on March 5, 1781, at the age of 35. Father Arriquibar, on the other hand, lived to a very old age. After serving at Tumacácori for five years, he moved to San Ignacio and afterwards to Tucson as military chaplain. Always close to the Ramírez family (beginning with Tubac Militia Captain Juan Crisóstomo Ramírez), he was taken care of by Teodor Ramírez, grandson of Juan Crisóstomo and son of Juan Joseph, an interpreter at Tumacácori. Father Arriquibar left his estate to Teodoro upon his death in 1820, which gave the Ramírez family considerable status thereafter.

Father Arriquibar was fortunate to live out his life on the frontier; protection of missionaries and settlers did not improve after Teodoro de Croix moved their head-quarters to Arizpe. A dozen Apaches had killed Captain Miguel de Urrea, ambushing him near Altar, while another Apache war party of about thirty killed Father Francisco Perdigon, chaplain of the Tucson garrison, on his way to Bacanuchi for the festival of St. John on June 23, 1780. Father Perdigon's body was found covered with wounds from head to foot.

Another missionary to arrive at Tumacácori during these difficult times was Baltazar Carrillo from Fitero in southern Navarra. Born around 1734, Carrillo grew up in a picturesque town with its houses crowded on a small hill on the broad plain of the Río Alhama. He joined the Franciscan order in 1752 in the city of Logroño, about sixty miles northwest of Fitero. After seventeen years serving the order in Spain, Baltazar volunteered from Pamplona to join the other recruits going to the Franciscan college at Querétaro. His first assignment was to replace Fray Antonio de los Reyes at Cucurpe. When the Queretarans left La Pimería Baja, Carrillo went to San Ignacio with Fray Francisco Sánchez Zuniga. In early 1780, when Father Pedro de Arriquibar left Tumacácori to replace Sánchez Zuniga, Carrillo went to Tumacácori. During his first year there, Apaches killed several friendly Native Americans and continued their hostile raids.

WAR WITH ENGLAND, 1778

On July 4, 1776, the English colonies in North America declared war on the mother country. As the Americans fought against what they considered the tyranny of George III, they asked France and other European mercenaries to join their effort. Because of long-standing grievances against England throughout the eighteenth century, and especially as a result of the war ending with the Treaty of Paris in 1763, France by 1778 was eager to assist the Americans. Because of the alliance of the Bourbon monarchs, Spain had an obligation to make a formal declaration of war against England in the summer of 1779, even though the country was already extended beyond its resources on the Mississippi valley and Gulf Coast frontiers. In order to raise money for Spain's offensive, Carlos III appealed to his American colonies for a donation of 2 pesos from each Spaniard and 1 peso from each Indian. Captain Allande made a concerted effort to raise the money on the Sonoran frontier and continued the effort until his departure in 1786.

To the inhabitants of Hispanic Arizona, the Apaches seemed to be a much greater threat than the war with England. In May 1780, Jacobo de Ugarte y Loyola, military governor of Sonora, and Lieutenant Jerónimo de la Rocha of the Army Corps of Engineers agreed that Oconor's plan to move the presidios beyond the former line of defense had been a mistake. Thus the Fronteras garrison, isolated and ineffective in the valley of San Bernardino, was to be moved back to its original site. The Terrenate garrison after its transfer north to the Río Santa Cruz had lost two captains and more than eighty men in five years. It would have to be pulled back. However, much as the residents of Tubac continued to ask for the return of the soldiers from Tucson, it remained impossible because they were then needed for the protection of the Gila-Colorado River road to California.

SETTLEMENT OF THE RÍO COLORADO

The establishment of a mission among the Yuma Indians on the Colorado continued as a priority for Father Garcés and Salvador Palma. After his visit to Mexico City with Anza, Palma—Olleyquotequiebe of the Yumas—had returned to Arizona with thrilling stories. He told his fellow tribespeople that he had seen the capital with its markets and wide streets; had ridden in a carriage and been baptized in a great cathedral; had worn the uniform of a Spanish officer with a large medal of a principal chief gleaming upon his breast. He promised the Yumas that the soldiers would come to build them a presidio, help them against their enemies and bring them trade and presents. The missionaries would bless the people. But where were they? Two years had passed without any sign of the proposed establishments. Palma began to lose face. He rode to Altar and begged Captain Pedro Tueros, interim military governor, to at least send gifts.

Croix had received the royal orders of February 10 and 14, 1777, approving the missionaries and presidio at Yuma, and directing the continued gratification of Palma. But he had Apache and Comanche problems on his mind and decided Yuma could wait. Finally on February 5, 1779, at the urgent request of Captain Tueros, Croix, then ill in Chihuahua, asked Father Garcés to take a companion and go to the Colorado to assure Palma and his people that something would soon be done. The Colegio of Querétaro chose Father Juan Marcelo Díaz to accompany Garcés. Díaz, a native of Sevilla, had accompanied Anza on his first expedition to California in 1774. The missionaries requested that at least a dozen married soldiers, all with their wives, and a carpenter, along with three months' provisions and gifts for the Indians, be sent. Garcés wanted family men with their own crops and domestic animals so they would create no additional burden on the Yuma economy. He spent the summer and spring trying to get the project organized. Handicapped by an inadequate budget, the final blow was a decision by Governor Corbalán that the wives should not go along because they might be coveted by the Indians. The missionaries were then to see to it that the lonely Spanish soldiers did not covet the Indians' wives. Garcés begged Viceroy Bucareli for alms to buy gifts for the Indians, but the generous Bucareli died before the missionary's plea reached the capital.

Knowing that they had insufficient support, but believing that additional help would come later, Garcés decided to go ahead with the journey. He, along with Father Díaz and twelve soldiers, started out across the desert for Yuma in August 1779—the worst month to travel. All but Garcés and two soldiers turned back, and the trio's arrival was hardly a cause for excitement among the Yumas. Their few gifts of tobacco, cloth, and glass beads were not enough to satisfy the Indians who had been promised great things by Palma for so long. The arrival of ten more unhappy soldiers and another priest in October only added more mouths to feed. Garcés knew that the Yumas were not going to remain friendly for long under these circumstances. More Spaniards were needed, especially muleteers and carpenters, and all should have wives in order to build a stable, self-sufficient community. When letters alone brought no action, Father Díaz rode to Arizpe to appeal to Croix in person, warning that without more troops and more funds the friars could not keep peace.

Croix finally provided for two Spanish mission settlements among the Yumas, one with eleven soldiers and the other with ten. Each would have sixteen subsidized civilian settlers, among whom would be artisans and interpreters. Each mission would have two friars and all soldiers would be married and required to bring their families along. The heads of families would be allotted lands in accordance with the *Recopilación de leyes de las Indias*, with one tract reserved for use in common and another for the benefit of the church. The Yumas would share in the land distribution either in individual lots or in one large grant in common. Father Díaz thought all Indians who wished to have individual plots should since they were accustomed to agriculture. Asesor Pedro Galindo Navarro feared the consequences of disturbing the existing Indian land-use patterns before the Spaniards could gain a clearer understanding of their practices.

Problems with the Yuma Settlement

According to the Franciscan Father Juan Domingo Arricivita, Teodoro de Croix was creating an impossible situation. He was ordering two Spanish towns to be set up in the midst of 3,000 unhappy Yuma Indians 250 miles beyond the closest presidio. The missionaries, with limited authority, were to instruct, baptize, and persuade the Yumas to join the Spanish settlements. There were no precedents for such a move.

Ensign Santiago de Islas, a native of Italy, would command the new settlements. He had come up through the ranks of the Dragoon Regiment of Mexico and had participated in nine attempts to run down Apache war parties. Ensign Islas asked for volunteers at the settlement around the former presidio of Tubac telling them that the Yumas were friendly and were eager for a mission. In addition to land and water, the colonist families would receive 10 pesos a month for the first year, a yoke of oxen, two cows, one bull, two mares, and tools. Artisans were being hired to help them build new homes and corrals.

Manuel Barragán, long a community leader, and his wife Francisca Olguin were the first to come forward and volunteer. Joseph Olguín and María Ignacia Hurtado with their three small children also offered to go. Others signed up and packed their meager possessions to join the caravan to the Colorado. Some of the recruits were from Tucson and some of the soldiers had already been to Yuma with Anza. It seemed like a good idea; the water was plentiful and the watermelons were abundant.

As Santiago de Islas prepared his group for travel, the situation at Yuma had worsened. Father Díaz wrote Croix from La Purísima Concepción del Río Colorado that food was critically short and that the Yumas had just raided a neighboring tribe. Because they had failed to keep their promises, Ignacio Palma, brother of Salvador, was inciting the Indians to kill the Spaniards. Nevertheless, the colonists under Islas arrived two days after Christmas with children, cattle, horses, and bleating sheep. Islas began laying out the colony and by mid-January 1781, there were two settlements, both on the California side. La Purísima Concepción was just across from today's Yuma, and San Pedro y San Pablo de Bicuñer was four leagues upstream.

Two more friars, Juan Antonio Joaquín de Barreneche, a native of the village of Lacazor in Navarra and Joseph Matías Moreno, born in Almarza, arrived to join Garcés and Díaz. Father Barreneche, born in 1749, had gone to Cuba as a youth and in 1768 enrolled in the Convent of Havana. Father Moreno, born in 1743 or 1744, became a Franciscan at Logroño in the Holy Province of Burgos. Both were attached to the Colegio at Querétaro and neither had experience with frontier conditions.

The Yumas became increasingly hostile toward the Spaniards when the newcomers took Yuma lands, let their stock graze over Yuma crops and mesquite trees, introduced forms of punishment, and in general treated the Indians with contempt. The settlement failed to meet Indian needs as imagined under the early promises of Salvador Palma; in addition, the friars could not control the behavior of unruly soldiers. To make matters even worse, a smallpox epidemic began to spread through Mexico and travel to the north. Father Carrillo at Tumacácori buried twenty-two bodies during a five-week period from the end of May to early July 1781.

THE YUMA DISASTER, 1781

Meanwhile, at this very time, Teodoro de Croix was working on his general report to José de Gálvez in which he praised his own effort in establishing successful low-cost establishments on the Río Colorado. The flourishing settlements with their crops and herds, he said, would protect the road to California. In fact, Captain Fernando de Rivera y Moncada was currently marching to the Colorado with settlers, soldiers, stock, and supplies for the proposed pueblo of Los Angeles. As Croix worked on his report, a rider from Tucson brought the terrible news—the friars, settlers, and soldiers on the Colorado were dead. Rivera and the men who had stayed behind while others were sent ahead were also dead.

The final insult to the Yumas had occurred in early July 1781 when a wagon train of forty families crossed Yuma country en route to California to settle in the new pueblo of Los Angeles. Captain Rivera saw his charges safely across the Colorado and then came back across the stream with a dozen soldiers and camped to let his animals rest and graze before moving them on to California. He had already made the mistake of distributing too few gifts, and now his cattle were ravaging the mesquite trees that were vital to Yuman subsistence. By Tuesday morning, July 17, 1781, the Yumas could take no more. Father Garcés was celebrating mass at Concepción when both settlements were overrun. Ensign Islas was killed early and his mangled body thrown into the river; Fathers Garcés and Barreneche at first were spared and tried to calm the Indians.

Upriver at Bicñuer, Father Juan Díaz and Father Joseph Matías Moreno both died in the initial onslaught; someone had chopped off Moreno's head with an ax. Holding the women and children captive, on Wednesday, July 18, the Indians massacred Rivera and all of his soldiers. Father Garcés warned the women and children to stay together and not to resist capture; he insisted that the Yumas would not harm them. Within two or three days, the Indians decided not to spare Fathers Garcés and Barreneche. Even though many were against killing their long-time friends, the enemies of Palma won out. The tragedy was complete.

Anza Gets the Blame

Croix, vulnerable to criticism for mishandling settlement among the Yumas, placed the blame on Anza and Garcés for misleading him about the power and responsibility of Salvador Palma, as well as the productivity of Yuma lands. He ordered Felipe de Neve, governor of California, and Lieutenant Colonel Pedro Fages, a veteran frontiersman who had served as lieutenant governor of California at Monterey from 1770 to 1774, to take an expedition to the Colorado to assess the damage and regain the captives at any price. Croix ordered Fages to pay any ransom, but once the captives were safe, the soldiers were to take back everything given. Fages gave no punishment and took no rebel leaders, but in exchange for tobacco and other goods managed to ransom seventy-four captives, mostly women and children. The number of dead reached 104.

The Spaniards at Tumacácori had known many of the victims in addition to their well-loved friars. Among the dead were Manuel Barragán and his wife Francisca Olguín, Joseph Olguín, Francisco Castro, and Juan Romero, whose wife and three children perished with him. Some of the rescued women and children went to Tucson where they joined relatives who had previously been at Tubac. The bodies of the four slain missionaries were packed in a couple of empty cigarette crates and shipped on muleback to Tubutama. Father President Francisco Barbastro buried his companions under the sanctuary floor on the gospel side. Years later they were dug up and returned to the college at Querétaro where the entire community joined in funeral rites on July 19, 1794, thirteen years after their deaths. Those attending knew their brother Franciscans had achieved martyrdom, the order's highest honor.

Croix continued to blame Anza for the Yuma disaster, ignoring the fact that Anza had warned from the earliest discussions of the project that it would be foolish to establish a colony without an ample garrison, and without adequate provisions so as not to strain the fragile Yuma economy. Anza also had insisted upon a scrupulous respect for Indian rights in order to have both groups live in peace. And, even though he had enjoyed a long period of success on the frontier, Anza was blamed too for not keeping the Apaches under control.

Ironically, Croix, mainly responsible for the Yuma disaster, was appointed viceroy of Peru the next year. Felipe de Neve, who was appointed to succeed Croix as comandant general, was apparently influenced by Croix or did not like Anza for other reasons, since he launched a campaign to oust him from the governorship of New Mexico. Neve even went so far as to forbid Anza from listing the discovery of the overland route to California on his service record. Well along in gathering evidence to use against Anza, Neve died in 1784, and Anza did receive the support he deserved from veteran officers of the Provincias Internas. After leaving the governorship of New Mexico, Anza returned to the provisional command of the military forces of Sonora.

The friars never recovered from the disaster of 1781. They were disenchanted with the government of the Provincias Internas for the next forty years of its existence. They begged that La Pimería Alta be returned to the viceroy's jurisdiction, believing that he better represented the king's desire to convert the Native Americans. Unfortunately, the missionaries did not convince the king of their position.

THE FOUNDING OF LOS ANGELES, 1781

In the meantime, first among the projects undertaken during California's second decade of settlement was the expansion of its civilian population. Governor Felipe de Neve's original plan of 1777 had proposed two pueblos in the province. By 1781, San José on the Guadalupe River seemed permanent, so Neve proceeded with the founding of his second town. Aware of the need for an adequate water supply, he chose a site near the banks of the Porciúncula (Los Angeles) River—the location that Father Crespí and Miguel Costansó had admired during their travels with Portolá in 1769–1770. According to Neve's survey, the Porciúncula was the only stream in southern California whose water was unfailing, which flowed steadily, and could be easily diverted. The governor had obtained necessary approval for founding the town from Commandant Teodoro de

Croix of the Provincias Internas, and sent instructions to his lieutenant governor, Fernando de Rivera, to recruit prospective settlers in Sonora and Sinaloa. After some difficulty, Captain Rivera assembled about half the requested number—a mixed group of forty-six persons. They departed on February 2, 1781, from Alamos, Sonora, under two of Rivera's officers, Lieutenant José de Zuniga and Ensign Ramon Lasso de la Vega. Those whom Rivera accompanied personally became involved in the Yuma uprising in July.

The more fortunate colonists sailed across the Gulf of California to Loreto and then to San Luis Gonzaga Bay. They continued overland by way of Mission San Fernando Velicatá, and reached their destination at Mission San Gabriel in Alta California on August 18. Though suffering from sickness and exhaustion, the party recovered successfully at the mission after a few weeks of rest. Governor Neve ordered distribution of equipment and, on August 26, 1781,

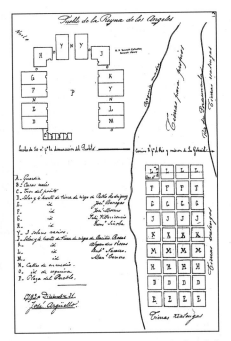

Map 11.1. Map of Pueblo of Los Angeles founded September 4, 1781. Courtesy The Bancroft Library.

signed the explicit instructions for founding "El Pueblo de Nuestra Señora la Reina de los Angeles de Porciúncula" (The Town of Our Lady the Queen of the Angels of Porciuncula). Led by Corporal José Vicente Feliz, the townspeople were to mark out a pueblo site near the river that was "slightly elevated and freely open to North and South winds," construct a *saca de agua* (diversion dam), and run a large irrigation ditch to the farm lands. They were to build a plaza 200 by 300 feet long, reserving the area looking east across the square for the church and government buildings. (Ms., The Bancroft Library) After a town lot and four farming tracts were assigned to each settler, certain communal lands for pasture, firewood, and recreation were to be set aside. The corporal was also to designate the lands reserved for eventual assignment to new settlers, and mark out the *propios*—land belonging to the town for revenue purposes. Neve did not set the outer boundaries of Los Angeles, although new pueblos under the Laws of the Indies generally encompassed four square leagues (about thirty-six square miles).

On September 4, 1781, eleven heads of families—two Spaniards, two African-Americans, one mestizo, two mulattos, and four Indians—traveled with their wives and children (forty-four total) from Mission San Gabriel to the level grassy area indicated by Corporal Feliz near the Porciúncula River. Not far away they could see low, brown hills covered with a scattering of chaparral and cactus clumps. In the distance rose the high San Gabriel Mountains—clearly visible from the town. Corporal Feliz assigned lots to each settler according to the "drawing of lots" held at the mission. (The Spanish word *suerte* used for lot also means "chance" or "luck.")

After drawing their lots, the party made a temporary camp and began building their adobe, thatched-roof houses. Thus the city of Los Angeles—today the nation's largest in area and third-ranking in population—came into being inauspiciously. Five years after its founding, on September 4, 1786, Ensign José Dario Argüello of the Santa Barbara presidio, established in 1782, confirmed nine of the original settlers in formal possession of their lands. None of the new owners could write, so each made a cross acknowledging his document of title and cattle brand certification. The marks were witnessed by Corporal Feliz and Private Roque de Cota of Santa Barbara.

FAGES RETURNS TO CALIFORNIA, 1782

As previously noted, a number of settlers recruited for the pueblo of Los Angeles by Captain Rivera in Sonora and Sinaloa perished at Yuma in July 1781. Lieutenant Colonel Pedro Fages, former governor of California then serving in Sonora, traveled to the Colorado River in an attempt to rescue or ransom the captives and recover the bodies of the martyred priests. The Spaniards did not gain peace with the Yumas but succeeded in their mission. Yuman tribal organizations by this time had been sufficiently disrupted to prevent further war, but the Anza trail was closed to further travel during the remainder of the Spanish occupation of the Southwest and California.

Pedro Fages left the Colorado River in April 1782, and, after completing a survey of remaining Yuma strength, headed across the Laguna Mountains to Mission San Diego. He visited with the padres while looking over the mission's new site, inspected the presidio, and then proceeded to Mission San Gabriel. Fages sent word of his arrival to Governor Neve at the new Santa Barbara presidio, expecting to receive instructions for returning to Yuma with the governor and additional troops. Neve replied instead that the trip to the Colorado River would be postponed until mid-August. Fages thus began a tour of California's establishments, renewing old—and this time more pleasant—acquaintances with the Franciscan fathers. At Carmel, after inspecting the northern missions, Fages amiably discussed provincial matters with Father Serra until Neve was ready to depart.

Finally en route to Yuma late in August with a company of sixty men, Neve and Fages were overtaken by a courier with news from Teodoro de Croix that Neve had been appointed inspector general of the Provincias Internas and Fages elevated to the post of governor of California. Both promotions were provisional, but royal confirmation was subsequently received. Without delay, Neve formally relinquished his office, signing instructions to Fages at Saucillo de la Santa Catalina on September 7, 1782. Neve proceeded to the Colorado River while Governor Fages returned to Monterey to resume command of the province that he had been forced to relinquish in 1773.

PRESIDIO OF SANTA BARBARA

Governor Neve had decided that a fourth presidio should be located midway between San Buenaventura and Point Concepción since the coastline in that area was most vulnerable to landing by a foreign power. Because the presidio also had to be near a protected harbor with a sandy bottom for proper anchorage, as well as near an available water supply, Santa Barbara was chosen. The specific site, slightly elevated and inland, was distant from the main Indian village and provided a good view of incoming ships. Neve reported to Croix that there was abundant water, wood, and stone, and the

Indians were cooperative. Their chief, Yanonalit, had control over thirteen rancherías and his friendship, carefully cultivated, proved to be a great advantage. Father Serra assumed that a mission would be founded simultaneously in April 1782, but Neve refused, preferring to keep the Indians living in their own rancherías. Baptisms and marriages of the soldiers would continue at Mission San Buenaventura.

In order to assure Indian cooperation, Neve wrote to Lt. José Ortega on June 30, 1782, asking that a guard be posted to watch merchandise being unloaded from the supply ships *Princesa* and *Favorita* when they arrived at Santa Barbara in order to prevent the sailors from bothering the Indians. Neve knew the Indians would be curious when they saw the landing of a cargo in their bay and knowing that they were not happy about having strangers in the area, wanted to make sure they were protected from any unnecessary harassment. The governor was most anxious to have the building of the presidio go smoothly.

Neve appointed Captain Felipe Antonio de Goycoechea, of Basque descent, as commander of the Santa Barbara Company in 1783. Goycoechea, born in 1747 in Real de Cozala, a small town ninety miles southeast of Culiacán in Sinaloa, Mexico, had served at the presidios of Fronteras, southeast of Tucson, at San Buenaventura, southwest of El Paso, and at Loreto in Baja California during his first year of service. He received rapid promotions and had reached first lieutenant at the time of his assignment to Santa Barbara. Even though he remained a bachelor, Goycoechea fathered a boy at Santa Barbara by the widow of one of the presidio soldiers.

THE DEATH OF FATHER SERRA

When Fages returned to the governorship of California in 1782, he experienced few of his previous difficulties with the aging father-president. Indeed, Father Serra realized that Fages was easier to get along with than had been either Rivera or Neve. Serra's zeal to build missions and promote Indian welfare had consistently come up against equally strong wills of the military governors to proceed differently. With Felipe de Neve, trouble arose in 1777 over the amount of rations at the three new missions, and about the type of future mission establishments. As governor, Neve constantly opposed Serra's desire to be consulted on matters affecting the missions, and even questioned Serra's authority to administer the rite of confirmation to the Indians. For five years he delayed the founding of Mission San Buenaventura, finally achieved on March 31, 1782, and refused to give in to Serra's request for a mission at Santa Barbara. But despite his differences with Serra, when Neve became commandant general of the Provincias Internas, he praised the missionary work done in Upper California:

> ... *[the Franciscans] who administer the missions in California, have surpassed expectation in developing them. In every respect they are enormous when one compares them with their beginnings. ... In a word they have brought to those establishments that state of progress they enjoy today, compared to which there are no other missions like theirs in all these provinces. They have made fertile and fecund a portion of land they found as uncultivated wastes.* (Neve to Reyes, Dec. 29, 1783, in Geiger, *The Life and Times of Fray Junipero Serra*, pp. 368–69)

Toward the end of August 1784, the venerable Fray Junípero Serra, already past 70, suffered a fatal illness. He sent for Father Palóu to administer last rites, and shortly after taking communion on August 28, passed away. He was buried the next day beside Father Crespí at his beloved Mission San Carlos Borromeo on the Carmel River. The Father Superior at the College of San Fernando in Mexico relayed the news of Serra's death to the order at Palma de Mallorca, commenting that the father president's kindness was well recognized by people in general as well as by persons of high standing. Three years after Serra's death, Governor Fages, who once considered Serra despotic and opposed to rightful measures of government, wrote the following about the missionaries in California during the first years:

> ... *[they] commenced the grand work amid the poverty, penury and want which are inseparable from such undertakings in newly discovered countries. ... Nevertheless, these religious have placed their institutions on a solid basis. If we must do justice to all, as is obligatory, we must confess that the rapid, agreeable, and interesting progress in spiritual as well as in temporal affairs ... is the glorious effect of the apostolic zeal, activity, and indefatigable efforts of these religious.* (Fages 1787 Report on California in Geiger, *The Life and Times of Fray Junipero Serra*, p. 333)

Serra's attention to detail coupled with constant hard work made the mission enterprise fruitful. He firmly believed he was giving the Indians a better life.

FATHER LASUÉN AND THE CALIFORNIA MISSIONS

The man who replaced Junípero Serra as father-president of the California missions deserves recognition equal to his predecessor for achievement. But Father Fermín Francisco de Lasuén came second—a position always to remain in the shadow of number one. In addition, the prolific writings of Father Palóu, Serra's devoted companion and biographer, have served to further this imbalance, since there was no one of similar stature to chronicle the events of Lasuén's administration. Yet time has altered this circumstance as historians have uncovered the events of Lasuén's early life and recreated his significant role in California's development.

Lasuén, a native of Vitoria in Spain's Basque province of Alava, was born on July 7, 1736. His family had resided in that northern area for several generations. At the age of 14, Lasuén became a novice in the Franciscan monastery of Vitoria and made his profession as a Franciscan on July 7, 1752, his 16th birthday. Recruited by a Franciscan missionary from New Spain, Lasuén left for Mexico on March 6, 1759, with a band of eighteen candidates for overseas service. After a year's residence at the College of San Fernando in Mexico, Lasuén served as a missionary in the Sierra Gorda region. He traveled to Baja California under Father Serra in 1767 and was placed in charge of the Jesuit Father Linck's northerly Mission San Francisco Borja, just inland from the Bahía de Los Angeles.

Father Lasuén's mission philosophy emphasized the improvement of the Indians' material welfare first, with the hope that more willing conversion would follow. The Franciscan priest believed that generous provisions of food and clothing could convince the natives of Christianity's rewards better than words they did not understand. Lasuén, a well-educated and intelligent administrator, was also kind and hardworking— all of which contributed to his success in the mission field.

The soldiers placed in charge of Mission San Francisco Borja after the Jesuit expulsion from Baja California had limited experience in agriculture and had allowed crops to die, fields to grow over, animals to wander away, and Indians to become scattered throughout the mountains. Shortly after Lasuén's arrival, José de Gálvez advised the priest to prohibit gambling and suggested that the natives be given tobacco to gain their friendship. Lasuén replied that San Borja's need was neither reform nor tobacco but food and clothing. Gálvez finally agreed. Lasuén, always working alone, little by little repaired the run-down mission, and by 1771 had converted or baptized all the Indians in the district. Even with a scarcity of water, the good-natured Basque supervised the planting of vineyards, fig and pomegranate trees, and some cotton. He taught the Indians to manufacture shawls and weave woolen blankets. When the Dominicans assumed control of Mission San Borja in May 1773, the result of five years' work showed 1,000 Christian residents, 648 cattle, 387 horses and mules, 2343 sheep, and 1,003 goats. This was a substantial achievement since all fourteen missions of Baja California had a combined total of 4,268 Indians and 14,716 domestic animals.

Lasuén's Assignments

Lasuén's first assignment in Upper California was at Mission San Gabriel in September 1773. The previous eight months had been a period of famine in the district and supplies were dangerously low. Nevertheless, Lasuén managed to ward off starvation and even to offer provisions to Anza's first expedition, which arrived in March 1774. Conditions improved when a relief ship arrived from New Spain, and San Gabriel's Indians finally harvested a crop of grain. In October 1775, Lasuén and Father Gregorio Amurrio inaugurated Serra's sixth mission at San Juan Capistrano, but the Indian uprising at Mission San Diego in November of that year forced Capistrano's official founding to be delayed until November 1, 1776. In the meantime, Serra reassigned Lasuén to the partially destroyed Mission San Diego where he brought affairs at the troubled mission under control. Lasuén remained at the southernmost post until his appointment as father-president.

All of Lasuén's previous experience pointed toward his ability to fulfill Serra's job as administrative head of the California missions. No selection could have been more fortunate. Palóu's interim presidency ended with his departure for Mexico in September 1785, where he became father superior of the College of San Fernando the next year. Although Lasuén's appointment was dated February 6, 1785, it did not reach California until the following September, when the new executive left San Diego to begin his eighteen-year term as father-president. Lasuén's accomplishments covered all fields—from architecture to scientific surveys, and from administrative reform to replacing thatched roofs with hand-made tiles.

Lasuén and the Military

Cooperation between the military and religious arms of the state began slowly. Lasuén first had to consider charges levied against the missions by Pedro Fages in 1785 that

Fig. 11.2. Leather-jacket soldier Gabriel Moraga stationed at Monterey presidio, drawn by José Cardero in 1791. Courtesy Museo Naval, Madrid.

had been answered in part by Father Palóu. Some of these were complaints of long standing and had been aggravated by differences between Serra and previous governors. Fages accused the padres of not performing chaplain duty at the presidios, charging unwarranted prices for mission produce, refusing to render inventories, and failing to solicit permission to leave the province. Palou had replied that chaplain duty was a favor, not a requirement and should be paid for and that prices were determined by supply and demand. He said nothing about inventories and insisted that only one priest had to be at a mission, so permission for one to depart was not necessary. Lasuén levied a few charges against the government, especially that the soldiers were wrongly accusing the Indians of petty crimes in order to demand their services at the presidios, and that the soldiers were mostly doing work other than performing their military duties. Because of Lasuén's nature, he was able to discuss matters easily with Fages, and the differences between the two arms of Spanish government were soon smoothed over.

Indian Policy

Spain's Indian policy, humanitarian in intent, was effectively continued under Lasuén and Governor Fages. As Neve had instructed him in 1782, Fages was to bear in mind that the principal objective of California's governor was to preserve peace and maintain Indian friendship through kindness, gentleness, good treatment, and gifts. Besides its purely Christian motives, the Spanish government had cogent reasons for not provoking hostility or revolt: its resources were slender, its manpower limited, and its forces already overextended. Control of the North Pacific coast and protection of California settlements from European aggression required Spain to maintain peace with the various tribes of Indians and keep the new mission converts happy and content. Any kind of prolonged Indian war would have been fatal to its policy of expansion in California. Father Lasuén well understood the means to peace and friendship when he issued this statement:

> ... the following are the principles we follow: The first principle is patience, and the second is patience, and the third is patience, and so are all the others. ... Before recourse is had to severity (it should be kept to the minimum; just as little as possible), first exhaust every effort that is mild, as would a father of a family who is affectionate and considerate towards

*his children. Use punishment as an effective method of correcting, never as
an instrument to harass the offender.* ... (Lasuén to José Gasol, "Refuta-
tion of Charges," June 19, 1801, quoted in Kenneally, trans. and ed.,
Writings of Fermín Francisco de Lasuén, vol. II, p. 221)

New Missions

During his father-presidency from 1785 to 1803, Lasuén was responsible for the founding
of nine missions, equaling Serra's nine and nearly completing the Upper California
chain from San Diego to San Francisco. Lasuén also devoted energy to the repair and
expansion of Serra's original missions. He ordered some to be completely reconstructed
on better sites and gave thought to improving their architectural design. At Lasuén's
request, Governor Fages obtained Spanish artisans to supervise the Indians in building
mission structures like those restored today. The father-president founded his first mission in December 1786, at Santa Barbara about a mile and a half northeast of the
presidio. The site, called Tanayan by the Indians and Pedregosa (Rocky Point) by the
Spaniards, encompassed a striking view of the valley and channel. Two dams were built
on the Río Pedregosa (today's Mission Creek) and its eastern tributary to provide sufficient water for domestic needs and irrigation. Diverted into stone aqueducts, the waters converged northeast of the mission and flowed into a storage reservoir built below.
Father Lasuén planned each of his new missions with the same care, but Santa Barbara
remained his favorite.

THE ARIZONA PIMAS

Meanwhile, the Pimas living along the Santa Cruz and San Pedro Rivers had become converted and lived under the direction of Franciscan missionaries. They planted
crops and took up the Spanish way of life because they had no choice. On the other
hand, the Pimas along the Gila River were not subjected to control by the missionaries,
but they did become acculturated to a certain degree. The introduction of wheat brought
about a number of modifications in their life. They abandoned their former settlement
pattern and grouped their houses more closely together in order to cultivate their fields
and to protect their harvest from the Apaches. The Gila River Pimas acquired efficient
iron farming tools and the ox-drawn plow. The addition of beef, poultry, fruits, and
vegetables into their diet changed their eating habits. Their contact with Hispanic culture introduced them to commerce in place of gift trading. Manufactured goods and
food surpluses were marketed, and the Pimas became skilled in assessing relative val-
ues for trading purposes.

Despite the efforts of missionaries such as Kino and Garcés to establish a peaceful,
stable church-centered Spanish civilization in Arizona, their efforts were never entirely
successful. The Spanish crown tried to hold the Indians in check to allow settlers to
move in and exploit the resources of the region, but that proved impossible until the
Apaches were restrained. The reports of the padres were generally optimistic, but many
of the Indians lived outside the sphere of mission influence and consequently were
hostile. Even the peaceful Pimas and Yumas rebelled several times and put to death the
very missionaries who had worked among them on their behalf.

PEDRO VIAL IN NEW MEXICO, 1786

While stability was being achieved in California and the area remained free from outside, alien influence, such was not the case in New Mexico, where the shadow of foreigners loomed on the eastern frontier. A key figure interested in New Mexico was an ex-Frenchman who, after 1763, became a Spaniard. His exploits, imperfectly known previously, have recently been uncovered in the American and European archives. He was Pierre Vial, also known as Pedro Vial, and he was born in Lyons, France. He arrived early in the Southwest but appeared actively on the scene in 1786 as an explorer sent to open a trail from San Antonio in Texas to Santa Fe. By then he was an experienced frontiersman. There is no certain knowledge of what his capacity was, but it is clear that he was not a military officer, nor was he associated with the clergy, nor was he a regularly appointed civil servant. He was different and this difference has fostered interest. He was a man who in his many travels seemed to prefer going alone or at best with small groups. He was occasionally listed as a translator and was always called Don Pedro, implying that he belonged to the upper class of regional society. He had access to important people in obtaining various commissions.

In 1786 Vial proceeded north to the Red River at the Taovaya villages, which had earlier been a target for both trade and missionary activity in Texas. From there he ascended the Red River and cut directly across country to Santa Fe. En route he had contact with the Comanches with whom he maintained close association. Of this trip he drew a pair of maps and submitted a report to New Mexico's governor. For the next twenty years Vial traveled the Southwest in various expeditions. In 1787 he opened a route from Santa Fe, across the Texas Panhandle, down the same Red River, but past the Taovaya villages to Natchitoches and then on to New Orleans. He was the forerunner of trade that would someday develop in that area. From New Orleans, Pedro Vial went to San Antonio and then from San Antonio de Béxar he traveled overland almost directly to Santa Fe. His journals are never precise enough to follow him exactly, but on the basis of the existing facts, Vial apparently traversed some 2,377 miles in a period of fourteen months of travel.

In 1792–1793 the enigmatic Vial made the first transit of the Santa Fe Trail, traveling 867 leagues round trip from Santa Fe to St. Louis. On this occasion he, who usually got along very well with the aborigines, was bothered by some of the natives and finally captured by the Kansa Indians. They threatened Vial with death and kept him as a naked prisoner for six weeks, during which time he suffered terrible sunburn. The subsequent speed of Vial's return from St. Louis (twenty-five days), led New Mexican authorities to a realization that Santa Fe and the newly born United States were not really far apart and the two groups were uncomfortably close to possible confrontation.

Subsequently, in 1795 Vial acted as an explorer for the governor of New Mexico on a peace mission to the Pawnees, but by 1797 he was living with the Comanches. He was later reported to be residing near St. Louis. Upon Spanish intelligence of the planned western exploration of the United States by the Lewis and Clark expedition from St. Louis to the Pacific Ocean, Vial was sent to solidify relations with the Plains Indians. Later his kaleidoscopic career found him requesting a license to stay in the United States Louisiana Territory after its purchase from France. It is known that he made numerous other expeditions, details of which have not come to light, and that he was alternately thought by the Spaniards to be a great asset and a considerable liability. In 1814, he died in Santa Fe, nearly at the end of Spanish sovereignty.

TRENDS IN NEW MEXICO

New trends emerged with the reconquest of New Mexico. After 1700 until the end of the Spanish period, loose collections of small farms termed ranchos became the typical unit of colonization. This may have been a result of a marked decrease in Pueblo Indian population and to an increase in the number of Spanish colonists, whose arrival created a heavy demand for farmlands in the old core area of the Río Grande Valley. With the reconquest there were new concerns. Missions had to be reestablished and the capital at Santa Fe had to be reoccupied and utilized as a central base for eventual distribution of new settlers to outlying areas. After a survey was made of abandoned habitation sites, lands were distributed to both old and new colonists. Some Spanish sites had been preempted by the Pueblo Indians, who were moved out to make way for the reoccupation. Despite orders from higher authority to keep settlers congregated, Vargas and his successors authorized settlements beyond areas that had earlier been held by Hispanic residents prior to the revolt.

New Mexico life was even more rural than before, with people living in dozens of small communities. As late as the eighteenth century there were still only four places rated as villas and probably none was really in that category. They were Santa Fe, Albuquerque, Santa Cruz de la Cañada, and El Paso del Norte. The comment of Father Francisco Domínguez made in 1776 concerning Santa Fe is representative of all four when he said: "Its appearance, design, arrangement, and plan do not correspond to its status as a *villa*." (Simmons, "Settlement Patterns and Village Plans in Colonial New Mexico," p. 12) He indicated that in other parts of New Spain there were pueblos that had far more to recommend them than Santa Fe, a place that in the final analysis lacked everything. Simmons asserts that Santa Fe's lack of order in its municipal plan was not owing to negligence of local officials, "but through the willful determination of Santa Fe citizens to place their residences close to their fields, which were spread along the narrow valley of the Santa Fe River. They desired not only convenient access to farm plots, but also wished to keep a constant surveillance over them to prevent the loss of crops to thieves and wild animals. As a result of this scattering, the lands of the villa measured about three leagues in circumference" by 1775. (Simmons, "Settlement Patterns and Village Plans in Colonial New Mexico," pp. 12–13)

Santa Fe's lack of conformity was apparent elsewhere, with the sole uniformity of all having a central plaza adjacent to the main church. Some homes of important vecinos were nearby, but the other houses and small businesses were randomly placed according to the needs or whims of the owners. Beneath the villas in importance and population were the *poblaciones* (a group of ranchos) and the *plazas* (sometimes called *placitas*). These were villages grouped as either socio-economic or defensive units. Extremely small places were at times referred to by the Spanish term *lugar*.

Ranchos were composed of one or more households located on their farm or orchard land. "The small agricultural plots were small and generally long and narrow as a result of the Spanish custom of subdividing among all the heirs." (Simmons, "Settlement Patterns and Village Plans in Colonial New Mexico," p. 13) Grants were allotted with reference to ditches (*acequias*) or streams. Some frontier ranchos were established informally, without government sanction, by poor family heads who owned no lands and did not want to abide by proper legal forms. Many began in that category, and if successful they could later apply for a formal grant. In this they were not unlike the U.S. squatters on public land who expected that their illegality would be rewarded rather than punished.

Defensive Towns

These scattered ranchos, both legal and illegal, came under severe pressure from Indian raids in the late eighteenth century, forcing rural dwellers to abandon their holdings and to congregate in small fortified towns (plazas). Governmental permission for such new defensive towns was generally granted, along with instructions for construction of fortifications. Thus there was continued in New Mexico a long Spanish tradition of walled towns, though the frontier ones were on a very small scale in comparison with their European counterparts. They often took the form of houses contiguous to a central plaza, with the outer walls devoid of windows and with livestock corralled in the interior square during attack. A single gate of access was securely barred against entry. The defensive capacity of these towns was frequently enhanced by construction of one or more *torreones,* small towers which were intended to insure safety.

Defensive plazas were known to exist at Chimayó, Truchas, Trampas, Taos, Ojo Caliente, and Cebolleta. Lesser fortifications were found in single family or extended family dwellings throughout the area. Isolated family units did at times give attention to the protection of their members and property. The result was a unique arrangement—a *casa-corral*, which consisted of a dwelling (usually the conventional one-story adobe structure), with a corral or yard for holding livestock adjoining it in the rear. The corral walls were frequently as high as the walls of the house and of one piece with it. A door led directly from the dwelling into the corral, and the general impression was of a small fortress with stout, high walls, few openings and a compact, economical design. Such casas-corrales were a modest attempt to follow the royal laws as called for in the Ordinances of 1573.

Indian Towns in New Mexico

New Mexican Indian towns were of three types: (1) the well organized towns of the Pueblo Indians; (2) settlements of the detribalized Indians known as genízaros; and (3) reducciones for the residential plan of nomadic Indians. The Pueblo Indian population had peaked by about A.D. 1,300 and was in decline at the time of and after the arrival of the Spanish. The number of villages had slowly decreased up to the Pueblo Revolt, which brought about further reduction and several changes of location of surviving groups. By the end of the eighteenth century, there was growth of the remaining Indian towns as a means of defense, a lesson that the Spaniards did not take seriously. Clearly reflected in their settlement patterns was the Pueblo Indians' concern about possible incursions by hostile Indians, while the Spanish settlers were slow to take defensive precautions.

At the far northern outpost of Taos Valley in the eighteenth century, the Hispanic settlers sought safety by residing at times in the much more defensible Taos Pueblo, and this because their own towns had proved incapable of providing necessary protection. The Indian pueblo was described by Father Domínguez who said that "its plan resembles that of those walled cities with bastions and towers that are described to us in the Bible." (Simmons, "Settlement Patterns and Village Plans in Colonial New Mexico," p. 15) He mentioned heavy gates, fortified towers, a very high wall, and solid blocks of houses. Taos was probably the best defended of all the

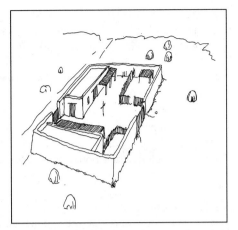

Fig. 11.3. Sketch of a casa-corral. Drawing by Jack S. Williams.

Indian pueblos, but almost all of the Pueblo Indian towns served as far more effective refuges than did the Spanish communities.

Genízaro Settlements

Settlements of the genízaros represented a special category. They consisted mostly of Indian captives or slaves of nomadic tribes who had been ransomed by the Spanish government. At first these people, who were not quite free and not quite slaves, were given to colonists to serve them as domestic servants or laborers. Most were given Spanish names, and some, those accorded ill-treatment, became fugitives or *cimarrones*. Others, eventually with the support of the Franciscans, were granted permission to found their own settlements. The first prominent genízaro settlement was created at the Cerro de Tomé south of Albuquerque. Similar settlements were established at Abiquiu on the Chama and at San José and at San Miguel del Bado (Vado) on the Pecos River to the east. Almost all genízaro town residents were once nomadic or descended from nomadic Indians, and therefore became very useful to the Spaniards as scouts, spies, and as auxiliary soldiers. The genízaro towns, situated as they were on the frontiers, became important barriers between the Spanish farmers and the hostile tribes beyond. Their innate knowledge of nomadic Indian techniques of warfare made them capable of repulsing such attacks.

From early colonial times, the Spanish of New Mexico tried to induce the nomadic natives to live in community life under supervision of religious and civil authorities. These reducciones, as they were called from early colonial times, aimed at nothing short of full social and cultural reorientation of Indian ways. In New Mexico because of the fierce independence of most of the natives, such reducciones or formal settlements depended on voluntary Indian submission. "At various times in the 18th century, the Spaniards responded to pleas from the Navajos, Apaches, and Comanches for aid in establishing their own [Indian] towns, but in the end the Indians returned to a roving life. Since the experimental reducciones were situated on the far frontiers, had they succeeded, the jurisdiction of New Mexico government would have been appreciably expanded and new areas might have been made safe for Spanish colonization." (Simmons, "Settlement Patterns and Village Plans in Colonial New Mexico," p. 15)

PRIVATE RANCHOS IN CALIFORNIA

In California after 1800, a fourth feature of Spain's colonization program rivaled missions, presidios, and pueblos for a position of prominence. The granting of large estates, called haciendas or ranchos, had been practiced since the first Spanish settlements were made in the region of Santo Domingo on the Island of Hispaniola. The Laws of the Indies provided that sites (*sitios*) of one square league—4,438.464 acres—of grazing land could be granted outside inhabited areas to persons owning a minimum of 2,000 cattle. (Book IV 17-5) Owners of 6,000 head could petition for two sites and of 10,000 or more cattle, a maximum of three. The grantee was further required to build a stone house on each site and provide a guard. Large private ranchos, as they were known in California, were a vital means whereby Spanish civilization could be extended into frontier areas throughout the Indies. Often they took on the characteristics of a small village.

Spanish settlers, coming from a country where the raising of cattle under semi-arid, plains conditions had long been a way of life, were particularly well suited to continue their ancient heritage in New Spain. The first cattle introduced into Santo Domingo multiplied rapidly and from there were taken to other islands and mainland regions. The Spanish also gave the New World horses, sheep, domesticated goats, and pigs. These animals made possible a large increase in the food supply of the Americas, although productivity soon outstripped potential demand and utilization. Herds of wild cattle became common in New Spain and the animals were killed primarily for their hides—a principal colonial export.

As California settlement achieved a measurable degree of permanence, several soldiers who had served in the province since the Portolá expedition of 1769 looked forward to retirement as independent cattle ranchers. Viceroy Bucareli's governmental reglamento of 1773 had envisioned that retired soldiers would be granted tracts of land within mission boundaries and thereby participate in the development of an integrated, carefully supervised civilian population. The first private grant was made in 1775 to Manuel Butrón, a soldier married to an Indian neophyte of Mission San Carlos. Butrón, however, soon abandoned his land, located near the mission, and no further applications were made for grants in the proximity of religious establishments.

Not until 1784 was the system of private ranchos truly inaugurated in California. In that year Governor Pedro Fages received petitions from three members of his old command who sought tracts of unoccupied grazing land beyond the boundaries of Mission San Gabriel. These grants, approved on November 20, 1786, were extremely large and covered a major portion of present-day Los Angeles and Orange Counties. Fages first assigned some sixteen square leagues, well over 75,000 acres, to Juan José Domínguez, a veteran of the San Diego presidio. Located to the southwest of Los Angeles between the San Gabriel River and some salt pits on Redondo Bay, the Domínguez estate, known as Rancho San Pedro, faced the Pacific Ocean on the south and west. Juan José, who spent little time on the rancho, built a typical adobe structure with a wooden roof covered with pitch, and increased his herds to "3,000 mares, 1,000 fillies, 1,000 colts, 700 cows, 200 heifers and 260 bulls" by 1805. (Cleland, *Cattle on a Thousand Hills: 1850–1880*, p. 9) José Dolores Sepulveda, a friend of the Domínguez ranch manager, was granted permission to run several hundred cattle on the western part of the original grant—a tract known as Rancho Palos Verdes. In later years, after the death of Juan José, the Sepulveda heirs received title to this valuable portion of the original grant.

The second grant, a triangular, 36,000-acre site encompassing a major portion of today's cities of Glendale and Burbank, was awarded to José María Verdugo, also of the San Diego presidio. Verdugo received the giant tract under Fages' simple decree of October 20, 1784, which conceded him "the permission which he solicits to keep his cattle and horses at the 'Arroyo Hondo' a league and a half distant from Mission San Gabriel. ..." When Verdugo came up for retirement in 1797, Governor Diego Borica ordered him to settle either at the pueblos of San José or Los Angeles or at the Villa de Branciforte, where he would serve on guard duty. The ex-soldier, "much afflicted with dropsy," found service at the pueblos impossible and petitioned the governor to settle with his six children and the family of his brother on the rancho granted to him by Pedro Fages. Borica, recognizing that Verdugo had "cleared fields, built a diversion dam for irrigation of the tract to La Zanja (later called San Rafael), and had a large number of major and minor livestock accustomed to pasturing upon the land," gave him permission and confirmed Fages's 1784 grant. (Cleland, *Cattle on a Thousand Hills: 1850–1880*, pp. 13–14)

The third rancho, the largest of the three granted by Governor Fages, was conceded to Manuel Pérez Nieto. Broadly interpreted, the boundaries of Nieto's property included all the land lying between the seacoast and the main road that led from San Diego to San Gabriel, and between the Santa Ana River and the San Gabriel River, which then emptied into the sea near the present Long Beach–Wilmington boundary. Thus defined the rancho contained nearly 300,000 acres, but the padres at Mission San Gabriel complained that Nieto's property encroached upon their land. The grant was reduced to 158,000 acres and later divided among Nieto's heirs as Ranchos Los Alamitos, Los Cerritos, Las Bolsas, Santa Gertrudes, and Los Coyotes. These ranchos lands today encompass the cities of Long Beach, Huntington Beach, Downey, Norwalk, Santa Fe Springs, Artesia, Westminster, Garden Grove, Talbert, and Fountain Valley.

The rancho grants made during the Spanish period in California, though few in number, have provided many historic place-names and include some of the state's most valuable property. Governor Borica, in 1795, granted Rancho Simi in the Santa Susana Mountains to Patricio and Miguel Pico; Rancho de Las Pulgas, site of present day Menlo Park, Atherton, Redwood City, San Carlos, Belmont, and part of San Mateo, to José Dario Argüello; and Rancho Buena Vista in the Salinas Valley to Joaquin Castro and José María Soberanes. In 1797, veteran leather-jacket soldier José Francisco Ortega received Rancho del Refugio, site of Gaviota, Gaviota Pass, and Refugio Beach just south of Point Conception. Grants made by Governor Arrillaga during the early 1800s were Rancho Los Feliz near Los Angeles to José Vicente Feliz; Rancho Las Virgenes, site of Agoura in the Santa Monica Mountains, to Manuel Ortega.

The final grant made while Spain still ruled its California province was to Luis María Peralta in 1820. Peralta, who accompanied Anza's expedition of 1775 as a 16-

year-old boy, retired after more than forty years' military service and received extensive lands east of San Francisco Bay. The Peralta estate, also called Rancho San Antonio, ran from present-day Richmond through Berkeley, Oakland, and Alameda to Emeryville. During the Mexican period (1821–1846), secularization of mission lands made possible the granting of upwards of 600 ranchos extending from San Diego to the region north of San Francisco and into the Central Valley. Though the number of ranchos increased, the life and activities of the rancheros remained essentially the same until the American conquest. Even after 1850, much of the Spanish heritage of California's rancho period was carried over into later agricultural development.

EARLY LAND GRANTS IN ARIZONA

In 1801, Lieutenant Mariano de Urrea, commanding the presidio in the absence of Captain Zuñiga, made a grant of Tucson land to settler Reyes Pacheco on the same terms as the assignment made earlier to Toríbio Otero at Tubac. Pacheco, one of few survivors of the Yuma Massacre, was listed in the 1797 census as a civilian settler of Tucson; he also appeared on a 1767 register of Tubac males.

The vecino population associated with the Tumacácori mission declined slightly after about 1802, but the number of gente de razon at Tubac increased substantially. As the possibility became ever greater that some of the settlers might try to establish ranches and farms on the lands of the long abandoned Guevavi and Calabazas communities, Father Narciso Gutiérrez decided the time had come to encourage the residents of Tumacácori and its environs to petition for a formal grant, or regrant, of mission lands and any other property that the original Jesuit missionaries might have acquired for raising livestock. Tumacácori Governor Juan Legarra headed a small delegation that traveled to Arizpe late in 1806 to confer with an attorney about obtaining title to lands the Indians were occupying and using. The attorney helped them draw up a petition which they presented to intendant governor Alejo García Conde. García Conde, who had been at Arizpe since the late 1790s had been sympathetic to the missionaries. Born in North Africa in 1741, García Conde began his military career at the age of 12 and had risen through the ranks to become a colonel.

A short time later, the governor responded favorably. It was the intention of Gutiérrez to ask that the residents of Tumacácori and environs be awarded legal title to mission lands and any additional acreage the Jesuits may have acquired for livestock grazing. The petition was granted on December 17, 1806, and Manuel de León, as comandante of the presidio of Tubac was instructed to survey and confirm the boundaries of the Tumacácori grant. The survey crew marked out a boundary that ran south along the river all the way to Calabazas. It was less than a half-mile wide but more than ten miles long. An additional grant of grazing land was surveyed south to Guevavi, bringing the total area to about 6,770 acres. When this work was completed, the Indians had title to a long strip of land beginning just south of Tubac and following the Santa Cruz River approximately to the present Mexican border. It included areas previously associated with all three mission communities: Tumacácori, Calabazas, and Guevavi.

The formal deed to the Tumacácori-Calabazas grant, dated April 2, 1807, included three special conditions. The first provided that claims by any other persons to lands within the grant would be considered if they were presented in due time and form. The second stated that the lands of the grant were to be cultivated, protected, and inhabited; if they should lie totally abandoned for three consecutive years, they would become subject to the claims of others. Finally, the document specified that if Calabazas were to be resettled by its former Indian inhabitants, that part of the grant would be segregated from the remainder. But as Father Gutiérrez was trying to make certain that the residents of Tumacácori were protected, Spain was being invaded and soon Mexico would be caught up in the turmoil of the War for Independence.

Five years after the award of the Tumacácori grant, another abandoned ranchería that had once been a visita of Guevavi became the object of a petition from one of the wealthy Spanish settlers of the area—Don Agustín Ortiz, a member of the same Arizpe family to which the wives of Mariano de Urrea and José de Zuñiga belonged. About 1800, if not slightly before, Agustín came to southern Arizona with his wife María Reyes Peña and a son Tomás. Not long after arriving in their new home, they had another boy named Ignacio. Sometime in 1812, while living in Tucson, Agustín Ortiz applied for a grant at the site of Arivaca, one of the oldest mining and ranching locations in the region. In accordance with the usual procedures, the petition was posted and persons opposing the grant were given an opportunity to be heard. When no objections were raised, the property was offered for sale at public auction. Don Agustín was the highest bidder and, according to testimony offered later, paid 747 pesos and 3 reales to the treasury at Arizpe. The Ortiz family lived and ranched on the grant for a generation thereafter.

The boundaries given for the Arivaca land grant were vague, even though the grant was for the specific quantity of two sitios. The landmark on the north was a high pointed hill that bordered on the Sierra de Buena Vista, on the south a low hill next to the canyon covered with trees, on the east a mesquite tree that had a cross cut in it and bordered on the Sierra de las Calaberas, and on the west a landmark standing at the Punta de Agua on a pointed hill opposite the Sierra del Baboquivari. Despite the lack of a definite location by survey, the Ortiz petition of 1833 was approved by Sonoran officials and a title was issued for two sitios of land for raising cattle and horses. Unfortunately, twenty years later, Arivaca became a part of the United States by the Gadsden Treaty and in 1902, the Supreme Court denied confirmation of the grant because of its uncertain location.

Another land grant made during the Spanish period was San Ignacio de la Canoa located in the fertile Santa Cruz valley. The Anza expedition stopped there in 1775 on its first night out of Tubac en route to California, and La Canoa was mentioned by both padres Garcés and Font as the site of a Pápago ranchería. It was named for a hollowed-out cottonwood log that resembled a canoe and was used as a watering trough. Captain Allande and other commanders from the presidios of Tucson and Tubac sometimes camped with their troops at that site. In September 1820 Tomas and Ignacio Ortiz, residents of Tubac, petitioned the intendente of Sonora and Sinaloa for four sitios of grassland around La Canoa for the purpose of raising cattle and horses. The survey was made under the supervision of Ignacio Elías González, the last comandante of the presidio of Tubac and the father-in-law of Tomás Ortiz. Elías González wrote that the rancho stretched from Tubac on the south to Saguarita on the north and that the vegetation consisted of mesquites, china trees, tamarisks, palo verdes, giant cactus, and a few

Fig. 11.4. Sanford Family at Rancho de los Peñasquitos. Courtesy County of San Diego.

cottonwoods and willows. The appraisers set the value of the land at only 30 dollars per sitio since there was no running water except during the rainy season.

The first publicized sale was on July 12, 1821, in Tubac. Father Juan Bano of San Xavier del Bac bid 210 dollars on behalf of Ignacio Sanches and Francisco Flores, residents of the mission. The proceedings were transferred to the capital at Arizpe and the final auction was held on December 13, 14, and 15. On the third day the property went to the Ortiz brothers for 250 dollars. Because of conditions in Mexico at that time, no title to the land was issued. In 1849, however, the Ortiz brothers were given a title at Rues in Sonora.

The Baron of Arizona

One other "grant" of the Spanish period turned out to be entirely fraudulent. A man by the name of James Addison Reavis who reached Arizona in 1880 invented a family lineage beginning with Don Nemecio Silva de Peralta de la Córdoba. According to the false data accumulated by Reavis, Peralta had been given the title of Baron de los Colorados by Fernando VI in 1748 and an extensive grant of land in northern Sonora to go with it. Reavis claimed he had acquired a deed to the land from Miguel Peralta, a poor descendant of the original Baron de los Colorados. To further complicate the matter, Reavis had married an orphan Mexican girl to whom he had given the title Baroness of Arizona. He forged church birth records to give her the name Sofia Loreta Micaela de Maso-Reavis y Peralta and make her the last surviving descendant of the Peralta family. She was therefore the heir to the giant land grant that started in New Mexico, was about seventy-five miles wide and had a southern boundary passing approximately twenty-five miles north of Tucson. In addition to Phoenix, it included the towns of Tempe, Mesa, Globe, Clifton, Solomonville, Casa Grande, and Florence, as well as the rich Silver King mine. Because the Americans of the 1880s believed there was truly a Baron de los Colorados and a Baroness of Arizona, they paid Reavis various amounts for deeds to their property. By 1889, however, an investigation by the United States office of the Surveyor General exposed the fraud and showed that the claim was spurious and should be rejected. The analysis of the documents showed several forgeries and historical inaccuracies that supported the conclusion. Therefore, the richest Spaniard of all, Don Nemecio Silva de Peralta, was just the clever invention of James Reavis, the only "Baron of Arizona."

Chapter Eleven
BIBLIOGRAPHIC ESSAY

Valuable for the final decades of the eighteenth century in the Spanish Southwest is John L. Kessell, *Friars, Reformers and Soldiers* (Tucson: University of Arizona Press, 1976). Other important works for this period are Max L. Moorhead, *The Apache Frontier: Jacobo Ugarte and Spanish-Indian Relations in Northern New Spain, 1769–1791* (Norman: University of Oklahoma Press, 1968); Michael C. Meyer, *Water in the Hispanic Southwest: A Social and Legal History, 1550–1850* (Tucson: University of Arizona Press, 1984); Albert Stagg, *The First Bishop of Sonora: Antonio de los Reyes, O.F.M.* (Tucson: University of Arizona Press, 1976) and Lino Gómez Canedo, ed., *Sonora hacia fines del siglo XVIII: Un informe del misionero franciscano Fray Francisco Antonio Barbastro, con otros documentos complementarios* (Guadalajara: Librería Font, 1971).

Eric Beerman has written *España y la independencia de los Estados Unidos* (Madrid: Editorial MAPFRE, Inc., 1992), explaining Spain's role in the American Revolution. See also John Caughey, *Bernardo de Gálvez in Louisiana, 1776–1783* (Berkeley: University of California Press, 1934).

Kieran McCarty, O.F.M., has translated and edited a number of documents pertaining to Arizona history during this period in *Desert Documentary: The Spanish Years 1767–1821* (Tucson: Arizona Historical Society, 1976). McCarty published "The Colorado Massacre of 1781: María Montielo's Report," in *The Journal of Arizona History*, 16 (autumn 1975): 221–25 in addition to "The Sonora Prophecy of 1783," *Journal of the Southwest*, 32 (autumn 1990): 316–20. Also important is Ronald L. Ives, "Retracing the Route of the Fages Expedition of 1781," *Arizona and the West*, 18 (spring and summer, 1966): 49–70; 157–70 and Ronald L. Ives, *José Velásquez: Saga of a Borderland Soldier* (Tucson: Southwestern Mission Research Center, 1984). Henry Dobyns, *Spanish Colonial Tucson* (Tucson: University of Arizona Press, 1976), chronicles the battle of May 1, 1782, in detail.

Alfred Barnaby Thomas, ed. and trans., *Forgotten Frontiers: A Study of the Spanish Indian Policy of Don Juan Bautista de Anza, 1777–1787* (Norman: University of Oklahoma Press, 1932) talks about Anza's later years as does Ronald J. Benes, "Anza and Concha in New Mexico, 1787–93: A Study in Colonial Techniques," *Journal of the West*, 4 (June 1965): 63–76. See also Adlai Feather, ed., "Colonel Don Fernando de la Concha Diary, 1788," *New Mexico Historical Review*, 34 (October 1959):285–304.

Basic to the founding of towns in the New World were the ordinances of Spanish King Philip II. These are contained in Zelia Nuttall, ed. and trans., "Royal Ordinances Concerning the Laying Out of New Towns," *Hispanic American Historical Review*, 4–5 (November 1921; May 1922): 743–53; 249–54. A comprehensive plan for the founding of towns is found in the Plan of Pitic of 1783. Its basic regulations were to apply to towns founded thereafter in the northern frontier region. Joseph P. Sánchez edited and transcribed a copy of the plan promulgated in 1789 entitled, "El Plan de Pitic de 1789 y las nuevas poblaciones proyectadas en las Provincias Internas de la Nueva España," *Colonial Latin American Historical Review*, 2 (fall 1993):449–67; Iris H.W. Engstrand clarified its date in "A Note on the Plan of Pitic," CLAHR, (winter 1994):73–78 and Jane C. Sánchez added, "The Plan of Pitic: Galindo Navarro's Letter to Teodoro de Croix, Comandante General de las Provincias Internas," CLAHR (Winter 1994):79–89.

Specific works on California towns are Francis F. Guest, "Municipal Institutions in Spanish California," *California Historical Society Quarterly*, 46 (December 1967):307–35 and "The Foundation of the

Villa de Branciforte," *CHSQ*, 41 (March 1962):29–50; Salomé Hernández, "No Settlement Without Women: Three Spanish California Settlement Schemes, 1790–1800," *Southern California Quarterly*, 2 (fall 1990):203–34. Harry Kelsey, "A New Look at the Founding of Old Los Angeles," *California Historical Quarterly*, 55 (Winter 1976):326–339 and Antonio Ríos-Bustamante, *Los Angeles, pueblo y región, 1781–1850* (México, D. F.: Instituto Nacional de Antropología e Historia, 1991) talk about the founding of Los Angeles. Maynard Geiger, *The Life and Times of Fray Junipero Serra*, 2 vols., (Washington, D.C.: Academy of American Francisco History, 1959) gives an account of missionary reaction to the founding of towns.

For New Mexico specifically, see Marc Simmons, "Settlement Patterns and Village Plans in Colonial New Mexico" in David J. Weber, ed., *New Spain's Far Northern Frontier: Essays on Spain in the American West* (Albuquerque: University of New Mexico Press, 1979); Charles F. Gritzer, "Hispanic Log Construction of New Mexico," *El Palacio*, 85 (winter 1979):20–29; Alicia Vidaurreta Tjarks, "Demographic, Ethnic and Occupational Structure of New Mexico, 1790," *The Americas*, 35 (July 1978):45–88 and Marc Simmons, "New Mexico's Smallpox Epidemic of 1780–1781," *NMHR*, 41 (October 1966):319–26. General works covering town founding and development under Spain is Dora P. Crouch, Daniel J. Garr, and Axel I. Mundigo, *Spanish City Planning in North America* (Cambridge: MIT Press, 1982) and Gilbert R. Cruz, *Let There Be Towns*, (College Station: Texas A&M Press, 1988).

Useful articles to understand trade routes and problems of Arizona and New Mexico are Carl Sauer, ed., "A Spanish Entrada into the Arizona Apacheria," *Arizona Historical Review*, 6 (January 1935):3–13; John L. Kessell, "The Puzzling Presidio: San Phelipe de Guevavi, alias Terrenate," *NMHR*, 41 (January 1966):21–46; George P. Hammond, ed., "The Zuñiga Journal, Tucson to Santa Fe: The Opening of a Spanish Trade Route, 1788–1795," *NMHR*, 6 (January 1931):40–65; Noel M. Loomis and Abraham P. Nasatir, *Pedro Vial and the Roads to Santa Fe*, (Norman: University of Oklahoma Press, 1967); Ray H. Mattison, "Early Spanish and Mexican Settlements in Arizona," *NMHR*, 21 (October 1946): 273–327; and Henry Dobyns, "The 1797 Population of the Presidio of Tucson," *Journal of Arizona History*, 13 (summer 1972):205–209.

Two important reports to Carlos IV in Spain were by Viceroy Conde de Revilla Gigedo, *Informe sobre las misiones, 1793*, and *Instrucción reservada al Márques de Branciforte, 1794*, edited with an introduction by José Bravo Ugarte (Mexico, D.F.: Editorial Jus., 1966), and Daniel S. Matson and Bernard L. Fontana have edited and translated *Friar Bringas Reports to the King: Methods of Indoctrination on the Frontier of New Spain 1796–97* (Tucson: University of Arizona Press, 1977).

For missionary activities in California during the period following the death of Serra in 1784 see Finbar Kenneally, ed. and trans., *Writings of Fermín Francisco de Lasuén*, 2 vols., (Washington, D. C.: Academy of American Franciscan History, 1965) and Francis F. Guest, *Fermín Francisco de Lasuén (1736–1803): A Biography* (Washington D. C.: Academy of American Franciscan History, 1973). Donald C. Cutter has edited and translated a Spanish document giving a firsthand report on Monterey in *California in 1792: A Spanish Naval Visit*, (Norman: University of Oklahoma Press, 1990). Lesley Byrd Simpson edited and Paul D. Nathan translated *The Letters of José Señan, O.F.M. Mission San Buenaventura, 1796–1823* (San Francisco: John Howell Books, 1962) detailing mission concerns.

Military affairs during the last decade of the eighteenth century are discussed in Edwin A. Beilharz, *Felipe de Neve* (San Francisco: California Historical Society, 1971); Manuel P. Servín, ed. and trans., "Costansó's 1794 Report on Strengthening New California's Presidios," *CHSQ*, 49 (September 1970):221–32; Max L. Moorhead, "Rebuilding the Presidio of Santa Fe, 1789–1791," *NMHR*, 69 (April 1974):123–42; Jack August, "Balance-of-Power Diplomacy in New Mexico: Governor Fernando de la Concha and the Indian Policy of Conciliation," *NMHR*, 56 (April 1981):141–60; Sidney B. Brinckerhoff, "The Last Years of Spanish Arizona, 1786–1821," *Arizona and the West*, 9 (spring 1967):5–20; and Donald Nuttall, "Los Gobernantes of Spanish Upper California," *CHQ*, 51 (fall 1972): 253–80.

Early rancho activities in California are covered in Robert Glass Cleland, *The Cattle on a Thousand Hills: 1850–1880* (San Marino: The Huntington Library, 1941) and Iris Engstrand, "California Ranchos: Their Hispanic Heritage," *Southern California Quarterly*, 67 (fall 1985):281–90. Special issues of the *Journal of the West* concerning land grants in the Southwest and also published separately are John R. and Christine M. Van Ness, eds., *Spanish and Mexican Land Grants in New Mexico and Colorado* (July 1980) and Malcolm Ebright, ed., *Spanish and Mexican Land Grants and the Law* (July 1988). See also bibliographic essay for Chapter 12.

Chapter Twelve

EXPANSION, SETTLEMENT, AND COMMERCIAL GROWTH: 1800–1810

CALIFORNIA IN 1800: AN OVERVIEW

*T*he dawn of the nineteenth century saw the gulf between Spain and her overseas provinces irreparably widen. Communications by sea existed at the mercy of British maritime strength, and constant smuggling along the coasts of Spanish America cut deeply into colonial revenues. The once-powerful mother country had become a nation with a glorious past but an uncertain future. Spain, whose power and Catholic ambition in the sixteenth century created the largest colonial empire the world had yet known, suffered in subsequent years a steady decline. Bourbon reforms and the careful guidance of Carlos III (1759–1788) arrested Spain's downward slide for a time during the eighteenth century, but the ineffectual Carlos IV (1788–1808) could not continue the administrative and economic progress initiated by his energetic predecessor.

The final plunge occurred in 1807, fewer than twenty years after the death of Carlos III. The country in that year for all practical purposes became a satellite of France, its fleet removed from the seas after the disaster of Trafalgar, its economy stagnant, and its fiscal situation hopeless. Spain, little able to strengthen control over its distant colonies after 1800, lost them completely by 1821. The success of the North American Revolution—supported, ironically, by Carlos III—and the ideological impact of the French Revolution in 1789 fanned a growing restlessness among members of the Spanish Creole aristocracy—those of pure lineage born in the New World. Mexico's fight to throw off peninsular control began as early as 1810, and during the next eleven years, colonial forces pressed steadily toward their goal of freedom. Even a highly competent monarch on the throne of Spain would have found the task of guiding his country's affairs through the first stormy decades of the nineteenth century a difficult undertaking. Carlos IV, though judged to be honest and well meaning, found the task to be impossible.

Special problems, stemming primarily from California's isolated coastal position, had complicated its general relationship with the Spanish crown since settlement was first accomplished in 1769. The supply base at San Blas could not successfully maintain the province with necessary provisions—both for lack of available goods and scarcity of ships able to tackle the often insurmountable headwinds along the California coast. Spain's involvement in the American and French revolutions and, more importantly, in the conflicts leading to its own wars for independence, subsequently aggravated the problem. Ships from San Blas were almost completely cut off after 1810. A number of California residents attempted to alleviate the pressing need for supplies by establishing a logical exchange with foreign merchants following the China route. Contraband trade advantageously served everyone on the local scene—the trader gained profits, colonists received needed and otherwise unattainable goods, and underpaid officials found cooperation lucrative.

During the period from 1800 until Mexico's successful bid for independence in 1821, California remained geographically apart from the revolutionary struggle. While forces in Mexico entered into armed conflict with Spanish royalists, California expanded her agricultural and commercial activities. Twenty missions, three pueblos, and numerous private ranchos flourished between San Diego and Sonoma. Military expeditions pushed inland to explore mountains and valleys covering the entire length of the province. Except for one outside attack, the final days of Spanish control in California were peaceful and prosperous—foretelling none of the chaotic conditions that lay ahead under an independent Mexico.

The romanticized concept of California's "days of dons" is perhaps best exemplified during these years. Though sparsely populated and dependent upon the sea for communication and trade, California entered a new era. The intensity of Yankee traders in the Pacific, driven by commercial necessity, sparked California's inevitable transition—a change heightened by the vulnerability of its giant coastline. New England merchants set the stage for future overland penetration into California from the United States. Within three decades another kind of trader—the mountain man—would slowly push his country's frontier westward across mountains, plains, and deserts to the Pacific Ocean. Hispanic California, caught between these sea and overland advances, eventually gave way to American occupation and outside influences, including technological advantages, were soon evident. Such change was not always good, nor always bad, but the proximity of the United States was a matter of concern.

THE RANCHO ECONOMY IN CALIFORNIA

Government regulations controlled Spain's cattle industry closely, even in outlying provinces such as California. A certain number of vaqueros were required to tend the cattle on unfenced ranges, and each animal, whether belonging to mission, pueblo, or individual, had to be branded with a mark recorded in the official Register of Brands. Definite dates were set in the spring for the annual *matanza* or slaughtering of cattle for hides, tallow, and beef. At the same time the *rodeo*, or roundup, was held for counting, sorting, branding, and selling of cattle to other rancheros. Cows were strictly protected and a tax of 2 reales (about 25 cents) was levied upon each of the cattle killed. This source of income aided the treasury and prevented unnecessary slaughtering of animals. Under this legislation, and because of abundant pasturage in California, the herds multiplied. By 1790 the number of cattle had increased from an original 200 to some 27,000 head, with nearly 20,000 belonging to mission herds. The missions were also tending approximately 26,000 sheep while most of California's 7,500 horses and mules were concentrated at the royal stock farms near the presidios and at the pueblos. At the end of the Spanish period, in 1822, the estimated livestock throughout California numbered 152,179 cattle, 200,646 sheep, and 20,508 horses.

Although cattle ranching was the mainstay of rancho economy, private landowners also engaged in varied agricultural pursuits. Verdugo planted a portion of Rancho San

Rafael with hemp and diverted water from the Los Angeles River to cultivate beans, corn, wheat, onions, potatoes, and vineyards. At Rancho Santa Ana, the Yorbas produced similar annual crops, taking water from the Santa Ana River for irrigation. They also built a water-powered grist mill in the river bottom that furnished the ranch with flour and meal. Some rancheros employed Indian laborers under a foreman or mayordomo who, if capable, may have been an Indian himself. Some Indians became expert farmers and, despite their previous lack of experience with stock animals, took naturally to handling both horses and cattle. Thus, the California rancho became, ideally, an integrated economic and social unit under the Spanish plan of frontier settlement.

Mission Progress in California, 1800–1810

The Franciscan chain of California missions, the dominant institution of cultural exchange between Spaniards and Indians, experienced unparalleled material progress during the decade from 1800 to 1810. The nineteenth mission, Santa Inés, was founded September 17, 1804, on a site today included within the Danish village of Solvang near Buellton. To achieve the architectural design of Santa Inés, Indian workers traveled forty-five miles into the mountains to cut pine, sycamore, and oak for ceiling beams. They bound the rafters together with rawhide strips because nails were scarce. Sea shells supplied lime and adobe walls which, protected by a gluey preparation of prickly cactus soaked in water, took on a smooth, whitewashed appearance.

Mission statistics from 1800 to 1810 reflect the activities of California's religious communities. The Franciscans baptized 22,000 Indians, of whom approximately 15,000 were converted adults and the rest children of neophytes. The number of deaths, mostly from disease, reached 16,000 or 72 percent of baptisms. The smallest number of deaths in any one year was 1,250 in 1810; the highest toll was 3,188 in 1806. Mission padres never understood the prevention or control of European epidemic diseases. The total gain in neophyte population was 5,300 for the ten-year period, with the greatest mission population recorded at 20,355 in 1805. Priests performed an average of 680 marriage ceremonies per year among mission converts; couples seldom had more than one or two children.

Measurable gains were made in almost all mission agricultural pursuits. Dams were built on nearby rivers and a network of irrigation ditches brought water to planted fields. Although methods of cultivation were primitive and Indian labor slow, the yearly mission produce averaged some 55,230 bushels of wheat; 11,400, barley; 12,360, corn; 1,740, beans; and 3,050, peas, lentils, and other minor grains. Indians harvested the grain with hand sickles and bound it in sheaves. For threshing, seventy-five to one hundred horses trampled the wheat on a flat, circular piece of dry, hard ground and winnowing was accomplished by the natives tossing the wheat against the wind. Grinding was done either by hand with stone mortars and pestles or by water-driven grist mills built by the padres. Olive trees and vineyards grew well in southern California and the missions became a source for olive oil and wine. Manufacturing was generally limited to the production of wool blankets, clothing, and furniture. Provisions and supplies sold to the presidios amounted to about 18,000 dollars per year.

New Mexico's Irrigated Agriculture

As mentioned earlier, one great contribution of Spain to native society in New Mexico was in the field of irrigated agriculture offering more complex and more fully developed conduit systems of zanjas and acequias. In addition, other aspects of rural activity were introduced. The Indians took quickly to elements that enriched their existence, ones that have been carried out to the present with great success. Both the Franciscan clergy and the lay settlers shared in this contribution to the local economy.

Corn, brought from Mexico, and wheat, which was found to prosper on the northern frontier (although it had not done well on a long term basis in the area to the south), placed New Mexico in a two-grain economy, with the concomitant benefits in variety of dishes, and in the health advantages therefrom. Fruits, particularly those of southern Spain—peaches, apricots, apples, quinces, grapes, and cherries—became local products of importance. Andalusian vegetables were found to yield well in areas of good soil and available water, with introduction of peas, chickpeas, cabbage, and certain types of beans.

As elsewhere in the New World, the transfer of crops was not strictly one way, but rather a matter of reciprocal borrowing. Indian agriculture continued to produce the earlier items of beans, squash, corn, and chiles. Over the period of many years, the agriculture of the two groups became fused and closely inter-related to the point that there was no hard and fast distinction. Indian foods and Spanish New Mexican foods are an area specialty, more similar to Mexican food than to Spanish cuisine, but having elements of three groups. In the critical area of cultural borrowing, one of the areas of quickest adaptation was that of agriculture, but in an area of limited water and minimal arable land the contest for control of the elements of food production led at times to conflict and has not ceased to be a factor in the local economy even in the late twentieth century.

Livestock from Europe

Of equal or even greater significance in altering the way in which New Mexico natives lived was the arrival with the Spaniards of European livestock, both major and minor. These imports moved into an area which was largely devoid of domesticated animals, and they prospered and multiplied from early times. The horse, associated in the beginning with cavalry and rapid personnel transport, had the greatest initial impact. Adapted to both Spanish and Indian agriculture, the horse became an essential partner in agrarian development, the burro taking a distant second place in such endeavor. Introduction of cattle became important, but without the great successes which were evident in the last half of the nineteenth century. Even in this regard, it is worthy of note that much of the traditions, methods, equipment, and even the language of the later Western American range cattle industry had major antecedents in the Spanish period of the area's history.

Early arrival of minor livestock was a prelude to the long period of sheep-raising, an economic activity of great importance in colonial New Mexico. Of the minor livestock of goats, pigs, and sheep, the latter became essential to survival on the frontier. Easily adaptable to the high desert environment, they became a mainstay of the local economy. Whereas in the beginning the Spanish colonists of the province withheld horses from the Indians because of the potential military threat posed thereby, sheep and other minor livestock were more rapidly in Indian ownership.

THE SHEEP INDUSTRY

The versatility of sheep as a frontier animal did much to guarantee its longevity in the area. It provided meat, milk, cheese, and wool. The meat of sheep contributed a lot toward the provincial diet with use in such dishes as roast lamb and posole. The wool impacted strongly not only Spanish culture and customs, but also Indian society, members of which became weavers of woolen blankets and garments. Both Spanish settlers and Indians have maintained this art, which in recent time has become a well-recognized and expensive form of folk art. Navajo and Pueblo weavers, as well as Hispanic-American makers of woolen materials, continue in this tradition, which for cultural and commercial reasons has not undergone great technological change despite mechanization and mass production of other handicraft items. The importance of sheep and the unique aspects of transhumance (the movement of animals from place to place and to different elevations in search of pasture) were gradually diminished by the replacement of ovine culture with cattle. This was in large measure due to dietary orientation of latecomers to New Mexico, and also because the sheep were considered, rightly or wrongly, as destructive of range grasses and incompatible with cattle in the same area.

The sheep industry had an important consequence on social development, one which lasted into the twentieth century. From sheep raising there developed a distinct class division between participants in the industry. An almost feudalistic system of exploitation resulted, with the *partido* system. A wealthy owner of sheep would entrust a flock, say 500 or more young animals, to a peon, or *partidario,* whereupon the *patrón* sent the shepherd to the open range with minimal supplies for an extended stay of many months' duration. The industry depended on transhumance. The contract, the partido, was the agreement whereby the shepherd invested his time and skill (coupled with such good luck as he might have), while the patrón invested the thing of monetary value, the flock of sheep. At the agreement's termination upon return of the partidario, the contract would be completed with repayment of the original herd and an established division of the increase, usually fifty-fifty. Some partidarios after several good years became patrones, but more frequently they became increasingly in debt to their original patrón, there developing as a result a type of debt servitude. Each year the shepherd's share of the increased flock went principally to pay off his earlier shortfall. Partido contracts did not involve Indian herders, though many of the shepherds involved in such agreements were detribalized natives who had assumed Spanish cultural orientation. In the twentieth century such partido contracts were made illegal; if any still exist, they would be oral agreements unenforceable in law.

From the sheepherding period, many of the folktales, much folk music, and various cultural mores of surviving vitality, emanate. It forms an important link between the Spanish past and a considerable segment of modern New Mexican society.

In addition to sheep, goats and pigs were a part of the first settlers' cultural baggage. All three of these minor livestock had a great impact on the diet of both Spaniards and Indians. They were optimally utilized, with almost all of the animal serving some useful purpose and resulting in a lasting dietary variety. In part transhumance became a victim of the reduction of the public domain to private ownership or to federal government control, since both the sheep and cattle industries for profitable existence needed unimpeded access to free land.

The 1801 Report on Communities in Arizona

As the nineteenth century began, Franciscans in La Pimería Alta were busy responding to new directives from the commandant of the Provincias Internas and from their religious superiors. These directives often called upon them to provide information about persons residing in mission communities under their jurisdiction. One such report, prepared in 1801, makes it clear that despite royal policy, the Indian villages continued to be settled by outsiders. Persons identified as coyotes, mestizos, and Indians of various tribes—along with others classified only as vecinos or gente de razón—were sharing land and water with the native inhabitants. The census prepared by Father Llorens of San Xavier del Bac in 1801 includes separate lists of the native Indians at Bac and its visita, El Pueblito. The priest classified as Pimas and Pápagos all 218 of those living at El Pueblito, notwithstanding the Sobaipuri ancestry of some. He lumped together the names of the non-natives residing in the two villages without indicating who lived where. Nevertheless, it can be taken for granted that outsiders were present at both locations. The total of thirty-nine vecinos in the two Indian communities included españoles, coyotes, mestizos, mulatos, and Yuma Indians.

Llorens listed more Spaniards than vecinos of any other type. In the home of a 29-year-old bachelor named Ygnacio Pacheco lived Pacheco's mother, María del Carmen Romero, daughter of pioneer Nicolas Romero. Literacy, almost unknown among women on the Sonoran frontier, was largely confined to upper-class Spanish males. Also listed were members of the León family. Joseph de León, seventeen and unmarried at the time, became Tucson's first elected mayor in 1825 and he, too, could read and write. Of the three persons shown as mulatos, two were women. From the beginning of Spain's rule in Mexico, the whole system of racial classification had been a highly arbitrary affair, and it became increasingly so toward the end of the colonial period. Father Francisco Iturralde of the Tubutama mission did not even attempt to record the origins of individuals in his jurisdiction that he listed as gente de razon, saying that he did not have this information at his disposal.

The Tumacácori census provided by Father Gutiérrez was equally vague. He counted twenty-nine persons in the vecino category, most of whom were apparently *peones* and *agregados*. Eleven of the twelve Yaquis reported living at Tumacácori in 1796 were no longer there, but the Cocospera census includes a sufficient number to make it clear that the Yaquis were still well represented in the region. Although the combination of the new Indian policy and the assignment of troops to Tubac made things considerably easier for the Hispanic residents and peaceful Indians of the Santa Cruz Valley after about 1790, the Apaches did not give up raiding altogether. In June 1801, a large number attacked Tumacácori and killed three mission residents who were tending their flocks of sheep close to the village. The villagers were afraid to go outside and retrieve the bodies because the raiders remained in the area. The next afternoon, a small force of Pima soldiers from Tubac came to the rescue.

Tumacácori, 1801

Sometime during 1801, Father Narciso Gutiérrez began work on a new church at Tumacácori to replace the crumbling ruin built by the Jesuits in 1757. He was hard pressed to sustain the effort, however, for there were few wealthy benefactors nearby. Nevertheless, he hired a master bricklayer to draw a set of plans. The church, with a five-foot thick foundation, would be in the shape of a cross, with a main entrance at the south end, a dome over the crossing, and barrel vaults over the nave, transepts, and sacristy. A southeast bell tower, one with foundations nine feet thick instead of five and with an interior stairway, would buttress the vaulted choir loft. The principal building material would be adobe.

Construction began in 1802. The master hired an assistant and eighteen to twenty skilled laborers to burn lime and make adobes, with unskilled labor coming from the village as needed. The crew dug foundation trenches to a depth of three feet. River boulders were hauled to the site and by the end of 1802, the cobblestone foundation was above ground, but all the money was spent. To protect the foundation from weathering, two courses of adobes were laid on top and the surfaces were plastered inside and out with decorative handfuls of crushed burned brick pressed into the wet plaster. While Father Gutiérrez might have raised money through the sale of cattle, which were plentiful at that time, livestock prices were down. Getting the church ready became a long, drawn-out affair. Father Gutiérrez could just continue to work on the walls.

Life of the Arizona Settlers

In the meantime, life among the settlers went on as usual. On August 4, 1803, the Bishop of Sonora dispatched a circular letter to the chaplains of the Pimería Alta presidios informing them that it would be their responsibility to see to the education of the children in their communities. The emphasis was primarily on religious and secular law, and obedience to their fathers. Teaching would take place on Sundays and religious holidays; on Saturdays, family heads would be required to send their servants and slaves, as well as their children, to learn Christian doctrine.

While the more peaceful conditions that prevailed in northern Sonora contributed to an increase in the civilian population, there were other factors that attracted settlers to the region. Early in October 1803, new gold discoveries were reported a few miles north of Cieneguilla, where the great strike of the 1770s had caused so much excitement. Father José María Paz y Goicochea reported in a letter to Bishop Rouset that Cieneguilla itself was all but abandoned. The miners were not returning to the town to attend mass, so the priest journeyed to the placer fields to carry the faith to them.

In June 1802, Carlos IV ordered an evaluation of the worth of the colonial outposts, such as those on the Sonoran frontier. It was late in the spring of 1804, however, before instructions for conducting this appraisal reached La Pimería Alta. Captain José de Zuñiga prepared the report for Tucson; Second Ensign Manuel de Leon did the same for Tubac. Zuñiga, with a full decade of Tucson service behind him, provided a detailed description of the presidio and its surroundings, including a statement about San Xavier mission. According to him, the only public work truly worthy of the report was the church at San Xavier del Bac; the other missions in the north just had chapels. Tucson's comandante provided a head count of all persons at the presidio and in the surrounding area. The total came to 1,015. Leon, who had replaced Erran as the commanding officer at Tubac, reported that his post included eighty-eight soldiers and their families, eight civilian Hispanic households, and twenty Indian families. The count of gente de razon at Tumacácori, although down somewhat from two years before, stood at eighty-two, equal to the population of Pimas and Pápagos.

PRODUCTS AND LIVESTOCK IN ARIZONA

By 1804, Southern Arizona was beginning to enjoy a measure of prosperity, at least compared to previous years. Leon noted that the Tubac district annually harvested about 600 bushels of corn and 1,000 of wheat. The presidio cattle herd consisted of 1,000 head, and there were 5,000 sheep. Tucson's corn crop was about the same size as that of Tubac, but the wheat harvest was larger—2,800 bushels. They grew about 300 bushels of beans and other vegetables and the Indians of the Tucson district produced cotton for their own use. Tucsonenses were raising more cattle than their southern neighbors, about 3,500, but they had only about half as many sheep. Captain Zuñiga reported some occupational diversity at his presidio: four individuals were operating pack trains and an unspecified number were engaged in making soap. The comandante lamented the absence of weavers, leather tanners, tailors, and saddle makers and also felt that the opportunity for cultivating grapes was being lost.

The larger sheep flock at Tubac had contributed to a weaving industry there. Leon observed that some 600 woolen blankets had been produced and sold at a price of slightly more than 5 pesos each. Over 1,000 yards of coarse serge had also been woven, and the sale price for this material was around half a peso per yard. Both Leon and Zuñiga noted that the settlers did not pay any sales or personal taxes. At Tubac, no tobacco taxes were collected either. Zuñiga reported that individuals within his jurisdiction at Tucson had paid out more than 2,000 pesos for this purpose. Soldiers and settlers bought their tobacco directly from the presidio paymaster, who was responsible for collecting the tobacco tax, or at the company store.

Both reports showed the dependence of Tucsonenses on the Sonoran capital of Arizpe, which had become the principal supply point for the northern presidios. Leon noted that there was no military store in Tubac and that merchandise from Spain was all brought in through Arizpe. According to him, both soldiers and settlers traveled frequently to the capital to make purchases. Zuñiga observed in his report that the paymaster, with a military escort, visited Arizpe in connection with his duties of delivering and picking up the mail. Leon mentioned that goods from Asia and China—even southern Mexico—did not reach his post. Zuñiga, on the other hand, stated that 500 pesos were spent each year on merchandise from the orient—presumably brought in from Arizpe. He commented that no products were received directly from Veracruz, Acapulco, or San Blas. Both commanding officers insisted that there were no smuggled goods within their jurisdictions. Despite peace throughout the region, it does not appear from either report that mining activities had been resumed to any significant degree by 1804. Zuñiga states quite positively that they had no gold, silver, lead, tin, quicksilver, copper mines, or marble quarries. There was an outcropping of lime twenty-five miles from the presidio that supplied local construction needs, but there were no salt beds. Leon did not mention the subject of mining at all.

TECHNOLOGY

Despite the modern attractiveness of going a long way off to get away from it all, life on the southwestern frontier was never easy. The farther one traveled, the less access there was to any technological advances that might have been easily available in centers of greater population. Comparatively, technology in a borderlands province such as New Mexico was almost non-existent. What little technol-

Fig. 12.1. Flume. Photo by Donald Cutter.

ogy there was depended upon the collective or individual past experiences of settlers and was motivated by great need. The pool of knowledge from which innovative ideas could be gleaned was limited, as were the physical resources.

Technological advance in the Provincias Internas had obvious limits. Save for the Franciscan missionaries and a few military officers, the level of education was low, and thus there had been minimal exposure to innovative ideas, restricting greatly even the mind set that often produces technological advance. Such developments as existed resulted from sheer necessity, being based on either memory of, or familiarity with, certain practical arts. With exceptionally limited outside contacts, and restricted by distance and cost from the latest innovations, frontier technology became a matter of developing local resources that were supplemented by a few alien influences.

Although many aspects of knowledge defined as technology resulted from Iberian experience and influence, there was also cultural borrowing from the Indians. In meat curing, most frequently buffalo beef, the Hispanics made use of the ancient Indian drying process in which sun and wind were employed to make jerky, a means by which protein was long preserved and could be transported great distances. This aided time and again in both providing supplies for extended trips and for survival in times of shortage, adding to the stability of life on an isolated frontier. The established practice of Indian basket making also was utilized by Spaniards, who became customers of Native American art by incorporating baskets into everyday life, though they made no great effort themselves to emulate either the artistic or the utilitarian basketry of the Native Americans. Nevertheless, the Spaniards utilized and developed a number of technologies that were crucial to survival in the Southwest.

ARMS AND AMMUNITION

A major area of Spanish technological advance was in the art and accouterments of warfare. Frontier arms and ammunition were usually out-of-date, but from the days of first contact with the Indians, Spaniards benefited from superiority in arms. In some ways this superiority was a drawback since at times it gave Spaniards excessive confidence that their capacity for warfare made them invincible. But the frontier experience altered Spanish military orientation at least somewhat as technological improvements were based on and conditioned by life there. Sheer necessity dictated change from the steel and chain mail armor of the early conquistadores to a new form of protection, as traditional equipment was scarce and the substitute gear practical. For example, the *cuera*, a short and heavy buckskin jacket of five to seven thicknesses of hide bonded together with animal glue, became the substitute for European armor. From this armor, used extensively in the Spanish Southwest, was derived the name for many of the frontier military as the *soldados de cuera*, whose unique protective equipment was nearly impervious to anything but a direct hit by a well-propelled arrow. Such was the confidence that the frontier soldier had in his armor that at times he was foolhardy in his dependence on it. Added to this was the *adarga*, an even more impervious buckskin shield, made of the same material as the jacket and replacing any metal shield, surpassing it in lightness and maneuverability. (A number of these old shields still exist in museum collections, their once brilliant colors muted by their antiquity.)

Firearms gave another advantage, and although the frontier weapons were second rate as compared to those available to soldiers near important centers of population and industry, they gave great superiority to the Spaniards. Colonial period arms had obvious limitations, including a scarcity and incompetence of needed gunsmiths who could repair faulty weapons. Another shortcoming was the time lapse needed for reloading arms, an interval sufficient for a native adversary to discharge multiple arrows. The obvious tactical answer to that drawback was to fire by the numbers, with rounds of one-third or one-fourth of the arms firing at one time, while others were held in reserve for discharge when battle conditions required, allowing time between uses for reloading.

Carretas

In New Mexico there was a notable lack of wheeled vehicles, particularly four-wheeled ones. The paucity of large wagons was made up for by use of two-wheeled carretas practical for carrying heavier freight and *recuas* (mule trains), that were used for carrying other materials. Colonial period documents indicate that in 1598, Juan de Oñate and his founding party brought with them a considerable number of wagons. Other documents reveal the use from time to time of four-wheeled wagons. It can be hypothesized that as those vehicles became damaged, they had to be discarded as the necessary expertise and the component parts for making wagon wheels were unavailable.

For the two-wheeled carretas, solid crosscuts of cottonwood trees of suitable roundness and size were utilized. Since lubrication of the wheels was essential, tallow was used, being the most available source of grease. Nevertheless, the squeaking noise of the carretas could be heard from a great distance as the massive wheels grated against wooden axles. All major parts of the carreta were made of wood, from the flat bed of

Fig. 12.2. Carreta in front of San Juan de los Caballeros, 1881. Photo by William H. Rau. Courtesy Museum of New Mexico. 99997.

pine to the upright stakes of uniformly sized small poles laced together with thongs and sturdy enough to prevent freight from slipping. In these vehicles long trips were made, as it was the major conveyance in use in the Southwest.

Other Arts

On the domestic scene, technology brought from elsewhere was used in making candles, a distinct quality-of-life advantage. Construction of beehive-shaped ovens for outdoor baking was an advance, one rapidly incorporated into Pueblo Indian life and still in continual use in the New Mexico pueblos among modern Indians. Beehive ovens were common on ranchos throughout the remainder of the Southwest.

The Indians of New Mexico were skilled in weaving prior to the arrival of the first Spaniards, and their talents and materials were suited to the manufacture of light cotton blankets, such as those acquired by explorer Antonio de Espejo when from the Hopi he received a gift of 4,000 blankets. This pre-existing capacity for weaving was transformed at a later date to the manufacture of woolen blankets. With the introduction of sheep, production of wool was almost immediate, and Spanish colonists and missionaries instructed local Indians in the more complicated techniques of floor looms for weaving of woolens, a direct lesson from Spain. Indian adoption of Spanish techniques altered their weaving orientation and permanently changed their craft ways in making blankets, rugs, and cloth. It would be hard to imagine today the Navajo and Pueblo Indians without their looms for woolens, but these were introduced by the Spaniards.

Lest it be thought that Indians alone did weaving, there is ample evidence that the art was maintained among Hispanic residents, and still is practiced in the areas of greatest Hispanic culture survival, such as Chimayó, Medenales, Truchas, and Trampas. The skill which still exists has been passed down form generation to generation in the manufacture of serapes, blankets, and woolen cloth of great utility. The hallmark of Spanish weaving in New Mexico is care and simplicity. Previously, folk-weaving produced items of practical and useful value, but today they are pieces of art with considerable monetary value.

In the late colonial period there was evident technological advance in the art of silversmithery. Though the Indians did not borrow this artistic endeavor at an early date, the tradition of modern Indian silver arts comes from the Spanish period, during which time it was confined mostly to Spanish sources, though it was not widespread. Today's Spanish-introduced Indian art in silver includes the popular squash blossom motif, which is really the pomegranate. The concho belt and other adornments such as bracelets and rings are highly prized today, and continue to be made by Indian, Spanish, and even latecomer artisans. Most are sold as indigenous to the area. Silver is usually associated with turquoise, the use of which was reasonably well developed in aboriginal times, and thus with turquoise the Spaniards became borrowers from the local Indians.

Building Methods

In building, Spaniards demonstrated technological skill that they brought with them to New Mexico. Construction expertise was already sufficiently established among the Pueblo Indians so that from the Spaniards they engaged only in selective borrowing. It is obvious that building depends greatly on native resources; to that limitation the Spaniards brought with them developed skills. Stone was available in considerable quantities in many parts of New Mexico, but was used mostly in footings or foundations. A major exception to this is the series of all-stone missions built in the Estancia Valley in the early seventeenth century, abandoned after they were repeatedly attacked by Apaches. Early examples of this colonial period stone construction can still be found in the buildings at Tajique, Abó, and Quarai, remains of the old missions that are today the Salinas Pueblo Missions National Monument.

Although building methods were pragmatic, they were as technologically advanced as frontier circumstances permitted. On rare occasions, experienced craftsmen were sent or decided to relocate on the frontier in New Mexico. Setting aside such notable exceptions, other Spaniards still introduced adobe and various construction methods associated with sun-dried bricks. As a building material, adobe was potentially available in abundance, with a sandy loam being considered best, with the earth tied together by straw, grass, weeds, and even manure. Adobe was early used in Spain, a Moorish import that derived its name from the Arabic word *atob*. From Spain it was exported to the New World and in New Mexico it was adapted to the local product. The Pueblo Indians had for centuries worked with a less manageable but similar material in constructing their buildings, the major difference having been the absence of a binder to hold the components together.

Adobe construction has definite advantages because of the availability of its component parts, its cheapness, its insulative properties, its immunity from infestation, and its fire- and sound-proof characteristics. But with these advantages there were some disadvantages. If there is too much sand, the adobe bricks crumble, whereas if the mixture has too much clay, adobe bricks shrink and crack. Another problem is their extreme susceptibility to melting; that is, to erosion by water or by wind. The melting factor is somewhat reduced by installing moisture-proof roofs and by frequently plastering the surfaces with gypsum. There is also a great downward pressure exerted by such heavy building materials.

In the manufacture of adobes a thorough mixing of the materials was essential, following which the mixture was placed in open, four-sided molds to dry. Bricks were characteristically fractions of the Spanish yard of thirty-three inches, with each brick weighing forty to sixty pounds. Curing time depended on the weather, but in the dry air of the Far Southwest, readiness time was minimal except during the rains of late summer.

Because building methods required many structural pieces of wood, much time was spent selecting, cutting, and transporting timbers of suitable size. Unless forests were near at hand, and frequently this was not the case, transporting timbers took some knowledge of terrain, much patience, and a great deal of manpower. Tree-ring dating and identification of timber has demonstrated that some timbers were carried several hundred miles to points of necessity. Most structural pieces were roughly shaped at the point of cutting to reduce the weight of material being moved, while small structural members were either dragged or moved by carreta or even by mule back.

Roofing was always complicated. Occasionally tiles were used, having been formed to the proper shape for laying over heavy beams. In most areas use was made of wattles, long a method in regular use in parts of Spain and still utilized there in rural areas. Wattle construction required many long, strong, and easily obtained rods of wood over which thatch could be laid. Iron for construction purposes was in scarce supply until quite late in the colonial period. "Windows" were merely openings in the wall with wooden gratings to prevent entry. Glass was sometimes substituted with mica, thinly scraped leather, or just a bare opening that could be closed in winter or rainy weather. As a substitute for nails, other hardware, and even some structural pieces, rawhide was often used, taking the place of spikes and hinges. Thongs were used instead of spikes to fasten together major structural members such as *vigas* (beams) and rafters. When tightly wound and tied, the rawhide contracted upon drying, making a rigid joint. Everywhere in the Southwest, rawhide was the universal plaster, or glue, for repairing ailing implements and meeting household requirements.

Water Supply

Conduction of water was necessary not only in agriculture, but for other purposes as well. Water was equally available to everyone so long as its use was not to the detriment of others. Practical frontier considerations of water utilization throughout the far Southwest required diversion and storage works. The semi-arid land brought a need for conservation whereby town and village residents were required to spend specific amounts of time working on a dam or on diversion ditches so that a year-round supply of water would be available.

Prior to the arrival of the Spaniards, the Pueblo Indians had established a series of gravity flow canals, particularly in the villages along the Río Grande. These diversion systems were made more complicated with establishment of acequias and zanjas of considerable extension. The Indians still use the old colonial system of a certain number of days of obligation in work on the irrigation system, prorated among the users and depending upon the amount of use by each.

In New Mexico's mountain villages, especially in the Sangre de Cristo range, an ingenious system for transporting water was developed during the colonial period, one which is still in limited use today. Trunks of trees were hollowed out, laid end to end, and through these *canoas* ran—and still runs—a copious flow of water. The hollow tree trunks, an inexpensive substitute for more complicated pipe conduits, are propped up by trestles to conduct water over canyons and gorges. Upkeep and maintenance factors restricted the log flumes to mountainous areas where both trees of appropriate size and untapped water supplies were available. There and elsewhere some water channels were diverted to power small, rudimentary grinding mills, to provide communal fountains and washing places, and to create storage tanks.

Spanish colonial law established the general principles relating to irrigation, and the development and public regulation of water usage were and continue to be rooted in the traditional legal codes of Spain. The superimposition of those Spanish traditions was greatly facilitated by the pre-existence among the Río Grande Pueblos of "a social organization which could mobilize and control a fairly large adult force and satisfy the irrigational needs of the society." (Simmons, "Spanish Irrigation in New Mexico," p. 2)

RELATIONS WITH THE UNITED STATES

By the beginning of the nineteenth century, the only real threat to the Spanish Southwest was the young, vigorous, expansionist United States. Its citizens, rather than the government itself, gave first notice of intending to break the long-established mercantilist policy. They were encouraged by New Mexico's need for trade goods, greatly increased by the insurgency and by uncertainty of northbound commerce via Durango, Chihuahua, and El Paso. Even at best, the few goods arriving in New Mexico via the Chihuahua trading trail were purchased very dearly. The potential markets of Taos and Santa Fe beckoned U.S. traders, and the probability of silver pesos for smuggled goods added greatly to their interest.

The western area of the United States was chronically short of specie and had a nearly insatiable demand for the silver coins to replace the fluctuating paper money issued haphazardly by western banks. So valuable was silver coinage that for many years Spanish, and later Mexican, pesos circulated as the most common and most acceptable monetary unit in much of the United States. Clearly the attraction of New Mexico was as a trading partner, the end result being Spanish hard money. For New Mexicans, trade was desirable except for those government employees whose duty it was to prevent this illicit commerce. It is obvious that illegal trade needs a favorable environment—traders cannot force goods on reluctant trading partners. There must be confederates within as well as suppliers on the outside. Commodities must be of small bulk and high value to defray the costs of transportation (but in this case, it was already true of things brought from central New Spain). Finally, the profits from smuggling must be great enough to compensate both seller and buyer for the risks involved in clandestine commerce. Variables are the amount of vigilance, the secrecy of such an illegal operation, and the relative scarcity or abundance of attractive goods.

The historian is at a great disadvantage in attempting to evaluate illegal trade. When it was successful, part of its success depended upon undercover activity, meaning minimal or no bookkeeping, a fact frequently in direct proportion to the favorable outcome of smuggling efforts. The best extant documentary records come from some unsuccessful efforts at illegal trade, men who were caught virtually in the act. Lists of their confiscated goods give some quantitative and qualitative idea of the trade, while the detention, interrogation, and sometimes incarceration of participants provide archival evidence of smuggling. Obviously, successful smugglers rarely if ever kept journals or logged daily illegal activities for fear of producing by their own hand conclusive evidence of guilt.

The real opening of massive trade with the western United States began during the twilight years of Spanish sovereignty and involved the Santa Fe Trade, whose commerce came over the semi-legendary Santa Fe Trail from Missouri, through Indian country to the ancient New Mexico capital. One precursor of this trade connection was the previously mentioned Pedro Vial whose travels demonstrated the relative nearness as well as the ease with which Spanish St. Louis (later U.S. St. Louis) and Santa Fe could become trading partners.

The Louisiana Purchase

In 1803, a major change in orientation for the Spanish Southwest began after the United States purchased from France the area of ancient Louisiana west of the Mississippi River, bearing in mind that France did not possess the area when the sale was negotiated. The expansive young American nation had already obtained the eastern portion of what had once been French Louisiana. The western portion, the trans-Mississippi West, was largely unknown save to a few hardy fur trappers and traders, men of transient national loyalties, but vigorous in pursuit of their private economic interests.

As for the United States, having acquired at bargain prices a territorial windfall, it was important to explore that area, particularly to ascertain the western limits of the great national addition of Louisiana. To that end, several early, military-led expeditions spread out in various directions, some of which came to the attention of Spanish authorities in Chihuahua and in New Mexico. United States President Thomas Jefferson, an advocate of national expansion, was surprised by how easy the acquisition had been, particularly by the favorable terms with which the Louisiana Purchase had been negotiated. He was also embarrassed by an official and even unofficial ignorance of its potential and of its extent. Jefferson wrote to various western figures, but got little authoritative response except from Dr. John Sibley, and even this concerned only the Red River. On the basis of the lack of information, the president requested and obtained a modest congressional appropriation permitting scientist William Dunbar and Dr. George Hunter to explore the Red River. Instead, however, in the winter of 1804–1805, they ascended the much shorter Ouichita River. Even so, the Spanish authorities in Chihuahua made known their objections, to which was added the reported hostility of the Osage Indians to any invasion of their lands. The expedition was a failure.

In the following year, 1806, the United States sent another expedition that actually did explore the Red River. It was led by a scientist, Thomas Freeman who went out accompanied by a small detachment of soldiers. Galvanized into action, the Spaniards of the northern frontier sent out a party from Nacogdoches under Francisco Viana to intercept and turn back the intrusive expedition. The United States exploring party was met some 600 miles upstream on the Red River by what was clearly a greatly superior party. Discretion became more important than fulfillment of orders, with the result that the Freeman party returned home, its mission incomplete.

Zebulon Pike, 1806

By far the most important and certainly the best known official explorer of the area was a young army officer, Zebulon M. Pike. His commanding general, the duplicitous James Wilkinson, a frontier military officer who served as a double agent in the generous pay of both Spain and the United States, not only provided Pike with multiple stories from which to choose in justification of his exploratory activities, but also informed the Spanish authorities concerning the Pike sortie. Whether this was in an effort to obtain a friendly reception or in fulfillment of his obligations as a spy, the Spanish authorities knew early on of the Pike enterprise.

Pike had recently returned from an unsuccessful effort to locate definitively the source of the Mississippi, and was thought to be ideal for the new command. He was the son of a military man, but had no formal training in military affairs prior to his enlistment at age 15. The avowed purpose of Pike's reconnaissance was to discover the source of the Red River and to ascertain the western boundary of the recently consummated Louisiana Purchase. He also had orders to return to their homes delegations of Osage and Pawnee Indians who had been to Washington, D.C., for a council meeting. Pike was also expected to act as a conciliator with other Plains Indians groups. Additional orders directed him to explore the Arkansas River and the area lying between it and the Red River. Pike was instructed to disguise the military identity of his small party consisting of twenty-three soldiers. When Pike got as far west as the Pawnee territory he was received with misgivings, for those Indians had been warned in advance by Spanish sources and had recently received Spanish flags and medallions, tokens of adhesion of those semi-nomadic Indians to Hispanic authorities in Santa Fe.

Proceeding westward across the Great Plains, Pike and his men explored well up on the Arkansas River, where they established a temporary headquarters at what is today Pueblo, Colorado. The leader and some of his men set out to ascend a "nearby" peak, which today bears his name, one of the best known geographical features of today's Colorado. They failed in the ascent, only arriving as far as the first ridge, the Front Range. Next Pike explored across the Sangre de Cristo Mountains, ending up on the banks of the Conejos tributary of the upper Río Grande, well to the north of the Spanish settlements. At that point Pike erected a hasty fortification and despite the fact that he was clearly on Spanish soil, he flew the United States flag. Although his intrusion on Spanish territory was passed off as a mistake in his geographical orientation, it was an unlikely error for an experienced explorer. If he were on United States soil, no fortification would have been necessary.

Spanish intelligence of Pike's activities resulted in mounting a large-scale party to intercept the small exploratory detachment. Six hundred men were mustered at Santa Fe, clearly the largest military party to have ever been sent out in New Mexico's long history, and perhaps the largest in Borderlands history. Entrusted to the leadership of Captain Facundo Melgares, the group consisted of 100 regular troops, supported by 500 men from local militia companies. The large army reflected a feeling that Pike was a maximum threat to the security of the Internal Provinces of the viceroyalty of New Spain. One adjunct member of the Pike party, Dr. John Robinson, a volunteer surgeon, set out independently for Santa Fe in an effort to collect a debt due to an Illinois merchant. Meanwhile, one of Melgares's detachments, one hundred strong, found Pike, took him and his party captive, and escorted them to the provincial capital at Santa Fe. There Governor Joaquín Real Alancaster was in a quandary concerning what to do with the interlopers. Was Pike's party hostile? Was he in Spanish territory by accident or by design?

As a prisoner, Pike was relieved of all of his notes and other papers, and was sent first to Chihuahua and then forwarded to Durango. While under guard Pike was able to make many mental and some written notes of the country traversed, probably gaining much more information as a prisoner than he would have had he been told simply to withdraw from his point of maximum penetration. For as a captive, he and his party visited not only El Paso, Chihuahua, Durango, Laredo, San Antonio, and Natchitoches, but also surreptitiously kept track of their travels. His earlier, more complete notes, had been taken and placed in the local archives where they rested undisturbed for almost exactly one hundred years. Interrogated by the Spanish authorities, using as interpreter a survivor of Philip Nolan's abortive invasion of Texas, the local officers learned little of value from Pike.

Even after his return home, Pike's journal, as recreated from memory and secret notes, did not picture his expedition and its results as a threat to New Mexico. To the contrary, Pike, though he had not accomplished his mission, left a discouraging report on the nature of the land he had traversed. He supported and even added to the concept of a Great American Desert of the trans-Mississippi West. His published report concerning the area was that "From these immense prairies may arise one great advantage to the United States; viz: the restriction of our population to some certain limits, and thereby the continuation of the Union. Our citizens being so prone to rambling and extending themselves on the frontier will, through necessity be constrained to limit their extent on the west to the borders of the Missouri and Mississippi, while they leave the prairies, incapable of cultivation to the wandering and uncivilized aborigines of the country." (Jackson, ed., *The Journals of Zebulon Pike with Letters and Related Documents*, vol. 2, p. 28)

For some years after Pike's expedition, United States involvement in war with England provided a hiatus in any official interest in New Mexico; nevertheless, despite his discouraging reports, Pike awakened frontier interest, if not in New Mexico, at least in neighboring Texas. Another precursor was the enigmatic Manuel Lisa—a long-time, well-known fur trapper and Indian trader of uncertain ethnic background and variable political orientation. Over a period of years Lisa and his associates attempted vainly to open trade with New Mexico.

The Coastal Trade

New Mexico was not the only area to attract U.S. attention. The Pacific Ocean provided an easy approach to the most isolated of New Spain's frontiers—California. Two factors—the existence of sea otter and the frequent appearance of New England merchants—significantly affected California's economic development during the early nineteenth century. The highly prized sea otter, an unsuspected determinant in world history, set into motion a chain of international events destined to reshape the course of Pacific Coast settlement. Because of its beautiful and valuable fur, Russia gained possession of Alaska, England sought a foothold on the Northwest Coast, and the United States first learned of the resources and advantages of California. The sea otter inhabited the coast from Alaska to Lower California, flourished especially on the Santa Barbara Channel islands, and for a time abounded in the harbors of the California mainland.

Asian markets served as the principal outlet for skins. Furs were inevitably popular in China since additional clothing took the place of household heating. A three-cornered trade between the Pacific Coast, Canton, and New England progressed rapidly once the advantages were known. Individual pelts brought as much as 120 dollars apiece in 1805, although competition during the next few years forced prices down to a low of 20 dollars. The later scarcity of sea otter restored prices to about 50 dollars per skin after 1812. Building upon the lucrative Chinese trade, Boston captains enlarged their activities by an exchange with Russians based in Alaska. They temporarily entered into a cooperative arrangement for Russian-American expeditions into Pacific waters.

As New England merchants moved southward along the coast, they challenged official Spanish control and were quick to profit from the political weakness of California. Unsettled world conditions at the turn of the century also enhanced the American position in the Pacific. The demands of the Napoleonic Wars, the War of 1812, and conflicting monopolies of the British East India Company and South Seas Company largely eliminated English competition; and the Russians were barred from Chinese ports. The *London Quarterly Review* noted in 1816 that direct trade with China from the Pacific Coast was almost entirely in American hands—a status achieved only by means of persistent, careful, and brazen smuggling. The Boston men, however, held the United States attitude that Spain did not "own" the Pacific and boasted:

> The conquest of their country [California] would be absolutely nothing; it would fall without an effort to the most inconsiderable force … [but] it would be as easy to keep California in spite of the Spanish, as it would be to wrest it from them in the first instance. (Coughlin, "Boston Smugglers on the Coast [1797–1821]: An Insight into American Acquisition of California," pp. 104–5)

The contribution of New England merchants toward Spain's loss of California was in reality a symptom rather than a cause of Spain's declining power. The Boston men encouraged, nevertheless, a growing United States interest in political acquisition of the province.

Boston Ships

The total extent of illegal American trading activities in California cannot be measured for lack of records. Spanish port documents, official correspondence, and Boston company accounts merely give an idea of Spanish contact with New England merchants. The first Boston ship to enter a California port was the 168-ton *Otter* under Captain Ebenezer Dorr.

Claiming distress, the ship remained in Monterey from October 29 to November 6, 1796, and received authorization to purchase fresh supplies. Captain Dorr also requested permission to disembark ten men and a woman—convicts who had "stowed away" at Botany Bay in New Zealand. Governor Borica refused, but Dorr secretly landed the group at gun point on the beach at Carmel. Borica's anger at such Yankee chicanery was calmed only when he found the men useful as skilled workmen—at 19 cents a day. California's governor was actually unhappy when royal orders required the convicts forwarded to New Spain.

Contact between New England and California prior to 1800 had been negligible, but during the first few years of the nineteenth century, Boston traders entered the Pacific with alarming frequency. Boldly putting into California ports with standard pleas for supplies and care of the sick, they side-stepped customs regulations in exchanging goods. Though Spanish officials recognized the Americans as smugglers, their lack of home support in terms of men and equipment made strong coastal defense impossible.

In August 1800, the 104-ton brigantine *Betsy*, commanded by 23-year-old Captain Charles Winship, put into the port of San Diego ostensibly to take on wood and water. Later, a letter in which Winship had described his trading activities with California Indians along the coast fell into Spanish possession. This firsthand evidence sparked a government effort to fight smuggling. Two months after the *Betsy* sailed from San Diego, it was forced to anchor in San Blas with a broken mast. Appearance of Spanish port officials occasioned the *Betsy*'s rapid departure; in fact, so great was its haste the ship's business agent, Joseph O'Cain, was left behind. O'Cain, who had been a pilot for the Spanish at San Blas in the 1790s, returned to Boston on another vessel, eventually to become an active coastal trader in his own right.

Also in 1800 the New York trading ship *Enterprise* arrived in San Diego asking for needed wood and provisions before sailing to Canton. It then proceeded southward along the Baja California coast—stopping at Ensenada, San Quintín, and San José del Cabo with a suspiciously identical story. The 167-foot *Alexander* reached San Diego under Captain John Brown in 1803 seeking help for some crewmen down with scurvy. While the men recuperated on shore, presidio commander Lieutenant Manuel Rodríguez ordered a search of the ship. Promptly confiscating 491 otter furs found on board, Rodríguez ordered the ship's immediate departure. Two letters resulting from this incident revealed Spanish cooperation in the illegal trade. One, from a priest at San Luis Rey, requested the return of 170 skins that the Indians had sold the Americans; and the second, from a corporal at the San Diego presidio, asked Governor Arrillaga that the 223 otter skins he had "pretended" to sell to the Americans be given back. This and considerable other evidence showed that Californians were exchanging furs for necessary goods.

Yankee Enterprise

One of the most active Boston trading ships operating off the California coast in 1803 was the 175-ton, Virginia-built brig *Lelia Byrd* commanded by William Shaler, later an American consul, and Richard Cleveland. These enterprising men confidently approached Lieutenant Rodríguez with a proposition to purchase the skins confiscated from the *Alexander*. Rodríguez not only refused, but when he learned the Americans had surreptitiously obtained some furs on shore, he opened fire on the ship as it fled undamaged from the harbor. The local skirmish became known as the "Battle of San Diego." After a trip to China, Shaler returned to California with the *Lelia Byrd* in 1804 and for several months carried on a considerable volume of trade—carefully avoiding official contact. Even though Spain's tightened policy after 1803 blocked the *Lelia Byrd*'s entrance into regular ports, Shaler maintained a close relationship with California civilians. He wrote in 1804:

> *For several years past, the American trading ships have frequented this coast in search of furs, for which they have left in the country about 25,000 dollars annually, in species and merchandise. The government have used all their endeavors to prevent this intercourse, but without effect … .*
> (Coughlin, "Boston Smugglers on the Coast [1797–1821]: An Insight into American Acquisition of California," p. 111)

A diminishing supply of furs in California after 1804 curtailed smuggling activities, and more rigid port controls were effective against Boston ships ostensibly seeking "supplies and care of the sick." The guardian of the College of San Fernando also warned the Franciscan missionaries not to trade with foreigners, and the priests themselves began to prohibit Indian participation when they saw their charges exploited by both soldiers and traders. New Englanders, therefore, turned toward another profitable source of furs.

Joseph O'Cain, who had been stranded in San Blas by the *Betsy*, reappeared in the Pacific with the 280-ton *O'Cain*, armed with eighteen guns, and sailed to Kodiak Island off the Alaskan Coast. He entered into an agreement with the Russian American Fur Company whereby the Americans supplied shipping and provisions and the Russians provided experienced Aleut hunters and necessary equipment. They would divide the furs equally. The Russian-American venture proved successful and California coastal waters were again invaded. Though fighting back whenever possible, Spanish officials were relatively helpless in effectively patrolling the mainland and channel island coasts.

GOVERNOR ARRILLAGA OF CALIFORNIA

Bids for California's highest office were opened once again with the retirement of Governor Diego de Borica in 1800. The impressive qualifications of Lieutenant Governor José Joaquín de Arrillaga, commander of the Loreto presidio and interim California governor from 1792 to 1794, brought him the post. A native of the Basque province of Guipuzcoa, Arrillaga served as a captain in Texas until his appointment to Baja California in 1783. Upon his arrival on the lower peninsula, the new executive sought to improve the difficult conditions faced by Dominican missionaries and revitalize Loreto's small military force of twenty-one men. Within a year, Arrillaga obtained 8,000 dollars worth of supplies from the mainland. Early in 1785, when his tour of inspection revealed that a drought had ruined all crops, food was scarce, shops and artisans were non-existent, and that mining had been suspended, Arrillaga initiated plans for reform.

Although the best lands of Baja California were monopolized by existing missions, Arrillaga made some grants to civilian settlers and authorized the founding of new missions that would fill in the gap between the peninsular settlements and those of Upper California. In cooperation with Lieutenant José Francisco Ortega of the San Diego presidio, he had proposed the sites for Dominican missions Santo Tomás and

San Miguel south San Diego. At this time his plans were interrupted by the death of Governor José Antonio Romeu in 1792, and Arrillaga served two years at Monterey as acting governor, primarily reforming military procedure.

Returning to Loreto in 1794, Arrillaga was promoted to lieutenant colonel and spent the next six years touring settlements and exploring for a possible land route to Sonora. Arrillaga recommended in 1796 that the two Californias—which in 1792 had been removed from the Provincias Internas and returned to the direct jurisdiction of the viceroy—be separated into distinct governmental entities. Governor Borica supported the measure, and while no opposition seems to have been aroused, effective division was delayed in official channels until 1804.

Acting first as interim governor, Arrillaga continued residence at Loreto, and Pedro de Alberni, veteran captain of the Spanish establishment at Nootka Sound, assumed military command of California at Monterey. When Alberni died in March 1802, Arrillaga prepared to journey northward. Before reaching the capital, he received word of another sad death. Father Fermín Francisco de Lasuén, for eighteen years father-president of the Upper California missions, had died on June 26, 1803, and was buried at Mission San Carlos. The devoted priest, whose passing was deeply mourned by all, was praised by his fellow Franciscans for his temporal and spiritual accomplishments. The father-presidency passed into the experienced hands of Father Esteban Tapis, a native of Coloma de Farnes in Catalonia, who had served as a missionary in California since 1790. The College of San Fernando had awarded Father Tapis a provisional *patente* in 1798 that allowed his immediate succession to the presidency upon Lasuen's death.

The royal order dividing the Californias into separate provinces reached Governor Arrillaga at Loreto on November 16, 1804. The boundary was set at a place called Barrabas, or the stream and ranchería of Rosario, near the line between Franciscan and Dominican mission jurisdiction since 1772. The order designated Arrillaga as political and military governor of Upper California at a salary of 4,000 pesos per year, and acting governor of Lower California until a replacement could be named. Leaving Loreto in the summer of 1805, Arrillaga journeyed northward by land, suggesting along the way measures to strengthen the defenses of both provinces. At this time there were twenty missions and few towns on the peninsula. Reaching Monterey on January 20, 1806, he immediately ordered the cooperation, selection, and enrollment of men, chiefly in the pueblos, to serve in local militias. The new executive also requested an armed vessel to patrol the coastline.

EXPLORER GABRIEL MORAGA

During the early years of California settlement, the pressing problems of survival and stabilization occupied the full attention of Spanish forces. Discoveries and settlements had been confined to coastal valleys, with few forays into the interior. Those in command knew that a great valley lay inland from the San Francisco Bay region, and that southern California was backed by an expanse of rugged mountains and inhospitable deserts, but exploration had been limited to coastal regions. Not until after 1800 did California enjoy a military population sufficient to permit penetration into these uncharted areas.

When Governor Arrillaga's arrived in Monterey in 1806 he called for a full-scale inspection of the interior. Arrillaga, fresh from his own explorations in Baja California, ordered four separate inland expeditions in 1806 and assigned Franciscan priests to serve as chaplains and diarists for each journey. The clergy willingly participated in a desire to extend their missionary activities into the central valley—with the potential end product of a parallel chain of inland missions. This would facilitate large numbers of new converts and remove an existing asylum for runaway mission Indians.

Foremost explorer of Spanish California was Gabriel Moraga, an ensign of the San Francisco presidio who had served as *comisionado* of the Villa de Branciforte. Moraga, born in 1767 at the presidio of Fronteras, Sonora, just missed being killed in the Yuma Massacre when he and his mother accompanied the ill-fated Rivera expedition to California in 1781. Gabriel, son of José Joaquín Moraga, second in command of Anza's colonizing party of 1776, at 16 joined the company of leather-jacket soldiers and soon won fame as an Indian fighter. He achieved more lasting recognition, however, in exploration. By the time of his retirement, Moraga's record consisted of forty-two expeditions and campaigns during forty-one years of military service.

In 1805 Moraga traveled to the central and southern San Joaquin Valley, exploring chiefly along the west side. He crossed the Tulare Lake region and named the river that he found El Río de los Santos Reyes (River of the Holy Kings—later shortened to Kings River). On a second expedition ordered by Arrillaga in the fall of 1806, Moraga explored the entire length of the San Joaquin Valley. After crossing the valley to the eastern slope of the Sierra Nevada and passing a river which they named Nuestra Señora de la Merced, the expedition came upon an area abundant with moths that they called Las Mariposas (moths or butterflies). They also visited an Indian ranchería of Tahualamne on the present Toulumne River. Traveling again to Kings River, Moraga continued southward and led his party through Tejon Pass in the Tehachapi Mountains to Mission San Fernando on November 2, 1806. Chaplain and diarist Father Pedro Muñoz reported that 141 Indians were baptized on the trip and prepared a list of rancherías visited and number of inhabitants in each one.

Governor Arrillaga, on September 13, 1808, ordered another expedition to search inland for new mission locations, capture runaway Indians, and look for Indian rancherías. No priest accompanied the small military force that set out from Mission San José. Moraga, as commander of the fourteen-man party, kept his own diary. By the fifth day out, the explorers reached a river that they named San Francisco (the Cosumnes) and then turned north-northwestward. The next day Moraga wrote, "after about 5 leagues I found a river which runs from north to south. It carries more water than any of the others except the San Joaquín." (Cutter, ed., *Diary of Ensign Gabriel Moraga's Expedition of Discovery in the Sacramento Valley, 1808*, pp. 17–18) He called the river Las Llagas (the wounds) to commemorate the suffering of Christ on being crowned with thorns. It is today's American River.

Moraga's party discovered the next very wide river and decided it should be known as the Sacramento. This name remained for the lower course of the combined rivers, but the one to which Moraga referred in 1808 was renamed Rio de las Plumas (Feather River) by Luis Argüello in 1820 because of feathers floating in it. The men saw many Indians on the river and an unfortunate minor skirmish resulted in the death of one of the natives. Continuing north-northwest upstream, Moraga's party encountered thirty armed Indians. After a friendly exchange by means of their interpreter, a San Francisco mission Indian, the Spaniards dismounted and the Indians loosened their bows. Commented Moraga, "They were greatly amazed by our horses, and many of them gave us their weapons so that we would allow them to look at our horses. I didn't permit such payment ... ." (Cutter, ed., *Diary of Ensign Gabriel Moraga's Expedition of Discovery in the Sacramento Valley, 1808*, p. 20) The soldiers finally reached a river which they named Jesús María (the Upper Sacramento) and there, since provisions were low, decided to turn back. Returning along the eastern slope of the valley, they continued southward to the Merced River, crossing the San Joaquin Valley near the river's mouth. They reached Mission San José on October 23, 1808. Though far from complete, Moraga's twenty-nine day survey was satisfactory for its day and served as the basis for information concerning the upper valley during the next thirteen years.

Moraga resumed his military duties at San Francisco and in 1812 headed an unsuccessful expedition against the Russians at Fort Ross. His last major exploratory expedition took place in southern California in 1819, designed primarily to capture fugitive Indians and punish the Mojaves for inciting a fight at Mission San Buenaventura. Two Spaniards, one mission Indian, and ten Mojaves had been killed. A force of fifty-five soldiers, with Father Joaquín Pascual Nuez serving as chaplain and diarist, headed eastward from Mission San Gabriel through Cajon Pass into the Mojave desert. They continued to a spot near the eastern boundary of California, perhaps into Nevada, but sparse grass and water forced their return. Little was accomplished on Moraga's last known campaign and the veteran lieutenant sought retirement. Moraga, a man whose exploits spanned a significant period of California development, died in active service on June 15, 1823, and was buried in the Santa Barbara mission cemetery.

CALIFORNIA EARTHQUAKE OF 1812

At a time when life in California had settled into a normal routine little beset by outside disturbances, a series of earthquake shocks in 1812 caused severe damage to church and rancho buildings. Minor quakes had been felt since the days when Portolá's expedition reported the "temblores" near the Santa Ana and San Gabriel Rivers in 1769, and the Indians talked of the demon who knocked down high walls. In 1808 San Francisco was rudely shaken but damage was slight. These and other earth movements were merely a prelude to the violent tremors which devastated portions of the southern missions between December 1812, and February 1813. Father José Señan, successor to Esteban Tapis as father-president in 1812, reported the disaster in a letter of April 9, 1813:

> *These quakes will form an epoch in history for their great destructiveness. ... There must be built anew the churches of San Fernando and Santa Barbara. ... At Purisima the quake was so violent that it caused the bells to swing till they rang forth their chimes. In a few brief moments the building was reduced to fragments and ruins, presenting the spectacle of Jerusalem destroyed. ...* (Richman, *California Under Spain and Mexico,* p. 208)

Apparently the earthquakes caused no damage at San Diego nor San Luis Rey; but on December 8, 1812, the bell tower at San Juan Capistrano crashed down upon the

Fig. 12.3. Mission San Juan Capistrano. Courtesy San Juan Capistrano Mission Archives.

vaulted roof of the chapel and within seconds the entire mass of stone and mortar fell upon the congregation. Thirty-nine Indians were buried in the mission cemetery and records indicate the later discovery of four more bodies. At San Gabriel tremors cracked the church, felled the top of the tower, and damaged most of the buildings. No shocks were reported at San Fernando until December 21, when the church was partially destroyed. Further north, earth movements apparently began on the 21st and continued intermittently for several months. The inhabitants of San Buenaventura evacuated the mission site, fearful of the sea's encroachment, and remained inland until April. The long series of shocks damaged both the Santa Barbara mission and presidio, and residents were afraid that some springs of *chapapote* (asphaltum) that formed along the ocean's shore were new openings of a supposed subterranean volcano. Inland at Santa Ines a corner of the church, a fourth of the houses, and all of the mission roofs were destroyed. At La Purísima Concepción, located near present-day Lompoc, the earth shook violently in two quakes, bringing down the church and nearly all the adobe buildings. Several Indians were wounded but none killed. Heavy rains completed nature's destruction, causing the water pipes to burst. The mission was subsequently rebuilt on another site. The destructive force of earthquakes would continue, but the more ominous events of war soon became the major factor in disturbing the tenuous peaceful existence of the Spanish Southwest.

Chapter Twelve
BIBLIOGRAPHIC ESSAY

Studies on rancho life and the rancho economy in California include Iris H. W. Engstrand, "An Enduring Legacy: California's Ranchos in Historical Perspective," in *Spanish and Mexican Land Grants and the Law,* edited by Malcolm Ebright (Manhattan, Kans.: Sunflower University Press, 1989), and Robert Glass Cleland, *The Cattle on a Thousand Hills: Southern California, 1850–1880* (San Marino: The Huntington Library, 1977). Robert C. Cowan, *Ranchos of California* (Fresno: Academy Library Guild, 1956) lists all of the land grants from 1775 to 1846; W. W. Robinson *Ranchos Become Cities* (Pasadena: San Pascual Press, 1939) concerns the Los Angeles area; and Cecil Moyer, *Historic Ranchos of San Diego* (San Diego: The Copley Press, 1969) gives a brief history of those ranchos. Terry G. Jordan has written a general study called *North American Cattle Ranching Frontiers: Origins, Diffusion and Differentiation* (Albuquerque: University of New Mexico Press, 1993) and the first chapter of Jay J. Wagoner, *History of the Cattle Industry in Southern Arizona, 1540–1940* (Tucson: University of Arizona Press, 1952) discusses the Spanish period. See also Yjinio F. Aguirre "Echoes of the Conquistadores: Stock Raising in Spanish-Mexican Times," *Journal of Arizona History*, 16 (autumn 1975):267–86.

For New Mexico see G. Emlen Hall, *Four Leagues of Pecos: A Legal History of the Pecos Grant, 1800–1933* (Albuquerque: University of New Mexico Press, 1984); Malcolm Ebright, *Land Grants and Lawsuits in Northern New Mexico* (Albuquerque: University of New Mexico Press, 1994); Iris H. W. Engstrand, "Land Grant Problems in the Southwest: The Spanish and Mexican Heritage," *New Mexico Historical*

Review, 53 (October 1978):317–36; Gilberto Espinosa, "About New Mexico Land Grants," *Albuquerque Bar Journal,* 7 (September 1967):5–15; Myra Ellen Jenkins, "Spanish Land Grants in the Tewa Area," *NMHR,* 47 (April 1966):85–114.

The sheep industry is covered in John O. Baxter, *Las Carneradas: Sheep Trade in New Mexico, 1700–1860* (Albuquerque: University of New Mexico Press, 1987). Marc Simmons talks about the movement of water in "Spanish Irrigation in New Mexico," *NMHR,* 47 (April, 1972):135–50. A colorful sketch about sheep is Winifred Kupper, *The Golden Hoof: The Story of the Sheep of the Southwest* (New York: A. A. Knopf, 1945).

John L. Kessell, *Friars, Soldiers and Reformers* (Tucson: University of Arizona Press, 1976) gives an excellent summary of the negotiations on behalf of the Tumacácori Indians to gain a grant of land. His work also covers the role of the frontier soldiers in the Mexican War for Independence. Henry Dobyns, *Spanish Colonial Tucson* (Tucson: University of Arizona Press, 1976) details the action of those stationed at Arizona presidios in remaining loyal to Spain in the early years of independence. His work contains census data on the Native American population of Tucson and San Xavier del Bac in 1801. The history of the early land grants in the Arizona area are contained in Jay J. Wagoner, *Early Arizona* (Tucson: University of Arizona Press, 1975).

The final days of mission life in California under Spanish control are discussed in Robert Archibald, *Economic Aspects of the California Missions* (Washington, D.C.: Academy of American Franciscan History, 1978); Francis F. Guest, "Cultural Perspectives on California Mission Life," *Southern California Quarterly,* 65 (spring 1983):1–65; Irving B. Richman, *California Under Spain and Mexico, 1535–1857.* (Boston: Houghton Mifflin Co., 1911); and Lesley B. Simpson, ed., and Paul Nathan, trans., *Letters of José Señan* (San Francisco: John Howell Books, 1962). Manuel P. Servín, gives background on the secularization movement in "The Secularization of the California Missions: A Reappraisal," *SCQ,* 47 (June 1965):133–150, while Gerald J. Geary covers the topic in greater detail in *The Secularization of the California Missions—1810–1846* (Washington, D.C.: Catholic University of America, 1934). See also Clement W. Meighan, "Indians and the California Missions," *SCQ,* 69 (fall 1987):187–201. Roger G. Kennedy, *Mission: The History and Architecture of the Missions of North America* (Boston and New York: Houghton Mifflin, 1993) gives an excellent summary of mission architectural influence with abundant photographs by Michael Freeman.

Roy F. Nichols, *Advance Agents of American Destiny* (Philadelphia: University of Pennsylvania Press, 1956), treats the career of Boston trader William Shaler, while the hunt for California sea otters is the subject of Adele Ogden, *The California Sea Otter Trade, 1784–1848* (Berkeley: University of California Press, 1941) and "New England Traders in Spanish and Mexican California," in *Greater America: Essays in Honor of Herbert Eugene Bolton* (Berkeley: University of California Press, 1945). Magdalen Coughlin, "Boston Smugglers on the Coast (1797–1821): An Insight into the American Acquisition of California," *California Historical Society Quarterly,* 46 (June 1967):99–120.

During the final decades of Spanish control in California, expeditions were made into the interior. Regarding the travels of Gabriel Moraga, see Donald C. Cutter, *Diary of Ensign Gabriel Moraga's Expedition of Discovery in the Sacramento Valley, 1808* (Los Angeles: Dawson's Book Shop, 1957). See also S. F. Cook, *Colonial Expeditions to the Interior of California's Central Valley, 1800–1820* (Berkeley: University of California Press, 1960). Surprisingly little information exists on José Joaquín de Arrillaga despite his long tenure as governor. There are few secondary studies that cover the lives of Spanish or Mexican governors of California. The various archival depositories and Bancroft's *History of California* remain the best sources.

On Zebulon Montgomery Pike, see Donald Jackson, ed. *The Journals of Zebulon Montgomery Pike with Letters and Related Documents,* 2 vols. (Norman: University of Oklahoma Press, 1966); John Upton Terrell, *Zebulon Pike: The Life and Times of an Adventurer* (New York: Weybright and Talley, 1968) and W. Eugene Hollon, *The Lost Pathfinder: Zebulon Montgomery Pike* (Norman: University of Oklahoma Press, 1966).

Some final thoughts on frontier conflict are in Thomas D. Clark and John D. W. Guice, *Frontiers in Conflict: The Old Southwest, 1795–1830* (Albuquerque: University of New Mexico Press, 1989). For California, see Antonia I. Castañeda, "Gender, Race, and Culture: Spanish-Mexican Women in the Historiography of Frontier California," *Frontiers: A Journal of Women's Studies,* 11 (Novermber 1990):8–30.

Chapter Thirteen

THE END OF AN ERA: 1821–1848

ERA OF INDEPENDENCE

*T*he Wars for Independence in Spanish America resulted from what many considered the oppressive nature of the colonial system, the growing resentment of criollos and other classes against the peninsular Spaniards who held positions of power in the church and state, the infiltration of ideas of the Enlightenment, and the successful examples of the American and French Revolutions. In addition, conditions in Spain led to further dissension. Though residents of the Spanish Southwest knew that movements toward independence had been occurring throughout Spanish colonies further to the south for nearly a decade, they had little first-hand knowledge of either side's progress. Geographically isolated from actual participation, they remained nominally loyal to the mother country until Spain's defeat in 1821.

The revolution in Spanish America, deeply rooted in the injustices created by a landed minority and a powerful aristocracy of church and state, was further kindled by dissension within Spain. When Napoleon installed his brother Joseph Bonaparte on the Spanish throne in 1808, civil war broke out. Many people remained loyal to Carlos IV, who was a captive of Napoleon, and to his son Fernando VII, in whose favor the king had abdicated. Nevertheless, preliminary steps toward independence were taken in Argentina, Chile, Venezuela, and Mexico.

Miguel Hidalgo, a parish priest in Dolores, Mexico, led the first revolt in New Spain in 1810. Instilled with French ideas of natural rights, and inspired by the success of the American Revolution, Hidalgo organized a band largely of Indian peasants and abortively attempted to overthrow the Spanish regime. His initial thrust, begun by the Grito de Dolores at midnight of September 15–16, 1810, is celebrated in Mexico as Independence Day. Captured and executed in 1811, Hidalgo became a martyr to the cause of independence and a hero of the revolutionary struggle. Others then took up the fight in Central Mexico while Californians felt the effect of this preliminary protest indirectly. A decrease in supply ships from San Blas and the stopping of salaries to officials, soldiers, and missionaries forced them to rely upon their own produce, illegal trade, and assistance from the existing missions.

THE EARLY YEARS: 1810–1811

The people in the region of Sonora and Arizona remained relatively isolated from information about outside events and, like California, the area was not caught up in the developments leading to the Mexican independence movement of 1810. The Grito de

Dolores shocked the civil, military, and religious authorities of Sonora and Sinaloa, and they moved quickly to affirm their loyalties to the Spanish crown, as well as to encourage others within their jurisdictions to oppose the revolt. Had it not been for the presence of the presidios in their midst, the Hispanic residents of southern Arizona might have escaped the independence movement altogether, since most of the fighting took place between Guanajuato and Guadalajara in central Mexico. As it was, however, the soldiers of the presidial garrisons were among the most experienced troops Spain could call upon, and these units were deemed of critical importance in putting down the revolt. Alejo García Conde, the 59-year-old intendant-governor of Sonora and Sinaloa when the rebellion began, was the same man who had assisted the Pimas and Pápagos of Tumacácori in obtaining title to their lands a few years before.

Noting the early successes of Hidalgo's followers in central Mexico, García Conde took steps to keep the rebellion from spreading into areas under his jurisdiction. He chose Lieutenant Colonel Pedro Sebastián de Villaescusa, commandant at Buenavista, to lead the first contingent of troops southward. In the years following his service at Tubac, Villaescusa had moved slowly up the ranks, while acquiring considerable fame as an Indian fighter. By 1794, he had been wounded several times. Villaescusa's forces consisted primarily of troops from his own post, but soldiers from both Tucson and Altar were included. The orders from García Conde called for the Sonorans to take up positions in the plaza of the important Sinaloa mining town of El Rosario, where they were to await the arrival of an insurgent army headed northward from Guadalajara.

Leader of the revolutionary force for campaigns in Sinaloa and Sonora was José María González de Hermosillo, a native of Jalisco, to whom Father Hidalgo had given the rank of lieutenant colonel. (The town of Pitic was renamed for him in 1828.) He set out from Guadalajara on December 1, 1810, with a small force. By the time the insurgents reached El Rosario, their army had increased to several thousand. Heavily outnumbered, Villaescusa was unable to defend the plaza, which fell to the insurgents before the end of the first day of battle. The Sonoran commander himself was captured, but González de Hermosillo allowed him his freedom, along with a small escort, and promised him safe conduct in returning to his home. Villaescusa took advantage of this situation by dispatching messengers to García Conde to inform him of the defeat and request reinforcements. Convinced that the situation was more serious than he had first thought, García Conde decided to assume personal command of the presidial forces. Ordering several units southward to slow the advance of González de Hermosillo, García Conde assembled the remaining forces and began his march.

Toward the end of the first week of February 1811, García Conde reached a spot on the outskirts of the Sinaloan town of San Ignacio Piaxtla. Villaescusa had arrived there earlier and had taken up a defensive position opposite the troops of González de Hermosillo, which were deployed on the other side of town. The soldiers under Villaescusa's command included a few who had been with him at El Rosario, but most were reinforcements from the presidios sent ahead by García Conde. Sharing the direction of the Royalist forces with Villaescusa was Captain Manuel Ignacio Arvizu who, following his service on the southern front, would become the commandant of the Tucson presidio. In command of the Royalist artillery under Arvizu's direction was

Antonio Leyva, ensign of the Tucson post. García Conde arrived on February 5, and after taking a quick look at the situation decided to initiate a major offensive against the enemy troops and chose the morning of February 9 for the attack. Meanwhile, however, González de Hermosillo was making similar plans. Perhaps aware of García Conde's intentions, the insurgent leader decided to send his forces into action on the morning of the 8th.

González de Hermosillo might have been better off to wait, as he was disastrously defeated. More than 500 were killed, and the number of wounded exceeded 1,000. The survivors fled in disorder. Contributing importantly to the Royalist victory were Opata soldiers from Sonora who ambushed 400 of the rebels. In March 1811, just a month after the Battle of San Ignacio, Father Miguel Hidalgo was captured and brought before a military court that ordered his execution. One member of that court was Captain Simon Elías González, then commander of military forces at the Villa de Chihuahua that, a few years before, had served in the garrisons of both Tucson and Tubac. On July 31, 1811, Father Hidalgo was put to death in Chihuahua, yet despite his execution and the defeat suffered by González de Hermosillo, the revolutionary effort continued. Leadership of the movement was assumed now by Father José María Morelos in the area of Chilpancingo.

CORTES OF CÁDIZ, 1812–1813

As noted, many colonials remained loyal to Carlos IV, who had abdicated the throne in 1808, and in turn delegated his power to his exiled son Fernando VII after the French invasion. During this period, Spanish-American delegates participated in the *cortes* of Cádiz, helping to adopt the liberal Constitution of 1812 which was to be effective when the French were driven out. In 1813, the cortes also decreed that certain of the pueblo and mission lands of the New World would be reduced to private property, and provided for the conversion of missions into civil pueblos. When the French were finally driven out of Spain in 1814, and Fernando VII assumed the throne in May, the liberal gains made in favor of the Americas were discontinued. The new king unfortunately proceeded to undo most of what the forward-thinking cortes had done, thereby adding fuel to the already smoldering revolutionary fires overseas. Movements toward independence were rekindled not only in Mexico but in South America. When Father Morelos was captured and executed by Royalist forces in 1815, lesser leaders did take his place, but the country was tranquil for the next several years.

The troubled years of war, first the United States–British War of 1812, which ended in the Treaty of Ghent of 1815, and the Greater American Revolution that swept Spain's colonial empire between 1810 and 1822, created uncertainty in the Spanish Southwest. The socio-political composition of the area, coupled with long decades of isolation, created no great enthusiasm for political independence from the mother country of Spain. To the contrary, the area had always been under the leadership of military governors and ministered to by Franciscan priests, with both groups professing and demonstrating loyalty to the nation that had placed them there and paid their salaries. As distant frontier provinces, New Mexico, Arizona, and California had little contact with new ideas of democracy, but were rather comfortable under the paternalistic system of nearly absolute monarchy. As a result, there were no stirrings of revolt from within, and only very limited contact from outside.

New Mexico's Isolation

During the period of independence movements that swept the heart of New Spain, New Mexico was largely neglected, since its adherence to or separation from Spain was of no concern to either the loyalists or the insurgents. It was during this period that one of the scions of an important New Mexico family had the chance to make his mark in the world. He was Pedro Bautista Pino, New Mexico's delegate to the outside world and more specifically to the liberal Spanish government that had permitted colonial representation. His story is summarized as follows:

> *After being elected to the Spanish Cortes, which occurred about the year 1810, in company with his private secretary and one or two other persons, he took passage through the port of Vera Cruz, Mexico, for Madrid [really Cádiz], Spain. He was absent from home about three years; and on his leisurely return he "took in" Paris and London, sojourning several weeks in each of these great capitals. At the English metropolis he purchased a very costly landau [a four wheeled carriage] which he brought home through the port from which he sailed. He continued to use this beautiful carriage for many years, and frequently invited his friends to share it with him; no one being so poor as to be refused when a seat was vacant. Of what Don Pedro accomplished for his constituents while abroad, but little could then be said. Soon after his return home some one, of a happy turn of mind, hit upon a rather pleasing little couplet that might be said to contain the whole history of his doings as a Cortezian, as far as known at that time:*
> 　　*Don Pedro Pino fué:*
> 　　*Don Pedro Pino vino.* (Carroll and Haggard, eds., *Three New Mexico Chronicles*, p. xix)

The meaning was clear, Pino had gone and he had returned, that was all that he had accomplished, but the ditty was heard repeated over the next twenty years at least. But Pedro Pino did not mind, he was the richest and about the most respected man in New Mexico. While in Spain he had contributed to the literature of his province by writing a forty-eight-page booklet published in Cádiz in 1812 entitled *Exposición sucinta y sencilla de la provincia del Nuevo México: Hecha por su diputado en cortes ... con arreglo a sus instrucciones*. It is clear that Pedro Pino was not a great asset as a representative, but there is no reason to believe that he failed to try.

New Mexico traders, 1812

The year 1812 brought to Santa Fe a trio of traders, James Baird, Samuel Chambers, and Robert McKnight, who arrived with a substantial amount of merchandise for sale. They felt that the revolt led by Father Miguel Hidalgo at Dolores might have loosened trade restrictions concerning New Mexico. They were wrong. They were jailed and spent nine years in prison in Santa Fe and were not released until after the success of Agustín Iturbide and the implementation of his Plan of Iguala, which made Mexico independent in 1821. With that the Spanish period was over, but the trio's case is representative of the severe punishment meted out to some unsuccessful illegal traders, even late in the colonial period.

CHOUTEAU-DEMUN VENTURE, 1815

Another notable attempt to open trade with Mexico was one in which Auguste P. Chouteau was involved in association with Julius Demun. The former, a Frenchman who had become a U.S. citizen, was a nephew of the famous Auguste Chouteau, one of the founders of St. Louis. Demun was the brother of the secretary of the French Legation in Washington, D.C. Their trade approach to New Mexico was tentative, beginning in 1815 when they obtained merchandise, provisions, munitions, and suitable equipment to engage in commerce with the Indians. This effort brought them to the upper waters of the Arkansas River in what is now Colorado, but what was then felt by New Mexicans to be part of their province. From there Demun went to Taos and on to Santa Fe where he talked with Governor Alberto Maynez, motivating his return with Chouteau to New Mexico the following year. When they did, to their surprise they were greeted with suspicion by a new governor (Allande), who being uncertain of their intentions ordered them to leave. They then went back to the Arkansas River area, from which point Demun was on the verge of departing to St. Louis with a valuable collection of furs, when both he and his partner were arrested by Sergeant Mariano Bernal, sent out by the Spanish governor to detain the fur traders as poachers.

While awaiting trial in Santa Fe, Chouteau and Demun were confined for forty-eight days on the charge that they had failed to leave New Mexico as previously ordered. As a result of their trial they were again ordered out of the province and were permitted to take with them only their horses and weapons, leaving behind their large harvest of furs. But being men of political connections in their home country, they sought recompense for their losses, basing their claim on the fact that they had a license from the governor of Missouri to trade and hunt for furs and that the New Mexican governor's seizure had been a breach of international law. Their claim was at first rejected, because private claims for damages were not included as part of the 1819 Adams-Onis treaty between Spain and the United States that had settled the boundary between the two nations. Demun and Chouteau continued to press their claim despite the change of sovereignty that made the area part of Mexico. Finally, in 1851 a claims payment was made, after a hearing before a United States commission, but the original petitioners did not benefit. By then the two men were dead and their heirs became the beneficiaries.

BOUCHARD EXPEDITION, 1818

California also remained relatively isolated from events taking place in central Mexico. The uprisings of Hidalgo and Morelos merely meant a slowdown in supply ships and a lack of pay for soldiers. Finally, two ships of the "patriots navy of Argentina" carried out an unexpected attack on California in 1818. The *Argentina* was commanded by Frenchman Hipólito de Bouchard, a hero of the Argentine cause for independence, and the smaller *Santa Rosa* by Peter Corney, an English veteran of the California fur trade picked up by Bouchard in Hawaii. The "navy" consisted of some 350 revolution-aries, a mixture of Malaysians, Portuguese, Spaniards, Hawaiians, Australians, and En-glishmen hoping to profit from the dissolution of the Spanish empire. Bouchard had letters of marque from José de San Martin, liberator of Chile, to blockade Spanish ships off the South American coast. Broadly interpreting his powers, the erstwhile French-man headed for Hawaii to recruit volunteers and then sail to California. Stopping briefly at Fort Ross for provisions, Bouchard's men launched an attack against Monterey late in October 1818. The *Santa Rosa* entered the harbor first and demanded supplies from Governor Solá, who refused. Corney's crew then opened fire on the presidio and re-ceived a brisk return volley. Second officer Joseph Chapman and two sailors went ashore to arrange a truce, but were taken prisoners. Bouchard moved in with the *Argentina* and the presidio's forty soldiers were no match for the combined forces of both ships. Solá refused to surrender and, gathering up the provincial archives and some ammunition, ordered a withdrawal to the royal stock-farm near present-day Salinas. The privateers sacked and burned the town of Monterey, destroying even the orchards and gardens.

The ships sailed southward to Rancho del Refugio which was owned by José Ortega, a resident of California since 1769. A force from the Santa Barbara presidio under Sargent Carlos Antonio Carrillo intercepted the revolutionaries and lassoed three of Bouchard's men. According to Corney they burned Ortega's rancho in revenge and then headed for Santa Barbara, where Bouchard agreed to spare the presidio in exchange for the prisoners. Commandant José de la Guerra y Noriega received a rebuke from Gover-nor Solá for having negotiated with "pirates." Anchoring next in the cove sheltered by today's Dana Point, Bouchard moved against San Juan Capistrano.

The Spaniards at the mission refused Bouchard's request for provisions, offering instead a supply of powder and shot. Unhappy with the compromise, the attackers pillaged the town, seizing provisions and a large supply of wine. José de la Guerra, protesting his alleged mishandling of affairs at Santa Barbara, soon arrived with rein-forcements from Los Angeles and drove off the revolutionaries. San Diego hustled its women and children off to the inland sub-mission of San Antonio de Pala and mar-shaled its defenses, but Bouchard bypassed the southern port. Leaving the Californias, he returned to South America and became commander of the Peruvian navy. After indepen-dence he received a cocoa and spice plantation in Peru, and was finally killed by a rebellion of his own slaves in 1837. California played no further role in the war for independence except to complain about its exposed position. It finally received reinforcements consist-ing of two companies of largely unsatisfactory troops sent by a reluctant viceroy.

DIFFICULTIES ON THE FRONTIER, 1818

Troops from Tucson and Tubac were tied up in the south until about 1818, leaving the frontier area unprotected. Tucson-born Ignacio Zuñiga, writing in 1835, asserted that the beginning of the Mexican independence movement sounded the death knell of the Apache peace settlements created around the presidios by the Indian policy initi-ated in 1786. Transfer of troops to the south, plus the drain on the Royal Treasury to fight the insurgents, set in motion a chain of conditions and events that weakened the capacity of the frontier forts to subjugate and control the hostile Indians. The impact of these developments was slow, however, in reaching its full effect on Tucson and Tubac. While Apache raids and forays against the raiders continued to be regular events for the troopers between 1812 and 1820, these were small-scale affairs compared with those of thirty years before. The sacramental registers do not assign the Apaches responsibility for many deaths, Hispanic or Indian, during this period. The fact that the *establecimientos de paz* were still functioning institutions in La Pimería Alta at the close of the colonial era is demonstrated to some extent by the decision of Pinal Apache chief Chilitipage and seventy-eight of his followers to settle near the Tucson post early in 1819. Because of the enmity between members of this Pinal band and other Apaches already at the post, Antonio Narbona, overall military commander for Sonora, arranged to transfer some of the original group to Santa Cruz.

More deadly than the Apaches in the early years of the nineteenth century were epidemics that continued to sweep through the area. Father Narciso Gutiérrez of Tumacácori buried twenty-five Indians from his jurisdiction during the final two months of 1816, fifteen of them children. The pestilence had struck first at San Ignacio in August, then spread northward. Its impact was probably heavy among the Indians of Tucson and San Xavier, as well as among those at Tumacácori; the Native American population at those locations declined by 209 between 1804 and 1818. The vecinos fared somewhat better than the mission Indians in maintaining their numbers during the final two decades of Spanish control over southern Arizona. Father Arriquibar's 1797 census of Tucson included seventy-nine civilians counting children; in 1819 the total was sixty-eight. At Tumacácori Father Gutiérrez reported seventy-five vecinos in 1820, compared with eighty-two counted by the same priest sixteen years before. The relative peace that prevailed on the northern frontier in the early 1800s gave rise to some increase of the vecino population in mining and ranching areas away from the presidios and missions.

SANTA FE TRADE

The last full year of declining Spanish power was 1821, which also marks the real beginning of the organized Santa Fe Trade. Thomas James and John McKnight (brother of the incarcerated Robert) arrived in Santa Fe with inferior merchandise, but with great hope of trade stimulated by a national economic panic that had been plaguing the United States since 1819. James was not well impressed with New Mexico but was pleased with his substantial profits. Converging on Santa Fe almost simultaneously were Hugh Glenn and Jacob Fowler who had left Glenn's Ferry on the lower Arkansas River, which they followed northwestward, crossing the Rockies and descending the Río Grande. In New Mexico commerce was lively and they sold all of their goods at a handsome profit.

William Becknell, 1821–1822

An American trader, William Becknell of Franklin, Missouri, also set out westward in 1821 with the intention of bartering with the Plains Indians. Instead, he made a significant detour southward and entered New Mexico via Raton Pass. In exchange for his merchandise, he obtained a load of silver pesos, returning to the United States where he was welcomed with enthusiasm. Up to this point, all trade had been carried out on pack animals, but Becknell's success led to another much more highly organized effort utilizing covered wagons which he and Braxton Cooper led in 1822. By that time, the traders were received by authorities representing a new sovereign—Mexico.

One overall effect of the newly established trading orientation was to extend, via the ancient Chihuahua trade trail, the impact on northern Mexico of United States trade goods. For Santa Fe it was a blessing by making it an essential entrepot for collection and dispersal of goods. In its new position as a middleman, New Mexico shared in profits rather then being the focal point of an exploitative system that had been long in effect.

SPAIN'S DEPARTURE FROM THE SOUTHWEST

Spain's departure from the Spanish Southwest was not merely a changing of the guard. It involved far more than simply lowering Spain's red and yellow flag with castles and lions and raising a new green and white Mexican emblem with an eagle and a serpent. Some who participated in the transfer of sovereignty, and many who were absent, were not convinced that this was the end of the colonial period. There was feeling among the committed royalists that this was just a temporary setback and that Spain would recover its empire following a restoration of a fully stable monarchy in the homeland. The great changes that had resulted from Napoleon's strong military conquest were viewed as a passing phase. Others did not know much of European matters, but were not convinced that being shorn of the mother country's protection was change for the good.

Lingering doubts about the political orientation of Spanish-American colonists probably triggered measures to ensure the political loyalty of the northern provinces, for certainly they had not contributed to the movement for independence. Many, perhaps most residents, had no reason for disloyalty to the crown and had compelling motives for adherence to old Spain. Some reasons were economic, because people's income derived from the king, some were sentimental, while others were based in fear of what change might bring. Texas, on the eastern flank of the Borderlands, was the area of greatest concern to the newly born nation, and it was the only province that saw even minimal action in the military uprising.

Certainly, the unexpected governmental change did not bring with it all of the advantages that had been hoped for by many, nor was it easy to implement the promises contained in the revolutionary Plan of Iguala with its democratic Three Guarantees: Independence, the Catholic faith, and racial equality.

AGUSTÍN ITURBIDE AND MEXICAN INDEPENDENCE

The opportunity for further strikes at independence presented itself with the appointment of Colonel Agustín de Iturbide as military commander of southern Mexico. Iturbide was born in Valladolid, Mexico (renamed Morelos), the son of a wealthy Basque merchant and a Creole mother. He fought against Hidalgo, but in 1815 was accused of wrongdoing in financial matters. A year later he retired from the army. Despite this poor record, Iturbide received the appointment to command the royalist forces.

From the very beginning, Iturbide seemed determined to gain the good will of his former adversary, the insurgent leader Vicente Guerrero. Guerrero was suspicious of his overtures, but finally agreed to meet with Iturbide when the royalist commander announced on February 24, 1821, his program for Mexican independence. Just a short time later, the two sides joined forces and by August the plans were complete. Iturbide rode into Mexico City as liberator on September 27, his 38th birthday. As it turned out, he did not last long in his position of power, and the troubles of an independent Mexico began. General Alejo García Conde agreed to uphold the Plan de Iguala on August 24, 1821, and remained with the frontier provinces until July 1, 1822, when he was transferred to Mexico City and was appointed inspector general of cavalry.

Within a few months, the same Agustín Iturbide, author of the statement of independence, set aside the new democracy and instead reinstituted a monarchy with himself as Agustín I, Emperor of Mexico. Officials in the northern borderlands were in a quandary. Should they wait for a possible third change? They found themselves required to swear allegiance to an entirely new form of government, even though conditions on the frontier did not really change rapidly. Iturbide sent to the north a personal representative and commissioner, Father Agustín Fernández de San Vicente, prebend of the cathedral of Durango, who went first to California and subsequently to New Mexico to begin facilitating changes that he feared might be difficult to institute.

Although there was no great evidence of unbridled enthusiasm, in neither area did opposition rear up, even though a few of the old Franciscans were unwilling to swear to a change that did away with control by their beloved Spain. One Franciscan refused to comply on the basis that the new government gave him the liberty to swear or not to swear and he chose the latter option. Though not everyone was overjoyed, the commissioner from the new Mexican government made one thing clear—no lingering loyalty to Spain would be tolerated. It did seem for a while that the Franciscan priests' leadership was safe in both New Mexico and California, but this influence was gradually whittled away. In time, major steps were taken toward the secularization of the California mission chain still administered by the priests of the College of San Fernando, and many felt that the exile of European-born priests from both areas was necessary.

The expulsion was not similar to the Jesuit expulsion from the Spanish colonies in 1768, and some elderly Franciscans on the basis of age held out against forced departure. But the mission lands, held by the Franciscans in trust for their Indian wards, became prime targets for usurpation and subsequent distribution to democratic, patriotic, or merely covetous aspirants. When turned over to secular administration and with some of the land distributed to the Indians, there would be less need for regular priests accompanied by their diminished control over former Indian charges. Meanwhile, Mexico fluctuated between a poorly understood democracy and an oligarchy of wealthy landholders supported by the military powers that had brought independence to fruition. Those residents who held title to land under the prior sovereignty of Spain suffered no losses as a result of the successful outcome of the war for independence.

CALIFORNIA: YEARS OF TRANSITION

The success of settlement in Alta California had been the final burst of glory in Spain's efforts to settle the Pacific coast of North America. Missions had reached the height of their productivity, retired soldiers were developing vast private ranchos, and civilian towns were slowly taking shape. Ironically, even though the mother country had paid scant attention to the province after 1810, California's location on the sea had insured its economic survival. Sustained for a decade by illegal maritime trade, commerce with non-Mexican vessels became legal under the new government and would become a significant factor in California's future. Nevertheless, some Californios had misgivings. Father José Señán at Mission San Buenaventura even asked God that foreigners not take too much of a liking to the province.

But foreigners did take a liking to the province, entering California first by sea and later by overland trails from the United States. At the time of Mexican independence from Spain, there were approximately 3,500 persons of Hispanic descent (two-thirds of whom were women and children), 20 foreigners, 20,000 mission Indians, and perhaps another 100,000 Indians living throughout the province. During the twenty-five year span of Mexican control, the non-Indian population of California increased from about 3,500 to some 14,000—but significantly most of the newcomers were foreigners, so that in 1846 only about 7,000 were Spanish-speaking.

The other 7,000 consisted primarily of Americans who entered California first as individual traders and then, after 1841, as members of organized immigrant wagon trains that arrived yearly. When Mexico became involved in a war with the United States in 1846, these Americans were naturally sympathetic to the cause of their own country and worked with some success to win the native Californios over to the American cause. They pointed to the political turmoil characteristic of the Mexican regime in California and praised the benefits of becoming a part of the expanding and progressive United States. They criticized the autocratic methods of Mexico's central government on the one hand, and commented on the lack of effective support and control on the other.

Foreign Immigrants

California's Mexican citizenry generally liked and accepted the early foreign immigrants—a composite group including men of American, British, French, German, and other nationalities—who married the Spanish-speaking daughters of local families and participated in the economic, social, and political life of the province. In 1830 about 120 foreigners lived in California, reaching 380 by 1840. Not until the Americans arrived in large wagon trains, with their own families, did the Californios mistrust and resent their intrusion, although even then the first "*yanqui rancheros*" softened the blow of United States infiltration and conquest.

Some writers have minimized the importance of Mexico's influence over California during the years from 1822 to 1846, commenting as did historian Charles Chapman in 1921 that "strictly speaking, there was no Mexican period in California history." (*History of California*, p. 455) Although American economic influence was indeed strong under the Mexican regime, Mexico's role in directing provincial affairs cannot be dismissed lightly. Problems of distance continued to prevent close communication and supervision, but California suffered no lack of administrative personnel, official directives, nor legislative pronouncements emanating from Mexico City. In addition, Mexican colonization laws of 1824 and 1828 allowed for a strictly Hispanic pattern of settlement and set California's development apart from territories of the United States. The

Mexican government in California essentially continued to operate under laws of the liberal Spanish cortes of 1813, modified slightly by ideas of self-rule espoused during the movement for independence. The result was a period of experiment frequently accompanied by turmoil, but a period nevertheless Mexican.

Transfer of Loyalty

Upon swearing allegiance to Mexico in April 1822, ex-Spanish Governor Pablo Vicente de Solá and his advisory junta devised procedures for electing California's representative to the new Mexican congress. The electors, chosen from pueblo settlers and mission neophytes—soldiers and priests were excluded from candidacy—decided in favor of former Governor Solá. Before Solá could depart, however, special envoy Agustín Fernández de San Vicente arrived in Monterey in 1822 to supervise the changeover to Mexican rule. Fernández, a jovial card-playing priest, was able to win over the decidedly loyalist Spanish clergy. Tactfully, but with an appropriate flourish, he substituted the eagle of Mexico for the lion of Castile. He proclaimed the rule of Iturbide, now Agustín I of the Mexican empire, and called for the organization of a six-member provincial legislature called the *diputación territorial*. The demise of Spain's control was clear when Father Fernández overturned the all-but-certain election of Spanish-born José de la Guerra y Noriega to the governorship and ensured the election of Luis Argüello, a native-born military leader. Inconsistent with this surprising move was the naming of the outgoing Spanish governor, Pablo Vicente de Solá, as representative from California to the Mexican legislature, possibly because he was a known liberal.

Fernández had included the Russians on his itinerary so he quickly traveled northward to Fort Ross. Initiating an agreement with the Russian American Fur Company to hunt otter on shares, he finally approved a contract on January 1, 1823, whereby the English firm of McCulloch, Hartnell and Company would purchase, for three years at a stipulated price, all the hides and tallow of the province. Fernández then toured California and, amid many toasts to the new republic, repeated the transfer ceremony. Juana Machado, the young daughter of San Diego presidial soldier José Manuel Machado, later recalled the change of flag in Alta California's southernmost settlement with vivid detail:

> There came from the north (I do not recall whether by sea or land) a prebendary [canon] called Don Valentín [sic] Fernández de San Vicente, who brought with him a chaplain or secretary. ... The prebendary wore a garment of a color resembling red. This gentleman was the agent of the Mexican empire to establish here the new order of things. I well recall that when some woman or girl, excited by the richness and the colors of his dress, which were really very showy and handsome, would ask, "Who is this gentleman?" someone would answer, "The prebendary." (Brandes, ed., "Diary of Juana Machado," pp. 201–2)

Juana continued to explain that the infantry, cavalry, and a few artillery troops were ordered to form in the plaza of the presidio. They placed the cannon outside the plaza pointing toward the ocean and waited for the flag raising.

THE PUEBLOS IN NEW MEXICO

Once Mexico had proclaimed its government, far-off residents of the Spanish Southwest scarcely heard the rumblings of change, which seemed hardly more than a murmur. The structure of government did not change greatly in New Mexico; a governor still ruled with a strong hand, while locally recruited military forces supported by Indian auxiliaries protected the province from possible outside attack. Town-dwelling Indians, mostly Pueblos, continued to live on their traditional tribal lands, although they began to feel increased pressure from non-Indians who were seeking land grants, concessions of land that were much larger in the Mexican period than they had ever been in the Spanish era.

Fig. 13.1. Portrait of Juana Machado de Wrightington, circa 1860. Courtesy Ray Brandes.

ARIZONA: THE FINAL YEARS OF INDEPENDENCE

The war for independence took an unusual turn in the Arizona area when a group of officers in Spain on January 1, '1820, proclaimed the liberal constitution, which had been approved by the cortes in 1812, to be in effect. When the church learned that it was facing a serious attack on its privileges and possessions, the high ecclesiastical authorities in New Spain thought that the church might save itself by aiding the establishment of an independent Mexico. An alliance with the army, or part of it, might allow them to accomplish their goal. Nevertheless, the transition from Spanish to Mexican nationality did not affect the Arizona region uniformly. The people on the frontier were only vaguely aware of the struggle for independence and did not begin to feel the effects until conditions began to deteriorate. Some of the Spanish officials in Arizona simply took the oath of allegiance to the new government and continued in office throughout the first part of the Mexican period. Civil government and institutions did not change. Local alcaldes continued throughout the state of which Arizona was a part and the presidial soldiers stayed at their posts. Their pay, supplies and equipment, however, soon became inadequate to fight off the reopened hostility of the Apaches.

Apache Raids Resurface

Even though the missionaries criticized the military policy instituted by Viceroy Bernardo de Gálvez during the late 1780s, it produced results. From 1790 to 1820, the Apaches were generally at peace, and settlers began to locate in and near Tubac and Tucson. By the end of the Spanish period, Ignacio Pérez was running large herds of cattle, and other settlers had received grants of land for grazing. Several thousand head of cattle, sheep, and horses plus crops of corn, beans, wheat, and vegetables were found throughout the area. Mining activities and extended farming around Tubac and Tucson increased as the Mexican era began.

Unfortunately, ten years after Mexican independence, the Apaches once more began their depredations. They attacked Calabazas, where they burned buildings, and raided the San Pedro Ranch, stealing large numbers of livestock. Tucson alcalde Francisco Ortega indicated that the Tucsonenses were ready to aid in defending the frontier. Among those volunteering to campaign against the Apaches were brothers Teodoro, Antonio, and Pedro Ramírez, the latter two having served as presidial soldiers. Former alcaldes Juan Romero and José Leon also offered their services as did residents José Herreras, Clemente Telles, and Saturnino Castro. In all, twenty-eight settlers plus twenty Pimas from the Tucson pueblito and eighteen from San Xavier del Bac agreed to campaign against the hostile Indians.

MEXICAN CONGRESS OF 1823

The national congress that assembled in Mexico following independence favored a republican form of government and deposed "Emperor" Agustín I on March 19, 1823. Iturbide went into exile but returned the following year only to be promptly executed. Delegates from throughout Mexico met in the fall of 1823 to adopt a new form of government. In November, Argüello's government in Monterey recognized the new Mexican congress and, pending the arrival of some plan of federation including California, devised a local system of government. A national charter—Acta Constitutiva— approved on January 31, 1824, became a part of the Federal Constitution of the United States of Mexico on October 4, 1824. Under the new liberal-federalist constitution, made effective in 1825, Alta and Baja California, lacking sufficient population for statehood, became territories entitled severally or jointly to a governor, and severally to a legislature and a non-voting delegate to the Mexican congress. A special advisory council called the Board of Development for the Californias functioned from 1825 until the end of 1827; several of its numerous recommendations and measures were eventually put into effect in the territories.

California's government was divided between two theoretically independent officers—the *comandante general* in charge of military affairs and the *jefe político* who served as civil governor. The elected representatives—*diputados*—of the various presidial and pueblo districts were advisers to the civil governor rather than legislators. These diputados ratified the Mexican Constitution of 1824.

Colonization Act of 1824

An important piece of legislation enacted by the new Mexican government was the Colonization Act of August 18, 1824. In order to populate distant provinces such as California, New Mexico, and Texas, the act appealed to foreign immigration, offering those who became Mexican citizens up to a total of eleven square leagues of free land: one square league that could be considered irrigable, four for dry farming, and six for grazing. The land could not be within twenty leagues of an international boundary nor within ten leagues of the coast. Although native Mexican citizens, especially veterans, received preference in the distribution of land, the act specified that foreigners who met citizenship requirements were to be given equal treatment. An additional colonization act of 1828 supplemented the decree of 1824 by outlining proper procedures for obtaining a grant through the governor of the respective territory. Allocations were to be approved by the territorial *diputación,* or by the Mexican congress in the case of colonization grants to *empresarios* for the settlement of many families. These new decrees led to a tremendous increase in the number of private ranchos granted, especially in California.

Expulsion of the Spaniards, 1828

Because Spain refused to recognize an independent Mexico, there were rumors that Fernando VII might try to reclaim it. An order was issued in Concepción de Alamos by the governor of the state of Occidente José María Gaxiola on February 15, 1828, expelling "all those serving in the militia of the Spanish government in the year 1821, who have not decided to lend the same service to our cause of Independence, will leave the territory of the State, in the precise and decisive term of thirty days counted from the publication of this law in the respective municipalities." (Ms., Arizona Historical Society, Tucson) Also covered under the law were "Spaniards of whatever class, state and conditions, notoriously opposed to independence and the present form of government" and "all the Spaniards who have obtained from the state any form of public, civil or ecclesiastic employment." (Ms., Arizona Historical Society, Tucson) Therefore, the Spanish-born missionaries had to go.

Captain Pedro Villaescusa of Tucson informed Father Ramón Liberos of Tumacácori that he had three days in which to get the affairs of the mission in order. He named Ramón Pamplona, half Pápago and half Yaqui Indian born at the mission in 1785, as administrator; Pamplona had been one of the representatives with the land grant delegation in 1806. During the second week in April 1828, the last resident friar left Tumacácori. The church was nearly finished, but now it would begin a downhill slide to abandonment and decay. Only four native-born priests were left in La Pimería Alta: José Pérez Llera at San Ignacio, Faustino Gonzáles at Caborca, Juan Maldonado for Oquitoa and Tubutama, and Rafael Díaz at Cocospera. Díaz was also charged with looking after Tumacácori, San Xavier, and the presidios of Santa Cruz, Tubac, and Tucson. The years following were marked by dissension, difficulty, and decline.

CONDITION OF THE MISSIONS

Two reports in 1843 summarize the condition of the missions in that year. The Tubac justice of the peace noted that the Tumacácori church was in a good state of repair but that portions of the adjacent convent, built in 1821, were falling down. The mission fields were overgrown with mesquite trees and other scrubby vegetation, and the one lying most distant from the village was visited only occasionally by a few Indians who went there to irrigate small plots. None of the fields was being rented to outsiders and none had been sold. The Calabazas pastures and fields were abandoned, as were those at Guevavi and Sonoita. Only wild livestock grazed on the hillsides.

The situation at San Xavier del Bac was not much better. The church was still in good condition, although the arches were fissured and weather-beaten from the heavy rains of summer and the steady drizzle of winter. The humidity had caused the paint to deteriorate, and the Tucson justice of the peace expressed concern that if no priests were appointed to supervise repairs, the ruin of the church was imminent. The convent was already being destroyed. In two of the rooms, the galleries had collapsed, roof beams were broken, and the matting over the beams was rotting away. The wall surrounding the priest's orchard and garden had fallen away, and the fruit trees were no longer bearing. The San Xavier governor was cultivating a part of the garden and only about one-eighth of the acreage previously devoted to growing crops was being used. The report blames Father Díaz, who had died a short time before, for neglecting the church and other buildings and for carrying away some of the furnishings. A few Indians remained at El Pueblito, and the mission fields were being cultivated by six Indians, the only ones still left.

HIDE AND TALLOW TRADERS IN CALIFORNIA

The priests at the California missions remained at their posts. In fact, one final mission—San Francisco Solano—was founded in 1823 under Mexico as a protective barrier against Russian encroachment. The cattle industry continued to flourish throughout the area so that by the beginning of the Mexican period, Californians could not use all of the available hides. The missions and a few ranchos tanned a small amount of leather and cured rawhide for local use; they extracted tallow for soap and candle making. A few ships had gone back and forth between California and Lima, Peru during the Spanish period so that by the early 1820s, after independence, trade was well established. The first permanent foreign arrivals were Hugh McCulloch and William E. P. Hartnell, representatives of the English house of John Begg and Company, which had agents in Chile and Peru. With a small stock of goods from Lima, they sailed from Callao to California on the ship *John Begg* to open up trade with the missions.

The English had an early commercial advantage, although within a month after the arrival of McCulloch and Hartnell, the first American hide trader appeared. William Gale, resident agent for the Boston firm of Bryant and Sturgis and a veteran dealer in seal and otter furs, gave the English some competition despite their exclusive contract. Nevertheless, McCulloch and Hartnell traveled up and down the coast from mission to mission. By the spring of 1823, McCulloch sailed for South America with a shipload of hides, but competition from the Americans would continue to plague the company. After expiration of the original contract, the English advantage disappeared and New Englanders took up more than half the trade.

Hartnell eventually became a good friend of Father Luis Martínez of San Luis Obispo and simultaneously fell in love with Teresa de Jesús Guerra y Noriega, daughter of presidio commandant José de la Guerra of Santa Barbara. Hartnell was officially baptized into the Catholic church in October 1824, and married his sweetheart the following April. It was a huge wedding and Hartnell took his bride to Monterey where they settled down. Unfortunately, Hartnell, basically an intellectual, was never very successful as a trader or businessman.

Fig. 13.2. San Xavier del Bac. Photo by Iris Engstrand.

As new ships arrived from Boston, they paid port duties at Monterey if they wished to remain within the law, or took their chances at bribing customs officials. They brought furniture, cloth, ready-made clothing, and other welcome articles from the east in exchange for California products. Their agents went ashore and visited missions and ranchos to arrange for the purchase of hides and tallow. San Diego offered the best port for easy access of hides and became a popular depot for curing them. San Pedro, however, was difficult to approach, and sailors sometimes had to row some three miles into shore.

To the east, in New Mexico, the end of the Spanish period coincided with the dawn of United States commercial penetration, reflected by the Santa Fe Trade with its laden wagons and its widespread influence. The trail, which was considerably less than a clearly marked highway, became a land bridge between the sparsely populated western frontier of the United States and the even more sparsely settled northern outposts of Mexico. Both the Boston maritime commerce and the Santa Fe Trade created a significant economic interdependency, one that weakened the Mexican connection and increased an alien orientation.

In California this foreign activity resulted in gradual settlement there of U.S. (and other) merchants who married into prominent Californio families, and soon became permanent local residents and progenitors of important families. They became hispanicized socially and sometimes culturally, but seldom economically, as most held on to the New England work and profit ethic that had propelled them to California in the first place. Those who came to New Mexico also reaped the benefits of intermarriage and establishment of entrepreneurial enterprises, but the shorter distance of immigration gave opportunity for some to bring their families. Conversely, St. Louis, origin of highly prized merchandise, became a place to which bicultural families sent their

Fig. 13.3. Sketch of Mission San Luis Rey de Francia made during the visit of French trader Auguste Bernard du Haut-Cilly in 1827.

children to seek greater educational opportunities than New Mexico or even the rest of the Mexican nation offered. Because of its isolation, Arizona experienced fewer changes during this period.

In New Mexico the early local impact of Manifest Destiny was largely positive. Benefits included a greater supply of trade goods, an outlet for local products, and a gradual transformation of the province to the position of middleman rather than that of final consumer in a trade network that stretched from Missouri to Chihuahua and Durango. Even the once scarce hard money, silver pesos, came to Santa Fe, although they did not stay long before being transported to the insatiable commercial centers of Missouri. The losers in the new commercial network were those to the south and particularly the Mexican national government, nearly powerless to control the easily evaded regulations that resulted in unpaid customs duties and taxes.

THE MEXICAN-AMERICAN WAR

International questions in the Southwest were not easily solved. As diplomatic relations between Mexico and the United States worsened over the annexation of Texas and the location of the state's southern boundary, troops from both countries moved into the disputed area. Hostilities broke out in late April 1846, and on May 9, President Polk called for a declaration of war against Mexico. The war's immediate cause proved less important than the feeling among many Americans that the United States's Manifest Destiny called for occupation of the entire continent from coast to coast.

The War in New Mexico

Although the war would bring about significant changes, New Mexico was not a target area for American expansion. At most it was a secondary objective, one of minor concern. In fact, in New Mexico the threat of being taken over by the "Yankees" was not viewed with universal dread. Some residents must have viewed it as just another change, as was certainly the case in California. Others had their fears mollified by United States Army Brigadier General Stephen Watts Kearny's promise that the United States would respect the persons and property of the conquered area, and that the inhabitants would be granted immediate citizenship in the invading nation. More reassuring was the willingness of the U.S. Army to pay for supplies requisitioned by the invasion forces. Even though Kearny as conqueror had no authority either in international law or under martial law to make such sweeping guarantees, he did have the authority to institute a rather mild occupation policy, one which had little negative economic impact. If anything, it made entry of goods even freer, as they could simply accompany the military invasion, and at the same time could leave the territory with U.S. traders that had come as part of the invasion force.

Kearny's promises of respect for Mexican rights, coupled with the subsequent terms of the peace treaty signed at Guadalupe Hidalgo in 1848, left open to peaceful New Mexican residents a citizenship option. Under the Mexican leadership of Guadalupe Miranda, a resident of long standing, those who wanted to preserve their Mexican citizenship were permitted to recolonize downstream on the Río Grande around Mesilla near Las Cruces, which was then part of Mexico. Some families availed themselves of the removal offer, not wishing to lose their national identity, but most local residents felt a closer allegiance to their *patria chica*, the limited area to which they had a long-standing attachment. Those who did change their area of residence shortly thereafter found that the Mexican national domain lands that they had been given underwent an unanticipated change of sovereignty. In an effort to clarify the elusive national boundary between Mexico and the United States and to ensure an easy access, all-weather route from the east to the rapidly developing area of California, the United States arranged with Mexico the Gadsden Purchase, including Mesilla, in 1853.

The War in Arizona

Arizona was little affected by the war between the United States and Mexico. In 1846 there were only two principal towns in the area: Tubac and Tucson, each with an army presidio. Since the work of the missionaries with the Pimas along the Gila, San Pedro, and Santa Cruz rivers had accustomed the Native Americans to foreign visitors, the military expeditions that crossed Arizona experienced few difficulties. The Arizona corridor established by the Spanish padres and Juan Bautista de Anza continued to be used by military men who crossed through it on their way to and from California. First, General José Castro, leader of Mexican resistance in California, crossed over into Sonora in 1846. Kit Carson followed in the same direction when he carried news about the war to the east. Shortly after the conquest of New Mexico, General Stephen Watts Kearny followed the Gila River trail to the Colorado junction and California. He was followed by the Mormon battalion under Lieutenant Colonel Philip St. George Cooke. The area of Arizona north of the Gila River became a part of the United States as a result of the Treaty of Guadalupe Hidalgo, ending the war with Mexico on February 2, 1848.

Post-War Arizona

The wagon route opened by the Mormon battalion was used immediately by the gold-seekers on their way to California in 1849. United States military men also used the Arizona corridor on different missions, but it was not until the 1853 Gadsden Purchase which brought the land south of the Gila River to its present boundary with Sonora, that any of those who traveled through Arizona remained to settle there. As part of the Pacific Railroad survey, southern Arizona was explored by Lieutenant A. W. Whipple and his party in 1853, acquainting more Americans with the area.

The long Hispanic period of Arizona came to an end in 1855 when the boundary commission determined the limits of Mexico and the United States. For another year, however, Tucson and that part of Arizona that had been settled by rancheros and farmers would still be under the protection of the Mexican garrison at the presidio in Tucson. Eight years after cessation of hostilities, in March 1856, Hilarion García withdrew the Mexican troops from Tucson, much to the unhappiness of American and Hispanic residents who were now left exposed to the threat of Apache raids. Not until November did the United States First Dragoons take over the presidio and raise the American flag over Tucson for the first time. Arizona, although peaceful in terms of European wars, was one of the most active in Indian warfare. The transition from Spain to Mexico was fairly smooth and occupation by the United States had only to wait until the international line was agreed upon and the Mexican garrison withdrawn.

The War in California

Although many Americans and other foreigners criticized California's progress under the Mexican regime, they did appreciate certain aspects of the area's slower-paced lifestyle and its rancho economy. The abundance of land had given rise to a pattern of activity that differed greatly from that of the bustling Northeast, and the temperate climate contrasted sharply with the harsh winters and hot summers of the Midwest, where pioneers struggled to build homes and cultivate the soil. The dominant Catholic faith, however, had evoked a prejudiced view from many Protestants who came in contact with former Spanish lands. After 1841 individual American travelers as well as wagon trains followed the trails to California. It became well known that the Mexican government allowed foreigners to apply for land grants, and opportunities for settlement existed near Sutter's Fort. Most of the new settlers made their homes in the areas near Sacramento and San Francisco. Lieutenant John Fremont of the United States Topographical Engineers happened to be traveling in California on a mapping expedition in the spring of 1846 when his presence near Sutter's Fort afforded him a pivotal role in the American takeover of California. Fremont supported a group of Americans who led an uprising in northern California against Mexican officials and declared the independence of "The Bear Flag Republic" in June 1846. Additional fighting in California was sporadic, and the Mexicans did their best to defend the province against combined military forces of the United States Navy, Army, and Marine Corps.

After a seemingly easy victory over native Californios, Kit Carson carried the news to General Stephen Watts Kearny's Army of the West on its thousand-mile march overland to California from Fort Leavenworth, Kansas. Kearny sent 200 of his 300 dragoons back to Santa Fe and proceeded optimistically along the southern route. Near present-day Escondido, California, he met the California lancers, who made a final effort to defend their ground at the Battle of San Pascual on December 6, 1846. The war in California ended with the Capitulation of Cahuenga agreed to by Mexican and American forces on January 13, 1847.

As mentioned, the Treaty of Guadalupe Hidalgo signed on February 2, 1848, promised perpetual peace between the United States and Mexico. Article V set the boundary line between the two countries, and Article VIII guaranteed the Mexican residents of California and other conquered territories the right to become U.S. citizens and to retain title to their land. Many of these people became citizens though not all obtained clear title.

THE FAR SOUTHWEST AFTER 1848

In California, statehood was quickly achieved. Several factors hastened the acceptance by the Thirty-First Congress of the thirty-first state, which broke the long-existing sectional balance between North and South and favored the North with admission of the Golden State as a free state. The immense population increase from the gold rush made California clamorous for inclusion as a full partner in the Union. And, when things were going unfavorably, California threatened to form a new nation, a Pacific Republic. Such a threat, impractical as it now seems, was in fact effective since the United States did not want to lose the great windfall of mineral wealth that the Mexican War had left. After mollifying the southern states by promising that the new territories would be organized without the prohibition of slavery, California was admitted to statehood on September 9, 1850.

The Territory of New Mexico had no such leverage; there was nothing that they could use to coerce the government to act. When statehood was delayed time after time, the opportunity for Hispanics to participate politically at any high level was minimized. Although there were many ascribed reasons for over sixty years' delay from conquest to final statehood, one of the most germane was the problem of assimilating a non-English-speaking population. Arizona, as part of New Mexico, was first made a part of Doña Ana County and later designated as the County of Arizona. After a long and difficult fight, Arizona achieved separate territorial status in 1863. Many residents of both New Mexico and Arizona continued to speak Spanish and maintain the laws and customs of their previous governments, especially in the sharing of scarce water resources. Even though the road to statehood was long and arduous, both New Mexico and Arizona were admitted to the union in 1912.

THE HISPANIC LEGACY IN NEW MEXICO

The Spanish legacy, strongest in New Mexico, was not merely a matter of accommodation. It is part of a dual heritage. This inheritance is frequently found in politics and in law, but there is also much evidence of it visible to the casual observer. Place-name geography, including names of towns, counties, streets, districts, shopping centers; plus geographical terminology: foods, celebrations, local dress, customs, and religious observances, continue to give testimony to the fact that Spanish settlers once walked those mesas and climbed those sierras, drank water from those rivers and springs, held rodeos and drove sheep up those arroyos, camped at the *parajes* (stopping places) negotiated La Bajada (the descent) between the Río Arriba and Río Abajo (the upper and lower reaches of the Río Grande), and placed an indelible stamp on the Land of Enchantment.

The richness of the Hispanic legacy makes New Mexico a unique area as the colors of colonial Spain were never truly erased. With the passage of time and an increasing awareness of the positive value of a mulitcultural society, the Hispanic past has increasingly enriched the present. Some of the many positive steps are evident in the Santa Fe building code that restricts the height of edifices and encourages a "Santa Fe" style; in the creation of a much visited Spanish Village at the State Fair; and in the development of a colonial period museum created by the Colonial New Mexico Historical Foundation at the Rancho de las Golondrinas southwest of Santa Fe. The museum is situated

Fig. 13.4. Carving of Santiago de Compostela (Matamoros). Carving by Max Roybal, Albuquerque.

along the Camino Real of yesterday and the Inter-American Highway of today. State-sponsored celebrations and cultural activities both preserve and add to a heritage that has long since passed the risk of oblivion.

The Spanish legacy gained some nostalgic favor in light of the neglect experienced during Mexico's sovereignty. Older people began to look back on the good old days of Spain's control. Any similar sentiment about Mexico was not evident after the transfer of sovereignty to the United States from Mexico. Spanish speakers in territorial New Mexico were more apt to recall the days of Spanish control, even when such feelings were based on events that they had not personally experienced, but instead had been passed down from their ancestors.

When finally with the passage of time, some things Spanish became considered economic assets, it was old Spain that often provided the model. Population increase was mostly locally generated. In California, the process was more greatly mixed; but in New Mexico, with its mountain enclaves where antiquated verb forms of old Spanish could still be heard, and in the little river valleys where the saints of Franciscan New Mexico were still active, the role model could be found in colonial Spain or even in its Iberian precedents.

Santeros, Bultos, and Retablos

It is felt that the emergence of the first religious folk artists in New Mexico dates from the third quarter of the eighteenth century. Their work followed the example of their more learned brethren as they copied directly from sophisticated models found in mission churches. In what seems to be an effort to meet demands created by a scarcity of statuary, most early work by folk artists was in the form of *bultos* (statues) rather that flat painting. Interesting evidence of this survival of older religious practices is found in

Fig. 13.5 Carving of Nuestra Señora de Guadalupe. Carving by Max Roybal, Albuquerque.

the *santero*, a carver of saints or religious figures, and his art. The santero, though he doubtless existed in the colonial period, came into prominence in the Mexican and territorial periods. His importance was proportionate to the decline of organized, authorized, supervised religion, and his fabricated images of saints were found in most rural and many urban households. Some *santos*, the name for santero art, were paintings of Jesus, Mary, or one of the saints, on a flat piece of wood, usually pine. This style of santo is called a *retablo*. Of greater frequency and merit were the saints carved in the round and painted usually with native earth pigments. They were called *bultos*. In all cases the art of the santero was primitive, appropriate to the frontier conditions that gave vitality to his work. Size and shape of santos varied greatly and proportion was of minimal importance. Cottonwood, as a result of its special characteristics, was almost always used, whether the root or the trunk of the tree or its branches.

The santero served the community as a quasi theologian, sometimes inventing traits of saints and at other times preserving through oral and iconographic tradition the customary attributes. Among the most frequently reproduced saints both in the past and today are what one might expect. Saints with rural orientation such as San Isidro Labrador (Saint Isidore the Husbandman) are often found, as is Santiago (Saint James) of close association with all of Spanish history. San Francisco (Saint Francis of Assisi), because of his affinity to nature and because in the colonial period New Mexico had been served exclusively by Franciscans, is often depicted. Other frequently carved saints are of San Antonio, patron saint of lost articles; the Santo Niño de Atocha, to protect travelers and prisoners, and Jesús of Nazareth.

The efficacy of these household santos, and of the santero who made them, was a matter of great importance. Santos were expected to respond favorably to the veneration in which they were held and to the fervency of family or individual prayers. Some santos, having been particularly responsive, were lent to neighbors, brought out on special occasions, and shown great respect. Saints failing to respond were punished by being turned to face the wall or being shut up in a closet. In extreme cases the Baby Jesus was taken from the arms of the Madonna until she became more responsive. The faith of many New Mexican people was often simple and direct.

During times when a special favor was to be requested, the image of a saint was set up in the main room of the house and neighbors and friends were invited to a night of prayer. This was (and is) called *velorio de santo*, night watch for a saint. At midnight refreshments were served to give the watch an element of celebration. In periods of water scarcity the image of the local patron saint was carried through the fields, a custom of long standing throughout the world. In New Mexico the santos most used in time of drought were San Isidro and Nuestra Señora de Guadalupe. This practice has produced a number of traditional tales, some borrowed from other Hispanic areas, and others developing locally as folk customs. In some cases, fragments of images were thrown into a field as an offering for an abundant harvest, or parts of an image were burned and the ashes used for the same purpose. Pieces of burned santos were also used in the ceremony for Ash Wednesday. Finally, when an image was broken or damaged beyond repair, it was completely burned and the ashes gathered for the purposes mentioned.

As for the santero, his acceptance by the faithful made him a subject of special concern, for not just anyone could become one. Artistic talent, at least in moderate degree, was required; but a virtuous life was a crucial asset, as was some notion of theology. As an art, the skill was often handed down from father to son. Even up to the present there are still a few santeros of the old style, and their pieces, made in the traditional colonial manner, are sought by collectors; genuine antique santos of the nineteenth century have taken on such great value that today most of them are museum pieces.

HISPANIC LIFE AND LEGACY IN ARIZONA

Anglo-Americans came to Arizona after 1848, but Hispanic culture did not disappear. Businessmen like Jesús and José Redondo made a good living by raising cattle near Yuma and driving them to the California gold fields. Estevan Ochoa, a native of Chihuahua, became prominent in New Mexico and Arizona in the mercantile business and in politics. Well-known rancheros who owed their heritage to the Spanish days were the families of Otero, Robles, Carrillo, Pacheco, Robledo, Aro, and Aguirre. The last three generations of Aguirres in Arizona—Pedro, Epifanío, and Yjinio—have had cattle ranches covering as much as twenty-seven sections of the state.

The heritage of Spain is particularly notable in mining, ranching, and agriculture. Also, many of the laws that Arizona included in its constitution were drawn almost verbatim from the Spanish code, and many of the practices in the life of early Arizona were those of the Spanish-Mexican settlers. Hispanic women in the families of Elías González, Soza, Carrillo, Aguirre, and Romero, as well as those who married Americans such as Teofila León who became the wife of Mark Aldrich, alcalde of Tucson, also contributed to the social and intellectual life of Arizona. Sisters Petra and Atanacia Santa Cruz, who married Hiram S. Stevens and Samuel Hughes, also notably bridged the gap between two cultures.

Mexicans in Tucson after 1856 continued to be merchants, politicians, artists, and intellectuals, forming a middle-class Mexican society in the United States. Men like Estevan Ochoa, who became mayor of Tucson, Jesús María Elías, Mariano Samaniego, and Federico Ronstadt, who ran businesses and ranches, were respected leaders throughout Arizona. Mexican-Americans served on the Tucson city council, on the Pima County board of supervisors, and in the territorial legislature. They pioneered both in private and public education; for example, Francisco León served on the first board of education in Tucson and Estevan Ochoa donated the land for the Congress Street School. Tucsonenses founded the Teatro Carmen and published newspapers such as *El Fronterizo* and *El Tucsonense*. Mexican food, art, and music were extremely popular among all segments of the population and continue to be today.

Arizona was the first state in which official contact was made in the area now called the Spanish Southwest. Since it was the land that fired the imagination of Fray Marcos de Niza and the land where Esteban, the ambitious Moor, met his death, Arizona has always had a special appeal to historians. It was the gateway to Coronado's misguided undertaking but where the Grand Canyon presented a breathtaking sight. Father Eusebio Kino paved the way for Jesuit missions and established the first step in peaceful native contact. Father Francisco Garcés and Juan Bautista de Anza explored the region and opened the route to California. Because of its large Spanish-speaking population and cultural ties to the Hispanic world, Arizona maintains a close relationship with the Mexican state of Sonora. Many of the early families have close relatives on both sides of the border, and practical business ties are also maintained.

United States President Theodore Roosevelt declared the mission church at Tumacácori a national monument in 1908. Since that time, the building has been preserved; five of the statues taken to San Xavier del Bac for safekeeping in 1848 were returned to Tumacácori in 1973. San Xavier, again an active Franciscan mission to the Pápago Indians, is also a registered National Historic Landmark, and is fully functional. Part of Tubac's presidio ruins became Arizona's first state park in 1958. A statue of Father Eusebio Kino, sculpted by Julian Martinez, a Spaniard living in Mexico City, graces Kino Boulevard in Tucson.

These physical remains, plus the very active Hispanic families, offer an important balance to Arizona's Anglo-American heritage of later decades. Approximately 25 percent of the population of Arizona is Spanish-speaking and the percentage of persons with Hispanic surnames is steadily increasing. The imprint of Spain's early occupation of the area lives on in place names, landmarks, and cultural identity.

CALIFORNIA'S HISPANIC LEGACY

In California today—as new developments with historic names such as Rancho de los Peñasquitos, Rancho Jamul, Mission Viejo, and Rancho Córdova dot the landscape with mission-revival type homes and shopping centers, the heritage of Spain has become a popular theme. Newcomers to the state marvel at the abundance of Hispanic names along busy freeways and can perhaps imagine the tranquil days when there were cattle ranches instead of condominiums on the rolling hillsides. Although times have changed and California life has given way to a more frantic pace, this colorful heritage and a growing Hispanic population has kept the state in touch with its historic past.

The Hispanic legacy begins in San Diego with the Junípero Serra Museum in Presidio Park, a mission-revival building constructed on the site where Spanish soldiers and Franciscan missionaries first camped in 1769. Archeological work has uncovered remains of the original presidio structure. Just below the hill is Old Town State Historic Park commemorating the civilian pueblo of San Diego founded by Spanish soldiers and their families and formally organized under Mexico in 1835. Other reminders of Spain's presence include the Cabrillo National Monument on Point Loma, marking the spot where the first explorers landed in 1542, and Balboa Park, named for the discoverer of the Pacific Ocean. Several Spanish Renaissance-style buildings and gardens were built in the park in 1915 to celebrate completion of the Panama Canal.

North of San Diego, the present freeway follows the route of Spain's El Camino Real through towns named San Dieguito and Encinitas. Restored missions include San Luis Rey de Francia near Oceanside and San Juan Capistrano, home of the legendary swallows that return each year. The city of Los Angeles, whose population contains a high percentage of persons of Hispanic descent, still retains many place-names attesting to its Spanish heritage. The original town plaza and church are located near the mission-style Santa Fe Railroad depot, and streets called Olvera, Alameda, Figueroa, Pico, and Sepulveda run nearby. The ensigns of Castile and León appear in the city's coat-of-arms and the courthouse employs over 200 Spanish interpreters.

El Camino Real, which has been basically replaced by the Pacific Coast Highway, duplicates for the most part the route taken northward by soldiers and priests. Travelers pass through Ventura (named for San Buenaventura) and Santa Barbara, site of both mission and presidio. Santa Barbara's unusual mission facade, based on Roman architectural influences, gives evidence of Franciscan sophistication during the late eighteenth century. The mission, still under Franciscan control, houses a fine collection of archival documents from the Spanish and Mexican periods.

Monterey, first capital of California, honors Gaspar de Portolá, a native of Lérida, Spain, as its founder, and citizens have restored the original presidio chapel. A number of original adobe homes are open as museums in the downtown area. The mission of San Carlos Borromeo occupies a site five miles south of Monterey on the Carmel River, and like most other California missions, it fell into near ruin after secularization in 1836. Rebuilding began in 1882 and the former mission, headquarters of Father Serra, became a parish church in 1933. Alta California's first city—San Jose (de Guadalupe)— was founded in 1777 under orders of Governor Felipe de Neve and has grown from a small farming community into a sprawling metropolis in just over 200 years. From San Jose, El Camino Real continues north along a peninsula that separates ocean from bay and ends at the city of San Francisco. Again, Spanish place names abound—Palo Alto, San Mateo, San Bruno, and San Carlos. First families include the names of Moraga, Estudillo, Peralta, Argüello, and Grijalva.

The first archbishop of San Francisco was Monsignor José Sadoc Alemany, a Catalan Spaniard who helped reclaim much of the former mission lands for the Catholic Church. Pope Pius IX appointed him bishop of Monterey in 1850 and archbishop of San Francisco in 1853. When he arrived in San Francisco there were 500 Catholics and three

Fig. 13.6 Interior of the chapel at Asistencia San Antonio de Pala today on the Pala Indian Reservation in San Diego County. Courtesy Library of Congress.

priests; at his death in 1887, there were 250 priests overseeing a flock of 250,000. Statues of El Cid, Miguel Cervantes, and Father Serra stand in Golden Gate Park.

Two missions are located north of San Francisco—San Rafael founded in 1817 near the end of the Spanish period, and San Francisco Solano, founded under Mexico in 1823 as a buffer against Russian expansion. Ironically, it was Russians at Fort Ross, located near the coast, who provided bells for the new church. The Spaniards founded no settlements north of Sonoma nor in the great central valley of California. There, however, explorers left additional place-names such as Merced, Mariposa, Modesto, Sacramento, and San Joaquin. There are forty-one towns bearing the names of saints, and one—San Ardo—honors a saint that had to be created. Historically the small town was named San Bernardo, but postal authorities forced it to become San Ardo to avoid confusion with San Bernardino.

Final Impact

The impact of Spain's legacy in the far Southwest is of major significance, but difficult to assess. Certainly the Native Americans have cause for complaint, but disruption of their culture by newcomers was inevitable. With hindsight, especially with later knowledge of disease control, cultural contact could have been less destructive. Many aspects of life readily assimilated and now taken for granted by Indians—horses, domestic animals, wool blankets, wheat, certain religious ceremonies, a written language, styles of pottery and clothing, and even weapons—were introduced by Spaniards who believed their way of life offered many advantages. For every cruelty levied against the Indians, there were acts of kindness. The number of priests who achieved martyrdom shows that men were willing to give their lives to save the souls of others. The Spaniards who settled the far Southwest, as well as the Native Americans who greeted them, accepted them, or fought them, were products of their heritage and their times. Historians should not attempt to justify or rationalize actions that have taken place. Their role is to give as honest an account as possible of what happened. Figures of the past can only be what they were, not what they might or should have been.

——————————— *Chapter Thirteen* ———————————
Bibliographic Essay

Documents concerning the period of Mexican rule in the Southwest are found in the Archivo General de la Nación in Mexico as well as in The Bancroft Library at the University of California, Berkeley; the State Archives of New Mexico; the Southwestern Mission Research Center in Tucson; and in various local depositories such as The Huntington Library in San Marino, California, and the Santa Barbara Mission Archives also in California. The library of the Arizona Historical Society in Tucson has several significant documents on microfilm such as the decree for the expulsion of Spaniards of February 15, 1828, by José María Gaxiola and also a similar decree of January 16, 1833, by Manuel Gómez Pedraza. Some specialized articles are Karen Sikes Collins, "Fray Pedro de Arriquibar's Census of Tucson, 1820," *The Journal of Arizona History,* 11 (spring 1970):14–22, Ray H. Mattison, "Early Spanish and Mexican Settlements in Arizona," *New Mexico Historical Review,* 21 (October 1946):273–327, and Raymond S. Brandes, trans., and ed., "Times Gone By in Alta California: Recollections of Señora Doña Juana Macado Alipaz de Ridington (Wrightington)," *Historical Society of Southern California Quarterly,* 41 (September 1959):201–3.

James E. Officer, *Hispanic Arizona 1536–1856* (Tucson: University of Arizona Press, 1987) gives excellent coverage of the Mexican community after independence from Spain and details the arrival of American fur traders during the 1820s and 1830s. Also important on this subject is David J. Weber, *The Taos Trappers: The Fur Trade in the Far Southwest, 1540–1846* (Norman: University of Oklahoma, 1971) and David J. Weber, *Northern Mexico on the Eve of the United States Invasion: Rare Imprints Concerning California, Arizona, New Mexico and Texas, 1821–1846* (New York: Arno Press, 1976).

For activities in New Mexico during the early nineteenth century, see Pedro Bautista Pino, *Exposición sucinta y sencilla de la provincia de Nuevo México hecha por su diputado en cortes con arreglo a sus instrucciones* (Cádiz, n.p., 1822) in H. Bailey Carroll and J. Villasana Haggard, eds., *Three New Mexico Chronicles* (Albuquerque: Quivira Society, 1942); Arthur Gómez, "Royalist in Transition: Facundo Melgares, the Last Spanish Governor of New Mexico, 1818–1822," *NMHR,* 68 (October 1993):371–388; George S. Ulibarri, "The Chouteau-Demun Expedition to New Mexico, 1815–1817," *NMHR,* 36 (October 1961):263–73. For life in Mexico, see Ruth R. Olivera and Liliane Crété, *Life in New Mexico Under Santa Anna, 1822–1855* (Norman: University of Oklahoma Press, 1991).

American infiltration into the west and California has been the subject of extensive writing. For the Pike expedition, see Donald Jackson, ed., *The Journals of Zebulon Montgomery Pike,* 2 vols. (Norman: University of Oklahoma Press, 1966). John A. Hawgood, "The Pattern of Yankee Infiltration in Mexican California, 1821–1846," *Pacific Historical Review,* 27 (February 1958):27–37, is a brief overview of the Americans who came to California. David J. Weber, *The "Californios" versus Jedediah Smith, 1826–1827: A New Cache of Documents* (Spokane: Arthur H. Clark, 1990) offers primary documents concerning the first American overland traveler to enter the province. For hide and tallow and other traders see Adele Ogden, *The California Sea Otter Trade, 1784–1848* (Berkeley: University of California Press, 1941), and Susanna B. Dakin, *The Lives of William Hartnell* (Stanford: Stanford University Press, 1949). Frank A. Knapp, Jr., "The Mexican Fear of Manifest Destiny in California," in Thomas E. Cotner and Carlos E. Castañeda, eds., *Essays in American History* (Austin: University of Texas Press, 1958).

Because of the extensive writings on the Mexican-American War of 1846, it is important to consult Norman E. Tutorow, ed., *The Mexican-American War: An Annotated Bibliography* (Westport, Conn.: Greenwood Press, 1981) for primary sources, periodical literature and some Mexican archival materials. More recent books include Neal Harlow, *California Conquered: War and Peace on the Pacific, 1846–1850* and Leonard Pitt, *The Decline of the Californios, 1846–1890* (Berkeley: University of California Press, 1982 and 1966).

For life among the Mexican families in California, see Arthur P. Botello, trans., *Don Pío Pico's Historical Narrative* (Glendale, Calif.: Arthur H. Clark, 1973). *Mexican California,* edited by Carlos E. Cortes (New York: Arno Press, 1976), is a collection of essays that includes descriptions of California in 1828 and 1832 plus several other articles on the Mexican period. George Hammond edited *The Larkin Papers: Personal, Business, and Official Correspondence of Thomas Oliver Larkin, Merchant and United States Consul in California,* 10 vols. (Berkeley: University of California Press, 1951–1968). For revealing impressions of Mexican California by Americans, one should look at the narrative of William Heath Davis, *Seventy-Five Years in California*, edited by Douglas S. Watson (San Francisco: John Howell, 1929).

For the problems and aftermath of secularization in California and the Southwest, see Robert H. Jackson, "The Impact of Liberal Policy on Mexico's Northern Frontier: Mission Secularization and the Development of Alta California, 1812–1846," *Colonial Latin American Historical Review*, 2 (spring 1993):195–225; Manuel P. Servin, "The Secularization of the California Missions: A Reappraisal," *Southern California Quarterly* (June 1965):133–50; George H. Phillips, *Chiefs and Challengers: Indian Resistance and Cooperation in Southern California* (Berkeley: University of California Press, 1975). David J. Weber, "Failure of a Frontier Institution: The Secular Church in the Borderlands under Independent Mexico, 1821–1846," *Western Historical Quarterly*, 12 (April 1981):125–43.

In New Mexico, the traditional religious-based folk art continued. For santos and santeros, see Thomas J. Steele, *Santos and Saints: The Religious Folk Art of Hispanic New Mexico* (Santa Fe: Ancient City Press, 1982); William Wroth, *Images of Penance, Images of Mercy: Southwestern Santos in the Late Nineteenth Century* (Norman: University of Oklahoma Press, 1991); Donald C. Cutter, *Arte Popular de Nuevo México* (Madrid: Instituto de Cooperación Iberoamericana 1984); and José E. Espinosa, *Saints in the Valleys: Christian Sacred Images in the History, Life, and Folk Art of Spanish New Mexico* (Albuquerque: University of New Mexico Press, 1967). For the legacy in literature, see J. Manuel Espinosa, ed., (Aurelio Espinosa) *The Folklore of Spain in the American Southwest: Traditional Spanish Folk Literature in Northern New Mexico and Southern Colorado* (Norman: University of Oklahoma Press, 1985), and Cecil Robinson, *With the Ears of Strangers: The Mexican in American Literature*, revised as *Mexico and the Hispanic Southwest in American Literature* (Tucson: University of Arizona Press, 1963 and 1977).

For the Hispanic legal heritage, see Donald C. Cutter, "Algunas influencias concretas de lo hispánico en la legislación de los Estados Unidos," in *Las Culturas Hispánicas en Los Estados Unidos* (Madrid: Asociación Cultural Hispano Norteamericana, 1978); Charles R. Cutter, *The Legal Culture of Northern New Spain* (Albuquerque: University of New Mexico Press, 1995); Iris H. W. Engstrand, "The Legal Heritage of Spanish California," *SCQ*, 75 (fall/winter 1993):205–36; Lewis Grossman, "John C. Fremont, Mariposa, and the Collision of Mexican and American Law," *Western Legal History*, 6 (winter/spring, 1993):17–50; David Langum, *Law and Community on the Mexican California Frontier: Anglo American Expatriates and the Clash of Legal Traditions, 1821–1846* (Norman: University of Oklahoma Press, 1987); Donald C. Cutter, ed. and trans., "The Legacy of the Treaty of Guadalupe Hidalgo" *NMHR*, 50:4 (October 1978):305–15; Richard Griswold del Castillo, *The Treaty of Guadalupe Hidalgo: A Legacy of Conflict* (Norman: University of Oklahoma Press, 1990).

Good general works on the legacy of Spain are Bernard L. Fontana, *Entrada: The Legacy of Spain & Mexico in the United States* (Tucson: Southwest Parks and Monuments Association, 1994); Arthur L. Campa, *Hispanic Culture in the Southwest* (Norman: University of Oklahoma Press, 1979); and Carlos Fernández-Shaw, *The Hispanic Presence in North America* (New York: Facts on File, 1987). C. L. Sonnichsen, *Tucson: The Life and Times of an American City* (Norman: University of Oklahoma Press, 1982) summarizes early Tucson and covers the transition from an Hispanic city occupied by Americans after the "Yanqui invasion" of 1846. Richard Nostrand, *The Hispano Homeland* (Norman: University of Oklahoma Press, 1992) and "The Century of Hispano Expansion," *NMHR*, 62 (October 1987):361–386, give excellent coverage of Spanish settlement patters from the sixteenth to the nineteenth centuries. Thomas L. Sheridan, *Los Tucsonenses: The Mexican Community in Tucson, 1854–1941* (Tucson: University of Arizona Press, 1986) follows the lives of Hispanic families to the beginning of World War II. Photographs of early Hispanic families are found in the library of the Arizona Historical Society in Tucson.

Glossary

A

acequia—irrigation ditch or canal

acequia madre—main irrigation ditch

adarga—oval bullhide or leather shield (lighter and more maneuverable than a metal shield

adelantado royal official with a contract for exploration or conquest; in Spain (formerly) governor of a province

agregados—recent settlers of a community

alcalde—mayor, magistrate

alcalde mayor—royal official appointed to govern districts into which colonized territories were divided; civil, military and judicial authority

alcaldía mayor—administrative jurisdiction of an alcalde mayor within a province

álferez—ensign in the Spanish Army, the lowest rank of commissioned personnel; army officer with approximately the rank of second lieutenant

alguacil—bailiff, court-officer

alguacil mayor—executive officer of the court; chief constable

Apachu—enemy or robber

arroba—Spanish weight of approximately 25 pounds

atob—Moorish word for adobe

atole—porridge made of the pith extracted from corn kernels, and tortillas

audiencia—royal court of appeals, judicial tribunal; could serve as a committee of government

auto de fé—sentence of the Inquisition

B

Bajada, La—geographical dividing line between the upper and lower Río Grande; literally "the descent"

barranca—ravine or gorge

belduques—large all-purpose knives; usually used in trade

biscochuelos—hard rolls made of corn flour, sugar, and milk

bolas de plata—free silver in large pieces

bultos—religious images carved in the round

C

cabildo—town council

cabos—corporals

canoas—hollowed out trunks of trees, laid end to end; they were a substitute for pipe conduits that conducted water over canyons and gorges

capitán mayor a la guerra—war captain; substitute for a regular military officer

carretas—two-wheeled carts; predominant transportation vehicle

casa-corral—adobe dwelling with adjoining corral in rear

casas reales—government buildings

castizos—one quarter or less mixture of Indian ancestry

casto—beaver

cédula—decree or order

chapapote—asphaltum forming along the ocean's military

chubasco—squall; thunderstorm

cimarrones—fugitives

ciudad—city (involved a royal grant of rank, privileges, and a coat of arms)

colegio—college or secondary school

comandante general—commandant general

comisarios—agents of the Inquisition

comisionado—commissioned; in towns of New Spain a soldier directed to supervise officials and activities; in charge of Indian relations, pueblo guards, etc.

compadrazgo—kinship; spiritual affinity

compadres—godparents; benefactors; intimate friends

compañía volante—mobile or "flying" company; cavalry troops

convento—community or dwelling place of religious men or women

cortes—Spanish legislative body

coyote—racial mixture of a Spaniard and Indian; in New Mexico the offspring of Anglo and Hispano parents (cobos); also used for the youngest child in a family

criollo—Creole or an American-born Spaniard

cuera—a laminated leather jacket worn by soldiers on the frontieras; a substitute for European armor

custos—a vice-provincial in the Franciscan order who substituted for the provincial when the latter was absent or unable to perform the duties of his office

D

dehesa—pasture land, grazing land; name applied to pasture land assigned for the common benefit of settlers within town boundaries

despoblado—unoccupied expanse of land

dictamen—official opinion

diputación territorial—territorial commission

diputado—elected representative of a presidial or pueblo district, acting as an advisor to the civil governor rather than a legislator

doctrina—mission; district under religious instruction

doctrineros—missionary assistants

donados—Indian lay brothers

ducados—ducats; old form of Spanish gold coin

ℰ

ejido(s)—commons; tract of land outside the center of a town held in common for the use and convenience of all settlers; within the exterior boundaries of the town

empresarios—grantees of large parcels of public land to be subdivided to individual owners

encomendar—to entrust

encomendero—holder of an encomienda; an institutional device to protect, civilize, and exploit native labor

encomienda—patronage conferred by the king over a portion of natives that imposed certain obligations to them in exchange for their labor; not a grant of land

entrada—expedition into unexplored or little known land

estancia—livestock ranch; landed property

estero—tidal inlet or salt marsh

estufa—kiva; ceremonial center

explorador—scout or explorer

ℱ

fanega—grain measure (about 1.6 bushels; in Mexico about 2.5 bushels); land measure (about 1.59 acres)

fiscal—legal advisor to the government

flota—fleet of merchant ships

fuero—decree, law, charter, or a code granted by the sovereign; in a specific sense it represented the documents granted by a king to a province securing to it certain rights and privileges

ℋ

genízaros—detribalized non-Pueblo Indians, or often any Indian not living a traditional life

gente de rázon—literally, "people of reason;" term used to distinguish Spaniards and civilized, Christian from unconverted Indians

gentiles—non-converted Indians

gran despoblado—vast unoccupied area of central Arizona

Grito de Dolores—Cry of Dolores; beginning of Mexican independence movement

ℋ

hacienda—large privately owned estate of rural nature

hechiceros—shamans; sorcerers; native healer

hidalgos—persons of the lowest rank of nobility
hijos de la mision—sons of the mission; native converts

J

jefe político—political chief; used in reference to the Mexican governor of California
juez—judge, magistrate
junta—committee of government, meeting, assembly, council
junta de guerra—war council or meeting of military officials
justicia mayor—chief magistrate

K

kivas—semi-subterranean ceremonial centers for communal and religious affairs

L

licenciados—persons with an advanced degree, usually in law
lobos—mixture of Indians and African-Americans
lugar—place, settlement, town, village, hamlet; term generally used in Spain to denote
   a small town

M

maestre de campo—commander; high-ranking military official
mantas—blankets
Mar del Sur—Pacific Ocean, though literally "South Sea"
matanza—slaughtering of cattle for hides, tallow, and beef
mestizaje—result of mixed marriages between racial or ethnic groups
mestizo—a person of mixed blood
milpas—planted corn fields
monte(s)—wood(s), forest(s) used for firewood; also means mountain
mulato—a person of mixed blood with Spanish and African ancestry

N

novena—a nine-day period of prayer
nutria—usually means sea otter; in New Mexico means beaver

O

obraje—factory or workshop
oidores—judges of the audiencia

P

palo colorado—redwood; giant evergreen trees
parajes—stopping places; campsites

partido—district; a pueblo or station with a resident missionary and generally attached to it several smaller settlements (*visitas*)

patente—writ conferring an exclusive right or privilege

patria chica—small area of one's origin

patrón—patron; boss; political protector

peones—day laborers; workers

pinole—any kind of gruel or paste made of ground seeds, nuts, acorns, grain, or the like

planchas de plata—large, flat outcroppings of silver

plaza de armas—main square or plaza in center of a town; military parade grounds

plazas—small fortified towns; open squares in the center of Spanish towns

poblaciones—collection of houses

posole—soup of corn, meat, and seasoning

propios—land belonging to the town for revenue purposes

Provincias Internas—Interior Provinces

pueblo—small, unincorporated town

Q

quintal—hundred weight

quinto—the royal share of sub-surface mineral wealth as a prerogative of the king's ownership

quinto real—royal fifth of all proceeds or profits from mining enterprise

R

ramadas—brush huts

ranchería—Indian village

rancho—privately owned farm or estate

real—royal; monetary unit; 1/8 peso

rebozo—shawl

Reconquista—Reconquest of the Iberian Peninsula from the Moslems

recuas—mule trains

reduccion(es)—reduction(s); settlement(s) of converted Indians commonly referred to as missions in California

regidor—member of municipal council

Regimiento de America—American Regiment consisting of Spanish troops and mercenaries who served as training units for the armies of New Spain

reglamento—regulation, ordinance, statute, by-laws, rules, and regulations

Relación(es)—account(s)

remuda—horse herd; often extra or replacement horses

repartimiento—allotment of forced native labor

residencia—investigation of an official at the end of his term

retablo—religious image painted on a flat wooden board

Río Abajo—downriver region along Río Grande, south of La Bajada

Río Arriba—upriver region along Río Grande at its tributaries north of La Bajada
rodeo—cattle round-up; detour

S

saca de agua—dam, point at which water is diverted from a river
santero—image maker; often a woodcarver
santos—carved or painted sacred images
sargento mayor—army officer of intermediate rank
sitios—sites; also a measure of land one league square
solar—lot, parcel, or piece of ground, building lot
soldados de cuera—leather-jacket soldiers
suerte—piece of ground separated by landmarks; in the Indies used to designate farming lands of a settler within a town

T

temescal—native sweat house
toloache—plant (jimsonweed) whose juice causes hallucinations or sometimes, if improperly taken, death
torreones—small towers intended to insure the safety of a town
tular—swamp area containing many "tules" (reeds)

V

vara—Spanish yard (33 inches)
vecino—head of a family, owner of a house lot; in general, resident, inhabitant, citizen
veloes—low clouds
velorio de santo—a wake
vigas—structural beams
villa—status or title given to a settlement that allowed certain privileges, a higher rank
 than a pueblo
visita—outlying mission having resident converted Indians, but no resident missionry
 (it was attended by the nearest missionary
visitador—inspector
visitador general—inspector general

Y

yanqui rancheros—American ranchers

Z

zanja—ditch, canal
zanjero—watermaster

A Commentary on Sources

*O*ver the years, the interpretation of Spain's role in the Southwest has changed considerably. Scholarly writings on the subject began during the late nineteenth century with the contributions of some early historical writers who recognized the value and uniqueness of the field of southwestern study. First to mind comes that great collector and publisher of North American materials, Hubert Howe Bancroft. Using teams of writers and assembly-line techniques, he published his monumental, thirty-nine-volume *Works of Hubert Howe Bancroft* (San Francisco: A. L. Bancroft and Co., 1882–1900). The emphasis of his work was California, though Bancroft ranged from Central America to Alaska and eastward to Texas. His great collections later became the nucleus of what is today the Bancroft Library of the University of California. His work on California has been made more accessible by Everett and Anna Marie Hager, eds., *The Zamorano Index to the History of California by Hubert Howe Bancroft*, 2 vols. (Los Angeles: University of Southern California, 1985).

Bancroft was not a professional historian and his work suffered from great inconsistency, lacking the perceptive analysis that characterizes later study. Nevertheless, most southwestern history begins with Bancroft and the voracious collecting mania that motivated him. Spanish efforts in discovery, exploration, and settlement are particularly emphasized in the following Bancroft volumes: *History of California*, vols. 1 and 2; *The North Mexican States and Texas*; *Arizona and New Mexico*; and the early chapters of both *Oregon* and *The Northwest Coast* in the series mentioned above. Each massive tome was accompanied by extensive and detailed footnotes and a useful bibliography. Some of Bancroft's compilers and writers should also receive credit for being in the vanguard of southwestern historiography, for they were probably more conversant with the history of the area than was the mastermind who collected and organized the material for subsequent writing. Bancroft is also noteworthy for his use of oral history, which consisted of dictated pioneer reminiscences in both Spanish and English; these are housed in the library that bears his name.

In summary, Bancroft was the first to develop an organized study of what popularly became known as the Spanish Borderlands, and his bibliography has been fundamental to subsequent efforts of both past and present research. The Bancroft Library has kept pace with the expansion of the field, adding many manuscript and microfilm collections from foreign and domestic archives. Because of the Library's resources, the history department at the University of California was able to hire Herbert E. Bolton in 1911 and then recruit, through the years, a number of producing scholars such as

Herbert I. Priestley, Charles E. Chapman, and subsequently Lawrence Kinnaird and George P. Hammond.

In writing of the northern extension of Spanish settlement, the early pioneer was retired mining engineer Henry Raup Wagner, bibliophile and collector, who published *Spanish Voyages to the Northwest Coast of America in the Sixteenth Century* (San Francisco: California Historical Society, 1929), *Cartography of the Northwest Coast of America*, 2 vols. (Berkeley: University of California Press, 1937), and *Spanish Explorations in the Strait of Juan de Fuca* (Santa Ana, Cal.: Fine Arts Press, 1933).

Outside of the Bancroft influence, but also highly motivated to contribute an understanding of the Hispanic role in the Southwest, were other non-professionals Adolph F. A. Bandelier, a Swiss-born, midwestern-raised banker, and Charles Fletcher Lummis, a journalist. Both men began their fruitful writings about Indian and Hispanic New Mexico at a time when few were interested in the area and when the availability of documentation and the opportunity for field work were unparalleled. Later in life Bandelier was joined in his interests by his second wife, Fanny, who translated the story of Alvar Núñez Cabeza de Vaca.

As a popularizer of the Southwest and its Hispanic and Indian heritage, Lummis divided his writing between history, fiction, and ethnography. After contributing from time to time to the magazines of his day, Lummis wrote his first book in 1891, *A New Mexico David and Other Stories and Sketches of the Southwest* (New York: Chas. Scribner's Sons, 1891), followed almost immediately by *Pueblo Indian Folk Tales* later released as *The Man Who Married the Moon* (New York: The Century Company, 1894). His *Land of Poco Tiempo* (New York: Chas. Scribner's Sons, 1925) won the plaudits of his contemporaries and *Spanish Pioneers* (Chicago: A.C. McClurg and Co., 1893) was a corrective to the prevalent misconception of rapaciousness of the Iberian conquest.

Though the phrase "Spanish Borderlands" has been used frequently to describe the area under consideration herein, the catchall title was not actually invented until 1921. It is not surprising that Herbert Bolton was involved, though there is reason to believe that he was not the originator of the expression. Rather, it seems that the phrase came out of the editorial office of the Yale Chronicles of America series, to which Bolton was at that time under contract to produce a small volume. This work, *The Spanish Borderlands: A Chronicle of Old Florida and the Southwest* (New Haven: Yale University Press, 1921) brings a large body of detailed factual material into a sweeping synthesis. Certainly it did not treat comprehensively the vast field of southwestern history, but it did introduce the concept of an area study by the man whose name would long be associated with the history of the border region between Mexico and the United States.

As an outgrowth of scholarly interest in the Spanish Southwest, the Quivira Society was formed in 1929. Responsible for a number of outstanding publications, the society has been an important force in southwestern history. One of Bolton's most capable students, George P. Hammond, was the impetus for the Quivira Society Publications, which between 1929 and 1958 added much to the bibliography of the Southwest. The list embraced eleven appropriate volumes as follows: George P. Hammond, *Diego Pérez de Luxán, Expedition into New Mexico made by Antonio de Espejo, 1582–83* (Los Angeles, 1929); Marguerite E. Wilbur, *Sigismundo Taraval, The Indian Uprising in*

Lower California (Los Angeles, 1931); Irving A. Leonard, *Carlos de Sigüenza y Góngora, The Mercurio Volante* ... (Los Angeles, 1932); Gilberto Espinosa, *Gaspar Pérez de Villagrá, History of New Mexico* (Los Angeles, 1933); Fritz L. Hoffman, *Francisco Céliz, Diary of the Alarcón Expedition into Texas, 1718–1719* (Los Angeles, 1935); Carlos E. Castañeda, *Juan Agustín Morfi, History of Texas, 1673–1779*, 2 vols. (Albuquerque, 1935); Henry Raup Wagner, *The Spanish Southwest: An Annotated Bibliography*, 2 vols. (Albuquerque, 1937); Hammond and Agapito Rey, *Juan de Montoya, New Mexico in 1602* (Albuquerque, 1938); H. Bailey Carroll and J. Villasana Haggard, *Three New Mexico Chronicles* (Albuquerque, 1942); Donald Worcester, *Instructions for Governing the Interior Provinces of New Spain by Bernardo de Gálvez* (Berkeley, 1951); and Nicolás de Lafora, *The Frontiers of New Spain* (Berkeley, 1958).

Hammond's direction of the Coronado Cuarto Centennial Publications series of the University of New Mexico Press resulted in a similar set of volumes concerning the Spanish Southwest. These included: Herbert E. Bolton, *Coronado and the Turquoise Trail* (1949); Hammond and Agapito Rey, *Narratives of the Coronado Expedition , 1540–1542* (1940); Hammond and Rey, *The Rediscovery of New Mexico, 1580–1594* (1966); Frederick W. Hodge, Hammond, and Rey, *The Benavides Memorial of 1634* (1945); Hammond and Rey, *Don Juan de Oñate, Colonizer of New Mexico, 1595–1628* , 2 vols. (1953); Charles W. Hackett and Charmion Shelby, *Revolt of the Pueblo Indians of New Mexico and Otermín's Reconquest, 1680–1682*, 2 vols. (1942); J. Manuel Espinosa, *The First Expedition of Vargas into New Mexico* (1940); Alfred B. Thomas, *The Plains Indians and New Mexico, 1751–1778* (1940); and Theodore E. Treutlein, *Pfefferkorn's Description of Sonora, 1756–1767* (1949). France V. Scholes, long associated with the University of New Mexico, was also a contributor who, in turn, trained a number of top scholars in the history of New Spain.

Particularly important in the matter of archival research were those guides and inventories of foreign archives that listed documents concerning the history of the United States. While Bolton was yet at the University of Texas in the first phase of his career, J. Franklin Jameson asked him to prepare a guide to the Mexican archives for the Department of Historical Research of the Carnegie Institution. Bolton's efforts south of the border resulted in his still useful *Guide to Materials for the History of the United States in the Principal Archives of Mexico* (Washington, D.C.: Carnegie Institution of Washington, 1913). A companion volume in spirit though not in sponsorship or format, was compiled by one of Bolton's first doctoral candidates, Charles E. Chapman. This catalog of more than 6,000 items of manuscript material in Sevilla was published in 1919 as *Catalogue of Materials in the Archivo General de Indias for the History of the Pacific Coast and the American Southwest* (Berkeley: University of California Press, 1919). Oriented strongly toward California, the book lists the Spanish archival holdings that are the core of the Bancroft Library Foreign Microfilm Collection of AGI materials. Newer systems of computer cataloguing have since been implemented in many archives.

A recent comprehensive summary, not in the detail of the Bolton or Chapman catalogs but of far-reaching importance, is Henry Putney Beers, *Spanish and Mexican Records of the American Southwest: A Bibliographical Guide to Archive and Manuscript Sources* (Tucson: University of Arizona Press, 1979). Broken down into individual states, the book provides an easement to archival repositories at all levels from the upper echelons of government to the modest holdings of administrative subunits. Both the focus and the comprehensiveness of Beers's work make it indispensable. Finally, mention must be made of an extremely thorough work by senior librarian Robert Leroy Santos at California State University, Stanislaus entitled *A Bibliography of Early California and Neighboring Territory through 1846* (Turlock: privately printed, 1992), which includes articles and books covering not only the Spanish and Mexican periods in California, but in Arizona and New Mexico as well.

The task of writing an overview of the Borderlands was undertaken by Bolton student Father John Francis Bannon, S.J., then professor of history at St. Louis University. The book was part of the Holt, Rinehart and Winston series, Histories of the American Frontier, under the general editorial supervision of Ray Allen Billington; its title was simple: *The Spanish Borderlands Frontier, 1513–1821* (New York: Holt, Rinehart and Winston, 1970). It is a comprehensive survey of the Borderlands, well documented with a useful bibliography of published and unpublished works. In addition to David Weber's *Spanish Frontier in North America* and Bernard Fontana's *Entrada* noted in the introduction, others who have focused on the Southwest in survey style include Odie B. Faulk, *Land of Many Frontiers* (New York: Oxford University Press, 1968); W. Eugene Hollon, *The Southwest: Old and New* (New York: A. A. Knopf, 1961); Lynn I. Perrigo, *Our Spanish Southwest* (New York: Banks, Upshaw and Company, 1960), and *The American Southwest: Its Peoples and Cultures* (New York: Holt, Rinehart and Winston, 1971). In a more literary vein is David Lavender's *The Southwest* (New York: Harper and Row, 1980) as well as Richard Francaviglia and David Narrett, eds., *Essays on the Changing Images of the Southwest* (College Station: Texas A&M, 1994). To date, however, the Spanish era in the Southwest has not effectively penetrated national textbooks, despite a rather large body of appropriate literature.

An outstanding Spanish contributor to a study of the Southwest is Luis Navarro García of the Universidad de Sevilla, an institution that is almost literally in the shadow of the Archivo General de Indias, the largest single repository of original documentation for southwestern history. His oft-cited *Don José de Gálvez y la Comandancia General de las Provincias Internas del norte de Nueva España* (Sevilla: Escuela de Estudios Hispano-Americanos, 1964) is massive, well documented, and includes a large collection of maps of the Spanish Borderlands. The same author has also produced *Las Provincias Internas en el siglo XIX* (Sevilla: Escuela de Estudios Hispano-Americanos, 1965), *Sonora y Sinaloa en el siglo XVII* (Sevilla: Escuela de Estudios Hispano-Americanos, 1966), and *La Conquista de Nuevo Mexico* (Madrid: Ediciones Cultura Hispánica, 1978). Mario Hernández Sánchez-Barba of the Universidad Complutense de Madrid is another notable Spanish contributor, especially in his *La Ultima expansión española en América* (Madrid: Instituto de Estudios Políticos, 1957) and *Juan Bautista de Anza: un hombre de frontera* (Madrid: Editorial Gráfica Espejo, 1962). A brief bibliography of works in several languages is contained in Francisco Morales Padrón, *Historia del descubrimiento y conquista de América* (Madrid: Editorial Nacional, 1963). Also from Spain, the documentary series *Chimalistac* has many volumes dealing with Spain in the Southwest. Published by José Porrúa, these limited editions of significant research materials, with notes frequently added, provide source documents for regional study. An example is volume 13, *Documentos para servir a la historia del Nuevo México, 1538–1778* (Madrid: Ediciones José Porrúa Turanzas, 1962).

In 1992, to celebrate the Columbus quincentennial, a leading Spanish insurance company in Madrid undertook to produce in a series called *Colecciones MAPFRE 1492* a significant number of books concerning the Americas from discovery to the end of the Spanish period of influence. Published by Editorial MAPFRE, the volumes totaled 280 with several concerning specific regions of the Spanish Southwest or dealing with related areas. These were Donald Cutter, *España en Nuevo México*; Iris Engstrand, *Arizona Hispánica*; Sylvia L. Hilton, *La Alta California Española*; David J. Weber, *La Frontera Norte de México, 1821–1846*; David Arias, *Las Raíces Hispanas de los Estados Unidos*, María Antonia Sainz, *Descrubrimiento y conquista*; Eric Beerman, *España y la independencia de Estados Unidos*; Mario Hernández Sánchez–Barba, *El Mar en la historia de América*; and María Pilar San Pío, *Expediciones Españolas del siglo XVIII*.

Among its many publications in western history, the Arthur H. Clark Company has one series dedicated specifically to Borderlands history. This series, Spain in the West, has contributed fourteen volumes since its inception in 1914. Significant titles and authors include: Herbert E. Bolton, ed., *Kino's Historical Memoir of Pimería Alta*, 2 vols. (1919); Marguerite Eyer Wilbur (ed. and trans.), *Juan María de Salvatierra of the Company of Jesus by M. Venegas*, (1929); Herbert I. Priestley, *Franciscan Explorations in California* (1946); Peter Gerhard, *Pirates on the West Coast of New Spain, 1575–1742*, (1960); Maurice G. Holmes, *From New Spain by Sea to the Californias, 1519–1668*, (1963); Michael E. Thurman, *The Naval Department of San Blas: New Spain's Bastion for Alta California and Nootka, 1767 to 1798* (1967); Janet R. Fireman, *The Spanish Royal Corps of Engineers in the Western Borderlands, 1764 to 1815* (1977); and Fay Jackson Smith, *The Captain of a Phantom Presidio: A History of the Presidio of Fronteras, New Spain, 1686–1735* (1993).

The prominent University of Oklahoma Press at Norman has two series listings in which important southwestern studies have appeared. The Civilization of the American Indians series includes two books by Alfred B. Thomas: *Forgotten Frontiers: A Study of the Indian Policy of Juan Bautista de Anza, Governor of New Mexico, 1777–1787* (1932), and *After Coronado: Spanish Exploration Northwest of New Mexico, 1696–1727* (1935). In Oklahoma's American Exploration and Travels series, Thomas also edited *Teodoro de Croix and the Northern Frontier of New Spain, 1776–1783* (1941); Abraham P. Nasatir and Noel Loomis wrote *Pedro Vial and the Roads to Santa Fe* (1967); and Donald Cutter, *The California Coast: A Bilingual Edition of Documents from the Sutro Collection* (1969). Notable contributors of single volumes from the same press, though not included in any series format, are included in the chapter bibliographic essays.

Dealer-publishers with an interest in the Southwest have produced important works, generally in limited editions and geared in large measure for the collector's market. Glen Dawson of Los Angeles has published a fifty-title series of small books called Early California Travels and more recently has been involved in the Baja California Travel series of an even greater number of titles. Warren Howell, of John Howell Books in San Francisco, has published some of the most elegant examples of the art of fine printing.

Aided by collector-author-editor John Galvin, Howell has published a series of luxury editions on various phases of regional history.

The California Historical Society, with books by W. Michael Mathes and Edwin A. Beilharz, and the Arizona Historical Society (formerly known as the Arizona Pioneers' Historical Society), with titles by Fathers Peter M. Dunne, Ernest J. Burrus, Charles Polzer, and Kieran McCarty, have long been involved in publishing in the Borderlands field. In Washington, D.C., the Academy of American Franciscan History has produced such significant studies as Francis F. Guest, *Fermín Francisco de Lasuén* (1973) and the several works of Maynard Geiger on Father Junípero Serra. A major effort has been under way at the academy to publish the collected writings of all of the father presidents of the California Franciscan missions. To date, the most notable are the writings of Serra, Lasuén, and Mariano Payeras, translated and edited by Antonine Tibesar (1955), Finbar Kenneally (1965), and Donald Cutter (1995), respectively.

Other noteworthy contributors to regional colonial study have appeared in the major journals concerning the region. Although many of these are included in the chapter essays, of particular general interest is James W. Byrkit's essay entitled "Land, Sky, and People: The Southwest Defined," in the *Journal of the Southwest,* 34 (autumn 1992): 257–387. An important contribution to women's history is Antonia Castañeda, "Women of Color and the Rewriting of Western History: The Discourse, Politics, and Decolonization of History," *Pacific Historical Review,* 61 (November 1992):501–33.

Bibliography

Adams, Eleanor B. *Bishop Tamerón's Visitation of New Mexico*. Albuquerque: Historical Society of New Mexico, 1954.

———, ed. "Fray Silvestre and the Obstinate Hopi," *New Mexico Historical Review*, 38 (April 1963):97–138.

Adams, Eleanor B., and Angelico Chávez, eds. and trans. *The Missions of New Mexico, 1776: A Description By Fray Atanasio Domínguez*. Albuquerque: University of New Mexico Press, 1956.

Adams, Eleanor B., and France V. Scholes. "Books in New Mexico, 1598–1680," *New Mexico Historical Review*, 13 (July 1942):226–70.

Aguado Bleyes, Pedro, and Cayetano Alcázar Molina. *Manual de Historia de España*. 3 vols. Madrid: Espasa-Calpe, 1964.

Aguirre, Yjinio. "Echoes of the Conquistadores," *Journal of Arizona History*, 10 (autumn 1969):267–86.

Aiton, Arthur Scott. *Antonio de Mendoza: First Viceroy of New Spain*. Durham: Duke University Press, 1927.

Alegre, Francisco Javier. *Historia de la Provincia de la Compañía de Jesus de Nueva España*, ed. by Ernest J. Burrus, S.J., and Felix Zubillaga, S.J. 4 vols. Roma: Institutum Historicum Societatis Jesu, 1956–60.

Archer, Christon I. "The Army of New Spain and the Wars of Independence, 1790–1821," *Hispanic American Historical Review*, 61 (November 1981):705–14.

———. "To Serve the King: Military Recruitment in Late Colonial Mexico." *Hispanic American Historical Review*, 55 (May 1975):226–50.

Archibald, Robert. "Acculturation and Assimilation in Colonial New Mexico," *New Mexico Historical Review*, 53 (July 1978):205–17.

———. *Economic Aspects of the California Missions*. Washington, D.C.: Academy of American Franciscan History, 1978.

———. "Price Regulation in Hispanic California," *The Americas*, 33 (April 1977):613–29.

Arrillaga, José Joaquín. *Diary of His Surveys of the Frontier, 1796*. Fray Tiscareno, trans. and John W. Robinson, ed. Los Angeles: Dawson's Book Shop, 1969.

August, Jack. "Balance of Power Diplomacy in New Mexico: Governor Fernando de la Concha and the Indian Policy of Conciliation," *New Mexico Historical Review*, 56 (April 1981):141–60.

Axtell, James. "Europeans, Indians, and the Age of Discovery in American History Textbooks," *American Historical Review*, 92 (June 1987):621–32.

Baegert, Johann Jakob, S.J. *Observations in Lower California*, ed. and trans. by M. M. Brandenburg and Carl L. Baumann. Berkeley: University of California Press, 1952.

Baldwin, Gordon C. *The Ancient Ones: Basketmakers and Cliff Dwellers of the Southwest*. New York: W. W. Norton, 1963.

Baldwin, Percy M. "Fray Marcos de Niza and His Discovery of the Seven Cities of Cibola," *New Mexico Historical Review*, 16 (April 1941):233–43.

Ballesteros Gaibrois, Manuel, ed. *Bibliotheca Indiana: Viajes y Viajeros por Norteamerica*. Madrid: Aguilar, 1958.

Bancroft, Hubert Howe. *History of Arizona and New Mexico, 1530–1888*. San Francisco: The History Company, 1889.

———. *History of California, 1542–1890*. 7 vols. San Francisco: The History Company, 1887–1890.

———. *History of the North Mexican States and Texas, 1531–1889*. 2 vols. San Francisco: The History Company, 1884–1889.

Bandelier, A. F. *The Gilded Man (El Dorado) and Other Pictures of the Spanish Occupancy of America*. New York: D. Appleton, 1893.

Bannon, John Frances. *The Mission Frontier in Sonora, 1513–1821*. Albuquerque: University of New Mexico Press, 1974.

———. *The Spanish Borderlands Frontier, 1513–1822*. New York: Holt, Rinehart and Wilson, 1970.

Barbier, Jacques A. "The Culmination of the Bourbon Reforms, 1787–1792," *Hispanic American Historical Review*, 57 (February 1977):51–68.

Barnes, Thomas C., Thomas H. Naylor, and Charles W. Polzer. *Northern New Spain: A Research Guide*. Tucson: The University of Arizona Press, 1981.

Barrett, Ellen C. *Baja California, 1535–1956*. Los Angeles: Bennett and Marshall, 1957.

———. *Baja California II, 1535–1964*. Los Angeles: Westernlore Press, 1967.

Baxter, John O. *Las Carneradas: Sheep Trade in New Mexico, 1700–1860*. Albuquerque: University of New Mexico Press, 1987.

Beck, Warren. *New Mexico: A History of Four Centuries*. Norman: University of Oklahoma Press, 1962.

Beck, Warren A., and Ynez Haase. *Historical Atlas of California*. Norman: University of Oklahoma Press, 1974.

Beerman, Eric. *España y la independencia de Estados Unidos*. Madrid: Editorial MAPFRE, S.A., 1992.

———. "The Death of an Old Conquistador: New Light on Juan de Oñate," *New Mexico Historical Review*, 54 (October 1979):305–19.

Beilharz, Edwin A. *Felipe de Neve, First Governor of California*. San Francisco: California Historical Society, 1971.

Benavides, Alonso de. *Revised Memorial of Fray Alonso de Benavides, 1634*, trans. and ed. by F. W. Hodge, G. P. Hammond, and Agapito Rey. Albuquerque: University of New Mexico Press, 1945.

———. *The Memorial of Alonso de Benavides of 1630*, trans. by Peter P. Forrestal. Washington, D.C.: Academy of American Franciscan History, 1954.

Benes, Ronald J. "Anza and Concha in New Mexico, 1787–1793," *Journal of the West*, 4 (January 1965):63–76.

Beninato, Stefanie. "Popé, Pose-yemu, and Naranjo: A New Look at the Leadership in the Pueblo Revolt of 1680," *New Mexico Historical Review*, 65 (October 1990):417–35.

Blakeslee, Donald J. "The Mallet Expedition of 1739," *Wagon Tracks: Santa Fe Trail Association Quarterly*, 5 (February and May 1991):15–18; 14–16.

Bleser, Nicholas J. *Tumacacori: From Rancheria to National Monument*. Tucson: Southwest Parks and Monuments Association, n.d.

Bloom, Lansing. "The Vargas Encomienda," *New Mexico Historical Review*, 14 (October 1939): 366–417.

———, ed. and trans. "Fray Estevan de Perea's Relación," *New Mexico Historical Review*, 8 (July 1933):211–35.

———, ed. and trans. "The Royal Order of 1620 to Custodian Fray Esteban de Perea," *New Mexico Historical Review*, 5 (July 1930):288–98.

Boas, Franz, and Elsie Clews Parsons. "Spanish Tales from Laguna and Zuni, N. Mex.," *Journal of American Folk-lore*, 33 (1920):47–72.

Bobb, Bernard E. *The Viceregency of Antonio Maria Bucareli in New Spain, 1771–1779*. Austin: University of Texas Press, 1962.

Bolton, Herbert Eugene. *Coronado on the Turquoise Trail: Knight of Pueblos and Plains*. Albuquerque: University of New Mexico Press, 1949.

———. *Guide to Materials for the History of the United States in the Principal Archives of Mexico*. Washington, D.C.: Carnegie Institution, 1913.

———. *Historical Memoirs of New California*. 4 vols. Berkeley: University of California Press, 1926.

———. "The Mission as a Frontier Institution in the Spanish-American Colonies," *American Historical Review*, 23 (October 1917):42–61.

———. *Rim of Christendom: A Biography of Eusebio Francisco Kino, Pacific Coast Pioneer*. New York: Macmillan, 1936.

———, ed. *Anza's California Expeditions*. 5 vols. Berkeley: University of California Press, 1930.

———, ed. *Spanish Exploration in the Southwest, 1542–1706*. New York: Charles Scribner's Sons, 1916; reprinted New York: Barnes and Noble, 1952.

———, ed. and trans. *Fray Juan Crespi: Missionary Explorer on the Pacific Coast*. Berkeley: University of California Press, 1927.

———, ed. and trans. *Historical Memoir of Pimeria Alta*. 2 vols. Berkeley: University of California Press, 1927.

————, ed. and trans. *Pageant in the Wilderness: The Story of the Escalante Expedition to the Interior Basin, 1776, Including the Diary and Itinerary of Father Escalante.* Salt Lake City: Utah State Historical Society, 1950.

Botello, Arthur P., ed. and trans. *Don Pio Pico's Historical Narrative.* Glendale, Calif.: Arthur H. Clark Co., 1973.

Bowman, J. N., and Robert F. Heizer. *Anza and the Northwest Frontier of New Spain.* Los Angeles: Southwest Museum, 1967.

Brading, D. A. *The First America: The Spanish Monarchy, Creole Patriots and the Liberal State, 1492–1867.* Cambridge, Mass.: Cambridge University Press, 1991.

Brady, Ralph Hamilton. "The Franciscans in Pimería Alta," M.A. thesis, University of California, Berkeley, 1925.

Brandon, William. *Quivira: Europeans in the Region of the Santa Fe Trail, 1540–1820.* Athens: Ohio University Press, 1990.

Brayer, Herbert O. *Pueblo Indian Land Grants of the "Río Abajo," New Mexico.* Albuquerque: University of New Mexico Press, 1938.

Briggs, Walter. *Without Noise of Arms: The 1776 Domínguez-Escalante Journal: Their Expedition through Colorado, Utah, Arizona, and New Mexico in 1776.* Provo, Utah: Brigham Young University Press, 1976.

Brinckerhoff, Sidney B. "The Last Years of Spanish Arizona," *Arizona and the West,* 9 (spring 1967):5–20.

Brinckerhoff, Sidney B., and Odie B. Faulk. *Lancers for the King.* Phoenix: Arizona Historical Foundation, 1965.

Broughton, William H. "The History of Seventeenth-Century New Mexico: Is It Time for New Interpretations?" *New Mexico Historical Review,* 68 (January 1993):3–12.

Burrus, Ernest J., S.J. *Kino and the Cartography of Northwestern New Spain.* Tucson: Arizona Pioneers' Historical Society, 1965.

————. *Kino and Manje, Explorers of Sonora and Arizona: Their Vision of the Future: A Study of Their Expeditions and Plans.* Rome: Jesuit Historical Institute, 1971.

————. *Kino's Plan for the Development of Pimería Alta, Arizona, and Upper California.* Tucson: Arizona Pioneers' Historical Society, 1961.

————. *La Obra Cartográfica de la Provincia Mexicana de la Compañía de Jesús 1567–1967.* Madrid: Ediciones José Porrúa Turanzas, 1967.

————. *Misiones Norteñas Mexicanas de la Compañía de Jesús 1751–1757.* Mexico D.F.: Antigua Librería Robredo, 1963.

————. "Rivera y Moncada, Explorer and Military Commander of Both Californias, in the Light of His Diary and Other Contemporary Documents," *Hispanic American Historical Review,* 50 (November 1970):682–92.

————, ed. *Correspondencia del P. Kino con los Generales de la Compañía de Jesús, 1682–1707.* Mexico, D.F.: Editorial Jus, 1961.

————, ed. *Diario del Capitán Comandante Fernando de Rivera y Moncada con un apéndice documental.* 2 vols. Madrid: Ediciones José Porrua Turanzas, 1967.

————, ed. *Kino Reports to Headquarters: Correspondence of Eusebio F. Kino, S.J., from New Spain with Rome.* Roma: Institutum Historicum Societatis Jesu, 1954.

————, trans. and ed. *Wenceslaus Linck's Diary of His 1766 Expedition to Northern Baja California.* Los Angeles: Dawson's Book Shop, 1966.

Byrkit, James W. "Land, Sky, and People: The Southwest Defined," *Journal of the Southwest,* 34 (autumn 1992):257–387.

Calderon Quijano, José Antonio, ed. *Los Virreyes de Nueva España en el reinado de Carlos III.* 2 vols. Sevilla: Escuela de Estudios Hispano-Americanos, 1967–1968.

Campa, Arthur L. *Hispanic Culture in the Southwest.* Norman: University of Oklahoma Press, 1979.

Campbell, Leon G. "The Spanish Presidio in Alta California During the Mission Period, 1769–1784," *Journal of the West,* 16 (October 1977):63–77.

Carlisle, Charles R., and Bernard L. Fontana. "Sonora in 1773: Reports by Five Jaliscan Friars," *Arizona and the West,* 11 (spring and summer 1969):39–56; 179–90.

Carlson, Alvar W. *The Spanish-American Homeland: Four Centuries in New Mexico's Río Arriba.* Baltimore: Johns Hopkins University Press, 1991.

Carroll, H. Bailey, and J. Villasana Haggard. *Three New Mexico Chronicles.* Albuquerque: The Quivira Society, 1942.

Castañeda, Antonia I. "Gender, Race, and Culture: Spanish-Mexican Women in the Historiography of Frontier California," *Frontiers: A Journal of Women Studies,* 11 (November 1990):8–30.

———. "Presidiarias y Pobladoras: Spanish-Mexican Women in Frontier Monterey, Alta California, 1770–1821," Ph.D. Dissertation, Stanford University, 1990.

———. "Women of Color and the Rewriting of Western History: The Discourse, Politics, and Decolonization of History," *Pacific Historical Review,* 61 (November 1992):501–33.

Castañeda, Carlos E., and Jack Autrey Dabbs. *Guide to the Latin American Manuscripts in the University of Texas Library.* Cambridge: Harvard University Press, 1939.

Castetter, Edward F., and Willis H. Bell. *Pima and Papago Indian Agriculture.* Albuquerque: University of New Mexico Press, 1942.

Caughey, John. *Bernardo de Gálvez in Louisiana, 1776–1783.* Berkeley: University of California Press, 1934.

Chapman, Charles E. *A History of California: The Spanish Period.* New York: Macmillan, 1921.

———. *Catalogue of Materials in the Archivo General de Indias for the History of the Pacific Coast and the American Southwest.* Berkeley: University of California Press, 1919.

———. *The Founding of Spanish California: The Northwestward Expansion of New Spain, 1687–1783.* New York: Macmillan, 1916.

Chávez, Angelico. *Coronado's Friars.* Washington, D.C.: Academy of American Franciscan History, 1968.

———. *Our Lady of the Conquest.* Santa Fe: Historical Society of New Mexico, 1948.

———. "Pohé-Yemo's Representative and the Pueblo Revolt of 1680," *New Mexico Historical Review,* 42 (April 1967):85–126.

Chávez, Thomas. "The Segesser Hide Paintings: History, Discovery, Art," *Great Plains Quarterly,* 10 (spring 1990):96–109.

Chávez, Thomas E. *An Illustrated History of New Mexico.* Niwot: University Press of Colorado, 1992.

Chipman, Donald E. *Spanish Texas, 1519–1821.* Austin: University of Texas Press, 1992.

Christiansen, Paige W. "The Presidio and the Borderlands: A Case Study," *Journal of the West,* 8 (January 1969):29–37.

Clark, Thomas D., and John D. W. Guice. *Frontiers in Conflict: The Old Southwest, 1795–1830.* Albuquerque: University of New Mexico Press, 1989.

Cleland, Robert Glass. *The Cattle on a Thousand Hills: 1850–1880.* San Marino: The Huntington Library, 1941.

Colahan, Clark. *The Visions of Sor María de Agreda: Writing Knowledge and Power.* Tucson: University of Arizona Press, 1994.

Collins, Karen Sikes. "Fray Pedro de Arriquibar's Census of Tucson, 1820," *The Journal of Arizona History,* 11 (spring 1970):14–22.

Cook, Sherburne F. *Colonial Expeditions to the Interior of California's Central Valley, 1800–1820.* Berkeley: University of California Press, 1960.

———. *The Conflict Between the California Indian and White Civilization.* Berkeley: University of California Press, 1976.

———. "Diseases of the Indians of Lower California in the Eighteenth Century," *California and Western Medicine,* 43 (December 1935):1–6.

———. "Smallpox in Spanish and Mexican California, 1770–1845," *Bulletin of the History of Medicine,* 2 (February 1939):153–91.

Cook, Warren L. *Flood Tide of Empire: Spain and the Pacific Northwest, 1543–1819.* New Haven: Yale University Press, 1973.

Coombs, Gary B., and Fred Plog. "The Conversion of the Chumash Indians: An Ecological Interpretation," *Human Ecology,* 5 (December 1977):309–28.

Cordell, Linda S., and George J. Gumerman, eds. *Dynamics of Southwest Prehistory.* Washington: Smithsonian Institution Press, 1989.

Cortes, Carlos E., ed. *Mexican California.* New York: Arno Press, 1976.

Coues, Elliott, ed. *The Expeditions of Zebulon Montgomery Pike.* Minneapolis: Ross and Haines, 1965.

———, ed. and trans. *On the Trail of a Spanish Pioneer: The Diary and Itinerary of Francisco Garcés in His Travels through Sonora, Arizona, and California, 1775–1776; Translated from an ... Original Spanish Manuscript.* 2 vols. New York: Francis P. Harper, 1900.

Coughlin, Magdalen, C.S.J. "Boston Smugglers on the Coast (1797–1821): An Insight into the American Acquisition of California," *California Historical Society Quarterly,* 46 (June 1967):99–120.

Cowan, Robert G. *Ranchos of California. A List of Spanish Concessions 1775–1822 and Mexican Grants 1822–1846.* Fresno, Calif.: Academy Library Guild, 1956.

Creamer, Winifred. "Re-examining the Black Legend: Contact Period Demography in the Rio Grande Valley of New Mexico," *New Mexico Historical Review,* 69 (July 1994):263–80.

Creer, Leland H. "Spanish-American Slave Trade in the Great Basin, 1800–1853," *New Mexico Historical Review,* 24 (July 1949):171–83.

Crosby, Harry. *Antigua California: Mission and Colony on the Peninsular Frontier, 1697–1768.* Albuquerque: University of New Mexico Press, 1994.

Crouch, Dora P., Daniel J. Garr, and Axel I. Mundigo. *Spanish City Planning in North America.* Cambridge: MIT Press, 1982.

Crow, John. *Spain: The Root and the Flower: An Interpretation of Spain and the Spanish People.* Berkeley: University of California Press, 1985.

Crown, Patricia L., and W. James Judge, eds. *Chaco & Hohokam: Prehistoric Regional Systems in the American Southwest.* Santa Fe: School of American Research Press, 1991.

Cruz, Gilbert. *Let There Be Towns.* College Station: Texas A&M Press, 1988.

Cutter, Charles R. *The Legal Culture of Northern New Spain, 1700–1810.* Albuquerque: University of New Mexico Press, 1995.

Cutter, Donald C. "Algunas influencias concretas de lo hispánico en la legislación de los Estados Unidos," in *Las Culturas Hispánicos en Los Estados Unidos.* Madrid: Asociación Cultural Hispano Norteamericana, 1978.

———. "An Anonymous Statistical Report on New Mexico in 1765," *New Mexico Historical Review,* 50 (October 1979):347–52.

———. *Arte Popular de Nuevo México.* Madrid: Gráficas Alocen, 1984.

———. *The California Coast: A Bilingual Edition of Documents from the Sutro Collection.* Norman: University of Oklahoma Press, 1969.

———. *California in 1792: A Spanish Naval Visit.* Norman: University of Oklahoma Press, 1990.

———. *Diary of Ensign Gabriel Moraga's Expedition of Discovery in the Sacramento Valley, 1808.* Los Angeles: Dawson's Book Shop, 1957.

———. *España en Nuevo Mexico.* Madrid: Editorial MAPFRE, 1992.

———. "The Legacy of the Treaty of Guadalupe Hidalgo," *New Mexico Historical Review,* 53 (October 1978):305–15.

———. "With a Little Help from Their Saints," *Pacific Historical Review,* 53 (May 1984):123–48.

———. *Malaspina and Galiano: Spanish Voyages to the Northwest Coast.* Vancouver: Douglas & McIntyre/Seattle: University of Washington Press, 1991.

———. "Plans for the Occupation of Upper California: A New Look at the 'Dark Age' from 1602 to 1769," *Journal of San Diego History,* 24 (Winter 1978):78–90.

———. "Prelude to a Pageant in the Wilderness," *Western Historical Quarterly,* 8 (January 1977):5–14.

———. "Technology: The Spanish Borderlands," *Encyclopedia of the North American Colonies,* 3 (1977):247–52.

———, ed. and trans. *The Defenses of Northern New Spain: Hugo O'Conor's Report to Teodoro de Croix, July 22, 1777.* Dallas: Southern Methodist University Press, 1994.

———, ed. and trans. *Writings of Mariano Payeras.* Santa Barbara: Bellerophon Books, 1995.

Dailey, Martha LaCroix, "Symbolism and Significance of the Lincoln Canes for the Pueblos of New Mexico," *New Mexico Historical Review,* 69 (April 1994):127–43.

Dakin, Susanna B. *The Lives of William Hartnell.* Stanford: Stanford University Press, 1949.

Dale, Edward Everett. *The Indians of the Southwest: A Century of Development under the United States.* Norman: University of Oklahoma Press, 1949.

Dantin Cereceda, Juan. *Exploradores y conquistadores de las Indias Occidentales, 1492–1540: Relatos geográficos.* Madrid: Consejo Superior de Investigaciones Científicas, 1964.

Davis, William Heath. *Seventy-Five Years in California,* ed. by Douglas Watson. San Francisco: John Howell Books, 1929.

Day, A. Grove. *Coronado's Quest: The Discovery of the Southwestern States.* Berkeley: University of California Press, 1940.

Díaz del Castillo, Bernal. *A True History of the Conquest of New Spain, 1517–1521,* trans. by A. P. Maudslay. New York: Farrar, Straus and Giroux, 1966.

DiPeso, Charles C. *The Upper Pima of San Cayetano del Tumacacori: An Archaeohistorical Reconstruction of the Ootam of Pimería Alta.* Dragoon, Ariz.: Amerind Foundation, 1956.

Dobyns, Henry F. "Indian Extinction in the Middle Santa Cruz Valley, Arizona," *New Mexico Historical Review,* 38 (April 1963):163–81.

————. "Military Transculturation of Northern Piman Indians, 1782–1821," *Ethnohistory,* 19 (fall 1972):323–43.

————. *Spanish Colonial Tucson: A Demographic History.* Tucson: University of Arizona Press, 1976.

Dockstader, Frederick. *The Kachina and the White Man: The Influences of White Culture on the Hopi Kachina Cult.* Albuquerque: University of New Mexico Press, 1985.

Dolbee, William B. "The Privilege to Mark Out the Way: American Mission, Mexico, and the Road to Santa Fe," *New Mexico Historical Review,* 68 (July 1993):227–245.

Donahue, J. Augustine. *After Kino: Jesuit Missions in Northwestern New Spain 1711–1767.* Rome: Jesuit Historical Institute, 1969.

————. "The Unlucky Jesuit Mission of Bac," *Arizona and the West,* 2 (summer 1960):127–39.

Ducrue, Benno. *Account of the Expulsion of the Jesuits from Lower California (1767–1769),* ed. by Ernest J. Burrus, S.J. Rome: Jesuit Historical Institute, 1967.

Dunbier, Rodger. *The Sonoran Desert: Its Geography, Economy, and People.* Tucson: University of Arizona Press, 1968.

Dunn, Oliver, and James E. Kelley, Jr., eds. and trans. *The "Diario" of Christopher Columbus's First Voyage to America, 1492–93, Abstracted by Fray Bartolomé de las Casas.* Norman: University of Oklahoma Press, 1991.

Dunne, Peter M. *Black Robes in Lower California.* Berkeley: University of California Press, 1952.

————. *Pioneer Black Robes on the West Coast of New Spain.* Berkeley: University of California Press, 1940.

————. *Pioneer Jesuits in Northern Mexico.* Berkeley: University of California Press, 1952.

————, ed. and trans., *Jacobo Sedelmayr: Missionary, Frontiersman, Explorer in Arizona and Sonora.* Tucson: Arizona Pioneers' Historical Society, 1955.

————, ed. and trans. *Juan Antonio Balthasar, Padre Visitador to the Sonora Frontier, 1744–1745.* Tucson: Arizona Pioneers' Historical Society, 1957.

Ebright, Malcolm. *Land Grants and Lawsuits in Northern New Mexico.* Albuquerque: University of New Mexico Press, 1994.

————, ed. *Spanish and Mexican Land Grants and the Law. Journal of the West* special issue (July 1988). Manhattan, Kans.: Sunflower University Press, 1989.

Eckhart, George B. "A Guide to the History of the Missions of Sonora, 1614–1826," *Arizona and the West,* 2 (summer 1960):165–83.

Elliott, J. H. *Imperial Spain, 1469–1716.* Harmondsworth, England: Penguin Books, 1975.

————. *The Old World and the New.* Cambridge, Mass.: Cambridge University Press, 1970.

Ellis, Richard N. *New Mexico Past and Present: A Historical Reader.* Albuquerque: University of New Mexico Press, 1971.

Engelhardt, Zephyrin, O.F.M. *Missions and Missionaries of California.* 4 vols. San Francisco: James H. Barry, 1908–1915.

Engelhardt, Zephyrin, O.F.M. *The Franciscans in Arizona.* Harbor Springs, Mich.: Holy Childhood Indian School, 1899.

Engstrand, Iris H. W. *Arizona Hispánica.* Madrid: Editorial MAPFRE, 1992.

————. "California Ranchos: Their Hispanic Heritage," *Southern California Quarterly,* 67 (fall 1985):281–90.

————. "The Enlightenment in Spain: Influences on New World Policy," *The Americas,* 61 (April 1985):436–44.

————. *Joaquín Velázquez de León: Royal Officer in Baja California, 1768–1770.* Los Angeles: Dawson's Book Shop, 1976.

————. "A Note on the Plan of Pitic," *Colonial Latin American Historical Review,* 3 (winter 1994):73–78.

———. "The Legal Heritage of Spanish California," *Southern California Quarterly,* 75 (fall/winter 1993):205–36.

———. *Spanish Scientists in the New World: The Eighteenth Century Expeditions.* Seattle: University of Washington Press, 1981.

Espinosa, Aurelio. *The Folklore of Spain in the American Southwest: Traditional Spanish Folk Literature in Northern New Mexico and Southern Colorado,* ed. by J. Manuel Espinosa. Norman: University of Oklahoma Press, 1985.

Espinosa, Gilberto. "About New Mexico Land Grants," *Albuquerque Bar Journal,* 7 (September 1967):5–15.

Espinosa, J. Manuel. *Crusaders of the Río Grande: The Story of Don Diego de Vargas and the Reconquest and Refounding of New Mexico.* Chicago: Institute of Jesuit History, 1942.

———, ed. and trans. *First Expedition of Vargas into New Mexico, 1692.* Albuquerque: University of New Mexico Press, 1940.

———, ed. and trans. *The Pueblo Indian Revolt of the 1696 and the Franciscan Missions in New Mexico.* Norman: University of Oklahoma Press, 1988.

Espinosa, José E. *Saints in the Valleys: Christian Sacred Images in the History, Life, and Folk Art of Spanish New Mexico.* Albuquerque: University of New Mexico Press, 1967.

Euler, Robert C., and Henry F. Dobyns. *The Hopi People.* Phoenix: Indian Tribal Series, 1971.

Ewing, Russell C. "Investigations into the Causes of the Pima Uprising of 1751," *Mid-America,* 23 (April 1941):138–51.

———. "The Pima Outbreak in November, 1751," *New Mexico Historical Review,* 13 (October 1938):337–46.

Ezell, Paul. "The Hispanic Acculturation of the Gila River Pimas," *American Anthropologist,* 63 (October 1961):1–171.

Farriss, N. M. *Crown and Clergy in Colonial Mexico, 1759–1821: The Crisis of Ecclesiastical Privilege.* London: Athlone, 1968.

Faulk, Odie B. *The Leather Jacket Soldier: Spanish Military Equipment and Institutions of the Late 18th Century.* Pasadena, Calif.: Socio-Technical Press, 1971.

———. "The Presidio: Fortress or Farce?" David Weber, ed. *New Spain's Far Northern Frontier.* Albuquerque: University of New Mexico Press, 1979.

Favata, Martín, and José B. Fernández, eds. *La "Relacion" o "Naufragios" de Alvar Nuñez Cabeza de Vaca.* Potomac, Md.: Scripta Humanistica, 1986.

Feather, Adlai. "Origin of the Name Arizona," *New Mexico Historical Review,* 39 (April 1964):89–100.

———, ed. "Colonel Don Fernando de la Concha Diary, 1788," *New Mexico Historical Review,* 34 (October 1959):285–304.

Fernández-Shaw, Carlos. *The Hispanic Presence in North America.* New York: Facts on File, 1987.

Fireman, Bert M. *Arizona: Historic Land.* New York: Alfred A. Knopf, 1982.

Fireman, Janet R. *The Spanish Royal Corps of Engineers in the Western Borderlands: Instrument of Bourbon Reform, 1764 to 1815.* Glendale, Calif.: The Arthur H. Clark Co., 1977.

Fisher, Lillian Estelle. "Teodoro de Croix," *Hispanic American Historical Review,* 9 (November 1929):488–504.

Fitzhugh, William W., ed. *Cultures in Contact: The European Impact on Native Cultural Institutions, A.D. 1000–1800.* Washington, D.C.: Smithsonian Institution Press, 1985.

Flagler, Edward K. "From Asturias to New Mexico: Don Francisco Cuervo y Valdés," *New Mexico Historical Review,* 69 (July 1994):127–44.

Flint, Richard, and Shirley Cushing Flint. "The Coronado Expedition: Cicuye to the Rio de Cicuye Bridge," *New Mexico Historical Review,* 67 (April 1992):123–38.

———. "Coronado's Crosses: Route Markers Used by the Coronado Expedition," *Journal of the Southwest,* 35 (summer 1993):207–16.

Fontana, Bernard L. "Biography of a Desert Church: The Story of Mission San Xavier del Bac," *The Smoke Signal,* no. 3, Tucson, The Westerners, 1961, rev. 1963.

———. *Entrada: The Legacy of Spain & Mexico in the United States.* Tucson: Southwest Parks and Monuments Association, 1994.

Forbes, Jack D. *Apache, Navajo, and Spaniard.* Norman: University of Oklahoma Press, 1960.

———. "Melchior Díaz and the Discovery of Alta California," *Pacific Historical Review,* 27 (November 1958):351–57.

———. *Warriors of the Colorado: The Yumas of the Quechan Nation and Their Neighbors.* Norman: University of Oklahoma Press, 1965.

Forest, Earle R. *Mission and Pueblos of the Old Southwest: Their Myths, Legends, Fiestas and Ceremonies, with Some Accounts of the Indian Tribes and Their Dances; and of the Penitentes.* Cleveland: Arthur H. Clark Co., 1929.

Francaviglia, Richard, and David Narrett, eds. *Essays on the Changing Images of the Southwest.* College Station: Texas A&M Press, 1994.

Gabriel, Kathryn. *Roads to Center Place: A Cultural Atlas of Chaco Canyon and the Anasazi.* Boulder, Colo.: Johnson Books, 1991.

Gallegos, Bernardo P. *Literacy, Education, and Society in New Mexico, 1693–1821.* Albuquerque: University of New Mexico Press, 1992.

Gálvez, Bernardo de. *Instructions for Governing the Interior Provinces of New Spain, 1786,* ed. and trans. by Donald E. Worcester. Berkeley: The Quivira Society, 1951.

Galvin, John, ed. *The First Spanish Entry into San Francisco Bay 1775.* San Francisco: John Howell Books, 1971.

Galvin, John, and Adelaide Smithers, trans. *The Coming of Justice to California: Three Documents Translated from the Spanish.* San Francisco: John Howell Books, 1963.

Garate, Donald T. "Basque Names, Nobility, and Ethnicity on the Spanish Frontier," *Colonial Latin American Historical Review,* 2 (winter 1993):77–104.

Garcés, Francisco. *A Record of Travels in Arizona and California, 1775–1776,* ed. by John Galvin. San Francisco: John Howell Books, 1967.

———. *In the Trail of a Spanish Pioneer: The Diary and Itinerary of Francisco Garcés (Missionary Priest) in His Travels Through Sonora, Arizona, and California, 1775–1776,* ed. by Elliot Coues. 2 vols. New York: Francis P. Harper, 1900.

Garr, Daniel. "Planning, Politics and Plunder: The Missions and Indian Pueblos of Hispanic California," *Southern California Quarterly,* 54 (winter 1972):291–312.

Garrahy, Stephen T., and David J. Weber. "Francisco de Ulloa, Joseph James Markey, and the Discovery of Upper California," *California Historical Society Quarterly,* 50 (March 1971):73–77.

Geary, Gerald J. *The Secularization of the California Missions 1810–1846.* Washington, D.C.: Catholic University of America, 1934.

Geiger, Maynard J., O.F.M. *Franciscan Missionaries in Hispanic California, 1769–1848: A Biographical Dictionary.* San Marino, Calif.: The Huntington Library, 1969.

———. *The Kingdom of St. Francis in Arizona (1539–1939).* Santa Barbara, Calif.: Mission Santa Barbara, 1939.

———. *The Life and Times of Fray Junípero Serra, O.F.M.* Washington, D.C.: Academy of American Franciscan History, 1959.

Gerald, Rex E. *Spanish Presidios of the Late Eighteenth Century in Northern New Spain.* Santa Fe: Museum of New Mexico Research Records, no. 7, 1968.

Gerhard, Peter. *The Northern Frontier of New Spain.* Norman: University of Oklahoma Press, 1993.

———. *Pirates on the West Coast of New Spain, 1575–1742.* Glendale, Calif.: Arthur H. Clark Co., 1960.

Gibson, Charles. *The Aztecs under Spanish Rule: The Indians of the Valley of Mexico, 1519–1810.* Stanford: Stanford University Press, 1964.

Gillingham, Robert C. *Rancho San Pedro,* ed. by Judson Grenier. Los Angeles: Museum Reproductions, 1983.

Gómez, Arthur. "Royalist in Transition: Facundo Melgares, the Last Spanish Governor of New Mexico, 1818–1822," *New Mexico Historical Review,* 68 (October 1993):371–88.

Gómez Canedo, Lino, O.F.M. *Los archivos de la historia de America, periódo colonial español.* 2 vols. Mexico, D.F.: Instituto Panamericano de Geografía e Historia, 1961.

———, ed. *Sonora hacia fines del siglo XVIII: Un informe del misionero franciscano Fray Francisco Antonio Barbastro, con otros documentos complementarios.* Guadalajara: Librería Font, 1971.

González Flores, Enrique, and Francisco R. Almada, eds. *Informe de Hugo de O'Conor sobre el estado de las Provincias Internas del Norte, 1771–76.* Mexico, D.F.: Editorial Cultura, 1952.

Goodwin, Grenville. *The Social Organization of the Western Apache.* Chicago: The University of Chicago Press, 1942.

Greenleaf, Cameron, and Andrew Wallace. "Tucson: Pueblo, Presidio, and American City: A Synopsis of Its

History," *Arizoniana,* 3 (summer 1962):18–24.

Greenleaf, Richard E. "Land and Water in Mexico and New Mexico, 1700–1821," *New Mexico Historical Review,* 47 (April 1972):85–112.

Griffen, William B. "The Chiricahua Apache Population Resident at the Janos Presidio, 1792 to 1858," *Journal of the Southwest,* 33 (summer 1991):151–99.

Griswold del Castillo, Richard. *The Treaty of Guadalupe Hidalgo: A Legacy of Conflict.* Norman: University of Oklahoma Press, 1990.

Gritzer, Charles F. "Hispanic Log Construction of New Mexico," *El Palacio,* 85 (winter 1979):20–29.

Grivas, Theodore. "Alcalde Rule: The Nature of Local Government in Spanish and Mexican California," *California Historical Society Quarterly,* 40 (March 1961):11–32.

Guest, Francis F., O.F.M. "An Examination of the Thesis of S. F. Cook on the Forced Conversion of Indians in the California Missions," *Southern California Quarterly,* 61 (spring 1979):1–78.

———. *Fermín Francisco de Lasuén (1736–1803): A Biography.* Washington, D.C.: Academy of American Franciscan History, 1973.

———. "Mission Colonization and Political Control," *Journal of San Diego History,* 24 (winter 1978):97–116.

———. "Municipal Institutions in Spanish California," *California Historical Quarterly,* 46 (December 1967):307–35.

Gumerman, George J., ed. *Exploring the Hohokam: Prehistoric Desert Peoples of the American Southwest.* Albuquerque: University of New Mexico Press, 1991.

Gutiérrez, Ramón A. *When Jesus Came, the Corn Mothers Went Away: Marriage, Sexuality, and Power in New Mexico, 1500–1846.* Stanford: Stanford University Press, 1991.

Habig, Marion A. "The Builders of San Xavier del Bac," *Southwestern Historical Quarterly,* 41 (October 1937):154–66.

Hackett, Charles W. *Historical Documents Relating to New Mexico, Nueva Vizacaya, and Approaches Thereto.* 3 vols. Washington, D.C.: Carnegie Institution, 1923–1937.

Hackett, Charles W., and Charmion C. Shelby. *Revolt of the Pueblo Indians of New Mexico and Otermín's Attempted Reconquest, 1680–1682.* Albuquerque: University of New Mexico Press, 1942.

Hager, Everett, and Anna Marie Hager, eds. *The Zamorano Index to the History of California by Hubert Howe Bancroft.* 2 vols. Los Angeles: University of Southern California, 1985.

Hague, Harlan. *The Road to California: The Search for a Southern Overland Route, 1540–1848.* Glendale, Calif.: Arthur H. Clark Co., 1978.

Hall, G. Emlen. *Four Leagues of Pecos: A Legal History of the Pecos Grant, 1800–1933.* Albuquerque: University of New Mexico Press, 1984.

Hallenbeck, Cleve. *Alvar Nuñez Cabeza de Vaca: The Journey and Route of the First European to Cross the Continent of North America, 1534–1536.* Glendale, Calif.: The Arthur H. Clark Co., 1940.

———, ed. *The Journey of Fray Marcos de Niza.* Introduction by David J. Weber and illustrations by José Cisneros. Dallas: Southern Methodist University Press, 1987.

Hammond, George, and Agapito Rey. *Don Juan de Oñate: Colonizer of New Mexico, 1595–1628.* 2 vols. Albuquerque: University of New Mexico Press, 1953.

———. *Narratives of the Coronado Expedition, 1540–1542.* Albuquerque: The University of New Mexico Press, 1940.

———. *The Rediscovery of New Mexico, 1580–1595.* Albuquerque: University of New Mexico Press, 1966.

Hammond, George P. *The Larkin Papers: Personal, Business, and Official Correspondence of Thomas Oliver Larkin, Merchant and United States Consul in California.* 10 vols. Berkeley: University of California Press, 1951–1968.

———. "Oñate's Effort to Gain Political Autonomy for New Mexico," *Hispanic American Historical Review,* 32 (August 1952):321–30.

———. "Pimería Alta after Kino's Time," *New Mexico Historical Review,* 4 (July 1929):220–38.

———. "The Zuñiga Journal, Tucson to Santa Fe, the Opening of a Spanish Trade Route, 1788–1795," *New Mexico Historical Review,* 6 (January 1931):40–65.

Hanna, Warren L. *Lost Harbor: The Controversy over Drake's California Anchorage.* Berkeley: University of California Press, 1979.

Harlow, Neal. *California Conquered: War and Peace on the Pacific, 1846–1850.* Berkeley: University of California Press, 1982.

———. *Maps and Surveys of the Pueblo Lands of Los Angeles.* Los Angeles: Dawson's Book Shop, 1976.

———. *Maps of the Pueblo Lands of San Diego, 1602–1874.* Los Angeles: Dawson's Book Shop, 1988.

Haskell, Marion. "A Review of Rubí's Inspection of the Frontier Presidios of New Spain, 1766–1768," Historical Society of Southern California *Annual Publications,* 11 (1918):33–44.

Hastings, James Rodney. "People of Reason and Others: The Colonization of Sonora to 1767," *Arizona and the West,* 3 (winter 1961):321–40.

Heizer, Robert F. *Elizabethan California.* Ramona, Calif.: Ballena Press, 1974.

———. *Francis Drake and the California Indians.* Berkeley: University of California Press, 1947.

———, ed. *Handbook of North American Indians: California. Vol. 8.* Washington, D.C.: The Smithsonian Institution, 1978.

———. "The Impact of Colonization on the Native California Societies," *Journal of San Diego History,* 24 (winter 1978):121–39.

———. *Languages, Territories, and Names of California Indian Tribes.* Berkeley: University of California Press, 1966.

———. *The Indians of California: A Critical Bibliography.* Bloomington: University of Indiana Press, 1976.

Heizer, Robert F., and M. A. Whipple. *The California Indians: A Source Book.* Berkeley: University of California Press, 1951.

Hendricks, Rick. "Pedro Rodríguez Cubero: New Mexico's Reluctant Governor, 1697–1703," *New Mexico Historical Review,* 68 (January 1993):13–39.

Henige, David. *In Search of Columbus: The Sources for the First Voyage.* Tucson: University of Arizona Press, 1991.

Hernández, Salomé. "No Settlement without Women: Three Spanish California Settlement Schemes, 1790–1800," *Southern California Quarterly,* 72 (fall 1990):203–34.

———. "*Nueva Mexicanas as Refugees and Reconquest Settlers, 1680,*" in *New Mexico Women: Intercultural Perspectives,* ed. by Joan M. Jensen and Darlis A. Miller. Albuquerque: University of New Mexico Press, 1986.

Hernández y Sánchez-Barba, Mario. "Frontera, Población y Milicia (Estudio estructural de la acción defensiva hispánica en Sonora durante el siglo XVIII)," *Revista de Indias,* 16 (1956): 9–49.

———. *Juan Bautista de Anza, un hombre de fronteras.* Madrid: Publicaciones Españolas, 1962.

———. *La ultima expansión española en América.* Madrid: Instituto de Estudios Politicos, 1957.

Herrera, Antonio de. *Historia general de los hechos de los Castellanos en las islas i tierra firme del mar oceano.* 12 vols. Madrid, 1601–1615; ed. by Antonio Ballesteros y Beretta, Madrid: Tipografía Archivos, 1934–1953.

Herring, Hubert H. *A History of Latin America from the Beginning to the Present.* New York: Alfred A. Knopf, 1965.

Herring, Patricia Roche. "Tucsonense Preclaro (Illustrious Tucsonan): General José C. Urrea, Romantic Idealist," *The Journal of Arizona History,* 34 (autumn 1993):307–20.

Hilton, Sylvia L. *La Alta California Española.* Madrid: Editorial MAPFRE, 1992.

Hittell, Theodore H. *History of California.* 4 vols. San Francisco: N. J. Stone and Co., 1897–1898.

Hodge, Frederick W., and Theodore H. Lewis, eds. *Spanish Explorers in the Southern United States, 1528–1543.* 1907. Reprint, New York: Barnes and Noble, 1965.

Hollon, W. Eugene. *The Lost Pathfinder: Zebulon Montgomery Pike.* Norman: University of Oklahoma Press, 1949.

Holmes, Maurice G. *From New Spain by Sea to the Californias, 1519–1668.* Glendale, Calif.: Arthur H. Clark Co., 1963.

Hurtado, Albert L. *Indian Survival on the California Frontier.* New Haven: Yale University Press, 1988.

———. "The Underside of Colonial New Mexico: A Review Essay," *New Mexico Historical Review,* 68 (April 1993): 181–88.

Ivancovich, Byron. "Juan Bautista de Anza: Pioneer of Arizona," *Arizoniana,* 1 (winter 1960): 21–24.

Ives, Ronald L. *José Velásquez: Saga of a Borderland Soldier.* Tucson: Southwestern Mission Research Center, 1984.

——. "The Quest for the Blue Shells," *Arizoniana*, 2 (spring 1961): 3–7.

——. "Retracing the Route of the Fages Expedition of 1781," *Arizona and the* West, 8 (spring–summer 1966):49–70; 157–70.

Ivey, James E. "'The Greatest Misfortune of All': Famine in the Province of New Mexico, 1667–1672," *Journal of the Southwest*, 36 (spring 1994): 76–100.

Jackman, Jarrell C. *Felipe de Goicoechea, Santa Barbara Presidio Comandante.* Santa Barbara, Calif.: Anson Luman Press, 1993.

Jackson, Donald, ed. *The Journals of Zebulon Montgomery Pike with Letters and Related Documents.* 2 vols. Norman: University of Oklahoma Press, 1966.

Jackson, Earl. *Tumacacori's Yesterdays.* Globe, Ariz.: Southwest Parks and Monuments Association, 1973.

Jackson, Robert H. "The Changing Economic Structure of the Alta California Missions—A Reinterpretation," *Pacific Historical Review*, 61 (August 1992):387–415.

——. "The Impact of Liberal Policy on Mexico's Northern Frontier: Mission Secularization and the Development of Alta California, 1812–1846," *Colonial Latin American Historical Review*, 2 (spring 1993):195–225.

Jackson, Robert H., and Edward Castillo. *Indians, Franciscans and Spanish Colonization: The Impact of the Mission System on California Indians.* Albuquerque: University of New Mexico Press, 1995.

Jacobs, G. Clell. "The Phantom Pathfinder: Juan María Antonio de Rivera and His Expedition," *Utah Historical Quarterly*, 60 (summer 1992):200–23.

Jenkins, Myra Ellen. "Spanish Colonial Policy and the Pueblo Indians" in Charles H. Lange, ed., *Southwestern Culture History: Collected Papers in Honor of Albert H. Schroeder.* Santa Fe: Ancient City Press, 1985.

——. "Spanish Land Grants in the Tewa Area," *New Mexico Historical Review*, 47 (April 1966): 85–114.

John, Elizabeth A. H. *Storms Brewed in other Men's Worlds: The Confrontation of Indians, Spanish and French in the Southwest, 1540–1795.* College Station: Texas A&M Press, 1975.

Jones, Oakah L. *Los Paisanos: Spanish Settlers on the Northern Frontier of New Spain.* Norman: University of Oklahoma Press, 1979.

——. *Pueblo Warriors and Spanish Conquest.* Norman: University of Oklahoma Press, 1966.

——. "Rescue and Ransom of Spanish Captives from the Indios Bárbaros on the Northern Frontier of New Spain," *Colonial Latin American Historical Review*, 4 (spring 1995): 129–48.

——. *The Spanish Borderlands: A First Reader.* Los Angeles: Lorrin L. Morrison, 1974.

Jordan, Terry G. *North American Cattle-Ranching Frontiers: Origins, Diffusion, and Differentiation.* Albuquerque: University of New Mexico Press, 1993.

Kamen, Henry. *Spain, 1469–1714: A Society of Conflict.* New York: Longman, 1991.

Kelly, Henry W. "Franciscan Missions of New Mexico, 1740–1760," *New Mexico Historical Review*, 15–16 (October 1940; January and April 1941): 345–68; 41–69; 148–83.

Kelsey, Harry. "Did Francis Drake Really Visit California?" *Western Historical Quarterly*, 21 (November 1990): 445–62.

——."A New Look at the Founding of Old Los Angeles," *California Historical Quarterly*, 55 (winter 1976): 326–39.

——. *Juan Rodriguez Cabrillo.* San Marino, Calif.: The Huntington Library, 1986.

——. "Mapping the California Coast: The Voyages of Discovery, 1533–1543," *Arizona and the West*, 26 (winter 1984): 307–34.

Kendrick, T. D. *Mary of Agreda: The Life and Legend of a Spanish Nun.* London: Routledge and Kegan Paul, 1967.

Kenneally, Finbar, ed. and trans. *Writings of Fermín Francisco de Lasuén.* Washington, D.C.: Academy of American Franciscan History, 1973.

Kennedy, Roger G. *Mission: The History and Architecture of the Missions of North America.* Boston and New York: Houghton Mifflin, 1993.

Kessell, John L. "Father Ramón and the Big Debt: Tumacácori, 1821–1823," *New Mexico Historical Review*, 44 (January 1969): 53–72.

——. "Friars, Bureaucrats, and the Seris of Sonora," *New Mexico Historical Review*, 50 (January 1975):73–95.

——. *Friars, Soldiers, and Reformers: Hispanic Arizona and the Sonora Mission Frontier 1767–1856.* Tucson: The University of Arizona Press, 1976.

———. "Friars versus Bureaucrats: The Mission as a Threatened Institution on the Arizona-Sonora Frontier, 1767–1842," *The Western Historical Quarterly,* 5 (April 1974):151–62.

———. *Kiva, Cross, and Crown: The Pecos Indians and New Mexico, 1540–1840.* Washington D.C.: National Park Service, 1979.

———. "Making of a Martyr: The Young Francisco Garcés," 4 *New Mexico Historical Review,* 45 (July 1970):181–96.

———. "Miracles or Mystery: María de Agreda's Ministry to the Jumano Indians of the Southwest in the 1620s," in Ferenc Morton Szasz, ed., *Great Mysteries of the West.* Golden, Colo.: Fulcrum Publishing, 1993.

———. *Mission of Sorrows: Jesuit Guevavi and the Pimas, 1691–1767.* Tucson: University of Arizona Press, 1970.

———. "The Puzzling Presido: San Phelipe de Guevavi, alias Terrenate," *New Mexico Historical Review,* 41 (January 1966):21–46.

———, ed. "Anza Damns the Missions: A Spanish Soldier's Criticism of Indian Policy," *The Journal of Arizona History,* 13 (spring 1972):53–63.

———, ed. "San José de Tumacacori—1773: A Franciscan Reports from Arizona," *Arizona and the West,* 6 (winter 1964):303–12.

Kessell, John L., and Rick Hendricks, eds. *By Force of Arms: The Journals of don Diego de Vargas, New Mexico, 1691–93.* Albuquerque: University of New Mexico Press, 1992.

Kessell, John L., Rick Hendricks, and Meredith D. Dodge, eds. *To the Royal Crown Restored: The Journals of don Diego de Vargas, New Mexico, 1692–94.* Albuquerque: University of New Mexico Press, 1995.

Kessell, John L., Rick Hendricks, Meredith D. Dodge, Larry D. Miller, and Eleanor B. Adams, eds. *Remote Beyond Compare: Letters of don Diego de Vargas to His Family from New Spain and New Mexico, 1675–1706.* Albuquerque: University of New Mexico Press, 1989.

Kinnaird, Lawrence. *The Frontiers of New Spain. Nicolas LaFora's Description, 1766–1768.* Berkeley: The Quivira Society 1958.

———. "The Spanish Tobacco Monopoly in New Mexico, 1766–1767," *New Mexico Historical Review,* 21 (October 1946):328–39.

Kino, Eusebio Francisco, S.J. *Historical Memoir of the Pimería Alta,* trans. by Herbert E. Bolton. Berkeley: University of California Press, 1948.

Kintigh, Keith W. *Settlement, Subsistence, and Society in Late Zuni Prehistory.* Tucson: University of Arizona Press, 1985.

Knapp, Frank A. "The Mexican Fear of Manifest Destiny in California," in Thomas E. Cotner, and Carlos E. Castañeda, eds., *Essays in American History.* Austin: University of Texas Press, 1958.

Kroeber, Alfred E. *Handbook of the Indians of California.* Washington, D.C.: The Smithsonian Institution, 1925.

Kupper, Winifred. *The Golden Hoof: The Story of the Sheep of the Southwest.* New York: Alfred A. Knopf, 1945.

LaFora, Nicolas de. *Relación del viaje que hizo a los presidios internos situados en la frontera de la America Septentrional perteneciente al Rey de España,* ed. by Vito Alessio Robles. Mexico, D.F.: Editorial Pedro Robredo, 1939. Translated and edited by Lawrence Kinnaird as *The Frontiers of New Spain: Nicolas de LaFora's Description, 1766–1768.* Berkeley: The Quivira Society, 1958.

Lamar, Howard R. *The Far Southwest, 1846–1912: A Territorial History.* New Haven: Yale University Press, 1966.

Langum, David. "The Caring Colony: Alta California's Participation in Spain's Foreign Affairs," *Southern California Quarterly,* 62 (fall 1980):217–28.

———. *Law and Community on the Mexican California Frontier: Anglo American Expatriates and the Clash of Legal Traditions, 1821–1846.* Norman: University of Oklahoma Press, 1987.

Leon Portilla, Miguel. *The Broken Spears: The Aztec Account of the Conquest of Mexico.* Boston: Beacon Press, 1992.

Lewis, David Rich. *Neither Wolf nor Dog: American Indians, Environment & Agrarian Change.* New York: Oxford University Press, 1994.

Loomis, Noel M. "Commandants–General of the Interior Provinces, A Preliminary List," *Arizona and the West,* 11 (autumn 1969):261–68.

Loomis, Noel M., and Abraham P. Nasatir. *Pedro Vial and the Roads to Santa Fe.* Norman: University of Oklahoma Press, 1967.

Madariaga, Salvador de. *Hernán Cortés, Conqueror of Mexico.* New York: Macmillan Company, 1941.

Magnaghi, Russell M. "Plains Indians in New Mexico: The Genízaro Experience," *Great Plains Quarterly,* 10 (spring 1990):86–95.

Manje, Juan Matheo. *Unknown Arizona and Sonora, 1693–1721,* trans. by Harry J. Karns and Associates. Tucson: University of Arizona Press, 1954.

Martínez, Pablo L. *History of Lower California.* México, D.F.: Editorial Baja California, 1956.

Mason, Bill. "The Garrisons of San Diego Presidio: 1770–1794," *Journal of San Diego History,* 24 (fall 1978):399–424.

Mathes, W. Michael. "Baja California Indians in the Spanish Maritime Service, 1720–1821," *Southern California Quarterly,* 62 (summer 1980):113–126.

——. "Sebastián Vizcaíno and San Diego Bay," *Journal of San Diego History,* 18 (April 1972):1–7.

——. *Vizcaíno and Spanish Expansion in the Pacific Ocean.* San Francisco: California Historical Society, 1968.

——, ed. and trans. *The Conquistador in California, 1535: The Voyage of Fernando Cortés to Baja California in Chronicles and Documents.* Los Angeles: Dawson's Book Shop, 1973.

Matson, Daniel S., and Bernard L. Fontana, eds. *Friar Bringas Reports to the King.* Tucson: University of Arizona Press, 1977.

Matson, Daniel S., and Albert H. Schroeder, eds. "Cordero's Description of the Apache—1796," *New Mexico Historical Review,* 32 (October 1957):335–56.

Matson, R. G. *The Origins of Southwest Agriculture.* Tucson: University of Arizona Press, 1991.

Mattison, Ray H. "Early Spanish and Mexican Settlements in Arizona," *New Mexico Historical Review,* 21 (October 1946):273–327.

Maughan, Scott Jarvis. "Francisco Garcés and New Spain's Northwestern Frontier, 1768–1781," Ph.D. dissertation, University of Utah, 1968.

McAlister, Lyle. "Social Structure and Social Change in New Spain," *Hispanic American Historical Review,* 43 (August 1963):349–70.

McCarty, Kieran, O.F.M. "Bernardo de Gálvez on the Apache Frontier: The Education of a Future Viceroy," *Journal of the Southwest,* 36 (summer 1994):103–30.

——. *A Spanish Frontier in the Enlightened Age: Franciscan Beginnings in Sonora and Arizona, 1767–1770.* Washington, D.C.: American Academy of Franciscan History, 1981.

——. "The Colorado Massacre of 1781: Mariá Montielo's Report," *The Journal of Arizona History,* 16 (autumn 1975):221–25.

——. *Desert Documentary: The Spanish Years, 1767–1821.* Historical Monograph no. 4. Tucson: Arizona Historical Society, 1976.

——. "Franciscan Beginnings on the Arizona–Sonora Desert, 1767–1770," Ph. D. dissertation, Catholic University of America, 1973.

——. "The Sonora Prophecy of 1783," *Journal of the Southwest,* 32 (autumn 1990):316–20.

McClintock, James H. *Arizona: Prehistoric, Aboriginal, Pioneer, Modern.* 3 vols. Chicago: The S. J. Clarke Publishing Company, 1916.

Meighan, Clement. "Indians and California Missions," *Southern California Quarterly,* 69 (summer 1987):187–201.

Meigs, Peveril. *The Dominican Mission Frontier of Lower California.* Berkeley: University of California Publications in Geography, vol. 7, 1935.

Meinig, D. W. *The Southwest: Three Peoples in Geographical Change, 1600–1970.* New York: Oxford University Press, 1971.

Meyer, Michael C. *Water in the Hispanic Southwest, A Social and Legal History, 1550–1580.* Tucson: The University of Arizona Press, 1984.

Milich, Alicia R. *Relaciones of Father Zárate Salmerón.* Albuquerque: University of New Mexico Press, 1966.

Miller, Robert Ryal. "New Mexico in Mid–Eighteenth Century: A Report Based on Governor Vélez de Cachupín's Inspection," *Southwestern Historical Quarterly,* 79 (October 1975):166–81.

Minge, Ward Alan. *Acoma: Pueblo in the Sky.* Albuquerque: University of New Mexico Press, 1976.

Miranda, Gloria E. "Gente de Razón Marriage Patterns in Spanish and Mexican California: A Case Study of Santa Barbara and Los Angeles," *Southern California Quarterly,* 63 (spring 1981):1–22.

——. "Hispano–Mexican Child–rearing Practices in Pre–American Santa Barbara," *Southern California Quar-*

terly, 65 (winter 1983):307–20.

———. "Racial and Cultural Dimensions of Gente de Razón Status in Spanish and Mexican California," *Southern California Quarterly,* 70 (fall 1988):265–78.

Moes, Robert J. "Smallpox Immunization in Alta California: A Story Based on José Estrada's 1821 Postscript," *Southern California Quarterly,* 61 (summer 1979):125–46.

Moorhead, Max L. *The Apache Frontier: Jacobo Ugarte and Spanish–Indian Relations in Northern New Spain, 1769–1791.* Norman: University of Oklahoma Press, 1968.

———. *New Mexico's Royal Road: Trade and Travel on the Chihuahua Trail.* Norman University of Oklahoma Press, 1958.

———. *The Presidio: Bastion of the Spanish Borderlands.* Norman: University of Oklahoma Press, 1975.

———. "Spanish Deportation of Hostile Apaches: The Policy and the Practice," *Arizona and the West,* 17 (autumn 1975):205–20.

———. "Spanish Transportation in the Southwest, 1540–1846," *New Mexico Historical Review,* 32 (August 1957):107–22.

Morison, Samuel Eliot. *Admiral of the Ocean Sea.* Boston: Little, Brown Co., 1942.

Moyer, Cecil. *Historic Ranchos of San Diego.* San Diego: The Copley Press, 1969.

Muldoon, James. *The Americans in the Spanish World Order: The Justification for Conquest in the Seventeenth Century.* Philadelphia: University of Pennsylvania Press, 1994.

Navarro García, Luis. *Don José de Gálvez y la Comandancia General de las Provincias Internas del Norte de Nueva España.* Sevilla: Escuela de Estudios Hispano–Americanos, 1964.

———. "El Marques de Croix (1766–1771)," in *Los virreyes de Nueva España en el reinado de Carlos III,* ed. by José Antonio Calderón Quijano. 2 vols. Sevilla: Escuela de Estudios Hispano–Americanos, 1967–1968, vol. I, pp. 161–381.

Nelson, Howard J. "The Two Pueblos of Los Angeles: Agricultural Village and Embryo Town," *Southern California Quarterly,* 59 (spring 1977):1–12.

Nentuig, Juan, S.J. *Rudo Ensayo, by an unknown Jesuit padre, 1763.* Tucson: Arizona Silhouettes, 1951.

Neuerburg, Norman. *The Decoration of the California Missions.* Santa Barbara, Calif.: Bellerophon Books, 1987.

Nichols, Roy F. *Advance Agents of American Destiny.* Philadelphia: University of Pennsylvania, 1956.

Nostrand, Richard L. *The Hispano Homeland.* Norman: University of Oklahoma Press, 1992.

Nunis, Doyce B. Jr., ed. *Southern California's Spanish Heritage: An Anthology.* Los Angeles: Historical Society of Southern California, 1992.

Nuttall, Donald A. "The Gobernantes of Spanish Upper California: A Profile," *California Historical Quarterly,* 51 (fall 1972):253–80.

———. "Light Cast Upon Shadows: The Non–California Years of Don Pedro Fages," *California Historical Quarterly,* 56 (fall 1976):250–69.

Nuttall, Zelia, ed. and trans. "Royal Ordinances Concerning the Laying Out of New Towns," *Hispanic American Historical Review,* 4–5 (November 1921; May 1922):743–53; 249–54.

O'Keefe, Timothy, ed. *Columbus, Confrontation and Christianity: The European–American Encounter Revisited.* Madison, Wis.: Forbes Mills Press, 1993.

Obregón, Baltasar de. *Historia de los descubrimientos antiguos y modernos de la Nueva España,* ed. by Mariano Cuevas. Mexico, D.F.: Secretaría de Educación, 1924.

Officer, James E. *Hispanic Arizona, 1536–1856.* Tucson: University of Arizona Press, 1987.

———. "Kino and Agriculture in the Pimería Alta," *The Journal of Arizona History* 34 (autumn 1993):287–306.

Ogden, Adele. *The California Sea Otter Trade, 1784–1848.* Berkeley: University of California Press, 1941.

Olivera, Ruth R., and Liliane Crété. *Life in New Mexico Under Santa Anna, 1822–1855.* Norman: University of Oklahoma Press, 1991.

Ortíz, Alfonso, ed. *Handbook of North American Indians. Southwest.* Vols. 9 and 10. William C. Sturtevant, general editor. Washington, D.C.: The Smithsonian Institution, 1979.

———. *New Perspectives on the Pueblos.* Albuquerque: University of New Mexico Press, 1972.

Page, Donald W. "Tucson, Pre-Traditional Times to the Founding of the Presidio," in Frank C. Lockwood, *Tucson, The Old Pueblo.* Phoenix: Manufacturing Stationers, 1930.

Palóu, Francisco. *Life of Fray Junípero Serra,* ed. by Maynard J. Geiger. Washington, D.C.: Academy of American Franciscan History, 1955.

Park, Joseph F. "Spanish Indian Policy in Northern Mexico, 1756–1810," *Arizona and the West,* 4 (winter 1962):325–44.

Parsons, Elsie Clews. *Pueblo Indian Religion.* 2 vols. Chicago: University of Chicago Press, 1939.

Pérez de Ribas, Andrés. *Historia de los Triumphos de Nuestra Santa Fe entre Gentes las mas Bárbaras y fieras del Nuevo Orbe.* Madrid, 1645; reprinted in Mexico: Editorial Layac, 1944.

Pérez de Villagrá, Gaspár. *Historia de la Nueva México, 1610,* trans. and ed. by Miguel Encinias, Alfred Rodríguez, and Joseph P. Sánchez. Albuquerque: University of New Mexico Press, 1993.

Pfefferkorn, Ignaz. *Sonora: A Description of the Province,* ed. and trans. by Theodore E. Treutlein. Albuquerque: University of New Mexico Press, 1949.

Phillips, George Harwood. *Indians and Intruders in Central California, 1769–1849.* Norman: University of Oklahoma Press, 1993.

Pino, Pedro Bautista. *Exposición sucinta y sencilla de la provincia de Nuevo México hecha por su diputado en cortes con arreglo a sus instrucciones.* Cádiz, Spain: n.p., 1822.

Pitt, Leonard. *The Decline of the Californios, 1846–1890.* Berkeley: University of California Press, 1966.

Polzer, Charles W., ed. "The Franciscan Entrada into Sonora, 1645–1652: A Jesuit Chronicle," *Arizona and the West,* 14 (autumn 1972):253–78.

Poster, Corky. "Sombra, Patios, y Macetas: Modernism, Regionalism, and the Elements of Southwestern Architecture," *Journal of the Southwest,* 35 (winter 1993):461–500.

Pourade, Richard. *Anza Conquers the Desert.* San Diego: The Copley Press, 1971.

Powell, Philip W. "Presidios and Towns on the Frontier of New Spain, 1550–1580," *Hispanic American Historical Review,* 24 (May 1944):179–200.

———. *Soldiers, Indians and Silver: The Northward Advance of New Spain, 1550–1600.* Berkeley: University of California Press, 1952.

Pradeau, Alberto Francisco. *La Expulsión de los Jesuitas de las Provincias de Sonora, Ostimuri y Sinaloa en 1767.* Mexico, D.F.: Antigua Librería Robredo de José Porrua e Hijos, 1959.

Preston, Douglas. *Cities of Gold: A Journey Across the American Southwest in Pursuit of Coronado.* New York: Simon and Schuster, 1992.

Priestley, Herbert I. *José de Galvez, Visitor-general of New Spain, 1765–1771.* Berkeley: University of California Press, 1916.

Radding de Murrieta, Cynthia. "The Function of the Market in Changing Economic Structures in the Mission Communities of Pimería Alta, 1768–1821," *The Americas,* 34 (October 1977):155–69.

Rawls, James J. *Indians of California: The Changing Image.* Norman: University of Oklahoma Press, 1984.

Recopilación de leyes de los reynos de las Indias. 4 vols. Madrid: Julián de Paredes, 1681; facsimile reprint, Madrid: Ediciones Cultura Hispánica, 1973.

Reeve, Frank D. "Navaho–Spanish Wars, 1680–1720," *New Mexico Historical Review,* 31 (July 1958):200–35.

Reff, Daniel T. *Disease, Depopulation, and Culture Change in Northwestern New Spain, 1518–1764.* Salt Lake City: University of Utah Press, 1991.

Remacha, José Ramón. "Traces of the Spanish Legal System in New Mexico," *New Mexico Historical Review,* 69 (July 1994):281–94.

Revilla Gigedo, Conde de. *Informe sobre las misiones, 1793, e Instrucción reservada al Marques de Branciforte, 1794,* introduction and notes by José Bravo Ugarte. Mexico, D.F.: Editorial Jus, 1966.

Richman, Irving B. *California Under Spain and Mexico, 1535–1857.* Boston: Houghton Mifflin Co., 1911.

Riley, Carroll L. "Las Casas and the Benavides Memorial," *New Mexico Historical Review,* 58 (July 1973):209–22.

———. "Early Spanish–Indian Communication in the Great Southwest," *New Mexico Historical Review,* 46 (October 1971):285–314.

Ríos–Bustamante, Antonio. *Los Angeles, pueblo y región, 1781–1850.* México, D.F.: Instituto Nacional de Antropología e Historia, 1991.

Robinson, Cecil. *With the Ears of Strangers: The Mexican in American Literature.* Tucson: University of Arizona Press, 1963.

———. *Mexico and the Hispanic Southwest in American Literature.* Tucson: University of Arizona Press, 1977.

Robinson, W. W. *Ranchos Become Cities.* Pasadena, Calif.: San Pascual Press, 1939.

Rock, Rosalind Z. "Mujeres de Substancia—Case Studies of Women of Property in Northern New Spain,"

Colonial Latin American Historical Review, 2 (fall 1993):425–40.

———. "Pido y Suplico: Women and Law in Spanish New Mexico, 1697–1763," *New Mexico Historical Review,* 65 (April 1990):145–59.

Rowland, Donald Winslow. "The Elizondo Expedition Against the Indian Rebels of Sonora, 1765–1771," Ph.D. dissertation, University of California, Berkeley, 1930.

Sánchez Albornoz, Claudio. *Spain: A Historical Enigma.* 2 vols. Madrid: Fundación Universitaria Española, 1975.

Sánchez, Jane C. "Spanish–Indian Relations during the Otermín Administration, 1677–1683," *New Mexico Historical Review,* 58 (April 1983):134–37.

———. "The Plan of Pitic: Galindo Navarro's Letter to Teodoro de Croix, Comandante General de las Provincias Internas," *Colonial Latin American Historical Review,* 3 (winter 1994):79–89.

Sánchez, Joseph P. "Old Heat and New Light Concerning the Search for Coronado's Bridge: A Historiography of the Pecos and Canadian Rivers Hypotheses," *New Mexico Historical Review,* 67 (April 1992):101–14.

———. "Pedro Fages in Sonora, 1767–1768 and 1777–1782," *New Mexico Historical Review,* 51 (October 1976):281–94.

———. *Spanish Bluecoats: The Catalonian Volunteers in Northwestern New Spain, 1767–1810.* Albuquerque: University of New Mexico Press, 1990.

———, ed. and trans. "El Plan de Pitic de 1789 y las nuevas poblaciones proyectadas en las Provincias Internas de la Nueva España," *Colonial Latin American Historical Review,* 2 (Fall 1993):449–67.

Sandos, James A. "Levantamiento!: The 1824 Chumash Uprising Reconsidered," *Southern California Quarterly,* 67 (summer 1985):109–33.

Santiago, Mark. *The Red Captain: The Life of Hugo O'Conor.* Tucson: Arizona Historical Society, 1994.

Sauer, Carl. "The Credibility of the Fray Marcos Account," *New Mexico Historical Review,* 16 (April 1941):233–43.

———, ed. "A Spanish Entrada into the Arizona Apacheria," *Arizona Historical Review,* 6 (January 1935):3–13.

Scholes, France V. *Church and State in New Mexico, 1610–1650.* Historical Society of New Mexico Publications in History, vol. 7. Albuquerque: University of New Mexico Press, 1942.

———. "Civil Government and Society in New Mexico in the Seventeenth Century," *New Mexico Historical Review,* 10 (April 1935):71–111.

———. "The First Decade of the Inquisition in New Mexico," *New Mexico Historical Review,* 10 (July 1935):195–241.

———. "Royal Treasury Records Relating to the Province of New Mexico, 1596–1683," *New Mexico Historical Review,* 50 (January and April 1975):5–23; 139–64.

———. "The Supply Service of the New Mexico Missions in the Seventeenth Century," *New Mexico Historical Review,* 5 (January, April, and July 1930):93–115; 186–210; 386–410.

———. *Troublous Times in New Mexico, 1659–1670.* Historical Society of New Mexico Publications in History, vol. 11. Albuquerque: University of New Mexico Press, 1942.

Scholes, France V., and Lansing P. Bloom. "Friar Personnel and Mission Chronology, 1598–1629," *New Mexico Historical Review,* 19–20 (October 1944; January 1945):319–36; 58–82.

Schroeder, Albert H. "The Locale of Coronado's Bridge," *New Mexico Historical Review,* 67 (April 1992):115–22.

———. "A Re–analysis of the Routes of Coronado and Oñate onto the Plains in 1541 and 1601," *Plains Anthropologist,* 7 (February 1962):2–23.

Schurz, William L. *The Manila Galleon.* New York: E. P. Dutton, 1939.

Señán, José. *The Letters of José Señán, O.F.M., Mission San Buenaventura, 1796–1823,* Leslie Byrd Simpson, ed., and Paul D. Nathan, trans. San Francisco: John Howell Books, 1960.

Servín, Manuel P. "Costansó's 1794 Report on Strengthening New California's Presidios," *California Historical Society Quarterly,* 49 (September 1970):221–32.

———. "The Secularization of the California Missions: A Reappraisal," *Southern California Quarterly,* 47 (June 1965):133–50.

Shea, John G. *The Expedition of Don Diego De Peñalosa, Governor of New Mexico from Santa Fe to the Río Mischipi ... in 1662.* Albuquerque: Horn and Wallace, 1964.

Sheridan, Thomas E. *Arizona: A History.* University of Arizona Press, 1995.

———. "Kino's Unforseen Legacy: The Material Consequences of Missionization among the Piman Indians of Arizona and Sonora," *Smoke Signal,* 49–50 (spring and fall 1988):151–67.

———. *Los Tucsonenses: The Mexican Community in Tucson, 1854–1941.* Tucson: University of Arizona Press, 1987.

Simmons, Marc. *Albuquerque: A Narrative History.* Albuquerque: University of New Mexico, 1982.

———. *Coronado's Land: Essays on Daily Life in Colonial New Mexico.* Albuquerque: University of New Mexico Press, 1991.

———. *The Last Conquistador: Juan de Oñate and the Settling of the Far Southwest.* Norman: University of Oklahoma Press, 1991.

———. "New Mexico's Smallpox Epidemic of 1780–1781," *New Mexico Historical Review,* 41 (October 1966):319–26.

———. "New Mexico's Spanish Exiles," *New Mexico Historical Review,* 59 (January 1984):67–79.

———. "Settlement Patterns and Village Plans in Colonial New Mexico," in David Weber, ed., *New Spain's Far Northern Frontier.* Albuquerque: University of New Mexico Press, 1979, pp. 96–115.

———. "Spanish Attempts to Open a New Mexico–Sonora Road," *Arizona and the West,* 17 (spring 1975):5–20.

———. *Spanish Government in New Mexico.* Albuquerque: University of New Mexico Press, 1968.

———. "Spanish Irrigation in New Mexico," *New Mexico Historical Review,* 47 (April, 1972):135–50.

———. "Tlascalans in the Spanish Borderlands," *New Mexico Historical Review,* 39 (April 1964):101–10.

———, ed. *Indian and Mission Affairs in New Mexico, 1773 by Pedro Fermín de Mendinueta.* Santa Fe: Stagecoach Press, 1965.

Simmons, Marc, Donna Pierce, and Joan Myers. *Santiago: Saint of Two Worlds.* Albuquerque: University of New Mexico Press, 1991.

Simpson, Lesley B., ed., and Paul Nathan, trans. *Letters of José Señán. O.F.M. Mission San Buenaventura, 1796–1823.* San Francisco: John Howell Books, 1962.

Simpson, Leslie Byrd., ed. *Journal of José Longinos Martínez: Notes and Observations of the Naturalist of the Botanical Expedition in Old and New California and the South Coast, 1791–1792.* San Francisco: John Howell Books, 1961.

Sizelove, Linda. "Indian Adaptation to the Spanish Missions," *Pacific Historian,* 22 (winter 1978):313–402.

Smith, Watson. "Seventeenth–Century Spanish Missions of the Western Pueblo Area," *The Smoke Signal,* no. 21. Tucson Corral of the Westerners, 1970.

Sonnichsen, C. L. *Tucson: The Life and Times of An American City.* Maps by Donald H. Bufkin. Norman: University of Oklahoma Press, 1987.

Spicer, Edward H. *Cycles of Conquest: The Impact of Spain, Mexico, and the United States on the Indians of the Southwest, 1533–1960.* Tucson: University of Arizona Press, 1962.

———. "Persistent Cultural Systems," *Science,* 174 (November 1971):795–800.

Stagg, Albert. *The Almadas and Alamos, 1783–1867.* Tucson: University of Arizona Press, 1978.

———. *The First Bishop of Sonora: Antonio de los Reyes, O.F.M.* Tucson: University of Arizona Press, 1976.

Steele, Thomas J. *Santos and Saints: The Religious Folk Art of Hispanic New Mexico.* Santa Fe: Ancient City Press, 1982.

Stoetzer, O. Carlos. "Tradition and Progress in the Late Eighteenth–Century Jesuit Rediscovery of America: Francisco Javier Clavijero's Philosophy and History," *Colonial Latin American Historical Review,* 2 (summer 1993):289–324.

Stoner, Victor R. "Fray Pedro de Arriquivar, Chaplain of the Royal Fort at Tucson," ed. by Henry F. Dobyns, *Arizona and the West,* 1 (spring 1959):71–79.

Sweet, Jill D., and Karen E. Larson. "The Horse, Santiago, and a Ritual Game: Pueblo Indian Responses to Three Spanish Introductions," *Western Folklore,* 53 (January 1994):69–84.

Szasz, Ferenc Morton, ed. *Great Mysteries of the West.* Golden, Colo.: Fulcrum Publishing, 1993.

Taylor, William B. "Land and Water Rights in New Spain," *New Mexico Historical Review,* 50 (July 1975):182–212.

Teggert, Frederick J., and Adolph van Hemert-Engert. *The Narrative of the Portolá Expedition 1769–1770.* Berkeley: University of California Press, 1910.

Terrell, John Upton. *Zebulon Pike: The Life and Times of an Adventurer.* New York: Weybright and Talley, 1968.

Thomas, Alfred Barnaby. *After Coronado: Spanish Exploration Northeast of New Mexico, 1696–1727; Documents from the Archives of Spain, Mexico and New Mexico.* Norman: University of Oklahoma Press, 1935.

——. *The Plains Indians and New Mexico, 1751–1778.* Albuquerque: University of New Mexico Press, 1940.

——. *Teodoro de Croix and the Northern Frontier of New Spain, 1776–1783.* Norman: University of Oklahoma Press, 1941.

——, ed. and trans. *Forgotten Frontiers: A Study of the Spanish Indian Policy of Don Juan Bautista de Anza, Governor of New Mexico, 1777–1787; from the Original Documents from the Archives of Spain, Mexico and New Mexico.* Norman: University of Oklahoma Press 1932; 1969.

——, ed. and trans. *Teodoro de Croix and the Northern Frontier of New Spain, 1776–1783: From the Original Document in the Archives of the Indies, Seville.* Norman: University of Oklahoma Press, 1941.

Thomas, David Hurst, ed. *Columbian Consequences.* 3 vols. Washington, D.C.: Smithsonian Institution Press, 1989–1991.

Thrower, Norman J. H. *Sir Francis Drake and the Famous Voyage, 1577–1580: Essays Commemorating the Quadricentennial of Drake's Circumnavigation of the Earth.* Berkeley: University of California Press, 1984.

Thurman, Michael. *The Naval Department of San Blas: New Spain's Bastion for Alta California and Nootka, 1767–1798.* Glendale, Calif.: Arthur H. Clark Co., 1967.

Tibesar, Antonine, ed. and trans. *The Writings of Fray Junípero Serra.* 4 vols., Washington, D.C.: Academy of American Franciscan History, 1955–1966.

Tjarks, Alicia Vidaurreta. "Demographic, Ethnic and Occupational Structure of New Mexico, 1790," *The Americas,* 35 (July 1978):45–88.

Tobias, Henry J. *A History of the Jews in New Mexico.* Albuquerque: University of New Mexico Press, 1990.

Tomkins, Walter A. *Santa Barbara's Royal Rancho.* Berkeley: University of California Press, 1960.

Treutlein, Theodore E. *San Francisco Bay: Discovery and Colonization, 1769–1776.* San Francisco: California Historical Society, 1968.

——, ed. *Missionary in Sonora: The Travel Reports of Joseph Och, S.J., 1755–1767.* San Francisco: California Historical Society, 1965.

Trimble, Stephen. *The People: Indians of the American Southwest.* Santa Fe: School of American Research Press, 1993.

Tutorow, Norman E., ed. *The Mexican–American War: An Annotated Bibliography.* Westport, Conn.: Greenwood Press, l981.

Twitchell, Ralph E. *The Leading Facts of New Mexico History.* 5 vols. Cedar Rapids, Iowa: Torch Press, 1911–1917.

Tyler, Daniel. *The Mythical Pueblo Rights Doctrine: Water Administration in Colonial New Mexico.* El Paso: Texas Western Press, 1990.

——. "The Spanish Colonial Legacy and the Role of Hispanic Custom in Defining New Mexico Land and Water Rights," *Colonial Latin American Research Review,* 4 (spring 1995):149–66.

Udall, Stewart L. *To the Inland Empire: Coronado and our Spanish Legacy.* Garden City, N.Y.: Doubleday and Company, 1987.

Ulibarri, George S. "The Chouteau–Demun Expedition to New Mexico, 1815–1817," *New Mexico Historical Review,* 36 (October 1961):263–73.

Underhill, Ruth. *The Papago Indians of Arizona and Their Relatives the Pima.* Lawrence: University of Kansas, 1941.

Van Ness, John R., and Christine M. Van Ness, eds. *Spanish and Mexican Land Grants in New Mexico and Colorado. Journal of the West* special issue, July 1980.

Vaux, W. S. W., ed. *The World Encompassed by Sir Francis Drake, Being His Next Voyage ... Collated with an Unpublished Manuscript of Francis Fletcher, Chaplain to the Expedition.* London: The Hakluyt Society, 1589; reprinted 1854.

Vehik, Susan C. "Oñate's Expedition to the Southern Plains: Routes, Destinations and Implications for Late Prehistoric Cultural Adaptations," *Plains Anthropologist,* 31 (February 1986):13–33.

Wagner, Henry R. *Cartography of the Northwest Coast of America to the Year 1800.* 2 vols. Berkeley: University of California Press, 1937.

——. *Sir Francis Drake's Voyage Around the World: Its Aims and Achievements.* San Francisco: California Historical Society, 1926.

——. *The Spanish Southwest, 1542–1794: An Annotated Bibliography.* 2 vols. Los Angeles: The Quivira Society, 1967.

————. *Spanish Voyages to the Northwest Coast of America in the Sixteenth Century.* San Francisco: California Historical Society, 1929.

Wagoner, Jay J. *Early Arizona: Prehistory to Civil War.* Tucson: University of Arizona Press, 1975.

————. *History of the Cattle Industry in Southern Arizona, 1540–1940.* Tucson: University of Arizona Press, 1952.

Walker, Billy D. "Copper Genesis: The Early Years of Santa Rita del Cobre," *New Mexico Historical Review,* 54 (January 1979):5–20.

Warner, Ted. "Felix Martínez and the Santa Fe Presidio," *New Mexico Historical Review,* 45 (October 1970):269–310.

————. "Frontier Defense," *New Mexico Historical Review,* 41 (January 1966):5–19.

Warner, Ted, ed., and Angelico Chávez, trans. *The Domínguez–Escalante Journal: Their Expedition through Colorado, Utah, Arizona and New Mexico in 1776.* Provo, Utah: Brigham Young University Press, 1976.

Weaver, Thomas, ed. *Indians of Arizona: A Contemporary Perspective.* Tucson: University of Arizona Press, 1974.

Weber, David J. *The "Californios" versus Jedediah Smith 1826–1827: A New Cache of Documents.* Spokane, Wash.: Arthur H. Clark Co., 1990.

————. "Failure of a Catholic Institution: The Secular Church in the Borderlands under Independent Mexico, 1821–1846," *Western Historical Quarterly,* 12 (April 1981):125–43.

————. "Fray Marcos de Niza and the Historians," in David J. Weber, ed., *Myth and the History of the Hispanic Southwest.* Albuquerque: University of New Mexico Press, 1988.

————. "Mexico's Far Northern Frontier, 1821–1854: Historiography Askew," *Western Historical Quarterly,* 7 (July 1976):279–93.

————. *Northern Mexico on the Eve of the United States Invasion: Rare Imprints Concerning California, Arizona, New Mexico and Texas, 1821–1846.* New York: Arno Press, 1976.

————. *The Spanish Frontier in North America.* New Haven: Yale University Press, 1992.

————. *The Taos Trappers: The Fur Trade in the Far Southwest, 1540–1846.* Norman: University Oklahoma Press, 1971.

————, ed. *New Spain's Far Northern Frontier: Essays on Spain in the American West.* Albuquerque: University of New Mexico Press, 1979.

Weber, Francis. "Sources for Catholic History of California: A Biblio–Archival Survey," *Southern California Quarterly,* 57 (fall 1975):321–35.

Weddle, Robert S. *Wilderness Manhunt: The Spanish Search for LaSalle.* Austin: University of Texas Press, 1973.

West, Robert C. *Sonora: Its Geographical Personality.* Austin: University of Texas Press, 1993.

White, Leslie A. "Punche: Tobacco in New Mexico History," *New Mexico Historical Review,* 18 (October 1943):386–93.

Whitehead, Richard S. "Alta California's Four Fortresses," *Southern California Quarterly,* 65 (spring 1983): 67–94.

Willey, Richard R. "La Canoa: A Spanish Land Grant Lost and Found," *The Smoke Signal,* no. 38, Tucson: Corral of the Westerners, 1979.

Williams, Jack S. "San Agustín del Tucson: A Vanished Mission Community of the Pimería Alta," and "The Presidio of Santa Cruz de Terrenate: A Forgotten Fortress of Southern Arizona," *The Smoke Signal,* nos. 47 and 48 (combined), Tucson Corral of the Westerners, 1986.

Wilson, John P. "Before the Pueblo Revolt: Population Trends, Apache Relations and Pueblo Abandonments in Seventeenth Century New Mexico," in Nancy Fox, ed., *Prehistory and History in the Southwest.* Santa Fe: Ancient City Press, 1985.

Winship, George P., ed. and trans. *The Journey of Coronado, 1540–1542.* Reprinted, Golden, Colo.: Fulcrum Publishing, 1990.

Worcester, Donald. *The Apaches: Eagles of the Southwest.* Norman: University of Oklahoma Press, 1979.

Wroth, William. *Images of Penance, Images of Mercy: Southwestern Santos in the Late Nineteenth Century.* Norman: University of Oklahoma Press, 1991.

Wyllys, Rufus Kay. *Arizona: History of a Frontier State.* Phoenix: Hobson & Herr, 1950.

————. "Padre Luis Velarde: Relación of Pimería Alta," *New Mexico Historical Review,* 6 (April 1931):111–57.

————. *Pioneer Padre: The Life and Times of Eusebio Francisco Kino.* Dallas: Southwest Press, 1935.

Zambrano, Francisco, S.J., and José Gutiérrez Casillas, S.J. *Diccionario Bio–Bibliográfico de la Compañía de Jesús en México.* México, D.F: Editorial Jus, 1977.

INDEX